One Book/Five Ways

One Book/Five Ways

THE PUBLISHING PROCEDURES OF FIVE UNIVERSITY PRESSES

Foreword by Joyce Kachergis

Introduction by Chandler Grannis

Afterword by William Kaufmann

WILLIAM KAUFMANN, INC.   Los Altos, California 94022

Library of Congress Cataloging in Publication Data
Main entry under title:

One book/five ways.

   Originally published as a workbook for use at the 1977 annual meeting of the Association of American University Presses.
   Bibliography: p.
   1. Scholarly publishing--United States--Case studies.
2. University presses--United States--Case studies.
I. Association of American University Presses.
II. Title.
Z479.O63   070.5'94   78-9505
ISBN 0-913232-53-X
ISBN 0-913232-54-8 pbk.

Copyright © 1977 by
The Association of American University Presses, Inc.

Copyright © 1978 by
William Kaufmann, Inc.

All rights reserved.
This book or any part thereof
may not be reproduced in any form
whatsoever, whether by graphic, visual, electronic,
filming, microfilming, tape recording
or any means, except in the case of brief passages
embodied in critical reviews and articles,
without the prior written permission of the publisher.

Write to: Permissions Department,
WILLIAM KAUFMANN, INC.
One First Street
Los Altos, California 94022

Printed in the United States of America

Cover photo by Robert Sulkin

Table of Contents

Foreword by Joyce Kachergis
Acknowledgments
Introduction by Chandler Grannis

The University of Chicago Press / 1

Acquisitions and Administration / 3
Editorial / 17
Production and Design / 41
Sales and Promotion / 53

The MIT Press / 57

Acquisitions and Administration / 59
Editorial / 75
Production and Design / 97
Sales and Promotion / 113

The University of North Carolina Press / 121

Acquisitions and Administration / 123
Editorial / 127
Production and Design / 162
Sales and Promotion / 173

University of Texas Press / 187

General Statement / 189
Acquisitions and Administration / 190
Editorial / 198
Production and Design / 226
Sales and Promotion / 237

University of Toronto Press / 251

Acquisitions and Administration / 253
Editorial / 260
Production and Design / 272
Sales and Promotion / 286

Afterword:
  What Do You Make of a "Make-believe" Book? / 307
  by William Kaufmann

One Book Six Ways:
  The University of Oklahoma Press / 317

Bibliography / 331

Foreword

These logs record the publishing history of an experiment in comparative publishing procedures in which a single manuscript was submitted for publication to five different university presses: The University of Chicago Press, The MIT Press, The University of North Carolina Press, University of Texas Press, and University of Toronto Press. The procedures followed by each press are shown here with the pertinent correspondence, budgets, forms, layouts, and specifications. It is possible to follow the manuscript as it was processed by the administrative, acquisitions, editorial, design, production, and sales departments.

These logs are surprising in their thoroughness. To be sure, some of the individual presses' presentations are not as complete as they would be if the manuscript were actually to be published. There is necessarily some difference in the emphasis placed upon a manuscript accepted for publication and a make-believe project such as this.

It must be emphasized, too, that *No Time for Houseplants* does not fit the usual scholarly publishing list. For all its scholarly aspects, it is essentially a trade book, more properly published by a commercial house. Yet as a fanciful project, *No Time for Houseplants* had advantages that the normal scholarly manuscript might not have. It allowed the participating presses the freedom to think of new design solutions to new problems and created challenges to our marketing people which took them beyond their normal routines.

The concept of several presses processing the same manuscript was Hilary Marshall's idea and the child of the Education and Training Committee of The Association of American University Presses. A special Project Committee worked for two years towards its completion. The university presses that participated were asked because of their divergent geographical locations, their representations of public and private universities, and the quality with which they perform publishing functions.

The logs were published as a workbook for a session at the 1977 Annual Meeting of The Association of American University Presses hosted by The University of North Carolina Press in Asheville, North Carolina, and dummies of the proposed final versions of the book were exhibited at that session.

Here one can see how a book is published, compare the procedures of five professional scholarly publishers, and see the differences and similarities between equally valid and startlingly different solutions.

Joyce Kachergis
14 April 1977

Acknowledgments

These logs were planned and assembled over a two-year period by a special Project Committee of The Association of American University Presses comprised of

MURIEL COOPER, *The MIT Press*

RICHARD HENDEL, *University of Texas Press*

JOYCE KACHERGIS, *Chairwoman, The University of North Carolina Press*

HILARY S. MARSHALL, *University of Toronto Press*

CAMERON POULTER, *The University of Chicago Press*

BRUCE YOUNG, *The University of Chicago Press*

In addition to the Project Committee those individuals who contributed their particular talents to these logs are:

Chicago: Joseph Alderfer / Richard DeBacher / Penelope Kaiserlian / Catharine Seybold / Kimberly Wiar

MIT: Mary Collins / Robin Cruise / Mario Furtado / Nancy Greenhouse / Arthur Kaplan / Patricia A. Mahon / Donna Schenkel

North Carolina: Gwen Duffey / Martha Farlow / Anne Geer / Johanna M. Grimes / Rebecca Johnson / Malcolm MacDonald / Sally McMillan / John Rollins / Ann Sulkin

Texas: Dohn Barham / Nancy Burton / Suzanne Comer / Chris Gray / Shirley Knop / Kathryn Stevens / Eje Wray / Carolyn Cates Wylie

Toronto: Jean Jamieson / Audrey Livernois / Jean Melusky / Barbara Plewman / Pauline Potts / William Rueter

We acknowledge with appreciation the suggestions and assistance given by J. G. Bell, Stanford University Press, and Edward King, University of Missouri Press, at the inception of the project.

Support and counsel were given by Willard A. Lockwood, President of The Association of American University Presses; John B. Putnam, Executive Director of The Association of American University Presses; and Jerome J. Lewis, Managing Director of American University Press Services.

The completion and publication of these logs would not have been possible without the continuing advice, dedication, and work of Carol Franz, Assistant Director of The Association of American University Presses.

J.W.K.

Introduction

In this unusual book about publishing, five university presses show in step-by-step detail how each would proceed with an identical manuscript from first consideration up to the point of manufacturing. In doing so, they demonstrate that (1) there is more than one way to make a book and (2) the operating principles of several highly competent presses are rather similar. They show also that a group of publishers is willing to devote great amounts of time and effort to a cooperative project and that they can have some fun along the way. The AAUP's tradition of sedate spoofery continues to be a lively creative force.

Above all, the cooperating presses provide here a body of instruction that is at least as illuminating for general trade as for scholarly books. The experimental but wholly plausible manuscript in question presents a number of publishing problems: making partly technical materials attractive to a popular audience; copy-editing and dealing with an author; handling extensive illustrations; setting up special segments for useful reference; postulating markets and the channels to them; deciding on the optimum means of printing and binding; determining budgets and setting prices in line with cost estimates and sales projections; finally, planning an economical means of effective promotion.

The basic idea of the project was for each participating press to make a log of the entire day-to-day process, with all the supporting documents. In effect, the documents constitute the log. The steps are listed in the table of contents of each press's contribution to this volume.

Among the items are: the inquiries, memos, and forms leading to the decision to publish; contracts or letters of agreement; preliminary publishing schedules; transmittal forms; style instructions; editorial checklists; minutes of meetings; correspondence with the author; design specifications; orders regarding illustrations; production cost estimates; manufacturing orders and schedules; sales plans and budgets; promotional calendars; catalog, publicity, and jacket copy. Included by each press are Chapters II and IV of the proposed book, showing copy-editing and author's reactions, also layouts for typical pages and for jackets.

The five treatments have some elements in common. All call for a first printing of 7,500 copies (although alternative estimates are computed); all will employ the VIP composition system (that of The University of North Carolina Press is the model); and all involve standard arrangements for royalties, rights, and trade discounts.

To compare differences among the logs is especially interesting. Each plan looks as if it would work. Each one, however, contains its own points of emphasis. Among those worth examining might be:

 ★The different estimates of total pages, trim sizes, unit costs, and prices.

 ★North Carolina's paperback with slipcase, compared with Chicago's spiral-bound volume, Toronto's unjacketed book with preprinted cloth cover, and the jacketed hardcover books of MIT and Texas.

 ★The five contents pages—some detailed, some succinct.

 ★How the responsibility for supplying illustrations is decided.

 ★Doubts about the title: Is North Carolina right about wanting a question mark after the main title? Is Chicago right in wishing to emphasize that the book is for beginners?

★Conflicting views about the volume's book club possibilities.

Some of the participants provide narrative accounts of some areas. Texas precedes its collection of documents with an essay about the entire process and later describes correspondence, not documented, that would be conducted with the Library of Congress, the author, the illustrator, and others. North Carolina presents an example of copy prepared for Optical Character Recognition. All the presses write proposals for low-budget promotion programs. MIT suggests heavy advance distribution of reading copies; 500 will go to retailers.

The implied question "Who is Purvis Mulch?" pervades the logs. Each press has its own image of the author, described almost as if Anthony Trollope were describing some friend of the Pallisers. Most interesting, perhaps, is the view of Toronto, which imagines at first that Mulch is a man—a rather mossy type—and finally discovers the writer is a woman, "an attractive, articulate person in her early 40s." This greatly enhances the promotion program; Toronto will send her on tour for demonstrations and personal appearances—which will not be too expensive because she will stay with some of her many friends and relatives in cities en route.

One Book/ Five Ways will give working publishers many practical points on which to compare notes and will bring reality and a touch of humor into many an instructional workshop. It is a valuable contribution to the literature of education for publishing.

Chandler Grannis
17 April 1977

THE UNIVERSITY OF CHICAGO PRESS

Table of Contents

Acquisitions and Administration

Acquisitions Procedures | 3
Author and Manuscript Inquiry Form | 5
Suggestions for the Reader | 7
Editorial Preliminary Cost Estimate | 8
Editorial Preliminary Financial Analysis | 9
Contract Abstract | 10
Contract | 11
Book Transmittal | 14
Editorial and Production Procedures | 15

Editorial

Preproduction Meeting Minutes | 17
Edited Manuscript | 18
Correspondence with Author | 38
Transmittal of Edited Manuscript | 40

Production and Design

Type Specifications | 41
Layouts | 42
Manufacturing Cost Estimate | 44
Sample Pages | 45
Book Order and Production Schedule | 51
Book Estimate and Release | 52

Sales and Promotion

Promotion Plan | 53
Cover Copy | 54
Catalog Copy | 54
Author Questionnaire | 55
Review List | 56

Acquisitions Procedures

When a manuscript is received, the editor's assistant sends an acknowledgement card to the author or the editor writes a personal note. The author's name, the author's address, the title of the manuscript, date received, number of copies received, and house (acquisitions) editor's initials are entered on two copies of a log card (p. 7), one for a master file and one for the house editor's file. The status of the manuscript is recorded on this card, names of readers, fees paid, etc. A book folder is prepared, and usually an Author and Manuscript Inquiry (pp. 5-6) is sent. The manuscript is walleted and labeled, with the author's name, the title, and date received.

Each manuscript is reviewed in the house, either by the editor, the editor's assistant, or a part-time reader. If the evaluation is favorable, the manuscript is sent to a scholar for review, usually with a page of suggestions (p. 7). Given a favorable first review, the house editor then must circulate a "house editor's statement," the reader's report, any response to the report, a preliminary cost estimate (p. 8) and a preliminary financial analysis (p. 9) to the senior editor, the editor-in-chief, and the director, requesting permission to obtain a second report. If the second report is approved and is also favorable, the earlier editorial reports, the second report and any response to it, a biographical note on the author, and the table of contents are circulated to the senior editor, the editor-in-chief, and the director, requesting approval to present the project to our faculty Board of University Publications. We do not present cost estimates or financial analyses to the Board, nor do we present projects that we do not wish to publish. The Board seldom rejects a project, but if there is doubt about the advisability of our publishing any manuscript submitted, it may request a third report, usually suggesting a reader's name.

If the Board approves publication, a contract abstract (p. 10) is circulated to the senior editor, the editor-in-chief, and the director for approval of the terms of the contract. The cost estimate and financial analysis accompany the abstract. If approved, the contract (pp. 11-13) is typed and sent to the author.

If necessary, the author may be asked to make final substantive revisions and to have the manuscript prepared according to the specifications in our Manual of Style. When the final version of the manuscript is in hand, the house editor completes a Book Transmittal form (p. 14) and the first (editorial) section of the Book Estimate and Release, eventually completed by the production controller, marketing manager, business manager, and director (p. 52). These forms and two copies of the manuscript are then transmitted to the managing editor.

THE UNIVERSITY OF CHICAGO PRESS

5801 ELLIS AVENUE
CHICAGO, ILLINOIS
60637

Author and Manuscript Inquiry

Would you be good enough to give us the following information in order to help us consider your manuscript for publication here?

Author and co-authors, if any:

```
                                    ,                              USA
------------------------------------------------------------------------
Name                Address                              Citizenship
```

Title of manuscript: **NO TIME FOR HOUSE PLANTS: A Busy Person's Guide to Indoor Gardening**

Is this manuscript an unrevised version of your dissertation? **no**
Is this manuscript a revised version of your dissertation? **no**
If revised, what is the nature of the revision?

Has your manuscript or part of your manuscript been previously published (ie. distributed). Were these parts copyrighted by you, University Microfilms or any other party? **no**

Is your manuscript presently being considered for publication by another publisher? **no**

Characteristics of the final manuscript:

Estimated words per typewritten page: **250**

Total number of typewritten pages: **144**

Number of tables **15** maps **0** line drawings **undetermined**

photographs **38**

Are you prepared to submit the whole manuscript for review at this time? If not, what would remain to be submitted later? **whole ms submitted**

PR167-1M-6-75

Please summarize in a few sentences the essence or theme of your manuscript:

This is meant to be a book for the casual grower of house plants--the home owner or apartment dweller who wants to raise several dozen attractive house plants while spending only a few minutes a day in caring for them. This book tells everything that is necessary to know in order to achieve success. Most house plant books are apparently written by enthusiasts who spend unending hours in careful watering, potting, repotting, propagating, tying up, inducing to flowering, humidifying, bathing, and even talking to plants in an effort to get them to grow. This book cuts care instructions to a bare minimum for the non-enthusiast who still wants the company of healthy house plants.

Please name a few scholars working in your field and therefore competent to read your manuscript. Indicate (*) if any of these scholars have already read it.

1.
2.   (not applicable)
3.

Has your manuscript been read by others whose opinions you care to send us?

   no

Please list any outstanding books on the subject of your work:

   There are hundreds.

Please give us a brief curriculum vitae: your university affiliations, graduate school, advanced degrees, and the titles of any previous books you have published.

University of Iowa, B.A., 1961; author, A Wisconsin Garden Guide, Wisconsin House, Ltd., 1975, 362 pp., 15,000 copies in print, 3 printings; contributor, The Encyclopedia of Organic Gardening, Rodale Press; book in progress, The Earthworm Book, Rodale Press contract for 1977 publication; author of more than 50 articles in Organic Gardening, House Beautiful, Mother Jones, Camping Journal, other magazines; contributing garden editor & monthly column (currently) in Countryside magazine.

What are your current research interests?

Organic gardening and farming; earthworms; solid waste management; environmental issues

NOTE: If invited to submit your manuscript for review, you should retain a completed copy in case of loss or damage in the mails.

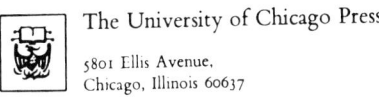

The University of Chicago Press

5801 Ellis Avenue,
Chicago, Illinois 60637

To the Reader:

Please be completely frank in giving us your critical judgment of this manuscript. Your report is solely for the guidance of the editors of the Press and the Board of University Publications, and your name will not be revealed to the author without your express permission. To protect you and us, as well as to avoid undue work and expense for the author, in case our decision is to decline publication of the manuscript, we ask you please to write any notes or queries on a separate sheet, not on the manuscript pages.

The questions below concern matters in which we are particularly interested. We shall be grateful if in the course of your comments you try to answer each of them for us.

1. Is the author's work original? Is his scholarship sound? What has he tried to accomplish, and to what degree has he succeeded? (A brief summary in your own words of the content and thesis, or argument, of the manuscript will be helpful.)

2. Is this a work of importance to specialists in its field? To what audience, or what particular groups, will it appeal?

3. What are the chief books already published on this subject, and how do they compare with this manuscript? (We should like as detailed a comparative bibliography as you can provide without inconvenience.)

4. Is the manuscript written in a clear, readable style? Is its organization suitable and effective? Does it contain unnecessary repetition? Could it be cut without loss of effectiveness, or is it about the right length for its essential content and purpose?

5. How could the manuscript be improved? (Please cite specific sections or chapters that need revision.)

Thank you for your helpful advice.

THE EDITORS
THE UNIVERSITY OF CHICAGO PRESS

LOG CARD

Author: Turvil Mulch   Address: AAUP ROJECT
Title: NO TIME FOR HOUSE PLANS
Date MS recvd: 5/14/76   Editor: IS/

Date	Reader	Amt	Sent	Rpt In	Ms In	Paid
Out						
In	Transmitted 9/29					
Out						
In						
Out						
In						
Out						
In						
Out						
In						

PR151

SIMPLIFIED COST ESTIMATE FOR AN AVERAGE BOOK

1. Cast off: count the number of words in the manuscript. Include everything -- text, notes, extracts, bibliography. Estimate the extent of a missing preface or appendix. Divide the total by 400 to obtain printed text pages.

   Number of printed text pages ... **90**
   Display prelims (add 4 pages) ... **4**
   Dedication or epigraph (2 each) .. **2**
   Contents (usually 2) ... **3**
   Index (1/50 to 1/20 of text) ... **3**
   + 41 illus, 1 table
   TOTAL PRINTED PAGES ... **143**

2. Figure the number of 32-page forms in the book. Divide total printed pages by 32. Ignore a remainder of 8 or less, but count any larger remainder as an additional form:
   NUMBER OF FORMS ... **5**

3. Record the desired print run:
   PRINT RUN ... **7,500**

These three figures are used below in making the cost estimate.

PLATE COSTS   41 illus. @ 10.— ea.   410
                        1 table   35
   Composition (total printed pages X $12.50*) 1263
   Other one-time costs (# of pages X $3 + $200) 629
            TOTAL PLATE COSTS........................ **2337**

STOCK COSTS

   Paper

   Number of sheets needed (print run X number of forms
           divided by 2)   18,750
   Spoilage (add 15 percent)   1,875
      Total number of sheets to be used   20,625
      COST OF PAPER (at $75.00 per 1,000 sheets) **1,547**

   Presswork

   Number of forms X print run + 15%. Divide by 4000
           and multiply product by $100
   TOTAL PRESSWORK **1,078**

   Binding

   Basic charge per copy   ...... $ .75
   Number of forms X .03 15
      Binding cost per copy   .90
      TOTAL BINDING COST (print run X cost per copy).... **6,750**

   Jacket printing

   Charge for first 1,000 jackets   ...... $ 300.00
   Additional 1,000s (at $50.00 per 1,000)   ...... 325.—
      TOTAL JACKET PRINTING **625**
            TOTAL STOCK COSTS........................ **10,000**

                  TOTAL MANUFACTURING COST................................... **12,337**

* or $15.00 for a more elaborate book

11/23/76

Financial Analysis

Date: 8 Sept 76   ☒ Original   ☐ Superseded Version

Author/Editor: Purvis Mulch   Title: No Time for House Plants

Series: _____   Trim Size: _____   No. of Pages: est. 143 p+tol

Discount Class: Cloth	Trade			
Paper				
Royalty Terms:	10% NR	1st 2500; 12½% NR next 2500; 15% NR thereafter		

Manufacturing Cost: Plate Cost	2337				Discount Actual Average %
Stock Cost	10 000				First year:
Total Mfg. Cost	12 327				Second Year:
Unit Mfg. Cost	1.645				Add 1% cushion to Highest Figure:
Subsidy					Reciprocal %:
Total Mfg. Cost After Subsidy					
Unit Mfg. Cost After Subsidy	1.645				

No. copies produced	7500			
No. copies pre-sold				
No. frees	250			
No. on hand to sell	7250			

Pricing Without Subsidy

List Price	$ 7.50				
Average discount %	36%				
Net Price	$ 4.80				
Less unit cost	$ 1.645				
Less Average Royalty	$ .57				
Gross Margin	$ 2.585				
% Gross Margin	54%				

Unit $ required for overhead	$				
Unit $ available for overhead	$				
Unit (Loss) or Gain $	$				
Net Sales Revenue (Multiply # units available for sale, + or (-))	$				
% Return on Investment					

	1973-74	This Year
Budgeted Overhead	48.7%	____%
Gen'l Press Admin.	4.66%	____
Interest Rate on Borrowed Money	2.3%	____
Translation Expense	.2%	____
Write-Off Expense	4.6%	____
Total:	60.46%	____%

CONTRACT ABSTRACT

Type of contract:
- ☒ Author
- ☐ Translator
- ☐ Import
- ☐ Proprietor (translation)
- ☐ Series
- ☐ Revised edition
- ☐ Letter of intent
- ☐ Other _____

Author: Purvis Mulch

Contract with (Author/~~Editor/Translator/Proprietor~~):

Address (and affiliation):

Box 1379

BUP approval: ✓
Contract date: 15 Sept 76
Contract number: 9728

Title of work: NO TIME FOR HOUSE PLANTS: A BUSY PERSON'S GUIDE TO INDOOR GARDENING

Series title and editor:

Copyright by: University of Chicago

Rights limitations:

Market: World

Delivery date of MS: In hand

Length of MS: 156 pp. + 1 table

Illustrations: 41 photographs

Index: yes   Within ___15___ days

Subsidy:

Author's alterations: 5%

Royalty terms: 10% NR first 2500; 12½% next 2500; 15% thereafter

Advance

Author's frees (clothbound/paperback): 10/5

Clauses to be deleted:

Special clauses/Remarks:

Previous Contracts relating to this work (Series/Letter of intent/ _____)

Contract with:

Contract number:

Royalty terms or fees:

House editor: KW
PR 114 rev. 71 5C 4-76

Approval: (MP) 9/15

10 / Chicago / Administration / Acquisitions

Memorandum of Agreement made this 15th day of September,

A.D. 19 76, between THE UNIVERSITY OF CHICAGO, a corporation organized under the laws of the State of Illinois, of Chicago, Illinois, hereinafter referred to as the "University," its successors and assigns, and

Purvis Mulch

hereinafter referred to as the "Author," his heirs, executors, administrators, successors, and assigns, WITNESSETH:

In consideration of the covenants and agreements of the University hereinafter set forth, the Author covenants and agrees with the University as follows:

1 To grant and assign and he does hereby grant and assign exclusively to the University for its use any and all rights of whatsoever kind or nature now or hereafter protected by the Copyright Laws (common or statutory) of the United States and all foreign countries in all languages in and to a Work, the subject or title of which, subject to change by agreement of both parties, presently is: **Grant**

NO TIME FOR HOUSE PLANTS: A BUSY PERSON'S GUIDE TO INDOOR GARDENING

for any and all purposes, and by any means of communication and distribution, including the power to cause the same to be translated, abridged, dramatized, serialized and otherwise adapted, and other rights of every kind and nature now or hereafter during the term of this Agreement recognized as the property of the Author in said Work or in any parts thereof, for the United States of America and elsewhere for the respective term of the copyrights in the United States of America and elsewhere, and any permitted renewals thereof.

2 That the University shall have the exclusive right in its name, ~~or in the name of the Author,~~ to secure copyright for said Work and all subsidiary rights therein in the United States and elsewhere, and the renewal of copyrights, and the University shall be the sole owner thereof; that the Author hereby irrevocably appoints the University, its successors and assigns, his attorney in fact with power of substitution in the name of the University to take out in his name or otherwise but for the exclusive use of the University any renewal or extension of original copyright and to execute in his behalf any and all documents necessary to secure to the University any renewal or extension; and said Author agrees to execute all papers necessary to secure to the University such renewals or extensions of such copyright. **Copyright**

3 That the Author warrants the Work is original and that he is the sole Author and owner of the said Work and has full power to make this Agreement and grant; that the said Work or any part thereof has not heretofore been published (except as may be set out in a rider annexed hereto and signed by the University) and no agreement to publish is now outstanding; that it contains no matter libelous or otherwise unlawful or which invades individual privacy or which infringes any proprietary right at common law or any statutory copyright; that he will hold harmless and indemnify the University, its licensees and distributees, or any of them, against any and all suits, claims, demands, or recoveries, including damages, costs, expenses, and attorneys' fees, which may be made, taken, or incurred at any time by or against the University, its licensees and distributees, or any of them, which are based upon any of the following allegations: invasion of privacy, violation of proprietary right or copyright, libelous or injurious matter contained in said Work. **Warranty and Indemnity**

4 To deliver to the University on or before 30 September 19 76, time being of the essence, two legible, double-spaced typewritten copies of the complete manuscript (with all illustrations, charts, graphs, and other material for the said Work, reproducible without redrawing or relettering), in a form and content and with subject matter satisfactory to the University for publication, it being understood that the length of the manuscript shall be approximately 156 typewritten pages ~~xxxx~~, and the illustrations, etc., shall be as follows: approximately 41 photographs. **Manuscript**

Acquisitions / Administration / Chicago / 11

5 To read, correct, and return promptly galley and page proofs of the said Work submitted to the Author by the University, and that in the event of the Author's failure to return corrected proofs within sixty (60) days after the mailing thereof by the University, the University shall be free to proceed with the manufacture and publication of the said Work without waiting for the return of corrected proofs, and may deduct from royalties accruing to the Author or charge his account for any expense incurred by the University on this account. **Proofs**

6 To pay the University within thirty (30) days after receipt of statement, at the current rates charged by its University Press, for all alterations made by or caused to be made by the Author in galley and page proofs in excess of five (5%) per cent of the cost of the original composition thereof. **Alterations**

7 To revise the first and subsequent editions of the Work at the request of the University and to supply any new matter necessary from time to time to keep the said Work up to date, and provided that if the Author shall neglect or be unable to revise or supply new matter, the University may engage some other person or persons to revise or to supply such new matter and may deduct the expenses thereof from royalties accruing to the Author on such revised subsequent editions, it being understood that if such revisions be not made by the Author, the University shall cause such fact to be evident in the revised subsequent edition. The University shall have all of the rights in connection with all subsequent editions that it is entitled to in the original Work. **Subsequent Editions**

8 To make the University the first offer of publication of his next full-length book. If the University fails to exercise this option by executing a publishing agreement within 90 days of receipt of the next completed manuscript, the Author shall be under no further obligation under this option and shall be free to cause its publication elsewhere. **Option**

9 To prepare and deliver to the University index copy and such other similar matter as may be required by the University in connection with the publishing of the said Work, within fifteen (15) days after final page proofs are mailed to the Author by the University. In the event the University shall not receive such index copy and other matter in a form acceptable to it, within the time specified above, it may have such copy and other matter prepared at the expense of the Author. All permissions necessary to publish the Work are to be acquired by the Author at his own expense. **Index** **Permissions**

10 That the Author will not, during the continuance of this Agreement, furnish to any other publisher any work on the same subject of competing character or material therefor. **Competing Material**

In consideration of the foregoing covenants and agreements on the part of the Author, the University covenants and agrees with the Author as follows:

11 As soon as practicable after receipt of the final manuscript, and following its formal acceptance by the University Board of Publications, to publish the said Work in the English language through its University Press, at its own cost and expense (except as otherwise provided in the memorandum annexed hereto), in such manner and style as the University deems best suited to the sale of the Work, and to reprint whenever in its judgment demand for the Work justifies reprinting, and, as long as the Work is in print and this Agreement is in effect, to offer the Work for sale at such prices as the University may from time to time determine. **Acceptance by Board**

12 To pay to the Author, during the continuance of this Agreement, on the actual cash receipts or net price of the Work (net price being defined as list price less standard discounts), the following royalties from sales (less returns and refunds) of any one edition of the said Work published by the University: **Royalties**

  a. 10% on the first 2500 copies sold; 12½% on next 2500; thereafter 15% on all sales of any clothbound edition in the continental United States of America; and outside the United States, two-thirds thereof respectively;

  b. 7½% on sales of any paper-bound edition if published by the University;

  c. 7½% on sales by mail and coupon advertising outside regular bookstore channels;

  d. 50% from the licensing by the University of any right in the Work protected by copyright, including the licensing of a cheap or paper-bound reprint or book-club edition, and the right to reprint portions thereof. In the event the Work be included in an omnibus edition and no specific sum be fixed for said use, then the University shall fix a pro rata reasonable sum therefor, 50% of which shall be paid to the Author.

  e. 50% from the licensing by the University of any right in the Work or Revised Work not specifically in this paragraph set out.

Provided, however, that after two (2) years from date of first publication, the University shall be free to offer for sale, and to sell at reduced prices, retail or wholesale, any or all of the stock of this Work which in its judgment constitutes overstock, and, as become royalties and when payable hereunder, the rate of royalty payable to the Author on the sale of copies at such reduced prices shall be ten per cent (10%) of the actual receipts therefrom, except that on all copies sold at less than the manufacturing cost incurred or paid by the University, no royalty shall be payable to the Author; it being understood that no royalty shall be paid on free copies furnished to the Author, or on copies used for promotion of sales, review, advertising, samples, or like purposes, or on damaged copies, or on copies sold in any fiscal year of the University ending June 30th in which fewer than fifty (50) copies are sold, and that sales statements shall be made annually for the fiscal year ending as aforesaid, and that royalty payments due as set forth in such statements shall be made on or before August 15th following.

13 To present to the Author __ten (10) clothbound & five (5) paperback__) free copies of the said Work upon publication, and __five (5)__ (............) free copies of any revised edition hereafter published; it being understood that additional copies will be supplied at the regular wholesale price prevailing at the time of such purchase. **Free Copies**

It is mutually understood and agreed by and between the parties hereto as follows:

14 That the University shall have the right after three (3) years from the date of first publication of the said Work to terminate this contract by giving the Author notice by registered mail of its intention to do so. The Author shall have the right within three (3) months from the date of the mailing of said notice to take and pay for the remaining stock and plates, if any, at cost, but the Author shall not in the sale and distribution of the said stock, or in printing from said plates, use the name of the said University. If the Author does not exercise this right, the University shall be free at the expiration of the said three (3) months' period to dispose of all stock and plates remaining on hand for waste paper or otherwise as it may determine, without incurring any obligation to the Author for payment of royalty thereon. This Agreement and the obligation of the parties hereunder shall terminate at the expiration of said three (3) months' period. The University will at any time after notifying the Author as provided above assign the copyright to the Author if he so requests subject to the exercise of any rights theretofore granted by the University. **Termination of Contract**

15 That in every case where, under the provisions of this Agreement, it shall be required or permitted for either party to give or serve any demand or notice to or upon the other party hereto it shall be sufficient: To deliver or cause to be delivered a written or printed copy of any such demand or notice to the said party, or to send a written or printed copy of such notice or demand by registered mail, with postage prepaid and duly addressed to "The University of Chicago Press, ~~5750 Ellis Avenue~~* Ellis Avenue, Chicago ~~37~~* Illinois,"*and to the Author at **Notices** *5801

60637

or at such other place as either party may designate to the other by written notice.

16 That the word "Author" as used herein, and the reference thereto by the masculine singular pronoun, shall be understood to include and designate all authors or editors who may be party to this Agreement. **Definition of Author**

17 That amendments to this Agreement shall not be valid unless in writing and signed by both parties. **Amendments**

18 That the rights herein granted shall inure to the University, its successors, assigns and licensees. **Succession**

19 That the submission by the University of unsigned copies of this document to the Author for his signature shall confer no rights on said Author, and this document shall not become effective unless and until it is executed by both parties hereto.

In Witness Whereof *the University has caused these presents to be signed under the hand of the Director of the University Press, and the Author has hereunto set his hand and seal the day and year first above written.*

THE UNIVERSITY OF CHICAGO

By..
Director of the University Press

....
Purvis Mulch

....
Soc. Security No.

Book Transmittal	Date: 29 Sept. 1976
	House editor: KW

Author: Purvis Mulch

Full title: NO TIME FOR HOUSE PLANTS: A BUSY PERSON'S GUIDE TO INDOOR GARDENING

General: Author's background and our reasons for publishing book: Mulch is a former editor of <u>Organic Gardening</u>, author of 50-odd articles on gardening, published in <u>Org. Gardening</u>, <u>Mother Jones</u>, <u>HouseBeautiful</u>, etc. His WISCONSIN GARDEN GUIDE sold 15,000 copies in 1½ years.

Mulch argues here that there are two basic secrets to raising house plants successfully: choosing the right plants in the first place and providing a "proper basic environment" for them. The right plant, he says, if given the right conditions for growth, will thrive even if the owner must necessarily be frequently inattentive. This is not a book that presents a wealth of new material on raising house plants; rather, the author has selected from the masses of material available on house plants those suggestions that are most helpful for the person with little time to spend on indoor gardening. The reader without much experience will find it especially helpful. Illustrated with some forty-one halftones, the book could be an attractive coffee table item and will make an excellent gift.

Checklist — Herewith [x] / To come [date]

- Half title X
- Series title
- Title page X
- Copyright page X
- Dedication
- Epigraph
- Contents X
- List of illustrations
- List of tables
- Foreword
- Preface X
- Acknowledgments
- Introduction
- Complete text X
- Notes
- Appendix(es)
- Glossary
- Bibliography
- Index .... w/p.prf.
- All illustrations .. X
- Tables X
- Boxes X

Contract

Contract no.: 9728 Series: Series contract no.:

[X] Book represents all new work by one or more authors under contract to us.
[ ] Category of book as follows:

Manuscript Editing

Manuscript and proof to:

Index to be done by: Author

Rights and Permissions

[X] We have world rights, all languages, all editions. [ ] Rights specified below
[X] Author(s), editor(s), translator(s) citizens of U.S. [ ] Specifics below
[X] No permissions needed [ ] Permissions in, free to Press [ ] Details below

Design and Production

[X] Duplicate MS attached Words or MS pages: 156 pp. If reprint, no. pages:
No. line drawings: No. maps: No. photos: 41
[X] All straight composition [ ] Special sorts (see below) No. tables: 1
[ ] Standard trim size OK [X] Special trim (see below) [ ] Offprints needed
Proposed del. date: March 77

Marketing

Publishing season: Fall 77 Subject codes: ODE, OJD *
Proposed price and discount— Cloth: 7.50 trade Paper:

Remarks/Explanations

Trim size: Depending on how we decide to handle the illustrations and market the book, a special oversize format may be needed.

(* NB: i.e. Botany, Horticulture, Floriculture, & Ornamentals)

PR 133-500-1/76

Editorial and Production Procedures

The managing editor on receiving a manuscript with its accompanying forms (see p. 4) obtains an ISBN, makes a first assessment of the editorial and production problems presented by the work, and sends the two copies of the manuscript to the chief manuscript editor and production manager, respectively. Copies of the Book Transmittal (p. 14) are sent to various persons throughout the Press at this time as a signal that the book is going into work, and the title is added to the agenda of the next preproduction meeting.

Preproduction meetings are held at intervals of one to four weeks to make decisions on such questions as trim size, binding, type of jacket, mode of composition, press run, and discount, to discuss preliminary marketing plans, and frequently to agree on a target delivery date. Persons concerned with the editing, production, and marketing of the book attend, as well as department heads and the director. Meetings are chaired by the managing editor. Minutes of the meeting on each book discussed (p. 17) are distributed to all who attend. Later, the managing editor, chief manuscript editor, assistant production manager, and chief designer--working back from the target delivery date if one has been assigned--assign other key target dates, and these are recorded on the schedule card (p. 51) from which preproduction and production schedules are made up.

Manuscript editing and design usually begin after the preproduction meeting, the editor using the ribbon copy and the designer the second copy. Edited manuscript (pp. 18-38) is always sent to the author for approval, and by the time it has come back, the book design (pp. 42-44) should have been completed and circulated, and the manuscript can be marked up for setting. With the design completed, the production controller also obtains a manufacturing estimate (p. 44), and if this is satisfactory, it is added to the Book Estimate and Release (p. 52), which is sent to the marketing manager for pricing, and the book is ordered.

Meanwhile, the promotion section of the marketing department has been furnished with prelim copy and other descriptive matter on the book and writes jacket or cover copy (p. 55) in time to meet production deadlines assigned earlier.

The progress of every book in work (100-150 titles) is checked every two weeks by a "tracking" committee consisting of the editor-in-chief, managing editor (chairman), senior editor, chief manuscript editor, production manager, assistant production manager, chief designer, and head of the in-house typesetting facility. If books have fallen behind, remedial action is agreed upon or future target dates are adjusted.

Author/TITLE   Purvis Mulch   MS/pr pp.: 36,040 words
               NO TIME FOR HOUSE PLANTS?: A BUSY PERSON'S   est. 143 Mid-Jan.
               GUIDE TO INDOOR GARDENING   Target del. date: June '77
KW/BY:CS

Description/Importance? KW: frustrated with title because it didn't really provide time-savers. Felt photos were good. Boxes arranged by plant needs were the best feature. CP: liked boxes that showed where things grew best and the provision of English and Latin names.

Market? Limited to beginners. PK: many on market, most cloth at $7.95. Not a bookclub possibility because it is a beginner's book, not coffeetable or library.

Title OK? Change subtitle: A BEGINNER'S GUIDE... (KW check with author). Other suggestions: Dig This; Houseplants--Chicago Style; The Hows and Whys of House Plants. Should clearly indicate that it is a book for beginners.

Jacket: Modular? Special points? Use back as chart? Put design, not copy, on the back cover since we have nothing like this to advertise.

Trim size? 5¼ x 8? Est. on spiral binding--like handbook of cat musculature. Waterproof cover would look more practical. Consider plastic coating, large pullout chart, paper over boards.

Special machinework?   No

Illustrations or Tables?   41 illustrations
                                  special boxes: straight prose & tabular

Anything missing in MS?   no list of illus.

Press run? 7500 Estimate on spiral book with bound-in pullout chart, also on 6 x 9
               trim. Part dividers are also possible.

Sugg. price & discount?   Aim for minimum cost: $1.50 unit or less; $7.50 or less, trade
                              discount. Price est. on our standard royalty terms.

Editorial Problems
                              Illus. interspersed or grouped?
                              CS to edit chapters 2 and 4.

Preproduction meeting: 14 October 1976

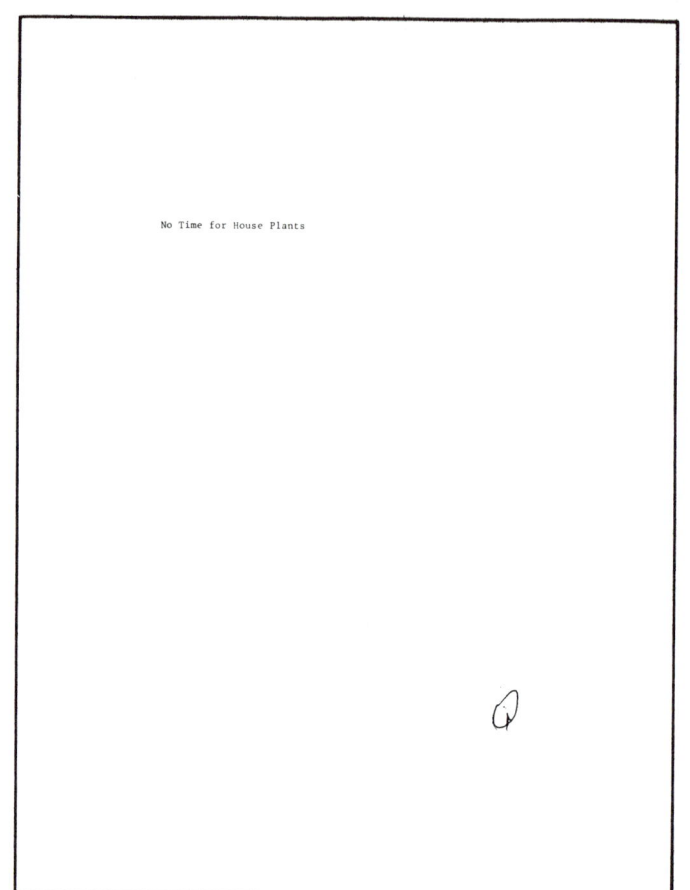

No Time for House Plants

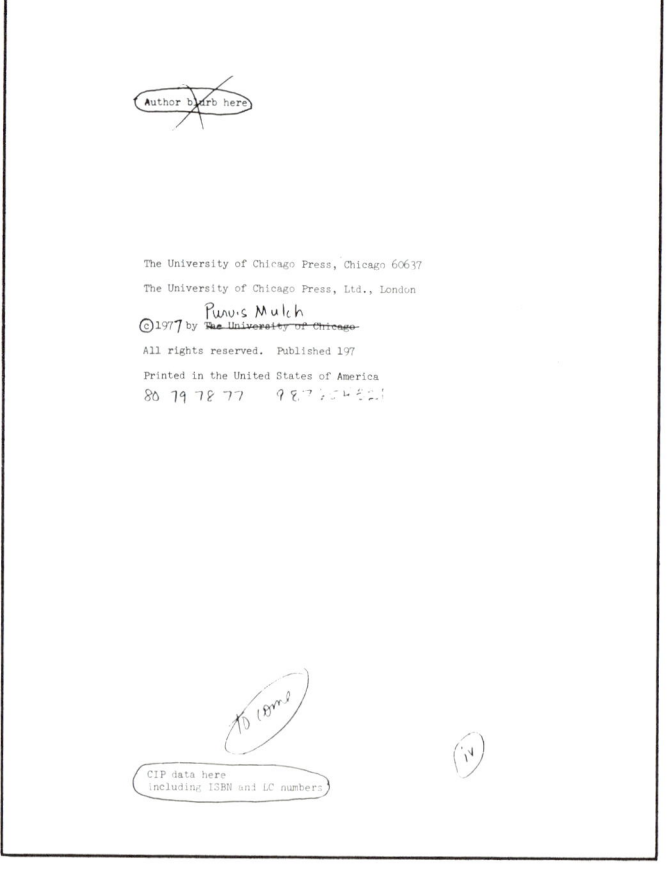

CONTENTS

Preface P-1
CHAPTER 1: THE SECRETS OF NO-WORK HOUSE PLANT
          SUCCESS I-1
CHAPTER 2: UNDERSTANDING HOUSE PLANTS II-1
    The Basic House Plant II-1a
    How a Plant Feeds II-1c
    Parts of the Plant II-1f
    Soil II-1h
    Acidity/Alkalinity II-2a
    Potting Mixtures II-3
    Nutrient Maintenance II-4
    Containers II-5
    Watering II-6
    Humidity II-8
    Ventilation II-10
    Temperature II-11
    Light II-12
    Pruning and Training II-12
    Repotting II-14
    Propagation II-16
CHAPTER 3: PLANT TROUBLES AND CURES III-1
    Improper Handling and Care III-1
    Insect Foes III-3
    Diseases III-8

---

contents, add 1

CHAPTER 4: INTRODUCING THE FOLIAGE PLANTS IV-1
    Where to Buy House Plants IV-3
    Foliage Plants IV-5
CHAPTER 5: CACTI AND OTHER SUCCULENTS V-1
    Care of Cacti and Succulents V-3
    Potting Soil for Cacti V-5
    Introducing the Cacti V-5
    The Unusual Succulents V-7
CHAPTER 6: FLOWERING HOUSE PLANTS VI-1
    Forcing Spring Bulbs VI-12
    Care of Gift Plants VI-17
CHAPTER 7: SPECIAL INDOOR GARDENS VII-1
    Dish Gardens and Planters VII-1
    Bottle Gardens and Terrariums VII-3
    House Plants from Kitchen Scraps VII-7
    An Indoor Kitchen Garden VII-11

SPECIAL BOXES

    1: The ABCs of Artificial Light
    2: Should You Send Your Plants to Summer Camp?
    3: Can Your Plants Survive Your Vacation?
    4: Plants for Cool Conditions
    5: Plants for Medium Temperatures
    6: Plants for High Temperatures
    7: Plants of Greatest Tolerance

---

contents, add 2

    8: Plants for Dry and Semi-Dry Conditions
    9: Vines and Trailing Plants for Totem Poles
    10: Plants for Hanging Baskets
    11: Suggestions for Large-Tubbed Specimens
    Guide to Plant Requirements
    Bibliography
    Suggested Symbols
    Key to Symbols
    Index

II - 1

CHAPTER 2

UNDERSTANDING HOUSE PLANTS

Every plant has its own preferences and requirements for soil, light, temperature, ventilation, humidity, and several other factors that are within our power to control, or at least to mitigate. It is vitally important for you, as a busy indoor gardener, to understand the basics of each, since a prior understanding will enable you to avoid much work later on while achieving routine success in growing plants.

In addition to understanding these basic needs, you will want to know something about pots and other containers, repotting plants, propagation, and a few matters that, while not vital to immediate success, will help you to gain further enjoyment in raising better plants.

THE BASIC HOUSE PLANT

The major difference between a house plant and an outdoor plant is one of location. All house plants could live and flourish outdoors, in the proper climate. All are derived from forebears that lived, reproduced, and died in the outdoors, whether it was on a forest floor in Central Europe or in the bough of a tree in a South American rain forest. Over many centuries of adaptation and evolution, each plant species embraced those characteristics that enabled it to survive; and even today, every house plant carries within its genetic structure the characteristics of its distant progenitors. Thus the Maranta may lose some of its leaves each autumn, even though autumn's weather does not come to the top of the bookshelf where the plant rests, and a cactus, no matter how long we have been feeding and watering it with unfailing regularity, will continue to hoard food and water within its swollen stems. In plants, old habits might recede, but they are never forgotten.

At no time are these innate plant characteristics more noticeable than during the autumn and winter, when many plants—particularly those from temperate regions—enter a period of dormancy. Then, new growth ceases and the plant takes on a listless and washed-out appearance. Other plants, including many of tropical origin, will maintain their bright appearance but will stop growing completely for several months each year, emulating the natural rest periods of their forebears. You will do well to watch for these signs of dormancy and rest, and respond to each plant's needs at that time. When any plant enters a dormant or rest period, water should be reduced and fertilizer withheld completely, until new growth once again begins, usually in the late winter or early spring. At that time, water the plant freely and give it normal doses of fertilizer once again, in order to encourage new growth. By your proper treatment of the plant at this time, you will emulate the advent of spring, working with the plant in carrying out its rhythmic cycles.

Some plants also are naturally short-lived, and will last no more than a year or two in your home despite your careful attention, because their genetic structure dictates a finite life span. Garden annuals, for instance, will germinate, grow to maturity, flower, produce seeds, and die, all in as little as six months. For this reason, very few annuals are selected as house plants. Although a few short-lived plants are cultivated indoors for their unusual characteristics, such as the Sensitive Plant, which is easily grown from seed, the house plants that we have cultivated over the generations are most often those that will give years of pleasure. Some house plants, in fact, live to be hundreds of years old.

Still other house plants are attractive when young, but grow ungainly or otherwise unattractive when they approach maturity. The only plants of this kind I have chosen for inclusion in this book are those that are very easy to propagate from cuttings, so that the parent plant may be discarded after a year or two, and be replaced by its children.

From the hundreds of thousands of plant species in the world, those traditionally cultivated as house plants are the relatively few that have shown a wide tolerance to conditions of heat, light, moisture, humidity, and ventilation—in other words, those that can withstand a human environment. They are both attractive to the eye and tough. Still, if we are looking for success with house plants—and particularly success without working hard at it—then we should spend some time to learn the characteristics of each plant, so that we can recognize individual needs and fulfilling them to the best of our ability.

HOW A PLANT FEEDS

A plant manufactures nearly all of its food by itself—not from the "plant food" that you buy for it. Commercial plant food is no more than a combination of certain chemicals (sometimes in an organic base) that are essential to the plant's basic functioning, much as vitamins are essential to human nutrition. But the bulk of a plant's food—the sugar it uses for energy and growth—is manufactured by the plant itself. In the presence of light, the leaves of the plant draw carbon dioxide from the air and water from the roots, converting these into sugar that is then used for producing energy or stored for future use.

During this sugar-manufacturing process, known as photosynthesis, several other things happen within the plant. While carbon dioxide is being absorbed, oxygen is being released from the pores of the leaf surface. (Plants produce not only all of the world's food but most of its atmospheric oxygen as well.) During the darkness hours, the process is reversed; some of the atmosphere's oxygen is recaptured by the plant and used to convert stored sugar to energy for growth. Generally, a plant manufactures growth food during the day and does its actual growing at night.

Often, the plant converts its newly manufactured sugar to starch and stores it, reconverting it to sugar as the need arises. Although the starch can be stored in almost any area of the plant, certain plants have developed specialized storage areas just for this purpose. Cacti and succulents have enlarged stems and leaves for the greatest above-ground storage capacity of any house plant, while others have developed underground storage apparatus for this purpose, including bulbs, tubers, corms, and rhizomes. A bulb is simply an enlarged underground bud, such as is found with hyacinths, tulips, and onions. A tuber is nothing more than an enlarged root; a common potato is a tuber; gloxinias, caladiums, dahlias, and many other common plants are grown from tubers. →

A corm is the enlarged base of a stem. And a rhizome is a laterally growing, enlarged, underground stem. All are used by the plant for food storage, and all can also be used to propagate plants.

Water is constantly being drawn up through the plant. As it transpires through the stomata (pores) of the leaves, a "pulling" action draws more water up through the roots. The water carries with it mineral salts, including all the elements which the plant needs to carry out its complex chemical processes. The transpiration which takes place in the leaves is similar to perspiration in humans and it serves a similar purpose: to cool the plant. With house plants, it would be difficult for you to notice this cooling effect. But it is readily apparent when a group of large trees carry out the transpiration process. The cool and fresh feeling you enjoy in a thick woods in summer is not primarily the product of the shade itself, but the transpiration of the millions of leaves overhead.

A plant usually cannot absorb too much water, since its vessels and cells can accommodate only so much at a given time; however, the overwatering of a plant can exclude oxygen from the root system, ironically causing wilting of the top portion of the plant. When water is withheld, the plant's cells will gradually collapse, causing wilting of the entire plant. All plants do have protective mechanisms that conserve water in times of drought, however, and can withstand a temporary dry spell. Most wilted house plants will quickly spring back to a normal state when they are watered.

PARTS OF THE PLANT

Stem. The stem serves to support the plant and to contain and direct the vessels that transport water from the roots, and food from the leaves, to every other part of the plant. Most house plants, including Philodendron, Ivy, and Spider Plant, have soft stems. Such plants must either climb or crawl, since their stems are not strong enough to support an upward-growing structure of significant height. Other plants have soft but thick stems that enable them to attain good height, although their stems are apt to be subject to breakage. Woody-stemmed plants, such as the Avocado, Poinsettia, and Boxwood, are far more sturdy, and are usually derived from trees or shrubs of the temperate region. Canes are thick stems with hollow or pithy centers. Bamboo is an example of a cane with which we all are familiar; among house plants, Dieffenbachia and Ti Plant are good examples.

Some plants have a distinct main stem, while others send up many stems, none dominant. A side shoot is a smaller stem growing out from the main stem. A petiole is a leaf stalk, the stem-like structure from which a leaf grows. A node is a joint on the main stem from which a leaf or side shoot grows.

Leaf. The major purpose of the leaf is, as we have seen, to manufacture food for the plant's growth and reproduction. Considering its total mass, the leaf has a remarkably large surface area, ideally designed for the efficient absorption and diffusion of gases through its thousands of stomata.

After the basic functions of the leaf are understood, its proper care is not difficult to appreciate. The stomata must be kept fairly clean, free of dust and oil that might hinder their efficient operation. Leaves must also be given the freest access to light and ventilation, according to the individual preferences of each plant. Never crowd plants to a point where they are competing for light and air.

Roots. Roots serve two main purposes: to anchor the plant in the ground and to supply, from the soil, water and the mineral salts which accompany water. Bulbs, corms, rhizomes, and tubers serve much the same purposes, as well as acting as food storage areas. Roots, just as the above-ground parts of plants, may be pruned without injuring the plant in any way. Roots are often trimmed to prevent a plant from growing too large for the convenience of the grower, just as top growth is cut back. If roots are cut back, however, be certain to cut back top growth to about the same percentage, or the reduced roots might be unable to supply the plant with sufficient amounts of water. The major precaution in caring for roots is, as I will mention several times in these pages, to avoid overwatering.

Flowers. The plant's flowers contain its sexual apparatus. Pollination occurs when male pollen is deposited onto female stigmata, thus fertilizing the plant and allowing the formation of seeds. The fruit of any plant is, in reality, the ovary which swells to protect the seeds. In nature, most plants produce flowers. For the purposes of cultivating house plants, only certain ones, which in this book are listed as flowering house plants, can be depended upon to produce, under home conditions, blossoms of sufficient size, profusion, and beauty to warrant our attention. The plants which we grow for their attractive foliage often cannot produce flowers indoors because of insufficient light or because of a pollination failure. In nature, pollen is transferred either by insects or wind, both of which are lacking in the home. Where indoor pollinization is essential, it can be accomplished by transferring the pollen from one flower to another, using a soft camel's hair brush. This process is described fully in most books devoted only to flowering house plants.

SOIL

Since the house plant you bring home from the shop will already be rooted in soil (presumably the shop knows its business), you might wonder why you have to consider this need at all. The answer is that your house plant will,

II-2

assuming hoped-for longevity, someday need repotting, and you will want to provide it with a potting mixture that will serve its special needs. You might even wish to propagate some of your favorite house plants at some later time, to share with friends and to give as gifts. In any case, a basic knowledge of potting mixtures and soils is essential to a complete understanding of all your plants.

Two simple definitions are in order here, to avoid any confusion later on. <u>Soil</u>, when mentioned here, refers to garden loam, that combination of mineral matter, organic matter, air, and water commonly found outside, in your garden or under your lawn. A <u>potting mixture</u> is soil with the addition of other materials, such as sand, compost, peat moss, limestone, and bone meal, that together form an ideal environment for the roots of your house plants.

The easiest way to assure your plants of a perfect loam is to buy prepackaged sterile potting soil from your garden or flower shop. This soil (will have not only) the proper texture, but it will also be free of disease organisms, insects (some too small to be seen), and weed seeds. To this loam you will add the other ingredients which together will form an ideal potting mixture. You may also buy packaged potting mixture at the store, but if you do, read the package carefully to ascertain the ingredients, making sure that the mixture is right for your plants.

It is, of course, far less expensive to make your own potting mixture from your own garden loam (free), sand (free or next to free), and small amounts of purchased ingredients. If you choose this route, it is important that you be able to make at least a cursory analysis of the garden loam that will form the basis of the potting mixture. Texture is important. A heavy clay soil will hold water for too long a time, encouraging disease and root rot, and it will bake cement-hard when dry. On the other hand, a coarse sand will not hold water well, nor will it hold nutrients long enough for the plant's roots to absorb them. Strive, then, for a happy medium—a good loam, containing both clay and sand, which will hold both water and nutrients, yet offer adequate drainage.

II - 2a

To this basic loam, we usually add one or more of other materials—peat moss, to increase water-holding capacity and to add organic matter; compost, for organic matter and nutrients; sand, to open up the soil to air; and some form of supplemental mineral fertilizer, usually bone meal and lime. Chemical fertilizer can be used, although it is not necessary to add it to the potting mixture, since the other ingredients will supply all the nutrients the plant can use for several months.

ACIDITY/ALKALINITY

A discussion of soils and potting mixtures would not be complete without some mention of acidity and alkalinity, and of the pH scale, which is the scientific measure for acidity and alkalinity. The pH scale runs from 0 to 14. A soil with a pH of 7 is neutral—neither acid nor alkaline. Numbers above 7 indicate an alkaline soil; those under 7, an acid soil. Most house plants, as most garden plants, will do best in a slightly acid soil (a pH of 6.0 to 7.0). Most garden soils are within this range, and so you should not worry unduly about the pH of the garden loam you dig for use in the potting mixture. In this book, all the house plants listed will do well in this normal range, unless special notations to the contrary are made.

If you question your soil's pH, or are simply curious, call your county agricultural agent and ask for directions on having a pH test made. The cost will be nominal. Any soil may be made more acid with the addition of peat moss, or less acid with the addition of ground limestone

II - 3

POTTING MIXTURES

There are as many different basic potting mixtures as there are plant experts—probably more. Perhaps the most common one, however (and one which can be trusted), calls for two parts loam, one part finely screened compost (or a mixture of peat moss and compost) and one part builder's sand (not sea sand). To this is added a small amount of bone meal (about one teaspoon for a five-inch pot) and a pinch of ground limestone. Other recommendations call for more of one ingredient and less of another. Do a little experimenting of your own. After a while, you will doubtless come upon your own favorite mixture, which you can recommend to others.

And now that you have the basic mixture formula well in mind, we will consider the exceptions:

1. Acid-loving plants such as azaleas, camelias, gardenias, and heathers should have no lime, since they are acid-loving. They should, in fact, have some form of acid organic matter—acid peat moss or oak leafmold.

2. Foliage plants need somewhat more compost in the mixture, although half of this compost should be peat moss (which will not overstimulate the plant).

3. Fast-growing and hungry plants need more bone meal and lime, since they use them up so quickly.

4. Some plants, such as cacti, succulents, and orchids, have very special soil requirements, described later in the discussions of individual plants.

II - 4

NUTRIENT MAINTENANCE

The mineral nutrients contained in any fresh potting soil or mixture, whether it is homemade or a sterilized commercial brand, should be sufficient for your plant's needs for the first four to six months. After that, you should begin to replenish those nutrients on a regular and carefully measured basis.

All plants need substantial amounts of three elements—nitrogen (N), phosphate (P_2O_5), and potash (K_2O), and lesser amounts of a dozen or more others, called "trace minerals" or "trace elements." In grower's language, the three major elements are referred to as N, P, and K, and on the label of any commercial fertilizer, the percentages of each are given in N-P-K order. A 5-10-5 fertilizer, for instance, will contain 5 percent nitrogen, 10 percent phosphate, and 5 percent potash. A so-called "balanced" fertilizer contains a balance of all three in the amounts needed for the proper growth of most plants. The fertilizer may be either a chemical or an organic preparation, according to your preference. The chemical kind are quick-acting, easy to use, and tidy. Organic fertilizers, on the other hand, are slow to release their nutrients, providing a gentle and steady supply. Chemical mixtures come in liquid, tablet, and even spray form (the last applied directly on the foliage). Organic fertilizers may be purchased commercially in balanced formulas (fish emulsion, made from fish wastes, is a popular one for house plant use) or may be made at home from a combination of ingredients. Blood meal is a good

II - 4a

choice for supplying substantial amounts of nitrogen (its NPK formula is 15.0%-1.3%-0.7%), while bone meal (4.0%-21.0%-0.2%) is good for phosphate and wood ashes (0.0%-1.5%-7.0%) are high in potash content. A combination of one part blood meal, one part bone meal, and two parts wood ashes will make a 5-6-4 formula, which is a good one for house plants.

How often should plants be fertilized? There is wide disagreement on this point, some experts believing in weekly feedings of full strength (the dosage recommended on the label), others fertilizing no more than once a month, and even less often during the winter ~~plant's dormant or rest period~~. In the end, you will probably have to come to your own policy by way of experimentation. In the beginning, however, it is better to err on the conservative side, since far more plants have been injured from overfertilization than from nutrient starvation. If you use a commercial chemical or organic formula, I suggest that you feed your plants as often as recommended on the label, but only half the recommended dosage. (Manufacturers tend to overstate the need for their product.) If the plant shows a spurt of active growth in late winter or early spring, increase the dosage to the manufacturer's recommendation. During a dormant or rest period, withhold fertilizer entirely. If you are using a home-made organic fertilizer, such as the one suggested above, use it sparingly at first. A level teaspoon of the blood meal/bone meal/ wood ash formula, applied monthly, should be plenty for a plant in a five-inch pot. You may also put some of the mixture in a

II - 4b

bottle, fill the bottle with water, and use this "tea" to water your house plants. A mild tea solution, applied weekly, will give all your plants a continuing and gentle supply of the essential nutrients.

Last, remember never to apply a chemical fertilizer if the soil is dry. The quick action of the chemicals can easily injure the roots.

II - 5

~~balanced house plant fertilizer, which should be applied sparingly. Chemical preparations should be applied according to the manufacturer's directions.~~

Ⓐ OK

CONTAINERS

Nearly any container that offers adequate drainage and doesn't leak (except from a drainage hole) is suitable for house plants. After checking a container quickly for leakage, consider drainage carefully. If the container has a hole in its bottom, there is no problem. If not, then you should put coarse gravel or broken crockery in the bottom of the container to fill one-fourth to one-fifth of its depth. In this way, you will avoid the liklihood of waterlogging your plants and encouraging root rot.

The traditional terra cotta clay pot offers definite advantages. It is inexpensive, easily replaced, and—most important—allows air to be exchanged through its porous walls. This same porosity, however, allows water to evaporate fairly quickly, necessitating more frequent watering. If a plant's location makes it awkward to water, you will save yourself some effort by choosing a glazed or otherwise impervious container.

Some metal containers, notably copper, may produce adverse chemical reactions with soil and fertilizer elements, injuring plants therein. Most copper planters, however, are usually lacquered to prevent such reactions.

Wooden tubs and boxes are ideal for very large house plants. You can make any wooden container watertight by lining it with

II - 6

several sheets of heavy-gauge plastic or, for permanent results, sheet metal.

Last, if you want the best advantages of both a terra cotta pot and a decorative container, place the former inside the latter, leaving a quarter-inch or more of space for air circulation around the walls of the inner pot. Sometimes sphagnum moss is inserted here to help preserve moisture. A base of gravel in the decorative pot can provide good drainage while lifting the inner pot to the level of the outer container.

Ⓐ

WATERING

More house plants are killed by overwatering than by any other cause. This killing with kindness can be avoided, if you learn to understand just when your plants need water and when they should be left alone.

The best rule of thumb is that a plant should be watered when the soil surface is dry to the touch. Then, water thoroughly, either by adding water to the soil surface, or by immersing the entire pot in a larger container of water.

Certain plants, such as the African violets and other woodsy varieties, need more water than most, while cacti and succulents need far less than the average. Aside from the specific preferences of individual varieties, there are many conditions which call for more or less water, this are indicated in Table 1.

Table 1

Immersion, provided the pot is porous, is the best method of watering because it is the surest. The soil in any pot may tend to form water channels which, upon receiving water from the surface, will rush it to

Table 1. WATERING NEEDS OF PLANTS UNDER VARIOUS CONDITIONS

Plants will need more water when...	Plants will need less water when...
They are in a period of active growth	They are in a period of rest (usually during winter)
They are in bright light	They are in dim light or under artificial light
Room humidity is low	Room humidity is high
Room temperature is high	Room temperature is under 70°
They are contained in small pots	They are in large pots
They are in clay pots	They are in non-porous pots
They are fast-growing varieties	They are slow-growing varieties
They are planted in sandy soil	They are planted in heavy soil
They are in flower or about to go into flower	

II - 7

the bottom of the pot and out the drainage hole, leaving large parts of the soil bone-dry. Then, some potting soil mixtures will shrink when drying, leaving many spaces along the wall of the pot where water can run through. Immersion is the one sure way to soak the soil thoroughly, provided that the pot is porous. You will do it in any large container, or even a sink or bathtub. Set the pots in the water, but do not let the water flow over the lips of the pots. After the surface of the potting mixture has become moist— ten to thirty minutes—remove the potted plant, drain off any excess water, and put it back in its place. Never go out for the afternoon, leaving your plants standing in water.

If you water from the top, remember to remove any excess water from the saucer. Plants should never be allowed to stand in water, lest they develop root rot. In time, you should learn to give each plant just enough water to soak it thoroughly, with very little excess drainage.

Some other watering tips:

1. Do not let water sit in the crown (where the roots and stem merge at the soil line) of any plant; wet crown will encourage decay.

2. Never use very cold water, especially for tropical plants. Keep an open jar of water at room temperature for your house plants. Not only will the proper temperature be assured, but some of the chemicals in the water will have been dissipated by the time it is given to plants.

3. Water which is artificially softened may be detrimental to plant growth. If you can, use rainwater, or

---

II - 8

water that has not been softened. Fluorine and chlorine, on the other hand, are not thought to pose any problems.

4. If your water is especially hard, lime salts may cause trouble with such acid-loving plants as Orchids, Primulas, Rhododendrons, Azaleas, and other plants whose natural soil is woodsy (indicating a high organic content) and acid. Either choose plants which prefer a more neutral range in the pH scale, or plan to collect rainwater for your calcifuges (lime-haters).

HUMIDITY

Much of our trouble with house plants, especially in wintertime, can be traced to insufficient moisture in the air. Except for the cacti and succulents, nearly all house plants thrive best in a relative humidity of between 60 and 80 per cent, while that of most heated homes in winter is under 50 per cent—often, considerably under 50 per cent. House plants cry for moisture in these conditions, and it is incumbent upon you to answer that cry.

There are several ways to add moisture to the air in your home. The more expensive include the adding of a humidifying device to your furnace, if you live in a house, or installing an electric humidifier. This step will benefit not only the plants but everyone living in the house as well. But there are less expensive ways of bringing moisture to your plants:

II - 9

1. *The pebble tray.* Line the bottom of a waterproof tray with decorative pebbles and arrange your plants, in pots, on top of the pebbles. Keep the tray filled with water, being sure that the pots' drainage holes are above it. Change the water weekly to keep it fresh.

2. *Decorative containers.* If you keep a clay pot inside a decorative container (double-potting), keep a pool of water in the bottom of the larger vessel. Again, provide some means of support for the clay pot so that it is not resting in water at any time.

3. *Standing water devices.* Water left standing in a room will gradually evaporate, meaning that the lost moisture is added to the room atmosphere. If your home is particularly dry during cold weather, take the trouble to place pans of water on tops of radiators; grow ivy, philodendron, or wandering Jew in containers of water; maintain an aquarium; rotate plants so that each can spend an afternoon in the bathroom each week, where the air is humid. Change standing water weekly.

4. *Bathing and showering.* Most house plants will respond favorably to a brief shower every day, or at least as often as you can manage to provide the treat. Little brass-plated atomizers are ubiquitous in mail order catalogs, but more dependable (albeit less decorative) are the plastic sprayers available wherever house plant supplies are sold. These hold a pint or quart of water, and they feature an adjustable shower head, affording an entire range of water action from a sharp jet capable of carrying twenty feet all the way to a fine mist. Your plants, of course, will like

II - 10

the fine mist. Remember to fill the container after every use, so that the next day's spray will be at room temperature. Remember also to avoid spraying plants which have been standing in direct sunlight (the shock is great) and those which have been subjected to very cool temperatures (perhaps spending the autumn on a cold sunporch).

Rubber plants and others with large leaves should be cleaned thoroughly and gently with a damp cloth about once a week. The leaf polish sold commercially is permissible, if you want really stunning looking, large-leafed plants, but never use oil of any kind. Ivies and other rugged small-leafed plants can be held under the gentle stream of a faucet for their weekly bath.

5. _Grouping._ Plants will maintain a moist surrounding air (leaves not touching) with greater facility if they are grouped together rather than separated. During the coldest part of winter, you might want to group most plants on a pebble tray under a light window, to take advantage both of maximum light and greatest humidity.

VENTILATION

Plants, like people, benefit from fresh air. Like people, also, they react badly to drastic changes in air movement and temperature. Provide adequate ventilation for your house plants, but do not subject them to sharp winds, winter drafts, or heat arising directly from a radiator. Think of your own comfort, in this respect, and you will

II - 11

know what will be best for please your plants. If, in autumn, you bring your plants in from a summer outdoors, help them to adjust to indoor conditions gradually by placing them by an open window for the first several days. Gradually lower the window day by day, keeping a watchful eye on night temperatures.

TEMPERATURE

The temperature requirements of house plants vary widely, according to the natural habitat of their forebears and also according to other conditions. Many cool-weather plants prefer a range of 50°-60° F. and cannot tolerate temperatures above 70°, while tropicals may thrive in a moist 70°-75°. Know the temperature preferences of any house plant before you adopt it, and then place it in the best possible temperature location in your home. You might find, for instance, that a cool-loving aspidistra will do best in a back bedroom, while tropical plants thrive happily next to (but not above) a living room heat vent. The temperature needs of plants are included in their descriptions throughout this book. Heed them well, make liberal use of an indoor thermometer, and do not be afraid to experiment by placing different plants in different locations for a week at a time. You might notice in your plants distinct preferences for particular locations throughout the house, and their preferences will not always corroborate expert advice.

II - 12

LIGHT

Light and temperature needs are closely related. In their native surroundings, many tropical plants can thrive in higher temperatures because they receive long hours of sunlight. In the home, and especially during winter's short days, they do not receive enough light to enable them to stand high house temperatures.

Except for cacti and succulents, house plants should not be placed in windowsills where they will receive long periods of direct sunlight. Simply place a thermometer in this position and you will soon see that your plants can be literally cooked to death, even in the dead of a Minnesota winter. Strive, instead, for a bright spot with a few hours of filtered sunlight each day, at least for most plants.

Individual varieties differ, of course, in their light needs, and these needs are specified in the descriptions of individual plants in the following pages. Again, do not be afraid to experiment with different locations for different plants. I have a _Philodendron scandens_—one of the most popular and most common of all house plants—which has thrived for years in a dim corner, when actually it is supposed to require a bright spot out of direct sun. Plants, I am afraid, sometimes exhibit unmistakable individual characteristics which we have yet to understand.

PRUNING AND TRAINING

Some plants should be pruned and pinched back occasion-

II - 13

ally, in order to encourage bushy and stocky growth, while trailing plants such as philodendrons and ivies need gentle support to guide them into pleasing growth patterns.

Many people hesitate to prune at all, feeling somehow that they are hurting the plant or interfering with its natural development. Actually, plants will respond to judicious pruning with new and vigorous growth. Plants such as geraniums, coleus, and begonias should be pinched back routinely, in order to encourage lateral growth. The process is quite simple: with a sharp knife, cut back perhaps one-half inch of the central growing tip. The plant should respond by sending out side shoots below the central tip, and the main stem of the plant should then become thicker and sturdier. If this is done several times a year, the plant should eventually attain the vigorous and well-rounded form many you desire. Without this pruning, it may well grow "leggy" with a weak main stem and requiring some kind of support. Many older plants, as well as the young ones, will benefit from occasional pinching back or shearing of outside growth. Do not, however, prune or pinch back African violets, gloxinias, flowering bulbs, ferns, or cyclamen.

Vines and trailing plants often need some kind of support, unless you prefer to let them cascade from a hanging basket. The usual practice is to sink a slab of cork or tree bark into a pot, then to train the vines of the plant to grow around and up the support, eventually concealing it.

RIGHT—SLABS ARE COMMONLY USED.

II - 14

Another effective device is the sphagnum moss cylinder. Pack the moss fairly tightly around a stake and secure it in a cylinder of the proper size for the pot. The cylinder can be made easily from either chicken wire or green plastic material made for this purpose. If you wish, sink a small clay pot into the top of the cylinder, so that you can add water regularly to keep the moss damp. (Otherwise, the moss will require regular spraying.) Tie the vines gently to the cylinder as they grow; eventually, philodendrons and similar plants will anchor themselves to the moss with their aerial rootlets, making other support unnecessary.

REPOTTING

The temptation to repot plants often is a strong one, but should be strongly resisted. A plant needs repotting only when it has become potbound—when the roots have filled the entire container and are creeping out of the drainage hole. Choose a new pot only one size larger than the old, for a house plant will not do well in a pot that is too large. If the larger pot has been used before, scrub it thoroughly to remove any possibility of disease. new clay pots soak it for a few hours in water so that they become saturated. Then, with ample potting soil, gravel, and a tongue depresser or similar wood tool, set to work.

To remove the plant from its old pot, slide your hand over the top of the pot, index and second fingers cradling

II - 15

the plant stem. Turn the pot upside-down, thus supported, and tap the lip of the pot sharply on the edge of a bench or table. After a few taps the entire soil ball, ringed with plant roots, should come out easily, in one neat piece. Set it aside. Take the larger pot and line the bottom with a layer of coarse gravel or broken crockery, to provide good drainage. Then add potting soil on top of the gravel, placing the plant with its soil ball into the new pot several times as you add soil you few enough, to see when it reach to the proper depth. (The soil should reach to about one-half inch below the lip of the new pot, a four-inch pot, and one inch below the lip of an eight-inch pot, to leave room for watering.) When enough soil has been added to raise the plant to its proper height, center it well and begin to pack soil around the sides (A cork impaled with a stick handle is also effective.) of the soil ball, using the tongue depresser. Take your time in doing this, for it is the most crucial part of the entire operation. It is important to pack the soil firmly, so that no air spaces are left when the job is finished. Roots cannot draw nutrients in air spaces and many of them will thus be injured or die, affecting the health of the entire plant. When the new soil is finally brought up to a level even with the top of the soil ball, the job is finished. You might want to add just a little soil over the top of the root ball, especially if roots have been forced up to the soil surface, but don't add any more than you must, for you do not want to change the planting depth of the plant. Repotting is shock enough, for many plants, without altering the plant-

II - 16

ing depth. Water it thoroughly and return the plant to its usual location.

How often should you repot? Obviously, only as each plant indicates a need. For slow-growers, this may be once every two or three years; a mature slow-grower may go for many years without repotting, if new growth is cut back. For fast-growing and very young plants, repotting may be needed once or twice a year for the first several years. Plants that do not need repotting after one year should have the top one-half to one inch of soil replaced annually, to keep the soil fresh.

PROPAGATION

There will come a time when you will want to start your own house plants, to increase your own plant population, to use as personal gifts for friends and family, or to replace a short-lived plant or one that has become ungainly with age. The propagation of most house plants is not difficult, and it is most rewarding.

There are two general methods of doing the job: by the collecting and planting of seeds, and by the cutting and rooting of plant parts—stems, leaves, or underground structures. The first way (sexual reproduction) is often difficult, always time-consuming, and likely to produce unsatisfactory results. Propagation from seed is ideal for garden annuals, but not for most house plants. Special equipment is required, and daily attention is essential, making the activity an unlikely one for

II - 16a

anyone who professes "no time for house plants." In addition, the seeds from hybrid plants are likely to produce plants vastly inferior to the parent plant. (A hybrid, incidentally, is any plant produced by cross-pollinating two plants of different species or genera.) Last, many house plants do not flower and produce seeds under home conditions, requiring the house plant gardener to purchase seeds from specialty houses. The one advantage of growing house plants from seed is that you can create new hybrids by the cross-pollination of plants. This can be an exciting and fascinating hobby for house plant enthusiasts, but is unlikely to appeal to those who cannot afford to devote a lot of spare time to it.

Far more simple, and yielding far more reliable results, is the propagation of plants by the cutting and rooting of plant parts. Less care is required, and the offspring will look just like the parent, even when the parent is a hybrid.

Plants may be propagated at any time of year, although it is best to avoid tackling the job when the plant is going into a dormant period. In early spring, just before active growth begins, is perhaps the ideal time.

Cuttings. The most common method of propagating is by taking stem cuttings, which are then rooted in either water or some sterile rooting medium such as perlite, vermiculite, or sand. If you have never rooted a cutting before, begin with African violet, coleus, Dracaena, Fuchsia, gardenia, geranium, Impatiens, ivy, Philodendron, wandering Jew, or wax begonia. These are the easiest, because all can be rooted in water. Simply take a cutting from an actively growing tip of the plant, containing four to six leaves, severing the stem just below a joint with a clean razor blade. Place the cutting (you may take several at a time, from the same plant if you wish) so that the bottom portion is submerged in water—a colored or clear bottle is fine—remembering only to keep the leaves above water. (Cut off the bottom leaf or two, if necessary, to get more of the stem into the water; about a third of the entire length should be in water.) Place the container in diffused light—not direct sun—and wait until vigorous roots appear. When they have, the little plant may then be removed from the water and potted in a small pot, using the potting mixture recommended earlier in this chapter. Be sure to pack the potting mixture firmly around the roots of the plant, to avoid any air spaces, and water thoroughly afterwards.

Stem cuttings which cannot be rooted in water may be rooted in perlite, vermiculite (both available wherever house plant

supplies are sold) or builder's sand.

The process is basically the same as for rooting in water. The cuttings are inserted in the moist medium, which may be contained in a small clay pot or, for larger numbers of cuttings, a shallow plastic tray. The planted container is then placed in a plastic bag which is tied shut (the zip kind, used for food storage, is convenient, effective, and reusable) and placed in diffused light at a temperature of 65 to 70°. You can tell whether the cuttings have developed roots by testing them weekly. Open the bag and pull gently on a plant. If it moves easily, then the roots have not yet formed; if it resists your gentle tug fairly well, the roots probably are mature enough to stand repotting. The rooting process can take as little as two weeks, or as long as several months, depending upon the variety of the plant and the size of the cutting. When the roots are strong and vigorous, pot the plant in a small pot and treat it as you would any other plant.

Plants that have (hollow or pithy stems), canes (including Chinese ever-

---

*You may by now be wondering why, throughout this book, builder's sand is recommended for potting purposes while sea sand is cautioned against. The answer is that builder's sand, which comes from inland locations, has irregular and sharp surfaces, allowing good soil drainage. Sea sand, having been washed smooth over the years, packs too snugly and leads to a compacted soil and resultant drainage problems.

---

green, Dracaena, and Dieffenbachia, which look much like the eyes of a potato, can be propagated by taking cuttings of the canes, which have discernible "eyes." Press each cane section (containing one eye) into moist sphagnum moss, eye up, secure it with wooden clothes pins at each end so that the cane does not pop out, seal it in a plastic bag, and put it in a cool place out of direct sun. In six to eight weeks, move it into a warm place (70 to 90°), still out of direct sun. Soon, a shoot will grow from the eye. When the shoot has grown four or more leaves, the cane may be cut close to the shoot on both sides, and the new plant may be lifted from the moss and potted.

Plants that with fleshy leaves are best propagated by taking leaf or leaf-petiole cuttings. (A petiole is a leafstalk, or stem.) Leaf cuttings work well when large and mature leaves are available. Cut the leaf close to the stem of the parent plant, using a razor blade for a clean cut so that the cells. The leaf may then be cut horizontally into smaller sections, with the main vein running from top to bottom along the center of the leaf section. One leaf from a long-leafed plant such as (cape primrose) Sansevieria and Streptocarpus may be cut into as many as ten sections, each of which will produce an individual plant. Each leaf section is sunk halfway into the rooting medium, after which the process is the same as that described for stem cuttings.

Smaller leaves may be rooted by taking leaf-petiole cuttings. Cut one leaf stem close to the main stalk and sink the stem into the rooting medium, so that the leaf nearly but

not actually touches the medium. African violets, begonias, piggy-back plants, and Peperomia all respond well to leaf-petiole cuttings.

Underground division. Older plants with thick main roots can be propagated by root cuttings. Cuttings are usually taken when the plant is being repotted. Cut about one inch of the main root, making sure that it has at least one eye. Cover this with one-half inch of rooting medium and treat it as you would any other cutting.

Thick-rooted perennials may be propagated simply by the process of root division, in which the entire plant, including the root mass, is simply forced apart into two or more clumps, each of which is then repotted.

Plants which produce rhizomes (underground stems) may be propagated by dividing the rhizome into pieces and planting so that one leaf bud is contained on each piece, and planting the pieces under one-half inch of rooting medium. Plants which produce potato-like tubers can be propagated by cutting the tubers apart with a sharp knife, keeping one eye to each section, and planting the sections in the rooting medium, eyes up.

Some plants produce "suckers," small plants that grow up from an underground stem or root. These may be separated from the parent plant and potted in soil immediately.

Anyone who has seen strawberries grow outdoors knows what runners are—the baby plants that grow from a long stem coming

II-21

from the base of the parent plant. Among house plants, Boston fern and spider plant both produce runners, which can be severed from the parent and started in a rooting medium.

Other methods of underground division include the separation and replanting of baby bulbs and corms which are produced by the mother bulb or corm.

Air layering. A fairly simple (and most impressive) way of propagating larger or woody-stemmed plants is by air layering. Here, a sharp cut is made into the stem, perhaps a third of the way in, and into which a toothpick is placed horizontally to keep the cut open. That stem section is then wrapped with moist sphagnum moss and covered with clear plastic, tied top and bottom so that moisture cannot escape. Roots will form from the incision and will soon show through the plastic. When a fair number of them have appeared, cut through the stem below the plastic wrap, remove both plastic and moss, and pot the new plant immediately in potting soil.

As you might imagine, the propagation of plants can often be integrated with the cutting back, pruning, and shaping of older plants. It seems a shame to throw away plant parts when they can be used to produce more plants, and it is precisely this attitude of thrift which, if not controlled, can lead to a frightening multiplication of house plants. The answer, of course, is to share plants with friends, thus encouraging still more enthusiasts and still more house plants.

IV-1 / II-22

How about moving IV-1-2-3-4 back to the end of Chapter 2, and inserting a new subhead--"Choosing House Plants"--to begin this section? All this material applies to Chapters 3, 4, & 5, and really does fall under "understanding house plants." -jm

CHAPTER 4

INTRODUCING THE FOLIAGE PLANTS

CHOOSING HOUSE PLANTS

The number and variety of house plants available for your consideration is staggering. For every combination of conditions your home can offer—including heat, light, and humidity—there are literally thousands of suitable house plant varieties, offering almost limitless selection of sizes, forms, colors, textures, growth patterns, and flowering habits. You survey the conditions that your home can offer, and then make your plant selections, within those limits, to suit your own tastes.

The house plants I have selected for inclusion in this chapter are only representative of the many available far greater. I have included nearly all of the most common plants, and I have tried to avoid those difficult to grow. The old favorites are here, as well as some newer varieties and unusual plants which can add zest to your collection.

II-23

I have divided into three broad groups: foliage plants, flowering plants, and cacti and succulents. Within each group, individual plants are listed alphabetically by their common names, followed by (in parentheses) their scientific (or Latin) designations. The scientific name comprises both the genus and species names. For example, the scientific name for the common boxwood is Buxus (the genus) sempervirens (the species). After a genus name is introduced, it is thereafter abbreviated. Thus Buxus sempervirens, if mentioned again, becomes B. sempervirens. Last, there may be a third part to the scientific name which designates a further subdivision of the species, usually called a subspecies or a variety. The popular Japanese boxwood, for example, is B. microphylla japonica.

Although I have attempted to maintain an informal tone in these pages, by using common names whenever possible, the scientific nomenclature has obvious benefits. Many species are known by different common names in different parts of the country; different species of a genus are often called by a single common name; and a single common name may be applied even to varieties of completely different genera. The only sure way to identify any plant, then, is by referring to its scientific name.

For each plant listed, you will find symbols that indicate its preferences for growing temperature, light, soil moisture and air humidity, and window placement.

II-24 / IV-3

Please remember that these are rough guides and not inflexible demands. Many plants have a wide range of tolerance, and conditions will thrive in a variety of them. Many plants which are said to prefer an east window will do just as well in a shaded south or a west location. Do not hesitate to try a plant you like because you cannot provide its exact needs—but neither should you attempt a new plant if you can provide none of them. Experimentation is both valuable and enjoyable.

WHERE TO BUY HOUSE PLANTS

The best place to buy a house plant is from someone who grows his own stock. He will know his plants and you will be able to rely on his advice. If there is no grower in your area, the next best source is your local flower shop or nursery center. Whichever place you choose, talk to the owner or his representative about house plants. Ask for precise identification of a plant that interests you. Ask for specifications of the plant's needs for light, soil, temperature, and humidity. Ask how large the plant is apt to become, and whether or not it produces flowers, even if you know the answers to these questions. If it becomes apparent that he doesn't know very much about the plant, or about house plants in general, then ask to talk to someone who can answer your questions in greater detail, or seek another source.

Plants found in supermarkets and discount houses are usually not bad, although many you see flowering in the store may have been grown quickly and forced into bloom under ideal greenhouse conditions that you cannot hope to match in your home. However, most plants offered by these sources are likely to be common varieties that are quite tolerant of adverse conditions. It is hard to go wrong with grape ivy or a climbing philodendron.

Plants stored outside at garden centers or in shopping centers may carry insects or disease, particularly if they are resting close to flats of outdoor vegetable or flower seedlings. Examine them closely before purchasing, and isolate them for one or two weeks at home before putting them with other house plants.

Wherever you buy your plants, look for young and sturdy specimens with rich color and a generally healthy appearance. Examine particularly carefully large and mature plants which carry high price tags. These may have been growing for too long a time in ideal conditions. Generally, you will have better luck with a younger plant, and you will have the added pleasure of bringing it along to maturity in your own home.

Larger plants offered at bargain prices are often severely under-rooted.

---

4 FOLIAGE PLANTS

In this chapter, we will survey many of the house plants grown primarily for their foliage. Some of them, under favorable conditions, will flower from time to time, although few should be selected for their flowering abilities. Nearly all of these plants are fairly easy to grow and maintain, giving even the beginner a wide variety of plants from which to choose.

The plants are listed in alphabetical order, according to their common or popular names. If there is no popular name for a plant, or if there are more than one, but no dominant name, then the plant is listed by its scientific or Latin name. The index, which includes both common and scientific names, provides a convenient means of cross-checking names.

The special symbols accompanying each plant name will provide a quick and convenient guide to that plant's requirements (see key, pg 000). Remember, however, that these are guides and not sharp demands. Many of these plants are tolerant by nature, and will take to an east window as well as a west window, and can tolerate some direct sunlight even if none is recommended. Most crucial, perhaps, are the guides to humidity and moisture, since overwatering is one thing that almost no plant will tolerate.

IV - 6

African Boxwood (*Myrsine africana*)

This slow-growing boxwood has red stems, but otherwise is similar to regular Boxwood (q.v.). Many people think it is even more graceful. African Boxwood is a good plant for terrariums, if the atmosphere is not too hot.

Aralia (*Fatsia japonica*)

Sometimes sold as *Aralia sieboldii*. Beautiful, bright green, leathery, maple-like leaves highlight this cheerful plant. In appearance, it is similar to the castor oil plant, and in fact is sometimes called False Castor Oil Plant. It thrives in a cool spot. Aralia can easily grow leggy, and so it should be pruned annually in order to encourage it into bushy growth. *It will attain a height of four feet at maturity.*

A striking hybrid, *Fatshedera lizei*, crosses *F. japonica* and ivy (*Hedera*) forming a climbing plant with maple-shaped leaves, which is tolerant of adverse conditions.

There is also a plant called False Aralia, which has graceful and feathery foliage. It bears no resemblance to the true Aralia and is difficult to grow.

Asparagus

There are two kinds of Asparagus suitable for growing as house plants. *A. plumosus*, with slender, needle-like dark green leaves, forming a feathery appearance, and *A. sprengeri* (Emerald Feather) which has thicker yellow-green leaves and drooping stems. The latter makes a good

---

IV - 7

plant for hanging baskets, and produces red berries at Christmastime. Both like some sun in the summer and full sun in the winter, and both can grow to a height of about two feet.

Australian Laurel (*Pittosporum tobira*)

A tolerant and slow-growing plant whose leaves, glossy and leathery, resemble those of the Rhododendron. Australian Laurel will grow vigorously bushy and does not require much attention. Florists often use the leaves in floral arrangements.

An interesting variegated form is *P. tobira variegata*.

Australian Umbrella Tree (*Schefflera actinophylla*)

Here is a very attractive and vigorous-growing tree with rich and glossy leaves that radiate like an umbrella from the ends of the leaf stalks. It is a tough and rewarding plant, growing to six feet and can be propagated by air-layering.

Australian Umbrella Tree is also sold as *Brassaia actinophylla*. A dwarf variety, *B. actinophylla compacta*, is also available.

Baby's Tears (*Helxine soleirolii*)

This low creeper is also called Irish Moss. It likes a constantly moist (but not soggy) soil, and higher than average humidity. It makes a good ground cover for terrariums but will also grow in a pot if adequate humidity is provided. Baby's Tears may appear to die in the colder months, but

IV - 8

an adequate rest period it will spring back to life.
#

Black Pepper (Piper nigrum)   A-C-B-C

This is not a ~~terribly~~ very attractive plant, but it produces real peppercorns which you may use at the table, and is a good conversation piece for that reason. The plant's berries ~~begin as~~ green, later turn red, then dry up and turn black. Pick the dried-up black corns, dry them thoroughly for several weeks in an open spot, then use them in your pepper grinder. ~~The~~ Care for Black Pepper is the same as that required for Philodendron. It is not a demanding plant.
#

Boxwood (Buxus)   C-A-B-B

The same plant which grows the most prized hedges outdoors *with glossy, bright-green leaves* can make a very attractive house plant. Boxwood is slow-growing *the ancient Oriental art of growing dwarf trees and shrubs.* and dependable, a good subject for bonsai. *It has glossy,* ~~bright-green leaves.~~ B. sempervirens and B. microphylla japonica (Japanese Boxwood) are the two popular species.

(Bromeliaceae) #
Bromeliads   A-B-C   *eighteen hundred*

There are more than ~~1,800~~ varieties of this popular group, many of which are suitable for growing as house plants. Some of them produce attractive flowers, but most are grown for their striking and variegated leaf patterns. One distinctive feature of the Bromeliads is the rosette leaves ~~which~~ *forming* a small water cup, which the plant uses to hold reserve

IV - 9

supplies of water in its natural habitat. ~~Since the plant lives in~~ the crotches of trees in Central and South America, ~~the water cup is~~ an evolutionary survival characteristic. In the home, keep the cup filled with water, changing it weekly to keep it fresh.

A few of the more common Bromeliads are Aechmea, Ananas (Pineapple), Billbergia, Cryptanthus (Zebra Plant), Dyckia, Tillandsia (Spanish Moss), and Vriesia.
#

Caladium   A-B-B-C

Caladiums, with their spectacularly-colored and variegated leaves, are equally at home in the garden or on the window sill. They are ideal additions to plant groupings on porch or patio in the summer and early autumn. Give them bright light, but not long periods of direct sun, ~~especially~~ in summer, if you want the brightest leaf colors.

Caladiums are grown from tubers, which can be divided easily to produce new plants. Start the tubers in regular potting soil at a very warm temperature--80° to 90°--and move the young plants to a cooler spot when they have appeared. *They will attain a height of about one foot.*
#

Cast Iron Plant (Aspidistra elatior)   A-C-B-C

This is perhaps the easiest plant in the world to grow, as its name suggests. It is virtually impossible to neglect it to death. It is also called Saloon Plant, since it was one of the few that could survive in Victorian taverns, and it was made immortal by George Orwell in his novel Keep the

IV - 10

Aspidistra Flying. If you cannot grow the Aspidistra, you may safely conclude that you have a purple thumb, hopelessly irredeemable *as a gardener* ~~and are~~. ~~The~~ *which grows about two feet tall,* Cast Iron Plant seems to thrive even better when kept slightly pot-bound, and it will appreciate having its leaves washed occasionally. A white-striped species is called A. variegata.
#

Chamaeranthemum igneum   A-B-A-C

This low, spreading herb has attractive, dark green leaves with reddish-yellow veins. It is suitable for hanging baskets or as a low contrast in large plant groupings. It does like warm temperatures and high humidity, however, and might not be suitable for dry apartments.
#

Chinese Evergreen (Aglaonema)   A-B-B-A
and low-growing
Here is an attractive plant that is very easy to grow. It will stand abuse almost as easily as Cast Iron Plant.

There are at least ten commonly found species of the Aglaonema, the most popular of which, A. modestum, has interestingly mottled leaves. Perhaps the most attractive, however, is A. pseudobracteatum, which is sometimes difficult to find in stores and greenhouses.

IV - 11
#

Cissus   A-B-B-C

Cissus is a vine plant ~~which~~ *that* offers a number of interesting and attractive species. Most are vigorous climbers, suitable for training on a trellis or for adding to hanging baskets.

Among the more popular species are C. rhombifolia (Grape Ivy), which is one of the most popular of all house plants; C. antarctica (Kangaroo Vine), which prefers a small pot; C. antarctica minima (Miniature Kangaroo Vine); C. rotundifolia; and C. discolor (Begonia Ivy), which is perhaps the most spectacular of the genus, although difficult to grow.

Of all the Cissus, Grape Ivy is the easiest to grow, which doubtless accounts for a large share of its popularity.
#

Coleus   A-A-A-B

This old favorite has velvety leaves sporting bright splashes of reds, pinks, purples, and yellows. There is a seemingly endless number of varieties of Coleus, nearly all of them interesting, *most growing twelve to eighteen inches in height.*

Coleus is equally happy outdoors, grown as an annual in the North, or in ~~the~~ window garden. It can be grown easily from seed, and stem tip cuttings can be taken from established indoor plants. If you grow Coleus outdoors in summer, take some cuttings before the first autumn freeze and root them for growing as house plants.

The soil for Coleus should be kept damp, but not soggy. Pinch back plants often to encourage bushy growth.

IV - 12

#

Copper Leaf (*Acalypha wilkesiana*)

These are members of the Spurge family, which feature copper-colored foliage. A close relative, *A. hispida*, is described in this book under flowering plants.

Copper Leaf may be propagated easily by taking cuttings late in the summer. The plant is susceptible to attack by spider mites, and proper precautions should be taken against this menace.

~~Croton (*Codiaeum*)~~

~~Here is a genus that is not particularly easy to grow, but well worth the effort, since it is perhaps the most colorful of all the foliage plants. There are dozens of suitable varieties, nearly all of them sporting bright, variegated, and multi-colored leaves, in a variety of shapes.~~

~~Croton needs full sun, except in the heat of summer, and warm temperatures to keep it happy.~~

#

Dichorisandra reginae

This is an attractive and slow-growing plant with interesting leaf markings. It resembles Wandering Jew, except that it grows upright. Give it warm temperatures and not too much direct light, but do watch room humidity.

IV - 13

#

Dieffenbachia

There are many species of this popular plant, often called Dumbcane. It is prized for its large leaves with interesting markings, usually variations of cream and white on dark green. *Dieffenbachia* is a fairly tough plant, not too difficult to grow. Most varieties attain a height of eighteen to twenty-four inches, although growth is slow.

D. arvida 'Exotica' is very popular because it is even more durable than other members of the family. Other well-known species include *D. picta*, *D. amoena*, *D. sequina*, and *D. bowmannii*.

There are no special cultural requirements, although *Dieffenbachia* does like a warm spot and will appreciate having its foliage cleaned regularly. The plant may be propagated by taking stem cuttings and rooting them in moist and warm peat.

Caution: Eating or nibbling on the leaves of *Dieffenbachia* can cause severe swelling of the tongue and mouth tissues, hence its popular name, Dumbcane. It is not a plant to grow in a home with toddlers.

#

Dracaena

There are many available species of *Dracaena*, which vary so greatly in appearance that some appear to be unrelated. Most grow tall—five feet or more—on sturdy stalks.

IV - 14

They are very tough plants, tolerant of a surprising amount of neglect, all in all one of our most dependable house plants.

Some varieties to investigate are *D. deremensis* 'Warnecki,' *D. fragrans* (which has corn-like leaves), *D. fragrans massangeana* (whose leaves feature yellow stripes), *D. marginata* (a truly exciting plant, with grass-like, cream-colored foliage, edged in red—sometimes sold as *D. marginata tricolor*), *D. sanderiana* (with white-banded leaves), *D. godseffiana*, *D. draco* (the Dragon Tree of the Canary Islands), and many others, some of which will doubtless be offered by any good supplier. Those mentioned, however, are some of the most attractive and also some of the easiest to grow.

Episcia

This genus, which offers many species and subspecies, is related to the African Violet and requires largely the same culture, although it does demand a little more light. *Episcia* is not really one of the easiest plants to grow successfully, and should be tried only after success with some of the others listed in these pages. The leaves are a rich green, most varieties tinged with copper, some with variations of silver, blue, purple, and bronze. The veins often offer striking color contrasts. *Episcia* is a trailing plant, a natural selection for hanging baskets. It sends out runners that may be used for propagation.

IV - 15

Most species of *Episcia* produce small and attractive flowers, in the color range of red-orange-yellow, but the plant is generally grown for its delightful foliage. If you do not wish to strive for blossoms, a north window will suit *Episcia* well enough.

The most popular species is *E. cupreata* (Flame Violet), which has soft and hairy copper-tinged leaves, and comes in several attractive varieties. Also investigate *E. dianthiflora*, which produces white flowers, and *E. lilacina* 'Cuprea,' with lavender-colored flowers. Many other species and subspecies are available, all of which have fascinating foliage variations and some of which will bloom quite profusely.

Fatshedra (see *Aralia*)

Fatsia japonica (see *Aralia*)

Ferns

The fern is the oldest plant, on the evolutionary scale, that you are likely to cultivate. Its family is predated only by the algae and the mosses. Everyone knows and admires ferns for their graceful and feathery fronds. They are one of the few house plants that reproduce themselves by spores rather than seeds. Some ferns grow regally upright, while others trail with modesty and grace. There are many sizes of ferns, from miniature plants suitable for the window sill, all the way to the seven-foot tub plants that can add a touch of class

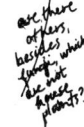

to entryways, patios, and conservatories.

The secret to the successful raising of ferns is in offering them an environment matching, as nearly as possible, that of their natural habitat. They need warmth, a decent degree of room humidity (not under thirty percent), and a moist and humusy soil (at least fifty per cent organic matter). They appreciate bright light, but will be affected adversely if allowed to stand for long periods of time in direct sun.

There are a great many ferns from which to choose. Among the smaller ones are:

<u>Adiantum</u>, the Maidenhair Fern, which is available in several varieties; it sends forth fragile-looking fronds in sprays; needs good light and high humidity.

<u>Asparagus plumosus</u> (Asparagus Fern), the most popular of the small "ferns," is really not a fern at all but a member of the lily family. It is treasured for its delicate, hair-like leaves.

Other smaller ferns ~~of popularity~~ include <u>Asparagus medeoloides</u> (Smilax), a trailer; <u>A. sprengeri</u> (Emerald Feather), a climber; <u>Pteris multifida</u> (Brake Fern); <u>Woodwardia orientalis</u> (Chain Fern), <u>Polypodium aureum</u> (Hare's Foot Fern); and many, many others.

Among the larger ferns are:

<u>Cyrtomium falcatum</u> (Holly Fern), which has holly-shaped fronds.

<u>Asplenium nidus</u> (Bird's Nest Fern), with broad lance-shaped fronds.

<u>Nephrolepis exaltata</u>, which has long, sword-shaped fronds and is often called Sword Fern.

<u>N. exaltata</u> "Bostoniensis,' the ever-popular Boston Fern.

<u>Platycerium bifurcatum</u> (Staghorn Fern), whose fronds are usually attached to a piece of bark or other support, and which can become parched quite easily in a dry atmosphere.

The world of ferns is a large one, full of interest, and extremely rewarding. No house plant collection should be without at least one or two representatives of this proud family.

<u>Ficus</u>   B-C-C-C

This large group of indoor plants, whose best-known member is the Rubber Plant, offers species ranging from large, tree-like plants, down to small-leafed trailers. Although they are not difficult plants to grow, the large species are especially sensitive to both overwatering and sudden temperature changes, and will react to either by dropping their leaves.

There has been much improvement in the Rubber Plant (<u>F. elastica</u>) since World War II. The best now is perhaps <u>F. elastica</u> 'Robusta,' which is remarkably trouble-free. There are many decorative varieties, as well, including <u>F. elastica</u> 'Doescheri,' which has light and dark green patched leaves and cream-colored leaf margins, and <u>F. elastica</u>

'Schryveriana,' another mottled-leafed variety. <u>F. elastica</u> 'Decora,' from which 'Robusta' was developed, is still a popular slow-growing variety. Rubber plants will grow as tall as any room, but may be cut back to encourage bushiness.

Chinese Banyan (<u>F. retusa</u>), another tree-like <u>Ficus</u>, showers forth with a profusion of small, leathery leaves. <u>F. retusa nitida</u> (Indian Laurel) resembles mountain laurel.

The Fiddle-Leaf Fig (<u>F. lyrata</u>) is a tough and attractive tree-like species, with large, dark green, fiddle-shaped leaves. It needs warmer conditions than other <u>Ficus</u>. Weeping Fig (<u>F. benjamina</u>) is another <u>Ficus</u> tree which has small, densely-growing foliage.

There are, as well, many small plants in the genus. Most popular, perhaps, is Creeping Fig (<u>F. pumila</u>), a small-leafed creeper that has been developed to include several variations—<u>F. pumila minima</u> (slower-growing and smaller), and <u>F. pumila variegata</u>, a variegated variety. All will adhere to rough surfaces, sending out aerial roots similar to those of ivy, and are thus easily trained.

The tree-type <u>Ficus</u> are propagated by air-layering, while the small-leafed climbers and trailers may be reproduced easily by simple division.

German Ivy (<u>Senecio mikanioides</u>)   C-B-B-C

Here is an easy-to-grow plant that is similar to the true ivies in both appearance and requirements. A handsome relative is <u>S. macroglossus variegatus</u> (Cape Ivy). Treat them in every way like Ivy (q.v.) for success.

Ginger (<u>Zingiber officinale</u>)   A-A-A-B

This is the same ginger that is used in cooking, which makes the plant even more interesting than its appearance would indicate. The untreated rhizomes sold in specialty food and gourmet shops can be planted directly in potting soil to produce plants—or, established plants may be divided easily. The plants have reed-like stems and interesting grassy foliage, truly exotic in appearance. Successful as a house plant depends upon giving it plenty of sunlight and warm temperatures. Keep the soil constantly damp but never soggy for long periods of time. As an added bonus, healthy plants will bear colorful clusters of flowers.

Golddust Plant (<u>Aucuba japonica</u>)   C-B-B-C

This modest plant features dark green leaves spotted with yellow-gold markings. Its main attribute is that it will withstand very cool temperatures, all the way down to freezing, and ~~still come up smiling~~. It is good for unheated winter porches in all but the coldest parts of the country. Two popular varieties are <u>A. japonica variegata</u> and <u>A. japonica goldeana</u>.

Ivy (<u>Hedra</u>)   C-B-B-C

Here is surely one of the most popular of house plant species, both easy to grow and cheerful and attractive in appearance. There are a great number of varieties, with new improvements coming along all the time.

English Ivy (Hedera helix) is the most popular of the true ivies, and is available in more than fifty varieties to suit nearly any taste. There are varieties with large leaves and small, fast or slow growing habits, plain green or variegated. The best way to choose an English Ivy to your liking is to visit some flower shops and greenhouses, or to beg a few cuttings from a friend who has a plant that appeals to you.

Propagation of Ivy is easily; and in fact the plant does half of the job for you. Small rootlets will form on the stem of the plant, just below the leaves, which the Ivy uses to attach itself to rough surfaces, helping it to climb. Make cuttings just below the roots and plant these cuttings directly in potting soil or a sterile rooting medium.

It would be the sheerest folly to attempt to recommend all the good varieties of English Ivy. For a starter, however, you might investigate H. helix conglomerata (Japanese Ivy), an upright-growing plant with small and densely-growing leaves; "Curlilocks" and 'Ivalace' with curled leaf margins; 'Green Ripples,' 'Maple Queen,' 'Merion Beauty,' 'Needlepoint,' 'Pittsburgh,' 'Pixie,' 'Rochester,' H. helix cutifolia, and 'Shamrock,' the last of which likes more than average moisture and which is good for terrariums.

Among the variegated English Ivies, try 'Golddust,' 'Glacier,' and 'Goldheart,' the last of which has dark green leaves with sharply contrasting bright yellow centers.

Canary Islands Ivy (Hedera canariensis) is another easy-to-grow Ivy, which has larger leaves than English Ivy. It is often trained around a piece of bark, much like a Philodendron, to form a striking plant with a very bushy appearance. More popular than the basic green-leafed variety is the variant H. canariensis variegata, also known as 'Glorie de Marengo,' whose leaves are slate-green to cream in color.

Joseph's Coat (Alternanthera)   A-B-B-B

These are low-growing, dwarf plants that are good for terrariums. Their multicolored foliage adds interest to any plant grouping. Joseph's Coat needs warm temperatures and a moist soil to be happy.

(Note: Codiaeum is also called Joseph's Coat, because it, too, has colorful foliage. But Codiaeum grows to a height of ten feet.)

Maranta   A-C-A-C

Here is a genus of plants that has striking foliage. It is easy to grow and impressive in appearance. Marantas will grow to about eight inches in height. M. leuconeura kerchoveana (Prayer Plant) is perhaps the most popular of the Marantas, and is so named because its leaves fold up at night, as if in prayer. The leaves are large and oval-shaped, and the plant requires a fairly humid atmosphere. In the autumn, the leaves may begin to die out.

If so, do not be alarmed. Cut off the affected leaves and reduce watering until late winter, when new growth begins; then water normally.

A red-veined variety, even more striking, is M. erythroneura. Another with red veins is M. leuconeura erythrophylla (Jungle Plant), which has olive-green leaves. Still another striking variation is offered by M. leuconeura massangeana.

Most house plant growers will want to include at least one Maranta among their collections. The key to success with this plant is in giving it lots of bright light, but no direct sun at all.

Miniature Holly (Malpighia coccigera)   C-B-B-B

This is not a true holly, but a bushy evergreen shrub with dense holly-like foliage. The leaves are shiny, dark green, and have spiny teeth. Miniature Holly does produce small flowers, but it is grown primarily as a foliage plant. It is propagated easily from cuttings.

Nephthytis (Arrowhead)   A-C-B-A

This is an attractive plant, but difficult to identify, since there is great confusion over what is and what is not a Nephthytis. Experts tell us that many Syngoniums are mistaken for Nephthytis. Other experts say that most plants sold as Nephthytis are really Syngoniums. Since the two plants are difficult to tell apart, however, no one cares very much except

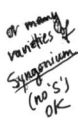
or many varieties of Syngonium (no s's) OK

the experts. Whatever they are, they are tough plants, able to withstand adverse conditions. Nephthytis have large, heart-shaped leaves, and are either trailers or climbers. Used as climbers, they will have to be offered some support, such as that used by Philodendron. Propagation may be achieved by taking stem cuttings.

Among several available species, the most popular is Syngonium podophyllum (Goosefoot Plant).

Norfolk Island Pine (Araucaria excelsa)   A-B-B-C

This popular evergreen, graceful and symmetrical, is seen with increasing frequency. It will hold up well under adverse conditions, although its branches will droop in dim light. Give it a damp, but not soggy, soil, for it is very susceptible to overwatering. It seems to do well when kept slightly potbound.

Norfolk Island Pine is a slow grower, and should never be pruned. It will grow gracefully to a height of about six feet, after which it tends to become ungainly.

Palms   B-C-B-B

Here is a plant family full of nostalgia for many of us. In Victorian times and right up through the 1930s and 1940s, the potted palm was a symbol of exotic elegance, bringing a bit of the tropics to shivering Northerners. No movie made before 1950 was complete without a detective peering out from behind a potted palm.

The elegant palms lost much of their allure after

IV - 24

World War II, but now they are making a modest comeback. You can achieve success with palms, by giving them bright light (even though they will endure shade), little water, and no plant food during the winter months. Palms actually seem to thrive on inattention, doing well when slightly potbound. They are slow-growing, in any case.

The palms are a plant family—Palmaceae is the scientific name—which comprises many genera and far more species. Few, however, are both attractive and manageable as house plants. Among the palms you might wish to investigate are:

Chamaerops (European Fan Palm) has fan-shaped leaves on long stalks, and will become quite large at maturity.

Cocos is an attractive dwarf coconut palm, the best species of which is C. wedelliana.

Howea is the Palm Court Palm, the most popular of all indoor large palms. H. belmoreana, the most attractive species, will eventually grow to ten feet or more in height.

Neanthe is an attractive and easy-to-grow dwarf which can tolerate a dry room.

Phoenix, the Date Palm, can be grown easily from the stone of a fresh date. Plant the stone in potting soil, keep it warm (70° to 80°) and it should germinate in about a month. It is slow-growing during the first year or so, but within ten or fifteen years it will reach the ceiling.

IV - 25

Pellonia   A-B-A-B

This is a colorful, slow-growing, creeping plant, fine for hanging baskets and a good filler plant for groupings. It features small, oval-shaped leaves with interesting variegated patterns. There are two popular varieties—P. daveauana and the more compact P. pulchra.

Pellonia is not difficult to propagate. As it creeps along the soil it sends down roots from the stems. Just cut the stems into sections and root them in potting soil.

Peperomia   A-C-B-C

There are many varieties of this popular and cheerful little plant (eight inches or less in height), most of which are low and upward-growing, with deeply ridged leaves. It is the ridging that gives Peperomia its distinction in a world of larger and more spectacular house plants. They are tough plants, tolerant of most conditions, although they will rot at the groundline if the top of the soil is not allowed to dry out between waterings. Peperomia like bright light, but not direct sun in the summer.

Among the more popular varieties are:

P. caperata (Emerald Ripple Peperomia) has deeply ridged heart-shaped leaves; the tops of the ridges are green and the valleys are brown, giving an interesting effect.

P. rotundifolia is a low grower with light green and thick leaves.

P. obtusifolia (Ovalleaf Peperomia) has solid green

IV - 26

leaves, while P. obtusifolia variegata is the variegated form of the same species.

P. Sandersii (Watermelon Peperomia) is identified by its red petioles and silver-striped leaves.

P. griseo argentea hederaefolia has ridged, glossy leaves, silver-hued, and purple-olive veins.

There are many other varieties of Peperomia, many of which may be found at your local flower shop or greenhouse.

Philodendron

These plants constitute what is probably the most popular group of house plants in America today. There are many, many species and varieties, with leaves ranging from small to very large, in an interesting variety of shapes offered by no other house plants. Most are climbers, and will appreciate a support that can be kept moist, such as that described on page 00.

Philodendron are not difficult plants to grow, unless you disregard the rules. Growth will be stunted by poor light, and the leaves can turn yellow and drop from lack of water, too much water, too small a pot, low temperatures, or poor drainage. They will appreciate a monthly washing with a mild soap (not detergent) solution. Cut back the growing tips if you wish to encourage bushy growth, and use the tip cuttings to form new plants.

IV - 27

Some of the more popular varieties include:

P. scandens (Sweetheart Vine), a very popular climber which can withstand the dry air of a typical apartment.

P. oxycardum, the most commonly grown form, which has heart-shaped leaves very similar to P. scandens. It is often grown in water or wet moss.

P. dubium (Cut-Leaf Philodendron) is a slow grower with star-shaped leaves.

P. panduraeforme (Fiddleleaf Philodendron) has irregularly shaped, olive-green leaves.

P. pertusum has perforated leaves, irregularly shaped. The adult form, known as Monstera deliciosa, has broad and thick leaves with many perforations.

P. squamiferum (Anchorleaf Philodendron) has leaves and petioles that are covered by red hairs. The leaves are shaped like daggers.

P. bipinnatifidum (Twice-Cut Philodendron) is a large-leafed variety; the leaves resemble the smaller P. dubium in shape, but are more deeply notched.

P. selloum is another cut-leaf variety, the cuts becoming more pronounced as the plant reaches maturity. This species will tolerate temperatures down to freezing with no apparent harm.

P. wendlandi is another large-leafed species, very tolerant of a wide range of temperature and humidity. Its leaves are long and narrow.

IV - 28

Piggy-Back Plant (Tolmiea menziesi)   B-B-A-A

Here is a native to the West Coast of the United States, a modest-sized plant that can be grown outdoors/in the warmer regions of the country. Its name is derived from its unusual habit of bearing young plantlets from the junction of the leaf and the petiole. These can be rooted easily to grow new plants. The leaves are toothed and lobed, covered in down. It is an easy plant to grow, although not considered especially attractive by some.

Pilea   A-B-B-B

There are at least four cultivated house plants in this interesting group, none of which grows more than a foot in height. They are rather unusual looking plants, not liked by everyone. All like moist soil, warm temperatures, and full sun in the winter. The plants become less attractive as they grow older, but cuttings are easily made, so that older plants may be discarded when desired. Fertilize Pilea liberally when growth is active.

P. cadierei (Aluminum Plant) has dark green leaves with striking aluminum-colored markings. A dwarf variety, P. cadierei minima, is preferred by many, as is P. cadierei nana, a compact variety.

P. microphylla (Artillery Plant) is fine in texture with bright green, fern-like leaves. When its flowers are dry, pollen literally explodes from the blossoms, hence its common name.

IV - 29

P. involucrata (South American Friendship Plant) is bushy in growth and has coppery leaves. It can be made to look even more bushy, if several cuttings are taken, then rooted in the same pot, at the sides of the parent plant.

P. 'Silver Tree' has bronze-hued leaves with silver markings.

Plectranthus   A-C-A-B

Various species of this genus are often called Trailing Coleus or Swedish Ivy. Some are upright in growth, while others are trailers, making good subjects for hanging baskets.

P. australis (Swedish Ivy), a trailer, has waxy green leaves, round in shape with sawtooth edges.

P. australis variegatus, similar in leaf shape, with added white markings.

P. purpuratus is an upright growing plant with purple coloring on the undersides of its leaves.

There are other interesting varieties, including P. oertendahlii, a flowering trailer with bronze-hued leaves and silvery veins.

Pleomele   A-C-B-A

This is an interesting group of plants with cultural requirements similar to those of Philodendron.

P. reflexa variegata (Song of India) is now included in the genus Dracaena. Its attractive, spear-shaped leaves are gold and green striped, borne in clusters on branching stems. It will grow to tree size in ten or fifteen years.

IV - 30

P. reflexa gracilis has dense foliage; its recurved leaves have translucent edges.

P. thalioides has waxy green leaves, ribbed lengthwise.

Pothos (Scindapsus)   A-C-B-C

Pothos is very similar in appearance and growth habits to the heart-leaf Philodendron, P. scandens, except that it needs less water and warmer temperatures--not below 65°. It likes bright light, but cannot stand direct sun. Pothos is a natural trailer, although it can be trained upward along a support, again like Philodendron. The leaves are heart-shaped, green, with pale yellow markings. It is not as easy to grow as most plants listed in this book.

The most popular species is S. aureus, which offers several variegated varieties, some of which require even warmer temperatures.

Ruellia makoyana   A-C-A-C

This is an old favorite, not seen as often today as in the 1930s. It is a free-spreading plant, with glossy and pale green leaves with silvery veins. It likes a warm and moist environment, shaded from the sun.

Sanchezia nobilis glaucophylla   A-C-A-B

This is a member of the Acanthaceae family. It grows to a heighth of four feet and has large, glossy, sword-shaped leaves with yellow veins.

IV - 31

Screw Pine (Pandanus)   A-C-B-B

This old favorite will withstand most adverse conditions. It is recognized by its long, arching, sword-like leaves, which have saw-toothed edges.

P. veitchii has green and white striped leaves. Often preferred, however, is P. veitchii compactus, a dwarf variety with clearly variegated leaves. P. baptistii has no marginal spines, as do the other species. All Screw Pines like moist soil, but never soggy soil. They can take some direct sun, except in the heat of summer, although they do best in a bright location out of direct sun, altogether.

Selaginella   A-D-A-A

Among these fern-like plants are some small creepers, some upright-growing species, and some trailers. All offer bright green, feathery foliage. The conditions they require are the same as those for ferns.

S. kraussiana is a low creeper, perfect for terrariums.

S. emmeliana is an upright-growing plant.

S. willdenovii is a vigorous climber with unusual blue leaves, while S. apus is a trailer, good for hanging baskets.

Sensitive Plant (Mimosa pudica)   B-C-*-B

This is a fascinating plant for both adults and children

---

* Prefers dry soil but high room humidity.

IV - 32

because its delicate and feathery leaves and petioles droop
and fold up instantly (and temporarily) whenever it is touched,
or even if a lighted match is held close to it. Seeds are often
available in stores, from which plants will grow easily. It
becomes leggy and out of hand after about a year, but it is
not difficult to grow more plants at any time.

Silk Oak (Grevillea robusta)   C-B-B-C

This is a pleasant plant with graceful and feathery
foliage similar to that of the False Aralia. It will grow to three feet in height. The Silk Oak likes
cool and moist conditions, and can spend the summer outdoors
with benefit. It does tend to get leggy if unchecked, and
so it should be cut back at the growing tip fairly regularly.
The Silk Oak will react badly if its soil becomes very dry.

Snake Plant (Sansevieria)   A-C-B-A

The Snake Plant is actually a succulent, but few of us
think of it as such, and so we include it among the foliage
plants. It has long been very popular, probably because of
its great tolerance to adverse conditions. It is also called
Mother-in-Law Tongue and Bowstring. Like the Cast Iron Plant,
it can grow perfectly well in hot, dry, and dim locations
(including, it seems, most old hotel lobbies in the country).
The leaves are thick and sword-shaped, usually upright, growing to eighteen inches or more in height,
in some varieties ground-hugging. It is propagated easily by

IV - 33

division of the rootstock or by taking leaf cuttings. (Be
careful not to turn the leaf cutting upside down when setting
it in the rooting medium, for roots grow only from the downward
portion of the cutting.)

There are many varieties available, including:

S. trifasciata laurenti (Variegated Snake Plant) has
handsome yellow bands along its leaf margins.

S. trifasciata is similar in form, but without the yellow
bands.

S. trifasciata laurenti 'compacta' (Dwarf Congo Snake
Plant) has shorter leaves and yellow margins.

S. trifasciata 'hahni' (Hahn's Dwarf Snake Plant) has
light and dark green bands along the leaves.

There are many other interesting variegated varieties
of this old standby.

Spathe Flower (Spathiphyllum)   B-D-A-A

Here is an easy-to-grow, tough plant, suitable for the
homes of most novice green thumbs. It has sword-shaped and
glossy green leaves. White blossoms will sometimes surprise
you in the winter, but do not depend on their appearance.
There are two popular species—S. clevelandii and
S. floribundum.

Spider Plant (Chlorophytum comosum)   B-B-B-C

The Spider Plant is one of the most popular of house plants.

IV - 34

It has grassy leaves, variegated cream and green in color,
which arch gracefully from either pot or hanging basket.
Mature plants produce perfectly formed baby plants on the end
of long runners, which resemble spiders hanging from a thread.
Propagation is simply a matter of rooting one of the "baby
spiders" in a rooting medium. The Spider Plant can store
water in its tubers, and can take dry soil for a fairly long
time because of this characteristic.

Strawberry Geranium (Saxifraga sarmentosa)   C-B-B-B

This trailing plant, also called Strawberry Begonia and
Mother of Thousands, is good for both hanging baskets and
terrariums. All its really asks is a woodsy soil containing plenty of organic matter, and a cool
location. Leaves of the Strawberry Geranium resemble
those of the true geranium, and it sends out runners just
as strawberry plants do. The leaves of the standard variety
are deep olive in color, with silver-gray markings. An interesting variant, S. sarmentosa 'tricolor,' has dark green
leaves marked with white and pink, and is considerably more
difficult to grow.

Sweet Flag (Acorus gramineus)   A-C-A-C

Here is a moisture-loving plant that grows only two
inches tall. It is a pleasant little fellow, and will be
most happy in a terrarium.

IV - 35

Syngonium (see Nephthytis)

Ti Plant (Cordyline terminalis)   A-B-A-B

C. terminalis is only one of many species of Cordyline,
but is certainly the most popular. Also called Firebrand, it
will last for only one to three years and grow to two feet in height before dying out, but
its spectacular short life is certainly worth your placing
this plant on your list of house plant candidates. It has
long, upward-reaching leaves, cerise, purple, and green, which
grow from a cane trunk. Another popular species is C. australis,
which features long and slender leaves. The Ti Plant is very
popular in Hawaii, where its colorful grassy leaves are used
in making grass skirts. It is sold there in tourist shops as
a "Ti Log." In recent years, breeders have developed several
variations of the original plant, including a dwarf and a
variegated variety, which go under various names.

Umbrella Sedge (Cyperus alternifolius)   A-C-A-C

Here is a popular exotic plant with narrow, pointed,
grasslike leaves that grow in clusters. It will grow up to
two feet tall in a pot. Constant moisture is essential, and
propagation is a simple matter of root division.

Related species include C. papyrus, similar in appearance and requirements but which grows to seven feet in height,
and a dwarf variety, C. alternifolius gracilis.

IV - 36

Velvet Plant (Gynura)   A-B-B-B

This is a vigorous-growing plant with dark red, velvety leaves. It will offer a fine contrast to your green plants. It is best to train the Velvet Plant to some support, to keep it in bounds, or to pinch it back often to encourage bushy growth.

There are two common varieties: G. aurantiaca, which is upright in growth habit, and G. sarmentosa, a smaller and loosely-twining plant. The flowers of both have a bad scent and should be removed immediately upon their appearance.

Yew (Podocarpus)   C-B-B-B

Yews are prized outdoor plants in many parts of the country, but can be made into attractive house plants anywhere. These hardy evergreens can provide welcomed contrast to your tropicals. They are slow-growing and tolerant of adverse conditions. They will take low temperatures without a whimper, and may require frequent repotting because of vigorous growth. They can become quite large and bushy.

P. macrophylla angustifolia (Southern Yew) can be pruned to a pleasing shape and will respond with even more vigorous growth. Other similar species include P. macrophylla 'Nagai' and P. macrophylla 'Maki.'

Wandering Jew (Tradescantia)   C-C-B-C

Tradescantia and Zebrina both claim the common name of Wandering Jew, and the two genera are so similar that they are

---

IV - 37

commonly interchanged. All are easy-to-grow, tolerant, and vigorous trailers of many varieties, perfect for hanging baskets. Feed them regularly for good growth. Propagation is simplicity itself. Simply take cuttings of growing tips and root them in water.

Among many interesting species are:

T. fluminensis, the original Wandering Jew, has silver markings, but there are many variants of different markings and colors available today.

T. albiflora has bluish-green leaves with white stripes.

Z. pendula is an excellent house plant whose leaves have purple undersides. Again, there are several interesting variegated varieties.

BIBLIOGRAPHY   24 pt headliner 11/u

ARTIFICIAL LIGHT GARDENING
6 pt #

Bickford, Elwood D., and Stuart Dunn. Lighting for Plant Growth. Kent, Ohio: Kent State University Press, 1972. One of the best books on the subject; especially valuable to those who have had some experience in the area.

6 pt # between entries

Cherry, Elaine C. Fluorescent Light Gardening. New York: Van Nostrand Reinhold Co., 1965.

Elbert, George A. The Indoor Light Gardening Book. New York: Crown Publishers, Inc., 1975.

Fitch, Charles Marden. The Complete Book of Houseplants under Lights. New York: Hawthorn Books, 1975.

Kranz, Frederick H. and Jacqueline. Gardening Indoors under Lights. New York: Viking Press, rev. 1971.

13 pt #
BEGONIAS
6 pt #

Brilmayer, Bernice. All about Begonias. New York: Doubleday Publishing Co., 1960.

---

bibliography, add 1

Kramer, Jack. Begonias, Indoors and Out. New York: E. P. Dutton & Co., 1967.

13 pt #
BONSAI
6 pt #

Brooklyn Botanic Garden. Bonsai: Special Techniques. New York: Brooklyn Botanic Garden.

Chidamian, Claude. Bonsai: Miniature Trees. New York: Van Nostrand Reinhold Co., 1955.

BROMELIADS

Kramer, Jack. Bromeliads: The Colorful House Plants. New York: Van Nostrand Reinhold Co., 1965.

BULBS

Field, Xenia. Growing Bulbs in the House. New York: St. Martin's Press, Inc., 1966.

Peters, Ruth Marie. Bulb Magic in Your Window. New York: M. H. Barrows & Co., 1954.

Walker, Marion C. Flowering Bulbs for Winter Windows. New York: Van Nostrand Reinhold Co., 1965.

Key to Symbols

Explanation: Instead of saying, under each of 140 plants, "This plant requires a moderate temperature of 50° to 70°, will appreciate a bright spot out of direct sunlight, likes a high degree of humidity and constantly moist soil, and will do best in a west window," I suggest that we develop a series of symbols indicating these preferences.

I have seen letters used in other books, something like "A-B-A-C," and although this does save space, it is very inconvenient for the reader, since he can never memorize the symbols and must continually turn back to the explanation of the letters (if he can remember what page it's on). I will indicate the symbols in this way, in my ms copy, but better symbols should be used in the book. Other books use a one- or two-page chart, listing all the plants and then symbols for their environmental preferences. This accomplishes the same thing, but again the reader must flip back and forth to get full information. Indeed, unless he is familiar with the book, he might not even be aware that the chart is stuck in the back pages.

The answer, I think, is to adopt some easily-memorized symbols for use with each individual plant listing. I suggest:

TEMPERATURE PREFERENCE

A. warm, 60° - 80°
B. moderate, 50° - 70°
C. cool, 45° - 60°

BEST WINDOW

A. north
B. south or east
C. west

LIGHT NEEDS

A. full sun
B. tolerates some direct sun
C. bright spot with no direct sun
D. tolerates continuous shade

SOIL MOISTURE & HUMIDITY NEEDS

A. higher than room humidity, constantly moist soil
B. moderate humidity & soil moisture
C. tolerates dry conditions
D. low humidity & soil moisture required

In my copy, I will use the A-B-C indications, since I don't want to spend hours drawing symbols, but the actual symbols should be the job of the artist. Just for starters, I might suggest the ones on the following page. The object, of course, is that they should be immediately recognizable to the reader--a visual touchstone. OK, then...

---

15 November 1976

Dear

Enclosed are chapters 2 and 4, copy-edited, of your manuscript NO TIME FOR HOUSE PLANTS. I have made a few changes to avoid word repetition or to attempt further clarification for the layman, but no such change is sacred, of course. Following current practice in these matters, I have kept your italics and initial capitals for scientific Latin names but have lowercased common names and Latin names used as common names.

In chapter 2 I have suggested that the three subheadings following "Soil" should be sub-subheadings because they all relate to soil. Perhaps you would like to omit them instead, or set them as run-in sideheads at the beginning of a paragraph as you do similar headings under "Humidity."

In chapter 4 I suggest changing the title further by eliminating "Introducing the"--leaving "Foliage Plants" as the title, thus making it parallel with chapters 5 and 6. Also I have suggested moving the section "Where to Buy House Plants" back to chapter 1, since it does not seem to belong in this chapter devoted to foliage plants alone. You will note in this chapter that what you say on pages 2 and 5 is so similar that you will want to combine the material to avoid repetition.

Please check spelling of all scientific names carefully. By comparing with other books in the field, I found a number of errors, I think, in your typescript. I have not checked every one of them.

Finally, now is the time for you to make any changes you have in mind. Do not wait until you see proofs! We will go straight to pages--omitting--galleys--and any alteration other than correcting typographical errors will be enormously expensive.

- 2

Please return the manuscript to me by 1 December 1976, with all questions answered and all your final changes made. If this proves impossible for you, please let me know when you plan to return it so that I can revise the schedule for your book. My number is: 312 753 3326.

The designer is working on the problem of the symbols and the boxes. We'll let you know what the decision is.

Since I am something of an indoor gardener myself, I enjoyed reading your manuscript. And I learned something from it.

Very sincerely yours,

Catharine Seybold
Senior Manuscript Editor

THE UNIVERSITY OF CHICAGO

DATE 16 November 1976

TO   BY   DEPARTMENT
FROM   KW   DEPARTMENT
IN RE   NO TIME FOR HOUSE PLANTS: A Busy Person's Guide to Indoor Gardening

I have just heard from   about the title change we proposed for his book. He is quite emphatic in arguing for the above title and subtitle. Any other suggestions from anyone? If not, we might as well consider the above final.

KW:rhm

The Association of American University Presses, Inc.
One Park Avenue, New York, N.Y. 10016 · 212 889-6040

November 23, 1976

Ms. Catharine Seybold
Senior Manuscript Editor
THE UNIVERSITY OF CHICAGO PRESS
5801 Ellis Avenue
Chicago, Illinois 60637

Dear Ms. Seybold:

Thank you for your letter of the 15th and for the copy-edited manuscript. I have responded to the queries. Any changes that I have not commented on are fine with me.

I have suggested that the first four pages of chapter 4 be placed at the end of chapter 2. In this way, the general information contained in those pages will not be confined to the chapter on foliage plants but applied to the section that deals with all house plants. I hope that you agree with this suggestion.

I agree that, in chapter 2, the three subheadings following "Soil" should be run-in sideheads, since they all deal with soil and potting mixtures. I would suggest further that the subhead "Soil" be changed to "Potting Media," which would then properly include all three following sideheads.

I have checked scientific spellings as carefully as I can. There are some instances in which even scientists differ in their usage, and I don't suppose there is an omnipotent authority for this nomenclature. In any case, I do not think that any variances will interfere with communication, and this, after all, is paramount.

There are no more changes I will want to make, and I do thank you for an excellent job in copyediting. You have made many passages clearer for the reader, without interfering with my basic style or message. I appreciate this.

Last, I apologize for slandering your piggy-back plant. Please convey my sincere regret.

Sincerely,

UNIVERSITY OF CHICAGO PRESS
5801 S. Ellis Ave. / Chicago, Illinois 60637

AUTHOR: Purvis Mulch
TITLE: NO TIME FOR HOUSE PLANTS

Date: 5 January 1977
Manuscript Editor: CS
House Editor: KW

GENERAL INFORMATION

Number of chapters ... 7
Total number of MS pages
   Front matter
   Text
   End matter
Notes print at:
   Foot of page
   End of book
Subheads (how many levels?) ... 2
Reduced material
Halftones
   Print as figures on text paper
   Print as plates in special section(s)
Text figures ... x

HANDLING OF PROOF

Editor's Proofs
   Galleys ... sets
   Pages ... 1 ... sets

Author's Proofs
   Galleys ... sets
   Pages ... 2 ... sets
   Allow ___ wks for galleys out & back
   Allow 3 wks for pages out & back
   Allow 2 wks for index after last pages out

SPECIAL INSTRUCTIONS

EDITOR'S CHECK LIST

Items to be transmitted for this publication (✓)	Here-with	To come (date)	For printer's use
GENERAL			
Spine & cover layout			
Prelim layouts			
Text layouts			
Spine copy (2 copies)	x		
Running head copy	x		
List spec. characters			
PRELIMS			
Half title			
Series title			
Frontispiece			
Title	x		
Copyright	x		
Dedication			
Epigraph			
Contents	x		
List of illustrations			
List of tables			
List of abbreviations			
Foreword			
Preface	x		
Acknowledgments			
Introduction			
BODY OF BOOK			
Second half title			
Part half titles			
Text (all or part?)	x		
Tables (how many?)			
Plates (how many?)			
Figures (how many?)	50		
Legend copy			
Footnotes			
END MATTER			
Appendix(es)			
Notes			
List of Abbreviations			
Glossary			
Bibliography	x		
Index		x	
Chart	x		

Preliminary specification from The University of Chicago Press

AUTHOR *MULCH, PURVIS* Date: *25.*
TITLE *NO TIME FOR HOUSE PLANTS* Printer:
Series: First Printing No.

FORMAT
Trimmed size: *6 × 8"*
Size of paper:

MARGINS
Head (trimmed): *3½* pica ems
Back: *4* pica ems

PRELIMS
Allowance for prelims and other material not yet supplied
* = copy supplied. Please cast off and add to total below

Half title and Title:	pp.	List of illustrations:	pp.
Dedication:	pp.	Introduction:	pp.
Epigraph:	pp.	Author's note:	pp.
Foreword:	pp.	Acknowledgments:	pp.
Preface:	pp.	Abbreviations:	pp.
Contents:	pp.		

OTHER MATTER

Tables:
Appendixes:
Notes:
Bibliography:
Glossary:
Indexes:

Total to come = pp.
Any text figures or plates will be allowed for separately by The University of Chicago Press

COMPOSITION: MONO/LINO/PHOTO *COMPUGRAPHIC*
Text typeface: *GARAMOND*   Display typeface: *GARAMOND*

Measure: *20* pica ems.   page depth: *36* lines text, excluding running heads and folios

PARTS
New recto/recto or verso/separate half titles
Part-opening pages start recto/verso

CHAPTERS:
New pages/run on/recto or verso
Allow   lines for heading

~~RUNNING HEADS~~ & FOLIOS *9/13 GARAMOND*
verso:
recto:
Folios: Old Style/Modern/in running heads/at foot/centered/left/right/indented:
Number consecutively including prelims/Number prelims separately

Space between heading and text: pts.

TYPE SIZES
Main text: *11/13*
Quoted matter:
Poetry:
Tables:
Footnotes: Aligning figs./superior figs. / * † ‡ § etc.   Number consecutively through: page/section/chapter/book
Appendixes.
Notes:
Bibliography:
Indexes: Flush and hang/run-on

QUOTES: double quotes

HEADINGS All caps 14 pt. and above to be visually letterspaced. All smalls and caps below 14 pt. to be unit spaced: units

Part Nos:
Part headings:
Part drop:

Chapter Nos: *42 PT.*
Chapter headings: *24 PT.*
Chapter drop: lines

SUB-HEADINGS
A to occupy   lines in text. Set in:
B to occupy   lines in text. Set in:
C to occupy   lines in text. Set in:
D to occupy   lines in text. Set in:
E to occupy   lines in text. Set in:
F to occupy   lines in text. Set in:

SPECIMEN
Please trim to correct size and show margins specified
Please return copy and layouts with specimens
Specimen to consist of   pp. showing:

Designer: The University of Chicago Press

MANUFACTURING COST ESTIMATE

Author: Mulch
Title: No Time for House Plants
Quantity: 7500 cloth   paper:
         paper 50 W05
         sheets 43125

Trim size: 6"x8"
No. pages: 160
Series:
Compositor: In house
Printer: } P-D
Binder: }

PLATE COSTS

Text	Estimate	Estimate	Actual
Composition	1600		
5% Alterations	80		
*Addl Galley Proof			
*Addl Page Proof			
Repros			
Negatives	} 400		
Plates			
Blues	30		

Illustrations

Frontispiece			
Drawings/Photographs	1000		
Insert Plates			

Jacket/Cover

Design			
Composition	150		
Plates	125		

Miscellaneous

Printed Cloth Cover			
Dies			
3% Contingencies	102		
Total Plate Cost	3487		

*over two sets

Prepared by: CP
Date:

STOCK COSTS   Qty   Qty   Qty

Presswork	Estimate	Estimate	Actual
Text	766		
Illustrations			

Paper

Text: Sheet size 25"x38"
No. sheets: 43125   at   32.45 /M sheets

Cost	1400		

Illustration: Sheet size
No. sheets: at   /M sheets

Cost			

Binding

spiral at 230 /M	1725		

Jacket/Cover

Printing	200		
Paper	250		

Miscellaneous

coating Prntd Cloth Cover	100		

Freight

local Costs	30		
Total Stock Cost	4471		

Unit Costs

Plate	.4649		
Stock	.5961		
Total	1.0610		

44 / Chicago / Design / Production

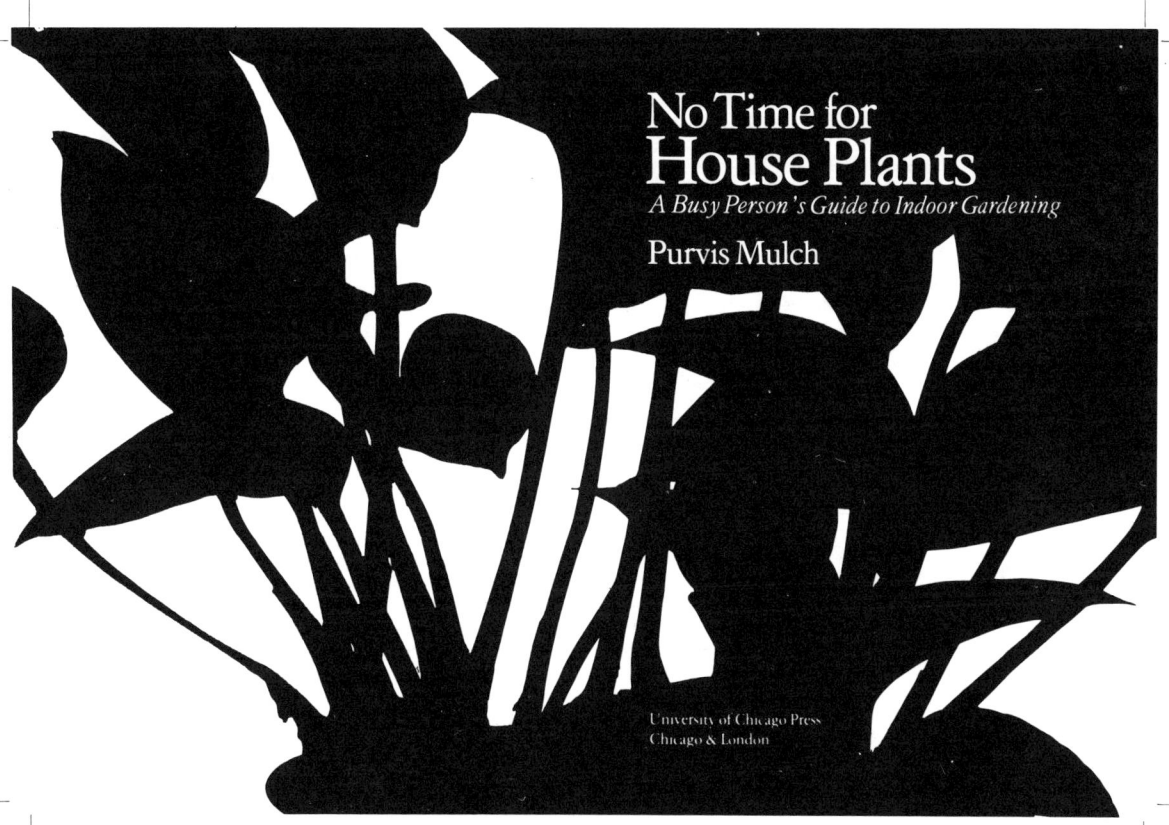

No Time for House Plants

No Time for House Plants

Designed to a trim size of 6 x 8 inches
by the design staff of the University of Chicago Press.
Composed by the University of Chicago Press
in Compugraphic Garamond with display lines
in Compugraphic Headliner Garamond.
Printed by Kingsport Press, Inc. on
60# Springhill Offset, wove finish.

PAGE 16

PAGE 1

REPEAT ON PAGE 7

The University of Chicago Press, Chicago 60637
The University of Chicago Press, Ltd., London

© 1977 by Purvis Mulch
All rights reserved. Published 1977

Printed in the United States of America
80 79 78 77   9 8 7 6 5 4 3 2 1

Library of Congress Cataloging in Publication Data
Mulch, Purvis
    No Time for House Plants
      1. Agriculture—United States. 2. Hobbies.
PQ000.000
ISBN 0-266-00000-0

Contents

Preface
1: **The Secrets of No-Work House Plant Success**

2: **Understanding House Plants**
    The Basic House Plant
    How a Plant Feeds
    Parts of the Plant
    Soil
    Acidity/Alkalinity
    Potting Mixtures
    Nutrient Maintenance
    Containers
    Watering
    Humidity
    Ventilation
    Temperature
    Light
    Pruning and Training
    Repotting
    Propagation

3: **Plant Troubles and Cures**
    Improper Handling and Care
    Insect Foes
    Diseases

PAGE 4

PAGE 5

4: **Foliage Plants**

5: **Cacti and Other Succulents**
  Care of Cacti and Succulents
  Potting Soil for Cacti
  Introducing the Cacti
  The Unusual Succulents

6: **Flowering House Plants**
  Forcing Spring Bulbs
  Care of Gift Plants

7: **Special Indoor Gardens**
  Dish Gardens and Planters
  Bottle Gardens and Terrariums
  House Plants from Kitchen Scraps
  An Indoor Kitchen Garden

Bibliography
Index

No Time for House Plants

4 Foliage Plants

In this chapter, we will survey many of the house plants grown primarily for their foliage. Some of them, under favorable conditions, will flower from time to time, although few should be selected for their flowering abilities. Nearly all of these plants are fairly easy to grow and maintain, giving even the beginner a wide variety of plants from which to choose.

The plants are listed in alphabetical order, according to their common or popular names. If there is no popular name for a plant, or if there is more than one, but no dominant name, the plant is listed by its scientific or Latin name. The index, which includes both common and scientific names, provides a convenient means of cross-checking names.

The special symbols accompanying each plant name will provide a quick and convenient guide to that plant's requirements (see key, p. 000). Remember, however, that these are guides and not sharp demands. Many of these plants are tolerant by nature, and will take to an east window as well as a west window, and can tolerate some direct sunlight even if none is recommended. Most crucial, perhaps, are the guides to humidity and moisture, since overwatering is one thing that almost no plant will tolerate.

African Boxwood (*Myrsine africana*)
This slow-growing boxwood has red stems, but otherwise is similar to regular boxwood (q.v.). Many people think it is even more graceful. African boxwood is a good plant for terrariums, if the atmosphere is not too hot.

Aralia (*Fatsia japonica*)
Sometimes sold as *Aralia sieboldii*. Beautiful, bright green, leathery, maplelike leaves highlight this cheerful plant. In appearance, it is similar to the castor oil plant, and in fact is sometimes called false castor oil plant. It thrives in a cool spot. Aralia can easily grow leggy, and so it should be pruned annually in order to encourage it into bushy growth. It will attain a height of four feet at maturity.

A striking hybrid, *Fatshedera lizei*, crosses *F. japonica* and ivy (*Hedera*) forming a climbing plant with maple-shaped leaves, which is tolerant of adverse conditions.

There is also a plant called false aralia, which has graceful and feathery foliage. It bears no resemblance to the true aralia and is difficult to grow.

Asparagus

There are two kinds of asparagus suitable for growing as house plants—*Asparagus plumosus* (fern asparagus), with slender, needle-like dark green leaves, forming a feathery appearance, and *A. sprengeri* ("emerald feather") which has thicker yellow-green leaves and drooping stems. The latter makes a good plant for hanging baskets, and produces red berries at Christmastime. Both like some sun in the summer and full sun in the winter, and both can grow to a height of about two feet.

Australian Laurel (*Pittosporum tobira*)
A tolerant and slow-growing plant whose leaves, glossy and leathery, resemble those of the rhododendron. Australian laurel will grow vigorously bushy and does not require much attention. Florists often use the leaves in floral arrangements.

An interesting variegated form is *P. tobira variegata*.

Australian Umbrella Tree (*Schefflera actinophylla*)

Here is a very attractive and vigorous-growing tree with rich, glossy leaves that radiate like an umbrella from the ends of the leaf stalks. It is a tough and rewarding plant, which grows to six feet and can be propagated by air-layering.

Australian umbrella tree is also sold as *Brassaia actinophylla*. A dwarf variety, *B. actinophylla compacta*, is also available.

Baby's Tears (*Helxine soleirolii*)

This low creeper is also called Irish moss. It likes a constantly moist (but not soggy) soil, and higher than average humidity. It makes a good ground cover for terrariums, but will also grow in a pot if adequate humidity is provided. Baby's tears may appear to die in the colder months, but after an adequate rest period it will spring back to life.

Black Pepper (*Piper nigrum*)
This is not a very attractive plant, but it produces real peppercorns which you may use at the table, and is a good conversation piece for that reason. The plant's green berries later turn red, then dry up and turn black. Pick the dried-up black corns, dry them thoroughly for several weeks in an open spot, then use them in your pepper grinder. Care for the black pepper is the same as that required for philodendron. It is not a demanding plant.

Boxwood (*Buxus*)
The same plant which grows the most prized hedges outdoors can make a very attractive house plant. Boxwood with glossy, bright-green leaves is slow-growing and dependable, a good subject for bonsai, the ancient Oriental art of growing dwarf trees and shrubs. *B. sempervirens* and *B. microphylla japonica* (Japanese boxwood) are the two popular species.

Bromeliads (*Bromeliaceae*)

There are more than eighteen hundred varieties of this popular group, many of which are suitable for growing as house plants. Some of them produce attractive flowers, but most are grown for their striking and variegated leaf patterns. One distinctive feature of the bromeliads is the rosette leaves forming a small water cup which the plant uses to hold reserve supplies of water in its natural habitat—the crotches of trees in Central and South America. In the home, keep the cup filled with water, changing it weekly to keep it fresh.

A few of the more common bromeliads are *Aechmea*, *Ananas* (pineapple), *Billbergia*, *Cryptanthus* (zebra plant), *Dyckia*, *Tillandsia* (Spanish moss), and *Vriesia*.

Caladium
Caladiums, with their spectacularly colored and variegated leaves, are equally at home in the garden or on the window sill. They are ideal additions to plant groupings on porch or patio in the summer and early autumn. Give them bright light, but not long periods of direct sun in summer, if you want the brightest leaf colors.

Caladiums are grown from tubers, which can be divided easily to produce new plants. Start the tubers in regular potting soil at a very warm temperature—80°–90°—and move the young plants to a cooler spot when they have appeared. They will attain a height of about one foot.

Cast Iron Plant (*Aspidistra elatior*)
This is perhaps the easiest plant in the world to grow, as its name suggests. It is virtually impossible to neglect it to death. It is also called saloon plant, since it was one of the few that could survive in Victorian taverns, and was made immortal by George Orwell in his novel *Keep the Aspidistra Flying*. If you cannot grow the aspidistra, you may safely conclude that you have a purple yellow thumb and are hopelessly irredeemable as a gardener.

The "cast iron plant," which grows about two feet tall, seems to thrive even better when kept slightly potbound, and it will appreciate having its leaves washed occasionally. A white-striped species is called *A. variegata*.

Chamaeranthemum igneum
This low, spreading herb has attractive, dark green leaves with reddish yellow veins. It is suitable for hanging baskets or as a low contrast in large plant groupings. It does like warm temperatures and high humidity, however, and might not be suitable for dry apartments.

Chinese Evergreen (*Aglaonema*)

Here is an attractive and low-growing plant that is very easy to grow. It will stand abuse almost as easily as the cast iron plant.

There are at least ten commonly found species of the *Aglaonema*, the most popular of which, *A. modestum*, has interestingly mottled leaves. Perhaps the most attractive, however, is *A. pseudo-bracteatum*, which is sometimes difficult to find in stores and greenhouses.

14

Cissus

Cissus is a vine plant that offers a number of interesting and attractive species. Most are vigorous climbers, suitable for training on a trellis or for adding to hanging baskets.

Among the more popular species are *C. rhombifolia* (grape ivy), which is one of the most popular of all house plants; *C. antarctica* (kangaroo vine), which prefers a small pot; *C. antarctica minima* (miniature kangaroo vine); *C. rotundifolia;* and *C. discolor* (begonia ivy), which is perhaps the most spectacular of the genus, although difficult to grow.

Of all the *Cissus,* grape ivy is the easiest to grow, which doubtless accounts for a large share of its popularity.

Coleus

This old favorite has velvety leaves sporting bright splashes of reds, pinks, purples, and yellows. There is a seemingly endless number of varieties of coleus, nearly all of them interesting, most growing twelve to eighteen inches in height.

Coleus is equally happy outdoors, grown as an annual in the north, or in a window garden. It can be grown easily from seed, and stem tip cuttings can be taken from established indoor plants. If you grow coleus outdoors in summer, take some cuttings before the first autumn freeze and root them for growing as house plants.

The soil for coleus should be kept damp, but not soggy. Pinch back plants often to encourage bushy growth.

Copper Leaf (*Acalypha wilkesiana*)

This is a member of the Spurge family, which features copper-colored foliage. A close relative, *A. hispida,* is described in this book under flowering plants.

Bibliography

Artificial Light Gardening

Bickford, Elwood D. and Stuart Dunn. *Lighting for Plant Growth.* Kent, Ohio: Kent State University Press, 1972. One of the best books on the subject; especially valuable to those who have had some experience in the area.

Cherry, Elaine C. *Fluorescent Light Gardening.* New York: Van Nostrand Reinhold Co., 1965.

Elbert, George A. *The Indoor Light Gardening Book.* New York: Crown Publishers, Inc., 1975.

Fitch, Charles Marden. *The Complete Book of Houseplants under Lights.* New York: Hawthorn Books, 1975.

Kranz, Frederick H. and Jacqueline. *Gardening Indoors under Lights.* New York: Viking Press, rev. 1971.

Begonias

Brilmayer, Bernice. *All about Begonias.* New York: Doubleday Publishing Co., 1960.

Kramer, Jack. *Begonias, Indoors and Out.* New York: E. P. Dutton & Co., 1967.

15

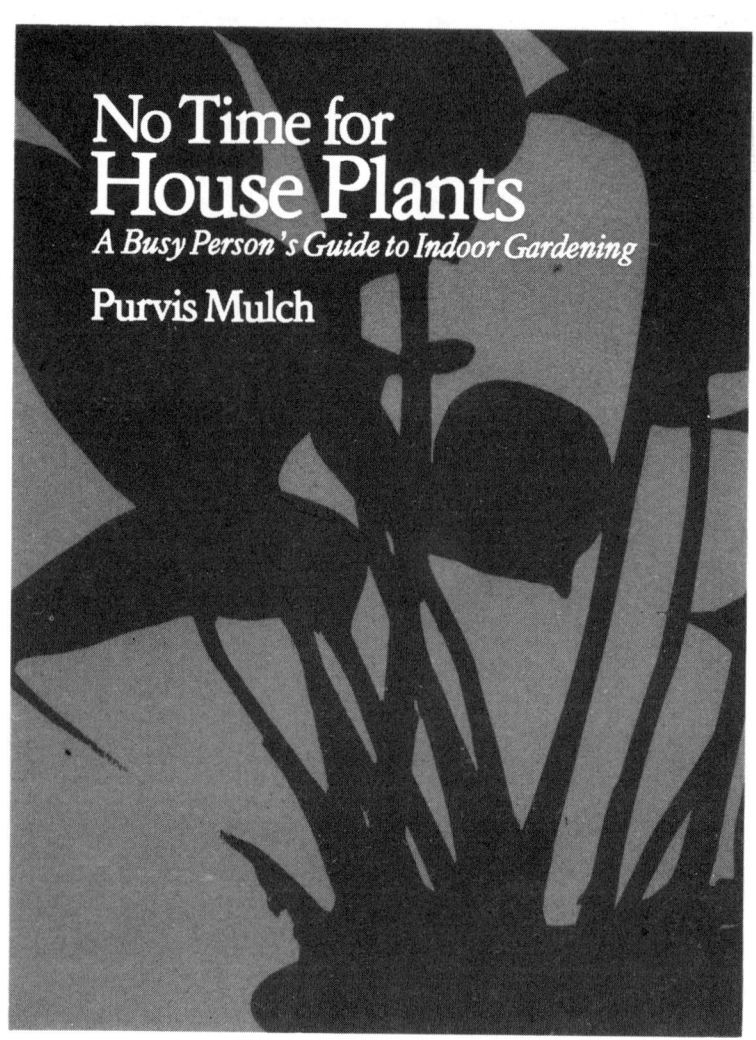

Book Order The University of Chicago Press, Ellis Avenue and 58th Street, Chicago, Illinois 60637

	Order No.	Date	Delivery
	Composition & repros		
	Printer		
	Binder		

Author/Editor
Title
Series — Edition — Impression
Print Quantity — Cloth — Bind — Flat
Print Quantity — Paper — Bind — Flat

Plate Cost $ — Charge to 4-9002-30-0501
Stock Cost $ — Charge to 0-0134-01-0501
Alterations — 10% to composition; balance to suspense 0-0124-04-0501

Paper Stock: Body — Sheet size — Trim size
Paper Stock: Cover — — Est. total pages
Inserts/Wraparounds/Frontispiece
Special/Labels

Typeface: Text — Quoted Matter
Poetry — Tabular
Footnotes — Appendixes
Bibliography — Legends
Index — Figs: OS/Mod.
Half titles — Chapters start — Type page
Running heads: verso — — Columns   Lines
Running heads: recto — — Head margin
Artwork, photographs, etc. — — Back margin
Printing process: (text): Offset/Letterpress/Other — Printing process: (illustrations): Offset/Letterpress/Other
Please note:

Binding — Rounded & backed — Flatback — Perfectbound
Boards — Stain — Headbands
Endsheets: Regular/Reinforced — Color — — Printed
Cloth — — 1 Piece — 2 Piece
— — 3 Piece
Stamping — Spine — Front — Back
Colors: Ink/Foil
Frontispiece — Wraparounds — Inserts — Tips
Jackets/Covers

Proofs
Sample Pages
Galleys — Pages
Repros — Blues
F & G's — Stamped sample case
Bound dummy for jacket art

Please note: — Page count:
— Prelims
— Text
— Illustrations
— Index
— Total

Mulch NO TIME FOR HOUSEPLANTS   KW:CS : IJ   PD   75CD
0-226-00000-0   TRADE Fall 77

MS rec'd	To MS ed	To author	From author	To prod	Pld for comp	Galleys rec'd	Galleys back	Pages rec'd	Pages back	Index typed	Repros ck	Blues ck	Sheets printed	Delivery
10/4	11/19	12/3	12/17					1/27	2/10	2/10	2/13	3/11	4/1	Late April
10/1	10/6	11/15	11/26	1/5	1/6			1/20	2/7					

Des MS to prod.	Design finished	Estimate in	Sample pages					Ja'cover copy in	Ja'cover design	Ja'cover printed	Ja'cover delivered	Sample case ok
eP/JEA	12/15							12/21	1/6	2/13	3/25	Apr
10/1	12/29	1/3	1/13					12/27	1/6			

NOTE: The card above forms part of the preproduction and production schedules, which are issued every three weeks and cover all books in work. The card is begun and carried through the preproduction stage by the manuscript editor, then transferred to the production controller, who records the manufacturing events. The upper rows of boxes are estimated target dates, the lower rows actual completion dates.

Early Fall 1977

[x] New Book
[ ] Revision
[ ] Reprint

Book Estimate and Release

Author Purvis Mulch   **Editor/Trans.**
Title NO TIME FOR HOUSE PLANTS: A Busy Person's Guide to Indoor Gardening
Series na   ISBN (cloth) 0-226-00000-0   (paper) 0-226-

Editor's Release
Royalties 10% n.r. 1st 2,500; 12½% n.r. next 2,500; 15% n.r. thereafter on domestic cloth; 2/3 thereof on foreign cloth; 7½% n.r. on paper and d.m.
Other fees or charges   none
Subsidy $ none   from   Copyright by   University of Chicago
Contract no. 9728   Market   world
Series contract no. na   Target pub. date   (cloth)   June 1977
BUP approval na   (paper)
Remarks   Codes: ODE-OJD-

Editor   Kimberly Wiar   Date   9/29/76
(KW) 9/30/76

Sales Release

	Print	Bind	Price	Discount	No. pages	Size	Pub. date
~~Cloth~~							
Paper - spiral	7500	all	$5.95	Trade (40% av)	160	6 x 8"	Sept. 77

Remarks   Spiral bound with stiff covers. Suggest fall publication when interest in houseplants revives.

Main code: H-ODE   Marketing Manager   P. Kaiserlian   Date   2/10/77

Financial Release and Estimate

	Cloth	Paper		Cloth	Paper
Plate cost	$	$ 3,486	No. copies sold		7,250
Stock cost 7,500 copies	$	$ 4,471	Mfg. break even		2,228
Royalties	$	$ 3,262	Total break even		3,142
Less subsidy	$	$ -	Net price per copy	$	$ 3.57
Total cost	$	$ 11,219	Less mfg. cost per copy	$	$ 1.06
Sales revenue	$	$ 25,882	Less royalty	$	$ .45
Contribution to operation	$	$ 14,663	Gross margin	$	$ 2.06
			Gross margin %		57.7

Remarks

On the terms set forth above this book meets/~~does not meet~~ current financial requirements of the Press

Business Manager   Date   2/14/77

Director's Release
Remarks

PR 156-1M-7/70   Approved Director   Date   2/15

DIRECTOR'S COPY

52 / Chicago / Design / Production

THE UNIVERSITY OF CHICAGO

DATE 15 November 1976

To PK   DEPARTMENT Marketing

FROM RD   DEPARTMENT Promotion

IN RE: Promotion plan for <u>No Time for Houseplants</u>

Despite its catchy title, we fear that NTFHP may appear to be only another "basic" houseplant book -- of which there are too many already. The "no time", "busy person's" handle helps distinguish it, but only to a point. Hawthorne Books has just published something called <u>The Office Gardener</u> and if the offices to which this book is intended are anything like ours, there's not much time for office plants either. NTFHP is entering a flooded market and may suffer (overwatering <u>is</u> the most common cause of ill health for houseplants) if an appropriate promotion strategy is not found.

Because we have chosen to enter these waters cautiously, a mass advertising campaign directed to consumers is out of the question. After all just about everyone considers him/herself busy these days, so the market is rather large. And nothing short of a fortune could buy NTFHP's way into the nation's consciousness as one of <u>the</u> basic houseplant books (such as <u>The New York Times Book of Houseplants</u>), or make it as ubiquitously resplendent as Sunset Books spinning racks of house and garden books.

Our promotional strategy is designed to capture those "busy houseplant novices" who take the time to go to a bookstore, looking for a basic guide and are confronted with an impossible number of books from which to choose. Overwhelmed, our customer turns to the friendly, informed clerk and inquires,"What would you recommend for someone who wants to grow a few plant but who really has no time for houseplants?" And our friendly, informed clerk will respond, "I have <u>just</u> what you're looking for," not only because NTFHP is just what the customer has in mind, but because our promotional plan has provided that clerk with good economic reasons to recommend our book above all others.

The aim, then of our promotional efforts is to make NTFHP attractive to booksellers to stock by making it easy for them to sell. The plan entails the following:
Total budget: $2,690

1. Space advertising: As I stated, one can go broke doing this sort of thing. We will place a single half-page ad in PW six to eight weeks before delivery of the book to announce its pub date and our special offers to booksellers (see below). Cost: $800

2. Statement stuffers. We will prepare 15,000 two color statement stuffers that can be imprinted with the bookseller's address at a later date. These will be offered to those who order 50 or more copies of the book. Minimum quantity of 500 statement stuffers for imprinting by the Press. Good booksellers know their customers and can direct these to likely buyers. They help generate larger bookstore orders and more frequent reorders. Cost: $450

3. Window posters: Since we planned to chart the Mulch "no time" system on a colorful wall poster, I shall ask the production department to overprint 1,000 posters for booksellers to use as window displays. Again, this makes our book stand out in the store. Always appreciated. Cost: $200

4. Ten copy pre-pack. We have offered our Spanish Dictionary in a 10-copy counter display pre-pack with good success and feel that a similar treatment would help NTFHP. A pre-pack can put the book in the spotlight in the store. This is especially important in a crowded field such as houseplant books. It makes it easy to display a title in other areas of the store, such as by the cash register, and pick up "impulse buyers" as they check out. (Just like the "supermarket trap"). One pre-pack qualifies the customer for full trade discount. They also make it easy for the warehouse to fill and ship orders quickly. Cost: $240

5. Co-op ads. $1,000 will be held in the advertising budget for co-op ads that will be arranged by the salesmen at their discretion. Once again, we're trusting the booksellers' knowledge of his/her area and customers.

THE UNIVERSITY OF CHICAGO

Date 17 November 1976

To RD
cc: VH, GT

Department Promotion

From PK

Department Marketing

In re Promotion plan for NO TIME FOR HOUSEPLANTS

Thank you for your promotional plan for this spring title. I think you have covered everything we discussed in our marketing meetings about the book.

Since that time I have had the cost estimates. With our spiral binding and paper cover (which incidentally will be quite sturdy) we are able to come up with an attractive low price of $5.95. I think this will help it in competing with other titles in the stores; we are not expecting much in the way of library sales because of LJ's usually cool reception to more houseplant books.

Because of the low price, we do not have much to work with in the way of an advertising budget, and can make best use of our money with the kind of program you suggest.

Other possibilities we've thought of at our meetings I'll note here as a reminder to publicity and the sales department: a display at the spring Garden Show at McCormick place when many gardening aids are for sale; informing garden-supply wholesalers of the book and our promotional aids--by mail since we will not have time to call on them for this one title.

Mulch back cover

No Time for Houseplants
Purvis Mulch

Here is a beautifully-illustrated, complete guide to houseplant care designed for people who have "no time for houseplants."

Purvis Mulch, who has been writing about gardening and plant care for more than twenty years, has written this book for the novice indoor gardener who simply hasn't much time to spend caring for sensitive, exotic houseplants. He has brought together everything you need to know to grow interesting and beautiful houseplants without really working at it.

The Mulch "no time" system of houseplant care is built upon two fundamental rules: (1) Choose plants that will tolerate adverse conditions. (2) Provide your plants with conditions that will encourage growth without your constant attention.

No Time for Houseplants provides the busy indoor gardener with a beautiful wall poster that is as useful as it is attractive. It charts the light, watering, humidity, and temperature requirements for more than 100 "no time" indoor plants. The book contains all the essential information on topics such as

*Choosing the right plant -- picking healthy specimens of those varieties that are easiest to grow
*Potting mixtures, fertilizers, and containers
*Pest control and other problems
*Propagation and repotting
*Terrariums, dish gardens, and even growing vegetables indoors

PURVIS MULCH is a graduate of the University of Iowa and a former editor of Organic Gardening. He is the author of The Wisconsin Garden Guide and some fifty articles on gardening.

Paper   ISBN:0-226-
The University of Chicago Press

Mulch catalog copy

No Time for Houseplants
A Busy Person's Guide to Indoor Gardening
Purvis Mulch

New books on houseplants and indoor gardening number in the dozens each publishing season. But most of these evermore specialized titles are written for green-thumbed enthusiasts who spend countless hours tending to their exotic flora. Until now no one has written a houseplant book for busy people -- and today, that includes most of us. Here is a beautifully illustrated guide to houseplant care designed for people who have "no time for houseplants."

Purvis Mulch, who has been writing about gardening and plant care for more than twenty years, has written this book for the busy, novice indoor gardener. He has brought together everything they need to know to grow interesting and beautiful houseplants without really working at it.

No Time for Houseplants includes a wall poster that is as useful as it is attractive. It charts the light, watering, humidity, and temperature requirements for more than 100 "no time" indoor plants. The book contains all the essential information on topics such as

*Choosing the right plant -- picking healthy specimens of those varieties that are easiest to grow
*Potting mixtures, fertilizers, and containers
*Pest control and other problems
*Propagation and repotting
*Terrariums, dish gardens, and even growing vegetables indoors

No Time for Houseplants may be ordered in a handsome 10-copy counter display pre-pack.

The University of Chicago Press
Marketing Department
Chicago, Illinois 60637
Since 1891 Publishers of Scholarly Books and Journals

Author Questionnaire

Your answers to the following questions will help us plan an effective advertising and promotion campaign for your work—and will be used in preparing jacket and catalogue copy and publicity releases, as well as in answering inquiries from libraries, booksellers, review media, and others. We urge you to expand upon your replies to any extent necessary to give us adequate information. Please return this questionnaire at the earliest possible date.

I. PERSONAL INFORMATION

Name (as you wish it to appear on title page): Jerry Minnich
Date: November 11, 1976

Title of manuscript: No Time for House Plants: A Busy Person's Guide to Indoor Gardening

Your date and place of birth: 7/6/33; Allentown, Pa.
Citizenship: USA

Home address (please include Zip Code): 315 N. Franklin St., Madison, WI 53703
Home telephone number: 608; 255-6065

Office address (please include Zip Code): Box 1379, Madison, WI 53701
Office telephone number: 608; 262-7756 (262-4928)

Married? Spouse's name? divorced
Children? 2

II. PROFESSIONAL INFORMATION

Present position: Asst. Dir., Univ. of Wisconsin Press, 1971-

Former positions:
Marketing Mgr., Univ. of Wisconsin Press, 1969-71
Journals Mgr., Univ. of Wisconsin Press, 1965-69
Editor, Vigor magazine, 1963-65
Assoc. Editor, Organic Gardening magazine, 1953-57; 1961-63

Colleges and universities attended (with dates and degrees, if any):
University of Iowa, B.A., 1961

Professional and other honors and offices:

Principal countries, cities, and states in which you have lived, with approximate dates:

Allentown, Pa., 1933-57; 1961-63
Iowa City, Ia., 1957-61
Newark, N.J., 1963-65
Madison, Wis., 1965-

Any other pertinent biographical data for use on book jackets, etc.:

(from jacket of my other book) Jerry Minnich has been gardening and writing about gardening for more than twenty years, the last ten in Wisconsin. He has published more than fifty articles on home gardening, most in Organic Gardening and Farming magazine, where he was formerly associate editor, but also in a number of other publications including House Beautiful. He has also contributed to several larger gardening books, including The Encyclopedia of Organic Gardening and The Complete Book of Compost (Rodale Press). Minnich was born and raised in Allentown, Pa., and was graduated from the University of Iowa. He is married [no longer], has two children, and has lived and worked in Madison since 1965.

Books published:
title (state whether author or editor) | publisher | year | approx. sales
(Please indicate book club adoptions, paperback reprints, serializations, and foreign editions)

A Wisconsin Garden Guide; Wisconsin House, Ltd.; 1975; 15,000

Other important published writings (journal articles, etc.):
title | where published | year

Am currently garden editor (contributing) for Countryside magazine; monthly column.

Currently working on The Earthworm Book (tentative title) to be published by Rodale Press in 1977.

Please enclose a glossy print of a recent photograph of yourself, if readily available. Be sure the photographer is willing to allow its reproduction without fee.

none available at present

III. MARKETING INFORMATION

Please describe the content of your manuscript and the *reasons for its importance* in 300 or more words. We hope you will bear in mind that *this information will be our primary source for preparing jacket, catalogue, and advertising copy*. Please do not refer us to your introduction, since this may not be available to us at the time information is needed. If it is available, we shall of course refer to it.

In 1973, with the purchase of a new house, I was determined to increase my house plant population. Still, I realized that, with my busy schedule, I would not have much time to devote to indoor plants. I was frequently gone for long periods of time, and many days, even while in town, I simply have no time to fuss with plants.

I therefore sought to find methods to raise interesting and beautiful house plants with the least amount of effort. All the house plant books I checked, however, were apparently written by enthusiasts who spent unending hours in careful watering, potting, repotting, propagating, tying up, inducing to flowering, humidifying, bathing, and even talking to their plants, in an effort to get them to grow. There was no book for the casual house plant grower.

There is now such a book. By researching many sources, and with the aid of personal experimentation and past experience, I have narrowed down the crucial requirements for a "no-time" indoor house plant population. The research yielded two cardinal rules: Choose plants that are tolerant of adverse conditions, and then give them the right conditions to grow without your constant attention.

The implementation of these rules form the crux of this book. I explain how to choose plants, tell which are the easiest to grow, and explain the conditions of light, soil moisture, humidity, and temperature that each of more than a hundred indoor plants requires. I explain, in short, how your house plants can live well without your constant attention and painstaking devotion.

The chapter on understanding house plants is critically important to the "no-time" system, since it details the initial requirements plants need for success, including potting mixtures, fertilizing, containers, watering, humidity, ventilation, temperature, light, and pruning. When these conditions are met at the very beginning, countless hours will be saved later in nursing plants or attempting to track down troubles.

There is a separate chapter devoted to plant troubles and cures, and special sections on artificial light, summer care, and lists of plants for various conditions of light and temperature. For those who wish to devote a little more time to raising house plants, there is detailed information on repotting, propagation, training, dish gardens, planters, bottle gardens and terrariums, kitchen scrap gardens, and growing vegetables indoors.

The bulk of the book, however, comprises listings of more than a hundred "easy" foliage plants, flowering plants, and succulents, including cacti, giving light, soil moisture, and humidity requirements for each.

For the home owner or apartment dweller who wants to raise several dozen attractive house plants while spending only a few minutes a day in caring for them, this book will tell everything that is necessary to know in order to achieve success.

Please list scholarly journals, magazines, and newspapers which you believe are most likely to carry a review of your book and be most suitable for possible space advertising:

(a) In the U.S.:

Organic Gardening and Farming
House Beautiful
Apartment Dweller
Mother Jones
Rolling Stone
Ms
(other general magazines going to single, affluent audience)

(b) Abroad:
none

Please list columnists, editorial writers, radio and television commentators, etc., who in your opinion would be interested in your book:

don't know of any

Please list, in order of importance, names and addresses of persons whose good opinion of the book might broaden its audience—those to whom, for instance, advance copies of the book might be sent by us for comments that could be quoted in advertising: (Please be selective)

Jeff Cox, Rodale Press, Inc.
Elvin McDonald, House Beautiful

Please list those professors and their institutions that should be approached with a view to the classroom adoption of the book:

none

Sales / Promotion / Chicago / 55

/PAPER/ Review Distribution List

Date: June 1977
Attn. Langley:
--Charge to Acct. # 4-9010-48-0501
--Enclose review with each book
--Special instructions

TITLE: NO TIME FOR HOUSEPLANTS

AUTHOR/ED.: Purvis Mulch

Approved by VH   Paper ISBN # 0-226- 00000-0

PLEASE SHIP AS SOON AS POSSIBLE   Virginia Heiserman 753-2594

Editor, Original Paperbacks
ALA BOOKLIST
Am. Library Assn.
50 East Huron
Chicago, IL 60611

Book Review Editor
AMERICAN HOME
641 Lexington Avenue
New York, NY 10022

Book Review Editor
AMERICAN HORTICULTURALIST
American Horticultural Society
Mt. Vernon, VT 22121

F. H. Hilner, Editor
AMERICAN NURSERYMAN
310 So. Michigan Avenue
Chicago, IL 60604

Bohdan S. Wynar, Editor
AMERICAN REFERENCE BOOKS ANNUAL
P. O. Box 263
Littleton, CO 80160

David Jordan, Editor
APARTMENT LIFE
Meredith Corp.
1716 Locust Street, Meredith Bldg.
Des Moines, IA 50365

Book Review Editor
APARTMENT LIVING
DeBare Publ. Co.
Box 1838
Wichita, KS 67218

Mr. John Barkham
JOHN BARKHAM REVIEWS
27 East 65th Street
New York, NY 10021

Book Review Editor
BETTER HOMES & GARDENS
1716 Locust Street
Des Moines, IA 50336

Book Review Editor
THE BOSTON PHOENIX
100 Mass. Avenue
Boston, Mass. 02115

Connie Dodds Devit, Editor
BUDGET DECORATING
Maco Publ. Co.
699 Madison Avenue
New York, NY 10021

Edith Proctor
CALIFORNIA SENIOR CITIZEN NEWS
2222 Albatros Drive
San Diego, CA 92101

Features Editor
CANADIAN HOMES MAGAZINE
Southstar Publ. Co.
401 Bay Street
Toronto, Ont. M5H 2Y8
CANADA

Book Review Editor
CANADIAN INTERIORS
Maclean-Hunter Ltd.
Toronto, Ont. CANADA M5W 1A7

The entire review mailing includes an additional five pages listing appropriate publications. A generous review mailing, the cheapest form of advertising, is consistent with our "less is more" approach to marketing this special book.

THE MIT PRESS

Table of Contents

Acquisition and Administration

General Statement / 59
Letter of Receipt of Manuscript and Log-In / 63
Readers' Reports / 64
Publishing Proposal / 65
Letter of Agreement / 68
Financial Projection and Publishing Log / 70
New Publication Information Sheet / 71
Turnover Form / 72
Marketing Plan / 74

Editorial

Editorial and Production Launch Reports / 75
Schedule Card and Bound Book List / 76
Edited Manuscript / 77
Covering Letter to Author and Style Sheet / 91
Transmittals of Proof and Sample Pages / 93
Transmittal to Production / 95

Production / Design

Preliminary Manufacturing Estimate / 97
Memo to Typesetter and Page Layout / 98
Composition Specifications / 99
Sample Pages / 100
Jacket Print Order and Design Specifications / 109
Production, Printing, and Binding Specifications / 110
Manufacturing Cost Estimate / 111
Final New Publication Information Sheet / 112

Sales and Promotion

Covering Letter to Author / 113
Author Questionnaire / 114
Covering Letter and Jacket Copy / 117
Promotion and Marketing Plan / 118

THE PUBLISHING PROCESS

At the MIT Press acquisition is not a passive or rote process. Increasingly, successful acquisition is the result of an active search process. The formulation of an idea for a publishing program may find its origin within the Press, or through exchange of ideas with faculty. While today the Press conducts a growing part of the acquisition process through the development and implementation of publishing plans for each of its area programs, it would be misleading to say the the Press deliberately acquires all the properties it wishes to publish within the context of definitive plans. A significant part of our program grows out of our alertness to opportunities and possibilities for publishing successfully. The Mulch book presented such an opportunity.

The Acquisition Department screens approximately 1000 proposals, outlines or partial manuscripts each year. Perhaps 90% of the unsolicited manuscripts are rejected, most before outside scholarly or professional review. After initial screening, promising manuscripts and proposals are thoroughly read by outside reviewers, including members of the MIT faculty. In most cases two or three critical reviews are obtained before it is determined that a proposal to publish should be written and presented to the Editorial Board for consideration and approval.

The proposal to publish presents a complete profile of the book: it identifies and informs about special considerations for the editorial, design, production, marketing, and financial staff at the Press. The Acquisition Editor reviews the proposal with departments and with the Director, then finalizes the proposal, appends reviews and samples of the manuscript, and sends the proposal to each of the 10 members of the Editorial Board, in advance of the meeting. The Board meets for a half-day every third week to discuss the proposals on the agenda. After discussion of each proposal, the Board may accept it for publication, defer it for further consideration, or reject it. The Board's rejection rate is quite low, but the threat of rejection is effective in assuring quality submissions by the editors.

Following the Editorial Board meeting, projects are entered onto a seasonal Publishing Log, which along with copies of the proposal is distributed to all departments of the Press. In the interval between signature of the contract and delivery of a complete and satisfactory manuscript, Acquisition Editors and members of the Editorial, Marketing, and Design Departments might be involved in discussions with authors regarding the special needs of the manuscript.

After the manuscript is delivered, it is reviewed again before the Acquisition Editor launches it into the publishing process. By the time he has completed the manuscript, the author has also filled out an Author's Questionnaire which is reviewed both by Marketing and Acquisition. By providing the Press with the author's view of the market and specific interested segments of it, where he feels the book should be reviewed, publicity activities he will participate in, etc., this questionnaire helps the formulation of a marketing strategy for the book.

As the book is launched into the system, the Acquisition Editor prepares a Turnover document and a Release form which accompany the manuscript to the Editorial, Design, and Production Departments within the Press. The Turnover form is a means of updating all important information presented in the original proposal. Its preliminary review by the Editorial, Design, and Production Departments results in more accurate estimates of editorial difficulty, copyediting time, and any special design and production problems. The Marketing Department revises its estimate for print runs and prices at this stage, a bound book date is established, and the book is placed on a seasonal list. All this new information is brought to a formal Launch meeting for the book and after discussion is incorporated into a launch document and a Publication Information Sheet that becomes the basic control mechanism through which schedules, costs, and other variables of the publishing process are monitored.

The Turnover document also includes a preliminary Marketing Strategy prepared by the Acquisition Editor. This strategy is reviewed by various members of the Marketing and Promotion staffs, and following the Launch, at a time during the editing, design, and markup stage, before the manuscript is committed to composition, a marketing meeting is held to detail our approach to selling the book through a variety of channels: direct mail, promotion, publicity, exhibits, adoptions, subsidiary rights, book clubs, etc. Because of the necessary lead time, implementation of the marketing plan begins well in advance of the book's availability.

The Release/Publication Information document itself is reviewed by the Director at the Launch meeting, then when the book is sent to the compositor, again when the book is sent to the manufacturer, and before the book is actually released to the warehouse for shipping to buyers. MIT Press books take from six weeks to 18 months to publish, with an average of eight months for the typical book and 12 for those with more complex typographical and design demands.

At the production end, once a manuscript is launched into the system, copies of it are sent simultaneously to the Design and Editorial Departments. The Editorial Department will be responsible for working with the author on developmental editing, copyediting, and proofreading, and generally for monitoring the proofing cycle. While the work is in process in the Editorial Department, the Design Department is producing design specifications and sample pages for each book. When the manuscript is out of editing and after it is checked by the author, the Design Department then marks the manuscript against design specifications for the compositor. At this point the Production Department takes over the monitoring of the schedule as it releases the book for composition. Galley proofs or page proofs are circulated back through the Editorial Department for proofing and checking, and then on to the Design Department. In some cases books with multiple illustrations or complex typography will require both dummying and mechanical layout which in many cases is provided by the Design Department. Finally, repro copy is released to the printer for printing.

Finished bound copies of the books are shipped to the warehousing and fulfillment facility, UNISERV, in Littleton, Massachusetts, to IBD Warehouse in London, and to the Book & Film warehouse in Sydney. UNISERV was established by The MIT Press and Harvard University Press to supply present and future needs, and potentially to provide warehousing service to other university presses.

New books are featured in advance seasonal catalogs published twice each year which present books in display format. These catalogs are sent to our largest wholesale and reatil customers, including libraries. About 12,000 of these catalogs are distributed domestically twice each year and through the London office (Europe, the Middle East, Africa) and through agents in the Far East, India, South America, Australia, and New Zealand. Books are simultaneously listed in a variety of book-trade reference publications.

Our direct mail program concentrates on eight subject matter catalogs in Architecture and Urban Studies, Linguistics and Language, Management and Business, Life Sciences, Physical Sciences, Engineering, Humanities, and Political Science and Social Science. These subject matter catalogs feature new, recent, and important titles from the backlist and contain descriptive listing of the entire backlist in each area covered. Books are cross-listed as well. Approximately 1,000,000 of these direct mail pieces are mailed each year, mostly to the domestic and Canadian markets.

In addition to the emphasis on direct mail selling, the Press field sales staff, both here and abroad, make personal calls on our largest wholesale and retail book buyers. The Press covers the eastern United States and Canada from its Cambridge office and shares field representatives in the midwest and the west with other university presses.

Supporting our marketing campaign, especially for books aimed at general audiences, is our Advertising Department which places about 100 space advertisements each year. The Publicity Department is concerned with a variety of activities aimed at bringing visibility to the Press's recently published books, especially by way of ensuring that an adequate number of copies are placed with reviewers for journals, newspapers, magazines, and other periodicals around the world. MIT Press books generate from 800 to 1000 reviews each year.

The Subsidiary Rights Department is responsible for selling translation rights to our books and maintains an ongoing dialogue with interested publishers around the world. The Press places about two dozen of its book with foreign publishers each year. Book club sales are significant for many of the Press's books, not only producing income but also allowing larger print runs which reduce the unit cost and thereby increase the margin on books sold directly. When books are finally in stock, sales and shipping are traced on a daily basis so that we can closely monitor our inventory.

Orders from all of our market channels (except London and Sydney, where full inventories are maintained for direct shipping to those regions of the world) come to the Press offices in Cambridge where they are edited and processed through the Press's own Ultimacc electronic data processing system to generate packing lists as well as invoices then shipped daily to UNISERV for processing. Units shipped and sales are reported on a daily basis and are posted in the office. Ultimacc also supplies a variety of other Press needs, including the maintenance of customer files, accounts receivable processing, generation of mailing lists, and a wide variety of sales and inventory information on daily, weekly, and monthly bases. Similar electronic data processing services are available through our other warehousing and shipping facilities in London and Sydney.

Author	Purvis Mulch			Title	NO TIME FOR HOUSEPLANTS	
Address						
Submitted by	author			Accepted		Date
				Declined		Date
				Returned for Revision		Date
Date Rec'd & Ack.	Editor	Copy Number	Pages	Miscellaneous		
11/18/76	FG	1	147	Preface, VI chapts, Appendix, photos		

READER INQUIRIES

Date Asked	Fee Off.	Reader's Name & Affiliation		Reply	Reply Date
11/20	$35	Cedric Crassula/MIT		yes	11/20
11/20	$35	Fern Boston/MIT		yes	11/20

MS ROUTING & CORRESPONDENCE

Sent	To (From)	Date Sent	Date Received Report	MS	Opinion	Date Paid
US mail	Crassula	11/20	11/30/76		yes, but in list?	11/30/76
US mail	Boston	11/20	11/28/76		yes & no	11/30/76

The MIT Press 28 Carleton Street Cambridge, Massachusetts 02142 Massachusetts Institute of Technology 617-253-5646

November 18, 1976

Purvis Mulch
PO Box 1379
USA

Dear Mr. Mulch:

Thank you for sending us your manuscript NO TIME FOR HOUSE PLANTS for publishing consideration.

As you may know, the MIT Press's list concentrates primarily on professional, scholarly, and reference books in the technical, scientific, business, and medical areas. As offshoots of those major interests, however, we have a small but significant trade list into which your work might well fit. Two of our titles related to NO TIME FOR HOUSE PLANTS -- both of which have enjoyed enormous success, I might add -- are Sauer's SEEDS, SPADES, HEARTHS AND HERDS (a history of gardening and farming on earth) and Preston's NORTH AMERICAN TREES (a complete, illustrated field handbook of all North American trees, now in its third edition).

We will, of course, have to submit your manuscript to outside referees for review and evaluation. We have a good retail network where there will be interest in NO TIME FOR HOUSE PLANTS, should it be evaluated as a good addition to our list. We would promote your work along with the two above titles from our backlist. All this, again, is contingent upon favorable review and approval by our faculty Editorial Board. In such a competitive market for plant books, I would like to rush along the decision process for the book. I'll put the work in the hands of reviewers as soon as possible, submit it to our Board if the reviews are favorable, and then I'll be in touch again.

Sincerely,

Flora Greenhouse
Flora Greenhouse
Acquisition Editor

FG/ddt

Ms. Flora Greenhouse
MIT Press
28 Carleton Street
Cambridge, Mass. 02142

Dear Ms. Greenhouse:

My first reaction upon skimming the manuscript you sent to me was "What! Another book on houseplants!" Having examined the book more closely, I repeat that exclamation, with a few modifications.

Mulch's manuscript first examines the basic necessities of growing healthy houseplants -- soil, water, light, air, etc. -- before proceeding to a plant-by-plant description with much particulars on each plant. The first three chapters are useful but not in any sense of the word unique or special: there are at least ten books on the market, in all ranges of price, format, and intellectual demand, which cover this same material with equal or greater facility and inclusiveness. Time/Life, for instance, has covered this ground with an elegance of design that the MIT Press could certainly equal, but probably not surpass.

It is in the second part of the manuscript -- the detailed individual description of literally hundreds of different plants -- that Mulch takes on real interest and gains value as a useful, marketable guide. Very few plant books that I've seen are so encyclopedic in their scope, and those that do include as many different species usually become unwieldy by virtue of this very magnitude. Mulch, on the other hand, manages to cover the field with admirable brevity and concision.

One question that arose in my mind was that of illustrations. Are the illustrations included with the manuscript the only ones planned for the book? The usefulness of the book would certainly be increased almost arithmetically with the number of illustrations included.

Finally, I must wonder what place this book would fill on the MIT Press list. But I imagine that is your problem, not mine. My opinion is that this book is partly superfluous, partly useful; and that when it is useful it is very useful, but when it is redundant....

Sincerely,

Fern Boston
MIT Botany Dept.

Ms. Flora Greenhouse
MIT Press
28 Carleton Street
Cambridge, MA 02142

Dear Ms. Greenhouse:

I have read and quite enjoyed Purvis Mulch's NO TIME FOR HOUSEPLANTS. I even revived a couple of my mysteriously ailing plants on Mr. Mulch's good advice.

One aspect of the book which is quite nice is the author's informal tone. He manages to impart his information by way of chatty, narrative instruction rather than formal, pedantic lesson-giving. One nice stylistic device is his frequent tone of address to the reader: "your plant" and "be sure that.." are examples.

He also engages in an appealing kind of personification of nature, which I think must appeal to the tender cultivator of little sprouts in Dixie cups on a kitchen windowsill. While referring to the plants as if they have energetic wills to thrive, to bear "children," Mr. Mulch gives just enough science to make it all legitimate. I would say that his technical level is exactly appropriate to the lay audience who have pretty much forgotten their post-sixth grade science.

Mr. Mulch does another handy and creative thing, which is to encourage the reader not to be taken in by plant-cult commercial gimmics. For instance, he gives approximate recipes for mixing one's own potting soil.

I do hope the book is to be well indexed. One of the consistent problems with plant books is that in case of a problem with a particular plant the reader is unable to locate it in the plant book organized topically rather than by plant type. Mr. Mulch seems to cover his subject from both angles of organization (general issues and specific types) and the book will suffer if not well indexed. It will function best, after all, as a kind of handbook.

I do think this book is worth publishing, but I don't quite see how it fits the MIT list.

Yours truly,

Daisy Dirt for Cedric Gazzola, MIT

The MIT Press
Publishing Proposal

Board Action: Date 12/8/76
Accepted ✓ Rejected ☐ Deferred ☐
Comments: _full steam ahead!_

Author(s) and Editor(s)
Names and Addresses:
Purvis Mulch

Discipline Gardening/Botanical Science
Title NO TIME FOR HOUSE PLANTS
Subtitle A Busy Person's Guide to Indoor Gardening
Series/editor
Delivery Dates Complete Ms. In House 12/76   **Recommended Pub. Date** fall 1977

Type of Project:
☒ New Manuscript ☐ Camera Ready ☐ Import ☐ Distribution ☐ Consignment ☐ Paperback ☐ Translation

Format Summary
Pages 176
Trim 4x6
Binding hard

Illustrations 38
Line Drawings
Half Tones

Recommendations for MIT Press to Publish (Basis and Reasons, Quantity, Retail Price, summation of P & L data)

It is recommended that the Press publish an edition of 7500 copies, paperback, priced at approximately $6.95T.

This book will be a useful and informative addition to the list of books on the plant lovers' market, no doubt crowding out much of the inferior work in this field. Moreover, this acquisition will fit into our burgeoning series on Home Crafts, thus strengthening the sales position of such new titles as BASKET WEAVING IN YOUR LIVING ROOM, THE BAYEUX TAPESTRY AT YOUR FINGERTIPS, and ISN'T MACRAME FUN?. I feel sure that the superb facilities of the MIT Press Design and Marketing Departments can turn this modest manuscript into the supersmash it deserves to be. It is hoped that the Board will concur.

_____ 12/8/76   Acquisitions Editor Flora Greenhouse   12/8/76
Director   Date   Date

The MIT Press
Publishing Proposal.
Description of Project

Author Mulch

(1) Contract Terms:
Royalty Terms 10% net on first 3000, 12½% net on next 3000, 15% net thereafter
Series Editor Override --
Advance $ --   Date   Purpose
Subsidy $ --   From whom

	Author Will Do	Author to Pay	Charge to Royalties	Charge to Edit.	Charge to Plant
Art Work	XX				
Permissions					
Index	XX				
Translation					

Special Terms (Promotional Commitments, Possible Cooperative Arrangements, Scheduling Suggestions, Guaranteed Sales)

(2) The Author(s) or Editor(s) (Full Description of qualifications, degrees, professional affiliations, previously published books, achievements in field, etc.)

Purvis Mulch, Master of B.S. (Botanical Science) from Plant Univ., has long been a recognized authority in the field of indoor agriculture. He teaches Watering and Advanced Air-Layering at Plant U., and has authored several standard texts in this field, the most recent of which -- I LIKE PLANTS -- was awarded the "Thalassa Cruso plant book of the week" award. Mr. Mulch also writes a weekly column on plants in the New York Review of Books.

(3) List of Readers (Attach readers' reports or reviews to page 3)

A. Cedric Crassula, MIT Botany

B. Felu Boston, MIT Botany

(4) Describe Condition of Manuscript at Board Presentation

Manuscript is complete, and relatively clean. Some editing will be needed.

The MIT Press
Publishing Proposal
Description of Project (continued)

Author: Mulch Page 3

(5) General Description of the Book and Special Features (Collection, reprints, conferences, thesis, original, etc.)

Mulch's book consists of seven (7) chapters. The first three describe the basic needs of house plants -- soil, water, containers, air, light, training, etc.-- as well as Mr. Mulch's radical suggestions as to plant care (e.g., "don't overwater").

After these three introductory chapters come several specialized sections on foliage plants, cacti & succulents, flowering plants, and special gardens such as terraria, kitchen gardens, and dish gardens.

One unique and intriguing characteristic of this manuscript is the use of boxed-in special supplements to introduce more advanced or specialized data on "The ABC's of Artificial Light," "Plants for Cool Conditions," etc. Skillful design will surely make these boxes an eye-catching lure to potential buyers.

(6) Elaboration on Recommendation to Publish (Attach table of contents and reviews)

This work is grounded in the latest, most innovative and thought-provoking work in the complex field of plant relations. The author has drawn on the standard texts in this area, but breaks new ground in digging up new solutions to old knotty problems. Many thorny matters are considered with surprisingly fresh insight; indeed, he makes some of this old plant material seem positively green again with the vibrancy and fervor of his style.

The MIT Press
Publishing Proposal
Market Potential

Author: Mulch Page 4

Describe Primary Market (who will buy this book)

Plant enthusiasts of every shape and size; there should be a large trade market for this book. Perhaps some course adoptions in botany schools for a subsequent paperback edition.

Describe Secondary Market

Rich people and people who just love to buy books. People with hobbies, or who like to look at pictures.

MIT Press Related Books

Author	Title	Pub. Date	Quantity	Pages	Price	Sales History
Heinrich Dieffenbach	/MY PLANT WORLD	11/71			$7.95	6000
Jerry Powers	/PUSHING DAISIES	6/74			7.95	4589
Carl Sauer	/SEEDS, SPADES,..	4/69			12.50	1422 hard
					3.45	15488 paper

Competitive Books from Other Publishers

Author	Title	Publisher	Pub. Date	Pages	Price	Sales History
Preston	/N. AMERICAN TREES		2/69		5.95	2018
many!			7/77 3/e			

Marketing Department (evaluation of publishing season, pricing for market, strategy for sales, costs, etc....)

Publicity ☒ Direct Mail ☒ Advertising ☒ Catalog ☒ Review Distr. ☒

I would recommend a first printing of 7500 and a list price of $6.95 with a trade discount.

This title is in a highly competitive market. While we might reasonably hope for a three-year sale of 10,000-15,000, we shouldn't count on it.

Marketing activities would be directed to the trade, with special emphasis on many reviews and moderate advertising. We will use our status as a university press to emphasize that this is an authoritative, though not stuffy, handbook.

It is unlikely that we would try to sell this title through the mail, although we might consider inserting inquiry/order cards into two related titles: Preston/NORTH AMERICAN TREES, and Sauer/SEEDS, SPADES...

Marketing Director: TLM Date: 12/8/76

The MIT Press
Publishing Proposal
Editorial and Media

Author: Mulch

Page 5

Editorial (Discuss editorial problems, time allocation, costs, directions to author)

About 30 editorial hours. No unusual difficulties.

Managing Editor: HO/rc   Date: 12/8/76

Media

Estimates based on:
- Manuscript pages 200 To make Book pages 176 Trim 4×6
- Front matter 3 Text 19 Notes Footnotes
- Chapter end Book end Bibliography 8 Appendixes
- Tables 10 Equations displayed In text
- Extracts Captions Heads 1 2 3 4
- Line drawings Camera ready To be drafted
- Halftones 38 Color
- Special Characteristics
- Design In Out Dummy, full, partial, none
- Scaling
- Format
- Composition (Film) Hot metal Cold
- Camera ready Partial Camera copy
- Offset Letterpress
- Estimates no. of hours No. of months

Plant Costs
Design	
Drafting	
Composition @ $6	1056
Alterations	106
Engravings/prints	--
Repros	--
C. & S. Ills. @ $8	304
Jackex C&S	226
Blues	62
Jacket Comp	100
Dies	30
Contingencies 6%	113
TOTAL PLANT	**1997**

Edition Costs — 7500
Makeready	248
Presswork	261
Paper	1457
Binding 75 M @ .62	4650
	M@
	M@
Jacket pw/paper	1650
Freight	300
Plates	67
Total Edition	**8633**
Total plant	1997
TOTAL COST	**10630**
TOTAL UNIT	1.42

Comments

Media Director: [signature]   Date: 12/8/76

The MIT Press
Publishing Proposal
Title Profitability Analysis

Page 6

Author/Title: Mulch/NO TIME FOR HOUSEPLANTS

Suggested List Price/Discount $6.95 T / 38%   Print Size 7500   Total Mfg Unit 1.42

SALES ESTIMATES

Source	Avg. Disc.	Avg. Net	1st yr sales Copies	1st yr sales $	2nd yr sales Copies	2nd yr sales $	3rd yr sales Copies	3rd yr sales $
Wholesalers & Jobbers	42%	$4.03	1000	$4030	400	$1612	200	$806
College & Univ. Bkstores	41%	$4.10	800	$3280	500	$2050	350	$1435
Retail Bkstores	41%	$4.10	1000	$4100	900	$3690	600	$2460
Direct Mail	--%	$6.95	100	$695	100	$695	30	$209
Libraries	10%	$6.26	100	$626	100	$626	30	$188
Other Domestic	--%	$		$		$		$
Foreign -- UK	35%	$4.52	300	$1356	300	$1356	140	$633
Foreign -- Other	35%	$4.52	200	$904	200	$904	150	$678
TOTALS	38%	$4.28	3500	$14991	2500	$10933	1500	$6408

S.O.P.

	1st Printing	2nd Printing
(5) Print size, incl. Comp. Copies	7500	
(6) Plant costs	$ 1997	$
(7) Less SUBV		
(8) Total plant (6-7)	$ 1997	$
(9) Edition cost	$ 8663	$
(10) MFG cost (8 + 9)	$ 10630	$
(11) Unit cost (10 ÷ 5)	$ 1.42	$
(12) MFG breakeven units (10 ÷ 2)	1947 copies	copies
(13) Royalty adv. breakeven units 17 + 2 (% R)		

The Massachusetts Institute of Technology Press

MASSACHUSETTS INSTITUTE OF TECHNOLOGY, CAMBRIDGE, MASSACHUSETTS 02142

Letter of Agreement

December 11, 1976

Purvis Mulch

Dear Purvis Mulch:

We welcome the addition of your Work tentatively entitled: NO TIME FOR HOUSE PLANTS to our list on the terms and conditions which follow, and we look forward to its publication.

1 By this letter you grant and assign to us exclusively for our use or disposition throughout the world, in all languages, during the term of copyright in each respective country (and renewal copyright where available), all rights in the Work and every part thereof, and any revisions thereof which you may make, protectible under each such country's respective common law and statutory copyright, for all purposes and adaptations, and by all means and methods of distribution and communication, be these graphic, audio-visual, or otherwise.

2 Upon its publication we will undertake to procure copyright for your Work, and any revisions thereof which you may make, in the United States and in all member countries of the Universal Copyright Convention in ~~either~~ our ~~or your~~ name; and in order to protect copyright for the renewal term in the United States, you appoint us or our designee as your attorney-in-fact with power of substitution to renew copyright in your name or in the name of your executors; and upon such renewal, the grants made to us are to continue during the renewal copyright term.

3 You warrant: (a) that the Work is original and that you are the sole author and owner of the Work and have full power to make the grants to us; (b) that neither the Work nor any part has been published before, nor is any agreement with respect thereto presently outstanding (except as you may set out in a rider that is attached to this letter and signed by both of us); (c) that the Work contains no unlawful or libelous material and does not invade the right of privacy or infringe upon the common law or statutory rights of anyone. You will hold us, our licensees, and our distributees harmless and indemnify us and them against liabilities, judgments, or decrees against us and them and against expenses and attorneys' fees that may be incurred by us or them resulting from any claim, action, or proceeding alleging facts that constitute a breach of any warranty enumerated in this paragraph.

4 You agree to deliver to us in substance, content, form, and style satisfactory to The M.I.T. Press Board, on or before December 1976 , time being of the essence, two clean and legible double-spaced typewritten copies of the complete manuscript of the Work, including double-spaced footnotes and references, illustrations, charts, etc., ready for the printer, without requiring redrawing or relettering, it being understood that the length of the manuscript shall be approximately _____ words and that illustrations and other supplementary material shall be as follows:

5 When galley and page proofs of the Work are submitted to you, you are to correct and return them to us promptly; if by any chance you do not return corrected proofs within sixty (60) days after our mailing them to you, we shall be free to proceed with the manufacture and publication of the Work without waiting for the return of the corrected proofs. If we decide to have the proofs read and corrected by another because of your delay, then the expense incurred in that connection is to be charged to your royalty account. If, when correcting the galley or page proofs, alterations are required by you, or by us because of your delay in correcting them, and such alterations cost us more than 10% of the cost of original composition, then you will pay us or we will charge to your royalty account at our option such excess within thirty (30) days after we furnish you with a statement of such excess cost. If we request an index in connection with your Work, you are to deliver the copy for the index to us within 14 days after final page proofs are mailed to you. If you fail to deliver the index as requested, you authorize us to have the index copy prepared by another, and the cost of such preparation will be charged to your royalty account. If permissions are necessary in order to publish the Work, you will undertake to acquire them for us at your expense.

6 As soon as practical after receipt of the final and complete manuscript, and after formal approval of the Work by the M.I.T. Press Board, we will publish the Work in the English language at our own cost and expense in such manner and style and at such price as appears to us best suited for the sale of the Work, and we will reprint the Work as long as in our judgment demand justifies.

7 We will pay to you during the continuance of this agreement on our actual cash receipts the following royalties on our sales (less returns and refunds) of the Work as published by us:

a ~~No royalty shall be paid to you on the sale of the first~~ 3000 ~~copies of any hard-bound edition;~~

b 10 % on sales of the first/~~next~~ 3000 copies of any hard-bound edition;

12.5 % on sales of the next ~~_____ copies of any hard-bound edition;~~

~~% on sales of the next _____ copies of any hard-bound edition;~~

15 % on all additional sales of this edition, in each case with respect to sales in the continental United States of America;

and on sales outside the continental United States, two-thirds thereof, respectively.

c One-half the hard-bound royalty schedule (7b) shall be paid on sales of any paperback edition if published by us.

d Five percent (5%) on all sales outside regular bookstore channels, by mail or coupon or other special solicitation advertising, in lieu of any other royalty.

e The prevailing English-language hard-bound or paperback royalties shall be paid on sales of any translation published by us after first recouping the cost of the translation.

f Ten percent (10%) of the amount we receive shall be paid on copies, bound or in sheets, sold for export at discounts of 50% or more.

g Fifty percent (50%) from licensing by us to others to exercise any right in the Work protectible by copyright, after first recouping any costs incurred by us to effect the license.

h In the event the Work is included in an omnibus edition and no specific sum is fixed for the use of this Work, we will fix a pro rata reasonable sum therefor, fifty percent (50%) of which will be your share.

68 / MIT / Administration / Acquisitions

14. In order that there may be no misunderstanding between us, there are to be no amendments to this agreement unless in writing signed by both of us. All the rights granted to us under this agreement shall inure to us and our respective successors, assignees, licensees, and permitees. (Your interest in royalties hereunder may be assigned, but only as a whole, and no such assignment shall be binding upon us until you have first given us in writing due notice and evidence thereof.)

15. The Press agrees to pay the cost of all alterations in galley proof made by the Author or his agent and varying from the manuscript as accepted for typesetting, up to an amount equal to ten (10) percent of the original cost of composition of the Work. Any amount in excess of the above allowance will be paid by the Author.

If the foregoing correctly reflects the agreement between us, will you please sign two copies in the place indicated below and return one to us within 7 days of the date hereof; upon your so doing, we will both be bound by the foregoing terms as an agreement.

Sincerely yours,

MASSACHUSETTS INSTITUTE OF TECHNOLOGY

by _____
Director, The M.I.T. Press

Accepted this 15th day of December, 19___

_____

---

i. We expect to distribute free copies of the Work for promotion of sales, review, advertising, samples, or like purposes; in such cases, and on copies furnished (or sold) to you, or damaged copies, no royalties shall be payable.

j. If at any time after two years from date of first publication of the Work, we find we are overstocked and sell your Work at reduced prices, either at retail or at wholesale, then the rate of royalty of such sales shall be calculated at five percent (5%) of our actual receipts from the sales, but if on such copies sold our receipts are less than our manufacturing cost, no royalty shall be payable, and no such royalty shall in any event reduce our receipts to less than our manufacturing cost.

8. Royalty statements and royalty payments in accordance with such statements will be made for each of our royalty years ending March 31 and will be mailed to you on or before the following thirtieth of June, except that, if the amount due you is less than $15.00, no payment will be required of us until a subsequent period ending March 31st when the amount has reached $15.00.

9. We will present to you 5 copies of your Work on publication by us. If you require additional copies for your own personal use, and not for resale, we will supply them to you at our wholesale price.

10. You grant permission for the use of your name, picture, and biographical data in connection with the distribution and publicizing of the Work and the exercise of other rights granted in paragraph 1 of this letter.

11. Any notice which either of us may desire to give to the other will be sufficient if addressed by prepaid certified or registered mail to our respective addresses above shown, or as last appearing on our records, or to such other place as either of us may designate by certified or registered mail notice to the other. Galley proofs and page proofs, statements, and remittances may be sent by ordinary mail. We should be addressed as The M.I.T. Press, Massachusetts Institute of Technology, Cambridge, Massachusetts 02142.

12. When requested by us, you are to revise the latest edition of the Work and provide us with any new matter necessary from time to time to keep the Work current and up to date. If for any reason you fail to do so, we may engage some other person or persons for that purpose and may deduct the cost of such revisions from royalties accruing to you on subsequent editions. If the revisions are made by others, such fact will be set forth in the revised edition. For all purposes the revised material will be deemed part of the original Work, except that the royalty provision on sales shall be calculated as if the revised Work were a new Work, unless the new material is less than 25% of the original Work.

13. As long as this contract is in force between us, it is understood that you may not contract for publication of a work that is competitive with the Work which is the subject of this agreement, unless our written consent is first obtained.

PUBLISHING LOG (Board approved titles not yet turned over)
Season: Late Fall 1977
Routing date: 12/8/76

	Board approved	contract signed	MS delivery projected	(MS) type	pp/ illust.	turnover projected
Editor: BHA						
Killian/SPUTNIK	12/8/76	pending	2/77	ms	300/10	2/15/77
Weaver/DECISION TO PROSECUTE	6/5/76	7/2/76	2/28/76	ms	250/0	3/5/77
Nelson/ZONING	3/11/76	3/20/76	4/15/77	most cc	175/18	4/20/77
Horowitz/SCIENCE, SIN...	1/8/76	2/1/76	2/15/77	ms	150/0	2/20/77
Greenberg/UNIVERSALS 2/e	1/74	2/74	3/15/77	cc+ms	218/0	3/10/77
Editor: FG						
Castells/URBAN QUESTION	7/6/76	8/10/76	books 9/1/77	import	215/27	to launch 1/77
Carr/PLANNING CITIES	12/8/76	pending	2/77	ms	350/30	2/15/77
Frieden/NEIGHBORHOODS	4/17/76	5/1/76	12/15/76	ms	400/22	12/20/76
Mulch/NO TIME FOR HOUSE PLANTS	12/8/76	pending	inhouse	ms	176/38	12/15/76
Editor: ABE						
Graves/RELATIVITY revised	10/71 & 11/8/76	1/72	new 3/77	ms+cc	180/9	3/5/77
Huxley/CRAYFISH	6/5/76	9/1/76	12/10/76	ms	360/30	12/12/76
Neyman/COPERNICUS	12/8/76	pending	2/7/77	ms	200/15	2/15/77
Shrock/GEOLOGY AT MIT	6/5/76	8/1/76	1/15/77	ms	400/0	1/25/77
Editor: FPS						
Harvey/ENVIRONMENT	11/8/76	pending	books 9/1/77	import	200/0	to launch 2/77
Hill/POWER GENERATION	8/1/76	9/16/76	2/1/77	ms	215/6	2/15/77
Kerrebrock/AIRCRAFT ENGINES	12/75	3/76	3/77	part cc	180/10	3/5/77
Wilson/ENERGY DEMAND STUDIES	10/7/76	11/6/76	2/1/77	ms	160/15	2/15/77
Zucker/CRISIS	7/6/76	8/3/76	1/15/77	ms	200/0	1/20/77

FINANCIAL PROJECTION

Date 12/8/76

Author/TITLE Mulch/NO TIME FOR HOUSEPLANTS   Editor Greenhouse
Binding hard Size 4x6 Est. # bk pgs 176   Subject Area Botany
Suggested list price/discount $6.95 T   Net price $4.28
Estimated print run 7500   Subsidy amount
Estimated annual sales: 1st yr 3500 2nd yr 2500 3rd yr 1500 TOTAL 7500 Source

	19 78	1979	1980	TOTAL	% sales
1. Income	14991	10933	6408	32332	
Variable & Title-Related Costs					
2. Plant costs net of subsidy (Plant unit .27)	1997			1997	
3. Manufacturing cost of sales (Edition unit 1.15)	8633			8633	
4. Royalty expense	1499	1367	961	3827	
5. Complimentary copies	142			142	
6. Direct Title Promotion	500			500	
7. Total 2 thru 6	12771	1367	961	15099	
8. Contribution to Press Overhead (1-7)	2220	9566	5447	17233	
Shared Operating Expense					
9. Acquisitions	1700			1700	
10. Editorial	600			600	
11. Production	425			425	
12. Design	785			785	
13. Basic Marketing	3000	225	240	3465	
14. Fulfillment	2500	1500	1000	5000	
15. G&A Allocation	1050	270	290	1610	
16. Total Operating Expense (9 thru 15)	10060	1995	1530	13585	
17. Cost Inflation Adjustments 7%		139	214	353	
18. Total Shared Expense (16 + 17)	10060	2134	1744	13938	
NET PROFIT/(LOSS) (8-18)	(7840)	7432	3703	3295	

NET PRESENT VALUE/DISCOUNTED CASH FLOW ANALYSIS

	Prepub. yrs. 19	Year 1 1977	Year 1 1978	Year 2 1979	Year 3 1980	TOTAL
Revenues						
1. Est. Sales Receipts			14991	10933	6408	32332
2. Subvention						
3. Total Revenues			14991	10933	6408	32332
Expenditures						
4. Author Advances/(Recovery)						
5. Royalty Expense		1997	1499	1367	961	2837
6. Plant Costs						1997
7. Edition Costs			8633			8633
8. Direct Title Promotion			500			500
9. Total Shared Expense (18 above)		4560	5500	2134	1744	13938
10. Total Expenditures		6557	16132	3501	2705	28895
Net Annual Cash Inflow/(Outflow) (3-10)		(6557)	(1141)	7432	3703	3437
Discount Factor @ 10 %	1.21	1.10	1.00	.909	.826	--
Net Present Value		(7212)	(1141)	6755	3058	1460

MIT PRESS

NEW PUBLICATION INFORMATION SHEET

Author or Editor: Purvis Mulch
Title (tentative): NO TIME FOR HOUSEPLANTS
Title (final): _____

☒ Hard ☒ Paper ☒ Press-owned ☐ Commission/Distrib. ☐ Import Disc: Short ☐ Trade ☒ Text ☐
Discipline code: SD144 Product line: Humanities Series Ed.: _____
Subsidy $: _____ Source: _____ Board approved 12/12/76 Contract date 12/15/76
Permissions cleared? yes Date ms. rec'd 12/18/76 2nd copy ms.? yes ~~Royalties to be charged~~ of author
Translation required? no Trans. est cost $ _____ Actual cost $ _____ How to be charged _____
Special sales anticipated: _____
Royalties X Net ___ List 10 % 0 to 3000 Payable to ☒ Author Ed. override ___ % (Net or List)
            12.5 % 3M to 6000   ☐ Other   Royalty advances _____
            15 % ___ to thereafter

Remarks:

Acquisitions Ed.: Greenhouse   Date: 12/19/76

Manuscript Data (Editorial Breakdown)

Type: ☒ ml/cc/pcc
Ms pages		No. Items		Illustrations	
153	FM	2	tables	58	no. fine drawings
	text	13	fits		☐ camera-ready
9	notes	4	equations		☐ draw and chg.au.h.
	bibliography		notes	58	no. halftones
	appendixes		legends		no. in color (line,HT)
207	Total ms pp.	3	1 heads		
		14	2 heads		
		80	3 heads		
			4 heads		

Remarks:

Managing Ed. _AC_

Production and Design

Trim size: 4x6 Total est. pp. 176   Scheduled dates
Dummy: ☐ Full ☒ Partial ☐ None ☐ Freelance? Cost Est.$ ___   1/13/77 edit. complete
Scaling: ☒ In-house ☐ Freelance Cost Est$ ___   2/1 au. check complete
Type comp: ☐ filmset ☒ hot metal ☐ cold type ☐ camera copy   ___ ms to Prod.
Remarks: 8pt $425 production unit   Editor assigned
          $85 design unit   ☐ by freelance
                                                          Cost: Est. 670 Actual $
Design Mgr. _____   Date _____   Hours: Est. 30 Actual $
                                                          Proofreading ☐ None ☒ Editor
                                                                       ☐ Freelance
                                                          Cost: Est ___ Actual ___
                                                          Index ☒ Author ☐ Freelance ☐ None
                                                          Chg. to ☐ Royalty ☒ Plant

APPROVAL OF MS. RELEASE TO COMPOSITION

Tentative Print Schedule   Design ☒ In-house ☐ Freelance   Cost Est $425 Actual $
Print _____   Actual $ _____   Freelance chg. to: _____
Bind _____ Hard ☐ Paper ☐   Actual $ _____
Tentative Price _____ Discount Cat.___ ☐ in-house composition
Director _____ Date _____   Production Mgr. _DW_   Date _____

APPROVAL OF FINAL PRICE AND PRINT QUANTITY

Final Print Schedule
Print _____
Bind _____   Hard ☐ Paper ☐
Final Price _____   Discount Cat. _____
Director _____   Date _____

Manufacturing Cost Estimates

Date of Estimate: _____
Book Specifications at: Board 200   Launch 207
Ms, pages   38   38
Illustrations   176   176
Book pages   5+180 = 8
Trim size   4x6   4x6
Type composition   VIP   VIP
Est. comp. cost   1997   1997

	Unit	Total	Unit	Total
Print 250 Bind 250 (H)	.27	1997	.38	1493
Plant	1.15	8633	1.15	8633
Edition	1.42	10630	1.42	10630
Total				
Print 400 Bind 400 (4)			.50	1493
Plant			.45	4452
Edition			1.31	6451
Total				

Print ___ Bind ___ (H/P)
Plant
Edition
Total

Remarks: H _____

Financial Projections
Sales copies (3 years)   7500
Suggested list price   6.95 T
Average discount   38%
NET RECEIPTS   32332
Est. price x est. cost x sales 8633
Royalties   38.27
CONTRIBUTION MARGIN   19872
Plant Expense (Net of SV)   1997
Free copies & spoilage   142
Direct promotion   500
NET CONTRIBUTION to OH   17233
Acquisition expense   1700
Editorial   600
Production   425
Design   785
Basic Marketing   3465
Fulfillment   5000
G&A Allocation   1610
Total Operating   13585
NET PROFIT/(LOSS)   3648
CM%
Return on Sales   11.3%

Acquisitions Department
Suggested Price   6.95 T
Suggested Quantity   7500
Maximum Price   8.95 T
← Sales Estimate   7500
Remarks:

Marketing Department
Suggested Price   8.95
Suggested Quantity   4000
Sales Estimate   _____
Remarks: Print 4000 ad. mgmt 3500

Financial Approval _____
Date _____

THE MIT PRESS TURNOVER FORM

07/30/76

PUB DATE WANTED Fall 1977   MS turnover date 12/20/76
XX New title ___ hard XX paper   Acq. Ed. Greenhouse/ajk
___ Paperback number   ISBN # _____ (hard)
___ Translation   ISBN # _____ (paper)
___ Import   Series _____
___ Camera-ready   Series Ed. _____
___ Revision   Board Approved '18/76
                        Contract Signed 11/21/76

Type of book:
___ Trade
XX Professional
___ Text

Principal Author/~~Editor~~ Purvis Mulch
Address _____
Telephone: Office _____
           Home _____
Title   NO TIME FOR HOUSEPLANTS
Subtitle A Busy Person's Guide to Indoor Gardening
Copyright: XX MIT ___ author ___ other _____

TERMS
Royalty   XX net ___ list   Editorial override royalty ___ net ___ list
           10 % to 3000   ___ % paid to _____
           12½ % XX on next 3000   Total Advance Royalty: $ _____
           15 % thereafter
Paid to   XX author ___ other _____   Date _____
Subvention $ -- from _____
Guaranteed sales # ___ @ ___ from _____

Brief description of content, market, and desired pub date:

This is a simple, comprehensive guide to growing and caring for indoor plants.
It will be thoroughly and charmingly illustrated, and cover every conceivable
aspect of this subject in a lucid but conversational style. As such, this
book will be immensely salable to a wide variety of readers -- indeed, anyone
who likes plants will want this book, and at $6.95 it will be quite a bargain.
It is suggested that the book be ready by Spring 1978 to catch the yearly
surge of interest in growing things.
This book will be an excellent entree for us into bookstores.

_____   Acquisition Editor Greenhouse/ajk (Hack)
Director   Date   12/20/76
Date

MANUSCRIPT TURNOVER: EDITORIAL SPECIFICATIONS

page 2

Trim size 5-3/8 x 8 **
Cover X hard ___ paper ___ other   Print 7500
                        Total MS pages: Total book pages:
Docket: ___   200   176 (est)
Turnover: ___   200   176 (est)
** this trim size may change after design has had a chance to look more carefully at material.

PERMISSIONS
File ___ copies with manuscript
     ___ missing
Charge to:
     ___ author royalty
     ___ book
     ___ other

FRONTMATTER
(in addition to title, copyright, and contents):
___ halftitle   ___ acknowledgments
___ frontispiece   ___ list of illustrations
___ series list   ___ list of maps
___ dedication   ___ list of tables
___ foreword   ___ other
 8 preface

PROOF/MS CHECK
Author to check ___ edited MS XX galley proof XX page proof ___ other
Extra galleys needed: amount ___ by ___ for _____
Index XX author ___ other ___ charge to ___ au. royalty ___ book
Reference style (scholarly field) _____
Editorial Suggestions from Acquisition Editor:
The manuscript may need some copy-editing and probably some substantive editing,
especially in the first parts.
Editorial Department Comments

(At Launch): ___ level of difficulty ___ no. hours ___ freelance ___ in-house

Managing Editor _____ Date 12/20/76

IMPORTS
Foreign pub. price _____
Foreign pub. date _____
MIT territory _____
                    ___ flat sheets   ___ bound books
                    ___ folded & gathered ___ jacketed
                        sheets
Foreign publisher _____
Co-publisher _____

TRANSLATIONS
From _____
___ MIT trans. $ ___ charge: ___ manufacturing
                                ___ other
Original publisher _____
Original provided? ___ yes ___ no
Translator's name & address _____
Co-publisher _____

CAMERA-READY MS
___ complete
___ running heads required
___ folios required
___ display composition required
___ drafting required

Author's alterations 10 % by contract

MANUSCRIPT TURNOVER: DESIGN SPECIFICATIONS   page 3

ILLUSTRATIONS   # Line B/W   # HFT B/W   # Comb. L/HFT/BW   # Line Color (2-3-4)   #HFT Color

Camera-ready by author   38

Camera-ready by author
except for labeling

To be redrawn by us   suggestion to
from roughs   draft about 30 line drawings of plants

Use film from present
edition (but if
camera-ready art is
available, list
above)

List missing illustra-
tions, itemized as
above, with date due

SUGGESTED DESIGN (comparable book, etc.)

Suggested typeface/size/leading

Notes: foot page _____ end chapter _____ end book
Jacket: yes X no   Suggested theme   PRINTED COVER OVER BOARDS

PRODUCTION/DESIGN ANALYSIS AT LAUNCH (by Media Department at Launch)

# MS pages	Est. # Book Pages	Trim Size	# Illustrations	Composition	Est. Unit Costs
207	176	5-3/8x8 upright	38 ht's supplied (supplementary 30 line drawings to be drafted)	VIP (on in-house system)	4000 @ 1.74 5000 @ 1.60 7500 @ 1.42

Estimated time from editorial complete to bound book   7   months.

COMMENTS FROM MEDIA:

This manuscript seems to present few unusual problems to production/design. The typesetting is very straightforward. Because of the number of illustrations (38 halftones and about 30 to 50 line drawings to be drafted to corespond to text) and their importance to the text, we will get galleys, provide a dummy, and then see pages. Projected manufacturing time from edited ms in production until bound books is about seven months.

The above costs are based on a 5-3/8 x 8 format. This may change after Design has had a chance to look more carefully at the material. Also, the above costs are based on printers scales and could therefore change when we get actual costs from outside based on a real format and castoff.
RAM.
production
12/30/77

Media Director _____
Date 12/30/77

MANUSCRIPT TURNOVER: MARKETING SPECIFICATIONS   page 4

	Acquisitions	Marketing (to be filled in at Launch)
Suggested price	$ 6.95	$ 6.95
Suggested Discount	T	T
Suggested Primary Market	___ Professional xx Trade ___ Text	___ Professional xx Trade ___ Text
Suggested Sales Estimate:	3500 # 1st year sales 2500 # 2nd year sales 1500 # 3rd year sales TOTAL 7500	2500 # 1st year sales 2000 # 2nd year sales 1500 # 3rd year sales TOTAL 6000

LIST OF PRIMARY MARKET SPECIFICS (professional organizations, names of courses and enrollments, lists available, etc.)
      Trade market, mainly bookstore sales. This effort should be directed
through jobbers.

Comparable/Competitive Books
Author/TITLE	Publisher (if different)	Pub Date	Price	Sales History
Cruso/MAKING THINGS GROW	Maple	7/77 (3/e)	5.95T	2018
Time/Life LIBRARY OF GARDENING T/L		h&p 1969	12.50, 3.45	1422 + 15488
Preston/N. AMERICAN TREES				
Sauer/SEEDS, SPADES....				

Suggested space advertising:
    Any mass media newspapers, magazines, etc. Perhaps concentrating on women's
magazines, Apartment Living, Pleasing Plants, and a variety of general-circulation media.
We should stretch a $500 budget.
Suggested reviewers/journals:
See above.

MARKETING DEPARTMENT COMMENTS (at Launch meeting by Marketing Manager):
    Design should reflect the authority of this university press book without
seeming forbidding or too scholarly. Book club possibilities should be
investigated thoroughly.

Marketing Manager TLM
                   Date 12/20/76

MARKETING PLAN by Acquisition Editor -- Flora Greenhouse

Author/Editor: Purvis Mulch
Title: NO TIME FOR HOUSEPLANTS: A Busy Person's Guide to Indoor Gardening
(Series)

List: Fall 1977   Pub. date: October 1977
List Price: Hard $6.95 (T)   Print size: (Trim 4x6
             Paper   Hard   7500
                                            Paper

I. Conceptual Outline of Book

This is a simple, comprehensive guide to growing and caring for indoor plants. The book consists of seven chapters. The first three describe the basic needs of house plants -- soil, water, containers, air, light, etc. -- and give sound, easily understood suggestions on how to meet them.

After these introductory chapters come several specialized sections on foliage plants, cacti & succulents, flowering plants, and special gardens such as terraria, kitchen gardens, and dish gardens. Mulch provides a wealth of usable material on these plants. One unique characteristic of this manuscript is the use of boxed special supplements to introduce more advanced or specialized data on "The ABC's of Artificial Light," "Plants for Cool Conditions," etc.

The book will appeal to plant lovers, more particularly to aspiring plant lovers -- those who enjoy looking at, living and working among houseplants, but who are either mystified by the process of care and feeding or misinformed about time and techniques. The book presents a genuinely new approach to keeping houseplants and will appeal to a significant part of a large but amorphous market. We can expect an appealing layout from the Design Department and an accessible text. The key to success will be getting this book on the shelves in bookstores.

II. Primary Market Focus

Retail bookstores, college bookstores, wholesaler and jobber accounts.

III. Marketing Functions

1. Direct Mail. The book should be featured as a special item of interest in all of the 8 subject matter catalogs and in season catalogs. There should be some interest among the many people receiving these catalogs, enough (it is hoped) to generate noticeable results. It'll be an interesting experiment -- is there some correlation between purchasers of professional and scholarly books, and plant lovers? No other direct mail program is planned.

2. Catalogs. The book will be featured in the Fall general catalog for both the domestic and London markets.

3. Space Ads. A budget of $500 has been allocated for specialty journals like Apartment Life, Apartment World, Plants Alive, Happy Houseplants, Plants & Gardens, Better Homes & Gardens, Avant Gardener,...

4. International Promotion. Graham reports that there will be excellent opportunities to sell in London if we can keep the price down.

5. Publicity. We have allocated at least 100 copies for distribution to reviewers in newspapers, popular magazines, and book review services. We should explore local possibilities in some of the gardening programs. Author might be willing to make appearances on local TV.

6. Endorsements. In the Boston area we have Jim Crockett and Thalassa Cruso -- both famous plant popularizers (and competition). Their names would be nice to emblazon boldly on jacket and/or ad, with a few kind words from each.

7. Exhibits. ABA, Globe Book Fair, CBA, other general exhibits.

8. Subsidiary Rights. Excerpts in McCalls, Better Homes? (The boxes lend themselves to magazine features.)

9. Field Sales. This should be the focus of our activity and we should attempt to place about 1500 copies through college bookstores, retail bookstores, and wholesaler and jobber accounts.

Launch report
12/30/76
Mulch/NO TIME FOR HOUSEPLANTS
Production/Design analysis

Ms.pages	Est.book pages	Trim size	Illustrations	Composition	Est.unit costs
207	176	5-3/8x8 upright	38 supplied (supplementary to be drafted)	VIP (on the in-house system)	4000 @ 1.74 5000 @ 1.60 7500 @ 1.42

General comments

This manuscript seems to present few unusual problems to production/design. The typesetting is very straightforward. Because of the number of illustrations and their importance to the text, we will get galleys, provide a dummy, and then see pages. Projected manufacturing time from edited manuscript in production until bound books is about seven months.

The above costs are based on a 5-3/8 x 8 format. This may change after Design has had a chance to look more carefully at the material. Also, the above costs are based on printer's scales and could therefore change when we get actual costs from outside based on a real format and castoff.

Launch Report
30 December 1976

No Time for House Plants: A Busy Person's Guide to Indoor Gardening, by Purvis Mulch,

Description: The author states in his preface that the book is "a guide to raising house plants for people who have no time to raise house plants." The opening chapters of the text discuss the basic needs of house plants--soil, water, containers, air, light, etc. Subsequent chapters deal with foliage plants, cacti and succulents, flowering plants, and unusual kinds of gardening. Special supplements illustrate more problematic topics such as the use of artificial light, special growing conditions, vines and trailing plants, large-tubbed speciments, etc. The simple, well-illustrated text makes the book a handy reference for all plant growers and will help them "to achieve house plant success without really working at it."

Contents: 12 pp. frontmatter, including half title, title, copyright, preface, content, symbols
133 pp. text, including 7 chapters
    31 no. 1 heads
    19 no. 2 heads
    80 no. 3 heads
    13 lists
    2 tables
    4 notes (page end)
38 pp. half tones with captions
15 pp. special boxes (appendixes)
9 pp. bibliography

207 total manuscript pages

Comments: Manuscript appears to be in good shape. It will require light copy editing. Design will have to pay special attention the the "special boxes"; these should possibly be handled as appendixes. No text references are included for the thirty-eight figures.

Level of Difficulty: 3

Editorial Hours: 30

FY78 TITLES, p. 1 of 6   bound books   notes

Allen/MANAGING THE FLOW OF TECHNOLOGY   July 1977
Beck/HEMATOLOGY h & pb   July
Preston/NORTH AMERICAN TREES rev'd   July

Newman/MARINE HYDRODYNAMICS   August 1977
SIPRI 1977   August
Taylor/INTERNAL COMBUSTION ENGINE I & II   August
WAES II & III   August

Bathe/FORMULATIONS & COMPUTATIONAL ALGORITHMS   September 27 1977
Bekefi & Barrett/ELECTROMAGNETIC WAVES   September 15
Bhagwati/NEW INTERNATIONAL ECONOMIC ORDER   September 16
Bronowski/SENSE OF THE FUTURE   September 21
Castells/URBAN QUESTION   September 15
Douglass/HUMID LAND FORMS   September 29
Fienberg/CROSSCLASSIFIED DATA   September 27
Harvey & Hallett/ENVIRONMENT AND SOCIETY   September 27
Hill/POWER GENERATION   September 27
Ivanaga/EDM   September 19
Killian/SPUTNIK   September 29
Mabbutt/DESERT LANDFORMS   September 16
Nelson/ZONING   September 28
Newman/COPERNICUS pb   September 2
Shrock/GEOLOGY AT MIT

Cantore/ATOMIC ORDER pb   October 4 1977
Graves/RELATIVITY THEORY pb   October 7
Greep & Koblinsky/FRONTIERS IN REPRODUCTION   October 23
Huxley/CRAYFISH pb   October 7
Kerrebrock/AIRCRAFT ENGINES   October 21
Lynch/GROWING UP IN CITIES   October 3
Mulch/NO TIME FOR HOUSEPLANTS   October 14
Sherman/MAMMALIAN EMBRYOGENESIS   October 28
Solomon/HOUSING THE URBAN POOR pb   October 4
Weaver/DECISION TO PROSECUTE   October 11
Zucker/CRISIS IN ISRAEL pb   October 28

Mulch/NO TIME FOR HOUSE PLANTS

Author/TITLE

Board approved 12/8/76
Contract signed 12/15/76
Turned over 12/20/76
Acq. Ed. FG

	12/30/76 LAUNCH	updates on: 2/1	3/1	4/1	6/1	8/1	9/1	FINAL
Edit. Complete	1/15/77	1/31						1/31
Design Samples	1/15	2/15						2/15
Release			2/28					2/28
To Comp.	2/1	2/21	4/1	4/15				4/15
Galleys In	3/1	3/21	4/7	4/15	6/1			5/1
Galleys Out	3/15	4/7	5/15	6/1	6/15			6/15
Pp In	4/15	5/7	6/15	7/1	7/15	7/30		6/30
Pp Out	5/15	6/7	6/15	7/1	8/1	7/15		7/30
Mech/Repro In	6/1	6/21	7/1	7/15	10/15	11/1		8/15
To Manu.	9/1	9/21	10/1				10/14	10/14
Bound Books								

COMMENTS: 12/30 - priority book! 1/1 - schedule OK. 3/1 - edited MS
late: author delay. 3/1 - MS late to comp; design pile up.
4/1 - galleys late - supplier overload. 5/1 - schedule OK.
6/1 - pages late. 7/1 - schedule OK. 8/1 - repro delayed.
9/1 - index. 10/1 - on schedule.

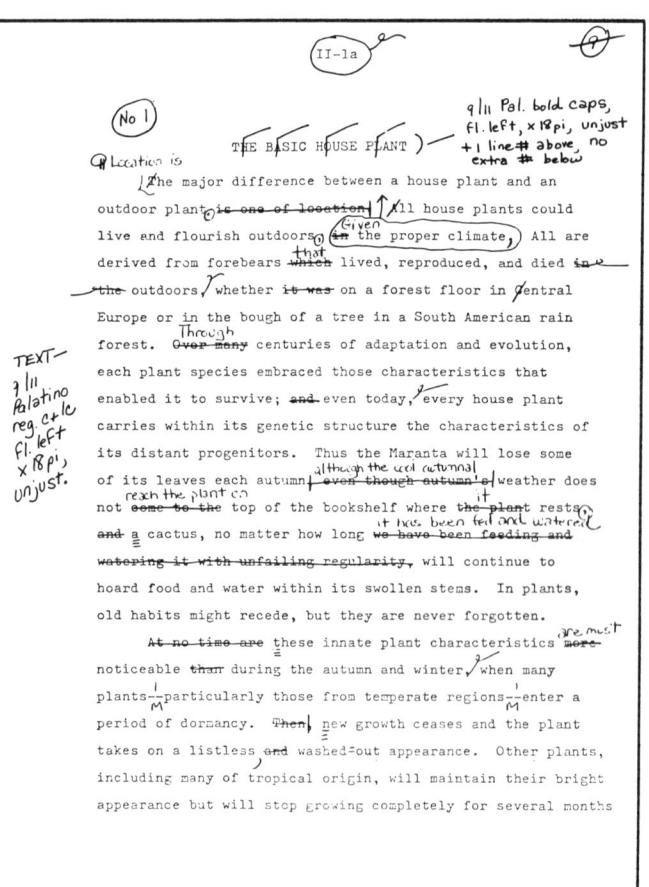

each year, thus emulating the natural rest periods of their forebears. You will do well to watch for these signs of dormancy and rest and should respond to each plant's needs at that time. When a plant enters a dormant or rest period, water should be reduced and fertilizer withheld completely, until new growth once again begins, usually in the late winter or early spring. At that time, resume watering and fertilizing the plant in order to encourage proper new growth. Treatment of the plant at this time will coincide with the advent of spring, and will support the plant in carrying out its rhythmic cycles.

Some plants are naturally short-lived and will last no more than a year or two in your home despite careful attention; their genetic structure dictates a finite life span. Garden annuals, for instance, will germinate, grow to maturity, flower, produce seeds, and die all in as little as six months. For this reason, very few annuals are selected as house plants. Although a few short-lived plants are cultivated indoors for their unusual characteristics, such as the Sensitive Plant which is easily grown from seed, the house plants that we have cultivated over the generations are most often those that will give years of pleasure. Some house plants, in fact, live to be hundreds of years old.

Other house plants are attractive when young, but grow ungainly or otherwise unattractive when they approach maturity. The only plants of this kind I have chosen for inclusion in this book are those that are very easy to propagate from cuttings; the parent plant may be discarded after a year or two to be replaced by its children.

From the hundreds of thousands of plant species growing in the world, those traditionally cultivated as house plants are the relatively few that have shown a wide tolerance to conditions of heat, light, moisture, humidity, and ventilation—in other words, those that can withstand a human environment. They are both attractive to the eye and tough. However, if we are looking for success with house plants—and particularly success without working hard at it—then we should spend some time learning the characteristics of each plant, recognizing its individual needs, and fulfilling them to the best of our ability.

No. 1   HOW A PLANT FEEDS

A plant manufactures nearly all of its own food, and not from the "plant food" that you buy for it. Commercial plant food is no more than a combination of certain chemicals (sometimes in an organic base) that are essential to the plant's basic functioning, much as vitamins are essential to human nutrition. But the bulk of a plant's food—the sugar it uses for energy and growth—is manufactured by the plant itself. In the presence of light, the leaves of the plant

draw carbon dioxide from the air and water from the roots, converting them into sugar that is then used for energy production or stored for future use.

This sugar-manufacturing process is known as photosynthesis. During photosynthesis several other processes are going on within the plant. While carbon dioxide is absorbed, oxygen is released from the pores of the leaf surface. (Plants produce not only most of the world's food but most of its atmospheric oxygen as well.) During darkness the entire process is reversed; some of the atmosphere's oxygen is recaptured by the plant and used to convert stored sugar to energy for growth. Generally, a plant manufactures growth food during the day and does its actual growing at night.

Often the plant converts its newly-manufactured sugar to starch and stores it, reconverting it to sugar as the need arises. Although the starch can be stored in almost any area of the plant, certain plants have developed specialized storage areas. Cacti and succulents. The enlarged stems and leaves of cacti and succulents equip them with the greatest above-ground storage capacity of any house plant. Others have developed underground storage apparatus for this purpose of hyacinths, bulbs, tubers, corms, and rhizomes. A bulb is characteristic of tulips, and onions, simply an enlarged underground bud. A tuber is nothing more than an enlarged root; a common potato is a tuber. Gloxinias, caladiums, dahlias, and many other common plants are grown from tubers.

A corm is the enlarged base of a stem. A rhizome is simply a laterally-growing, enlarged, underground stem. Each of these specialized structures is used by the plant for food storage, and each can be used to propagate new plants.

Water is constantly drawn up through the plant. As it transpires through the stomata (pores) of the leaves, a "pulling" action draws more water up through the roots. The water carries with it mineral salts, including all the elements needed by the plant to carry out its complex chemical processes. The transpiration that takes place in the leaves is similar to perspiration in humans and serves a similar purpose—to cool the plant. In house plants, it is difficult to notice this cooling effect; however, the results of the process are readily apparent when a group of large trees carry out transpiration. The cool and fresh feeling you enjoy in a thick woods in summer is not primarily the product of the shade but of the transpiration of the millions of leaves overhead.

A plant cannot absorb too much water, because the capacity of its vessels and cells is limited; however, the overwatering of a plant can exclude oxygen from the root system, ironically causing wilting of the top portion of the plant. When water is withheld, the plant's cells will gradually collapse, causing wilting of the entire plant. All plants do have protective mechanisms that conserve water in times of drought, however, and all can withstand a temporary dry spell. Most wilted house plants will quickly spring back to a normal state when watering is resumed.

PARTS OF THE PLANT

Stem The stem serves to support the plant and to contain and direct the vessels that transport water from the roots, and food from the leaves, to every other part of the plant. Most house plants, including Philodendron, Ivy, and Spider Plant, have soft stems. Such plants must either climb or crawl, because their stems are not strong enough to support an upward-growing structure of significant height. Other plants have soft but thick stems (susceptible to breakage) that enable them to attain good height. Woody-stemmed plants such as the Avocado, Poinsettia, and Boxwood, are far more sturdy and are usually derived from trees or shrubs of the temperate region. Canes are thick stems with hollow or pithy centers. Bamboo is a familiar example of a cane; among house plants, Dieffenbachia and Ti Plant are good examples of cane.

Some plants have a distinct main stem, while others send up many stems, none of which are dominant. A side shoot is a smaller stem growing out from the main stem. A petiole is a leaf stalk—the stem-like structure from which a leaf grows. A node is a joint on the main stem from which a leaf or side shoot grows.

Leaf The major purpose of the leaf is, as we have

---

to manufacture food for the plant's growth and reproduction. Given its total mass, the leaf has a remarkably large surface area and is ideally designed for the efficient absorption and diffusion of gases through its thousands of stomata. Keeping in mind the basic functions of the leaf, its proper care is not difficult to appreciate. The stomata must be kept fairly clean, free of dust and oil that might hinder their efficient operation. Leaves must also be given easy access to light and ventilation, according to the individual needs of each plant. Never crowd plants to a point where they are competing for light and air.

Roots Roots serve two main purposes—to anchor the plant in the ground and to supply, from the soil, water and mineral salts. Bulbs, corms, rhizomes, and tubers serve much the same purposes while simultaneously acting as food storage areas. Roots, like the above-ground parts of plants, may be pruned without injuring the plant in any way. Roots are often trimmed to prevent a plant from growing too large for the convenience of the grower. If roots are cut back, however, the top growth should be reduced by the same percentage to assure that the roots will be able to supply the plant with sufficient amounts of water. The major precaution in caring for roots is to avoid overwatering.

Flowers The plant's flowers contain its sexual apparatus. Pollination occurs when male pollen is deposited onto female stigmata, thus fertilizing the plant and allowing the formation of seeds. The fruit of any plant is, in essence, the ovary that swells to protect the seeds. In nature, most plants produce flowers. For the purposes of cultivating house plants, only certain ones—which in this book are listed as flowering house plants—can be depended upon to produce, under home conditions, blossoms of sufficient size, profusion, and beauty to warrant our attention. The plants that we grow for their attractive foliage often cannot produce flowers indoors because of insufficient light or because of a pollination failure. In nature, pollen is transferred either by insects or wind. Where indoor pollination is essential, it can be accomplished by transferring the pollen from one flower to another, by using a soft camel's hair brush. This process is described fully in most books devoted to flowering house plants.

SOIL

Since the house plant you bring home from the shop will already be rooted in soil, you might wonder why you have to consider this need at all. The answer is that your house plant will

---

someday need repotting, and you will want to provide it with a potting mixture that will serve its special needs. You might even wish to propagate some of your favorite house plants at some point, to share them with friends or to give as gifts. In any case, a basic knowledge of potting mixtures and soils is essential to a complete understanding of all your plants. A clear understanding of two simple definitions will help here to avoid confusion later. Soil, as mentioned here, refers to garden loam—that combination of mineral matter, organic matter, air, and water commonly found outside, in your garden or under your lawn. A potting mixture is soil combined with other materials, such as sand, compost, peat moss, limestone, and bone meal; these together form an ideal environment for the roots of your house plants.

The easiest way to assure your plants of a perfect loam is to buy prepackaged sterile potting soil from your garden or flower shop. This soil will have the proper texture, and will also be free of disease organisms, insects (some are microscopic), and weed seeds. When combined with the other ingredients outlined above, will form an ideal potting mixture. You may also buy packaged potting mixture at the store; however, the package should be read carefully to determine the ingredients included, making sure that the mixture is right for your plants.

It is, of course, far less expensive to make your own potting mixture from your own garden loam (free), sand (free or next to free), and small amounts of purchased ingredients. If you choose this route, it is important that you be able to make at least a cursory analysis of the garden loam that will form the basis of the potting mixture. Texture is important. A heavy clay soil will hold water for too long a time, thus encouraging disease and root rot, and it will bake cement-hard when dry. On the other hand, a coarse sand will not hold water well, nor will it hold nutrients long enough for the plant's roots to absorb them. Strive, then, for a happy medium—a good loam containing both clay and sand, which will hold both water and nutrients, and will offer adequate drainage.

To this basic loam, we usually add one or more of the other ingredients—peat moss, to increase water-holding capacity and to add organic matter; compost, for organic matter and nutrients; sand, to open up the soil to air; and some form of supplemental mineral fertilizer, usually bone meal and lime. Chemical fertilizer can be used; however, it is not necessary to add such fertilizer to the potting mixture, since the other ingredients will supply all the nutrients the plant can use for several months.

ACIDITY and ALKALINITY

A discussion of soils and potting mixtures would not be complete without some mention of acidity, alkalinity, and the pH scale, which is the scientific measure for acidity and alkalinity. The midpoint on the pH scale is 7. A soil with a pH of 7 is neutral—neither acid nor alkaline. Numbers above 7 indicate an alkaline soil, those under 7, an acid soil. Most house plants, as well as most garden plants, will do best in a slightly acid soil (a pH of 6.0 to 7.0). Most garden soils are within this range, and all the house plants discussed in this book will do well in this normal range, unless special requirements are indicated.

If you are worried about your soil's pH, or if you are simply curious about the pH level, call your county agricultural agent and ask for directions on having a pH test made. The cost will be nominal. The acidity of any soil may be increased by the addition of peat moss, or decreased by the addition of ground limestone.

POTTING MIXTURES

There are as many different basic potting mixtures as there are plant experts—probably more. Perhaps the most common one (and one which can be trusted), calls for two parts loam, one part finely-screened compost (or a mixture of peat moss and compost), and one part builder's sand (not sea sand). A small amount of bone meal (about one teaspoon for a five-inch pot) and a pinch of ground limestone are added to this basic mixture. Other recommendations call for more of one ingredient and less of another. Do a little experimenting on your own; you will eventually determine your own favorite mixture, which you can then recommend to others. Now that you have a sense of basic mixture formula, we will consider the exceptions:

1. Acid-loving plants such as azaleas, camelias, gardenias, and heathers should have no lime. They should, in fact, have some form of acid organic matter—acid peat moss or oak leafmold.

2. Foliage plants need somewhat more compost in the mixture, as half of it should be comprised of peat moss (which will not overstimulate the plant).

3. Fast-growing and hungry plants require more bone meal and lime, because they use them up so quickly.

4. Some plants, such as cacti, succulents, and orchids, have very special soil requirements; these are mentioned later in the discussions of the individual plants.

NUTRIENT MAINTENANCE

The mineral nutrients contained in any fresh potting soil or mixture, whether it is home-made or a sterilized commercial brand, should be sufficient for your plant's needs for the first four to six months. After this initial period, you should begin to replenish those nutrients on a regular and carefully measured basis.

All plants need substantial amounts of three elements—nitrogen (N), phosphate (P$_2$O$_5$), and potash (K$_2$O), as well as lesser amounts of a dozen or more "trace minerals" or "trace elements." In grower's language, the three major elements are referred to as N, P, and K, the label of any commercial fertilizer includes the percentages of each of these elements given in N-P-K order. A 5-10-5 fertilizer, for instance, will contain 5 percent nitrogen, 10 percent phosphate, and 5 percent potash. A "balanced" fertilizer contains a balance of all three elements in the amounts needed for the proper growth of most plants. The fertilizer may be either a chemical or an organic preparation. The chemical varieties are quick-acting, easy to use, and tidy. Organic fertilizers, on the other hand, are slow to release their nutrients, thus providing a gentle and steady supply. These mixtures come in liquid, tablet, and even spray form (the last applied directly on the foliage). Organic fertilizers may be purchased commercially in balanced formulas (fish emulsion, made from fish wastes, is a popular one for house plant use) or may be made at home from a combination of ingredients. Blood meal is a good

choice for supplying substantial amounts of nitrogen (its NPK formula is 15.00-1.30-0.70), while bone meal (4.00-21.00-0.20) is good for phosphate, and wood ashes (0.00-1.50-7.00) are high in potash content. A combination of one part blood meal, one part bone meal, and two parts wood ashes will make a 5-6-4 formula, a good one for house plants.

How often should plants be fertilized? There is wide disagreement on this question, some experts believe in weekly feedings at full strength (the dosage recommended on the label), others suggest fertilizing no more than once a month, and even less often during the winter. In the end, you will probably have to determine your own policy by way of experimentation. In the beginning, however, it is better to err on the conservative side, as far more plants have been injured from overfertilization than from nutrient starvation. If you use a commercial chemical or organic formula, I suggest that you feed your plants as often as recommended on the label; however, use only half the recommended dosage. (Manufacturers tend to overstate the need for their product.) If the plant shows a spurt of active growth in late winter or early spring, increase the dosage to the manufacturer's recommendation. During a dormant or rest period, withhold fertilizer entirely. If you are using a home-made organic fertilizer, use it sparingly at first. A level teaspoon of the blood meal/bone meal, wood ash formula, applied monthly, should be plenty for a plant in a five-inch pot. You may also put some of the mixture in a bottle, fill the bottle with water, and use this "tea" to water your house plants. A mild tea solution, applied weekly, will give all your plants a continuing and gentle supply of the essential nutrients. Finally, remember that a chemical fertilizer should never be applied to dry soil. The quick action of the chemicals can easily injure the roots.

→ Continue to II-5

A balanced house plant fertilizer, which should be applied sparingly. Chemical preparations should be applied according to the manufacturer's directions.

CONTAINERS

Nearly any container that offers adequate drainage and doesn't leak is suitable for house plants. After checking a container for leakage, consider drainage carefully. If the container has a hole in its bottom, there is no problem. If not, then coarse gravel or broken crockery should line the bottom of the container to fill one-fourth to one-fifth of its depth. In this way, the likelihood of waterlogged plants and root rot will be avoided.

The traditional terra cotta clay pot offers definite advantages. It is inexpensive, easily replaced, and—most important—allows air to be exchanged through its porous walls. This porosity, however, allows water to evaporate fairly quickly and necessitates frequent watering. If a plant's location makes its watering awkward, you will save yourself some effort by choosing a glazed or otherwise impervious container.

Some metal containers, (notably copper) can produce adverse chemical reactions with soil and fertilizer elements they contain, thereby injuring plants. Copper planters, however, are usually lacquered to prevent such reactions.

Wooden tubs and boxes are ideal for very large house plants. Any wooden container can be rendered water-tight by lining it with several sheets of heavy plastic or, for more permanent results, sheet metal.

Finally, if you want the best advantages of both a terra cotta pot and a decorative container, place the former inside the latter, leaving a quarter-inch or more of space for air circulation around the walls of the inner pot. Sometimes sphagnum moss is inserted here, to help preserve moisture. A base of gravel in the decorative pot can provide good drainage while lifting the inner pot to the level of the outer container.

WATERING

More house plants are killed by overwriting than by any other cause. Such killing with kindness can be avoided once you learn to understand exactly when your plants need water and when they should be left alone.

The best rule of thumb is that a plant should be watered when the soil surface is dry to the touch. Then, water the plant thoroughly, either by adding water to the soil surface, or by immersing the entire pot in a larger container of water.

Certain plants, such as African violets and other house plants woodsy varieties, need more water than most, while cacti and succulents require far less watering than average. Aside from the specific preferences of individual varieties, there are many conditions which call for more or less water; these are indicated in Table 1.

Immersion is the surest, and therefore the best, method of watering. The soil in any pot might tend to form water channels which, upon receiving water from the surface, will rush it to the bottom of the pot and out the drainage hole, leaving large parts of the soil bone dry. On the other hand, some potting soil mixtures will shrink when drying, leaving many spaces along the wall of the pot where water can run past. Provided that the plant container is porous, immersion is the one sure way to soak the soil thoroughly. A potted plant can be immersed in any large container, or even in a sink or bathtub. Set the pots in the water, but do not let the water flow over the lips of the pots. After the surface of the potting mixture has become moist—ten to thirty minutes—remove the potted plant, drain off any excess water, and put it back in its place. Never go out for the afternoon, leaving your plants standing in water.

If you water from the top, remember to remove any excess water from the saucer; allowing plants to stand in water encourages root rot. In time, you should learn to give each plant just enough water to soak it thoroughly, with very little excess drainage.

Some other watering tips:

1. Do not allow water to stand in the crown of any plant; this will encourage decay.

2. Never use very cold water, especially for tropical plants. Keep an open jar of water at room temperature for your house plants. Not only will the proper temperature be assured, but some of the chemicals in the water will have been dissipated by the time it is given to plants.

3. Artificially softened water may be detrimental to plant growth. If you can, use rainwater, or

water that has not been softened. Fluorine and chlorine, on the other hand, do not seem to pose any problems.

4. If your water is especially hard, lime salts might cause trouble with such acid-loving plants as Orchids, Primulas, Rhododendrons, Azaleas, and other plants whose natural soil is woodsy (indicating a high organic content) and acid. Either choose plants which prefer a more neutral range in the pH scale, or plan to collect rainwater for your calcifuges (lime-haters).

Insert Table 1 approximately here

HUMIDITY

Much of our trouble with house plants, especially in wintertime, can be traced to insufficient moisture in the air. Except for the cacti and succulents, nearly all house plants thrive best in a relative humidity of between 60 and 80 per cent, while that of most heated homes in winter is under 50 per cent—often, considerably under 50 per cent. House plants will virtually cry for moisture under these conditions, and it is incumbent upon you to answer that cry.

There are several ways to add moisture to the air in your home. The more expensive include the adding of a humidifying device to your furnace, if you live in a house, or installing an electric humidifier. This step will benefit not only the plants but everyone living in the house, too. But there are less expensive ways of bringing moisture to your plants:

1. *The pebble tray.* Line the bottom of a waterproof tray with decorative pebbles and arrange potted plants on top of the pebbles. Keep the tray filled with water, being sure only to avoid blocking the pots' drainage holes. Change the water weekly to keep it fresh.

2. *Decorative containers.* If you keep a clay pot inside a decorative container (double-potting), keep a pool of water in the bottom of the larger vessel. Again, provide some means of support for the clay pot so that it is not resting in water at any time.

3. *Standing water devices.* Water left standing in a room will gradually evaporate. If your home is particularly dry during cold weather, take the trouble to place pans of water on tops of radiators; grow ivy, philodendron, or wandering Jew in containers of water; maintain an aquarium; rotate plants so that each can spend an afternoon in the bathroom each week, where the air is humid. Change standing water every week.

4. *Bathing and showering.* House plants will respond favorably to a brief shower every day, or as often as possible. Small brass-plated atomizers are ubiquitous in mail order catalogs, but more dependable (albeit less decorative) are the plastic sprayers available in art supply stores. These hold roughly a pint of water, and feature an adjustable shower head, affording an entire range of water action from a sharp jet capable of carrying twenty feet to a fine mist.

Remember to fill the container after every use, so that the next day's spray will be at room temperature. Remember also to avoid spraying plants that have been standing in direct sunlight (the shock is great) and those that have been subjected to very cool temperatures.

Rubber plants and others with large leaves should be cleaned thoroughly and gently with a damp cloth once a week. The leaf polish sold commercially is permissible for producing stunning, large-leafed plants; however, as it can block the leaf pores and impede respiration, never use oil of any kind. Ivies and other rugged small-leafed plants can be held under the gentle stream of a faucet for their weekly bath.

5. *Grouping.* Plants will maintain a moist surrounding air (leaves not touching) with greater facility if they are grouped together rather than separated. During the coldest part of winter plants can be grouped on a pebble tray under a light window, to take advantage both of maximum light and greatest humidity.

VENTILATION

Plants, like people, benefit from fresh air and react badly to drastic changes in air movement and temperature. Provide adequate ventilation for your house plants, but do not subject them to sharp winds, winter draughts, or heat rising directly from a radiator.

If, in autumn, you bring your plants in from a summer outdoors, help them to adjust to indoor conditions gradually by placing them by an open window for the first several days. Gradually lower the window day by day, keeping a watchful eye on night temperatures.

TEMPERATURE

The temperature requirements of house plants vary widely, in accordance with the natural habitat of their forebears and other conditions. Many cool-weather plants prefer a range of 50 to 60° F. and cannot tolerate temperatures above 70°, while tropicals may thrive in a moist 70 to 75°. Know the temperature preferences of any house plant before you adopt it, and then place it in the best possible temperature location in your home. You might find, for instance, that a cool-loving aspidistra will do best in a back bedroom, while tropical plants thrive happily next to (but not above) a living room heat vent. Pay attention to the temperature preferences specified for your plants, make liberal use of an indoor thermometer, and do not be afraid to experiment by placing different plants in different locations for a week at a time. You might notice that your plants have preferences for particular locations throughout the house, and that their preferences will not always corroborate expert advice.

II - 12

No.1

LIGHT

Light and temperature needs are closely related. In their native surroundings, many tropical plants can thrive in higher temperatures because they receive long hours of sunlight. In the home, and especially during winter's short days, they cannot receive enough light to enable them to withstand high house temperatures.

Except for cacti and succulents, house plants should not be placed in windowsills where they will receive long periods of direct sunlight. Simply place a thermometer in this position and you will soon see that your plants can be literally cooked to death, even in the dead of a Minnesota winter. For most of your plants Strive, instead, for a bright spot with a few hours of filtered sunlight each day.

Include in Intro. Individual varieties vary in their light needs. Again, do not be afraid to experiment with different locations for different plants. One of the most popular house plants, Philodendron scandens, has thrived for years in a dim corner. Plants sometimes exhibit unmistakable individual characteristics which be completely have yet to understood.

No.1

PRUNING AND TRAINING

Some plants should be pruned and pinched back occasion-

II - 13

ally, in order to encourage bushy and stocky growth, while trailing plants such as philodendrons and ivies need gentle support to guide them into pleasing growth patterns.

Many people hesitate to prune at all, feeling that they are hurting the plant or interfering with its natural development. Actually, plants will respond to judicious pruning with new and vigorous growth. Plants such as geraniums, coleus, and begonias should be pinched back routinely, in order to encourage lateral growth. The process is quite simple: With a sharp knife, cut back perhaps one-half inch of the central growing tip. The plant should respond by sending out side shoots below the central tip, and the main stem of the plant should then become thicker and sturdier. If this is done several times a year, the plant should eventually attain the vigorous and well-rounded form you desire. Without this pruning, it might grow "leggy" with a weak main stem, and would soon require some kind of support. Many older plants also will benefit from occasional pinching back or shearing of outside growth. Do not, however, prune or pinch back African violets, gloxinias, flowering bulbs, ferns, or cyclamen.

Vines and trailing plants often need some kind of support, unless you prefer to let them cascade from a hanging basket. The usual practice is to sink a slab of cork or tree bark into a pot, training the vines of the plant to grow around and up the support, until they eventually conceal it.

II - 14

Another effective device is the sphagnum moss cylinder. Pack the moss fairly tightly around a stake and secure it in a cylinder of the proper size for the pot. The cylinder can be made easily from either chicken wire or green plastic material made for this purpose. A small clay pot can be sunk into the top of the cylinder, so that water can be added regularly to keep the moss damp. (Otherwise, the moss will require regular spraying.) Tie the vines gently to the cylinder as they grow; eventually, philodendrons and similar plants will anchor themselves to the moss with their aerial rootlets, making other support unnecessary.

No.1

REPOTTING

The temptation to repot plants is often a strong one, and should be resisted with strong will. A plant needs repotting only when it has become potbound—when the roots have filled the entire container and are creeping out of the drainage hole. Choose a new pot only one size larger than the old, for a house plant will not do well in a pot that is too large. If the larger pot has been used before, scrub it thoroughly to remove any possibility of disease. If it is a new clay pot, soak it for a few hours in water so that they became saturated. Then, with ample potting soil, gravel, and a tongue depressor or similar wood tool, set to work.

To remove the plant from its old pot, slide your hand over the top of the pot, index and second fingers cradling

---

II - 15

the plant stem. Turn the pot upside-down, thus supported, and tap the lip of the pot sharply on the edge of a bench or table. After a few taps the entire soil ball, ringed with plant roots, should come out easily in one neat piece. Set it aside. Take the larger pot and line the bottom with a layer of coarse gravel or broken crockery, as a provision for good drainage. Next, add potting soil on top of the gravel, placing the plant and soil ball on top of the new soil several times as a check to determine when it has reached the proper depth. (The top of the soil should be about one-half inch below the lip of the new pot, in a four-inch pot, and one inch below the lip in an eight-inch pot, to allow extra room for watering.) When enough soil has been added to raise the plant to its proper height, center it well and pack soil around the sides of the soil ball. Take your time in doing this, as it is the most crucial part of the entire operation. It is important to pack the soil firmly, so that no air spaces remain when the job is finished. Roots cannot draw nutrients in air spaces and many of them will thus be injured or die, thereby affecting the health of the entire plant. When the new soil is finally brought up to a level even with the top of the soil ball, the job is finished. You might want to add a little soil over the top of the root ball, especially if roots have been forced up to the soil surface, but don't add any more soil than necessary, since the planting depth of the plant must be maintained so as to alleviate shock to the repotted plant.

Water the plant thoroughly and return it to its usual location.

How often should you repot? The answer depends on the needs of each individual plant. For slow-growers, this might be once every two or three years; a mature slow-grower may go for many years without repotting, if new growth is cut back. For fast-growing and very young plants, repotting might be needed once or twice a year for the first several years. Plants that do not need repotting after one year should have the top one-half to one inch of soil replaced annually, to keep the soil fresh.

PROPAGATION

There will come a time when you will want to start your own house plants—to increase your own plant population, to use as personal gifts for friends and family, to replace a short-lived plant or one that has become ungainly with age. The propagation of most house plants is not a difficult task, and is most rewarding.

There are two general methods of doing the job: by the collecting and planting of seeds, or by the cutting and rooting of plant parts—stems, leaves, or underground structures. The first method (sexual reproduction) is often difficult, always time-consuming, and likely to produce unsatisfactory results. Propagation from seed is ideal for garden annuals, but not for most house plants. Special equipment is required, and daily attention is essential, thus making the activity an unlikely one for anyone who professes "no time for house plants." In addition, the seeds from hybrid plants (any plant produced by cross-pollinating two plants of different species or genera) are likely to produce plants vastly inferior to the parent plant. Finally, many house plants do not flower and produce seeds under home conditions; thus the house plant gardener must purchase seeds from specialty houses. The one advantage of growing house plants from seed is that new hybrids can be created by the cross-pollination of plants. The excitement of this activity creates a fascinating hobby for some house plant enthusiasts, but is unlikely to appeal to those who cannot afford to devote significant amounts of spare time to the activity.

Plants can be propagated far more simply and reliably by the cutting and rooting of plant parts. Less care is required, and the offspring will look identical to the parent, even when the parent is a hybrid.

Plants may be propagated at any time of year, although it is best to avoid tackling the job when the plant is going into a dormant period. Early spring, just before active growth begins, is perhaps the ideal time.

Cuttings. The most common method of propagating is by the taking of stem cuttings, which are then rooted in either water or a sterile rooting medium such as perlite, vermiculite, or sand. If you have never rooted a cutting before, begin with African violets, coleus, Dracaena, Fuchsia, gardenias, geraniums, Impatiens, ivy, Philodendron, wandering Jew, or wax begonia. These are the easiest, since they can all be rooted in water. Simply take a cutting from an actively growing tip of the plant, containing four to six leaves, severing the stem cleanly just below a joint with a clean razor blade. Place the cutting (several at a time can be taken from the same plant) so that the bottom portion is submerged in water, while the leaves remain above water. A colored or clear bottle is fine. If necessary, cut off the bottom leaf or two to get more of the stem into the water; about one-third of the entire length should be in water.) Place the container in diffused light, not direct sun. When new roots appear, the plant can be removed from the water and potted in a small pot, using the correct potting mixture. Be sure to avoid air spaces by packing the potting mixture firmly around the roots of the plant; water thoroughly after potting.

Stem cuttings that cannot be rooted in water are rooted in perlite, vermiculite (both available wherever house plant supplies are sold) or in builder's sand.*

The process is basically the same as for rooting in water. The cuttings are inserted in the moist medium, which may be contained in a small clay pot or, for larger numbers of cuttings, a shallow plastic tray. The container is then planted in a plastic bag which is tied shut (the zip kind often used for food storage, is convenient, effective, and reusable) and placed in diffused light at a temperature of 65 to 70°. You can tell whether the cuttings have developed roots by testing them weekly. Open the bag and pull gently on a plant. If it moves easily, the roots have not yet formed; if it resists your gentle tug, however, the roots probably are mature enough to stand repotting. The process can take as little as two weeks, or as long as several months, depending upon the variety of the plant and the size of the cutting. When the roots are strong and vigorous, pot the plant cutting in a small pot and treat it as you would any other plant.

Some plants that produce canes (hollow or pithy stems), including Chinese ever-

---

*. Throughout this book, builder's sand is suggested for potting purposes while sea sand is not recommended. Builder's sand, which comes from inland locations, has irregular and sharp surfaces and allows good soil drainage. Sea sand, having been washed smooth over the years, packs too snugly and leads to a compacted soil with resultant drainage problems.

green, Dracaena, and Dieffenbachia can be propagated by taking cuttings of the canes, which have discernable "eyes." Press each section (containing one eye) into moist sphagnum moss, secure it with wooden clothes pins at each end so that it does not pop up, seal it in a plastic bag, and put it in a cool place out of direct sun. In six to eight weeks, move it into a warm place (70 to 90°), still out of direct light. Soon, a shoot will grow from the eye. When the shoot has attained a respectable size, the cane can be cut close to the shoot on both sides, and the new plant can be lifted from the moss and potted.

Plants that have fleshy leaves are best propagated by taking leaf or leaf-petiole cuttings. (A petiole is a leafstalk, or stem.) Leaf cuttings work well when large and mature leaves are available. Cut the leaf close to the stem of the parent plant, using a razor blade for a clean cut that does not crush the cells. The leaf can then be cut horizontally into smaller sections, so that the main vein runs from top to bottom along the center of the leaf section. (Long-leafed plants such as Sanseveiria and Streptocarpus can be cut into as many as ten sections, each of which will produce an individual plant.)

Each leaf section is then sunk halfway into the rooting medium; at this point the growing procedure previously described for stem cuttings can be applied to the leaf sections.

Smaller leaves can be rooted by taking leaf-petiole cuttings. Cut one leaf stem close to the main stalk and sink the stem into the rooting medium, so that the leaf nearly (but not actually) touches the medium. African violets, begonias, snake plants, piggy-back plants, and Peperomia respond well to leaf-petiole cuttings.

Underground division. Older plants with thick main roots can be propagated by taking root cuttings. This is usually done when the plant is being repotted. Cut about one inch of the main root, making sure that it has at least one eye. Cover this with one-half inch of rooting medium and treat it as you would any other cutting.

Thick-rooted perennials can be propagated simply by the process of root division; the root mass is simply forced apart into two or more clumps, each of which is then repotted.

Plants that produce rhizomes (underground stems) can be propagated by dividing the rhizome so that one leaf bud is contained on each piece; the section is then planted under one-half inch of rooting medium. Plants that produce potato-like tubers can be propagated by cutting the tubers apart (one eye to each section) with a sharp knife, and planting the sections in the rooting medium just as one would plant potatoes in the open field.

Some plants produce "suckers," small plants that grow up from an underground stem or root. These can be separated from the parent plant and potted in soil immediately.

Anyone who has seen strawberries grow outdoors knows what runners are — baby plants that grow from a long stem coming from the base of the parent plant. Among house plants, Boston fern and spider plant both produce runners; these can be severed from the parent plant and started in a rooting medium.

Other methods of underground division include the separation and replanting of baby bulbs and corms which are produced by the mother bulb or corm.

Air layering. A fairly simple (and most impressive) way of propagating larger or woody-stemmed plants is by air layering. In such layering a sharp cut is made into the stem, perhaps a third of the way in, into which a toothpick is placed horizontally, to keep the cut open. The stem section is then wrapped with moist sphagnum moss and covered with clear plastic, and is tied at top and bottom so that moisture cannot escape. Roots will form from the incision and will soon show through the plastic. When a fair number of roots have appeared, cut the stem below the plastic wrap, remove both plastic and moss, and pot the new plant immediately in potting soil.

The propagation of plants can often be integrated with the cutting back, pruning, and shaping of older plants. It is a waste to throw away plant parts when they can be used to produce more plants, and it is precisely this thrifty attitude which, if uncontrolled, can lead to a frightening multiplication of house plants. The answer to such overwhelming plant production is to share plants with friends, thus encouraging still more enthusiasts and still more house plants.

(Appendix 1) **THE ABCs OF ARTIFICIAL LIGHT**

The recent introduction of fluorescent tubes designed specifically for plant growing has been a great boon for indoor gardeners. With the aid of artificial light, we can now grow lush, green plants in areas where they would never grow before. A windowless bathroom, which might offer ideal humidity and temperature conditions, can now be made into an ideal plant-growing environment. Plants growing on a drab northern window sill can now receive supplemental light during winter's short and dark days. Dim corners of any room can be transformed into green showplaces. Cuttings and seedlings can now make faster and surer progress than ever, under artificial light, and we can even grow vegetables in the dead of winter in the bedroom or kitchen. Artificial lighting is not essential for house plant success, but it certainly broadens growing horizons and increases chances for maximum rewards.

The outdated incandescent bulb still offers some help to plant growers, although the heat it produces makes it impossible to offer plants the amounts of light they need without drying them or burning the short spectrum of light wavelengths emitted by incandescent bulbs, falling far short of simulating the beneficial rays of the sun. Ordinary daylight or cool white fluorescent lights are far better for growing plants, since they have not only a wider and more effective light wavelength, but also produce light with three times as much efficiency as incandescent bulbs, thus reducing heat.

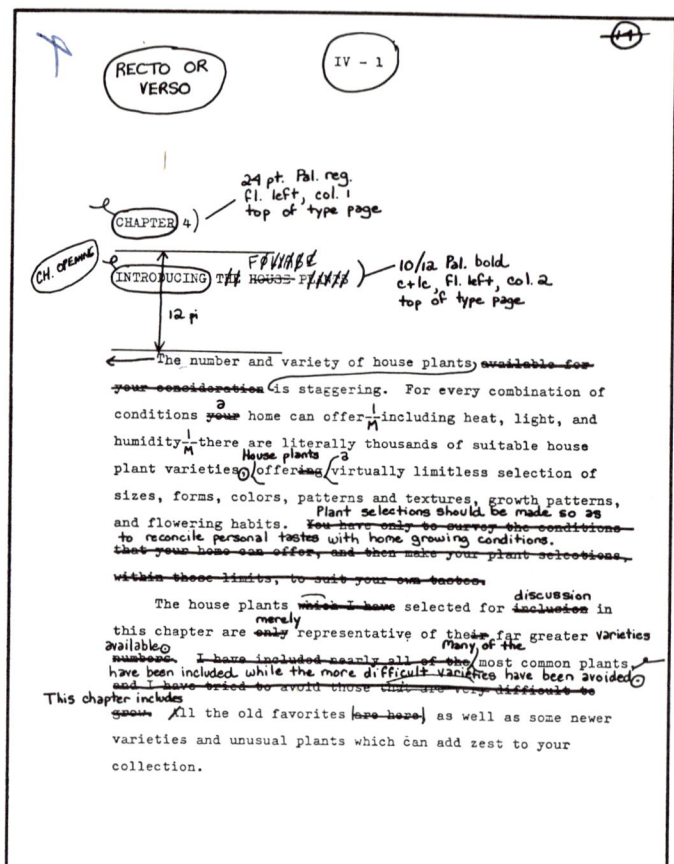

IV-4

house conditions that you cannot hope to match in your home. However, most plants offered by these sources are likely to be common varieties that are quite tolerant of adverse conditions. It is hard to go wrong with grape ivy or a climbing philodendron.

Plants stored outside at garden centers or in shopping centers may carry insects or disease, particularly if they are resting close to flats of outdoor vegetable or flower seedlings. Examine them closely before purchasing, and isolate them for one or two weeks at home before putting them with other house plants.

Wherever you buy your plants, look for young and sturdy specimens with rich color and a generally healthy appearance. Take particular care in examining large and mature plants that carry high price tags. These may have been growing for too long a time in ideal conditions. Generally, you will have better luck with a younger plant, and you will have the added pleasure of bringing it along to maturity in your own home.

Larger plants offered at bargain prices are often severely under-rooted.

IV-5

FOLIAGE PLANTS

9/11 Pal. bold caps, fl. left + 1 line # above no extra # below

In this chapter, we will survey many of the house plants grown primarily for their foliage. Some of them, under favorable conditions, will flower from time to time, although few should be selected for their flowering abilities. Most of these plants are fairly easy to grow and maintain, thereby providing even the beginner a wide variety of plants from which to choose.

The plants are listed in alphabetical order, according to their common or popular names. The scientific (or Latin) name is used for plants with no popular names or for plants with more than one popular name. The index, which includes both common and scientific names, provides a convenient means of cross-checking names.

The symbols accompanying each plant name provide a quick and convenient guide to that plant's requirements. Remember, however, that these are guides and not demands. Many of these plants are tolerant by nature and will take to an east window as well as a west window; many can tolerate some direct sunlight even when none is recommended. Most crucial, perhaps, are the guides to humidity and moisture, since virtually no plant will tolerate overwatering.

IV-6

No.3 African Boxwood (<u>Myrsine africana</u>) [B-C-A-C] DESIGN: USE SYMBOLS (See Boxwood.)

This slow=growing boxwood has red stems but is similar to regular Boxwood. Many people think it is even more graceful. African Boxwood is a good plant for terrariums, if the atmosphere is not too hot.

No.3 Aralia (<u>Fatsia japonica</u>) [C-B-B-C] SYMBOLS

Aralia is characterized by Sometimes sold as <u>Aralia sieboldii</u>, beautiful, bright green, leathery, maple-like leaves highlight. In appearance, it is similar to the castor oil plant, and in fact is sometimes called false castor oil plant. It thrives in a cool environment. Aralia can easily grow leggy; it should be pruned annually in order to encourage bushy growth. It can attain a height of four feet at maturity.

A striking hybrid, <u>Fatshedra lizei</u>, crosses <u>F. japonica</u> and ivy (<u>Hedra</u>), forming a hardy climbing plant with maple-shaped leaves.

There is also a plant called false Aralia, which has graceful and feathery foliage. It bears no resemblance to the true Aralia and is difficult to grow.

No.3 Asparagus [A-B-B-B] SYMBOLS

There are two kinds of Asparagus suitable for growing as house plants: M fern Asparagus (<u>A. plumosus</u>), with slender, needle=like, dark green leaves, which give the plant a feathery appearance, and <u>A. sprengeri</u> (Emerald Feather) which has thicker yellow=green leaves and drooping stems. The latter makes a good

IV-7

plant for hanging baskets, and produces red berries at Christmastime. Both like some sun in the summer and full sun in the winter, and both can grow to a height of about two feet.

No.3 Australian Laurel (<u>Pittosporun tobira</u>) [C-B-A-B] SYMBOLS

A tolerant and slow-growing plant with leaves resembling glossy, leathery, those of Rhododendron. Australian Laurel will grow vigorously bushy and does not demand much attention. Florists often use the leaves in floral arrangements.

An interesting variegated form is <u>P. tobira variegata</u>.

No.3 Australian Umbrella Tree (<u>Schefflera actinophylla</u>) [A-A-B-A] SYMBOLS

Here is an attractive and vigorous tree with rich=looking, glossy leaves that radiate umbrella-like from the ends of several leaf stalks. It is a tough and rewarding plant, growing to six feet, which can be propagated by air=layering.

Australian Umbrella Tree is sometimes sold as <u>Brassaia actinophylla</u>. A dwarf variety, <u>B. actinophylla compacta</u>, is also available.

No.3 Baby's Tears (<u>Helxine soleirollii</u>) [B-B-A-B] SYMBOLS

This low creeper is also called Irish Moss. It likes a constantly moist (but not soggy) soil, and more than average humidity. It makes a good ground cover for terrariums, but will also grow in a pot if adequate humidity is provided. Baby's Tears may appear to die in the colder months, but after an adequate rest period it will spring back to life.

No.3 Black Pepper (Piper nigrum) A-C-B-C Symbols
While Black Pepper
~~This~~ is not a terribly attractive plant, ~~but~~ it produces
  can be used   for this reason
real peppercorns which ~~you may use~~ at the table, and is an
excellent
~~good~~ conversation piece ~~for that reason~~. The plant's berries
                              and eventually
~~begin as~~ green, later turn red, then dry up and turn black.
Pick the dried=up black corns, dry them thoroughly for several
weeks in an open spot, then use them in your pepper grinder.
The care for Black Pepper is the same as that required for
Philodendron. It is not a demanding plant.

No.3 Boxwood (Buxus) C-A-B-B Symbols
                used as
The same plant ~~which grows~~ the most prized hedges outdoors
              with glossy, bright-green leaves
can make a very attractive house plant. Boxwood is slow-growing
the ancient Oriental art of growing dwarf trees and shrubs
and dependable, a good subject for bonsai. ~~It has glossy,~~
~~bright-green leaves.~~ B. sempervirens and B. microphylla
japonica (Japanese Boxwood) are the two popular species.

No.3 Bromeliads A-B-B-C Symbols
There are more than 1,800 varieties of this popular
group, many of which are suitable for growing as house plants.
Some of them produce attractive flowers, but most are grown
for their striking and variegated leaf patterns. One distinctive feature of the Bromeliads is the rosette leaves which
form a small water cup; ~~which~~ the plant uses to hold reserve
                                     these leaves

supplies of water in its natural habitat. Since the plant
lives in the crotches of trees in Central and South America,
the water cup is an evolutionary survival characteristic.
In the home, keep the cup filled with water, changing it
weekly to keep it fresh.

A few of the more common Bromeliads are Aechmea, Ananas
(Pineapple), Billbergia, Cryptanthus (Zebra Plant), Dyckia,
Tillandsia (Spanish Moss), and Vriesia.

No.3 Caladium A-B-B-C Symbols
Caladiums, with their spectacularly-colored and variegated
leaves, are equally at home in the garden or on the window sill.
They are ideal additions to plant groupings on porch or patio
in the summer and early autumn. Give them bright light, but
     for bright leaf colors avoid
~~not~~ long periods of direct sun, ~~especially~~ in summer. ~~if you~~
                                                         kill this plant
~~want the brightest leaf colors.~~
Caladiums are grown from tubers, which can be divided
easily to produce new plants. Start the tubers in regular
potting soil at a very warm temperature—80° to 90°—and move
the young plants to a cooler spot when they have appeared.
They will attain a height of about one foot.

No.3 Cast Iron Plant (Aspidistra elatior) A-C-B-C Symbols
                      one of
This is ~~perhaps~~ the easiest plants in the world to grow.
~~as its name suggests.~~ It is virtually impossible to ~~neglect~~
through neglect
~~it to death.~~ It is also called Saloon Plant, since it was one
of the few that could survive in Victorian taverns, and it
was made immortal by George Orwell in his novel Keep the

Aspidistra Flying. If you cannot grow the Aspidistra, you
                            hopelessly
may safely conclude that you have a purple thumb ~~hopelessly~~
~~irredeemable~~.
              , which grows about two feet tall,   best
Cast Iron Plant seems to thrive ~~even better~~ when kept
slightly pot=bound, and it will appreciate having its leaves
washed occasionally. A white=striped species is called A.
variegata.

No.3 Chamaeranthemum igneum A-C-A-C Symbols
This low, spreading herb has attractive, dark green
leaves with reddish=yellow veins. It is suitable for hanging
baskets or as a low contrast in large plant groupings. It
does like warm temperatures and high humidity, however, and
might not be suitable for dry apartments.

No.3 Chinese Evergreen (Aglaonema) A-C-B-A Symbols
                       and low-growing
Here is an attractive plant that is very easy to grow.
It will stand abuse almost as easily as Cast Iron Plant.
There are at least ten common ~~ly found~~ species of the
Aglaonema, the most popular of which, A. modestum, has
interestingly mottled leaves. Perhaps the most attractive,
however, is A. pseudobractaetum, which is sometimes difficult
to find in stores and greenhouses.

No.3 Cissus A-B-B-C Symbols
                          that
Cissus is a vine plant ~~which~~ offers a number of interesting and attractive species. Most are vigorous climbers,
suitable for training on a trellis or for adding to hanging
baskets.

Among the more popular species are C. rhombifolia (Grape
Ivy), which is one of the most popular of all house plants;
C. antartica (Kangaroo Vine), which prefers a small pot; C.
antartica minima (Miniature Kangaroo Vine); C. rotundifolia;
and C. discolor (Begonia Ivy), which is perhaps the most spectacular of the genus, although difficult to grow.

Of all the Cissus, Grape Ivy is the easiest to grow,
which doubtless accounts for ~~a large share of~~ its popularity.

No.3 Coleus A-A-A-B Symbols
This old favorite has velvety leaves sporting bright
splashes of reds, pinks, purples, and yellows. There is a
seemingly endless number of varieties of Coleus, nearly all
                           of which
of them interesting, most ~~growing~~ twelve to eighteen inches in height.

Coleus is equally happy outdoors, grown as an annual in
the North, or in the window garden. It can be grown easily
from seed, and stem=tip cuttings can be taken from established
indoor plants. If you grow Coleus outdoors in summer, take
some cuttings before the first autumn freeze and root them
for growing as house plants.

The soil for Coleus should be kept damp, but not soggy.
Pinch back plants often to encourage bushy growth.

EDITORIAL STYLE SHEET

The M.I.T. Press
28 Carleton Street
Cambridge, Mass. 02142

Date: _____

Name of Author(s)/Editor(s): MULCH, PURVIS

Title of Book (Tentative/Final): NO TIME FOR HOUSE PLANTS

Press Editor (In-House/Free-Lance): ROBIN CRUISE

Spelling and Compounding of Words

1. Use Webster's Third New International Dictionary. (Webster's New Collegiate Dictionary, 7th ed., may also be used.)
2. For spelling and alphabetizing of personal names use Webster's Biographical Dictionary. Also consult the following: _____.
3. For spelling of geographical names use Webster's Geographical Dictionary.
4. For spelling of technical terms use the following reference(s): —NONE—
5. For rules on compounding and hyphenating see A Manual of Style, 12th ed. (Chicago: University of Chicago Press, 1969).
6. Do not use hyphen with most prefixes (exceptions are before capitalized words, as in pre-Columbian; when two i's come together, as in semi-industrial; to distinguish homonyms as in re-cover).
7. See also Word List (attached) for examples, exceptions, and special terms.

Punctuation

1. Follow A Manual of Style for general rules.
2. Use a comma in a compound sentence unless both clauses are very short.
3. Use a comma before "and" or "or" in a series with three or more elements.
4. Use a comma after an introductory clause or a long introductory phrase.
5. Set off nonrestrictive phrases and clauses and parenthetical expressions by commas.
6. Do not use periods with abbreviations of units of measure. Two exceptions are inch (in.) and number (no.).
7. Periods and commas are placed inside quotation marks, semicolons and colons outside. Question marks and exclamation points are placed logically. Superscript references are placed outside all punctuation.
8. Do not separate a subject from a verb by a comma except to set off an intervening nonrestrictive clause or phrase.
9. Do not use an apostrophe to form the plural in dates (e.g., 1980s).

Capitalization

1. Follow A Manual of Style and/or Webster, but be consistent.
2. In most headings and titles capitalize the principal words, that is, first word and all others except articles, conjunctions, and prepositions. Capitalize first word of a subtitle.
3. Usually capitalize only the first word and proper names in legends.
4. In table headings and in stubs of columns, main words are capitalized; elsewhere within table only the first word in a cell is capitalized.

The MIT Press 28 Carleton Street Cambridge, Massachusetts 02142   Massachusetts Institute of Technology 617-864-6900

January 20, 1977

Mr. Purvis Mulch

Dear Purvis:

I have sent to you today (under separate cover) a copy of the edited manuscript for NO TIME FOR HOUSE PLANTS for a check of editing. I have also included a copy of the editor's style sheet and word list to clarify the editing. Your manuscript was exceptionally well prepared and you will find only light copy editing for your review.

Please go through the manuscript carefully and answer all questions posed by the editor, using a red or green pencil to distinguish the marks. Do keep in mind that this is the last chance for substantive changes as we will be proceeding directly to page proof with your manuscript. Changes in the page proof stage are prohibitively expensive and could disrupt our production schedule.

We will expect to have the manuscript returned to us with your comments by February 19 unless we hear from you to the contrary. If you do have questions, please get in touch with us.

Yours sincerely,

Robin Cruise
Editorial Assistant

Editorial Style Sheet (Cont.)

Other Notes on Style

1. Follow H. W. Fowler, A Dictionary of Modern English Usage, 2nd ed., revised by Ernest Gowers (New York: Oxford, 1965), for standard English usage.
2. In most cases use "that" to introduce restrictive clauses and "which" to introduce nonrestrictive clauses.
3. Usually avoid the authorial "we"; instead use "I" or "one" or reconstruct sentence.

Editorial Style Sheet (cont.)

Use of Numbers

1. Follow recommendations in A Manual of Style or ~~(specify)~~ _____.
2. Use words for round numbers and most other numbers below (specify).
3. In most cases use arabic (rather than roman) numbers for chapters, tables, figures, appendixes, and, when necessary, sections.
4. When footnotes (or references) are numbered, start a new series in each chapter.
5. When many cross references are used, follow a double-numbering system for figures, tables, equations, sections, and subsections, using chapter number and number of item within chapter (e.g., Figure 1.2, Table 3.1, Equation 2.2).
6. In numbers containing four digits use (do not use) a comma. Please specify.
7. In consecutive page references repeat the second page number in full (e.g., 101-102, 234-239, 569-573).
8. Use figures for percentages (e.g., 15 percent).

References, Footnotes, Bibliography

1. Follow recommendations in A Manual of Style or ~~in (specify)~~ _____.
2. When bibliographical references are repeated within a chapter, use a short form rather than op. cit. (see Chicago Manual for details).
3. Notes will be as follows (specify): (a) foot of page; (b) end of chapter; (c) end of book; (d) other: _NONE_
4. References will be handled as follows (specify): (a) as footnotes; (b) placed at end of ~~book~~ and arranged alphabetically (or in order of citation); (c) author's last name and date of publication in text or footnote and full reference in bibliography.
5. Samples of bibliographical style in footnotes for books and articles are:
   a)
   b)
6. Samples of style used in References or Bibliography are as follows:
   a)
   b)

Mathematics

1. Most algebraic letters, including subscripts and superscripts, are italic.
2. All physical units (g, cm, in., lb) are roman. Functions like sin, cos, log, exp, lim, det are roman.
3. All o, O, 0 are to be interpreted as zero unless otherwise noted.
4. Use sentence punctuation around displayed equations.
5. Do not use commas in expressions of apposition like "the energy E" or "the price P."
6. Use a comma after an introductory phrase ending with a mathematical expression.
7. Do not begin a sentence with an abbreviation or a figure; either spell out or recast sentence.

The MIT Press

February 8, 1977

Mr. Purvis Mulch

Dear Purvis:

Enclosed you will find sample pages for NO TIME FOR HOUSE PLANTS for your review and comments. Please bear in mind in looking over the sample pages that they should be reviewed in terms of layout and design and not in terms of content -- i.e., do not be concerned with typographical errors, sentence structure, etc., since the sample pages are simply indications of the types of design problems inherent in the book.

We must have your approval of the sample pages February 15 in order to proceed with our production schedule.

If you have any questions, please feel free to contact our Design Department. Mario Furtado will be handling the design of your book and can bereached at 617-253-1961.

Yours sincerely,

Robin Cruise
Editorial Assistant

Encs.

The MIT Press

April 16, 1977

Mr. Purvis Mulch

Dear Purvis:

I have sent to you today (under separate cover) the galley proof and original manuscript for NO TIME FOR HOUSE PLANTS for proofreading.

Please read through the galley proof, carefully noting all errors in red pencil in the margin. The galley proof will also be read here. We will need your proof returned to us by May 7 so that your corrections can be consolidated with those of our proofreader and the entire batch can be returned to the compositor by May 12.

If you have any questions, please feel free to call us.

Yours sincerely,

Robin Cruise
Editorial Assistant

The MIT Press 28 Carleton Street Massachusetts Institute of Technology
Cambridge, Massachusetts 02142 617-864-6900

June 15, 1977

Mr. Purvis Mulch

Dear Purvis:

I am enclosing the page proof for NO TIME FOR HOUSE PLANTS with all illustrations in place. I will need these pages back by July 7.

You will notice that I have also enclosed sample pages from an index as well as the indexing chapter from the Chicago Manual of Style; these are for your personal use and need not be returned to us. We must have your index no later than July 12. I realize that you have been compiling the entries for the index for some time now, so that filling in the correct page numbers (taken from the page proof) will not be terribly time consuming for you.

Please phone if you have questions.

Yours sincerely,

Robin Cruise
Editorial Assistant

Encs.

The MIT Press
28 Carleton Street
Cambridge, MA 02142

6/15/77
RC

INDEXING INSTRUCTIONS

Instructions for preparing indexes can be found in A Manual of Style, 12th edition (Chicago: University of Chicago Press, 1969), pp. 399-430, or in the booklet reprinted from this source. To a large extent we follow the principles outlined in this booklet. However, there are a few exceptions and a few preferences, which are listed here.

1. We prefer the indented form rather than the run-in style (see sections 18.12 and 18.90) because it is easier to pick out the subentries.

2. We use complete page numbers in inclusive references rather than the somewhat complicated system suggested in the book (see section 8.36). In other words, we would cite, for example, 3-10, 100-104, 107-108, 1002-1003, 321-325, 415-532 rather than as shown in the book.

3. We prefer to arrange subentries in alphabetical rather than chronological order (see section 18.76).

4. We like to have first names or initials as well as surnames listed in the index even when persons have been referred to in the text only by the surname. In the case of really obscure persons there can be a brief description in parentheses following the name (see section 18.40).

5. Either the letter-by-letter or word-by-word alphabetical arrangement of entries is acceptable (see sections 18.49 and 18.50), as long as one system is consistently followed.

6. We prefer not to use an entry such as the adjective "Indian" (see sections 18.3 and 18.4), we would use, for example, "Indian ceremonial dances" and "Indian food" or we would use the noun "Indians" as a main entry and use the subentries "ceremonial dances of" and "food of."

Important Note to Authors

The M.I.T. Press
MASSACHUSETTS INSTITUTE OF TECHNOLOGY
CAMBRIDGE, MASSACHUSETTS 02142

To ..DESIGN.&.PRODUCTION........ Date 2/20/77

We enclose the material listed below:

Author/Title: MULCH / NO TIME FOR HOUSE PLANTS
....
Manuscript pages ..207 pp. COMPLETE AND COPY EDITED
Galley proof .... INCLUDING FRONT MATTER AND
Cut dummy .... LIST OF RUNNING HEADS
Foul galley proof ....
Page proof ....
Foul page proof ....
Plate proof ....
Blueprints ....
Other ....
....

Signed ROBIN

Author: when marking the master proof which is to be returned to us, please use a color different from that already used by the editor or printer.

AUTHOR'S ALTERATIONS
(Changes ordered in type matter which differ from original copy)

Correction of type, because of the hand work involved, is extremely expensive: a change in a single line may involve as many as five people in a composing room. At the present compositors' rate of more than $.10 per minute, many changes will involve the author, if not in a bill for alterations, at least in a possible loss of sales through an increase in selling price. The author should, therefore, in his own and everyone else's interest, confine his alterations to those essential for accuracy.

The most expensive changes are those that cause overrunning of type from one line to another. At any time they should be avoided but more than ever on page proof. Lines may have to be carried over from one page to another, even to the end of a chapter. In so doing, running heads, extracts, and footnotes may have to be replaced or transposed, and changes may be necessary in the list of contents, list of illustrations, and index.

If insertions or deletions are inevitable, then the author should, wherever possible, make compensatory cuts and additions as close as possible to the point where the change has to be made. Only in this way will he avoid the greatest risks and the worst inflation of production costs.

QUERIES ON PROOF
(Questions to the author from editor or proofreader)

To answer a query affirmatively, cross out the question mark only. If you wish no change to be made, cross out the entire query.

FOUL MANUSCRIPT AND PROOF
(Ms. or proof superseded by a succeeding stage in production)

When you receive galley proof, please do not mark the foul manuscript in any way. Similarly, when you receive page proof, do not put any marks on the foul galleys.

Please return foul material to us.

TITLE

Pages text		1	3	3
Notes (pg/ch/end)			
Bibliography			9
Glossary			
Appendixes			
~~Index~~ Illustrations		3	8
Other (Boxes)		1	5
Frontmatter		1	2
Captions			
Total ms. pp.	2	0	7

F.M.BREAKDOWNS

halftitle X title X copyright X dedication __ epigraph __
foreword __ preface X contents X list of ~~illustrations~~ symbols X
introduction __ authors note __ acknowledgements __
abbreviations

HEADINGS	1	2	3	4	5 (Boxes)	6	7																	TOTALS
Part																								
Chapter	1	1	1	1	1	1	1																	7
Number 1		16	3	2	4	2	4																	31
Number 2		7			7	5																		19
Number 3				60	3	15	2																	80
Number 4																								
Number 5																								
pp. per chapt.	3	34	9	37	11	24	15	15																148
Lists		3		9		1																		13
Tables		1			1																			2
Equations																								
Notes		1	1	1		1																		4
Extracts																								
Poetry																								
Language																								
Legends																								
ILLUSTRATIONS																								
No. line dwgs.																								
camera ready																								
draw & charge au.																								
no. halftones																								
no. color (1-h.t.)																								38
placement in text																								
grouped																								
separate sig(s)																								

THE M.I.T. PRESS Manufacturing Cost Estimate

Author/Title: AAUP BOOK PRELIMINARY / LAUNCH **Date:** 12/20/76

Manuscript Description
- Ms total pages: 200
- No. halftones: 38
- No. line ills: 0
- No. tables: 0
- est. to make: ___ book pages
- est. to make: ___ book pages
- No. to be drawn: ___
- No. camera-ready: ___

Remarks: ___

Book Description
- Total pages: 176
- Trim size: 5¾ × 6
- Type page size: ___
- Paper: 4×6 60# white offset
- Binding: ☒ sewn (cloth) ☐ pgate bd ___ HARDCOVER
- ☐ Mono ☐ Lino No. forms: 2(615), 1(132),1/6 2.75/sig
- ☒ sht/84 ☐ Film (___) ☐ Type ☒ 0% ☐ L
- ☐ pd. ☐ paper cover

Plant Costs — Estimated | Actual | supplier

Item	Estimated			Actual		
Design						
Drafting						
Composition @ $/p	1054					
Alterations	106					
Engravings/prints	—					
Repros						
C. & S. ills. @ $6	304					
Plates (x)45	226					
Blues	63					
Jacket Comp	100					
Dies	30					
Contingencies 6%	113					
TOTAL PLANT	**1997**					

Edition Costs

				TOTAL	PAPER	CLOTH
Makeready	246	5000 248	2500 248			
Presswork	135	175	261			
Paper	784	971	1457			
Binding: 4 M @ $65	3200		4650			
5 M @ .64						
75 M @ .63						
Jacket pw/paper	910	1150	1650			
Freight	60	200	300			
Plate	67	67	67			
Total Edition	4454	6011	8633			
Total plant	1997	1997	1997			
TOTAL COST	6451	8006	10630			
Plant unit	.50	.40	.27			
Edition unit	1.24	1.20	.115			
TOTAL UNIT	1.74	1.60	1.41			
sell at about	$8.75	$8.00	$7.00			

ESTIMATE DETAIL:

Composition:
- pp FM @ ___
- pp text @ ___
- pp index @ ___
- pp ills @ ___
- TOTAL ___ pages (as ___)
- pp repros/negs @ ___
- Draft ___ line ills @ ___
- C. + S. ills: ___ line @ ___
- ___ halftone @ ___
- ___ loose prints @ ___
- **TOTAL C. + S.** $ ___

Plates: No. forms ___
- First @ ___
- Second + subs. @ ___
- Work + turn @ ___
- **TOTAL PLATES** $ ___

MR: No. forms ___
- First @ ___
- Second + subs. @ ___
- Work + turn @ ___
- **TOTAL MR** $ ___

Run:
- No. forms: ___ × ___ /M @ ___ $ ___
- No. forms: ___ × ___ /M @ ___ $ ___
- No. forms: ___ × ___ /M @ ___ $ ___

Stock: Sheet size = 2.75 ÷ 2 = 1.375 sheets/book
- No. forms ___ sheets/book × ___ M books = ___ M (basis) 5000 / 7500
- (or, no. forms = rms/M) plus ___ % spoil 4000
- TOTAL SHEETS = 6105 / 7563 / 11344
- × M weight = 367
- Total weight = 2240 / 2775 / 4163
- ¢ cost/lb. = .135
- Total cost = $ 784 / 971 / 1457

Sheets

The MIT Press

28 Carleton Street
Cambridge, Massachusetts 02142

Massachusetts Institute of Technology
617-253-5646

1 March 1977

M. Bradley
MIT In-House Media Computer Composition Group

Re: Mulch/NO TIME FOR HOUSEPLANTS

Enclosed is a marked edited manuscript of 176 pages, together with composition specifications and a page layout. Also herewith are marked sample pages (indicating any changes we have made in specifications).

There are 68 illustrations in this book. What we propose is that you supply us with four sets of galleys (one marked set included). We will prepare a dummy and return the dummy to you with marked galleys. You will then provide us with three sets of page proof (one marked set included). Finally, you will provide us with one set repro (with holes where illustrations will go).

Our projected schedule is as follows:

manuscript to composition   3/2/77
galleys at MIT Press   4/15/77
galleys with dummy to comp 5/18/77
pages at MIT Press   6/15/77
pages to comp   7/13/77
repro to MIT Press   7/29/77

Please let me know immediately if you foresee any problems with this schedule. We are looking for an October 1 book date and this schedule allows that.

Thank you very much and please let me know if there are any questions.

pat mahon

Mulch 4"x6"

- 3 pi head margin
- Folio 9½ pi
- Running Head
- 3 pi back margin
- col. 1
- col. 2
- chap. sink 13 pi
- Type page - 29⅔ pi deep
- Text page - 37 pi deep
- Text page - 18 pi wide

MIT PRESS COMPOSITION SPECIFICATIONS

Book code _____ **Date** 1/15/77

Author · Title Mulch/NoTime for House Plants

Composition In House ~~Linotype / Monotype / Film / Computer / IBM Composer / Typewriter~~

Format 4"x6" ~~Trim size · 5-3/8 · 6" / 6 · 9" / 7 · 10"~~

Margin Head 3 picas · Back 3 picas

Style

Typefaces - list by style, size, leading

Palatino bold + reg. - 10/12, 9/11, 8/10

24 pt, 20 pt. numbers

Special Requirements

Epigraphs - fl. left / indent 1cm # ~~space between~~

First para under heads, fl. left

Style figures - lining / ~~oldstyle~~

Spacing - French / between words / sentences tight

~~Justified~~ Unjustified - hyphenate to achieve good ragged right: x 18 pi

Word space tight

Makeup

~~Let column depth full~~

Type page overall - wide 18 pi deep 29½ pi

Text lines per page 30 excluding RH & folio

Text measure wide 18 pi deep 27 pi

One column / Two column / ~~Three column / Marginal column /~~
1 + 2 column formats, as indicated

Space between columns 1 pi

Pages run long / short / short or long f line only

Facing pgs match / ~~as they come~~ if possible. Do not add extra space.
~~Add extra space above and below figures / tables / extracts to make facing pages match where needed.~~

Text 9/11 Palatino reg. c+lc
fl. left x 18 pi, unjust

Lists 9/11 Pal. reg. c+lc, x 18 pi, unjust.
indent nos. 1em #, runovers fl. left

Heads indent / cantel / runovers

Footnotes superior figures / regular Insert ____ space between text and notes (max - min)
fl. l / indent Insert ____ rules above notes
Chapter / Book Insert ____ space between notes

Notes 9/11 Pal. reg. c+lc
Bibliography 9/11 Pal. reg. c+lc
fl. left x 18pi Runovers fl. left Insert 5p3 space between items

Appendices 9/11 Pal. reg. c+lc, fl. left x 18 pi, unjust.

Index

Captions 9/11 Pal. reg. c+lc fl. left x 8.2 pi, unjust.

Preliminaries

Part none
Number
Headline
Text

New recto / recto or verso / 2 page spread
Part sinkage ____ lines of text to part page
Folio · RH / none
Start text on new page R or V

Chapters

Number 24 pt Palatino reg. fl. left, top of type page
Headings 10/12 Palatino bold c+lc, indent 9.3 pi, following part title V / R / V or R
top of type page, runovers indent 9.3 pi ~~New recto / recto or verso / 2 page spread~~
Chapter sinkage 12 pi lines of text to chapter page 20
Galleys / Authors / Abstracts Start text on new page R or V
Text sinkage of 12 pi first words / first line Folio · RH / (none)

Front Matter

10/12, 9/11 Palatino reg. + bold

Subheads

1 9/11 Palatino bold, all caps
   fl. left x 18 pi, unjust. in text / mcrgn / run-in / fl.l / indent — 1 line space above 0 space below

2 9/11 Palatino bold c+lc
   x 18 pi In text / mcrgn / run-in / fl.l / indent 1 line space above 0 space below

3 9/11 Palatino bold c+lc
   indent 9.3 pi, x 8.2 pi In text / margin / run-in / fl.l / indent start new page - col. 3 space above 0 space below

4 _____ In text / margin / run-in / fl.l / indent

Running Heads

Verso 9/11 Pal. reg. c+lc, top of type page Booktitle / ~~part / chapter~~ / ~~no. / heads / sections~~ Head / ~~foot~~ / fl.l / ~~RH~~ / centered indent
indent 9.3 pi

Recto 9/11 Pal. reg. c+lc, top of type page Booktitle / part / chapter / no. / heads / sections Head / ~~foot~~ / fl.l / ~~RH~~ / centered / indent
indent

Folios

Verso 9/11 Palatino reg.
top of type page ~~OS~~ / Lining Head / ~~foot~~ / fl.l / ~~RH~~ / centered indent
Recto 9/11 Palatino reg.
top of type page Head / ~~foot~~ / fl.l / ~~RH~~ / centered / indent space between RH & folio

No Time for House Plants

No Time for House Plants
A Busy Person's Guide
to Indoor Gardening

Purvis Mulch

The MIT Press
Cambridge, Massachusetts, and London, England

Contents

Preface ix

1 The Secrets of No-Work House Plant Success 1

2 Understanding House Plants 6

The Basic House Plant 6
How a Plant Feeds 8
Parts of the Plant 11
Soil 12
Acidity and Alkalinity 14
Potting Mixtures 15
Nutrient Maintenance 17
Containers 18
Watering 19
Humidity 21
Ventilation 21
Temperature 22
Light 23
Pruning and Training 24
Repotting 25
Propagation 27

3 Plant Troubles and Cures 30

Improper Handling and Care 30
Insect Foes 32
Diseases 34

4 The Foliage Plants 37

Where to Buy House Plants 38
Foliage Plants 39

2
Understanding House Plants

Every plant has its own preferences and requirements for soil type, light, temperature, ventilation, humidity, and several other factors that are within our power to control, or at least to mitigate. It is vitally important for you, as a busy indoor gardener, to understand the basics of each plant's requirements. A prior understanding will enable you to avoid much work later and will help you to achieve routine success in growing plants.

In addition to understanding these basic needs, you will want to know something about containers, repotting plants, propagation, and other topics that will help you to gain further enjoyment in raising better plants.

THE BASIC HOUSE PLANT

Location is the major difference between a house plant and an outdoor plant. Given the proper climate, all house plants could live and flourish outdoors. All are derived from forebears that lived, reproduced, and died outdoors, whether on a forest floor in central Europe or in the bough of a tree in a South American rain forest.

Roots

Roots serve two main purposes—to anchor the plant in the ground and to supply water and mineral salts from the soil. Bulbs, corms, rhizomes, and tubers serve much the same purposes while simultaneously acting as food storage areas. Roots, like the aboveground parts of plants, may be pruned without injuring the plant in any way.

If you water from the top, remember to remove any excess water from the saucer; allowing plants to stand in water encourages root rot. In time, you should learn to give each plant just enough water to soak it thoroughly, with very little excess drainage.

Some other watering tips:

1. Do not allow water to stand in the crown of any plant; this will encourage decay.

2. Never use very cold water, especially for tropical plants. Keep an open jar of water at room temperature for your house plants. Not only will the proper temperature be assured, but some of the chemicals in the water will have been dissipated by the time it is given to plants.

3. Artificially softened water may be detrimental to plant growth. If you can, use rainwater, or water that has not been softened. Fluorine and chorine, on the other hand, do not seem to pose any problems.

Table 1 Watering Needs of Plants Under Various Conditions

Plants will need more water when:	Plants will need less water when:
They are in a period of active growth	They are in a period of rest (usually during the winter)
They are in bright light	They are in dim light or under artificial light
Room humidity is low	Room humidity is high
Room temperature is high	Room temperature is under 70°
They are contained in small pots	They are in large pots
They are in clay pots	They are in nonporous pots
They are fast-growing varieties	They are slow-growing varieties
They are planted in sandy soil	They are planted in heavy soil
They are in flower or about to go into flower	

4

The Foliage Plants

The number and variety of house plants is staggering. For every combination of conditions a home can offer—including heat, light, and humidity—there are literally thousands of suitable house plant varieties. House plants offer a virtually limitless selection of sizes, forms, colors, patterns and textures, growth patterns, and flowering habits. Plant selections should be made so as to reconcile personal tastes with home growing conditions.

The house plants selected for discussion in this chapter are merely representative of the far greater varieties available. Many of the most common plants have been included while the more difficult varieties have been avoided. This chapter includes all the old favorites as well as some newer varieties and unusual plants which can add zest to your collection.

The plants have been divided into four broad categories: foliage plants, flowering plants, fruiting plants, and cacti and succulents. Within each group, individual plants are listed alphabetically by their common names, followed (in parentheses) by their scientific (or Latin) designations. The scientific name comprises both the genus and species.

FOLIAGE PLANTS

In this chapter, we will survey many of the house plants grown primarily for their foliage. Some of them, under favorable conditions, will flower from time to time although few should be selected for their flowering abilities. Most of these plants are fairly easy to grow and maintain, thereby providing even the beginner a wide variety of plants from which to choose.

The plants are listed in alphabetical order, according to their common or popular names. The scientific (or Latin) name is used for plants with no popular names, or for plants with more than one popular name. The index, which includes both common and scientific names, provides a convenient means of cross-checking names.

The symbols accompanying each plant name provide a quick and convenient guide to that plant's requirements. Remember, however, that these are guides and not strict demands. Many of these plants are tolerant by nature and will take to an east window as well as a west window; many can tolerate some direct sunlight even when none is recommended.

Dieffenbachia

There are many species of this popular plant, often called Dumbcane. It is prized for its large leaves with interesting markings, usually variations of cream and white on dark green. *Dieffenbachia* is a hardy plant and is not difficult to grow. Although growth is slow, most varieties attain a height of eighteen to twenty-four inches.

D. arvida "Exotica" is popular because it is even more durable than other members of the family. Other well-known species include *D. picta*, *D. amoena*, *D. sequina*, and *D. bowmannii*.

While Dieffenbachia has no special cultural requirements, it grows best under warm conditions and appreciates having its foliage cleaned regularly. The plant may be propagated by rooting stem cuttings in moist, warm peat.

Caution: Eating or nibbling on the leaves of *Dieffenbachia* can cause severe swelling of the tongue and mouth tissues, hence its popular name, Dumbcane. It should not be grown in a home with toddlers.

Many plants, such as this *Dieffenbachia pieta*, grow better when slightly potbound.

Dracaena

The many available species of *Dracaena* vary so greatly in appearance that some appear to be unrelated. Most grow tall—five feet or more—on sturdy stalks. They are very tough plants, tolerant of a surprising amount of neglect, all in all one of our most dependable house plants.

Some varieties to investigate are *D. deremensis* "Warnecki," *D. fragrans* (cornlike leaves), *D. fragrans massangeana* (yellow-striped leaves), *D. marginata* (an exciting plant with grasslike, cream-colored foliage edged in red—sometimes sold as *D. marginata tricolor*), *D. sanderiana* (white-banded leaves), *D. godseffiana*, *D. draco* (the Dragon Tree of the Canary Islands), and many others, some of which will doubtless be available from a good supplier. The dracaena mentioned, however, are some of the most attractive examples and are among the easiest to grow.

Dracaena sanderiana, *D. fragrans*, and Zebra Plant (*Aphelandra*).

Appendix 1

The ABCs of Artificial Light

The recent introduction of fluorescent tubes designed specifically for plant growing has been a great boon for indoor gardeners. With the aid of artificial light, we can now grow lush, green plants in areas where they would never grow before. A windowless bathroom, which might offer ideal humidity and temperature conditions, can now be made into an ideal plant-growing environment. Plants growing on a drab northern window sill can now receive supplemental light during winter's short and dark days. Dim corners of any room can be transformed into green showplaces. Cuttings and seedlings can now make faster and surer progress under artificial light, and we can even grow vegetables in the dead of winter in the bedroom or kitchen. Artificial lighting is not essential for house plant success, but it certainly broadens growing horizons and increases chances for maximum rewards.

The outdated incandescent bulb still offers some

Bibliography

ARTIFICIAL LIGHT GARDENING

Bickford, Elwood D. and Dunn, Stuart. *Lighting for Plant Growth*. Kent, Ohio: Kent State University Press, 1972.

Cherry, Elaine C. *Fluorescent Light Gardening*. New York: Van Nostrand Reinhold Co., 1965.

Elbert, George A. *The Indoor Light Gardening Book*. New York: Crown Publishers, Inc., 1975.

Fitch, Charles Marden. *The Complete Book of Houseplants under Lights*. New York: Hawthorn Books, 1975.

Kranz, Frederick H. and Jacqueline. *Gardening Indoors under Lights*. rev. ed. New York: Viking Press, 1971.

BEGONIAS

Brilmayer, Bernice, *All about Begonias*. New York:

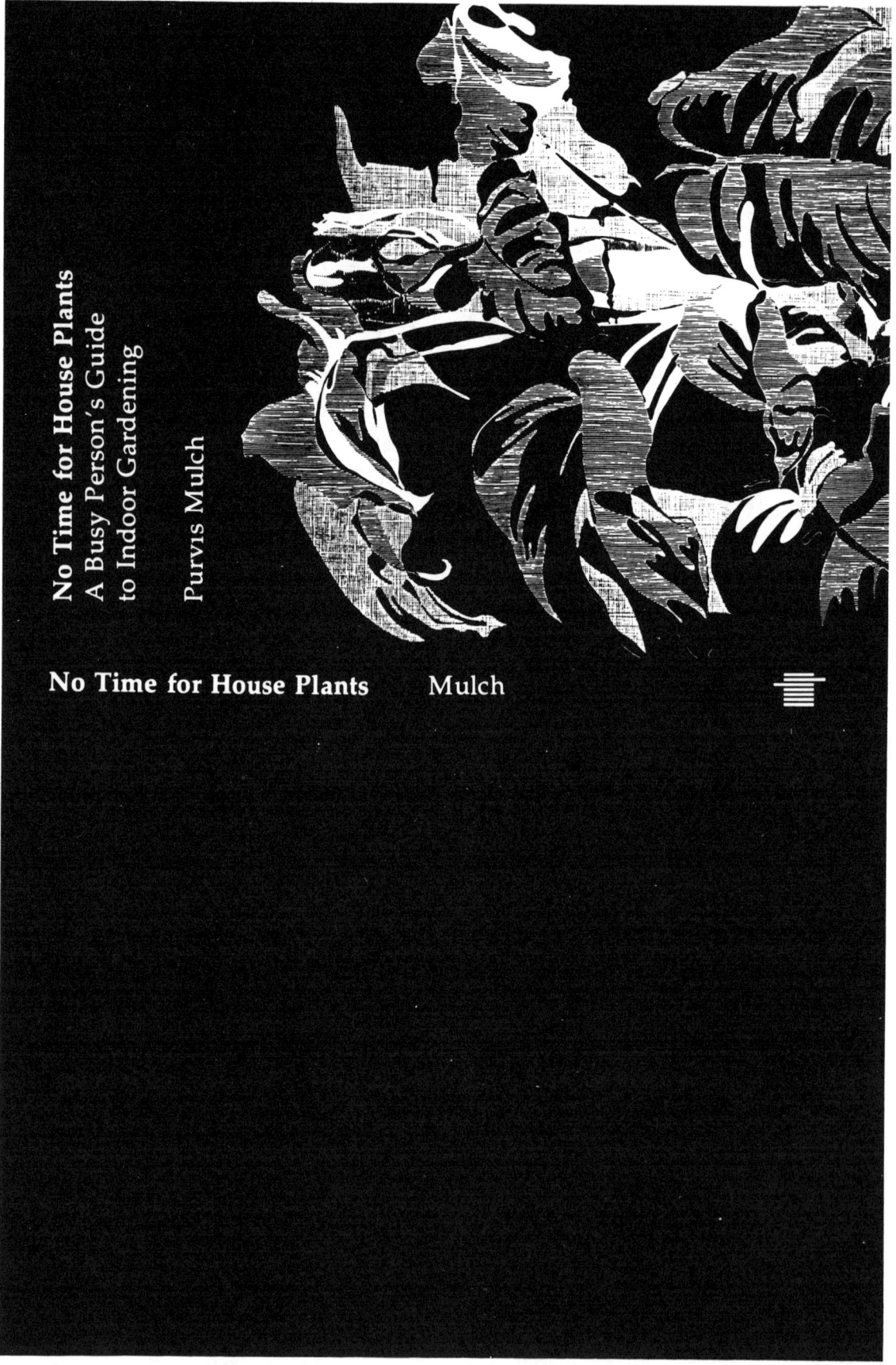

Background: PMS 354; Illustration: Black overprinting green; All type & colophon: Drop out white

The MIT Press

28 Carleton Street
Cambridge, Massachusetts 02142

Massachusetts Institute of Technology
617-253-5646

March 15, 1977

Note:

If flaps are to be included, please add 2 1/8" (PMS 354) to each side of mechanical.

Thank you very much.

The MIT Press
Massachusetts Institute of Technology
Cambridge, Massachusetts 02142

Date **March 14, 1977**
Our PO No. ___
Job No. ___

Book Jacket Printing Order

To **Arlington Lithograph** See your quotation of **Please call Pat Mahon 253-5640**
Author/Title **Mulch/No Time for House Plants** Include breakdown with estimate

Quantity **4700**

Dimensions
Spine **3/8"**
Front **4 1/4" x 6 1/4"**
Back **4 1/4" x 6 1/4"**
Flaps **4"**

☒ offset   ☐ letterpress

Trim size **12 7/8** inches wide x **6 1/4** inches deep   ☒ bleed, allow 1/8" for trim   ☐ no bleed

Copy **Herewith complete mechanical**

Proofs ___ sets salt prints   **1** sets 3M prints   imposition

Stock   Grade **offset coated**   Color **white**   Basis **80 lb.**
Size **(1 side)**   No. sheets ___
☒ supplied by printer   ☐ supplied by MIT

Ink   ☐ black only   ☒ black and **PMS 354**   ☐ no black

Coating   ☐ press varnish   ☐ plastic coat   ☐ none

Delivery **100** trimmed jackets to The MIT Press office
400 trimmed jackets to our warehouse at: The MIT Press
c/o UNISERV, Inc.
525 Great Road (Rte. 119)
Littleton, Mass 01460

4200 untrimmed jackets to binder:
Colonial Press
Plant #2 Adams Road
Clinton, MA

0 trimmed jackets to our London warehouse:
P.A.G.E.S.
17-21 Sunbeam Road
London N.W. 10
ENGLAND

Special Instructions   Please ship jackets by **3/28**
When the run is finished, please send us about 6 random press sheets that are representative of the run as a whole. Wait for our telephone OK before shipping sheets to the binder. Thank you.

Signed _Kenna Schenll_   The MIT Press

Production / Design / MIT / 109

MIT Press

28 Carleton Street
Cambridge, Mass. 02142

To Murray Printing Company
Author/Title Mulch/NO TIME FOR HOUSEPLANTS

BINDING SPECIFICATIONS

Date 3/16/77
Purchase Order G-5678

See your quotation of

SHEETS
Quantity 4000 To come on From your pressroom
Sheet size 33 x 50 Imposition yours
Quantity to bind 4000 (all) Hold balance as F&G's folded sheets

OTHER MATERIALS
Endpapers printed plain
Headbands white black other supplied by Murray; please match color white of text stock as closely as possible
Cloth
Board .080 binders .088 binders .040 red flex. other .070
Foil XXXXXXXXXXXXXXXXXXXXXXXXXXXXXXXXXXXXXXXXXXXX
XXXXXXXXXXXXXXXXXXXXXXXXXXXXXXXXXXXXXXXXXXXX
Covers printed paper nonwoven (to be adhered over boards) supplied by MIT Press

BINDING
Trim size 5⅜x8 6x9 7x10 other 4 x 6 upright Head margin 3 picas Gutter margin 3 picas
(On adhesive bound books, trim size and gutter margin are given as the full dimensions, before trimming the spine)
Pages 224 No. signatures 3/64's, 1/32 Bulk 9/16"
Cancel or inserts none
Style Smyth sewn hardcover Smyth sewn paperback adhesive paperback
Reinforcing none paper cambric Edges smooth rough Line one super two supers paper
Cover one-piece two-piece three-piece Spine round flat (Flat spines should not extend beyond front and back boards)

STAMPING none
Spine one hit two hits blind color
Front one hit two hits blind color
Back one hit two hits blind color
Submit two sample cases for approval (with covers glued over boards)

SPECIAL INSTRUCTIONS

PACKING SEE SEPARATE NOTICE ATTACHED
Pack books in 275-lb test, double-wall cartons. Mark each carton with:
Author MULCH
Title NO TIME
Books per carton please add
Code MNT

Pack cartons on skids which are to become the property of The MIT Press and must not exceed the following dimensions:
36" x 28"
7" to 9" clearance from floor to underside

Bound books due our warehouse

DELIVERY
23 copies to the MIT Press office
0 copies to T. D. Downing Co. for onward shipment to London for our London office. See our Letter of July 1, 1970.

Author's copies as follows (shipping labels attached):
10 copies to:
Purvis Mulch

Balance to: Technical Impex Corp.
Alex Bluid, 9. Union and Merrimack Streets
Lawrence, Massachusetts

Signed P.A.M. 8/1/76
production manager

---

28 Carleton Street
Cambridge, Mass. 02142

To Murray Printing Company
Author/Title Mulch/NO TIME FOR HOUSEPLANTS

PRINTING SPECIFICATIONS

Purchase order
See your quotation of 11/30/76

COPY
Text copy repros IBM Composer typewritten bound book negatives other mechanicals with salts in place for halftones and camera-
Text reduction (% of original) 100%
Illustration copy separate in text copy none copy in place for line drawings.
You have already shot halftones and have negs on hand. (38 in all)
We will see these in place in book blues.

(There are also 30 line drawings which are in place in mechanicals.)

Text blueprints complete 1st signature only

PLATES
Offset surface other
Letterpress plastic print from type other
Trim size 5⅜x8 6x9 7x10 other 4 x 6 upright Head margin Gutter margin
(On adhesive bound books, trim size and gutter margin are given as the full dimensions, before trimming the spine)
Pages 224 No. signatures Imposition yours
Cancel or insert none

PRESSWORK
Quantity 4000 Ink color Black only other
Text stock size 33 x 50 basis 50# vellum Mill brand R&E Book
No. sheets about 7800 sheets Supplied by MIT yes (on hand in lot number G-567) Supplied by printer

SPECIAL INSTRUCTIONS

SCHEDULE
Blues due MIT (Cambridge) Blues ret. to printer (Cambridge) Sheets due binder

DELIVERY
F&G's send 2 sets to The MIT Press with foul blues
(F&G's, with blueprints, must be sent immediately after job comes off press)

Flat sheets

Acceptance of this order will be considered as your agreement that the negative flats produced as part of this order become the property of The Massachusetts Institute of Technology Press.

Signed P.A.M. 8/1/76
production manager

M.I.T. PRESS Manufacturing Cost Estimate — RELEASE COST SHEET

Date: 2/15/77

Author/Title: **NO TIME FOR HOUSE PLANTS**

Manuscript Description
- Ms total pages: 207 (exclud) — No. halftones: 38 — est. to make: 38 — book pages
- No. tables: 2 — No. line ills.: 0 — est. to make: — book pages
- No. to be drawn: 0 — No. camera-ready: —

Remarks:

Book Description
- Total pages: 224 — trim size: 4x6 upright — No. forms: 7/32's
- Type page size: 33 x 50 — 60# offset — ☐ Mono ☐ Lino ☒ Film ( ) Type
- Binding: ☒ sewn (cloth — Digite Plysoptic bd ☐ paper cover
  - Diapre Plyoptic

Plant Costs — Estimated / Actual / supplier

	Estimated							Actual		TOTAL	PAPER	CLOTH
Design												
Dusting 36#pp x 2.50	95											
Composition 186 x 6.	1116											
Alterations	121											
Engravings/prints	—											
Repros	—											
C. & S. ills. 38 x 3.72	142											
Blues	67											
Jacket Comp	150											
Dies	30											
Contingencies 6%	103											
TOTAL PLANT	1824											

Edition Costs	4000	5000	7500									
Makeready	401	451	588									
Presswork	552	686	1012									
Paper 4 M @ .60	2400											
Binding 5 M @ .59		2950										
7.5 M @ .57			4275									
M @												
Jacket pw/paper	800	850	1125									
Freight	100	125	188									
Plates	387	387	387									

Total Edition	4640	5449	7575									
Total plant	1824	1824	1824									
TOTAL COST	6464	7273	9399									
Plant unit	.46	.36	.24									
Edition unit	1.16	1.09	1.01									
TOTAL UNIT	1.62	1.45	1.25									
4 wker 50# p bd	1.59	1.43	1.23									

ESTIMATE DETAIL:

Composition:
- pp FM @
- pp text @
- pp index @
- pp ills @

TOTAL ____ pages (as ____) $

C. + S. ills:
- Draft — line ills @
- pp repros/negs @
- line ills @
- halftone @
- loose prints @
- TOTAL C. + S. $

Plates: No. forms =
- First @
- Second + subs. @
- Work + turn @
- TOTAL PLATES $

MR: First @
- Second + subs. @
- Work + turn @
- TOTAL MR $

Run: No. forms: ____ x ____ M @ = $
- No. forms: ____ x ____ M @ = $
- No. forms: ____ x ____ M @ = $

Stock: Sheet size = 33 x 50, 60# — 4000 — 5000 M (basis) 7500
- No. forms ____ sheets/book x ÷ 2 = ____ M books ____ sheets/book
- (or, no. forms = rms/M) plus ____ % spoil

		Sheets	
TOTAL SHEETS =	7800	9700	14300 (acc. to print)
60# x M weight =	.208 m	.208 m	.208 m
Total weight =	1622.4	2017.6	2974.4
x cost/lb.	.34	.34	.34
Total cost = $	552.	685.98	1011.296

50#	.174 M	.174 M	.2833
	1357.2	1687.8	.34
	.34	.34	846.
	461.	574.	

112 / MIT / Design / Production

The MIT Press 28 Carleton Street Cambridge, Massachusetts 02142   Massachusetts Institute of Technology 617-253-5646

Purvis Mulch

8 January 1977

Dear Purvis Mulch,

We are enclosing a copy of our author questionnaire which is essential to our overall marketing plans for your book <u>No Time for House Plants</u>. As far as you are able to, please provide suggestions about advertising, the names of professional groups and/or industrial concerns whose mailing lists may be useful in promoting the book, the names of periodicals which are likely to review the book, in addition to your curriculum vitae.

We would appreciate it if you would fill out the enclosed questionnaire as completely and as soon as possible. Please return it to me at the above address.

Thank you for your prompt attention to this matter.

Sincerely,

Mary E. Collins

Mary E. Collins
Marketing Department

AUTHOR QUESTIONNAIRE

When completed, please return to:

Mary E. Collins
THE MIT PRESS
28 Carleton St.
Cambridge, Mass. 02142

TITLE OF BOOK AS IT IS TO APPEAR IN PRINT:

No Time for House Plants: A Busy Person's Guide to Indoor Gardening

The promotion of a book is necessarily a mutual effort: the author has the information, the publisher the organization. The effectiveness of our promotional copy -- for jacket, catalogue, publicity releases, flyers, brochures and space advertising -- depends directly upon the thoroughness with which you complete this questionnaire. We urge you to develop your replies to whatever extent necessary to give us adequate and useful information.

PLEASE RETURN THIS QUESTIONNAIRE AT THE EARLIEST POSSIBLE DATE.

Date: January 29, 1977

ABOUT THE AUTHOR:

Your name as you wish it to appear in print   Purvis Mulch

Home address and phone number

Present title and position   freelance garden writer, lecturer, and plant exorcist
Copyright information required:

   Your legal address

   Nationality U.S.

Education. Please list college, concentrations, degrees (with dates), and honors
Allentown Business College; certificate, payroll accounting, 1952
University of Iowa; B.A. (history), B.S. (repotting), 1961 (no honors)

Research. Please list any research, discoveries, and inventions, and publications reporting such work.

Research is not my forte. In 1958, I grew two coleus for a period of eight months, one of which was shut in a dark closet and given no water or food, the other in a sunny window where it was watered regularly and fertilized with a balanced formula according to directions. Both died.

---

page 2

Previous Books. Please give titles, publishers, and dates.

The Earthworm Book (contract, Rodale Press, Inc., 1977)

Affiliations. Please separate present from past, giving pertinent academic, business, and governmental affiliations; include professional and other honors, and relevant offices held.

President, Dane County (   ) chapter, American Gourd Society (1974-present)
Affiliate, Smithsonian Institution, 1972-73
Member, National Geographic Society, 1970-71
Member, Book-of-the-Month Club, 1969 (revoked)
Close friend of former Phi Beta Kappa member (1939)
Life member, American Red Cross Gallon Club (1957)

Other Biographical Information. Place of birth, marital status, children. Principal foreign countries lived in, etc., any notable information that may help fill out the picture.

Born of wealthy but honest parents in Allentown, Pa., 1933. Still bear scars of Great Depression. Ate insects in father's victory garden 1942-45. Grew first house plant in 1948 (eggplant). Average student in public school, brilliant but undisciplined in college, only history undergraduate at Univ. of Iowa. to ever pass Advanced Bridge and Crown course in dental school. Became intensely interested in gardening when, in post-college rooming house in Emmaus, Pa., mushrooms grew under bed. Investigation into causes led to general gardening inquiry, also clear understanding of Emmaus, Pa. housing code. From that point on, it was one thing after the other.

page 4

Description. In describing what your book is about, please cover these areas: PURPOSE, SUBJECT MATTER, WHAT MAKES YOUR BOOK UNIQUE? INTENSITY or EXTENSIVENESS OF TREATMENT, THE AUDIENCE INTENDED, APPROACH TO THE SUBJECT AREA COVERED, SPECIAL NEED FULFILLED BY THE BOOK, CONCLUSIONS.

Your response will provide us with our primary source of reliable information for use in all our advertising and promotional efforts on behalf of the book. WE URGE YOU, THEREFORE, TO BE AS COMPLETE AS POSSIBLE.

In 1973, with the purchase of a new house, I was determined to increase my house plant population. Still, I realized that, with my busy schedule, I would not have much time to devote to indoor plants. I was frequently gone for long periods of time, and many days, even while in town, I simply have no time to fuss with plants.

I therefore sought to find methods to raise interesting and beautiful house plants with the least amount of effort. All the house plant books I checked, however, were apparently written by enthusiasts who spent unending hours in careful watering, potting, repotting, propagating, tying up, inducing to flower, humidifying, bathing, and even talking to their plants in an effort to get them to grow. There was no book for the casual house plant grower.

There is now such a book. By researching many sources, and through past personal experience and experimentation, I have narrowed down the crucial requirements for a "no-time" indoor house plant population. The research yielded two cardinal rules: Choose plants that are tolerant of adverse conditions, and then give them the right conditions to grow without your constant attention.

The implementation of these rules forms the crux of this book. I explain how to choose plants, tell which are the easiest to grow, and explain the conditions of light, soil moisture, humidity, and temperature that each of more than a hundred indoor plants requires. I explain, in short, how your house plants can live well without your constant attention and painstaking devotion.

The chapter on understanding house plants is critically important to the "no-time" system, since it details the initial requirements plants need for success, including potting mixtures, fertilizing, containers, watering, humidity, ventilation, temperature, light, and pruning. When these conditions are met at the very beginning, countless hours will be saved later in nursing plants or attempting to track down troubles.

There is a separate chapter devoted to plant troubles and cures, and special sections on artificial light, summer care, and lists of plants for various conditions of light and temperature. For those who wish to devote a little more time to raising house plants, there is detailed information on repotting, propagation, training, dish gardens, planters, bottle gardens and terrariums, kitchen scrap gardens, and growing vegetables indoors.

The bulk of the book, however, comprises listings of more than a hundred "easy" foliage plants, flowering plants, and succulents, including cacti, giving light, soil moisture, and humidity requirements for each.

For the home owner or apartment dweller who wants to raise several dozen attractive house plants while spending only a few minutes a day

Artwork. Specify illustrations, figures, photos, etc., by figure or cut number if possible, that can be used in advertising to stimulate interest.

Any of the photographs or drawings submitted with the manuscript may be used for advertising purposes.

Endorsements. Who are considered leaders in the field (names and addresses) from whom we might solicit endorsements of your book after publication? Both foreign and domestic leaders should be considered.

M. C. Goldman, Managing Editor, Organic Gardening & Farming magazine
Jeffrey Klein, Editorial Board, Mother Jones magazine
Elvin MacDonald, Senior Editor, House Beautiful magazine
Heather Tischbein, Managing Editor, Countryside magazine

Reviews. List periodicals, domestic and foreign, which are most likely to review the book. Please star major journals.

The four listed above, plus NYTBR, Apartment Ideas, Apartment Life, Ms, Esquire, Better Homes & Gardens, Playboy, other magazines geared to the single and/or working life.

page 5

Advertising. Please list magazines and scholarly journals which accept advertising, where notice of your book might be especially effective.

The same magazines previously cited for review

Mailing lists. Please list the professional groups and industrial concerns whose mailing lists may be useful in promoting this book. Your efforts in this area can be especially valuable. Can you help us to secure the lists of any of these organizations? If so, please specify.

Subscription lists to the above magazines would be effective; also numerous garden clubs, e.g., African-Violet Society of America, American Fern Society, American Horticultural Society, Cactus and Succulent Society of America, etc.

Newspapers. Please list hometown or other newspapers to whom you or your books are news.

---

page 6

Competition with other books: Please give titles and dates of publication.

There are too many house plants books in print to attempt a listing here. However, there is none competing directly--none that instructs the busy working person in specific methods of caring for house plants with a minimum of time expended.

Courses. Please list courses for which your book might be used as text or collateral reading.

Probably extension or short courses in growing indoor plants.

The MIT Press

28 Carleton Street
Cambridge, Massachusetts 02142

Massachusetts Institute of Technology
617-253-5646 Telex 92-1497

Purvis Mulch

Dear Purvis Mulch,

Enclosed is the draft of an announcement of your book. This will be used on the flaps of the jacket and in our catalogue. Please return it with your corrections of fact and suggestions at your earliest convenience. If you have no changes, or only very minor ones, you may want to call either Randall Goff or myself at (617) 253-2884.

Sincerely,

Mary E. Collins
Mary E. Collins
Marketing Department
June 15, 1977

Enc.

Jacket copy -- Purvis Mulch/NO TIME FOR HOUSEPLANTS

Here at last is THE definitive, busy person's guide to raising, feeding, caring for, and loving houseplants -- a book so comprehensive and so comprehensible that no one who reads it need ever exclaim, "I have no time for houseplants!"

Three introductory chapters explain carefully and thoroughly the basic needs of your house plants -- soil, water, air, light -- and how you can meet those needs simply yet fully. Then come several specialized sections which show the best and easiest ways to make your particular plant healthy and happy -- whether it's a colorful flowering plant, a beautiful lush foliage plant, or a miniaturized terrarium collection.

Throughout the book, many photographs and sketches give you an exact idea of what to do and how best to do it.

Purvis Mulch is a columnist and houseplant lover, author of such books as I LIKE PLANTS and PLANTS ARE A LOT LIKE PEOPLE IN SOME WAYS.

The MIT Press 28 Carleton Street Massachusetts Institute of Technology
Cambridge, Massachusetts 02142 617-253-5646

Sketch of marketing plan

Direct mail

A sample copy would be sent to each of our 500 best retail accounts accompanied by a special order form quoting appropriate endorsements.

We would also compile a list of people in the trade (e.g. nurseries) to mail to.

An offer of a sample copy would be sent to all our bookseller customers.

Advertising

An announcement of the book would be included in our fall catalog.

This title would also be included in seasonal announcement ads in publications such as Publisher's Weekly and Library Journal.

Since we usually group books for ads, and this title could not be grouped with others on our list, individual advertisements would be very few, placed in horticultural magazines.

Review copies

We maintain our review list on a computer system such that we can order labels of publications based on subject matter and importance. In the case of this book we would choose review media coded as major newspapers, major general magazines, general science publications, including newspaper science writers, general biology publications, publications on botany, ecology horticulture, and phytopathology.

In addition to these, we would send additional copies to review media not on our standing review file, such as gardening magazines, home magazines, and women's magazines.

The approximate total number dispatched would probably be in the range of 180-240, probably closer to the latter.

PROMOTION AND DIRECT MARKETING FALL 1977

Promotion Expense '3070

Book   Bound date   Edition
NO TIME FOR HOUSEPLANTS   10/77   7500
by Purvis Mulch
4x6 -- 176 pp. -- $6.95T   Publication date
                                         11/15/77

Direct Mail 1800 (&'200)

Although this is primarily a trade title, it will also be featured in all 8 subject matter catalogs. In addition, it will play a prominent role in the Christmas Gift Treasury Catalog.

Space Advertising 500

Given the limitations of budget, we must stretch our advertising as far as possible. Ads will be placed in as many as of the following as is feasible:

PW   Plants Alive
New York Times   Boston magazine
Home Garden Magazine   Countryside
Apartment Life
Apartment World
Boston Globe
McCall's
House & Garden
Avant Gardener

Exhibits 50

MIT Booth: ABA
            CBA
Montreal Book Fair
Globe Book Fair

Seasonal Catalog 70

Announced in the Fall 1977 catalog mailed to bookstores, libraries, wholesalers, and the MIT community.

Review Copies 150

100 or so complimentary copies will include magazines listed under "Space Ads" above, plus:

        Esquire   Ms
        Cosmo   Mother Jones
        Playboy   Organic Gardening & Farming
        Countryside   House Beautiful
Boston Herald American   American Nurseryman
        Phoenix, Real Paper, etc.
          and to 10-20 plant "experts"

THE UNIVERSITY OF NORTH CAROLINA PRESS

Table of Contents

Acquisitions and Administration

Editorial and Marketing Estimate Requests / 123
Decision to Publish / 124
Contract / 125

Editorial

Manuscript Record and Covering Letter to Author / 127
Correspondence with Author and Editorial Notes / 128
Correspondence with Copy Editor / 131
Author's Memorandum / 132
Editing Notes and Style Sheet / 133
Edited Manuscript / 134
Production Notes / 154
Covering Letter and Book Plan / 155
Correspondence with Author / 156
Transmittal to Production and Editorial Checklist / 157
Proof Transmittal and Author's Response to Sample Pages / 160
Corrected Sample Pages / 161

Production and Design

Manuscript Castoff / 162
Production Cost Estimates / 163
OCR Typescript and Transmittal / 164
Composition Specifications / 165
Job Sheet and Sample Pages / 166
Printing and Binding Specifications / 168
Proof Transmittal and Schedule / 169
Final Job Cost Estimate and Transmittal / 170
Repros and Blues Check Sheet and Final Production Plan / 171
Print Order Request and Purchase Order / 172

Sales and Promotion

Edition Size and Title Memoranda / 173
Author's Biographical and Publicity Questionnaire / 175
Promotion Plan / 177
Marketing and Design Meeting Notes and Catalog Description / 178
News Releases / 179
Promotion and Advertising Schedules, Budgets, and Ads / 180
Ad Transmittal and Printing Quotation / 183
Circular / 184
Review List / 185

MEMO: Acquisitions / Administration

The Mulch manuscript was logged in by our editorial department in December 1975. At first our staff was skeptical at best about the appropriateness of a university press publishing, or even hypothetically publishing, a trade title like the Mulch. Our readers, two botanists and a plant store owner, were mixed in their reactions to the manuscript and shared some of our skepticism, but despite the divergent opinions of our readers and our initial misgivings, we soon warmed to the project and to the charm of Purvis.

The manuscript was returned twice to the author for revisions suggested by our readers and the editor-in-chief. Once revisions were completed, the next step was to prepare our decision-to-publish form, including the title budget, and present the project to our board of governors.

NO TIME FOR HOUSEPLANTS? is not a typical university press publication. In publishing the Mulch we were obviously entering a very crowded and highly competitive market in which an attractive price and a well-planned marketing approach would be critical to success. A low unit manufacturing cost, under $1.50, was a necessity.

Our manufacturing estimates were based on a print run of 7,500 copies, a figure that the director, editor-in-chief, marketing manager, and business manager nervously settled on after admitting that our resources and list of trade publications would limit our marketing effort to the southeast.

The completed decision-to-publish form, accompanied by the readers' reports and a statement from the sponsoring editor, was presented to our board of governors, whose editorial and finance committees consider the merit and financial factors associated with each project. Following acceptance by the board, a contract was drawn up with Ms. Mulch and the manuscript was sent for copyediting.

MEMO: Editorial Procedures

The managing editor was first exposed to the houseplant MS when the comptroller asked for an estimate for editorial overhead. The figure given was based on an average editorial cost figured from one year's experience in working with free-lance editors and was for the entire MS, not just the portion to be edited for the project. We had averaged $1.50 per MS page, which included the free-lance editing, the free-lance proofreading, and the in-house time spent on transferring marks, jacket preparation, and correspondence. In the few years immediately before working exclusively with free-lance editors, our editorial overhead had been approximately $4.00 per MS page.

The managing editor selected an experienced free-lance editor, and, when the MS was returned to the press, a photocopy was sent to the author for review. A covering letter was sent explaining that this was the appropriate time to make final changes, as he would see only page proof. Although we allow 5% of composition cost for author's alterations, this figure was not mentioned in the letter although it had appeared in the contract. The log reveals interesting differences in the percentage allowed for AAs: MIT allows 10%; Chicago 5%; Texas none; and Toronto budgets 20% of composition. When the photocopy was returned to the managing editor, she transferred the author's answers to queries and other changes to the original MS and, after preparing the editorial checklist, copy for running heads, and the frontmatter, gave the MS to the production manager for design and composition. The managing editor approved sample pages, and a production schedule was sent to the author. The original MS and two sets of proof were sent to the author for corrections, and the proof was also read by both production and editorial proofreaders. Revised pages and repros were checked by the managing editor, and the rest is history-- the history of One Book / Five Ways.

MEMO: Production / Design

In an effort to design and produce something that would compete in the book store with other trade titles--and, of course, we wanted the book to be attractive and readable--we did many things with this book that we would not ordinarily do with our usual scholarly monograph. One was the use of a photograph taken by the son of the production and design manager of a pathetic plant, a photo that demonstrates in its poignancy the theme of NO TIME FOR HOUSEPLANTS? Other factors in our planning had to do with the use of halftones, which are now so inexpensive to print, and the suggestion of a legibility study that a short measure containing just the phrase that the reader perceives with one eye movement is the most readable. Since it was impossible to produce a four-color trade jacket on our budget, we opted for a little bright green subliminal package that we hoped would attract the curious, sophisticated, busy, professional reader.

After layouts and specs were completed by the designer, the MS was turned over to a senior compositor who worked up the sample pages, and then the book went to the keyboard for corrections and line justification. Although the ragged right phrasing proved interesting, there were problems with ideal breaks. After galleys had been run through the VIP, they were pasted up, allowing a flexible column length for smoother layout work in placement of photos and headings. After paging, the book was proofread, line corrections were made, a quality check was made by four people in production and one in editorial, and the repros were off to the printer. Normally the book would have gone through a similar check in blues, and since this step was bypassed for the project, we failed to notice that the photo on the title page, which is also on the cover, was flopped. Our struggling plant must simply be reaching for the sun--wherever it may be.

MEMO: Sales/Promotion

In this project, North Carolina is the only press without sales representation. This was the controlling factor in our initial printing decision. It also controlled our promotion plans. We decided to focus our marketing effort on North Carolina, South Carolina, and Virginia, where our relationships with booksellers are well established, and in the author's home area--where she says she's well established. Our rather small marketing area is the major difference between North Carolina's promotion plan and those of other presses. We scheduled two "regional" ad campaigns, one on publication and the second during the Christmas season. Our only national ads are for Publishers Weekly. National advertising did not make much sense, we felt, because of the slim chance of having books available across the country. We have used "pre-pub" quotes in our sample ads to emphasize that we would secure advance quotes for this book. Our efforts would be directed to well-known and busy people, not houseplant experts.

Rather important, but not emphasized in the log, is our decision to send a majority of the newspaper review copies and news releases to lifestyle editors rather than book review editors. We have a better chance of getting publicity this way. Major buyers in our marketing area and wholesalers would receive reading copies. Advertising schedules (where relevant) and a brochure on the book would accompany reading copies. The brochure is important since the design of the book does not include jacket copy.

Finally, a comment on the title change. I did not like NO TIME FOR HOUSEPLANTS. Neither did anyone else at The UNC Press or the booksellers we queried. The title is negative and it is not clear. Adding the question mark seemed an appropriate solution and, to me, represents a real improvement.

Date: October 22, 1976

TO: Johanna Grimes
From: John Rollins
Request for Marketing Estimates

Title and Author: <u>No Time For House Plants-Purvis Mulch</u>

Number of Pages: <u>222</u>

Potential Market(s): <u>Urban ad Suburban adult</u>
<u>reading public. Primary Professionals Business People</u> (will sell)
Suggested Discount Classification: <u>Trade</u>

Initial Price Suggestions coupled with estimates of
associated demand: <u>Book is price sensitive</u>
<u>Suggest range of 5.95 to 7.95</u>

Marketing Cost Estimates:

Demand in units: 7,500
Advertising: $3,500
Direct Mail: $500
Direct Time: 3 weeks $1,500
Comp/Review Copies: $400
Other Direct Costs: $ —

Date: October 22, 1976

TO: Gwen Duffey
EDITORIAL ESTIMATES REQUEST

Title and Author: <u>NO TIME FOR HOUSE PLANTS-Purvis Mulch</u>

Number of Pages: <u>222</u>

Inhouse editing _____ or Freelance editing ✓

Estimate of direct hours needed to edit the manuscript: 53

Special editorial considerations: Many illustrations

Editorial Cost Estimates: $332   Editing: $266   Proof: $66

Please estimate for entire manuscript

DECISION TO PUBLISH: page 1

The University of North Carolina Press
P.O. Box 2288
Chapel Hill, North Carolina 27514
(919) 933-2105

Author: Purvis Mulch   Date: December 21, 1976
Title: NO TIME FOR HOUSEPLANTS?

Edition size: 7,500   Trim size: 5" x 7 3/8"   Number of Pages: 192
Cloth or Paper: cloth   Illustrations: 7 linecuts
                                        30 halftones
Acquisition Editor: PETE MOSS

Projected Markets: General adult reading public, with special emphasis on urban and suburban population in the southeast.

Discount Classification: Trade   Expected Discount: 42%

Special Funding Considerations: none

Sales Forecasts, in $ and in units:

Time Period	Estimated Sales for Period	Estimated Cumulative Sales
6 months	$10,142 - 2,200	$10,142 - 2,200
6-12 months	6,454 - 1,400	16,596 - 3,600
2nd year	9,220 - 2,000	25,816 - 5,600
3rd year	6,915 - 1,500	32,731 - 7,100
4th year		
5th year		

Expected Publishing Season: Fall 1977

DECISION TO PUBLISH: page 2

The University of North Carolina Press
P.O. Box 2288
Chapel Hill, North Carolina 27514
(919) 933-2105

Title Budget

Title: NO TIME FOR HOUSEPLANTS?   Author: Purvis Mulch
Printing: Initial printing and binding 7,500

INCOME FROM SALES:
                                                              Unit Figures
                                        Retail price $ 7.95
                                        Avg. discount $ 3.34
                                        Avg. net proceeds $ 4.61
$ 4.61 x 7,100 copies = net proceeds $ 32,731 $ 4.61

COST OF SALES:
Manufacturing:
  Plant Costs $ 2,027
  Running Costs   3,448
  Binding Costs   4,058
                              $ 9,533

Royalties:
  10% of retail on all
      copies sold $ 5,645 $ 1.34

GROSS MARGIN ON SALES: $ 15,178 $ .80
                                                             $ 2.14
SALE OF SUBSIDIARY RIGHTS: none foreseen $ 17,553 $ -- $ 2.47
                                        $ 17,553 $ 2.47

MARGINAL (OUT OF POCKET) DEPARTMENTAL EXPENDITURES:
  Editorial $ 332
  Marketing   4,000
  Order   (700)
  Shipping
  Other
                              $ 5,032 $ .71
CONTRIBUTION TO ADMINISTRATIVE AND FIXED OH: $ 12,521 $ 1.76

PRORATED SHARE OF ADMINISTRATIVE AND FIXED OH:
  Editorial $ 1,000
  Production   350
  Marketing   3,800
  Administrative   6,400
                              $ 11,550 $ 1.63

TITLE SURPLUS OR (DEFICIT): $ 971 $ .13

SUBSIDY: $ $

SUBSIDIZED SURPLUS OR (DEFICIT): $ $

MEMORANDUM OF AGREEMENT

Purvis Mulch

whose address is 13 Mouldering Way, Pemigewasett, Kansas
hereinafter described as the Author, and referred to by the masculine singular pronoun, and the University of North Carolina Press, Incorporated, of Chapel Hill, North Carolina, hereinafter described as the Press, agree as follows with respect to the publishing of a literary work, approximately

55,500   words in length and tentatively entitled

NO TIME FOR HOUSEPLANTS?

hereinafter described as the Work:

ARTICLE I. THE AUTHOR'S GUARANTEE

1. *Guarantee of Proprietorship.* The Author guarantees that the Work has not heretofore been published in book form, and that he is the Author Editor and, for the purpose of making this agreement, the sole proprietor of the Work.

2. *Guarantee Against Violation of Property Rights, Libel, or Unlawful Matter.* The Author guarantees that the Work is in no way whatever a violation of any existing copyright or other property right, and contains nothing libelous or otherwise unlawful; and that he will hold harmless and defend the Press from all manner of claims on the ground that the Work contains such violation, or anything libelous or otherwise unlawful; and that he will compensate the Press for any sums, including its attorney's fees, which it may find it necessary to pay in settlement of any claim or judgment against it, by reason of any violation of copyright or other property right or publication of libel or unlawful matter.

3. *Guarantee Against Conflicting Books by Author.* The Author agrees that during the life of this agreement he will not, without the consent of the Press, furnish to any other publisher any work on the same subject, of similar extent and character, which may conflict with the sale of the Work.

4. *Suits Against Others for Infringement.* The Author may bring against any other party for infringement of copyright or violation of other property right, and shall receive one-half of any damages or profits, less attorney's fees and disbursements, that may be recovered in any such suit; or the Author may, at his option, decline to participate in the risks and proceeds of any such suit, leaving both open to the Press.

ARTICLE II. CONDITIONS OF PUBLICATION

1. *Extent of the Press's License.* The Author grants to the Press and its successors, representatives, and assigns full, sole, and exclusive license to print, publish, and sell the Work in book form throughout the world, and to sell or lease such other rights as are enumerated in Article V hereunder, during the full term of the copyright of the Work, and any renewals thereof. Rights not specifically granted to the Press are reserved to the Author.

2. *Publication of the Work.* The Press shall within a reasonable time publish the Work, at its own expense (except as provided for in Articles III and IV), in such style and manner, and shall keep it in print as long, and at such times, as it shall deem expedient.

3. *Copyright.* The Press agrees to take out copyright in its own name in the United States, but it shall not be obligated to take out any copyright elsewhere. The Press shall also have the right to effect any renewals of copyright that may be provided by law, and the right to any assistance from the Author or his executor, administrator, heirs, or next of kin essential thereto.

ARTICLE III. AUTHOR'S RESPONSIBILITY FOR DELIVERY AND PREPARATION OF MANUSCRIPT, PROOF READING, AND NEW EDITIONS

1. *Delivery of Manuscript.* If the complete manuscript of the Work has not been delivered, the Author agrees to deliver a complete manuscript satisfactory to the Press not later than January 1, 1977

2. *Preparation of Manuscript.* If, in the judgment of the Press, the manuscript is not furnished properly prepared for composition, the Author shall have the option of preparing it properly or commissioning the Press to do so at the Author's expense.

3. *Illustrations.* If the Author and the Press agree that the Work requires illustrations, the Author agrees to deliver to the Press within a reasonable time such photographs, drawings, diagrams, maps, graphs, or charts as are necessary in a condition suitable to the Press for reproducing without retouching, redrawing, or additional art work.

4. *Permissions for Use of Copyright Material.* Pursuant to the guarantee of Article I, the Author agrees to deliver promptly to the Press written authorizations for the use of any copyright material included in the Work, or any other material for which an authorization is necessary; and the Author agrees to pay all fees required for the use of such material.

5. *Proof Corrections.* The Press shall submit to the Author such proofs as it and the Author agree are necessary. The Author agrees to read, revise, correct, and promptly return all proof sheets of the Work, and to pay the cost of alterations in proof required by the Author, other than printers' errors, in excess of   5%   of the cost of original composition. However, the Author shall pay the full cost of any changes which are necessary for the correction of actual errors, after the Press has made correction in conformity with the Author's directions on the last proof that the Press has agreed to submit to him.

6. *Index.* The Author shall promptly furnish copy for an index satisfactory to the Press, if it considers one desirable; or at his option the Author may commission the Press to prepare an index at his expense.

7. *New Editions.* Whenever the Press and the Author agree that it is necessary, the Author shall prepare material for new editions of the Work. In case of desiring a new edition, or new editions, after the Author's death or disability, the Press may engage competent persons to prepare them, and charge the expense against the Author's royalty.

ARTICLE IV.

The Press shall pay the author a royalty of 10% of the retail price on all copies sold of the regular edition except for such royalties as are specified in Article V hereinunder.

ARTICLE V. SPECIAL RIGHTS AND ROYALTIES

1. *Special Royalties on the Regular Edition.* In lieu of such royalties as may be specified in Article IV on the Press's regular editions of the Work, the following royalties shall be paid to the Author under the conditions specified:

a. On books, whether bound or in sheets, sold at a discount greater than forty-six per cent (46%) from the list price, the Press shall pay the Author ten per cent (10%) of the actual price received.

b. On books sold for export, whether bound or in sheets, the Press shall pay the Author a royalty of ten per cent (10%) of the actual price received.

c. *After two years from the date of the original publication, if the Press, in order to reduce an overstock of the Work, reduces the list price of its regular edition of the Work by fifty per cent (50%) or more, it shall pay the Author a royalty of five per cent (5%) of the list price of each copy sold at the reduced price.*

2. *Cheap Editions.* The Press shall have the right to publish under its own imprint cheap editions of the Work at a list price less than two-thirds of the original list price, and the Press agrees to pay the Author a royalty of 6% per cent (6 %) of the net price of each copy sold of such editions. The Press shall also have the right to license the cheap edition rights of the Work to a regular publisher of cheap editions, and in this case it shall pay the Author one-half of the sums received from the cheap edition publisher.

3. *Copies Exempt from Royalties.* No royalty shall be paid on free copies furnished to the Author, or on copies for review, sample, or other similar purpose, or on copies sold below manufacturing cost, or on books sold in any accounting period, as defined in Article VII, in which no more than five copies are sold.

4. *Permission to Reprint Selections from the Work.* The Press may permit others to publish such selections from the Work, for publicity, educational, or scholarly purposes, as it may consider appropriate, without charge; but if any fee is charged, the Press shall pay one-half of the fee to the Author.

5. *Second Serial, Syndication, Anthology, and Digest Rights.* The Press shall control second serial, syndication, anthology, and digest rights, and if such rights are sold or leased, the Press shall pay the Author one-half of the net sums received.

6. *Book Clubs.* If the Press sells the book-club rights of the Work to a recognized book club which pays a royalty or outright sum for a license to distribute the Work to its members or subscribers, the Press shall pay the Author one-half the net sums received.

7. *Foreign and Translation Rights.* The Press shall have exclusive right to arrange for publication of the Work in all foreign countries and for translations of the Work, on a royalty basis or for an outright fee, and it shall pay the Author three-fourths of the net proceeds of any such sale or license.

8. *Non-Book Rights.* The Press shall control dramatic, motion picture (sight and sound), radio, television, electrical recording, and microfilm rights, and if such rights are sold or leased the Press shall pay the Author three-fourths of the net proceeds of any such sale or lease.

ARTICLE VI. AUTHOR'S COPIES

The Press shall give to the Author on publication 12 copies of the Work, and the Author shall have the right to purchase further copies for personal use but not for resale at a discount of thirty-three and one-third per cent (33⅓%) from the list price.

ARTICLE VII. SETTLEMENT OF ACCOUNTS

The Press shall render a statement of account annually, on August 1, as of June 30th of each year, and shall make settlement in cash within three months after the date of the statement.

ARTICLE VIII. THE PRESS'S LIABILITY FOR LOSS OR DAMAGE

Except for loss or damage due to its own negligence, the Press shall not be responsible for loss or damage to any property of the Author in its possession or in the possession of its independent contractors, or in the possession of anyone else to whom delivery is made by the Press in the normal course of its operations.

ARTICLE IX. TERMINATION

If, at any time after two years from the date of publication, the Press shall be satisfied that the public demand does not justify a continued publication of the Work, or if for any other cause it shall deem the further publication of the Work improper or inexpedient, the Press shall have the right to terminate this agreement by sending written notice to the latest address given by the Author to the Press. Thereupon the Author shall have the right within ninety (90) days to take from the Press, as an entirety, the copyright, all bound copies and sheets on hand, and the stamps, electrotype plates, and engravings of illustrations (if any), at one-half their cost to the Press, including the composition. If the Author fails to exercise this option by paying for the same in cash, this agreement shall terminate, and the Press shall have the right to dispose of the property as it sees fit, free of any commission or royalty to the Author.

ARTICLE X. ASSIGNMENT

This agreement shall be binding upon the assigns, heirs, executors, or administrators of the Author, and upon the assign or successors of the Press.

ARTICLE XI.

In consideration of the respective undertakings herein set forth, the Author and the Press agree to all the provisions of this agreement, and in testimony thereof affix their signatures, this 1st day of January, 19 77, at Chapel Hill, North Carolina.

Witness to signature of _____

Purvis Mulch
AUTHOR

Witness to signature of _____

Matthew Hodgson, Director
THE UNIVERSITY OF NORTH CAROLINA PRESS, INC.

Memorandum of Agreement

Between

Purvis Mulch

and

THE UNIVERSITY OF NORTH CAROLINA PRESS

Made January 1, 19 77

at Chapel Hill, North Carolina

THE UNIVERSITY OF NORTH CAROLINA PRESS

Box 2288, Chapel Hill, N.C. 27514

4 December 1975

Dear

Joyce Kachergis gave me yesterday the original copy of your manuscript on house plants, together with your letter to her of November 25. I have had an opportunity to read quickly through the manuscript, and to discuss it with both Joyce and Matt Hodgson.

As you know, the Governors of the Press stipulate that we obtain two supportive readings, by disinterested senior specialists, of each complete manuscript that we recommend to them for acceptance. In your letter to Joyce you stated that you consider the manuscript to be in an unfinished state, and that you will be revising it. In my opinion, it would be prejudicial to the manuscript's chances for acceptance by the Press for us to obtain outside readings until you are satisfied that the manuscript is as good as you can make it.

Aside from your "suggested symbols," no illustrations accompanied the manuscript, although you did refer, in your letter to Joyce, to photographs and captions. Before we obtain our outside readings it will be necessary for us to have all the illustrations (in final form, if possible) that you plan to include.

I have taken the liberty of making a xerox copy of the manuscript, and I am returning the original to you separately. During the next three or four days I should like to read through (and mark up) the xerox copy in some detail, and I shall send it to you with my general observations.

I look forward to working with you on this project. May I suggest that all your correspondence about this project, for the time being, be directed to me? I shall make copies for Joyce's AAUP file.

With best wishes,

Sincerely yours,

Malcolm M. MacDonald
Assistant Director and Editor

MMM:kt

Received 3 December 1975   N° 09050

The University of North Carolina Press

I. MANUSCRIPT RECORD

Author...

Title.....THE SCHOLARLY HOUSE PLANT by Pruvis Mulch
141 pages   rec'd and acknowledged by MM
Returned to author for revision 1/24

Sent for reading   Date sent   Date ret'd

Form No. A-649

THE UNIVERSITY OF NORTH CAROLINA PRESS

Box 2288, Chapel Hill, N. C. 27514

8 December 1975

Dear

As I promised in my letter of December 4, I am returning separately the xerox copy of your manuscript on house plants. You will find a number of queries and suggestions in the margins of the manuscript, which are in addition to those on the attached sheets. As you plan to recast both your preface and first chapter, I began my annotations with chapter two.

In general, the manuscript reads well, although I believe chapters two and three are not as strong as chapters four-seven. In the earlier chapters you seem not to have your audience firmly in mind. I judge from your letter of November 25 that your book is intended for rank beginners; that is, for people who may have one or two plants (and no books on the subject) around the house. The main thrust of my annotations and separate comments is toward a clearer definition of your prospective reader and modifying the manuscript to meet his needs.

I agree with you that the preface and first chapter must be recast entirely. In the case of books, such as your own, intended for a broad general audience, the preface should be regarded as a selling tool. It should be brief (two or three double-spaced typewritten pages), and it should state clearly the audience for whom the book is written and how you have gone about helping that audience meet its plant-growing needs.

As my separate comments convey, I would like to see you introduce some elementary plant biology concepts into chapter one. Here, too, I think you would be wise to distinguish between indoor plants and outdoor plants. Such a distinction would enable you to lead right into the heart of the book, which deals with the special requirements of indoor plants. We are agreed, are we not, that references to scholarly publishing are not appropriate in a book of this kind?

As I mentioned in my earlier letter, it is essential that we receive all the illustrations with the final manuscript, as they form an integral part of the proposed book.

8 December 1975
Page Two

We recommend that you include an annotated bibliography, in which you list five or six books in each of your categories (foliage plants, plants grown for their flowers, cacti and other succulents, and perhaps florescent light gardening and indoor vegetable gardening). Please prepare the annotated bibliography according to the style recommended in the Chicago Style Manual; and we recommend that you include the pagination of each book.

An index will be essential for the book, and I hope you will be prepared to provide the index manuscript at the proper time.

In your "special boxes" you refer exclusively to a publication by Widmer. May I suggest that you obtain similar lists from other authors (there must be dozens of such lists available), as excessive reliance on a single authority may convey a misleading impression.

When you send us the final draft, please include an extended table of contents (one that incorporates your principal subheadings).

May I have your best estimate about when I may expect to receive the complete, final draft of your manuscript? As we are looking toward publication in the spring of 1977, time is a factor: would it be possible for you to have the manuscript to me by mid January?

I do not wish to conclude without telling you that I have derived both pleasure and information from going through your manuscript. As it happens, I have a few indoor plants, which I have grown only with common sense to guide me. Your graceful manuscript has already given me a greater appreciation for, and understanding of, these special friends; and I am looking forward to working further with you toward its ultimate publication.

With very best wishes,

Sincerely yours,

Malcolm M. MacDonald
Assistant Director and Editor

MMM:kt

The following comments and suggestions are intended to help you sharpen the focus of the book and, in some cases, to make it more precise. In each case, I refer to check marks in the left margins of manuscript pages.

II-1: I think you might amplify on the difference between house plants and plants found in nature. Are all house plants found in the wild, somewhere?

II-2: I confess to a long-standing personal bias against anthropomorphism, and I have flagged several examples throughout the manuscript (while leaving some others). I think you could take it out without violating your style, and I think further that your manuscript would be stronger as a result.

II-3: (top of page) Why treat potting mixtures and soils under separate headings?

II-4: (top of page) I believe all the potting soils I have bought are advertised as "sterile"; do they contain nutrients? You do not say enough about the methods of fertilizer application.

(middle & bottom of page) You sound as though you would like to launch into the chemical vs. organic controversy. Surprisingly, perhaps, some of us are vaguely aware of the "controversy." We look to this book for advice about growing house plants; why not recommend specific fertilizers for specific classes of plants. This entire brief section is in need of revision, for it is not informative.

II-7: You refer here, and at many other places in the manuscript, to a particular plant part. Somewhere in the book (I would prefer to see it in a first chapter) you should present enough botany (anatomy, physiology, and ecology) to enable the house-plant grower to understand, at a working level, what goes on in his indoor garden. A diagram showing the parts of plants is a must.

At several places in the manuscript, you refer to periods of dormancy and periods of rapid growth. These references cry out for greater explanation.

II-8: (first check) See comment under II-1.

(second check) I suggest you either explain pH or not use it. But if you introduce a technical term, you owe your reader a working definition.

II-9: Is it wise to encourage the use of standing-water devices, which may provide a habitat for organisms harmful to humans? I understand some hospitals prohibit the introduction of cut flowers into the rooms of patients because the water in which they are kept has been found to harbor alarming numbers of disease-causing bacteria. If one does grow plants in containers of water, should the water be changed periodically?

II-10: The term "microclimate." This could be a useful unifying concept to tie together everything you present under the headings of containers, watering, humidity, ventilation, temperature, and light. At the very least, you should define "microclimate."

II-13: See comment under II-7.

II-16: What is a "worn out plant"? Please reword.

(second check) Why dismiss propagation from seeds, which affords delight to many house plant growers? If you don't wish to discuss it,

-2-

perhaps you could refer the reader to a book that does. (third check) See comment under II-7.

II-17: Can you obtain vigorous roots this way? I had bad luck with coleus, as they developed long trailing roots that matted together when I removed them from the bottle. On the other hand, mine did well when rooted in moist vermiculite, which appeared to give the new roots something to "grab."

II-18: This sounds awkward. An illustration would help greatly here.

At bottom of page: the term "canes" brings me back to my earlier appeal for a section on the anatomy of plants.

II-19: Again, anatomical terms. You have referred earlier to the stem, or stalk of the plant; I believe you have used those terms interchangeably. Here you refer to leaf stems. It is confusing.

II-21: Anatomy again.

III-2: See comment under II-4.

III-5: (first check) Why single out government and university bulletins?

(second check) Another reference to the "organic-chemical controversy."

III-9: How does one Pasteurize potting soil? Do you Pasteurize yours? Really?!

(second check) Obviously, you live in a university community! Why not suggest a place people can mail their plants (or infected parts)? For example, to the county agent, or to the Department of Plant Pathology at any university within one's state that has a college of agriculture.

IV-3: Here you mention the mature size of plants, something you ought to stipulate in your discussions of the individual varieties. I expect the sizes will vary according to the treatment the plants receive; still the plant-grower should be given some indication about whether his plant will attain a height of eight inches, or three feet.

IV-13: Here you do give the size range of the mature plant. It is welcome information for the beginner!

V-5: If grafting is easy, perhaps the house-plant grower would like to try his hand. Is an explanation within the scope of your book?

"special box #1": What are the "special boxes" for? Where ought they to go in the finished book?

"special box #3", add 1": This procedure requires an illustration or sequence of illustrations. I simply cannot visualize the process from your description.

THE UNIVERSITY OF NORTH CAROLINA PRESS

Box 2288, Chapel Hill, N. C. 27514

19 December 1975

Dear

I was pleased to receive your letter of December 12, and to have your initial, general response to mine of December 8.

I like your new Preface. It not only defines your audience, but it tells the prospective reader what the remainder of the book is about.

I am sure you have already anticipated my reaction to the revised first chapter. I like your brief discussion of the natural environment and the home environment, and I shall look forward to seeing your extention of that chapter, where you will deal with some basiξ plant biology.

As you revise your manuscript, perhaps you could keep in mind that North Carolina is a southern university press, and that plants common to the South should not be excluded for that reason alone.

You state in your Preface that the book might serve as a useful companion when one visits his local florist or garden center. I agree thoroughly, and even in the brief period of time since I returned the manuscript to you, I have wished that I could refer to it while chosing plants to give as Christmas gifts. I believe that portability should be designed into the book, and we shall bring that to the attention to the designer at the appropriate time.

I am delighted that you are pushing ahead so well on this project, and I shall look forward to receiving the completed manuscript, with its illustrations, around the middle of next month.

With best wishes,

Sincerely yours,

Malcolm M. MacDonald
Assistant Director and Editor

MMM:kt

December 12, 1975

Mr. Malcolm M. MacDonald
Assistant Director and Editor
THE UNIVERSITY OF NORTH CAROLINA PRESS
Box 2288
Chapel Hill, North Carolina 27514

Dear Malcolm:

Thank you for your letter of the 8th, for the return of the manuscript, and for your detailed comments which I found very helpful.

Over the past several days I have recast entirely the preface and first chapter. I feel much better about the manuscript after having done this. As it stands now, the book is a straight-forward guide for the beginner, with no references to scholarly publishing. But now you present me with more work. Your recommendations regarding the preface have, I think, been carried out. The first chapter is improved, although it still needs a little more explanation of general biological concepts, as you point out. I will revise this further. Then, of course, I will address myself to the detailed comments, work up the bibliography, etc. I will be happy to prepare an index at the appropriate time.

I am sending my revised preface and first chapter to you at this time--not as final copy, but to give you an indication of the direction I am moving. As I said, these were revised without the benefit of your counsel, and they now are in for further revision.

I can see immediately that you are going to make me write a good book, and I am thankful for that. I will plan to send you the completed and revised ms. by January 15. After the readers' reports come in, there will doubtless be more revision in store, for which I am prepared.

Last, I might say that for the first time I am beginning to feel good about this whole project, especially knowing that you will be there to keep the train on the track.

Sincerely,

                                              3505 Hampton Hall Way NE
                                              Atlanta, Georgia 30319
                                              August 2, 1976

Gwen Duffey, Managing Editor
University of North Carolina Press
Box 2288
Chapel Hill, North Carolina 27514

Dear Gwen:

     Both your letter and the package containing the house
plants manuscript have arrived safely. What an interesting
project for the AAUP to do--seeing the results will be fun.

     I'm going to try to have this in the mail back to you
by August 25 (I'm allowing a little time off for a one-week
visit from my brother and his wife, or I'd have it back
sooner) and I can't imagine that this would be more than
$150 dollars, maybe less.

     Maybe working on this will help me save the maidenhair
fern I am now in the process of destroying. I'm known in
my neighborhood as The Purple Thumb (not quite black--for
philodendrons and one neanthebella palm are known to be
thriving in my house--but certainly not green, as this year
it took three plantings in my window boxes before I could
get marigolds to survive and everybody knows that you can't
kill marigolds!) I live amongst dozens of young suburbanites
whose houses are immaculate and whose house plants are
exotic, numerous, and healthy. I keep hoping their children
will turn out to be dope fiends or something, so that I can
feel a little less inadequate.

                                   Affectionately,

                                   Bobbie

                                   Barbara B. Reitt

---

                                              23 July 1976

Mrs. Barbara Reitt
3505 Hampton Hall Way NE
Atlanta, Georgia 30319

Dear Bobbie:

The manuscript that I mentioned to you on the phone this morning has now been
shipped to you. After looking over the material to be edited, please let me
know about when you might be able to get it back to us and approximately how
much the editing fee will be.

                                   Yours sincerely,

                                   (Mrs.) Gwen Duffey
                                   Managing Editor

---

                                              28 July 1976

House Plants MS

Mrs. Barbara Reitt   FIRST CLASS
3505 Hampton Hall Way NE   Registered (rrr)
Atlanta
Georgia 30319

AUTHOR'S MEMORANDUM

TO:
FROM: Barbara Reitt (copyeditor)
RE: No Time for House Plants, chapters II and IV

The text of your book reads well; directions and descriptions are concise, clear, and easy to follow. The overall organization of subjects is sensible and the use of symbols in the plant descriptions is particularly good.

The copyediting that has been done on the manuscript of your book has two purposes: to locate and correct any errors that might remain in the copy or in the organization of the book and to instruct the printer and his typesetter as to the details of the printing of the book. This reading has been intended to be as thorough as possible since corrections past this point are prohibitively expensive, as they would have to be made in type after it had been set.

Most of the marks you see on the manuscript pages are of a technical nature, instructing the typesetter, but some are corrections or queries to you, and all of these should be carefully reviewed by you at this time so that the Press can be assured that the manuscript as it now stands has your approval. Please feel free to question anything that has been done.

The few queries that need your attention have been signaled by a red check mark and should be easy for you to locate. I have followed as many of your style choices as possible ("style" in this sense refers to such choices as which of two alternate spellings to use, word compounding, use of figures or words for number amounts, capitalization, etc.). The Press follows the style recommended in the Chicago Manual of Style, which has been the guide used in the copyediting of your book. Webster's New Collegiate Dictionary is the authority used for spelling.

The few revisions that have been suggested have to do with the coherence and overall structure of the book; content has not been changed, only the order of some of the elements. In each case, logic and the reader's ease dictated the change. First, the footnote on p. 36, about builder's sand, seemed better placed on p. 18, where the reader is first instructed to use it.

Second, the opening section of chapter IV seemed to need some reworking. The explanations of symbols and nomenclature were repeated; these are now combined into one explanation for each instead of two. The section on buying plants seemed more appropriately placed early in chapter I, where one of the repeated ideas is that plant selection is a crucial part of plant-growing success. Moreover, as this material concerns all plants, not just foliage plants, it seemed wrong to place it in the chapter on foliage plants.

3505 Hampton Hall Way NE
Atlanta, Georgia 30319
August 24, 1976

Gwen Duffey, Managing Editor
University of North Carolina Press
Box 2288
Chapel Hill, North Carolina 27514

Dear Gwen:

I am sending today, by first class mail, the manuscript for the book and the accompanying notes. I am enclosing my statement with this letter.

I was not sure that any revisions of the organization of the book fell under the copyeditor's duties (it was the description of the project that boggled me a bit here) but I went ahead as I would have normally anyway. The two revisions in these chapters that I have recommended really were called for and I felt that the project's rather strict distinction between "editor" and "copyeditor" (maybe the distinction is more apparent than real anyway) need not be observed religiously.

I might add (nobody asked, but that isn't stopping me!) that if the whole book were to be undertaken by the Press for actual publication that quite a bit of revision would be necessary. A fair number of little pieces like the two I've suggested in these two chapters.

Hope this fills your bill. If you need anything else of me, let me know. Incidentally, it turns out to be hard to copyedit just a *part* of a book!

As ever,

Billie

3505 Hampton Hall Way NE
Atlanta, Georgia 30319
August 24, 1976

Account #22

University of North Carolina Press
Box 2288
Chapel Hill, North Carolina 27514

For copyediting chapters II and IV
of NO TIME FOR HOUSE PLANTS $150.00

Thank you,

Barbara B. Reitt

Style Sheet   No Time for House Plants, II & IV

air layering (no hyphen)   overfertilization
central Europe   potbound
dates: 1930s   q.v.
depressor   rainwater
draft   repotting
homemade   short-lived
life span   subdivision
-like: fernlike, maplelike   table 1 (textual reference)
North, the; northerner   watertight
numbers: 5-inch pot   windowsill
18 inches   World War II
5 feet tall
5 percent
50-60° F.

PLANT NAMES

A. Common and family names, others that are set in roman type:

African violet, avocado, Boston fern, boxwood, bromeliads, Chinese evergreen, false castor oil plant, geraniums, gloxinia, ivy, orchids, piggy-back plant, poinsettia, primulas, sensitive plant, snake plant, spider plant, spurge, ti plant, wandering Jew

B. Scientific names; genus or genus and species usually; all set in italic type:

Aspidistra, Azalea, Begonia, Caladium, Camellia, Coleus, Cyclamen, Dieffenbachia, Dracaena, Ficus, Fuchsia, Gardenia, Hedera, Impatiens, Maranta, Peperomia, Philodendron, Rhododendron

Philodendron scandens is abbreviated P. scandens in a second mention, for example.

Cultivated species are referred to as follows: D. arvida 'Exotica' and as 'Exotica' in subsequent references.

Editing Notes   No Time for House Plants, II and IV

1. Plant names: the style follows that prescribed by the Chicago Manual backed up, for details, by the Style Manual for Biological Journals of the Conference of Biological Editors. I have used Webster's and Kathryn Arthurs, ed., How to Grow House Plants as sources for doublechecking some of the spellings.
   The author tended to be inconsistent in his treatment of generic names. In casual speech or writing, "philodendron" would be acceptable, but in a work of this nature, the use of both "philodendron" and "Philodendron" would be slipshod and even confusing. The use of caps and itals for generic names has been applied consistently; likewise, the use of lc for common names (except elements within them that are normally capped--"Chinese" for example) has been applied consistently. The specific names, or at least many of them, are listed in the style sheet under "plant names."

2. The author was imprecise in his use of "that" and "which" and I have followed the recommendations of usage books in having him use "that" exclusively for the restrictive clauses and "which" with a comma for nonrestrictive.

3. I've explained carefully to the author in his memo why I am suggesting the revised order of a few passages in these chapters. The changes do improve the coherence greatly, and I hope he is pleased with the revision. No content has been deleted or altered in meaning.

4. An index will be essential to the book's usefulness, especially as a tool for cross-checking scientific and common names. Please note that the author refers to an index on p. 51; if you decide not to have an index, be sure to omit this sentence.

No Time for House Plants

A Busy Person's Guide to Indoor Gardening

The University of North Carolina Press

Chapel Hill

Copyright © 1977 by
The University of North Carolina Press
All rights reserved
Manufactured in the United States of America
ISBN 0-8078-0000-0
Library of Congress Catalog Card Number 00-0000

CONTENTS

Preface	P-1
CHAPTER 1: THE SECRETS OF NO-WORK HOUSE PLANT SUCCESS	I-1
CHAPTER 2: UNDERSTANDING HOUSE PLANTS	II-1
The Basic House Plant	II-1a
How a Plant Feeds	II-1c
Parts of the Plant	II-1f
Soil	II-1h
Acidity/Alkalinity	II-2a
Potting Mixtures	II-3
Nutrient Maintenance	II-4
Containers	II-5
Watering	II-6
Humidity	II-8
Ventilation	II-10
Temperature	II-11
Light	II-12
Pruning and Training	II-12
Repotting	II-14
Propagation	II-16
CHAPTER 3: PLANT TROUBLES AND CURES	III-1
Improper Handling and Care	III-1
Insect Foes	III-3
Diseases	III-8

---

contents, add 1

CHAPTER 4: INTRODUCING THE FOLIAGE PLANTS	IV-1
Where to Buy House Plants	IV-3
Foliage Plants	IV-5
CHAPTER 5: CACTI AND OTHER SUCCULENTS	V-1
Care of Cacti and Succulents	V-3
Potting Soil for Cacti	V-5
Introducing the Cacti	V-5
The Unusual Succulents	V-7
CHAPTER 6: FLOWERING HOUSE PLANTS	VI-1
Forcing Spring Bulbs	VI-12
Care of Gift Plants	VI-17
CHAPTER 7: SPECIAL INDOOR GARDENS	VII-1
Dish Gardens and Planters	VII-1
Bottle Gardens and Terrariums	VII-3
House Plants from Kitchen Scraps	VII-7
An Indoor Kitchen Garden	VII-11

SPECIAL BOXES

1. The ABCs of Artificial Light
2. Should You Send Your Plants to Summer Camp?
3. Can Your Plants Survive Your Vacation?
4. Plants for Cool Conditions
5. Plants for Medium Temperatures
6. Plants for High Temperatures
7. Plants of Greatest Tolerance

contents, add 2

8. Plants for Dry and Semi-Dry Conditions
9. Vines and Trailing Plants for Totem Poles
10. Plants for Hanging Baskets
11. Suggestions for Large-Tubbed Specimens

Bibliography
Index

P - 1

PREFACE

This is a guide to raising house plants for people who have no time to raise house plants.

Many of us—single people, working couples, harassed mothers, college students, anyone whose daily living pattern leaves precious little time for indoor gardening—would enjoy the beauty and companionship of bright, green house plants, especially through the drab winter months. Past failures, however, have led us to believe that we cannot raise indoor plants without giving them more time and attention than we can provide. Beautiful gift plants may have quickly withered and perished. The bright little English Ivy, bought on impulse at the supermarket, may never have made it past childhood at home. Then, the books and articles written by house plant experts present, in loving and extended detail, the special methods they use to achieve success—and it seems as though house plant growing must be a consuming hobby if it is to produce gratifying results.

Not so! The gift plant you received probably would not have survived in your home, no matter how much attention

P - 2

it received. The first secret of house plant success is in choosing the right plants in the beginning, and gift plants from the florist are very often the wrong plants entirely for home conditions. The English Ivy was perhaps given too little sun, or an atmosphere much too warm and dry, or too little growing room. Secret number two is in providing the proper basic environment for your plants. The right plant, given the right conditions for growth, will thrive despite your frequent inattention.

This book is meant not only for busy people, but also for busy people who have no long or extensive experience in growing house plants. The green-thumb grower with a collection of two hundred thriving exotic specimens will see at a glance that there are no revolutionary breakthroughs revealed in these pages, no closely-guarded secrets unveiled, but simply a collection of solid and practical information, trimmed of excess detail and shaped for a single purpose: <u>to help you to achieve house plant success without really working at it.</u>

Last, we have created this book to be a pleasant companion in itself, one which can provide a pleasant few hours of reading and also one which you may refer to time and time again for the answers to many questions about your house plants. It might even be your traveling companion, for it will serve as a guide to your choosing plant varieties at the florist shop or garden center. However it is used, I

P - 3

hope that this volume, modest in both size and scope, will lead you to success with house plants, and eventually to a love for them. Should that happen, it will have more than achieved its purpose.

*indicates reader's suggested change

II

CHAPTER 2

UNDERSTANDING HOUSE PLANTS

Every plant has its own preferences and requirements for soil type, light, temperature, ventilation, humidity, and several other factors that are within our power to control, or at least to mitigate. It is vitally important for you, as a busy indoor gardener, to understand the basics of each factor, since a prior understanding will enable you to avoid much work later on while achieving routine success in growing plants.

In addition to understanding these basic needs, you will want to know something about pots and other containers, repotting plants, propagation, and a few other matters that, while not vital to immediate success, will help you to gain further enjoyment in raising better plants.

II-A

THE BASIC HOUSE PLANT

The major difference between a house plant and an outdoor plant is location. All house plants could live and flourish outdoors, in the proper climate. All are derived from forebears that lived, reproduced, and died in the outdoors, whether it was on a forest floor in Central Europe or in the bough of a tree in a South American rain forest. Over many centuries of adaptation and evolution, each plant species embraced those characteristics that enabled it to survive; even today, every house plant carries within its genetic structure the characteristics of its distant progenitors. Thus the <u>Maranta</u> will lose some of its leaves each autumn, even though autumn's weather does not come to the bookshelf where the plant rests, and a cactus, no matter how long we have been feeding and watering it with unfailing regularity, will continue to hoard food and water within its swollen stems. In plants, old habits might recede, but they are never forgotten.

At no time are these innate plant characteristics more noticeable than during the autumn and winter, when many plants—particularly those from temperate regions—enter a period of rest or dormancy. Then, new growth ceases and the plant takes on a listless and washed-out appearance. Other plants, including many of tropical origin, will maintain their bright appearance but will stop growing completely for several months each year, emulating the natural rest periods of their forebears. You will do well to watch for these signs of dormancy and respond to each plant's needs at that time. When any plant enters a dormant period, water should be reduced and fertilizer withheld completely, until new growth once again begins, usually in the late winter or early spring. At that time, water the plant freely and give it normal doses of fertilizer once again, in order to encourage new growth. By your proper treatment of the plant at this time, you will emulate the advent of spring, working with the plant in carrying out its rhythmic cycles.

Some plants also are naturally short-lived, and will last no more than a year or two in your home despite your careful attention, because their genetic structure dictates a finite life span. Garden annuals, for instance, will germinate, grow to maturity, flower, produce seeds, and die, all in as little as six months. For this reason, very few annuals are selected as house plants. Although a few short-lived plants are cultivated indoors for their unusual characteristics, such as the sensitive plant, which is easily grown from seed, the house plants that we have cultivated over the generations are most often those that will give years of pleasure. Some house plants, in fact, live to be literally hundreds of years old.

Still other house plants are attractive when young, but grow ungainly or otherwise unattractive when they approach maturity. The only plants of this kind I have chosen for inclusion in this book are those that are very easy to propagate from cuttings, so that the parent plant may be discarded after a year or two, to be replaced by its children.

From the hundreds of thousands of plant species in the world, those traditionally cultivated as house plants are the relatively few that have shown a wide tolerance to conditions of heat, light, moisture, humidity, and ventilation—in other words, those that can withstand a human environment. They are both attractive to the eye and they are tough. Still, if we are looking for success with house plants—and particularly success without working hard at it—then we should spend some time to learn the characteristics of each plant, recognizing its individual needs and fulfilling them to the best of our ability.

HOW A PLANT FEEDS

A plant manufactures nearly all of its food by itself—and not from the "plant food" that you buy for it. Commercial plant food is no more than a combination of certain chemicals (sometimes in an organic base) that are essential to the plant's basic functioning, much as vitamins are essential to human nutrition. But the bulk of a plant's food—the sugar it uses for energy and growth—is manufactured by the plant itself. In the presence of light, the leaves or other green parts of the plant draw carbon dioxide from the air and water from the roots, converting these into sugar that is then used for energy production or stored for future use.

During this sugar-manufacturing process, known as photosynthesis, several other things happen within the plant. While carbon dioxide is being absorbed, oxygen is being released from the pores of the leaf surface. (Plants produce not only all of the world's food but most of its atmospheric oxygen as well.) During darkness hours, the process is reversed; some of the atmosphere's oxygen is recaptured by the plant and used to convert stored sugar to energy for growth. Generally, a plant manufactures growth food during the day and does its actual growing at night.

Often, the plant converts its newly manufactured sugar to starch and stores it, reconverting it to sugar as the need arises. Although the starch can be stored in almost any area of the plant, certain plants have developed specialized storage areas just for this purpose. Cacti and succulents have enlarged stems and leaves for the greatest above-ground storage capacity of any house plant, while others have developed underground storage apparatus for this purpose, including bulbs, tubers, corms, and rhizomes. A bulb is simply an enlarged underground bud, such as is found with hyacinths, tulips, and onions. A tuber is nothing more than an enlarged stem or modified stem; a common potato is a tuber; gloxinias, caladiums, dahlias, and many other common plants are grown from tubers.

A corm is the enlarged base of a stem. And a rhizome is simply a laterally growing, enlarged, usually underground stem. All are used by the plant for food storage, and all can be used to propagate plants, too.

Water is constantly being drawn up through the plant. As it transpires through the stomata (pores) of the leaves, a "pulling" action draws more water up through the roots. The water carries with it mineral salts, including all the elements that the plant needs to carry out its complex chemical processes. The transpiration that takes place in the leaves is similar to perspiration in humans and it serves a similar purpose: to cool the plant. With house plants, it would be difficult for you to notice this cooling effect. But it is readily apparent when a group of large trees carry out the transpiration process. The cool and fresh feeling you enjoy in a thick woods in summer is not primarily the product of the shade itself, but the transpiration of the millions of leaves overhead.

It is virtually impossible for a plant to absorb too much water, since its vessels and cells can accommodate only so much at a given time; however, the overwatering of a plant can exclude oxygen from the root system, ironically causing wilting of the top portion of the plant. When water is withheld, the plant's cells will gradually collapse, causing wilting of the entire plant. All plants do have protective mechanisms that conserve water in times of drought, however, and can withstand a temporary dry spell. Most wilted house plants will quickly spring back to a normal state when water is again provided.

PARTS OF THE PLANT

Stem. The stem serves to support the plant and to contain and direct the vessels that transport water from the roots, and food from the leaves, to every other part of the plant. Most house plants, including Philodendron, Ivy, and Spider Plant, have soft stems. Such plants must either climb or crawl, since their stems are not strong enough to support an upward-growing structure of significant height. Other plants have soft but thick stems that enable them to attain good height, although their stems are apt to be subject to breakage. Woody-stemmed plants such as the Avocado, Poinsettia, and Boxwood are far more sturdy and are usually derived from trees or shrubs of the temperate region. Canes are thick stems with hollow or pithy centers. Bamboo is an example of a cane with which we all are familiar; among house plants, Dieffenbachia and Ti Plant are good examples.

Some plants have a distinct main stem, while others send up many stems, none dominant. A side shoot is a smaller stem growing out from the main stem. A petiole is a leaf stalk—the stemlike structure from which a leaf grows. A node is a joint on the main stem from which a leaf or side shoot grows.

Leaf. The major function of the leaf is, as we have seen, to manufacture food for the plant's growth and reproduction. Considering its total mass, the leaf has a remarkably large surface area, ideally designed for the efficient absorption and diffusion of gases through its thousands of stomata.

After the basic functions of the leaf are understood, its proper care is not difficult to appreciate. The stomata must be kept fairly clean, free of dust and oil that might hinder their efficient operation. Leaves must also be given the freest access to light and ventilation, according to the individual preferences of each plant. Never crowd plants to a point where they are competing for light and air.

Roots. Roots serve two main functions: to anchor the plant in the ground and to supply from the soil water and the mineral salts which accompany water. Bulbs, corms, rhizomes, (all modified stems) and tubers serve much the same purposes, as well as acting as food storage areas. Roots, just as the above-ground parts of plants, may be pruned without injuring the plant in any way. Roots are often trimmed to prevent a plant from growing too large for the convenience of the grower, just as top growth is cut back. If you cut roots back, however, be certain to cut back top growth to about the same percentage, or the reduced roots might be unable to supply the plant with sufficient amounts of water. The major precaution in caring for roots is, as I will mention several times in these pages, to avoid overwatering.

Flowers. The plant's flowers contain its sexual apparatus. Pollination occurs when pollen is deposited onto stigmas, thus allowing the formation of seeds. The fruit of any plant is, in reality, the mature or ripened ovary which swells to protect the seeds. In nature, most plants produce flowers. For the purposes of cultivating house plants, only certain ones—which in this book are listed as flowering house plants—can be depended upon to produce, under home conditions, blossoms of sufficient size, profusion, and beauty to warrant our attention. The plants we grow for their attractive foliage often cannot produce flowers indoors because of insufficient light or other conditions. In nature, pollen is most often transferred either by insects or wind, both of which are lacking in the home. Where indoor pollinization is essential for seed or fruit production, it can be accomplished by transferring the pollen from one flower to another, using a soft camel's hair brush. This process is described fully in most books devoted to flowering house plants.

SOIL

Since the house plant you bring home from the shop will already be rooted in soil (presumably the shop knows its business), you might wonder why you have to consider this need at all. The answer is that your house plant will, assuming hoped-for longevity, someday need repotting, and you will want to provide it with a potting mixture that will serve its special needs. You might even wish to propagate some of your favorite house plants at some later time, to share with friends and to give as gifts. In any case, a basic knowledge of potting mixtures and soils is essential to a complete understanding of all your plants.

Two simple definitions are in order here, to avoid any confusion later on. Soil, when mentioned here, refers to garden loam, that combination of mineral matter, organic matter, air, and water commonly found outside, in your garden or under your lawn. A potting mixture is soil with the addition of other materials, such as sand, compost, peat moss, limestone, and bone meal, that together form an ideal environment for the roots of your house plants.

The easiest way to assure your plants of a perfect loam is to buy prepackaged, sterile potting soil from your garden or flower shop. This soil will have not only the proper texture, but it will also be free of disease organisms, insects (some too small to be seen), and weed seeds. To this loam you will add the other ingredients which together will form an ideal potting mixture. You may also buy packaged potting mixture at the store, but if you do, read the package carefully to ascertain the ingredients, making sure that the mixture is right for your plants.

It is, of course, far less expensive to make your own potting mixture from your own garden loam (free), sand (free or next to free), and small amounts of purchased ingredients. If you choose this route, then it is important that you be able to make at least a cursory analysis of the garden loam that will form the basis of the potting mixture. Texture is important. A heavy clay soil will hold water for too long a time, encouraging disease and root rot, and it will bake cement-hard when dry. On the other hand, a coarse sand will not hold water well, nor will it hold nutrients long enough for the plant's roots to absorb them. Strive, then, for a happy medium—a good loam, containing both clay and sand, that will hold both water and nutrients yet offer adequate drainage. Be sure, also, to sterilize the soil by spreading it out in a shallow pan and placing it in an oven (medium heat) for one hour.

To this basic loam we usually add one or more of other materials—peat moss, to increase water-holding capacity and to add organic matter; compost, for organic matter and nutrients; sand, to open up the soil to air; and some form of supplemental mineral fertilizer, usually bone meal and lime. Chemical fertilizer can be used, although it is not necessary to add it to the potting mixture, since the other ingredients will supply all the nutrients the plant can use for several months.

ACIDITY/ALKALINITY

A discussion of soils and potting mixtures would not be complete without some mention of acidity and alkalinity, and of the pH scale, which is the scientific measure for acidity and alkalinity. The midpoint on the pH scale is 7. A soil with a pH of 7 is neutral—neither acid nor alkaline. Numbers above 7 indicate an alkaline soil, those under 7, an acid soil. Most house plants, as most garden plants, will do best in a slightly acid soil (a pH of 6.0 to 7.0). Most garden soils are within this range, and so you should not worry unduly about the pH of the garden loam you dig for use in the potting mixture. In this book, all the house plants listed will do well in this normal range, unless special notations to the contrary are made.

If you have cause to worry about your soil's pH, or are simply curious, call your county agricultural agent and ask for directions on having a pH test made. The cost will be nominal. Any soil may be made more acid with the addition of peat moss, or less acid with the addition of ground limestone.

POTTING MIXTURES

There are as many different basic potting mixtures as there are plant experts—probably more. Perhaps the most common one, however (and one that can be trusted), calls for two parts loam, one part finely screened compost (or a mixture of peat moss and compost), and one part builder's sand (not sea sand).* To this is added a small amount of bone meal (about one teaspoon for a 5-inch pot) and a pinch of ground limestone. Other recommendations call for more of one ingredient and less of another. Do a little experimenting of your own. After a while, you will doubtless come upon your own favorite mixture, which you can recommend to others.

And now that you have the basic mixture formula well in mind, we will consider the exceptions:

1. Acid-loving plants such as azaleas, camellias, gardenias, and heathers should have no lime, since they are acid-loving. They should, in fact, have some form of acid organic matter—acid peat moss or oak leafmold.

2. Foliage plants need somewhat more compost in the mixture, although half of it should be composed of peat moss (which will not overstimulate the plant).

3. Fast-growing and hungry plants need more bone meal and lime, since they use them up so quickly.

4. Some plants, such as cacti, succulents, and orchids, have very special soil requirements; these are mentioned later under the discussions of individual plants.

See note p. 18A

★ 1. You may by now be wondering why, throughout this book, builder's sand is recommended for potting purposes while sea sand is cautioned against. The answer is that builder's sand, which comes from inland locations, has irregular and sharp surfaces, allowing good soil drainage. Sea sand, having been washed smooth over the years, packs too snugly and leads to a compacted soil and resultant drainage problems.

NUTRIENT MAINTENANCE

The mineral nutrients contained in any fresh potting soil or mixture, whether it is home-made or a sterilized commercial brand, should be sufficient for your plant's needs for the first four to six months. After that, you should begin to replenish those nutrients on a regular and carefully measured basis.

All plants need substantial amounts of three elements—nitrogen (N), phosphate (P_2O_5), and potash (K_2O), and lesser amounts of a dozen or more others, called "trace minerals" or "trace elements." In grower's language, the three major elements are referred to as N, P, and K, and on the label of any commercial fertilizer, the percentages of each are given in N-P-K order. A 5-10-5 fertilizer, for instance, will contain 5 percent nitrogen, 10 percent phosphate, and 5 percent potash. A so-called "balanced" fertilizer contains a balance of all three in the amounts needed for the proper growth of most plants. The fertilizer may be either a chemical or an organic preparation, according to your preference. The chemical kind are quick-acting, easy to use, and tidy. Organic fertilizers, on the other hand, are slow to release their nutrients, providing a gentle and steady supply. Chemical mixtures come in liquid, tablet, and even spray form (the last applied directly on the foliage). Organic fertilizers may be purchased commercially in balanced formulas (fish emulsion, made from fish wastes, is a popular one for house plant use) or may be made at home from a combination of ingredients. Blood meal is a good choice for supplying substantial amounts of nitrogen (its NPK formula is 15.00N-1.30P-0.70K), while bone meal (4.00N-21.00P-0.20K) is good for phosphate and wood ashes (0.00N-1.50P-7.00K) are high in potash content. A combination of one part blood meal, one part bone meal, and two parts wood ashes will make a 5-6-4 N formula, which is a good one for house plants.

How often should plants be fertilized? There is wide disagreement on this point, some experts believing in weekly feedings of full strength (the dosage recommended on the label), others fertilizing no more than once a month, and even less often during the winter. In the end, you will probably have to come to your own policy by way of experimentation. In the beginning, however, it is better to err on the conservative side, since far more plants have been injured from overfertilization than from nutrient starvation. If you use a commercial chemical or organic formula, I suggest that you feed your plants as often as recommended on the label, but only half the recommended dosage. (Manufacturers tend to overstate the need for their product.) If the plant shows a spurt of active growth in late winter or early spring, increase the dosage to the manufacturer's recommendation. During a dormant or rest period, withhold fertilizer entirely. If you are using a homemade organic fertilizer, such as the one suggested above, use it sparingly at first. A level teaspoon of the blood meal/bone meal/wood ash formula, applied monthly, should be plenty for a plant in a 5-inch pot. You may also put some of the mixture in a bottle, fill the bottle with water, and use this "tea" to water your house plants. A mild tea solution, applied weekly, will give all your plants a continuing and gentle supply of the essential nutrients.

Last, remember never to apply a chemical fertilizer if the soil is dry. The quick action of the chemicals can easily injure the roots.

balanced house plant fertilizer, which should be applied sparingly. Chemical preparations should be applied according to the manufacturer's directions.

CONTAINERS

Nearly any container that offers adequate drainage and does not leak is suitable for house plants. After checking a container for leakage, consider drainage carefully. If the container has a hole in its bottom, there is no problem. If not, then you should put coarse gravel or broken crockery in the bottom of the container to fill one-fourth to one-fifth of its depth. In this way, you will avoid the likelihood of waterlogging your plants and encouraging root rot.

The traditional terra cotta clay pot offers definite advantages. It is inexpensive, easily replaced, and--most important--allows air to be exchanged through its porous walls. This same porosity, however, allows water to evaporate fairly quickly, necessitating more frequent watering. If a plant's location makes it awkward to water, you will save yourself some effort by choosing a glazed or otherwise impervious container.

Some metal containers, notably copper, might produce adverse chemical reactions with soil and fertilizer elements, injuring plants therein. Copper planters, however, are usually lacquered to preventing such reactions.

Wooden tubs and boxes are ideal for very large house plants. You can make any wooden container watertight by lining it with several sheets of heavy-gauge plastic or, for permanent results, sheet metal.

Last, if you want the best advantages of both a terra cotta pot and a decorative container, place the former inside the latter, leaving a quarter-inch or more of space for air circulation around the walls of the inner pot. Sometimes sphagnum moss is inserted here, to help preserve moisture. A base of gravel in the decorative pot can provide good drainage while lifting the inner pot to the level of the outer container.

WATERING

More house plants are killed by overwatering than by any other cause. This killing with kindness can be avoided, if you learn to understand just when your plants need water and when they should be left alone.

The best rule of thumb is that a plant should be watered when the soil surface is dry to the touch. Then, water thoroughly, either by adding water to the soil surface or by immersing the entire pot in a larger container of water.

Certain plants, such as the African violets and other woodsy varieties, need more water than most, while cacti and succulents need less than the average. Aside from the specific preferences of individual varieties, there are many conditions which call for more or less water, as indicated in Table 1.

Immersion is the best method of watering because it is the surest. The soil in any pot might tend to form water channels which, upon receiving water from the surface, will rush it to

Table 1. WATERING NEEDS OF PLANTS UNDER VARIOUS CONDITIONS

Plants will need more water when:	Plants will need less water when:
They are in a period of active growth	They are in a period of rest (usually during winter)
They are in bright light	They are in dim light or under artificial light
Room humidity is low	Room humidity is high
Room temperature is high	Room temperature is under 70°
They are contained in small pots	They are in large pots
They are in clay pots	They are in non-porous pots
They are fast-growing varieties	They are slow-growing varieties
They are planted in sandy soil	They are planted in heavy soil
They are in flower or about to go into flower	

---

the bottom of the pot and out the drainage hole, leaving large parts of the soil bone-dry. Then, some potting soil mixtures will shrink when drying, leaving many spaces along the wall of the pot where water can run past. Immersion is the one sure way to soak the soil thoroughly, provided that the pot is porous. You can do it in any large container, or even in a sink or bathtub. Set the pots in the water, but do not let the water flow over the lips of the pots. After the surface of the potting mixture has become moist—ten to thirty minutes—remove the potted plant, drain off any excess water, and put it back in its place. Never go out for the afternoon, leaving your plants standing in water.

If you water from the top, remember to remove any excess water from the saucer. Plants should never be allowed to stand in water for fear of root rot. In time, you should learn to give each plant just enough water to soak it thoroughly, with very little excess drainage.

Some other watering tips:

1. Do not get water into the crown of any plant, for this will encourage decay.

2. Never use very cold water, especially for tropical plants. Keep an open jar of water at room temperature for your house plants. Not only will the proper temperature be assured, but if you use tap water, some of the chemicals will have been dissipated by the time it is given to plants.

3. Water that is artificially softened may be detrimental to plant growth. If you can, use rainwater, or

water that has not been softened.

4. If your water is especially hard, lime salts might cause trouble with such acid-loving plants as orchids, primulas, Rhododendrons, Azaleas, and other plants whose natural soil is woodsy (indicating a high organic content) and acid. Either choose plants that prefer a more neutral range in the pH scale, or plan to collect rainwater for your calcifuges (lime-haters).

HUMIDITY

Much of our trouble with house plants, especially in winter, can be traced to insufficient moisture in the air. Except for the cacti and succulents, nearly all house plants thrive best in a relative humidity of between 60 and 80 per cent, while that of most heated homes in winter is under 40 per cent—often, considerably under 40 per cent. House plants will virtually cry for moisture under these conditions, and it is incumbent upon you to answer that cry.

There are several ways to add moisture to the air in your home. The more expensive include the adding of a humidifying device to your furnace, if you live in a house, or installing an electric humidifier. This step will benefit not only the plants but everyone living in the house, too. But there are less expensive ways of bringing moisture to your plants:

The pebble tray. Line the bottom of a waterproof tray with decorative pebbles and arrange your plants, in pots, on top of the pebbles. Keep the tray filled with water, being sure only to avoid blocking the pots' drainage holes. Change the water weekly to keep it fresh.

Decorative containers. If you keep a clay pot inside a decorative container (double-potting), keep a pool of water in the bottom of the larger vessel. Again, provide some means of support for the clay pot so that it is not resting in water at any time. (Or, fill the space between the walls of the two pots with sphagnum moss and keep it constantly moist.)

Standing water devices. Water left standing in a room will gradually evaporate, meaning that the lost moisture is added to the room atmosphere. If your home is particularly dry during cold weather, take the trouble to place pans of water on tops of radiators; grow ivy, philodendron, or wandering Jew in containers of water; maintain an aquarium; rotate plants so that each can spend an afternoon in the bathroom each week, where the air is humid. Change standing water weekly.

Bathing and showering. Most house plants will respond favorably to a brief shower every day, or at least as often as you can manage to provide the treat. Little brass-plated atomizers are ubiquitous in mail order catalogs, but more dependable (albeit less decorative) are the plastic sprayers available in art supply stores. These hold a pint or quart of water, and they feature an adjustable shower head, affording an entire range of water action from a sharp jet to a fine mist. Your plants, of course, will do best with the fine mist. Remember to fill the container after every use, so that the next day's spray will be at room temperature. Remember also to avoid spraying plants that have been standing in direct sunlight (the shock is great) and those that have been subjected to very cool temperatures (perhaps spending the autumn on a cold sunporch).

Rubber plants and others with large leaves should be cleaned thoroughly and gently with a damp cloth about once a week. The leaf polish sold commercially is permissible, if you want really stunning looking, large-leafed plants, which can block the leaf's pores and impede respiration, but never use oil of any kind. Ivies and other rugged small-leafed plants can be held under the gentle stream of a faucet for their weekly bath.

Grouping. Plants will maintain a moist surrounding air (leaves not touching) with greater facility if they are grouped together, rather than separated. During the coldest part of winter, you might want to group most plants on a pebble tray under a light window, to take advantage both of maximum light and greatest humidity.

VENTILATION

Plants, like people, benefit from fresh air. Like people, also, they react badly to drastic changes in air movement and temperature. Provide adequate ventilation for your house plants, but do not subject them to sharp winds, winter drafts, or heat arising directly from a radiator. Think of your own comfort, in this respect, and you will know what will be best for your plants. If, in autumn, you bring your plants in from a summer outdoors, help them adjust to indoor conditions gradually by placing them by an open window for the first several days. Gradually lower the window day by day, keeping a watchful eye on night temperatures.

TEMPERATURE

The temperature requirements of house plants vary widely, according to the natural habitat of their forebears and also according to other conditions. Many cool-weather plants prefer a range of 50-60° F. and cannot tolerate temperatures above 70°, while tropicals may thrive in a moist 70-75°. Know the temperature preferences of any house plant before you adopt it, and then place it in the best possible temperature location in your home. You might find, for instance, that a cool-loving aspidistra will do best in a back bedroom, while tropical plants thrive happily next to (but not above) a living room heat vent. The temperature requirements or tolerances of plants are included in their descriptions throughout this book. Heed them well, make liberal use of an indoor thermometer, and do not be afraid to experiment by placing different plants in different locations for a week at a time. You might notice in your plants distinct preferences for particular locations throughout the house, and their preferences will not always corroborate expert advice.

LIGHT

Light and temperature needs are closely related. In their native surroundings, many tropical plants can thrive at higher temperatures because they receive long hours of sunlight. In the home, and especially during winter's short days, they cannot receive enough light to enable them to stand high house temperatures.

Except for most cacti and succulents, house plants should not be placed in windowsills where they will receive long periods of direct sunlight. Simply place a thermometer in this position and you will soon see that your plants can be literally cooked to death, even in the dead of a Minnesota winter. Strive, instead, for a bright spot with a few hours of filtered sunlight each day, at least for most plants.

Individual varieties vary, of course, in their light needs, and these needs are specified in the descriptions of individual plants in these pages. Again, do not be afraid to experiment with different locations for different plants. I have a Philodendron scandens, one of the most popular and most common of all house plants, that has thrived for years in a dim corner, when actually it is supposed to require a bright spot out of direct sun. Plants, I am afraid, sometimes exhibit unmistakable individual characteristics that we have yet to understand.

PRUNING AND TRAINING

Some plants should be pruned and pinched back occasionally, in order to encourage bushy and stocky growth, while trailing plants such as philodendrons and ivies need gentle support to guide them into pleasing growth patterns.

Many people hesitate to prune at all, feeling somehow that they are hurting the plant or interfering with its natural development. Actually, plants will respond to judicious pruning with new and vigorous growth. Plants such as geraniums, coleus, and begonias should be pinched back routinely, in order to encourage lateral growth. The process is quite simple: With a sharp knife, cut back perhaps one-half inch of the central growing tip. The plant should respond by sending out side shoots below the central tip, and the main stem of the plant should then become thicker and sturdier. If this is done several times a year, the plant should eventually attain the vigorous and well-rounded form you desire. Without this pruning, it might grow "leggy" with a weak main stem, requiring some kind of support. Many older plants, as well, will benefit from occasional pinching back or shearing of outside growth. Do not, however, prune Norfolk Island Pine, or pinch back African violets, gloxinias, flowering bulbs, or cyclamen.

Vines and trailing plants often need some kind of support, unless you prefer to let them cascade from a hanging basket. The usual practice is to sink a slab of cork or tree bark into a pot, then to train the vines of the plant to grow around and up the support, eventually concealing it.

Another effective device is the sphagnum moss cylinder. Pack wet moss fairly tightly around a stake and secure it in a cylinder of the proper size for the pot. The cylinder can be made easily from either chicken wire or green plastic material made for this purpose. If you wish, sink a small clay pot into the top of the cylinder, so that you can add water regularly to keep the moss damp. (Otherwise, the moss will require regular spraying.) Tie the vines gently to the cylinder as they grow; eventually, philodendrons and similar plants will anchor themselves to the moss with their aerial rootlets, making other support unnecessary.

REPOTTING

The temptation to repot plants too often is a strong one and should be resisted with strong will. A plant needs repotting only when it has become potbound—when the roots have filled the entire container and are creeping out of the drainage hole. Choose a new pot only one size larger than the old, for a house plant will not do well in a pot that is too large. If the larger pot has been used before, scrub it thoroughly to remove any possibility of disease. new clay pots, soak they become saturated for a few hours in water. Then, with ample moist potting soil, gravel, and a tongue depressor or similar wood tool, set to work.

To remove the plant from its old pot, slide your hand over the top of the pot, index and second fingers cradling the plant stem. Turn the pot upside-down, thus supported, and tap the lip of the pot sharply on the edge of a bench or table. After a few taps the entire soil ball, ringed with plant roots, should come out easily, in one neat piece. Set it aside. Take the larger pot and line the bottom with a layer of coarse gravel or broken crockery, to provide good drainage. Then add potting soil on top of the gravel, placing the plant and soil ball on top of the new soil several times in order to see when it has reached the proper depth. (The top of the soil should be about one-half inch below the lip of the new pot, in a 4-inch pot, and 1 inch below the lip in an 8-inch pot, to leave room for watering.) When enough soil has been added to raise the plant to its proper height, center it well and begin to pack soil around the sides of the soil ball, using the tongue depressor. Take your time in doing this, for it is the most crucial part of the entire operation. It is important to pack the soil firmly, so that no air spaces are left when the job is finished. Roots cannot draw nutrients in air spaces and many of them will thus be injured or die, affecting the health of the entire plant. When the new soil is finally brought up to a level even with the top of the soil ball, the job is finished. You might want to add just a little soil over the top of the root ball, especially if roots have been forced up to the soil surface, but don't add any more than you must, for you do not want to change the planting depth of the plant. Repotting is shock enough, for many plants, without altering the planting depth. Water the plant thoroughly and return it to its usual location.

How often should you repot? Obviously, only as each plant indicates a need. For slow-growers, this might be once every two or three years; a mature slow-grower may go for many years without repotting, if new growth is cut back. For fast-growing and very young plants, repotting might be needed once or twice a year for the first several years. Plants that do not need repotting after one year should have the top one-half to one inch of soil replaced annually, to keep the soil fresh.

PROPAGATION

There will come a time when you will want to start your own house plants—to increase your own plant population, to use as personal gifts for friends and family, to replace a short-lived plant or one that has become ungainly with age. The propagation of most house plants is not a difficult task, and it is most rewarding.

There are two general methods of doing the job: by the collecting and planting of seeds, and by the cutting and rooting of plant parts—stems, leaves, or underground structures. The first way (sexual reproduction) is usually a less satisfactory than the second. Propagation from seed is ideal for garden annuals, but not for most house plants. the seeds from hybrid plants are likely to produce plants vastly inferior to the parent plant. (A hybrid, incidentally, is any plant produced by cross-pollinating two plants of different species, varieties, or genera.) Last, many house plants do not flower and produce seeds under home conditions, requiring the house plant gardener to purchase seeds from specialty houses. The one advantage of growing house plants from seed is that you can create new hybrids by the cross-pollination of plants. The excitement of this activity creates a fascinating hobby for some house plant enthusiasts, but is unlikely to appeal to those who cannot afford to devote significant amounts of spare time to the activity.

Far more simple, and yielding far more reliable results, is the propagation of plants by the cutting and rooting of plant parts. Less care is required, and the offspring will look just like the parent, even when the parent is a hybrid.

Plants may be propagated at any time of year, although it is best to avoid tackling the job when the plant is going into a dormant period. In early spring, just before active growth begins, is perhaps the ideal time.

Cuttings. The most common method of propagating is by the taking of stem cuttings, which are then rooted in either water or some sterile rooting medium such as perlite, vermiculite, or sand. If you have never rooted a cutting before, then begin with African violets, coleus, Dracaena, Fuchsia, gardenias, geraniums, Impatiens, ivy, Philodendron, wandering Jew, or wax begonia. These are the easiest, because all can be rooted in water. Simply take a cutting from an actively growing tip of the plant, one containing four to six leaves, severing the stem cleanly just below a joint with a clean razor blade. Place the cutting (you may take several at a time, from the same plant if you wish) so that the bottom portion is submerged in water—a colored or clear green wine bottle is fine—remembering only to keep the leaves above water. (Cut off the bottom leaf or two, if necessary, to get more of the stem into the water; about a third of the entire length should be in water.) Place the container in diffused light—not direct sun—and wait until vigorous roots appear. When they have, the little plants may be removed from the water and potted in a small pot, using the potting mixture recommended earlier in this chapter. Be sure to pack the potting mixture firmly around the roots of the plant, to avoid any air spaces, and water thoroughly afterwards.

Stem cuttings that cannot be rooted in water are rooted in perlite, vermiculite (both available wherever house plant supplies are sold), or in builder's sand.

The process is basically the same as for rooting in water. The cuttings are inserted in the moist medium, which may be contained in a small clay pot or, for larger numbers of cuttings, a shallow plastic tray. The planted container is then placed in a plastic bag which is tied shut (the zip kind, used for food storage, is convenient, effective, and reusable) and placed in diffused light at a temperature of 65 to 70°. You can tell whether the cuttings have developed roots by testing them weekly. Open the bag and pull gently on a plant. If it moves easily, then the roots have not yet formed; if it resists your gentle tug fairly well, however, then the roots probably are mature enough to stand repotting. The process can take as little as two weeks, or as long as several months, depending upon the variety of the plant and the size of the cutting. When the roots are strong and vigorous, pot the plant in a small pot and treat it as you would any other plant.

Be sure that at least one node is below the surface of the potting medium.

Some plants that produce canes (hollow or pithy stems), (including Chinese ever-

---

*A node or eye is a point of the stem at which a leaf or root will emerge. It will appear as a little spot and may be slightly swollen, protruded, indented, or otherwise distinguished by coloration.

green, Dracaena, and Dieffenbachia, can be propagated by taking cuttings of the canes, which have discernable "eyes." Press each cane section (containing one eye) into moist sphagnum moss, secure it with wooden clothes pins at each end so that it does not pop up, seal it in a plastic bag, and put it in a cool place out of direct sun. In six to eight weeks, move it into a warm place (70 to 90°, still out of direct sun. Soon, a shoot will grow from the eye. When the shoot has attained a respectable size, the cane may be cut close to the shoot on both sides, and the new plant may be lifted from the moss and potted.

Plants that have fleshy leaves are best propagated by taking leaf or leaf-petiole cuttings. (A petiole is a leafstalk, or stem.) Leaf cuttings work well when large and mature leaves are available. Cut the leaf close to the stem of the parent plant, using a razor blade for a clean cut without crushing the cells. The leaf may then be cut horizontally into smaller sections, so that the main vein runs from top to bottom along the center of the leaf section. (Long-leafed plants such as Sansevieria and Streptocarpus may be cut into as many as ten sections, each of which will produce an individual plant.) Each leaf section is then sunk halfway into the rooting medium, after which the process is the same as that described for stem cuttings. Patience is required here, for this method is often a very slow one to produce results.

Smaller leaves may be rooted by taking leaf-petiole cuttings. Cut one leaf stem close to the main stalk and sink the stem into the rooting medium, so that the leaf nearly (but not actually) touches the medium. African violets, begonias, snake plant, piggy-back plant, and Peperomia respond well to leaf-petiole cuttings.

Underground division. Older plants that have thick main roots can be propagated by taking root cuttings. This is usually done when the plant is being repotted. Cut about one inch of the main root, making sure that it has at least one eye. Cover this with one-half inch of rooting medium and treat it as you would any other cutting. Coleus, ivy, Philodendron, and wandering Jew may be easily propagated in this

Thick-rooted perennials may be propagated simply by the manner process of root division, in which the root mass is simply forced apart into two or more clumps, each of which is then repotted.

Plants that produce rhizomes (underground stems) may be propagated by dividing the rhizome so that one leaf bud is contained on each piece, and planting the section under one-half inch of rooting medium. Plants that produce potato-like tubers can be propagated by cutting the tubers apart with a sharp knife, keeping one eye to each section, and planting the sections in the rooting medium just as one would plant potatoes in the open field.

Some plants produce "suckers," small plants that grow up from an underground stem or root. These may be separated from the parent plant and potted in soil immediately.

Anyone who has seen strawberries grow outdoors knows what runners are—the baby plants that grow from a long stem coming from the base of the parent plant. Among house plants, Boston fern and spider plant both produce runners, which can be severed from the parent and started in a rooting medium.

Other methods of underground division include the separation and replanting of baby bulbs and corms that are produced by the mother bulb or corm.

Air layering. A fairly simple (and most impressive) way of propagating larger or woody-stemmed plants is by air layering. Here, a sharp cut is made into the stem, perhaps a third of the way in, into which a toothpick is placed, horizontally, to keep the cut open. That stem section is then wrapped with moist sphagnum moss and covered with clear plastic, tied top and bottom so that moisture cannot escape. Roots will form from the incision and will soon show through the plastic. When a fair number of them have appeared, cut the stem below the plastic wrap, remove both plastic and moss, and pot the new plant immediately in potting soil.

As you might imagine, the propagation of plants can often be integrated with the cutting back, pruning, and shaping of older plants. It seems a shame to throw away plant parts when they can be used to produce more plants, and it is precisely this attitude of thrift which, if not controlled, can lead to a frightening multiplication of house plants. The answer, of course, is to share plants with friends, thus encouraging still more enthusiasts and still more house plants.

---

special box No. 3

CAN YOUR PLANTS SURVIVE YOUR VACATION?

What shall you do with your plants while you are gone for a long weekend, for a week, for a month?

The best solution is to have someone come in to water your plants for you. Be sure to give the volunteer specific instructions, however, since anyone unfamiliar with the needs of house plants might easily kill them with kindness by overwatering them.

A long weekend should present no problem whatsoever, except perhaps for vegetables and the few others that need daily watering. Simply soak your plants thoroughly by immersion, drain them, and they should last for four days with no problem. If you will be gone for a week, enclose each pot in a plastic bag and tie it snugly around the base of the plant stem. This device will cut surface evaporation greatly. Smaller plants can be enclosed completely in plastic bags, as long as some support is provided so that the plastic does not touch the foliage.

Water wicks will keep a plant happy for an even longer Wicks and pots are sold as units, usually called self-watering pots, but you can easily make your own at far less expense. Buy several yards of broad lamp wick. Cut off a 6- to 10-inch section for each potted plant, depending on the pot size. Invert the empty pot in a

---

special box No. 3, add 1

larger container of water, the water level coming to just below the top (well, the bottom, actually) of the inverted pot. Knock out the soil ball of the potted plant, insert the wick into the drainage hole, and flare out the end of the wick so that it covers as much of the bottom of the pot as possible. (The wick should spread out above the drainage gravel, just under the soil ball.) Replace the soil ball and plant. The bottom of the wick then goes through the drainage hole of the inverted bottom pot and into the water. Water the plant once, from above, and the action should be continuous from then on. Test this method on several plants while you are still at home, in order to determine just how well it works for you and how long you can afford to be away from home without worry. It is a most effective method.

NB: I am suggesting that the introductory part of this chapter be reorganized because the material explaining the symbols and the nomenclature of plants was repeated and the section of buying plants seemed more appropriate in the first chapter and not here under foliage plants (the advice concerns all plants and fits nicely with the theme of ch. 1). The insertions on pp. 51 and 52 came from the passages that were deleted as being redundant. Pp. 52-54 were retyped as one page after the removal of one section and revisions to eliminate repetition.

CHAPTER 4

INTRODUCING THE FOLIAGE PLANTS

The number and variety of house plants available for your consideration is staggering. For every combination of conditions your home can offer—including heat, light, and humidity—there are hundreds or thousands of suitable house plant varieties, offering virtually limitless selection of sizes, forms, colors, patterns and textures, growth patterns, and flowering habits. You have only to survey the conditions that your home can offer, and then make your plant selections, within those limits, to suit your own tastes.

The house plants I have selected for inclusion in this chapter are only representative of their far greater numbers. I have included nearly all of the most common plants, and I have tried to avoid those difficult to grow. All the old favorites are here, as well as some newer varieties and unusual plants that can add zest to your collection.

If there is no popular name for a plant, or if there is more than one, none dominant, the plant is listed by its scientific name. The plants are listed alphabetically by their common or popular names, followed by (in parentheses) their scientific (or Latin) names. The scientific name comprises both the genus name and the specific epithet. For example, the scientific name for the common boxwood is Buxus (the genus) sempervirens (the specific epithet). After a genus name is introduced, it is thereafter abbreviated. Thus Buxus sempervirens, if mentioned again, becomes B. sempervirens. Last, there may be a third part to the scientific name which designates a further subdivision, usually called a subspecies or variety. The popular Japanese boxwood, for example, is B. microphylla japonica.

Although I have attempted to maintain an informal tone in these pages, by using common names whenever possible, the scientific nomenclature has obvious benefits. Many species are known by different common names in different parts of the country; different species of a genus are often called by a single common name; and a single common name may be applied even to varieties of completely different genera. The only sure way to identify any plant, then, is to refer to its scientific name. The index, which includes both common and scientific names, provides a convenient means of cross-checking names.

For each plant listed, you will find symbols that indicate its individual preferences for growing temperature, light, soil moisture and air humidity, and window placement. Please remember that these are rough guides and not inflexible demands. Many plants have a wide range of tolerance and will thrive in a variety of conditions. Many plants said to prefer an east window will do just as well in a shaded south or west location. Most crucial, perhaps, are the guides to humidity and moisture, since overwatering is one thing that virtually no plant will tolerate. Do not hesitate to try a plant of your liking because you cannot provide its exact needs; but neither should you attempt growing a plant if you can provide none of them. Experimentation is both valuable and enjoyable.

In this chapter we will survey many of the house plants grown primarily for their foliage. Some of them, under favorable conditions, will flower from time to time, although few should be selected for their flowering abilities. Nearly all of these plants are fairly easy to grow and maintain, giving even the beginner a wide variety of plants from which to choose.

African Boxwood (Myrsine africana) B-C-A-C
This slow-growing plant has red stems but otherwise is similar to boxwood (q.v.). Many people think it is even more graceful. African Boxwood is a good plant for terrariums, if the atmosphere is not too hot.

Aralia (Fatsia japonica) C-B-B-C
Sometimes sold as Aralia sieboldii. Beautiful, bright green, leathery, maple-like leaves highlight this cheerful plant. In appearance, it is similar to the castor oil plant, and in fact is sometimes called False Castor Oil Plant. It thrives in a cool spot. Aralia can easily grow leggy, and so it should be pruned annually in order to encourage it into bushy growth. It will attain a height of 4 feet at maturity.

A striking hybrid, Fatshedra lizei (a cross between F. japonica and ivies (Hedera) forms a climbing plant with maple-shaped leaves, tolerant of adverse conditions.

There is also a plant called False Aralia (Dizygotheca elegantissima), which has graceful and feathery foliage. It bears no resemblance to the true Aralia and is difficult to grow.

Asparagus A-B-B-B
There are two common kinds of Asparagus suitable for growing as house plants: Fern Asparagus (A. plumosus), with slender, needle-like dark green leaves, forming a feathery appearance, and A. sprengeri (Emerald Feather) which has thicker yellow-green leaves and drooping stems. The latter makes a good plant for hanging baskets, and produces red berries at Christmastime. Both like some sun in the summer and full sun in the winter, and both can grow to a height of about 2 feet. A. meyeri, less common but equally attractive, has tiny fern-like leaves that arch out on long stems from the center of the plant.

Australian Laurel (Pittosporum tobira) C-B-A-B
A tolerant and slow-growing plant whose leaves, glossy and leathery, resemble those of Rhododendron. Australian Laurel will grow vigorously bushy and does not ask much attention. Florists often use the leaves in floral arrangements.

An interesting variegated form is P. tobira variegata, which grows quite large.

Australian Umbrella Tree (Schefflera actinophylla) A-A-B-A
Here is a very attractive and vigorous grower, a tree-like plant with rich-looking and glossy leaves that radiate like umbrellas from the ends of several leaf stalks. It is a tough and rewarding plant, growing to 4 feet, which can be propagated by air-layering.

Australian Umbrella Tree is also sold as Brassaia actinophylla. A dwarf variety, B. actinophylla compacta, is also available.

Baby's Tears (Helxine soleirollii) B-B-A-B
This low creeper is also called Irish Moss. It likes a constantly moist (but not soggy) soil, and higher-than-average humidity. It makes a good ground cover for terrariums but will also grow in a pot if adequate humidity is provided. Baby's Tears may appear to die in the colder months, but after

an adequate rest period it will spring back to life. It is most sensitive to fertilizer burn and salt accumulation.

Black Pepper (Piper nigrum)

This is not a very attractive plant, but it produces real peppercorns that you may use at the table and is a good conversation piece for that reason. The plant's berries with glossy, bright-green leaves later turn red, then dry up and turn black. Pick the dried-up black corns, dry them thoroughly for several weeks in an open spot, then use them in your pepper grinder. The care for Black Pepper is the same as that required for Philodendron. It is not a demanding plant. (Be sure that you have this plant and not one of the so-called Black Peppers of the Deadly Nightshade family!)

Boxwood (Buxus)

The same plant that grows the most prized hedges outdoors can make a very attractive house plant. Boxwood, with glossy, bright-green leaves, is slow-growing and dependable, a good subject for bonsai, the ancient Oriental art of growing dwarf trees and shrubs. B. sempervirens and B. microphylla japonica (Japanese Boxwood) are the two popular species.

Bromeliads

There are more than 1,800 varieties of this popular group, many of which are suitable for growing as house plants. Some of them produce attractive flowers, but most are grown for their striking and variegated leaf patterns. One distinctive feature of the Bromeliads is the rosette of leaves that forms a small water cup, which the plant uses to hold reserve supplies of water in its natural habitat. Since the plant lives in the crotches of trees in Central and South America, the water cup is an evolutionary survival characteristic. In the home, keep the cup filled with water, changing it weekly to keep it fresh.

A few of the more common Bromeliads are Aechmea, Ananas (Pineapple), Billbergia, Cryptanthus, Dyckia, Tillandsia (Spanish Moss), and Vriesia.

Caladium

Caladiums, with their spectacularly colored and variegated leaves, are equally at home in the garden or on the window sill. They are ideal additions to plant groupings on porch or patio in the summer and early autumn. Give them bright light, but not long periods of direct sun in summer, if you want the brightest leaf colors. They will not last through the year and should be treated as annuals.

Caladiums are grown from tubers, which can be divided easily to produce new plants. Start the tubers in regular potting soil at a very warm temperature—180° to 90°—and move the young plants to a cooler spot when they have appeared. They will attain a height of about 1 foot.

Cast Iron Plant (Aspidistra elatior)

This is perhaps the easiest plant in the world to grow, as its name suggests. It is virtually impossible to neglect it to death. It is also called Saloon Plant, since it was one of the few that could survive in Victorian taverns, and it was made immortal by George Orwell in his novel Keep the Aspidistra Flying. If you cannot grow the Aspidistra, you may safely conclude that you have a purple thumb, hopelessly irredeemable.

Cast Iron Plant, which grows about two feet tall, seems to thrive even better when kept slightly pot-bound, and it will appreciate having its leaves washed occasionally. A white-striped species is called A. variegata.

Chamaeranthemum igneum

This low, spreading herb has attractive, dark green leaves with reddish-yellow veins. It is suitable for hanging baskets or as a low contrast in large plant groupings. It does like warm temperatures and high humidity, however, and might not be suitable for dry apartments.

Chinese Evergreen (Aglaonema)

Here is an attractive plant that is very easy to grow. It will stand abuse almost as well as Cast Iron Plant.

There are at least ten commonly found species of the Aglaonema, the most popular of which, A. modestum, has interestingly mottled leaves. Perhaps the most attractive, however, is A. pseudobractaetum, which is sometimes difficult to find in stores and greenhouses.

Cissus

Cissus is a viny genus that offers a number of interesting and attractive species. Most are vigorous climbers, suitable for training on a trellis or for adding to hanging baskets.

Among the more popular species are C. rhombifolia (Grape Ivy), which is one of the most popular of all house plants; C. antartica (Kangaroo Vine), which prefers a small pot; C. antartica minima (Miniature Kangaroo Vine); C. rotundifolia; and C. discolor (Begonia Ivy), which is perhaps the most spectacular of the genus, although difficult to grow.

Of all the Cissus, Grape Ivy is the easiest to grow, which doubtless accounts for its popularity.

Coleus

This old favorite has velvety leaves (some sporting bright splashes of reds, pinks, purples, and yellows. There is a seemingly endless number of varieties of Coleus, nearly all of them interesting, most growing to eighteen inches in height.

Coleus is equally happy outdoors, grown as an annual in the North, or in the window garden. It can be grown easily from seed, and stem tip cuttings can be taken from established indoor plants almost any time of the year. If you grow Coleus outdoors in summer, take some cuttings before the first autumn freeze and root them for growing as house plants.

The soil for Coleus should be kept damp, but not soggy. Pinch back plants often to encourage bushy growth.

Copper leaf (*Acalypha wilkesiana*) A-A-A-B

These are members of the spurge family, which feature copper-colored foliage. A close relative, *A. hispida*, is described in this book under flowering plants.

Copper leaf may be propagated easily by taking cuttings late in the summer. The plant is susceptible to attack by spider mites, and proper precautions should be taken against this menace.

Dichorisandra reginae A-C-B-C

This is an attractive and slow-growing plant with interesting leaf markings. It resembles Wandering Jew, except that it grows upright. Give it warm temperatures and not too much direct light, but do watch room humidity.

Dieffenbachia A-C-C-C

There are many species of this popular plant, often called dumbcane. It is prized for its large leaves with interesting markings, usually variations of cream and white on dark green. *Dieffenbachia* is a fairly tough plant, not too difficult to grow. Most varieties attain a height of 18 to 24 inches, although growth is slow.

D. arvida 'Exotica' is very popular because it is even more durable than other members of the family. Other well-known species include *D. picta*, *D. amoena*, *D. sequina*, and *D. bowmannii*.

There are no special cultural requirements, although *Dieffenbachia* does like a warm spot and will appreciate having its foliage cleaned regularly. The plant may be propagated by taking stem cuttings and rooting them in moist and warm peat.

Caution: Eating or nibbling on the leaves of *Dieffenbachia* can cause severe swelling of the tongue and mouth tissues, hence its popular name, dumbcane. It is not a plant to grow in a home with toddlers.

Dracaena A-B-B-C

There are many species of *Dracaena*, which vary so greatly in appearance that some appear to be unrelated. Most grow tall—5 feet or more—on sturdy stalks. They are very tough plants, tolerant of a surprising amount of neglect, all in all one of our most dependable house plants.

Some varieties to investigate are *D. deremensis* 'Warneckii,' *D. fragrans*, *D. fragrans massangeana* (whose leaves feature yellow stripes), *D. marginata* (a truly exciting plant, with grasslike, cream-colored foliage, edged in red—sometimes sold as *D. marginata tricolor*), *D. sanderiana* (with white-banded leaves), *D. godseffiana*, *D. draco* (the Dragon Tree of the Canary Islands), and many others, some of which will doubtless by offered by any good supplier. These mentioned, however, are some of the most attractive and also some of the easiest to grow.

Episcia A-C-A-C

This genus, which offers many species and subspecies, is related to the African Violet and requires largely the same culture, although it does demand a little more light. *Episcia* is not really one of the easiest plants to grow successfully, and should be tried only after success has been attained with some of the others listed in these pages. The leaves are a rich green, most varieties tinged with copper, some with variations of silver, blue, purple, and bronze. The veins often offer striking color contrasts. *Episcia* is a trailing plant, a natural selection for hanging baskets. It also sends out runners that may be used for propagation.

Most species of *Episcia* produce small and attractive flowers, in the color range of red-orange-yellow, but the plant is generally grown for its delightful foliage. If you do not wish to strive for blossoms, a north window will suit *Episcia* well enough.

The most popular species is *E. cupreata* (Flame Violet), which has soft and hairy copper-tinged leaves, and comes in several attractive varieties. Also investigate *E. dianthiflora*, which produces white flowers, and *E. lilacina* 'Cuprea,' with lavender flowers. Many other species and subspecies are easily available, all of which have fascinating foliage variations and some of which will bloom quite profusely.

Fatshedra (see *Aralia*)

Fatsia japonica (see *Aralia*)

Ferns A-C-A-C

The ferns are the oldest plants on the evolutionary scale, that you are likely to cultivate. The ferns are predated only by the algae and the mosses. Everyone knows and admires ferns for their graceful and feathery fronds. They are one of the few house plants that reproduce themselves by spores rather than seeds. Some ferns grow regally upright, while others trail with modesty and grace. There are many sizes of ferns, from miniature plants suitable for the window sill, all the way to the 7-foot tub plants that can add a touch of class to entryways, patios, and conservatories.

The secret to the successful raising of ferns is in offering them an environment matching, as nearly as possible, that of their natural habitat. They need warmth, a decent degree of room humidity (not under thirty percent), and a moist and humusy soil (at least 50 per cent organic matter). They appreciate bright light, but will be affected adversely if allowed to stand for long periods of time in direct sun.

There are a great many ferns from which to choose. Among the smaller ones are:

Adiantum, the Maidenhair Fern, which is available in several varieties; it sends forth fragile-looking fronds in sprays and needs good light and high humidity. It is a rather difficult plant.

Asparagus plumosus (Asparagus Fern), the most popular of the small "ferns," is really not a fern at all but a member of the lily family and reproduces by seeds rather than spores. It is treasured for its delicate, hair-like leaves.

Other smaller "ferns" of this group include Asparagus medeoloides (Simlax), a trailer; A. sprengeri (Emerald Feather), a climber; Pteris multifida (Brake Fern); Woodwardia orientalis (Chain Fern); Polypodium aureum (Hare's Foot Fern); and many, many others.

Among the larger ferns are:

Cyrtomium falcatum (Holly Fern), which has holly-shaped fronds.

Asplenium nidus (Bird's Nest Fern), with broad lance-shaped fronds.

Nephrolepis exaltata, which has long, sword-shaped fronds and is often called Sword Fern.

N. exaltata 'Bostoniensis,' the ever-popular Boston Fern.

Platycerium bifurcatum (Staghorn Fern), whose fronds are usually attached to a piece of bark or other support, and which can become parched quite easily in a dry atmosphere.

The world of ferns is a large one, full of interest, and extremely rewarding. No house plant collection should be without at least one or two representatives of these proud families.

C) Ficus   B-C-C-C

This large group of indoor plants, whose best-known member is the Rubber Plant, offers species ranging from large, tree-like plants down to small-leafed trailers. Although they are not difficult plants to grow, the large species are especially sensitive to both overwatering and sudden temperature changes, and will react to either by dropping their leaves.

There has been much improvement in the Rubber Plant (F. elastica) since World War II. The best now is perhaps F. elastica 'Robusta,' which is remarkably trouble-free. There are many decorative varieties, as well, including F. elastica 'Doescheri,' which has light and dark green patched leaves and cream-colored leaf margins, and F. elastica

'Schryveriana,' another mottled-leafed variety. F. elastica 'Decora,' from which 'Robusta' was developed, is still a popular slow-growing variety. Rubber plants will grow as tall as any room, but may be cut back to encourage bushiness. Chinese Banyan (F. retusa), another tree-like Ficus, showers forth with a profusion of small, leathery leaves. F. retusa nitida (Indian Laurel) resembles mountain laurel.

The Fiddle-Leaf Fig (F. lyrata) is a tough and attractive tree-like species, with large, dark green, fiddle-shaped leaves. It needs warmer conditions than other Ficus. Weeping Fig (F. benjamina) is another Ficus tree that has small, densely growing foliage.

There are, as well, many small plants in the genus. Most popular, perhaps, is Creeping Fig (F. pumila), a small-leafed creeper that has been developed to include several variations—F. pumila minima (slower-growing and smaller), and F. pumila variegata, a variegated variety. All will adhere to rough surfaces, sending out aerial roots similar to those of ivy, and are thus easily trained.

The tree-type Ficus are propagated by air-layering, while the small-leafed climbers and trailers may be reproduced easily by simple division or cuttings.

C) German Ivy (Senecio mikaniodies)   C-B-B-C

Here is an easy-to-grow plant that is similar to the true ivies in both appearance and requirements. A handsome relative is S. macroglossus variegatus (Cape Ivy). Treat them in every way like Ivy (q.v.) for success.

C) Ginger (Zingiber officinale)   A-A-A-B

This is the same ginger that is used in cooking, which makes the plant even more interesting than its appearance would indicate. The untreated rhizomes sold in specialty food and gourmet shops can be planted directly in potting soil to produce plants—or, established plants may be divided easily. The plants have reed-like stems and interesting grassy foliage, truly exotic in appearance. Success as a house plant depends upon giving Ginger plenty of sunlight and warm temperatures. Keep the soil constantly damp but never soggy for long periods of time. As an added bonus, healthy plants will bear colorful clusters of flowers. A rest period is required for this plant.

C) Golddust Plant (Aucuba japonica)   C-B-B-C

This modest plant features dark green leaves spotted with yellow-gold markings. Its main attribute is that it will withstand very cool temperatures, all the way down to freezing, and still come up smiling. It is good for unheated winter porches in all but the coldest parts of the country. Two popular varieties are A. japonica variegata and A. japonica goldeana.

C) Ivy (Hedera)   C-B-B-C

Here is surely one of the most popular of house plant species, both easy to grow and cheerful and attractive in appearance. There are a great number of varieties, with new improvements coming along all the time.

IV-20

English ivy (<u>Hedera helix</u>) is the most popular of the true ivies, and is available in more than fifty varieties to suit nearly any taste. There are varieties with large leaves and small, fast or slow growing habits, plain green or variegated. The best way to choose an English ivy to your liking is to visit some flower shops and greenhouses, or to beg a few cuttings from a friend who has a plant that appeals to you.

Propagation of ivy is easy, and in fact the plant does half of the job for you. Small rootlets will form on the stem of the plant, just below the leaves, which the ivy uses to attach itself to rough surfaces, helping it to climb. Make cuttings just below the roots and plant these cuttings directly in potting soil or a sterile rooting medium.

It would be the sheerest folly to attempt to recommend all the good varieties of English ivy. For a starter, however, you might investigate <u>H. helix conglomerata</u> (Japanese ivy), an upright-growing plant with small and densely growing leaves; 'Curlilocks' and 'Ivalace' with curled leaf margins; 'Green Ripples,' 'Maple Queen,' 'Merion Beauty,' 'Needlepoint,' 'Pittsburgh,' 'Pixie,' 'Rochester,' <u>H. helix scutifolia</u>, and 'Shamrock,' the last of which likes more than average moisture and which is good for terrariums.

Among the variegated English ivies, try 'Golddust,' 'Glacier,' and 'Goldheart,' the last of which has dark green leaves with sharply contrasting bright yellow centers.

IV-21

Canary Islands ivy (<u>Hedera canariensis</u>) is another easy-to-grow ivy, which has larger leaves than English ivy. It is often trained around a piece of bark, much like a <u>Philodendron</u>, to form a striking plant with a very bushy appearance. More popular than the basic green-leafed variety is the variant <u>H. canariensis variegata</u>, also known as 'Glorie de Marengo,' whose leaves are slate-green to cream in color.

(C) Joseph's Coat (<u>Alternanthera</u>)   A-B-B-B

These are low-growing, dwarf plants that are good for terrariums. Their multicolored foliage adds interest to any plant grouping. Joseph's Coat needs warm temperatures and a moist soil to be happy.

(Note: <u>Codiaeum</u> is also called Joseph's Coat, because it, too, has colorful foliage. However, <u>Codiaeum</u> grows to a height of 10 feet.)

(C) <u>Maranta</u>   A-C-A-C

Here is a genus of plants that has striking foliage. It is easy to grow, and impressive in appearance. Marantas will grow to about eight inches in height. <u>M. leuconeura kerchoveana</u> (Prayer Plant) is perhaps the most popular of the <u>Marantas</u>, and is so named because its leaves fold up at night, as if in prayer. The leaves are large and oval-shaped, and the plant requires a fairly humid atmosphere. In the autumn, the leaves may begin to die out.

IV-22

If so, do not be alarmed. Cut off the affected leaves and reduce watering until late winter, when new growth begins; then water normally.

A red-veined variety, even more striking, is <u>M. erythroneura</u>. Another with red veins is <u>M. leuconeura erythrophylla</u> (Jungle Plant), which has olive-green leaves. Still another striking variation is offered by <u>M. leuconeura massangeana</u>.

Most house plant growers will want to include at least one <u>Maranta</u> among their collections. The key to success with this plant is in giving it lots of bright light, but no direct sun at all.

(C) Miniature Holly (<u>Malpighia coccigera</u>)   C-B-B-B

This is not a true holly, but a bushy evergreen shrub with dense holly-like foliage. The leaves are shiny, dark green, and have spiny teeth. Miniature Holly does produce small flowers, but it is grown primarily as a foliage plant. It is propagated easily from cuttings.

(C) <u>Nephthytis</u> (Arrowhead)   A-C-B-A

This is an attractive plant, but difficult to identify, since there is great confusion over what is and what is not a <u>Nephthytis</u>. Experts tell us that many <u>Syngoniums</u> are mistaken for <u>Nephthytis</u>. Other experts say that most plants sold as <u>Nephthytis</u> are really <u>Syngoniums</u>. Since the two plants are difficult to tell apart, however, no one cares very much except

IV-23

the experts. Whatever they are, they are tough plants, able to withstand adverse conditions. <u>Nephthytis</u> have large, compound at maturity but simple before that, arum-shaped leaves, and are either trailers or climbers. Used as climbers, they will have to be offered some support, such as that used by <u>Philodendron</u>. Propagation may be achieved by taking stem cuttings.

Among several available species, the most popular is <u>Syngonium podophyllum</u> (Goosefoot Plant).

(C) Norfolk Island Pine (<u>Araucaria excelsa</u>)   A-B-B-C

This popular evergreen, graceful and symmetrical, is seen with increasing frequency. It will hold up well under adverse conditions, although its branches will droop in dim light. Give it a damp, but not soggy, soil, for it is very susceptible to overwatering. It seems to do well when kept slightly potbound.

Norfolk Island Pine is a slow grower, and should never be pruned. It will grow gracefully to a height of about 6 feet, after which it tends to become ungainly.

(C) <u>Palms</u>   B-C-B-B

Here is a plant family full of nostalgia for many of us. In Victorian times and right up through the 1930s and 1940s, the potted palm was a symbol of exotic elegance, bringing a bit of the tropics to shivering Northerners. No movie made before 1950 was complete without a detective peering out from behind a potted palm.

The elegant palms lost much of their allure after

World War II, but now they are making a modest comeback. You can achieve success with palms, by giving them bright light (even though they will endure shade), little water, and no plant food during the winter months. Palms, actually, seem to thrive on inattention, doing well when slightly potbound. They are slow-growing, in any case.

The palms are a plant family—Palmae is the scientific name—that comprises many genera and far more species. Few, however, are both attractive and manageable as house plants. Among the palms you might wish to investigate are:

Chamaerops (European Fan Palm) has fan-shaped leaves on long stalks, and will become quite large at maturity.

Cocos is an attractive coconut palm, the best species of which is the dwarf C. wedelliana.

Howeia is the Palm Court Palm, the most popular of all indoor large palms. H. belmoreana, the most attractive species, will eventually grow to 10 feet or more in height, given many years and sufficient room.

Neanthe is an attractive and easy-to-grow dwarf that can tolerate a dry room.

Phoenix, the Date Palm, can be grown easily from the stone of a fresh date. Plant the stone in potting soil, keep it warm (70° to 80°) and it should germinate in about a month. It is slow growing during the first year or so, but within ten or fifteen years it will become as tall as any room.

Pellonia A-B-A-B

This is a colorful, slow-growing, creeping plant, fine for hanging baskets and a good filler plant for groupings. It features small, oval-shaped leaves with interesting variegated patterns. There are two popular varieties—P. daveauana and the more compact P. pulchra.

Pellonia is not difficult to propagate. As it creeps along the soil it sends down roots from the stems. Just cut the stems into sections and root them in potting soil.

Peperomia A-C-B-C

There are many species and varieties of this popular and cheerful little plant, most of which are low and upward-growing, some with deeply ridged leaves. They are tough plants, tolerant of most conditions, although they will rot at the groundline if the top of the soil is not allowed to dry out between waterings. Peperomia like bright light, but not direct sun in the summer.

Among the more popular varieties are:

P. caperata (Emerald Ripple Peperomia) has deeply ridged heart-shaped leaves; the tops of the ridges are green and the valleys are brown, giving an interesting effect.

P. rotundifolia is a low grower with light green and thick leaves.

P. obtusifolia (Ovalleaf Peperomia) has solid green leaves, while P. obtusifolia variegata is the variegated form of the same species.

P. sandersii (Watermelon Peperomia) is identified by its red petioles and silver-striped leaves.

P. grieseo-argentea hederaefolia has ridged, glossy leaves, silver-hued, and purple-olive veins.

There are many other varieties of the Peperomia, many of which may be seen at your local flower shop or greenhouse.

Philodendron B-C-B-C

These plants constitute what is probably the most popular group of house plants in America today. There are many, many species and varieties, with leaves ranging from small to very large, in an interesting variety of shapes offered by no other house plants. Most are climbers, and will appreciate a support that can be kept moist, such as that described on page CC.

Philodendron are not difficult plants to grow, unless you disregard the rules. Growth will be stunted by poor light, and the leaves can turn yellow and drop from lack of water, too small a pot, low temperatures, or poor drainage. They will appreciate a monthly washing with a mild soap (not detergent) solution. Cut back the growing tips if you wish to encourage bushy growth, and use the tip cuttings to form new plants.

Some of the more popular varieties include:

P. scandens (Sweetheart Vine), a very popular climber that can withstand the dry air of a typical apartment.

P. oxycardum, the most commonly grown form, which has heart-shaped leaves very similar to P. scandens. It is often grown in water or wet moss.

P. dubium (Cut Leaf Philodendron) is a slow grower with star-shaped leaves.

P. panduraeforme (Fiddleleaf Philodendron) has irregularly shaped, olive-green leaves.

P. pertusum has perforated leaves, irregularly shaped. The adult form, known as Monstera deliciosa, has broad and thick leaves with many perforations.

P. squamiferum (Anchorleaf Philodendron) has leaves and petioles that are covered by red hairs. The leaves are shaped like daggers.

P. bipinnatifidum (Twice-Cut Philodendron) is a large-leafed variety; the leaves resemble the smaller P. dubium in shape, but are more deeply notched.

P. selloum is another cut-leaf variety, the cuts becoming more pronounced as the plant reaches maturity. This species will tolerate temperatures down to freezing with no apparent harm.

P. wendlandi is another large-leafed species, very tolerant of a wide range of temperatures and humidity. Its leaves are long and narrow.

Piggy-Back Plant (<u>Tolmiea menziesi</u>) B-B-A-A

Here is a native to the West Coast of the United States, a modest-sized plant that can be grown outdoors in the warmer regions of the country. Its name is derived from its unusual habit of bearing young plantlets from the junction of the leaf and the petiole. These can be rooted easily to grow new plants. The leaves are toothed and lobed, covered in down. It is an easy plant to grow, although not considered especially attractive by some.

Pilea   A-B-B-B

There are at least four cultivated house plants in this interesting group, none of which grows more than a foot in height. They are rather unusual looking plants, not liked by everyone. All like moist soil, warm temperatures, and full sun in the winter. The plants become less attractive as they grow older, but cuttings are easily made, so that older plants may be discarded when desired. Fertilize <u>Pilea</u> liberally when growth is active.

<u>P. cadiere</u> (Aluminum Plant) has dark green leaves with striking aluminum-colored markings. A dwarf variety, <u>P. cadiere minima</u>, is preferred by many, as is <u>P. cadiere nana</u>, a compact variety.

<u>P. microphylla</u> (Artillery Plant) is fine in texture with bright green, fern-like leaves. When its flowers are dry, pollen literally explodes from the blossoms, hence its common name.

<u>P. involucrata</u> (South American Friendship Plant) is bushy in growth and has coppery leaves. It can be made to be even more bushy, if several cuttings are taken, then rooted in the same pot, to the sides of the parent plant.

<u>P.</u> 'Silver Tree' has bronze-hued leaves with silver markings.

Plectranthus   A-C-A-B

Various species of this genus are often called Trailing Coleus or Swedish Ivy. Some are upright in growth, while others are trailers, making good subjects for hanging baskets.

<u>P. australis</u>, a trailer, has waxy-green leaves, round in shape with sawtooth edges.

<u>P. australis variegatus</u>, similar in leaf shape, with added white markings.

<u>P. purpuratus</u> is an upright plant with purple coloring on the undersides of its leaves.

There are other interesting varieties, including <u>P. oertendahlii</u>, a flowering trailer with bronze-hued leaves and silvery veins.

Pleomele   A-C-B-A

This is an interesting group of plants with cultural requirements similar to those of <u>Philodendron</u>.

<u>P. reflexa variegata</u> (Song of India) is now included in the genus <u>Dracaena</u>. Its attractive, spear-shaped leaves are gold and green striped, borne in clusters on branching stems. It will grow to tree size in ten or fifteen years.

<u>P. reflexa gracilis</u> has dense foliage; its recurved leaves have translucent edges.

<u>P. thalioides</u> has waxy green leaves, ribbed lengthwise.

Pothos (<u>Scindapsus</u>)   A-C-B-C

Pothos is very similar in appearance and growth habits to the heart-leaf <u>Philodendron</u>, <u>P. scandens</u>, except that it needs less water and warmer temperatures—not below 65°. It likes bright light, but cannot stand direct sun. Pothos is a natural trailer, although it can be trained upward along a support, again like <u>Philodendron</u>. The leaves are heart-shaped, green, with pale yellow markings.

The most popular species is <u>S. aureus</u>, which offers several variegated varieties, some of which require even warmer temperatures.

Ruellia makoyana   A-C-A-C

This is an old favorite, not seen as often today as in the 1930s. It is a free-spreading plant, with glossy and pale green leaves with silvery veins. It likes a warm and moist environment, shaded from the sun.

Sanchezia nobilis glaucophylla   A-C-A-B

This is a member of the <u>Aphelandra</u> family. It grows to a heigth of 4 feet and has large, glossy, sword-shaped leaves with yellow veins.

Screw Pine (<u>Pandanus</u>)   A-C-B-B

This old favorite will withstand most adverse conditions. It is recognized by its long, arching, sword-like leaves, which have saw-toothed edges.

<u>P. veitchii</u> has green and white striped leaves. Often preferred, however, is <u>P. veitchii compactus</u>, a dwarf variety with clearly variegated leaves. <u>P. baptistii</u> has no marginal spines, as do the other species. All Screw Pines like moist soil, but never soggy soil. They can take some direct sun, except in the heat of summer, although they do best in a bright location out of direct sun altogether.

Selaginella   A-D-A-A

Among these fern-like plants are some small creepers, some erect-growing species, and some trailers. All offer bright green, feathery foliage. The conditions they require are the same as those for ferns.

<u>S. kraussiana</u> is a low creeper, perfect for terrariums.

<u>S. emmeliana</u> is an erect-growing plant.

<u>S. willldenovii</u> is a vigorous climber with unusual blue leaves, while <u>S. apus</u> is a trailer, good for hanging baskets.

Sensitive Plant (<u>Mimosa pudica</u>)   B-C-*-B

This is a fascinating plant for both adults and children

---

*Prefers dry soil but high room humidity.

because its delicate and feathery leaves and petioles droop
and fold up instantly (and temporarily) whenever it is touched,
or even if a lighted match is held close to it. Seeds are often
available in stores, from which plants will grow easily. It
becomes leggy and out of hand after about a year, but it is
not difficult to grow more plants at any time. It is very sensitive,
also, to mealybugs.

Silk Oak (Grevillea robusta)   C-B-B-C

This is a pleasant plant with graceful and feathery
foliage similar to that of the False Aralia. It will grow to three feet in height. Silk Oak likes
cool and moist conditions, and can spend the summer outdoors
with benefit. It does tend to get leggy if unchecked, so it should be cut back at the growing tip fairly regularly.
Silk Oak will react badly if its soil becomes very dry.

Snake Plant (Sansevieria)   A-C-B-A

The Snake Plant is actually a succulent, but few of us
think of it as such, and so we include it among the foliage
plants. It has long been very popular, probably because of
its great tolerance to adverse conditions. It is also called
Mother-in-Law Tongue and Bowstring. Like the Cast Iron Plant,
it can grow perfectly well in hot, dry, and dim locations
(including, it seems, most old hotel lobbies in the country).
The leaves are thick and sword-shaped, usually upright, growing to inches or more in height,
in some varieties ground-hugging. It is propagated easily by

division of the rootstock or by taking leaf cuttings. (Be
careful not to turn the leaf cutting upside-down when setting
it in the rooting medium, for roots grow only from the downward
portion of the cutting.)

There are many varieties available, including:

S. trifasciata laurenti (Variegated Snake Plant) has
handsome yellow bands along its leaf margins.

S. trifasciata is similar in form, but without the yellow
bands.

S. trifasciata laurenti 'compacta' (Dwarf Congo Snake
Plant) has shorter leaves and yellow margins.

S. trifasciata 'hahni' (Hahn's Dwarf Snake Plant) has
light and dark green bands along the leaves.

There are many other interesting variegated varieties
of this old standby.

Spathe Flower (Spathiphyllum)   B-D-A-A

Here is an easy-to-grow, tough plant, suitable for the
homes of most novice green thumbs. It has sword-shaped and
glossy green leaves. White blossoms will sometimes surprise
you in the winter, but do not depend on their appearance.
There are two popular species: S. clevelandii and
S. floribundum.

Spider Plant (Chlorophytum comosum)   B-B-B-C

Spider Plant is one of the most popular of house plants.

It has grassy leaves, variegated cream and green in color,
which arch gracefully from either pot or hanging basket.
Mature plants produce perfectly-formed baby plants on the end
of long runners, that resemble spiders hanging from a thread.
Propagation is simply a matter of rooting one of the "baby
spiders" in a rooting medium. The Spider Plant can store
water in its tubers, and can take dry soil for a fairly long
time because of this characteristic.

Strawberry Geranium (Saxifraga sarmentosa)   C-B-B-B

This trailing plant, also called Strawberry Begonia and
Mother of Thousands, is good for both hanging baskets and
terrariums. All it really asks is a woodsy soil, containing plenty of organic matter, and a cool
location. Leaves of the Strawberry Geranium resemble
those of the true geranium, and it sends out runners just
as strawberry plants do. The leaves of the standard variety
are deep olive in color, with silver-gray markings. An interesting variant, S. sarmentosa 'tricolor,' has dark green
leaves marked with white and pink, and is considerably more
difficult to grow. Strawberry Geranium can be easily
harmed by overfertilization.

Sweet Flag (Acorus gramineus)   A-C-A-C

Here is a moisture-loving plant that grows only 2
inches tall. It is a pleasant little fellow, and will be
most happy in a terrarium.

Syngonium (see Nephthytis)

Ti Plant (Cordyline terminalis)   A-B-A-B

C. terminalis is only one of many species of Cordyline,
but is certainly the most popular. Also called Firebrand, it
will last for only one to three years, and grow to 2 feet in height before dying out, but
its spectacular young life is certainly worth your placing
this plant on your list of house plant candidates. It has
long, upward-reaching leaves, cerise, purple, and green, which
grow from a cane trunk. Another popular species is C. australis,
which features long and slender leaves. The Ti Plant is very
popular in Hawaii, where its colorful grassy leaves are used
in making grass skirts. It is sold there in tourist shops as
a "Ti Log." In recent years, breeders have developed several
variations of the original plant, including a dwarf and a
variegated variety, which go under various names.

Umbrella Sedge (Cyperus alternifolius)   A-C-A-C

Here is a popular exotic plant with narrow, pointed,
grasslike leaves that grow in clusters. It will grow up to
2 feet tall in a pot. Constant moisture is essential, and
propagation is a simple matter of root division.

Related species include C. papyrus, similar in appearance and requirements but which grows to 7 feet in height,
and a dwarf variety, C. alternifolius gracilis.

Velvet Plant (Gynura)   A-B-B-B

This is a vigorous-growing plant with dark red, velvety leaves. It will offer a fine contrast to your green plants. It is best to train the Velvet Plant to some support, to keep it in bounds, or to pinch it back often to encourage bushy growth. The plants tend to become spindly and leggy with age.

There are two common varieties: G. aurantiaca, which is upright in growth habit, and G. sarmentosa, a smaller and loosely-twining plant. The flowers of both are horrible in scent and should be removed immediately upon appearance. The plant also tends to harbor mealybugs.

Yew (Podocarpus)   C-B-B-B

Yews are prized outdoor plants in many parts of the country, but can be made into attractive house plants anywhere. These hardy evergreens can provide welcomed contrast to your tropicals. They are slow-growing and tolerant of adverse conditions. They will take low temperatures without a whimper, and might require frequent repotting because of vigorous growth. They can become quite large and bushy.

P. marcrophylla angustifolia (Southern Yew) can be pruned to a pleasing shape and will respond with even more vigorous growth. Other similar species include P. macrophylla 'Nagai' and P. macrophylla 'Maki.'

Wandering Jew (Tradescantia)   C-C-B-C

Tradescantia and Zebrina both claim the common name of Wandering Jew, and the two genera are so similar that they are commonly interchanged. All are easy-to-grow, tolerant, and vigorous trailers of many varieties, perfect for hanging baskets. Feed them regularly for good growth. Propagation is simplicity itself; take cuttings of growing tips and root them in water.

Among very many interesting species are:

T. fluminensis, the original Wandering Jew, has silver markings, but there are many variants of different markings and colors available today.

T. albiflora has bluish-green leaves with white stripes.

Z. pendula is an excellent house plant whose leaves have purple undersides. Again, there are several interesting variegated varieties.

Production Notes   No Time for House Plants, II & IV

Display Lines: all chapter titles, headings, tables titles, etc. have been marked for u & lc as a guide for the designer in the event that he or she does not choose to use all caps or sc in these places.

Heads and Subheads: all are keyed by letter in manuscript margins, as follows:
1. A-level heads mark the major divisions of the text in chapter II (and other chapters in the manuscript); see pp. 8, 10, 13, 15, 17, 18, 19, 22, 23, 25, 27, 28, 29 (twice), 31, 33
2. B-level heads mark subdivisions of the major divisions of chapter II (and others in the manuscript); see pp. 13 (twice), 14, 26 (four times), 27, 35, 38, 39
3. C-level heads, which occur in chapter IV (and others in the manuscript), could be treated as A levels or as a completely separate series. They mark the descriptions of individual house plants and are quite numerous—often several per page. Each line includes not only the plant name(s) but also the set of four symbols described by the author in the "Key to Symbols" at the end of the manuscript. The symbols are here represented by the caps A, B, C, and D. These headings occur on pp. 55-86.

Extracts: none

Footnotes: all are signaled by asterisks and occur on pp. 18 and 80. None are citations of sources.

Unusual Characters and Accents:
degree sign: pp. 28, 36, 37, 58, 73, 79, all in text; ff. p. 23, in the table
subscript numbers: p. 19, in text

Cross-References: One by page number on p. 75; this will have to be filled in during the reading of page proofs.

Illustrations: suggestions for the placement of illustrations (those suggested by the author have been gathered in a separate section at the beginning of the manuscript) are written in the margins beside the relevant text. See pp. 13, 22, 24, 26, 30, 31, 32

Production Notes -2   No Time for House Plants, II & IV

Special Boxes: eleven of these highlighted topics are gathered at the end of the manuscript, and some might well be placed in these two chapters somewhere. I am assuming that the eleven will be fairly evenly distributed throughout the book. Numbers 1, 2, and 3 might go well in chapter II, as they directly concern plant-growing methods. Boxes 4-11 all list plants in various kinds of groups--those that have a predominance of foliage plants would be appropriate for chapter IV. The author can advise best the precise locations for these lists.

Tables: Table 1 should be placed near the text on p. 23. The table itself is on the sheet following that page, which contains a specific reference to it. The table has a title and a number; you might want to consider dropping the number, as the book contains only a handful. A reference in the text, in that case, would have to be changed from number to title. Note that the column heads had to be so marked so that they could be more easily distinguished from column items.

EDITORIAL DEPARTMENT
The University of North Carolina Press
BOOK PLAN

Author _____   Date __3 September 1976__

Front Matter
Title page (copy to appear in print, check carefully)

Title __No Time for House Plants__
Subtitle __A Busy Person's Guide to Indoor Gardening__
Author or Editor _____
Special imprint __None__
Copyright page __UNC Press 1977__
Permissions notice __We may need permissions for illustrative material not yet received__
Dedication page __None__
Foreword __None__
Preface __Yes, copy supplied__
Acknowledgments __None__
Table of Contents __Yes, copy supplied__
List of Illustrations __To be prepared when all illustrations have been provided__
List of Tables __None__
Introduction __None__
Other _____

Text
Part titles __None__
Chapter divisions __1-7__
Tables __None__
Other __11 special boxes__
Illustrations
Linecuts __Finished art work to be supplied__
Halftones __38 received; more to come__
Other _____

Back Matter
Appendixes __None__
Notes __Symbol notes to be set at the bottom of the page; not in backmatter__
Bibliography __Yes, copy supplied__
Index __To be prepared by author; approximately 6 finished pages__
Other _____

THE UNIVERSITY OF NORTH CAROLINA PRESS

Box 2288, Chapel Hill, N.C. 27514

3 September 1976

Dear

We are sending you today by first class mail the edited manuscript of NO TIME FOR HOUSE PLANTS.

Please review it with care, answering all editorial queries, and make certain that the text now stands exactly the way you wish to see it in type. You will see only page proof, and making changes at that time—other than the correction of typographical errors—can be costly. If changes are made at that time, beyond the barest minimum, the author will be charged. So please review the edited manuscript with the care you would give to first proof.

The copy of the edited manuscript you will receive is a xerox, and your changes will be transferred to the original manuscript, so please make all marks in a bright color for high visibility.

You will also find with the manuscript a style sheet that will come in handy during the process of author review and also later when you are reading the proof.

Accompanying the manuscript you will find two copies of our book plan. This form is only a record for both of us, indicating the elements that are to appear in the finished book. Please check this form, initial one copy, and return it to us with the manuscript. The other copy is for your files.

We would like to have the reviewed manuscript back in this office no later than 20 September. Please feel free to call me (919-933-2105) if you have any questions concerning the review of your manuscript.

Yours sincerely,

(Mrs.) Gwen Duffey
Managing Editor

P.S. I noted that 6 of the 38 halftones accompanying the manuscript have no credits stamped on the back. Are these also USDA photos?

The Association of American University Presses, Inc.
One Park Avenue, New York, N.Y. 10016 · 212 889-6040

November 11, 1976

Mrs. Gwen Duffey
Managing Editor
THE UNIVERSITY OF NORTH CAROLINA PRESS
Box 2288
Chapel Hill, NC 27514

Dear Mrs. Duffey:

Please excuse this extreme delay in responding to your letters of September 3 and October 11. I hope that I have not interfered too seriously with your production plans.

In any case, I enclose the manuscript with this letter, with my appreciation to Barbara Reitt for a superb job of copyediting. She struck a very fine balance that I appreciate greatly. I hope that I have responded properly to all of her queries.

I also enclose the Book Plan, initialed.

The biographical form was returned yesterday.

This should bring us up to date on the project, at least so far as I am concerned. If there is anything further I may do, please do not hesitate to write or call at

Thank you again, and best wishes.

Sincerely,

P.S. All the photos are USDA photos.

THE UNIVERSITY OF NORTH CAROLINA PRESS
Box 2288, Chapel Hill, N.C. 27514

11 October 1976

Dear

On 3 September we sent you copyedited chapters 2 and 4 of No Time for House Plants for review, with the request that the manuscript be returned to us by 20 September. Since we have not received it, I am concerned that it might have been lost in the mails. We were planning to start composition by mid-October, and this delay may well affect the scheduling of our other titles for spring. Please let me know at your earliest convenience when we may expect to receive the manuscript.

Yours sincerely,

(Mrs.) Gwen Duffey
Managing Editor

TO: Joyce
FROM: Gwen

M E M O

RE:

17 November 1976

Here is the _____ title ready for composition. Included you will also find the following:

    editorial checklist   illustrations
    copy for running heads   copy for legends
    style sheet   author's key to symbols
    production notes from editor
    copy for spine

Jacket copy will be prepared later--if we decide to have a jacket.

May I please see sample pages that include the following:

    text
    chapter opening
    subheads A, B, C
    footnote
    bibliography
    special box (if we are going to treat this material in this fashion)

Finished art work has not been provided by the author. May I assume that the production department will take care of this?

Since we shall not have color in this title, have you considered the possibility of printing in dark green on pale green stock? Would there be any advantage in doing this with a ring binder?

Memo

To Joyce
From Gwen

The free-lance editor suggested that Spriva Bayer 1, 2, and 3 be used again in Chap. II.

It seems to me that Pages 4-11 should be grouped at the back of the book.

Design decisions will be made: changes in Title as content warrants.

UNC PRESS   **Editorial Department**
The University of North Carolina Press
Chapel Hill, N.C. 27514

EDITORIAL CHECKLIST

Author (as name should appear on title page): _____

Mailing address for galleys and pages: _____

Title: No Time for House Plants: A Busy Person's Guide to Indoor Gardening

Number of pages in manuscript: 144

Check the kinds of typesetting: (If the kinds checked occur infrequently, please list MS pages)

  X Text   Part titles
     Quoted matter   Poetry
  X Footnotes   X Bibliography
     Endnotes   Appendix
  X Index   X Tabular (p. 23)
     Formula   Other

List special characters: math, foreign language, etc.; if infrequent, list MS pages

degree sign; subscript number _____

Front matter: (Please cross out any items not included)

    Other of special imprint   Table of Contents
    ~~Recto blank~~   Foreword
    Half title   Preface
    Verso blank   ~~Acknowledgments~~
    Title page   ~~List of Illustrations~~
    Copyright page   ~~List of Maps, Tables, etc~~
    Dedication page   Introduction
    ~~Verso blank~~

How many levels of subheads? 3 (A,B,C)

What copy is to come? _____ finished artwork; additional halftones

Will there be illustrations? yes   How many? ?   What kind? halftones and linedrawings   Frontispiece? no

Special problems of comment: (i.e., British spelling or punctuation, erratic spelling, special indents, etc.)

Editorial / UNC / 157

legends for illustrations with MS locations

22 A terrarium or bottle garden can be grown in nearly any clear glass container, as long as a top can be found to prevent moisture from escaping. Here a plastic coffee-can lid has been placed over a brandy snifter. (USDA Photo)

23 A good example of double potting. The sphagnum moss between the two pots reduces the need for watering. (USDA Photo)

26 Decorative containers without drainage holes can be used successfully if the plant is double potted. This prayer plant (Maranta) has been potted in a clay pot, which was then inserted into the decorative container on a layer of gravel. Moss occupies the space between the two pots, helping to assure constant moisture for the plant's roots. (USDA Photo)

26 Smaller house plants should be sprayed weekly for good health and a sparkling appearance. A strong spray will also remove many smaller insects from plants. (USDA Photo)

26 Large-leafed plants will appreciate an occasional bath. Use a mild soap solution and rinse thoroughly with clear water--both at room temperature. (USDA Photo)

27 Decorative planters are available in many shapes and sizes, many of them equipped with lighting of the correct intensity for stimulating vigorous plant growth. (USDA Photo)

30 Stem cuttings should be made just below a node--the point at which the leaf originates--since many plants have embryonic root systems at the nodes which develop rapidly when placed in water. For this purpose, a sharp pair of pruning shears is adequate, although a sharp single-edged razor blade is even better since it will not crush the stem. (USDA Photo)

legends, p. 2

31 Any plant and soil ball may easily be separated from its pot by turning it upside-down and rapping the rim of the pot sharply against the edge of the kitchen counter. If the plant is not sufficiently potbound to require repotting and this one is not—the soil ball may easily be replaced with no harm and little mess. (USDA Photo)

35 The cuttings of many house plants can be rooted easily in water. The roots of this aluminum plant are at a stage at which the plant can be potted. Many of these plants, including this one, can also be grown permanently in water. (USDA Photo)

57 A selection of bromeliads: left, living vase plant (Aechmea chantinii); center top, Vriesia carinata; center bottom, earth star (Cryptanthus zonatus); right, Neoregelia hybrid. (USDA Photo)

58 Cast iron plant (Aspidistra). (USDA Photo)

60 Coleus blumei, Dracaena sanderiana, and Iresine herbstii. (USDA Photo)

62 Many plants, such as this Dieffenbachia picta, grow better when slightly potbound. (USDA Photo)

62 Dracaena sanderiana, D. fragrans, and zebra plant (Aphelandra). (USDA Photo)

62 Dieffenbachia picta 'Rudolph Roehrs,' Dieffenbachia amoena, and Ficus pandurata. (USDA Photo)

72 Palm (Phoenix), fern (Nephrolepsis), and Scindapsus (S. aureus). (USDA Photo)

72 Moses-in-the-cradle (Rhoeo spathacea 'discolor'), Norfolk Island pine (Araucaria excelsa), and Philea coderie. (USDA Photo)

74 A bromeliad, earth star (Cryptanthus zonatus), Peperomia floridii, and Bromelia serra. (USDA Photo)

75 Philodendron dubium, P. pertusum, and P. panduraeforme. (USDA Photo)

THE UNIVERSITY OF NORTH CAROLINA PRESS

Box 2288, Chapel Hill, N.C. 27514

16 December 1976

Dear

At a recent staff meeting, it was suggested that the present title of your book is somewhat negative in tone. Our sales manager suggested that the addition of a question mark would give it more appeal. We are all in favor of this change, and I believe that our production department is already planning the title page with the question mark included. How does No Time for Houseplants? strike you? (We are also following Webster's Third on the preferred usage of one word for "houseplant.") If I do not hear from you to the contrary, we shall proceed with this variation on your original title.

Yours sincerely,

(Mrs.) Gwen Duffey
Managing Editor

---

legends, p. 3

75 Philodendron squamiferum and umbrella tree (Schefflera actinophylla.)
    (USDA Photo)

81 The snake plant (Sansevieria), in several interesting varieties, is one
    of the easiest of all house plants to grow.

81 Snake plant (Sansevieria tricaciata), croton (Codiaeum varigatum),
    rubber plant (Ficus elastica). (USDA Photo)

85 Calathea ornata, southern yew (Podocarpus macrophylla), and Chinese
    evergreen (Aglaonemas commutatum). (USDA Photo)

running heads for   HOUSE PLANTS

verso   recto

Preface   Preface
No Time for House Plants The Secrets of No-Work House Plant Success
No Time for House Plants Understanding House Plants
No Time for House Plants Plant Troubles and Cures
No Time for House Plants Introducing the Foliage Plants
No Time for House Plants Cacti and Other Succulents
No Time for House Plants Flowering House Plants
No Time for House Plants Special Indoor Gardens
Bibliography   Bibliography
Index   Index

February 3, 1977

Mrs. Gwen Duffey
Managing Editor
The UNIVERSITY OF NORTH CAROLINA PRESS
Box 2288
Chapel Hill, North Carolina 27514

Dear Gwen:

It was nice talking with you just now, and I must apologize once again for mixing up your sample pages with the Toronto material. I hope that I have not delayed things.

I enclose the pages, with the corrections we discussed.

Sincerely,

(answering for Purvis Mulch, who is out of sorts today)

THE UNIVERSITY OF NORTH CAROLINA PRESS
Box 2288

Chapel Hill, North Carolina 27514

Editorial Department   Date: 19 January 1977

To:
                                    Author: _____
                                    Title: HOUSEPLANTS

We have mailed to you today by

___ educational materials, insured
___ educational materials, special delivery, insured
_X_ first class mail
___ air mail
___ air parcel post, insured

2 sets of page proof (pages 1 - 14) and the edited manuscript. One set is to be corrected and returned to us with the manuscript. The other set of proof is for your own use.

___ our index style memo, with attached specifications for your index.

Remarks:

Please have the proof back in this office no later than 27 January.

Signed: *Gwen Duffey*
(Mrs.) Gwen Duffey
Managing Editor

Contents

Preface

1: The Secrets of No-Work Houseplant Success / 00

2: Understanding Houseplants / 00
The Basic Houseplant
How a Plant Feeds
Parts of the Plant
Soil
Acidity/Alkalinity
Potting Mixtures
Nutrient Maintenance
Containers
Watering
Humidity
Ventilation
Temperature
Light
Pruning and Training
Repotting
Propagation

3: Plant Troubles and Cures / 00
Improper Handling and Care
Insect Foes
Diseases

4: Introducing the Foliage Plants / 00
Where to Buy Houseplants
Foliage Plants

5: Cacti and Other Succulents / 00
Care of Cacti and Succulents
Potting Soil for Cacti

Introducing the Cacti
The Unusual Succulents

6: Flowering Houseplants / 00
Forcing Spring Bulbs
Care of Gift Plants

7: Special Indoor Gardens / 00
Dish Gardens and Planters
Bottle Gardens and Terrariums
Houseplants from Kitchen Scraps
An Indoor Kitchen Garden

Special Boxes
1. The ABCs of Artificial Light
2. Should You Send Your Plants to Summer Camp?
3. Can Your Plants Survive Your Vacation?
4. Plants for Cool Conditions
5. Plants for Medium Temperatures
6. Plants for High Temperatures
7. Plants of Greatest Tolerance
8. Plants for Dry and Semi-Dry Conditions
9. Vines and Trailing Plants for Totem Poles
10. Plants for Hanging Baskets
11. Suggestions for Large-Tubbed Specimens

Bibliography

Index

Spotlighting Houseplants I

African boxwood (*Myrsine africana*)
This slow-growing plant has red stems but otherwise is similar to boxwood (q.v.). Many people think it is even more graceful. African boxwood is a good plant for terrariums, if the atmosphere is not too hot.

Aralia (*Fatsia japonica*)
Sometimes sold as *Aralia sieboldii*. Beautiful, bright green, leathery, maplelike leaves highlight this cheerful plant. In appearance, it is similar to the castor oil plant, and in fact is sometimes called false castor oil plant. It thrives in a cool spot. Aralia can easily grow leggy, and should be pruned annually in order to encourage it into bushy growth. It will attain a height of 4 feet at maturity.

A striking hybrid, *Fatshedra lizei*, a cross between *F. japonica* and ivy or *Hedra*, forms a climbing plant with maple-shaped leaves that is tolerant of adverse conditions.

There is also a plant called false aralia (*Dizygotheca elegantissima*), which has graceful and feathery foliage. It bears no resemblance to the true aralia and is difficult to grow.

Asparagus
There are two common kinds of *Asparagus* suitable for growing as house plants—fern asparagus (*A. plumosus*), with slender, needlelike, dark-green leaves, forming a feathery appearance, and *A. sprengeri* (emerald feather) which has thicker yellow-green leaves and drooping stems. The latter makes a good plant for hanging baskets, and produces red berries at Christmastime. Both like some sun in the summer and full sun in the winter, and both can grow to a height of about 2 feet. *A. meyeri*, less common but equally attractive, has tiny fernlike leaves that arch out on long stems from the center of the plant.

14

PRINTER #1 — PRODUCTION COST ESTIMATE

Author: Mulch Title: NO TIME FOR HOUSEPLANTS?
Print 5000/7500. Bind 5000/7500 paper/cloth Trim size 5 x 7⁷⁄₈ Pages 192
Paper 60 lb. Publishers white Illustrations: lincuts 7, halftones 30, maps, etc.
                                              5000   7500

PLANT:			
Composition	1,023.28	1,023.28	
AAs	102.32	102.32	
Negatives/Plates	498.00	498.00	
Illus. Prep. and Engravings	250.00	250.00	
Dxxxx Photographer			
Lock-up	53.40	53.40	
Blues			
Extra proof/xeroxes	100.00	100.00	
Sample pages			
Miscellaneous			
TOTAL PLANT:	2027.00	2027.00	
RUNNING: Printing - text	382.00	487.00	
- illustrations			
Paper - text	1135.00	1731.00	
- illustrations			
Freight	500.00	750.00	
Jackets			
Paperback covers (print and paper)	270.00	375.00	
Rxxxxxxxxx Shrinkwrap	90.00	135.00	
TOTAL RUNNING:	2377.00	3478.00	1.433
SHEET COST	4404.00	5475.00	
fold, gather, sew			
BINDING: xxxxxxb slipcases- manufacturing	2050.00	3075.00	
slipcases-insert books	145.00	217.50	
Paper	565.00	765.00	
TOTAL ESTIMATED MANUFACTURING COST:	7164.00	9552.50	1.271

Date 12/20/76

PRINTER #2 — PRODUCTION COST ESTIMATE

Author: Mulch Title: NO TIME FOR HOUSEPLANTS?
Print 5000/7500. Bind 5000/7500 paper/cloth Trim size 5 x 7⁷⁄₈ Pages 192
Paper 60 lb. Publisher's Eggshell Illustrations: lincuts 7, halftones 30, maps, etc.
                                              5000   7500

PLANT:			
Composition	1,023.28	1,023.28	
AAs	102.32	102.32	
Negatives/Plates	1,113.00	1,113.00	
Illus. Prep. and Engravings	250.00	250.00	
Dxxxx Photographer			
Lock-up			
Blues			
Extra proof/xeroxes	100.00	100.00	
Sample pages			
Miscellaneous			
TOTAL PLANT:	2588.60	2588.60	
RUNNING: Printing - text	371.00	468.00	
- illustrations			
Paper - text	1124.50	1686.75	
- illustrations			
Freight	500.00	750.00	
Jackets			
Paperback covers (print and paper)	534.50	666.00	
Endsheets			
TOTAL RUNNING:	2530.00	3570.75	
SHEET COST	5118.60	6159.35	1.684
fold, gather, sew			
BINDING: xXXXx Slipcases- stock & print	519.00	685.50	
Paper	2781.00	4074.00	
TOTAL ESTIMATED MANUFACTURING COST:	8418.60	10,918.85	1.456

Date 12/20/76

MATERIAL TO BE SCANNED   DATE: 11/30/76

TO: Interstate Graphics
      P.O. Box 1163
      Charlotte, North Carolina 28201

      Attn. Bill Evans

FROM: UNC PRESS PRODUCTION DEPARTMENT
      P.O. Box 2288
      305 Bynum Hall, UNC Campus
      Chapel Hill, N. C. 27514

Title: Mulch, NO TIME FOR HOUSEPLANTS?   Typescript pages: 1-160

Return 6 level TTS paper tape to us as soon as possible. Use
key optics. Use our code sheet as follows:
                        NO INDENT
Standard code sheet: ___ 1 em ___ 2 em ___ 3 em paragraph indent
                                    Helvetica
                        kerning: xxxxxxxxxxxxxxxxxx or Sabon ___
                        Roman/Italic position: (1/2)   3/4 (circle one)

Please notify us of projected shipping date immediately upon receipt
of copy.

11/17 Mulch

Estimated for Helvetica, no ¶ indent — 1 line sp.

Frontmatter, tables, legends to be set at AEs
All text (+ preface) typed for scanner

— Symbols to be put in after setting

(typist will indent ¶, scanner will output
no indent and extra line space)

CUSTOMER _____ JOB NO. _____ TYPIST _____ SHEET NO. _____ DATE _____

→ ALIGN FIRST CHARACTER UNDER THIS ARROW

1 ↱MULCH Galley 23/1/1

Chapter 2

Understanding House Plants

Every plant has its own preferences and requirements for soil type, light, temperature, ventilation, humidity, and several other factors that are within our power to control, or at least to mitigate. It is vitally important for you, as a busy indoor gardener, to understand the basics of each factor, since a prior understanding will enable you to avoid much work later on while achieving routine success in growing plants.

In addition to understnading these basic needs, you will want to know something about pots and other containers, repotting plants, propagation, and a few other matters that, while not vital to immediate success, will help you to gain further enjoyment in raising better plants.

The Basic House Plant

The major difference between a house plant and an outdoor plant is location. All house plants could live and flourish outdoors, in the proper climate. All are derived from forebears that lived, reproduced, and died in the outdoors, whether it was on a forest floor in central Europe or in the bough of a tree in a South American forest. Over many centuries of adaptation and evolution, each plant species embraced those characteristics that enabled it to survive; even today, every house plant carries within its genetic structure■re the characteristics of its distant progenitors. Thus the ¶Maranta¶r will lose some of its leaves each autumn, even though autumn's weather does not come to the bookshelf where the plant rests, and a cactus, no matter how long we have been feeding and wHatering it with unfailing regularity, will continue to hoard

DO NOT TYPE BELOW THIS LINE

PRODUCTION DEPARTMENT
The University of North Carolina Press
P.O. Box 2288
Chapel Hill, North Carolina 27514
(919) 933-2163

COMPOSITION SPECIFICATIONS

Title NO TIME FOR HOUSEPLANTS?   Author Mulch

Trim size 5" x 7 3/8"   Text page (incl. r. head/feet) 24 x 40 1/2   Margins: Head 1 1/2 pi Gutter 3 pi

Typography Face Helvetica   2 col. per page (11 pi ea.)   Paragraph indent 1 line #

Text in 10 / 13 pt. Editor used A.B.C.
A. Subheads in text
  1. 10 pt. B.F. lc anc c fl. left
     Space above 3 lines   Space below 2 lines
  B. 2. 10 pt. ital runon
     Space above 1 line #   Space below no extra
  C. 3. 9 pt. bf lc and c fl. left
     Space above 1 line #   Space below no extra
  4. Space above

Extracts In / pt. Measure
  Style: fl left ___ ctr ___ fl. rt ___ indent ___

Poetry In / pt
  Style: fl left ___ ctr ___ fl. rt ___ indent ___

Tables Heads As marked   Subheads
  Body   Rules
  Style: fl left ___ ctr ___ fl. rt ___ indent ___

Legends Figures in 9 / 10 pt bf. fl. left
  Illustrations in 9 / 10 pt rom. and 6 pt. ital.

Appendixes In / pt None
  Subheads in appendices A
                          B

Bibli- In 9 /10 pt. 24 pi measure
ography
  Subheads in bibliography: A
                            B
  Hanging indent: 1 em

Footnotes   Foot of page: In 8 / 9 pt. measure 11 pi
  Standard paragraph indent
  Back of book: In / pt. measure

Index In 8 / pt. Set to 11 picas; 2 columns to page
  Initial letter: Cap. fl. l.   space above 1 line   space below no extra
  Hanging indent: 1 em

Running Recto none
Heads
/ Feet   Verso
  With rule / without rule
  Space between runninghead/foot and text

Folios In 9 pt.: Old style figure / Modern figure. Bracketed: bf.
  In running head/foot?   Dropped?   Outside / Inside / Centered
  1 pi from outside trim, 1 pi from bottom trim

Chapter Chapter no in in press type
Openings Titles in 24 pt. De Vinne Ornamented
  Sink 1 pi
  Sub chapter title

Other to be ragged ri.

Method Set at keyboard   Justified x *   Unjustified
  Paging keyboard   strip. x   combination
    During setting   first proof corrections   second proof corrections x
  * This does not mean lines are justified (they are ragged) but that
    the compositor makes line ending decisions at the keyboard

Preface

The recent introduction of fluorescent tubes meant especially for plant growing has been a great boon to indoor gardeners. With the aid of artificial light, we can now grow lush, green plants where they would never grow before. A windowless bathroom, which might offer ideal humidty and temperature conditions, can now be made into an ideal plant-growing environment. Plants growing on a drab northern windowsill can now receive supplemental light during winter's short and dark days. Dim corners of any room can be transformed into green showplaces. Cuttings and seedlings can now make faster and surer progress than ever under artificial light, and we can even grow vegetables in the dead of winter in the bedroom or kitchen. Artificial lighting is not essential for house plant sucess, but it certainly does broaden our horizons and increase chances for maximum rewards.

The old incandescent bulb offers some help to growing plants, although the heat it produces makes it impossible to offer plants the amounts of light they need without drying or burning them. Also, incandescent bulbs offer a very short spectrum of light wavelengths, falling far short of simulating the beneficial rays of the sun. Ordinary daylight or cool white fiuorescent lights are far better for growing plants, since they have not only a wider and more effective light wavelength but also produce light with three times as much efficiency as incandescent bulbs, thus reducing heat by fully two-thirds. Not until the past decade, however, have we had fluorescent tubes made to meet exactly the needs of growing plants. These lights, sold under such names as Gro-Lux, Plant-Gro, and Plant-Light, cost more than ordinary fluorescent tubes, but they are long-lasting and they can solve virtually any light

2. Understanding Houseplants

The old incandescent bulb offers some help to growing plants, although the heat it produces makes it impossible to offer plants the amounts of light they need without drying or burning them. Also, incandescent bulbs offer a very short spectrum of light wavelengths, falling far short of simulating the beneficial rays of the sun. Ordinary daylight or cool white fiuorescent lights are far better for growing plants, since they have not only a wider and more effective light wavelength but also produce light with three times as much efficiency as incandescent bulbs, thus reducing heat by fully two-thirds. Not until the past decade, however, have we had fluorescent tubes made to meet exactly the needs of growing plants. These lights, sold under such names as Gro-Lux, Plant-Gro, and Plant-Light, cost more than ordinary fluorescent tubes, but they are long-lasting and they can solve virtually any light problem for the indoor gardener. By attaching them to a twenty-four-hour timer, you can control light exposure perfectly, even for such tricky operations as forcing plants to bloom out of season.

Should You Send Your Plants to Summer Camp?

Nearly all houseplants will enjoy a summer outdoors, where they will become rejuvenated and make very active growth. There are dangers involved here, however, not unlike those a sheltered city child will encounter on his first trip to a wilderness camp, and special precautions must be taken.

Roots. Roots serve two main functions—to anchor the plant in the ground and to supply from the soil water and the mineral salts which accompany water. Bulbs, corms, rhizomes, and tubers (all modified stems) serve much the same purposes, as well as acting as food storage areas. Roots, just as the above-ground parts of plants, may be pruned without injuring the plant in any way. Roots are often trimmed to prevent a plant from growing too large for the convenience of the grower, just as top growth is cut back. If you cut roots back, however, be certain to cut back top growth to about the same percentage, or the reduced roots might be unable to supply the plant with sufficient amounts of water.

The old incandescent bulb offers some help to growing plants, although the heat it produces makes it impossible to offer plants the amounts of light they need without drying or burning them. Also, incandescent bulbs offer a very short spectrum of light wavelengths, falling far short of simulating the beneficial rays of the sun. Ordinary daylight or cool white fiuorescent lights are far better for growing plants, since they have not only a wider and more effective light wavelength but also produce light with three times as much efficiency as incandescent bulbs, thus reducing heat by fully two-thirds. Not until the past decade, however, have we had fluorescent tubes made to meet exactly the needs of growing plants. These lights, sold under such names as Gro-Lux, Plant-Gro, and Plant-Light, cost more than ordinary fluorescent tubes, but they are long-lasting and they can solve virtually any light problem for the indoor gardener. By attaching them to a twenty-four-hour timer, you can control light exposure perfectly, even for such tricky operations as forcing plants to bloom out of season.

PRINTING AND BINDING SPECIFICATIONS

PRODUCTION DEPARTMENT
The University of North Carolina Press
P.O. Box 2288
Chapel Hill, North Carolina 27514
(919) 933-2163

Date: 10 December 1976

Author: Mulch
Title: NO TIME FOR HOUSEPLANTS

Specifications
- Print 5000/7500 Bind 5000/7500 Case _____ Paper _____ All _____ F & G's _____
- Print by Offset
- Color black (one color) X others _____ Trim size 5 x 7 3/8 Text page size 24 x 38
- Margins (after trim) head _____ gutter _____
- No of pages 192 Inserts _____ 3
- Halftones 30 Linecuts 7 Bleeds _____

Copy
- Printed book _____ Repros X Negatives _____ Other _____
- We will supply linecuts and text in place; halftones will be sized with windows.

Paper
- Text stock 60 lb. white offset
- supplied by you to supply
- Illustration stock same
- supplied by you to supply
- Endsheet stock no endsheets
- supplied by _____ color(s) _____

Reprints No changes _____ Frontmatter changes _____ Changes throughout _____

Case Binding
- Binding material _____
- Boards _____ binders _____ pasted _____
- Smyth sew _____ Perfect bind _____
- Inserts outside tip _____ inside tip _____ center insert _____ wrap _____
- Edges smooth _____ plain _____ rough cut _____ stain _____
- Backing rounded and backed _____ flat back (reinforced) _____
- Lining crash and paper _____ headbands _____
- Stamping spine only _____ face and spine _____
- foil _____ ink _____

Paper Binding
- Perfect bind X Smyth sew _____ Saddle stitch _____
- We will supply negatives _____ original art X You to print covers X
- Cover stock see sample
- supplied by you to supply
- Colors black X others _____ spine _____ back _____ inside _____
- Varnish covers _____ Plastic coat covers _____
- Also, estimate box separately - see sample
- will be on bright green background

Wrap
- Shrink wrap X in multiples of 6
- Kraft wrap _____

Jackets
- We will supply: Original art _____ Negatives _____ Finished jackets _____
- Jacket stock _____
- Stock supplied by _____
- Varnish _____ Laminate _____
- Color(s): black _____ others _____
- Print _____ jackets. Ship _____ trimmed to us X

Proof We Want To OK
- Blues of cover X Blues of illustrations _____ Complete set of blues _____
- Blues of the following pages _____
- 3M color key of jacket X 3 M color key of cover _____
- Set of f & g's _____ Stamped sample case _____

We need this estimate immediately. Please call in your estimate before Christmas if at all possible.

Please note - no endsheets.

We would like a somewhat sturdier box - please suggest.

Please return sample.

Special Instructions

To: _____
From: Rebecca Johnson
Re: Project
Date: 10 December 1976

Enclosed please find specifications for the above project.
Please submit your estimate as soon as possible.

Please return the enclosed sample.

UNC PRESS PRODUCTION DEPARTMENT

SCHEDULE

Author: Mulch
No. of MS pages: 136
Editor: Gwen Duffey
First proofreader: Jane

Date: Dec. 21, 1976
Title: NO TIME FOR HOUSEPLANTS?
MS to prod: Nov. 17, 1976
Sample pages:
Compositor: Martha Farlow

Proof Information

Proofreader (1st proof): 1 sets with MS   Editor: 4 sets with MS   Sales: 1 sets

Scanner

FIRST x xxx ALL
Nov. 22, 1976 to typist
Nov. 30, 1976 to OCR
Dec. 7, 1976 to proofreader
Dec. 21, 1976 to production

SECOND PART

First Proof

FIRST PART
_____ to xerox
_____ to proofreader
_____ to production

SECOND PART
_____ to xerox
_____ to proofreader
_____ to production

THIRD PART

Green (corrected) Proof

FIRST x xxx All
Jan. 17, 1977 to xerox
Jan. 18, 1977 to editor & sales

SECOND PART
_____ to xerox
_____ to editor & sales

THIRD PART
_____ to xerox
_____ to editor & sales

Index

Feb. 21, 1977 MS to production
Feb. 28, 1977 page proof to editor & sales
March 7, 1977 page proof to production

Revises

Feb. 28, 1977 all page proof (green) to production with list of revises
March 14, 1977 revises and foul proof to editor
March 25, 1977 repros OK

Printing and Binding

March 25 repros to Printer
April 20 blues to UNC Press
April 22 blues to printer
May 11 l & g's to UNC Press
May 13 l & g's to printer
May 4 sample case to UNC Press
July 1, 1977 **BOOKS IN**

DATE: 1/18/77
TO: Gwen
FROM: PRODUCTION
TITLE: Mulch

NO. OF PAGES: 192
1st PROOFREADER: Jan McInroy
DATE DUE BACK
TO PRODUCTION: 2/28
_____ 1st PART _____ 2nd PART X ALL

PRODUCTION DEPARTMENT **Transmittal Form**

TO: Gwen DATE: 2/7/77
FROM: Martha
RE: Dutch cover & slipcase DATE NEEDED: 2/7/77

Please return this form with the above proof and check the proper space below.

___ Proof OK for paste-up ___ Browns (blues) OK to print ___ Sample case OK
___ Paste-up OK to print ___ Gathers OK to bind ___ Color key OK
✓ Jacket comprehensive OK ___ Stamping die proof OK
___ Please make corrections as marked and let me see revised proof: ___

Comments:

Date returned to Production Department:

FINAL JOB COST ESTIMATES

Author: Mulch Title: NO TIME FOR HOUSEPLANTS
Budgeted for Composition F.P.P. Mellon
Date Composition started ___ Ended ___
Operators ___ Ms. pages ___ Book pages 192
Operators' hourly rate ___ Total hourly rate ___

Composition

Month	Time	Cost
November	Scan/82.88	82.88
December	AKI/29.00 VIP/16.88	80.26
	PU/34.38	
January	AKI/290.00 VIP/124.89	469.58
	PU/54.69	
February	AKI/41.69 VIP/30.38	90.82
	PU/18.75	
March	AKI/52.56 VIP/20.23	85.28
	PU/12.49	

Total: ___ Total: 808.82

No. of lines corrected: Other costs:
 Graphic Repro
PEs ___ xDisplayxType 14.00
AAs ___ Proofreader 53.04
EEs ___ Xeroxes 48.00
 Other ___
Total AAs and EEs ___ Scanner 91.42
Author charged ___ Letraset 8.00
Difference between amount budgeted Total 1023.28
and actual cost ___ less author's AAs ___
Difference between budgeted plant subtotal ___
cost and actual plant cost ___ less ___ % AAs ___
Per page cost 5.33 actual cost 1023.28
Rates: Type- $6.50/hour VIP- $13.50/hour
 AKI- $7.25/hour PU- $6.25/hour

The University of North Carolina Press
FINAL PRODUCTION PLAN

Author: Mulch Title: NO TIME FOR HOUSEPLANTS? Date: 2/11/77
Print: 7500 Bind: 7500 Trim Size: 5 x 7⅜ No. of pages: 192
Paper: 60-lb. Publisher's White Illustrations: Linecuts: 7 Halftones: 30
Charts: Maps: Endpapers:

Stock No.:
Sales Price:

SUPPLIER	ESTIMATE		ACTUAL	
		Total	Unit	Amount	Check No.
Plant: Composition		~~1023.28~~ 102.32			
AA's					
~~Xerox negative~~ Negatives & Plates		498.00	1		
~~Corrections~~					
Lock-up					
~~Dies~~ Photographer		250.00			
Freight		100.00			
Miscellaneous		53.40			
Blues					
TOTAL PLANT		2027.00			
Running: Printing: Text		487.00	2		
Illustrations					
Other					
Paper: Text		1701.00	3		
Illustrations					
Other					
Binding: Jackets					
Freight		750.00	4		
Paperback covers		375.00	5		
Shrinkwrap		135.00			
TOTAL RUNNING		3448.00			
SHEET COST		5475.00			
Paper		765.00	8		
~~Jackets~~ ~~Slipcases~~ many		3075.00	6		
~~Boxes~~ Slipcases insert books		217.50	7		
GROSS MANUFACTURING COST		9532.50	1.271		
less subsidy:					
NET MANUFACTURING COST					

Stock Date: Publication Date:

REPROS AND BLUES CHECK

Date: 2/7/77 Title: No Time for Houseplants?
Author: Mulch
Compositor: Martha Editor: Gwen
Date scheduled to go to the printer: 2/8/77

REPROS: Please put an X after the item after you have checked. The lines below are to list the pages which need correcting in that particular category.

EDITOR: ✓ 1. Check each page for obvious blobs of black or obvious white spots in the lettering
   Sample pages OK — gd 2/7/77

2. Check contents page against chapter titles and folios

3. Check running heads (or running feet) and folios

4. Record any other flaws that leap from the page

ANN: 1. Check typography throughout: Clean !!! ✓
   Opaque & clean around "Preface" — l.c. f is broken ✓
   ~~All pages need cleaning~~ — cap. 13
   ✓ check page length
   OK viii — looks funny — is it OK? (column lengths)

3. Check chapter openings for clear definition of type and for sinkage need ~~cleaning~~ black spot (at trim) all
   Yes marks on all display pages — fix "e" in "TIME" p.iii;
   Window p.iii not cut (really straight upper left side
   LESLIE: Opaque with "e" counter p.v — right side of window (p.vi) doesn't run parallel to trim
   1. Check ~~frontmatter~~; see that it is there and complete. (over)

2. Return to compositor to correct. Items corrected should be checked off when complete.

JOYCE/REBECCA: Check all windows
   1. Final check l.c. G & T & F & R & C in ¶ sequence

THE UNIVERSITY OF NORTH CAROLINA PRESS
Box 2288, Chapel Hill, N.C. 27514

IMPORTANT
PLACE THIS NUMBER
1256
ON ALL PACKAGES, INVOICES AND CORRESPONDENCE

DATE 2-11-77

To   Dalton Press

PLEASE FURNISH AND DELIVER THE FOLLOWING, RENDERING INVOICE IN DUPLICATE.
FORM UM WT

Mulch: NO TIME FOR HOUSEPLANTS?

Negatives/plates	498.00
Printing 7500	487.00
Paper	1701.00
Paperback covers	375.00
Shrinkwrap	135.00
Slipcases - manu.	3075.00
Slipcases-insert books	217.50
Paper	765.00

Please ship by motor freight to our warehouse, Airport Rd., Chapel Hill, NC

_____
John Rollins, Controller
PURCHASING AGENT

Form No. A-636

PRINT ORDER REQUEST

To: Ann
From: Joyce
Re: Mulch- NO TIME FOR HOUSEPLANTS?
Date: February 11, 1977

Please issue a purchase order to:

    Printer #1

for:

    items 1-8

Delivery or shipping instructions:

UNC Press Warehouse
Chapel Hill, NC 27511

October 11, 1976

To: Johanna

From: John

Edition size for Mulch must be decided. Matt and I think 5,000 is a good edition. Talk to Matt, and then send memo to JK. I think everyone should know that price must be under $10.00, hence cost in the $2.50 to $3.00 range.

October 13, 1976

To JK

From JG

Re: Mulch estimates

Joyce, our alternate edition size will be 5,000 (p&b)

To GD

From JG

Re: Mulch

Gwen, I think we should add a question mark to the Mulch title--

No Time for House Plants?

This way, it seems less negative and even a bit clearer. Can we discuss this at next week's meeting?

November 3, 1976

To JK

From JG, SM

Re: Mulch

There are a lot (too many??) of books on houseplants. The book buyer at Rich's (Atlanta) said we would have to be nuts to do another. Books with full-color illustrations are available from $2.95 up.

Generally, we found some oversized books but most were 6 x 9. All cloth books had full color on jackets. Some of the books had only black and white illustrations. We were not particularly impressed with the photographs.

There is one book organized much like the Mulch : INDOOR GARDENING, by Krockmal and Krockmal (Drake, 186 pp., approx. 100 illus--b & w photos and line drawings). Chapter arrangement is similar to Mulch but this book does not share the time theme. It would be easy to top this book, but difficult to complete with others we saw at comparable prices.

I have serious doubts about our being able to market a book on houseplants unless ours has some characteristic that makes it stand out from its shelfmates. Even then, most people will prefer color.

Our preference is a 6 x 9 trim size, color on jacket or cover, and some "gimmick" that will help make our book different.

Finally, I object to the title, NO TIME FOR HOUSEPLANTS. It is negative. It is also not clear.

Mulch: Some Competing Titles

Trim	Publisher	Pages	Price	Illustrations	Jacket or Cover	Title	Edition
	A&W Visual Library	274	~~$5.95~~	over 100	Paper, Watercolors	New York Times Book of Houseplants	225,000
	Quadrangle		9.95	" "	Cloth, " "	" "	"
	Frederick Fell		1.95	35 pages color	Paper, Four color	Be Yuor Own Houseplant Expert	
	Alfred Knopf	xv, 257, viii	4.95	sparse, b/w line drawings	Paper, Color	Making Things Grow Indoors	very textual
	" "		8.95		Cloth, Color	" "	
	Sunset		2.45		Paper, Color	How To Grow Houseplants	
	McGraw Hill		4.95		Paper,	First Aid For Houseplants	
	" "		8.95		Cloth,	" "	"
7x9	Scribners	170 tight type	8.95	1200 photos, few color	Cloth, slick color jacket	Exotic Houseplants	
	Better Homes and Gardens	96	2.95	140 / 97 in color	Full color Coated Cardboard	Better Homes and Gardens Favorite Houseplants	150,000
	S & S	128	6.95	watercolor, loaded	Cloth	Women's Day Book of Houseplants	
8x9	Doubleday	vi, 179	7.95	line, photos b+w 4pg insert of color	Cloth	Houseplants Are For Pleasure	
	Deribooks		3.95		Paper	Houseplants and Indoor Gardening	
	B & N		3.95		Paper	Houseplants and Indoor Landscaping	
	A.B. Morse		6.95		Cloth	"	"
	Delacorte		14.95		Cloth	Houseplants of the World	

Memorandum of meeting between JG, PM, JR, and MH to set edition size for NO TIME FOR HOUSEPLANTS

November 23, 1976

An edition size of 7,500 copies has been decided upon after a discussion that focused upon the capability of the Press to market NO TIME FOR HOUSEPLANTS? and the economics of the book.

Since we do not have a strong national trade list and do not use sales representatives it would be difficult to market this book nationwide. It was the consensus of those attending the meeting that we could be more effective by restricting our active marketing effort to the Southeast. In the Southeast our regional trade publications are well known and our relationships with booksellers well established. By restricting our geographic market the Press can concentrate its resources on outlets that are already aware of our existence.

Our recent experience with THE CAROLINA HOME GARDENER indicates that a printing of 7,500 copies should last us three to four years. A print run of 7,500 will allow us to price the book reasonably without incurring unacceptable risk.

jr/aj

Memo

To: JK
From: Jg
Date: November 23, 1976
Re: Edition size for the Mulch:NO TIME FOR HOUSE PLANTS

Please obtain complete manufacturing estimates for a run of 7,500 books. We will want to bind the entire printing.

The University of North Carolina Press
Box 2288
Chapel Hill, North Carolina 27514

AUTHOR'S BIOGRAPHICAL RECORD
And Publicity Questionnaire

The information supplied by you will be used in connection with the publication and publicizing of your book. Please be as accurate as possible and do not supply any information that you do not want made public. Please use a typewriter or print legibly. If more space is needed please use the back of the sheets.

Also, please return the completed sheets with two prints of a recent photograph of yourself--preferably a glossy, black-and-white, 5" x 7" photograph.

Date: November 11, 1976   Telephone:

Full name: Purvis Mulch

Name as it is to appear on title page of book: Purvis Mulch

Address: 19 Mouldering Way, Remigewasett, Kansas

Present position: Assistant Director

Date and place of birth: July 6, 19__, Pennsylvania
Citizenship: USA
(The above two lines of information will be used for copyright purposes only.)

Education (schools, colleges, and universities attended, with dates of attendance and degrees earned):

University of   1957-61, B.A.

Principal occupations, with approximate dates (if teaching, list institutions, with dates and positions held):

page 2

If employed by an educational or research institution, please give the name and address of the news bureau and/or public relations officer:

University of
News & Publications Office

List all honors, prizes, awards, etc., that you have received:

no rewards at all

List your other books (in addition to title, please give the publisher's name, the year of publication, and the type of book, e.g., history, literary criticism, poetry, fiction, etc.):

A _____ Garden Guide, _____ House, Ltd., 1975 (regional trade)

Periodicals to which you regularly contribute (including those for which you frequently review books):

Organic Gardening and Farming
Countryside

If any of the material in your book has been published previously in a copyrighted form (such as a scholarly journal) or if your book was derived from or forms a part of a copyrighted dissertation, give full details:

none

page 3

Please give a summary in 200 words or so of the contents of your book:

This book will give the casual grower of house plants all the information he needs to know to achieve indoor gardening success while spending the absolute minimum of time in caring for those plants. It is not essentially for "beginners," although beginners can use the book to great benefit; rather it is for those who might have had much experience, much of it bad. Most house plant books are written by enthusiasts who spend much time with house plants—careful watering, potting, repotting, propagating, tying up, training, inducing to flowering, humidifying, bathing, and in other ways nursing their plants to peaks of perfection. These authors seem to assume that the reader is willing or able to spend a similar amount of time in caring for their plants. This book makes no such assumption, but realizes that the reader wants the company of healthy indoor plants but does not want to spend more than a few minutes a day in the pursuit. This book tells how that may be done, in three different steps: (1) in explaining the workings of plants, so that the reader can have this basic understanding; (2) in establishing the proper conditions at the very beginning, in order to avoid later troubles; and (3) in listing more than a hundred house plants that will grow with little trouble. For the home owner or apartment dweller who wants to raise several dozen attractive house plants while spending only a few minutes a day in caring for them, this book tells all that is necessary to know.

Please specify the special contributions made by the book to its area of study. Also indicate the purpose(s) of the book and its advantages over competing books in its field.

I think these questions are answered in the foregoing statement.

---

page 4

Names and addresses of organizations to which you belong whose members will be interested in your book:

none

List any specialized mailing lists that you can make available for the promotion of your book. (To be usable all sizable lists should be available on labels):

none that I know of

Names and addresses of specialized reviewing media in the fields to which your book contributes:

The most likely reviewing media would be magazines whose audiences are largely single and affluent. These would include publications such as Apartment Ideas, Ms, Mother Jones, Rolling Stone, and others. I would not recommend garden magazines or shelter magazines.

Names and addresses of leading professional associates and other individuals engaged in work in your field who might influence the sales of your book:

none

Indicate the media you believe will be the most effective in advertising your book:

The same magazines mentioned for review purposes.

Note: We regularly send review copies of most of our new books to such publications as the New York Times, Saturday Review, North Carolina and major metropolitan area newspapers, etc.

December 9, 1976

Mulch Project

JR, JG, SM attending

1. Publication date will be September 15, 1977. (Stock date is July.) We are satisfied with this timing--people begin to think about indoor plants in the fall, and the book would make a grand Christmas gift.

2. We will distribute 375 review and comp copies--250 books to book review and "lifestyle" editors, and 125 to book buyers. Because there are so many houseplant books, quite a few book review editors will probably ignore this one. We hope to get good exposure in the lifestyle sections of newspapers. Also, it is important for book buyers to see this book. Sending comp copies to major buyers in our area is about the only way we can handle this.

3. Our major bookstore/promotion effort will be in North Carolina, South Carolina, Virginia and _____ (using Mulch's advice here). We also will make a special effort with some stores in New York, Atlanta, Washington, and Chicago.

4. We will distribute flyers to bookstores in the areas mentioned above. Where relevant, bookstores will also receive an advertising schedule.

5. Wholesalers will get a special 50% discount on orders of 100 or more books.

6. We will contact some plant stores in North Carolina. Probably, Mulch could help with some plant stores in his area.

7. News release will be sent to lifestyle editors in generally the same areas as mentioned above.

8. No Time for Houseplants? will be included in our Christmas '77 gifts books promotion for North Carolina bookstores. This campaign has a $1,800 budget and involves 12 titles--so $150 will be charged against the Mulch budget. Nationally, we will advertise No Time for Houseplants? and Marion Brown's Southern Cook Book around Christmas.

9. Autographing parties will be restricted to the _____ area, because of a lack of funds.

NO TIME FOR HOUSE PLANTS?

Memo, Phone Conversation with Mulch, mid-November

For the most part, we discussed publicity in and around Mulch's home area.

He is willing to autograph books, and will send us a list of key stores. We will make the arrangements.

He likes the idea of an interview with the _____ newspaper--I prefer the lifestyle section. We will attempt to set this up.

Mulch will send a list of the important _____ newspapers and magazines. This will help with review copies and news releases.

We will send review copies fo Univ. of _____. _____ News Bureau and to Alumni Office at University of _____. _____ News Bureau may do a story--if pushed.

Mulch does not think advertising in _____ newspapers is important. We probably can get good publicity from our news releases and the interview.

He does think the PW ads are a good idea, since we do not have salesmen.

He promised to send a photograph of himself.

CATALOG DESCRIPTION

"For people who love plants--but love other things better."--Rogue

No Time for Houseplants?
A Busy Person's Guide to Indoor Gardening
by Purvis Mulch

A stunning collection of house plants does not have to take much time. One can, in fact, enjoy the company of nearly two dozen plants without spending more than two or three minutes with them every other day.

No Time for Houseplants? gives only the essential information for house plant success. Purvis Mulch has two rules--choose plants that are easy to grow and give them the conditions they must have to thrive. Neither rule is difficult because he recommends more than one hundred easy-to-grow plants and plant groups, comprising several thousand varieties, and gives the conditions required for each recommended plant. Mulch also describes his "bit and snatch" method of house plant care and gives a brief description of the inner workings of plants.

Most house plant books suggest that growing plants indoors must be a consuming hobby. Mulch disagrees. "The right plant, given the right conditions for growth, will thrive despite your frequent inattention," he says. His book is for busy people and for people who have had little experience growing house plants.

LC 77-0000   192 pp., illus.,boxed
ISBN 0-8078-1300-1 $7.95

Memo to: JK, JR
From: SM
RE: Marketing and Design meeting on the Mulch--Notes taken
Date: 6 January 1977

JK: Discussed plans to leave case unillustrated in order to produce a surprise effect when book is taken out. Opinions all around were that this is somewhat risky but very well may attract the eye when placed with garden & houseplant books and will make an attractive gift item.

JK: Cost of case is high compared to overall cost--approximately 1/3.

JK: Will get   to reduce former estimate on case, if at all possible. Is there any possibility of increasing the edition size?

JG: This is a problem because we don't have salesmen and unless the books are available in the bookstores, much of our advertising will be wasted.

SM: We can handle the regional sales, but national marketing will have to be limited to PW and a few others.

JG: Discussed ads written and ideas about "busy people" approach. Will send ads to JK Monday morning. Meanwhile, if we can get cost down, that means more for marketing or a more reasonable price.

JR: 40% of estimated cost for Mulch is manufacturing. Price probably cannot be lowered more than 45¢ or so. Discussed whether or not 7.50 is better gift price than 7.95.

JG: Suggested the idea of a gift card enclosed in some way. General agreement was that it was too costly, but some description was needed. Sticker?

SM: Shrink-Wrapping causes problems when no description of the book is on the outside--bookstores tend to leave books in the shrink-wrap. JK said this book will not be shrink-wrapped because of the case.

JR: Bookstores will be putting a price sticker on the book--could this mess up the design? Discussion. Put a price on the book? No, because gift item.

JK: Will set 2 or 3 lines of descriptive copy on the back and design a circle for the bookstore to use for price sticker.

NEWS RELEASE

9/15/77
For Immediate Release

SOME PLANTS PREFER BUSY PEOPLE!

NEW UNC PRESS BOOK TELLS HOW TO SELECT PLANTS THAT REQUIRE ALMOST NO CARE

CHAPEL HILL, N.C. --- A stunning collection of house plants doesn't have to take much of your time.

You can, in fact, enjoy the company of nearly two dozen plants without spending more than two or three minutes with them every other day.

In "No Time for House Plants? A Busy Person's Guide to Indoor Gardening," author Purvis Mulch provides only the essential information for house plant success. The book was just published by The University of North Carolina Press.

Mulch has only two rules of success---choose plants that are easy to grow and give them the conditions they must have to thrive.

Neither rule is difficult because more than 100 easy-to-grow plants and plant groups, comprising several thousand varieties, are recommended in "No Time for House Plants?" Also, the conditions required for each recommended plant are given.

-- more --

NEWS RELEASE

NEW UNC PRESS BOOK -2-2-2

"The right plant, given the right conditions for growth, will thrive despite your frequent inattention," says Mulch.

His book includes a section explaining how plants work--basic information that is easily understood in a few minutes. As for plant care, the author explains his own "bit and snatch" method of tending plants. Nearly all of the chores necessary to keep plants thriving are little ones, he says. If you work them into your daily schedule, you won't spend any time "tending house plants."

Most house plant books suggest that growing plants indoors must be a consuming hobby. Mulch disagrees with this approach and designed his book for busy people and for people who have had little experience growing house plants.

"Many of us--single people, working couples, harrassed mothers, college students, anyone whose daily living pattern leaves precious little time for indoor gardening--would enjoy the beauty and companionship of bright, green house plants," he says.

"No Time for House Plants?" is illustrated and *bored and sells for* $7.95. It is available at bookstores or from The UNC Press, Box 2288, Chapel Hill, NC 27514.

####

NO TIME FOR HOUSE PLANTS? /Promotion Schedule

Stock Date: July
Pub date: September 15

July 25: Review copies out
August 8: Comp copies and flyers to book buyers (chiefly regional)
           Advertising schedule included if relevant
August 15: PW ad
August 29: Fall Announcement Ads
September: Regional ads and distribution of news release
October: Remainder of flyers to individuals
October 24: PW Christmas ad (with Southern Cook Book)
October and November: Regional ads (with Southern Cook Book)
November: Christmas books promotion (North Carolina only; 11 other titles)

```
                    MULCH PROMOTION BUDGET

Ad # 1                          $2,140.06
Ad # 2 (with cookbook)           1,162.18
Ad composition &
  design (UNCP)                     35.76
Ad repros, negs                     31.00
Flyer composition
  and design (UNCP)                 56.97
Printing (2,500)                   235.00
Postage (2,000 at
  bulk rates)                       38.00
Christmas Bookstore
  Promotion                        150.00
Fall Announcement
  Ads                              125.00
                                _____
                                $3,973.97
```

Advertising Schedule, Ad # 1

NO TIME FOR HOUSE PLANTS?

NATIONAL

Publishers Weekly, mid-August, 1/3 page $555.00

REGIONAL NEWSPAPERS   (all 3 cols x 5")

Raleigh News & Observer/Times, Sept. 18/20   158.25
Charlotte Observer/News, Sept. 18/20   260.00
Greensboro Daily News/Record, Sept. 18/20   162.45
Richmond, Va., Times-Dispatch/News Leader, Sept. 18   294.00
Columbia, S.C., The State   234.36

REGIONAL MAGAZINES

N.C. * New East, Sept.-Oct. 1/3 page   116.00
   " * The State, Sept., 1/3 page   135.00

S.C.   Sandlapper, Sept., 1/3 page   225.00

Total: $2,140.06   all assigned to NO TIME FOR HOUSE PLANTS

* contract rate

180 / UNC / Promotion / Sales

Ad #2

Publishers Weekly
New East
The State (NC)
UNC University Report

Gifts for All Seasons

No Time for Houseplants?
A Busy Person's Guide to Indoor Gardening

by PURVIS MULCH

"A must for people who love plants—but love other things better!"—*Rogue*

"This little green book tells exactly how to select a stunning variety of house plants that require almost no care."
—*Publishers Monthly*

192 pp., illus., boxed
$7.95

Marion Brown's
SOUTHERN COOK BOOK

"Mrs. Brown shows in her selection from over 30,000 recipes the happy mixture of English, Continental and Mexican cooking with true South richness and downright goodness that makes for famous food."
—*New York Times Book Review*

Nearly one million copies sold

498 pp.
$7.95

THE
UNIVERSITY OF
NORTH CAROLINA
PRESS

Box 2288
Chapel Hill 27514

No Time for Houseplants?
A Busy Person's Guide to Indoor Gardening

by Purvis Mulch

Some plants prefer busy people.

"This little green book tells exactly how to select a stunning variety of house plants that require almost no care."—*Publishers Monthly*

"For people who love plants—but love other things better."—*Rogue*

192 pp., illus., boxed
$7.95

Publication: Sept. 15
Now Shipping

THE UNIVERSITY OF
NORTH CAROLINA PRESS
Box 2288   Chapel Hill 27514

Ad #1

Publishers Weekly
Raleigh News & Observer/Times
Charlotte Observer/News
Greensboro Daily News/Record
Richmond, Va., Times Dispatch
Columbia, S.C., The State
New East Magazine
The State Magazine
Sandlapper Magazine

~~~~~~~ *Gifts for All Seasons* ~~~~~~~

No Time for Houseplants?
A Busy Person's Guide to Indoor Gardening
by PURVIS MULCH

"A must for people who love plants—but love other things better!"
—*Rogue*

"This little green book tells exactly how to select a stunning variety of houseplants that require almost no care."
—*Publishers Monthly*

192 pp., illus., boxed
$7.95

Marion Brown's SOUTHERN COOK BOOK

"Mrs. Brown shows in her selection from over 30,000 recipes the happy mixture of English, Continental and Mexican cooking with true Southern richness and downright goodness that makes for famous food."
—*New York Times Book Review*

Nearly one million copies sold

498 pp.
$7.95

THE UNIVERSITY OF NORTH CAROLINA PRESS
Box 2288   Chapel Hill   27514

Ad #2

For:
Raleigh News & Observer   Greensboro Daily News/Record
Charlotte Observer/News   Richmond Times-Dispatch
Winston-Salem Journal/Sentinel   Columbia, S.C., The State

Advertising Schedule, Ad #2

NO TIME FOR HOUSE PLANTS?
Marion Brown's SOUTHERN COOK BOOK

NATIONAL
Publishers Weekly $555.00

REGIONAL MAGAZINES
*New East, Nov.-Dec., 1/3 page   116.00
*The State, Oct., 1/3 page   35.00
*UNC University Report, Oct., 2" x 10"   99.00

REGIONAL NEWSPAPERS (all 3 cols x 6" except Charlotte)
Raleigh News & Observer/Times, Nov. 27/29   189.90
Charlotte Observer/News, Nov. 27/29 (2 cols x 6")   312.24
Winston-Salem Journal/Sentinel, Nov. 27/29   165.60
Greensboro Daily News/Record, Nov. 27/29   164.45
Richmond, Va., Times-Dispatch, Nov. 27   352.80
Columbia, S.C., The State, Nov. 27   234.36

Total: $2,324.35 one-half ($1,162.18) assigned to NO TIME FOR HOUSE PLANTS?
                  one-half ($1,162.17) assigned to SOUTHERN COOK BOOK

*contract rate

QUOTATION

meredith-webb printing company, incorporated

TELEPHONE 226-0363 AREA CODE 919 □ 116 E. HOLT STREET, BURLINGTON, NORTH CAROLINA

We, the undersigned, for the consideration hereinafter mentioned, covenant and agree with

    Ms. Joyce Kachergis
    UNC Press
    Chapel Hill, N.C. 27514

to perform in a faithful and workman-like manner the following specified work.

2,500 8½x11 folders (Mulch circulars). Printed 2-colors ink -- 1-side. Fold to fit #10 Envelope. Camera-ready. $235.00

2,500 Camera-ready Envelopes #10. Printed 2-color ink. $105.00

Your acceptance in writing at the end of this agreement will complete the whole contract between us.

Dated at Burlington, N. C., this 3rd day of Feb. , 19 77

Accepted this _____ day of _____ , 19 _____

_____
Customer Signature

Clyde Swann
meredith-webb printing co.

Sales Ad Transmittal Form

UNC PRESS SALES DEPARTMENT

Ad # _____ Name: **MULCH Brochure**

From Sales to Production Date: **1/4/77**   Finished Repros to Sales Date: **1/18/77**

Size: **see below**   Number of Repros: _____   ☒ Major   ☐ Medium   ☐ Minor Importance

Assigned to Compositor: _____   Date: _____

Paste-up xerox to Sales: Date _____   Xerox to Production: Date _____

OK Repro to Sales: Date _____

Ad will be in the following: distributed to bookstores and to some individuals

Special Instructions:

1. one page (8½ × 11) to fold type side out, top panel should be showy
2. use sketch of book instead of photo
3. 2 colors, green & black
4. Estimates for 2,000 & 2,500. Also, estimates for envelopes with sketch & quote on outside left, 2 color. (See our rough.)

end

The Perfect Gift

"For people who love plants—
but love other things better."
—ROGUE

No Time for Houseplants?
A Busy Person's Guide to Indoor Gardening

by PURVIS MULCH

A stunning collection of houseplants does not have to take much time. One can, in fact, enjoy the company of nearly two dozen plants without spending more than two or three minutes with them every other day. **No Time for Houseplants?** gives only the essential information for houseplant success. Purvis Mulch has two rules—choose plants that are easy to grow and give them the conditions they must have to thrive. Neither rule is difficult because he recommends more than one hundred easy-to-grow plants and plant groups, comprising several thousand varieties, and gives the conditions required for each recommended plant. Mulch also describes his "bit and snatch" method of houseplant care and gives a brief description of the inner workings of plants.

Most houseplant books suggest that growing plants indoors must be a consuming hobby. Mulch disagrees. "The right plant, given the right conditions for growth, will thrive despite your frequent inattention," he says. **No Time for Houseplants?** is for busy people and for people who have had little experience growing houseplants.

LC 77-0000
ISBN 0-8078-1300-1
192 pp., illus., boxed
$7.95 Trade

Send orders to:
THE UNIVERSITY OF NORTH CAROLINA PRESS
Box 2288   Chapel Hill, North Carolina   27514

Mulch--Preliminary Review List--Newspapers and Local Magazines

South Carolina

Columbia STATE
Columbia RECORD
Charleston NEWS & COURIER
Charleston EVENING POST
Greenville NEWS-PIEDMONT
Spartanburg HERALD-JOURNAL

SANDLAPPER Magazine

Georgia

Albany HERALD
Athens BANNER-HERALD
Atlanta JOURNAL CONSTITUTION
Augusta CHRONICLE HERALD
Columbus LEDGER-ENQUIRER
Gainesville TIMES
Macon TELEGRAPH & NEWS
Marietta JOURNAL
Savannah NEWS-PRESS

COASTAL QUARTERLY Magazine
GEORGIA LIFE Magazine
BROWN'S GUIDE TO GEORGIA

Florida

Miami HERALD
Miami NEWS
Orlando SENTINEL-STAR
St. Petersburg TIMES-INDEPENDENT
Tampa TRIBUNE & TIMES

Tennessee

Chattanooga NEWS-FREE PRESS
Chattanooga TIMES
Knoxville JOURNAL
Knoxville NEWS-SENTINEL
Memphis COMMERCIAL APPEAL
Nashville BANNER
Nashville TENNESSEAN

Virginia

Charlottesville PROGRESS
Norfolk VIRGINIAN-PILOT
Richmond TIMES-DISPATCH
Richmond NEWS LEADER
Roanoke TIMES

District of Columbia

The GEORGETOWNER
WASHINGTON POST BOOKWORLD
Washington STAR-NEWS

New York

TIMES - Home Editor
TIMES BOOK REVIEW
TIMES Daily Book Section
VILLAGE VOICE
New York DAILY NEWS

NEW YORK MAGAZINE

California

Los Angeles TIMES
San Francisco EXAMINER & CHRONICLE

MOTHER JONES
ROLLING STONE

Pennsylvania

Philadelphia INQUIRER
Pittsburgh PRESS
Philadelphia BULLETIN

Illinois

Chicago SUN-TIMES SHOW-BOOK WEEK
Chicago NEWS
Chicago TRIBUNE

Mulch Review list--Preliminary Plans

Popular Magazines

AMERICAN HOME
APARTMENT LIFE
APARTMENT WORLD
BETTER HOMES AND GARDENS
FAMILY CIRCLE
FLOWER & GARDEN
GOOD HOUSEKEEPING
HOME LIFESTYLES
HOUSE BEAUTIFUL
HOUSE & GARDEN
HOUSE & HOME
HOME GARDEN MAGAZINE
INTERIORS
LADIES' HOME JOURNAL
McCALL'S MAGAZINE
MS.
SOUTHERN LIVING
SPHERE
WOMAN'S DAY
WOMEN'S LEAGUE OUTLOOK
MADEMOISELLE
GLAMOUR
TRAVEL & LEISURE
WORKING WOMAN
REDBOOK
WORKBASKET

NOTE: About 50 review copies will be distributed in North Carolina, and about 40 review copies, in the author's home state.

Southern Magazines

SOUTHERN EXPOSURE
SOUTHERN BOOKLORE
THE SOUTH MAGAZINE
SOUTHERN LIVING

Book Review Services & Syndicates

AB BOOKMAN'S WEEKLY
BEST-IN-BOOKS
CHOICE
KIRKUS REVIEWS
LIBRARY JOURNAL--BOOK REVIEW
PUBLISHERS WEEKLY--FORECASTS
JOHN BARKHAM REVIEWS
BOOK BEAT BY JOAN ORTH
LITERARY LANTERN

Television Programs Featuring Books (and/or Radio)

Critique (WITI-TV & WMVT-TV, Milwaukee)
Book Beat (WTTW-TV, Chicago)
Gamut (WFMT-FM, Chicago)
Peggy Mann Show (WTVD-TV, Durham, NC)
Ty Boyd Show (WBTV, Charlotte, NC)

UNIVERSITY OF TEXAS PRESS

Table of Contents

General Statement / 189

Acquisitions and Administration

Acquisitions and Editorial Procedures / 190
Contract / 194
Contract Abstract and Notice of Contract Signed / 196
Estimate and Release Form, Pricing Worksheet / 197

Editorial

Correspondence between Copy Editor and Author / 198
Edited Manuscript / 201
Copy Editor's Procedures / 222
Editorial Checklist / 223
Preproduction Meeting Notes / 224
Editorial–Production Transmittal Sheet, Editorial Fact Sheet / 225

Production and Design

Production Cost Estimates / 226
Composition Specifications / 227
Print and Bind Specifications, Schedule / 228
Schedule Card for Production Report / 229
Sample Pages / 230
Jacket Design / 234
Jacket Printing Specifications / 235
Work-in-Progress Cost Sheet / 236

Sales and Promotion

Promotion Plan / 237
Sample Advertisement / 238
Direct Mail Plan / 239
Catalog and Jacket Copy / 240
Advertising Plan / 242
Review List / 243
Author Form / 245
Book Club Rights / 249
Author Party / 250

University of Texas Press

No Time for Houseplants

No Time for Houseplants is not representative of the kind of book the University of Texas Press normally publishes. For that reason we were at some disadvantage in attempting to show our *normal* procedures for publishing. Throughout we have tried to deal with the manuscript as if it were actually being published by us and have made our decisions recognizing our regular financial constraints. Our solutions have been the ones we would have used in reality and we have made no attempt to edit, design, produce and market in any special or ideal manner.

In our first review of the project we decided that we had to do something to distinguish our plant care book from the others on the market. Since we could not afford the use of color, and preferred not to use photographs because there was no one in our area we could afford or who could realistically complete the job in the time schedule we needed, we decided to commission line drawings. We felt that the artist we selected had a unique approach and hoped that buyers would be as attracted by the drawing style as by the clarity of information provided.

The book would have been typeset and pasted up in-house. The illustrations would have been sized on our stat camera and put into place on the repros by us.

Only in the preparation of the jacket design did we feel we compromised what might have been done differently had we actually published the book.

LOG OF ACQUISITIONS PROCESS: <u>NO TIME FOR HOUSE PLANTS</u>

Texas Press receives a letter from author Purvis Mulch, descriptive of the manuscript. Acquisitions editor decides manuscript might be a good trade book for Texas Press, but wants further information about the manuscript. (Note: This situation is of course hypothetical. If the initial inquiry had been "real," the Press would in fact have declined consideration, recommending a commercial publisher.)

Acquisitions editor sends author letter expressing interest, and encloses Author and Manuscript Inquiry form, from which she/he (in this case Iris Hill, who is also the Senior Editor) derives information about original form of manuscript (was it a dissertation?), length of manuscript, whether it is under consideration by another press (if so, we will not consider manuscript till it is free), whether the manuscript has tables, maps, photos, etc. (which, with the estimated length, aids the editor in determining whether the manuscript may be too expensive to produce), other books on the subject (has the subject been covered to too great an extent elsewhere?), the background of the author, and names of scholars in the field who may have read the manuscript or may be able to read it for us and give us an expert opinion of its worth.

Acquisitions editor receives AMI from author. Mulch has a good background in the field. There are a number of other books on the topic, but editor feels (in this hypothetical situation) that the topic is always popular. Manuscript is not long, and Mulch can provide his own line drawings for it. Editor invites the manuscript, with the condition that it not be simultaneously under consideration by another press.

Manuscript arrives, is logged in on file cards for Editorial Department's records and for acquisition editor's records, and receipt is acknowledged by secretary by postcard.

Manuscript is screened in house by acquisitions editor. The information seems to be well presented, clear to the general reader, though Mulch's drawings are not the best that can be obtained. Perhaps we will provide our own line drawings. Acquisition editor decides to send the manuscript out for a first reading, and chooses a reader after consulting with advisors in botany. Writes this person, offering an honorarium in payment for the reading. (Honorarium varies with length and complexity of manuscript.) The manuscript is sent to this reader, whose identity is kept confidential. (Such is always the case except for rare instances when a reader asks to have his/her identity revealed to the author.)

Manuscript returns from reader with report. At this point, if the report is negative, the Press usually rejects the project. If it is all praise, the acquisition editor directs a memo (see next step below) to the Director and with his/her (at Texas Press, Philip D. Jones) approval proceeds to a second reading. In Mulch's case, the first reader's report is mixed: The code he uses throughout for light and temperature conditions needs clarifying, the reader believes, and some reorganization is needed. The acquisition editor sends a copy of this report to the Press Director, with a description of the project, the AMI, and an initial cost estimate (a rough one which she has figured on the basis of figures and calculations provided the acquisition editors by the Press Production Department). The Director is asked his opinion about the mixed report--what step to take next (the acquisition editor suggests getting Mulch's response, and if this is adequate, going on for a second reading), who he considers a likely second reader (the editor suggests a regional "plant person," who conducts a weekly program on educational television advising viewers on plant care--this to get a slightly different angle of vision than the first reader's, a scholar in the Botany Department of a northern university), and in general whether the project seems suitable to pursue. The Director responds in agreement with the editor, suggesting a second reader's report if Mulch's response to the criticisms is adequate. In this case, since the revisions are not extensive, Director also suggests going on for a second reading without Mulch's revising the manuscript. (If suggested revisions are extensive but there is nevertheless sufficient praise to balance, the Press may ask the author to revise before seeking a second report, and may in fact go back to the original reader for an opinion on the revision.)

Mulch is sent a copy of the reader's report, with the acquisition editor's criticism of the line drawings included as a revision the Press would also wish to have made. He responds adequately, saying that he had feared the coding might not be completely clear, agreeing that the Press provide its own illustrations, and also agreeing to make some of the organization changes that the reader felt were necessary. He disagrees with a few of the reader's points and argues his case convincingly, so the acquisition editor phones the regional plant person, who does indeed read the manuscript for the Press and reports favorably, having been advised by the editor that Mulch would make certain revisions (the illustrations, the organizational problems, etc.) before the Press would publish the manuscript.

(A note: If for some reason--for example, competition with another press in the acquisition of a manuscript--there is a rush, the Press occasionally arranges for simultaneous readings by two experts at once.)

At this point the acquisition editor again directs a memo on the status of the project to the Press Director, including copies of this second report and the previous cost estimate; the editor recommends taking the project to the Press's next Faculty Advisory Committee meeting for the Committee's approval, but suggests first, because of the unusual nature of the project (its position as a trade book, with a large number of illustrations, etc.), a meeting with Business, Marketing, and Production Departments to discuss the viability of the manuscript's publication by the Press, the costs, and so on. Director agrees and meeting is held, at which a tentative arrangement for the new illustrations is discussed, a tentative number of illustrations set and an illustrator suggested, and suggestions of pricing, marketing methods, and general approach for the book are made. Given the print run tentatively decided on, the price can be set so as to be acceptable to a fairly extensive popular audience. The book can be made more distinctive and more attractive to buyers, the Production Manager suggests, by striking new line drawings.

Director and acquisition editor agree that the manuscript may be taken before the Press's next Faculty Advisory Committee meeting. The Committee, made up of eleven faculty members, must approve all new manuscripts and reprints originating from other presses.

Docket materials begin to be prepared for presentation to the FAC. Docket has a key which identifies readers for Committee members. Docket goes to the FAC before the meeting, so that they may read it in advance. Included in the docket for this book are the following:

1. House editor's statement describing the project and the Press's reasons for wishing to publish it-in this case, the manuscript is a good potential trade book for the Press (not an acceptable reason in the actual normal process)

2. Biographical note on author

3. Table of contents

4. First manuscript report

5. Author's response to criticisms and suggestions in first manuscript report

6. Second manuscript report

7. (optional) Supporting statement (from well-known botanist who says Mulch's work is reputable, this work useful for beginning plant raisers)

The acquisition editor presents the project before the FAC meeting, and after some discussion the manuscript is approved (unlikely in reality). The acquisition editor notifies Mulch that evening by phone that his project has passed, and the next afternoon prepares a Contract Abstract. Royalty terms are figured on the basis of the house editor's estimate corrected by the later tentative decision for the Press to provide its own illustrations for the book, and have been discussed by the acquisition editor with the Press business manager. Terms are okayed by the Press's director, who signs the Contract Abstract, and contracts are prepared by the Press secretary. (A post docket meeting of all department managers and acquisition editors to discuss marketing, editorial, and production strategy also occurs shortly after FAC.) 3 copies of the contract signed by press Director are sent to Purvis Mulch for signing. He keeps one copy, and the others are returned, one for a master file at the Press, another for University records. The Director's secretary assigns contract number which is the date of the last signature on the contract.

The Director's secretary sends to the acquisition editor a Notice of Contract Signed. Others who receive copies of this are the Press managers, and the advertising manager of the Marketing Department. Once this notice is distributed, the acquisition editor, the head of Production, and the Marketing Manager meet to plan a tentative schedule for the book.

Mulch in the meantime has been revising his manuscript and now sends it on to the Press by date stipulated in contract. At this point, the acquisition editor transmits the manuscript to the Senior Editor (though not in this case, since here the acquisition editor is also the Senior Editor). (A note: Were the acquisition editor not also the senior editor, as here, all memos would pass from the acquiring editor to the senior editor for comments, and then to the Director, and the senior editor would be involved in all discussions of the project.)

The transmittal material includes (1) the file card that has been kept on the manuscript, listing the readers, the author's address, and so on; (2) the manuscript itself and if possible a duplicate copy for Marketing*(if not, this will come later); (3) the file the acquisition editor has kept on the manuscript; (4) the Transmittal Sheet, which is distributed to the Marketing Manager, with a copy also of the front matter and preface or introduction, the advertising manager, the direct mail manager, the production manager (who received the original of the Transmittal Sheets), the business manager, and the manuscript's copy editor; (5) the Fact Sheet, which is given to the marketing manager, the advertising manager, the direct mail manager, the production manager (again, the original), the business manager, the Press Director, the senior editor, the proofreader, and the copy editor; (6) the Estimate & Release form, which is distributed to the production manager (the original) and the copy editor; (7) the Editorial Schedule (for the copy editor); and (8) the Copyright Notice Form, also for the copy editor's use. At this point the editorial secretary assigns an ISBN to the book.

The senior editor's transmittal of this material (by means of the editorial secretary) is announced in the weekly Editorial Report, copies of which are given to all in the Editorial Department as well as to the marketing manager and the advertising manager, the business manager and two of his assistants, the Press director, the production manager and the other designer at the Press.

The manuscript now enters the actual copy editing process, and the copy editor's weekly progress on the manuscript is reported in the Editorial Report.

When the manuscript nears the time when it will enter the actual production stage, a Preproduction meeting is called.

*and Production

University of Texas Press

P. O. Box 7819   Austin, Texas 78712

DEAR Purvis Mulch:

This letter is our contract with you. It sets down the terms of our agreement to publish your book, presently entitled NO TIME FOR HOUSE PLANTS

It also represents the convictions that govern our relations with authors. We believe that a book belongs to its author; that the chief function of a publisher is to publish the author's work in appropriate form and to get it to as many readers as possible; that the author should be consulted in the disposition of book club and reprint rights. Finally, although we hope and expect that our association with each of our authors will extend through the publication of many books, we do not believe in requiring commitments for the future and so do not ask for options.

1. You grant to us during the term of the United States copyright, and during any renewal or extension thereof, the exclusive right to publish and sell, including the right to permit others to publish and sell, your work in book form in the English language throughout the world.

2. You shall deliver to us no later than   (date)   a typed copy of your work in final form, complete and ready for the printer and accompanied by all necessary permissions, licenses, and consents. If we both agree that photographs, maps, charts, or other illustrations are necessary to the book, you will provide them in final form, ready for reproduction without additional art work (maps and charts will first be furnished in draft form for editing). When page proofs are ready you will prepare or cause to be prepared and deliver to us within 3 weeks of your receipt of such proofs an index to the work, unless we have agreed beforehand that one will not be needed.

If you do not so deliver your work to us in acceptable form by the date specified or at another date to be agreed to by us in writing, we may terminate this agreement by notice to you (unless failure to deliver is caused by circumstances beyond your control). When your work has been copy edited it will be returned to you so that you can discuss with the editor any changes which have been made with which you are not in agreement. Queries from the editor will be made on "flyers" attached to the typescript pages and you will make any queries or suggest any changes on flyers; you will not make changes directly on the edited copy. When you receive edited copy, this will be your last opportunity to make any substantive changes in your book without cost to you. Page proofs will be sent to you, and reading them, will be your sole responsibility, although we will check all lines reset to make corrections. No changes may be made on page proofs other than for the correction of actual errors made by the printer or our staff, will be charged against your account.

(If your work is a collection of articles by several authors and you are its general editor, you will be responsible for distributing edited copy to the contributors and forwarding their suggested changes which you approve to the copy editor. You will also be responsible for reading page proofs or for getting the contributors to read them and, unless otherwise agreed upon, for providing an index.)

3. We shall publish your work at our expense in manner and style and at a price we believe appropriate as soon as circumstances permit.

4. We shall apply for copyright in our name in the United States (unless otherwise stipulated in writing) and you shall (though we may do so on your behalf) apply for renewal or extension of such copyright if this agreement is then in effect. We may apply for copyright in our name in other countries. We shall publish your work in the United States in a way that complies with the provisions of the Universal Copyright Convention. In general, it is agreed that both you and we shall take all steps necessary to secure and preserve a valid United States copyright in your work.

5. You represent and warrant to us, and to those to whom we may license or grant rights hereunder, that you are the sole owner of your work and that it has not previously been published in book form; that it is original, is not in the public domain, and does not infringe upon or violate any personal or property rights of others; that it contains nothing scandalous, libelous, in violation of any right of privacy, or contrary to law; and that you have all necessary permissions, licenses, and consents and the full power to enter into this agreement and to grant us the rights herein provided for.

6. You agree to indemnify and hold us harmless against any loss, damage, liability, or expense (including counsel fees reasonably incurred) arising out of any claim, action, or proceeding asserted or instituted on any ground which, if established, would be a breach of any of the warranties made by you in this agreement.

7. We shall pay to you:

A. On each copy of the trade edition or microfiche sold by us, less returns, a royalty of

```
5% net receipt proceeds 1-3000
7 1/2% net receipt proceeds 3001-5000
10% net receipt proceeds beyond 5000
```

B. On copies sold by us, at a special discount of 50% or more from the publisher's retail price through channels outside of the ordinary wholesale and retail trade (other than remainders as described in paragraph E), a royalty of 10% of the amount we receive. Such sales shall be accounted for separately and not included in other sales totals.

C. On copies sold by us for export (except as provided in paragraph F), a royalty of 10% of the amount we receive.

D. On copies of a paperback edition issued by us, a royalty of 7 1/2% of the net proceeds 6% of the publisher's retail price of such paperback edition.

E. On copies sold at a remainder price (any sale at a price at or below manufacturing cost, whether through normal trade channels or otherwise, being deemed a remainder sale for purposes of this clause), no royalty shall be paid.

F. On copies, bound or in sheets, sold for export at discounts of 60% or more, a royalty of 10% of the amount we receive.

G. On copies furnished without charge or for review, advertising, sample, promotion, or other similar purposes, no royalty.

8. We may publish or permit others to publish or broadcast without charge and without royalty such selections from your work for publicity purposes as may, in our opinion, benefit the sale of your work. We shall also be authorized to license publication of your work without charge and without royalty in Braille or by any other method primarily designed for the physically handicapped.

9. You grant to us the exclusive right on your behalf to license, sell or otherwise dispose of the following rights in your work: publication or sale of your work by book clubs; publication of a reprint edition of your work by another publisher; condensations; serializations in magazines or newspapers (whether in one or more installments and whether before or after book publication); dramatic, motion picture, phonograph, and broadcasting rights and electronic, mechanical, or visual reproduction rights; publication of your work in the British Commonwealth; publication of your work in foreign languages; publication of your work and selections therefrom in anthologies, compilations, and digests; picturized book versions; and microprint and microfilm versions. In order to afford you the opportunity to consult with us on book club or reprint rights before we dispose of these rights, we shall notify you before making any disposition of same.

In the case of each of the rights specified in this paragraph 9, the net proceeds of its disposition (after all commissions, foreign taxes, and other charges) shall be shared equally between us except that as to first serial, dramatic, motion picture, phonograph, and broadcas: uses the division of net proceeds shall be 90% to you and 10% to us. (If this work is a collection of contributions, we may permit others to publish or make use of separate contributions from it, as described above, but not without approval of the individual contributor, with whom proceeds from such permissions will be divided on the same basis as described above in this article.)

10. During the life of this agreement you will not, without our written consent, furnish to any other publisher any book on the same subject and of the same extent and character as the book covered by this agreement, publication of which would clearly conflict with the sale of our book. When in doubt about application of this article to a new work, you will confer with us to receive the necessary clearance.

11. On publication of your work we shall deliver to you ten copies without charge and you shall have the right to purchase further copies, for your personal use but not for resale, at a discount of 40% from the publisher's retail price. (If this work is a collection of contributions edited by you, we shall deliver to you five copies without charge and you shall have the right to purchase further copies, for your personal use but not for resale, at a discount of 40% from the publisher's retail price. We shall deliver to each contributor one copy without charge if there are more than five contributors, two copies if there are five or fewer contributors.)

12. A. We shall render to you in October of each year an annual statement of account as of the preceding August thirty-first. Each statement shall be accompanied by payment of all sums due thereon. If in any yearly period the total payments due are less than $10.00, we may defer the rendering of statements and payments until such time as the sum of $10.00 or more shall be due.

B. You may, upon written request, examine our books of account insofar as they relate to your work.

13. A. In case we fail to keep your work in print (and for all purposes of this paragraph the work shall be considered to be in print if it is on sale by us in any edition or if it is on sale in any edition licensed by us during the term of this agreement) and you make written request of us to keep it in print, we shall, within sixty days after the receipt of your request, notify you in writing whether or not we intend to do so, and if we elect to do so, we shall have six months thereafter in which to comply. If we fail to comply (unless the failure is due to circumstances beyond our control), or if we do not desire to keep your work in print, then this agreement shall terminate and all of the rights granted to us shall revert to you.

B. In case of such termination you shall have the right for thirty days thereafter on prior written notice to us to purchase negatives and plates, if any, of your work at one third of their manufacturing cost, including composition, and any remaining copies or sheets of your work at the manufacturing cost. If you fail to do so, we may dispose of all of them as we see fit, subject to the provisions of paragraph 7 of this agreement.

C. Nothing contained herein shall affect our right to sell remaining copies of your work on hand at the date of termination of this agreement, nor shall such termination affect any license or other grant of rights, options, or contracts made to or with third parties by either of us prior to the termination date, or the rights of either of us in the proceeds of such agreements.

14. Prior to remaindering your work under paragraph 7E, we shall make reasonable effort to notify you and afford you the opportunity to purchase all or part of such overstock at the remainder price.

15. You shall execute and deliver to us whatever documents and assignments of copyright or other papers as may be necessary to fulfill the terms and intent of this agreement.

16. Any rights in your work not specifically granted to us hereunder are reserved to you. You agree, however, not to exercise or dispose of any of your reserved rights in such a way as to affect adversely the value of any of the rights granted to us under this agreement.

17. No waiver or modification of this agreement shall be valid unless in writing and signed by both of us.

18. This agreement shall inure to the benefit of and be binding upon you and your heirs, personal representatives, and assigns and upon us and our successors and assigns. We shall not assign this agreement without your consent.

If the foregoing correctly states your understanding of our agreement, please sign the enclosed copy of this letter where indicated below and return it to us, whereupon it will constitute a binding agreement between us.

Very truly yours,

By UNIVERSITY OF TEXAS PRESS

Accepted and Agreed to:

Date

Home Address

Social Security Number

NOTICE OF CONTRACT SIGNED
University of Texas Press

Author: Purvis Mulch

Contract with (Author/Editor/Translator/Proprietor): _____

Address (an affiliation): _____

Title of work: NO TIME FOR HOUSE PLANTS

Series title and editor: n/a

Copyright by: UT Press

Rights limitations: none

Market: world

Delivery date of MS: August 1, 1976   Length of MS: 170 ms. pp. not including index & illustrations

Illustrations: yes, to be supplied by Press

Index: yes Within 21 days   Author's alterations: none

Subsidy: none

Clauses to be deleted:

Special clauses/Remarks:

Previous Contracts relating to this work (Series/Letter of intent/_____)

Contract with: _____   Contract number:

Royalty terms or fees:

House editor: ITH   Approval: _____ (Director)

Type of Contract:

XX Author
   Translator
   Import
   Proprietor (translation)
   Series
   Revised edition
   Letter of intent
   Other

FAC approval: July 15, 1976
Contract date: (last date on
Contract no.: 0000   contract)

CONTRACT ABSTRACT

Author: Mulch, Purvis

Contract with (Author/Editor/Translator/Proprietor): _____

Address (and affiliation): _____

Title of work: NO TIME FOR HOUSE PLANTS

Series title and editor: n/a

Copyright by: UT Press

Rights limitations: None

Market: world

Delivery date of MS: _____

Illustrations: to be supplied by Press

Index: yes Within 21 days

Subsidy: no

Royalty terms: 5% net receipt proceeds 1-3000
               7 1/2% net rec. proceeds 3001-5000
               10% net receipt proceeds beyond 5000

Advance: no

Author's frees (clothbound/paperback): 10/10

Clauses to be deleted: none

Special clauses/Remarks: none

Previous Contracts relating to this work (Series/Letter of intent/_____)

Contract with: _____   Contract number:

Royalty terms or fees:

House editor: _____

PR 114 rev. 71 5C 11-71

Type of contract:
☒ Author
☐ Translator
☐ Import
☐ Proprietor (translation)
☐ Series
☐ Revised edition
☐ Letter of intent
☐ Other

FAC approval: July 15, 1976
Contract date:
Contract number:

Length of MS: 170 ms. pp., not incl. index and illustrations

Author's alterations: no

Contract number:

Approval: _____

Book Estimate and Release

[X] New Book
[ ] Revision
[ ] Reprint

Author: Mulch, Purvis
Title: NO TIME FOR HOUSE PLANTS
Series: n/a

Editor/Trans.
ISBN (cloth) 0-292-   (paper) 0-292-

Editor's Release

Royalties: 5% net rec. proceeds 1-3000,
7 1/2% net rec. proceeds 3001-5000,
10% net rec. proceeds beyond 5000

Other fees or charges: none   from
Subsidy $: n/a
Series contract no.:
FAC approval: July 15, 1976
Remarks:

Copyright by UT Press
Market: world

Target pub. date (cloth)
(paper)

Editor: ITH   Date: Aug. 1, 1976

No. pages: 128   Size: 6 x 9"   Pub. Date

Marketing Manager: CDS   Date 8/17/76

Sales Release

	Print	Bind	Price	Discount Trade
Cloth	7,500	7,500	6.95	
Paper				

Remarks:

Financial Release and Estimate

	Cloth	Paper
Plant cost	$ 4400	$
Running cost 7500 copies	$ 8875	$
Royalties	$ 2275	$
Less subsidy	$ ---	$
Total cost	$15570	$
Sales revenue	$31275	$ SEE WORKSHEETS
Contribution to operation	$15705	$

No. copies sold		
Mfg. break even	3184	
Total break even	3735	
Net price per copy	$	$
Less mfg. cost per copy	$	$ SEE WORKSHEETS
Less royalty	$	$
Gross margin	$	$
Gross margin %		

Remarks: Due to royalty increases, overall edition return at 50%. Should be safe. Savings ~~A~~composition & illustrations on reprint should cover maximum royalty.
On the terms set forth above this book meets/~~does not meet~~ current financial requirements of the Press

Business Manager: DoB   Date 8/17/76

Director's Release

Remarks:

Approved Director: [signature] Philip Jones   Date 8/23/76

PRICING WORKSHEET

August 4, 1976

	Royalty rate—5% net 1-3000	7½% net 3001-5000	10% net 5001 up	1st Prtg. Total
$6.75				
Gross	$20,250	$13,500	$16,875	$50,625
Discount	40%	40%	40%	40%
Net	$12,150	$ 8,100	$10,125	$30,375
Cost	5,310	3,540	4,425	13,275
Royalty	608	608	1,013	2,229
Revenue	$ 6,232	$ 3,952	$ 4,687	$14,871
				49%
$6.95 ✓				
Gross	$20,850	$13,900	$17,375	$52,125
Discount	40%	40%	40%	40%
Net	$12,510	$ 8,340	$10,425	$31,275
Cost	5,310	3,540	4,425	13,275
Royalty	626	626	1,043	2,295
Revenue	$ 6,574	$ 4,174	$ 4,957	$15,705
				50.2%

# pages	128	128	128	128
per page	4¢	4.5¢	5¢	5.5¢	6¢
list	$5.12	$5.76	$6.40	$7.04	$7.68

unit cost	$1.77	$1.77	$1.77	$1.77
x	4	4½	5	3½
	$7.08	$7.97	$8.85	$6.20

List	$6.95	$6.50	$6.75
Discount	40%	40%	40%
Net	4.17	3.90	4.05
Unit	1.77	1.77	1.77
Royalty 5%	.21	.20	.20
Return	2.19	1.93	2.08
%	53%	49%	51%

Acquisitions / Administration / Texas / 197

4 August 1976

Dear

I am happy to have been chosen as the copy editor for Texas Press for <u>No Time for House Plants</u> and will be starting immediately on the editing of Chapters 2 and 4. I expect to have edited copy ready to send to you for checking and any final revisions by August 9 and will need to have it back again by August 23 if at all possible. Please let me know if there is any reason that you will be unable to check the edited copy at this time.

On preliminary reading the manuscript seems to be in very good shape. The notes will need to be retyped on separate pages from the text, but, since there are so few, we will be able to handle that here at the Press. Also, since there are so few notes, we will be able to set them as footnotes at the bottoms of the pages. (If there were more than one or two notes per chapter, we would put them all at the end of the book, just before the bibliography.)

There is one structural problem that I noticed in looking over the manuscript. The book seems to fall into two rather different parts: a discussion of house plants in general, consisting of Chapters 1-3, and a listing of detailed information on specific kinds of plants and plants for specific purposes, consisting of Chapters 4-7. The first sections of Chapter 4 are actually an introduction to the whole second part. I think it would be helpful to the reader to label the two parts and provide titles for them, in addition to the Chapter titles. The introductory sections now on pages 1-4 of Chapter 4 could then come after the part title for Part 2 but before the Chapter title, thus making it clear that they refer to all types of house plants, not just foliage plants. Chapter 4 would then begin on page IV-5 with the section now headed "Foliage Plants." Does this suggestion seem reasonable to you? What titles would you suggest for the two parts?

I'll hold any further questions until I send the edited copy.

I am enclosing a copy of our <u>Guide for Authors</u> for your information about

---

- 2 -

Texas Press style and policies, as well as our Author Information form. Please fill out and return the Author Information form as soon as possible, as the requested information will be needed by people in several departments of the Press.

With best wishes,

Carolyn Cates Wylie
Associate Editor

CCW:pj

Enclosures

<u>Note</u>:

Normally this first letter to the author would also include a reminder that the contract calls for the author to provide an index at the page-proof stage and a discussion of any obvious problems with the illustrations. If we were going to use the illustrations provided with the copy, we would have to have glossy prints of photos and originals of drawings, rather than xerox copies. The author would be asked to provide a typed list of captions (captions are now on the backs of the Xerox copies) and to number the illustrations for purposes of identification.

The time required for editing and for checking edited copy would of course be greater if the whole book were being edited rather than just two chapters. The suggested dates allow only one week for him to check the copy, plus one week for mailing time both ways (an optimistic estimate).

The <u>Guide for Authors</u> would normally have been sent earlier, by the acquiring editor.

August 9, 1976

Ms. Carolyn Cates Wylie
Associate Editor
UNIVERSITY OF TEXAS PRESS
P.O. Box 7819
Austin, TX 78712

Re: <u>No Time for House Plants</u>

Dear Ms. Wylie:

Thank you for your letter of the 4th, and for the author information form, which I enclose, completed.

Yes, I agree that the structural suggestion you propose will strengthen the manuscript. It seems obvious to me, now, and I thank you for making the suggestion.

The titles I propose for the two sections are "Understanding House Plants" and "Introducing the House Plants."

I look forward to your queries and to working with you in the completion of this project.

Best wishes.

Sincerely,

11 August 1976

Mr.

Dear

The editing took a little longer than I had expected, as a result of interruptions due to other projects, but the edited copy is now ready for you to check. Please read through it carefully and indicate any changes that may be needed. (This review of the edited copy is the last stage at which Texas Press authors can make stylistic or substantive revisions; at the proof stage no changes are allowed except correction of typesetter's errors.)

My questions about the book are written on gummed flyers attached to the pages, and a supply of blank flyers is enclosed for your use in answering the questions and adding any corrections, comments, or suggestions of your own. Please use flyers or separate pages to indicate any disagreement with the editing, add additional material, or make changes of any sort. We ask that you not write or erase anything on the edited pages themselves.

One of the readers had suggested editorial checking of common and scientific plant names in the book. I have edited the spelling of common names in accordance with Webster's Third International Dictionary and have checked the scientific names, insofar as possible, against Standardized Plant Names, ed. Harlan P. Kelsey and William A. Dayton, 2d ed., indicating on flyers where the SPN system disagrees with yours. Please recheck your own sources in these cases.

You will find a few flyers in Chapter 2 which suggest possible illustrations. The Texas Press plans for the book will include a list of illustrations we would use in the two edited Chapters--probably a number of line drawings and perhaps some photographs. Because of the special nature of this project, the matter of illustrations is being handled at a later time than would be normal; ordinarily the number, type, and source of illustrations would be agreed on at the acquisitions stage, although some modifications might be introduced during copy-editing. (Any such changes would require the approval of both the Press and the author.) In this case, you don't need to do anything about my suggestions other than comment on whether you consider them appropriate.

I need to have the edited copy back by August 25--sooner if possible. Please call me if for any reason you will be unable to return it by that date, or if you have any questions about the editing. The editorial department number is 512-471-4278.

The editing has been a very pleasant assignment, and I'll be looking forward to getting the copy back again.

With best wishes,

Carolyn Cates Wylie
Associate Editor

CCW:pj

Enclosures

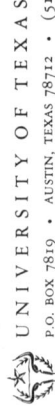

UNIVERSITY OF TEXAS PRESS
P.O. BOX 7819 • AUSTIN, TEXAS 78712 • (512) 471-7233

10 September 1976

Mr.

Dear

Thanks for returning the edited copy so quickly. I'm sorry to be so slow in answering your letter but have been tied up with a couple of urgent projects these past few weeks.

The second edition of Standardized Plant Names was published by the J. Horace McFarland Company of Harrisburg, Virginia, in 1942. The authors (editors?) are Harlan P. Kelsey and William A. Dayton. I don't know whether there is a newer edition that might still be in print. This was the only source I could find in the U.T. Biology Library that had names for a reasonable percentage of the plants in the book. Your own source is probably as good or better, and I haven't made any changes except the ones you authorized on the flyers.

So far there is no definite schedule for the plant project. If it were a regular Texas Press book, it would be in production by now, and I would be telling you when to expect galleys, indexing proofs, etc. But, since we aren't doing the whole book, things are happening somewhat out of the normal order, and in fact the copy is still awaiting a final reading, although I have removed the flyers and made the changes you suggested on them. I'll let you know when there are further developments.

With best wishes,

Carolyn Cates Wylie
Associate Editor

CCW:pj

August 18, 1976

Ms. Carolyn Cates Wylie
Associate Editor
UNIVERSITY OF TEXAS PRESS
Box 7819
Austin, Texas 78712

Dear Ms. Wylie:

Let me congratulate you on a keen bit of editing. I was amazed at the number of errors you picked up along the way, and I do appreciate the structural changes you suggested. I have no doubt that the manuscript is now stronger.

If I have one regret, it is that all my anthropomorphisms have been purged. Malcolm MacDonald plucked most of them during an earlier draft, and now you have flushed out the last remaining ones, poor fellows. I feel that most people who grow plants do impart human characteristics to them; they talk about their plants as if they were friends; they even talk to their plants; I even know one woman who insists that her plants talk back to her, in language that only she understands. With this attitude rampant among growers, I would think that my anthropomorphism friends might find a good home in the pages of a book on house plants. Alors.

I am returning the edited manuscript to you before leaving for a short camping trip to Rock Island, a pinpoint in Lake Michigan/Green Bay where there are no telephones, no TV, and no publishers. I will return on August 25.

Again, thank you for your careful and sympathetic work. I hope to hear from you soon.

Sincerely,

P.S. Can you give me the publisher and (if available) the current price of Standardized Plant Names?

Page 1 (top left):

No Time for Houseplants — 18/22 Goudy Bold clc

Page 2 (top right):

International Standard Book Number 0-292-FANTAS-Y
Library of Congress Catalog Card Number 76-PLANT
Copyright © 1977 by the University of Texas Press
All rights reserved
Printed in the United States of America

11/22 goudy old style
Flush left
line for line
sink to align with first text line

Page 3 (bottom left):

No Time for Houseplants — 18/22 GOUDY BOLD CLC
A Busy Person's Guide to Indoor Gardening — 18/22 GOUDY OLD STYLE CLC
by Purvis Mulch — 18/22 Goudy old style clc
University of Texas Press / Austin & London — 1/22 Goudy old style clc

Page 4 (bottom right):

12

II - 1

CHAPTER 2 — 10 goudy old style italic

Basic Needs of ~~UNDERSTANDING~~ HOUSE PLANTS — 16 goudy old style clc

Flush left

 Every plant has its own preferences and requirements for soil type, light, temperature, ventilation, humidity, and several other factors that are within our power to control, or at least to mitigate. It is vitally important for you, as a busy indoor gardener, to understand the basics of each, since a prior understanding will enable you to avoid much work later on while achieving routine success in growing plants.

 In addition to understanding these basic needs, you will want to know something about pots and other containers, repotting plants, propagation, and a few other matters which, while not vital to immediate success, will help you to gain further enjoyment in raising better plants.

11/11 goudy old style RAGGED RIGHT 14 pi max approx 12 pi min OK to hyphenate

Basic Needs of House Plants

THE BASIC HOUSE PLANT

The major difference between a house plant and an outdoor plant is one of location. All house plants could live and flourish outdoors, in the proper climate. All are derived from forebears which lived, reproduced, and died outdoors, whether on a forest floor in Central Europe or in the bough of a tree in a South American rain forest. Over many centuries of adaptation and evolution, each plant species embraced those characteristics that enabled it to survive; and even today, every house plant carries within its genetic structure the characteristics of its distant progenitors. Thus the Maranta will lose some of its leaves each autumn, even though autumn's weather does not come to the top of the bookshelf where the plant rests, and a cactus, no matter how long it has been fed and watered with unfailing regularity, will continue to hoard food and water within its swollen stems. In plants, old habits may recede, but they are never forgotten.

At no time are these innate plant characteristics more noticeable than during the autumn and winter, when many plants—particularly those from temperate regions—enter a period of dormancy. Then new growth ceases and the plant takes on a listless and washed-out appearance. Other plants, including many of tropical origin, will maintain their bright appearance but will stop growing completely for several months each year, emulating the natural rest periods of their forebears. You will do well to watch for these signs of dormancy and rest and respond to each plant's needs at that time. When any plant enters a dormant or rest period, water should be reduced and fertilizer withheld completely until new growth begins, usually in the late winter or early spring. At that time, water the plant freely and give it normal doses of fertilizer once again, in order to encourage new growth. By your proper treatment of the plant at this time, you will emulate the advent of spring, working with the plant in carrying out its rhythmic cycles.

Some plants also are naturally short-lived and will last no more than a year or two in your home despite your careful attention, because their genetic structure dictates a finite life span. Garden annuals, for instance, will germinate, grow to maturity, flower, produce seeds, and die, all in as little as six months. For this reason, very few annuals are selected as house plants. Although a few short-lived plants are cultivated indoors for their unusual characteristics, such as the Sensitive Plant, which is easily grown from seed, the house plants that have been cultivated over the generations are most often those that will give years of pleasure. Some house plants, in fact, can live to be hundreds of years old.

Still other house plants are attractive when young but grow ungainly or otherwise unattractive when they approach maturity. The only plants of this kind I have chosen for inclusion in this book are those that are very easy to propagate from cuttings, so that the parent plant may be discarded after a year or two, to be replaced by its children.

From the hundreds of thousands of plant species in the world, those traditionally cultivated as house plants are the relatively few that have shown a wide tolerance to conditions of heat, light, moisture, humidity, and ventilation—in other words, those that can withstand a human environment. They are both attractive to the eye and tough. Still, if you are looking for success with house plants—and particularly success without working hard at it—then you should take some time to learn the characteristics of each plant, recognizing its individual needs and fulfilling them to the best of your ability.

HOW A PLANT FEEDS ACTUAL

A plant manufactures nearly all of its food by itself—and not from the "plant food" that you buy for it. Commercial plant food is no more than a combination of certain chemicals (sometimes in an organic base) that are essential to the plant's basic functioning, much as vitamins are essential to human nutrition. But the bulk of a plant's food—the sugar it uses for energy and growth—is manufactured by the plant itself. In the presence of light, the leaves of the plant draw carbon dioxide from the air and water from the roots, converting these into sugar that is then used for energy production or stored for future use.

During this sugar-manufacturing process, known as photosynthesis, several other things happen within the plant. While carbon dioxide is being absorbed, oxygen is being released from the stomata (pores) of the leaf surface. (Plants produce not only all of the world's food but most of its atmospheric oxygen as well.) During darkness hours, the process is reversed; some of the atmosphere's oxygen is recaptured by the plant and used to convert stored sugar to energy for growth. Generally, a plant manufactures growth food during the day and does its actual growing at night.

Often, the plant converts its newly manufactured sugar to starch and stores it, reconverting it to sugar as the need arises. Although the starch can be stored in almost any area of the plant, certain plants have developed specialized storage areas just for this purpose. Cacti and succulents have enlarged stems and leaves for the greatest above-ground storage capacity of any house plant, while other plants have developed underground storage apparatus for this purpose, including bulbs, tubers, corms, and rhizomes. A bulb is simply an enlarged underground bud, such as is found with hyacinths, tulips, and onions. A tuber is nothing more than an enlarged stem (root); a common potato is a tuber; gloxinias, caladiums, dahlias, and many other common plants are grown from tubers.

A corm is the enlarged base of a stem. And a rhizome is simply a laterally growing, enlarged usually underground stem. All are used by the plant for food storage, and all can be used to propagate plants, too.

Water is constantly being drawn up through the plant. As it transpires through the stomata of the leaves, a "pulling" action draws more water up through the roots. The water carries with it mineral salts, including all the elements which the plant needs to carry out its complex chemical processes. The transpiration which takes place in the leaves is similar to perspiration in humans, and it serves a similar purpose to cool the plant. With house plants, it would be difficult for you to notice this cooling effect. But it is readily apparent when a group of large trees carry out the transpiration process. The cool and fresh feeling you enjoy in a thick woods in summer is not primarily the product of the shade itself but of the transpiration of the millions of leaves overhead.

A plant can seldom absorb too much water, since its vessels and cells can accommodate only so much at a given time; however, the overwatering of a plant can exclude oxygen from the root system, causing wilting of the top portion of the plant. If water is withheld, on the other hand, the plant's cells will gradually collapse, causing wilting of the entire plant. All plants do have protective mechanisms that conserve water in times of drought, however, and can withstand a temporary dry spell. Most wilted house plants will quickly spring back to a normal state when water is again provided.

PARTS OF THE PLANT

Stem. The stem serves to support the plant and to contain and direct the vessels that transport water from the roots, and food from the leaves, to every other part of the plant. Most house plants, including Philodendron, Ivy, and Spider Plant, have soft stems. Such plants must either climb or crawl, since their stems are not strong enough to support an upward-growing structure of significant height. Other plants have soft but thick stems that enable them to attain good height, although their stems are apt to be subject to breakage. Woody-stemmed plants, such as the Avocado, Poinsettia, and Boxwood, are far more sturdy and are usually derived from trees or shrubs of the temperate region. Canes are thick stems with hollow or pithy centers. Bamboo is an example of a cane with which we all are familiar; among house plants, Dieffenbachia and Ti Plant are good examples.

Some plants have a distinct main stem, while others send up many stems, none dominant. A side shoot is a smaller stem growing out from the main stem. A petiole is a leaf stalk—the stemlike structure from which a leaf grows. A node is a joint on the main stem from which a leaf or side shoot grows.

Leaf. The major purpose of the leaf is, as mentioned above, to manufacture food for the plant's growth and reproduction. Considering its total mass, the leaf has a remarkably large surface area, ideally designed for the efficient absorption and diffusion of gases through its thousands of stomata.

After the basic functions of the leaf are understood, its proper care is not difficult to appreciate. The stomata must be kept fairly clean, free of dust and oil that might hinder their efficient operation. Leaves must also be given the freest access to light and ventilation, according to the individual preferences of each plant. Never crowd plants to a point where they are competing for light and air.

Roots. Roots serve two main purposes—to anchor the plant in the ground and to supply from the soil water and the mineral salts which accompany water. Bulbs, corms, rhizomes, and tubers serve much the same purposes, as well as acting as food storage areas. Roots, like the above-ground parts of plants, may be pruned without injuring the plant in any way. Roots are often trimmed to prevent a plant from growing too large for the convenience of the grower, just as top growth is cut back. If roots are cut back, however, be certain to cut back top growth to about the same percentage, or the reduced roots may be unable to supply the plant with sufficient amounts of water. The major precaution in caring for roots is, as will be mentioned several times in these pages, to avoid overwatering.

Flowers. The plant's flowers contain its sexual apparatus. Pollination occurs when male pollen is deposited onto female stigmata, thus fertilizing the plant and allowing the formation of seeds. The fruit of any plant is, in reality, the ovary, which swells to protect the seeds. In nature, most plants produce flowers. But only a small percentage of house plants which in this book are listed as flowering house plants can be depended upon to produce, under home conditions, blossoms of sufficient size, profusion, and beauty to warrant attention. The plants which are grown for their attractive foliage often cannot produce flowers indoors because of insufficient light or because of a pollination failure. In nature, pollen is transferred either by insects or wind, both of which are lacking in the home. Where indoor pollination is essential, it can be accomplished by transferring the pollen from one flower to another, using a soft camel's-hair brush. This process is described fully in most books devoted to flowering house plants.

SOIL

Since the house plant you bring home from the shop will already be rooted in soil (unless you are growing a plant from seed), you might wonder why you have to consider this need at all. The answer is that your house plant will,

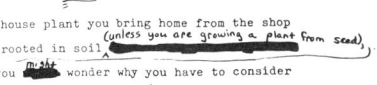

Editorial / Texas / 203

II-2

assuming hoped-for longevity, someday need repotting, and you will want to provide it with a potting mixture that will serve its special needs. You might even wish to propagate some of your favorite house plants at some later time, to share with friends and to give as gifts. In any case, a basic knowledge of potting mixtures and soils is essential to a complete understanding of all your plants.

Two simple definitions are in order here, to avoid any confusion later on. <u>Soil</u>, when mentioned here, refers to garden loam, that combination of mineral matter, organic matter, air, and water commonly found outside, in your garden or under your lawn. A <u>potting mixture</u> is soil with the addition of other materials, such as sand, compost, peat moss, limestone, and bone meal, that together form an ideal environment for the roots of your house plants.

The easiest way to assure your plants of a perfect loam is to buy packaged sterile potting soil from your garden or flower shop. This soil will have not only the proper texture, but will also be free of disease organisms, insects (some too small to be seen), and weed seeds. To this loam you will add the other ingredients which together will form an ideal potting mixture. You may also buy packaged potting mixture at the store, but if you do, read the package carefully to ascertain the ingredients, making sure that the mixture is right for your plants.

It is, of course, far less expensive to make your own potting mixture from your own garden loam (free), sand (free or inexpensive), and small amounts of purchased ingredients. If you choose this route, then it is important that you be able to make at least a cursory analysis of the garden loam that will form the basis of the potting mixture. Texture is important. A heavy clay soil will hold water for too long a time, encouraging disease and root rot, and it will bake cement-hard when dry. On the other hand, a coarse sand will not hold water well, nor will it hold nutrients long enough for the plant's roots to absorb them. Strive, then, for a happy medium—a good loam, containing both clay and sand, which will hold both water and nutrients, yet offer adequate drainage.

II - 2a

To this basic loam, one usually add one or more other materials—peat moss, to increase water-holding capacity and to add organic matter; compost, for organic matter and nutrients; sand, to open up the soil to air; some form of supplemental mineral fertilizer, usually bone meal and lime (if the soil is overly acid). Chemical fertilizer can be used, although it is not necessary to add it to the potting mixture, since the other ingredients will supply all the nutrients the plant can use for several months.

<u>ACIDITY/ALKALINITY</u>

A discussion of soils and potting mixtures would not be complete without some mention of acidity and alkalinity and of the pH scale, which is the scientific measure for acidity and alkalinity. The midpoint on the pH scale is 7. A soil with a pH of 7 is neutral—neither acid nor alkaline. Numbers above 7 indicate an alkaline soil; those under 7, an acid soil. Most house plants, like most garden plants, will do best in a slightly acid soil (a pH of 6.0 to 7.0).

In this book, all the house plants listed will do well in this normal range, unless special notations to the contrary are made.

If you have cause to worry about your soil's pH, or are simply curious, call your county agricultural agent and ask for directions on having a pH test made. The cost will be nominal. Any soil may be made more acid with the addition of peat moss, or less acid with the addition of ground limestone.

II - 3

POTTING MIXTURES

There are as many different basic potting mixtures as there are plant experts—probably more. Perhaps the most common one, however (and one which can be trusted), calls for two parts loam, one part finely screened compost (or a mixture of peat moss and compost), and one part builder's sand (not sea sand). To this is added a small amount of bone meal (about one teaspoon for a five-inch pot) and, unless the soil is alkaline, a pinch of ground limestone. Other recommendations call for more of one ingredient and less of another. Do a little experimenting of your own. After a while, you will doubtless come upon your own favorite mixture, which you can recommend to others.

And now that you have the basic formula well in mind, we will consider the exceptions:

1. Acid-loving plants such as azaleas, camellias, gardenias, and heathers should have no lime. In fact, they should have some form of acid organic matter—acid peat moss or oak leafmold.

2. Foliage plants need somewhat more compost in the mixture, although half of the total mixture should be comprised of peat moss (which will not overstimulate the plant).

3. Fast-growing and hungry plants need more bone meal and often more lime, since they use them up quickly.

4. Some plants, such as cacti and succulents, have very special soil requirements. these are mentioned later in the discussions of individual plants.

II - 4

NUTRIENT MAINTENANCE

The mineral nutrients contained in any fresh potting soil or mixture, whether it is homemade or a sterilized commercial brand, should be sufficient for your plant's needs for the first four to six months. After that, you should begin to replenish those nutrients on a regular and carefully measured basis.

All plants need substantial amounts of three elements—nitrogen (N), phosphate (P_2O_5), and potash (K_2O), and lesser amounts of a dozen or more others, called "trace minerals" or "trace elements." In grower's language, the three major elements are referred to as N, P, and K, and on the label of any commercial fertilizer the percentages of each are given in N-P-K order. A 5-10-5 fertilizer, for instance, will contain 5 percent nitrogen, 10 percent phosphate, and 5 percent potash. A "balanced" fertilizer contains a balance of all three in the amounts needed for the proper growth of most plants. The fertilizer may be either a chemical or an organic preparation, according to your preference. The chemical ones are quick-acting, easy to use, and tidy. Organic fertilizers, on the other hand, are slow to release their nutrients, providing a gentle and steady supply. Chemical mixtures come in liquid, tablet, and even spray form (the last applied directly on the foliage). Organic fertilizers may be purchased commercially in balanced formulas (fish emulsion, made from fish wastes, is a popular one for house-plant use) or may be made at home from a combination of ingredients. Blood meal is a good

II - 4a

choice for supplying substantial amounts of nitrogen (its NPK formula is 15.00-1.30-0.70), while bone meal (4.00-21.00-0.20) is good for phosphate, and wood ashes (0.00-1.50-7.00) are high in potash content. A combination of one part blood meal, one part bone meal, and two parts wood ashes will make a 5-6-4 formula, which is a good one for house plants.

How often should plants be fertilized? There is wide disagreement on this point, some experts believing in weekly feedings of full strength (the dosage recommended on the label), others fertilizing no more than once a month, and even less often during the winter. In the end, you will probably have to come to your own policy by way of experimentation. In the beginning, however, it is better to err on the conservative side, since far more plants have been injured from overfertilization than from nutrient starvation. If you use a commercial chemical or organic formula, I suggest that you feed your plants as often as recommended on the label, but only half the recommended dosage. (Manufacturers tend to overstate the need for their product.) If the plant shows a spurt of active growth in late winter or early spring, increase the dosage to the manufacturer's recommendation. During a dormant or rest period, withhold fertilizer entirely. If you are using a home-made organic fertilizer, such as the one suggested above, use it sparingly at first. A level teaspoon of the blood meal-bone meal-wood ash formula, applied monthly, should be plenty for a plant in a five-inch pot. Or you may use some of the mixture to fill a bottle

II - 4b

about one-fourth full, add water to the top of the bottle, and use the resulting "tea" to water your house plants. A mild tea solution, applied weekly, will give all your plants a continuing and gentle supply of the essential nutrients.

Last, remember never to apply a chemical fertilizer if the soil is dry. The quick action of the chemicals can easily injure the roots.

II - 5

CONTAINERS

Nearly any container that offers adequate drainage and doesn't leak is suitable for house plants. After checking a container for leakage, consider drainage carefully. If the container has a hole in its bottom, there is no problem. If not, then you should put coarse gravel or broken crockery in the bottom of the container to fill one-fourth to one-fifth of its depth. In this way, you will avoid the liklihood of waterlogging your plants and encouraging root rot.

The traditional terra cotta clay pot offers definite advantages. It is inexpensive, easily replaced, and most important, allows air to be exchanged through its porous walls. This same porosity, however, allows water to evaporate fairly quickly, necessitating frequent watering. If a plant's location makes it awkward to water, you will save yourself some effort by choosing a glazed or otherwise impervious container.

Some metal containers, notably copper, may produce adverse chemical reactions with soil and fertilizer elements, injuring plants therein. Copper planters, however, are usually lacquered to prevent such reactions.

Wooden tubs and boxes are ideal for very large house plants. You can make any wooden container watertight by lining it with

II - 6

several sheets of heavy-gauge plastic or, for permanent results, sheet metal.

If you want the best advantages of both a terra cotta pot and a decorative container, place the former inside the latter, leaving a quarter inch or more of space for air circulation around the walls of the inner pot. Sometimes sphagnum moss is inserted here to help preserve moisture. A base of gravel in the decorative pot can provide good drainage while lifting the inner pot to the level of the outer container.

Plastic containers are ideal for house plants. They do not allow air exchange through their walls, but, for this reason, they reduce the need for watering. Their light weight also suits them for hanging.

Nearly any container can be used for hanging plants, if you consider possible drainage problems. A cork can stop up a drainage hole to prevent floor and furniture damage, but then the advantage of the drain will be lost. Those hanging plastic pots that include a drip pan are ideal. You might also think of wire baskets, which are to be lined with sphagnum moss and then filled with the potting mixture. If possible, gather live sphagnum moss in a nearby bog and use that. It will continue to thrive in its natural green state, in sharp contrast to the dead, brown moss that your florist offers.

WATERING

More house plants are killed by overwatering than by any other cause. This killing with kindness can be avoided, if you learn to understand just when your plants need water and when they *should* be left alone.

The best rule of thumb is that a plant should be watered when the soil surface is dry to the touch. Then, water thoroughly, either by adding water to the soil surface or by immersing the entire pot in a larger container of water.

Certain plants, such as African violets and other woodsy varieties, need more water than most, while cacti and succulents need far less than the average. Aside from the specific preferences of individual varieties, there are many conditions which call for more or less water, as indicated in Table 1.

Immersion is the best method of watering because it is the surest. The soil in any pot *may* tend to form water channels which, upon receiving water from the surface, will rush it to

Table 1. WATERING NEEDS OF PLANTS UNDER VARIOUS CONDITIONS

Plants will need more water when:	Plants will need less water when:
They are in a period of active growth.	They are in a period of rest (usually during winter).
They are in bright light.	They are in dim light or under artificial light.
Room humidity is low.	Room humidity is high.
Room temperature is high.	Room temperature is under 70°.
They are in small pots.	They are in large pots.
They are in clay pots or wire baskets.	They are in nonporous pots.
They are fast-growing varieties.	They are slow-growing varieties.
They are planted in sandy soil.	They are planted in heavy soil.
They are in flower or about to go into flower.	

the bottom of the pot and out the drainage hole, leaving large parts of the soil bone-dry. Moreover, some potting soil mixtures will shrink when drying, leaving many spaces along the wall of the pot where water can run past. Immersion is the one sure way to soak the soil thoroughly, (provided that the pot is porous). You can do it in any large container, or even in a sink or bathtub. Set the pots in the water, but do not let the water flow over the lips of the pots. After the surface of the potting mixture has become moist— ten to thirty minutes—remove the pot, drain off any excess water, and put it back in its place. Never go out for the afternoon, leaving your plants standing in water.

If you water from the top, remember to remove any excess water from the saucer. Plants should never be allowed to stand in water for fear of root rot. In time, you should learn to give each plant just enough water to soak it thoroughly, with very little excess drainage.

Some other watering tips:

1. Do not get water into the crown of any plant (the portion where stem and roots meet, usually at the soil surface) for this will encourage decay.

2. Never use very cold water, especially for tropical plants. Keep an open jar of water at room temperature for your house plants. Not only will the proper temperature be assured, but some of the chemicals in the water will have dissipated by the time it is given to plants.

3. Water which is artificially softened may be detrimental to plant growth. If you can, use rainwater or

water that has not been softened. Fluorine and chlorine, on the other hand, are not thought to pose any problems.

4. If your water is especially hard, lime salts may cause trouble with such acid-loving plants as Orchids, Primulas, Rhododendrons, Azaleas, and other plants whose natural soil is woodsy (indicating a high organic content) and acid. Either choose plants which prefer a more neutral range in the pH scale, or plan to collect rainwater for your calcifuges (lime-haters).

HUMIDITY

Much trouble with house plants, especially in winter in the northern states, can be traced to insufficient moisture in the air. Except for the cacti and succulents, nearly all house plants thrive best in a relative humidity of between 60 and 80 percent, while that of most heated homes in winter is often considerably under 40 percent. In much of the West, the humidity is constantly lower than the range best for house plants. Where the problem is severe, it must be solved before general success with house plants can be expected.

There are several ways to add moisture to the air in your home. The more expensive include the adding of a humidifying device to your furnace, if you live in a house, or installing an electric humidifier. This step will benefit not only the plants but everyone living in the house as well. But there are less expensive ways of bringing moisture to your plants:

1. _The pebble tray._ Line the bottom of a waterproof tray with decorative pebbles and arrange your plants, in pots, on top of the pebbles. Keep the tray filled with water, being sure only to avoid blocking the pots' drainage holes. Change the water weekly to keep it fresh.

2. _Decorative containers._ If you keep a clay pot inside a decorative container (double-potting), keep a pool of water in the bottom of the larger vessel. Again, provide some means of support for the clay pot so that it is not resting in water at any time.

3. _Standing water devices._ Water left standing in a room will gradually evaporate, meaning that the lost moisture is added to the room atmosphere. If your home is particularly dry during cold weather, take the trouble to place pans of water on the tops of radiators or on stands placed above heat registers; grow ivy, philodendron, or wandering Jew in containers of water; maintain an aquarium; rotate plants so that each can spend an afternoon in the bathroom each week, where the air is humid. Change standing water weekly.

4. _Bathing and showering._ Most house plants will respond favorably to a brief shower every day, or as often as you can manage to provide the treat. Little brass-plated atomizers are ubiquitous in mail-order catalogs, but more dependable (albeit less decorative) are the plastic sprayers available in art-supply stores, garden shops, and many supermarkets. These hold perhaps a pint of water, and they feature an adjustable shower head, affording an entire range of water action from a sharp jet to a fine mist. Your plants, of course, should have

the fine mist. Remember to fill the container after every use, so that the next day's spray will be at room temperature. Remember also to avoid spraying plants which have been standing in direct sunlight (the shock is great) and those which have been subjected to very cool temperatures (perhaps spending the autumn on a cold sunporch).

Rubber plants and others with large leaves should be cleaned thoroughly and gently with a damp cloth about once a week. The leaf polish sold commercially is permissible, if you want really stunning looking large-leafed plants, which can block the leaf pores and impede respiration, but never use oil of any kind. Ivies and other rugged small-leafed plants can be held under the gentle stream of a faucet for their weekly bath.

5. _Grouping._ Plants will maintain a moist surrounding air (leaves not touching) with greater facility if they are grouped together, rather than separated. During the coldest part of winter, you might want to group most plants on a pebble tray under a light window, to take advantage of maximum light and greatest humidity.

VENTILATION

Plants, like people, benefit from fresh air. Like people, also, they react badly to drastic changes in air movement and temperature. Provide adequate ventilation for your house plants, but do not subject them to sharp winds, winter draughts, or heat arising directly from a radiator. Think of your own comfort, in this respect, and you will

know what will be best for your plants. If, in autumn, you bring your plants in from a summer outdoors, help them to adjust to indoor conditions gradually by placing them by an open window for the first several days. Gradually lower the window day by day, keeping a watchful eye on night temperatures. Reverse the process in spring.

TEMPERATURE

The temperature requirements of house plants vary widely, according to the natural habitats of their forebears and also according to other conditions. Many cool-weather plants prefer a range of 50°-60° F. and cannot tolerate temperatures above 70° while tropicals may thrive in a moist 70°-75°. Know the temperature preferences of any house plant before you adopt it, and then place it in the best possible temperature location in your home. You may find, for instance, that a cool-loving aspidistra will do best in a back bedroom, while tropical plants thrive happily next to (but not above) a living-room heat vent. The temperature needs of plants are included in their descriptions throughout this book. Heed them well, make liberal use of an indoor thermometer, and do not be afraid to experiment by placing different plants in different locations for a week at a time. You may notice in your plants distinct preferences for particular locations throughout the house, and their preferences will not always corroborate expert advice.

LIGHT

Light and temperature needs are closely related. In their native surroundings, many tropical plants can thrive at a high temperature because they receive long hours of sunlight. Indoors, especially during winter's short days, they cannot receive enough light to enable them to stand high house temperatures.

Except for cacti and succulents, house plants should not be placed on windowsills where they will receive long periods of direct sunlight. Simply place a thermometer in this position and you will soon see that your plants can be literally cooked to death, even in the dead of a Minnesota winter. Strive, instead, for a bright spot with a few hours of filtered sunlight each day, at least for most plants.

Individual varieties vary, of course, in their light needs, and these needs are specified in the descriptions of individual plants in these pages. Again, do not be afraid to experiment with different locations for different plants. I have a _Philodendron scandens_, one of the most popular and most common of all house plants, which has thrived for years in a dim corner, although it is supposed to require a bright spot out of direct sun. Plants sometimes exhibit unmistakable individual characteristics which we have yet to understand.

PRUNING AND TRAINING

Some plants should be pruned and pinched back occasionally, in order to encourage bushy and stocky growth, while trailing plants such as philodendrons and ivies need gentle support to guide them into pleasing growth patterns.

Many people hesitate to prune at all, feeling somehow that they are hurting the plant or interfering with its natural development. Actually, plants will respond to judicious pruning with new and vigorous growth. Plants such as geraniums, coleus, and begonias should be pinched back routinely, in order to encourage lateral growth. The process is quite simple: with a sharp knife, cut back perhaps one-half inch of the central growing tip. The plant should respond by sending out side shoots below the central tip, and the main stem of the plant should then become thicker and sturdier. If this is done several times a year, the plant should eventually attain the vigorous and well-rounded form you desire. Without this pruning, it might grow "leggy" with a weak main stem, requiring some kind of support. Many older plants, as well, will benefit from occasional pinching back or shearing of outside growth. Do not, however, prune or pinch back African violets, gloxinias, flowering bulbs, ferns, or cyclamen.

Vines and trailing plants often need some kind of support, unless you prefer to let them cascade from a hanging basket. The usual practice is to sink a slab of cork or tree bark into a pot, then to train the vines of the plant to grow around and up the support, eventually concealing it.

Another effective device is the sphagnum-moss cylinder. Pack the moss fairly tightly around a stake and secure it in a cylinder of the proper size for the pot. The cylinder can be made easily from either chicken wire or green plastic material made for this purpose. If you wish, sink a small clay pot into the top of the cylinder, so that you can add water regularly to keep the moss damp. (Otherwise, the moss will require regular spraying.) Tie the vines gently to the cylinder as they grow; eventually, philodendrons and similar plants will anchor themselves to the moss with their aerial rootlets, making other support unnecessary.

REPOTTING

The temptation to repot plants too often is a strong one and should be resisted with strong will. A plant needs repotting only when it has become potbound—when filled the entire container and are creeping out of the drainage hole. Indeed, some plants seem to thrive best when slightly potbound (these will be indicated in the section on individual plants.) When repotting is indicated, choose a new pot only one size larger than the old, for a house plant will not do well in a pot that is too large. If the larger pot has been used before, scrub it thoroughly to remove any possibility of disease. Soak new clay pots for a few hours in water so that they become saturated. Then, with ample potting soil, gravel, and a tongue depressor or similar wood tool, set to work.

To remove the plant from its old pot, slide your hand over the top of the pot, index and second fingers cradling the plant stem. Turn the pot upside down, thus supported, and tap the lip of the pot sharply on the edge of a bench or table. After a few taps the entire soil ball, ringed with plant roots, should come out easily, in one neat piece. Set it aside. Take the larger pot and line the bottom with a layer of coarse gravel or broken crockery, to provide good drainage. Then add potting soil on top of the gravel, placing the plant and soil ball on top of the new soil several times in order to see when it has reached the proper depth. (The top of the soil should be about one-half inch below the lip of the new pot, in a four-inch pot, and one inch below the lip in an eight-inch pot, to leave room for watering.) When enough soil has been added to raise the plant to its proper height, center it well and begin to pack soil around the sides of the soil ball, using the tongue depressor. Take your time in doing this, for it is the most crucial part of the entire operation. It is important to pack the soil firmly, so that no air spaces are left when the job is finished. Roots cannot draw nutrients in air spaces and many of them will thus be injured or die, affecting the health of the entire plant. When the new soil is finally brought up to a level even with the top of the soil ball, the job is finished. You might want to add just a little soil over the top of the root ball, especially if roots have been forced up to the soil surface, but don't add any more than you must, for you do not want to change the planting depth of the plant. Repotting is shock enough, for many plants, without altering the planting depth. Water the plant thoroughly and return to its usual location.

How often should you repot? Obviously, only as each plant indicates a need. For slow-growers, this might be once every two or three years; a mature slow-grower may go for many years without repotting, if new growth is cut back. For fast-growing and very young plants, repotting may be needed once or twice a year for the first several years. Plants that do not need repotting after one year should have the top one-half to one inch of soil replaced annually, to keep the soil fresh.

PROPAGATION

There will come a time when you will want to start your own house plants, to increase your own plant population, to use as personal gifts for friends and family, to replace a short-lived plant or one that has become ungainly with age. The propagation of most house plants is not a difficult task, and it is most rewarding.

There are two general methods of doing the job: by the collecting and planting of seeds, and by the cutting and rooting of plant parts—stems, leaves, or underground structures. The first way (sexual reproduction) is often difficult, always time-consuming, and likely to produce unsatisfactory results. Propagation from seed is ideal for garden annuals, but not for most house plants. Special equipment is required, and daily attention is essential, making the activity an unlikely one for anyone who professes "no time for house plants." In addition, the seeds from hybrid plants are likely to produce plants vastly inferior to the parent plant. (A hybrid is any plant produced by cross-pollinating two plants of different species or genera.) Last, many house plants do not flower and produce seeds under home conditions, requiring the house-plant gardener to purchase seeds from specialty houses. The one advantage of growing house plants from seed is that you can create new hybrids by the cross-pollination of plants. The excitement of this activity creates a fascinating hobby for some house-plant enthusiasts but is unlikely to appeal to those who cannot afford to devote significant amounts of spare time to the activity.

Far more simple, and yielding far more reliable results, is the propagation of plants by the cutting and rooting of plant parts. Less care is required, and the offspring will look just like the parent, even when the parent is a hybrid.

Plants may be propagated at any time of year, although it is best to avoid tackling the job when the plant is going into a dormant period. In early spring, just before active growth begins, is perhaps the ideal time.

<u>Cuttings.</u> The most common method of propagating is by the taking of stem cuttings, which are then rooted in either water or some sterile rooting medium such as perlite, vermiculite, or sand. If you have never rooted a cutting before, then begin with African violets, coleus, Dracaena, fuchsia, gardenias, geraniums, Impatiens, ivy, Philodendron, wandering Jew, or wax begonia. These are the easiest, because all can be rooted in water. Simply take a cutting containing four to six leaves, from an actively growing tip of the plant, severing the stem cleanly just below a joint with a clean razor blade. Place the cutting (you may take several at a time, if you wish) so that the bottom portion is submerged in water in a colored or clear bottle is fine, remembering only to keep the leaves above water. (Cut off the bottom leaf or two, if necessary, to get more of the stem into the water; about a third of the entire length should be in water.) Place the container in diffused light, not direct sun, and wait until vigorous roots appear. When they have, the little plants may be removed from the water and potted in a small pot, using the potting mixture recommended earlier in this chapter. Be sure to pack the potting mixture firmly around the roots of the plant, to avoid any air spaces, and to water thoroughly afterwards.

Stem cuttings which cannot be rooted in water are rooted in perlite, vermiculite (both available wherever house-plant supplies are sold), or builder's sand.

(You may by now be wondering why, throughout this book, builder's sand is recommended for potting purposes, while sea sand is cautioned against. The reason is that builder's sand, which comes from inland locations, has irregular and sharp surfaces, allowing good soil drainage. Sea sand, having been washed smooth over the years, packs too snugly and leads to a compacted soil and resultant drainage problems.)

Run in as for rooting in water. The process is basically the same. The cuttings are inserted in the moist medium, which may be contained in a small clay pot or, for larger numbers of cuttings, a shallow plastic tray. The planted container is then placed in a plastic bag which is tied shut (the zip kind, used for food storage, is convenient, effective, and reusable) and placed in diffused light at a temperature of 65° to 70°F. You can tell whether the cuttings have developed roots by testing them weekly. Open the bag and pull gently on a plant. If it moves easily, then the roots have not yet formed; if it resists your gentle tug fairly well, however, then the roots probably are mature enough to stand repotting. The process can take as little as two weeks or as long as several months, depending upon the variety of the plant and the size of the cutting. When the roots are strong and vigorous, pot the plant in a small pot and treat it as you would any other plant.

Some plants which produce canes, including Chinese evergreen, Dracaena, and Dieffenbachia can be propagated by taking cuttings of the canes, which have discernible "eyes." Press each cane section (containing one eye) into moist sphagnum moss, secure it with clothes pins at each end so that it does not pop up, seal it in a plastic bag, and put it in a cool place out of direct sun. In six to eight weeks, move it into a warm place (70° N 90° E), still out of direct sun. Soon, a shoot will grow from the eye. When the shoot has attained a respectable size, the cane may be cut close to the shoot on both sides, and the new plant may be lifted from the moss and potted.

Plants that have fleshy leaves are best propagated by taking leaf or leaf-petiole cuttings. Leaf cuttings work well when large and mature leaves are available. Cut the leaf close to the stem of the parent plant, using a razor blade for a clean cut without crushing the cells. The leaf may then be cut horizontally into smaller sections, so that the main vein runs from top to bottom along the center of the leaf section. (Long-leafed plants such as Sansevieria and Streptocarpus may be cut into as many as ten sections, each of which will produce an individual plant.) Each leaf section is then sunk halfway into the rooting medium, after which the process is the same as that described for stem cuttings.

Smaller leaves may be rooted by taking leaf-petiole cuttings. Cut one leaf stem close to the main stalk and sink the stem into the rooting medium, so that the leaf nearly (but not quite) touches the medium. African violets, begonias, snake plant, piggyback plant, and Peperomia respond well to leaf-petiole cuttings.

<u>Underground division.</u> Older plants which have thick main roots can be propagated by taking root cuttings. This is usually done when the plant is being repotted. Cut about one inch of the main root, making sure that it has at least one eye. Cover this with one-half inch of rooting medium and treat it as you would any other cutting.

Thick-rooted perennials may be propagated by the process of root division, in which the root mass is simply forced apart into two or more clumps, each of which is then repotted.

Plants which produce rhizomes may be propagated by dividing the rhizome so that one leaf bud is contained on each piece and planting the section under one-half inch of rooting medium. Plants which produce potato-like tubers can be propagated by cutting the tubers apart with a sharp knife, keeping one eye to each section, and planting the sections in the rooting medium just as one would plant potatoes in the open field.

Some plants produce <u>suckers</u>, small plants that grow up from an underground stem or root. These may be separated from the parent plant and potted in soil immediately.

Anyone who has seen strawberries grow outdoors knows what <u>runners</u> are — the baby plants that grow from a long stem coming from the base of the parent plant. Among house plants, Boston fern and spider plant both produce runners, which can be severed from the parent and started in a rooting medium.

Other methods of underground division include the separation and replanting of baby bulbs and corms which are produced by the mother bulb or corm.

<u>Air layering.</u> A fairly simple (and most impressive) way of propagating larger or woody-stemmed plants is by air layering. Here, a sharp cut is made into a stem, perhaps a third of the way in, and a toothpick is placed in the cut horizontally, to keep it open. That stem section is then wrapped with moist sphagnum moss and covered with clear plastic, tied top and bottom so that moisture cannot escape. Roots will form from the incision and will soon show through the plastic. When a fair number of them have appeared, cut the stem below the plastic wrap, remove both plastic and moss, and pot the new plant immediately in potting soil.

As you might imagine, the propagation of plants can often be integrated with the cutting back, pruning, and shaping of older plants. It seems a shame to throw away plant parts when they can be used to produce more plants, and it is precisely this attitude of thrift which, if not controlled, can lead to a frightening multiplication of house plants. The answer, of course, is to share plants with friends, thus encouraging still more enthusiasts and still more house plants.

[Chapter 3 would come here]

Part Two. Introducing the House Plants

18 Goudy Old Style
cle

Intro to 2nd half of book

IV - 1

The number and variety of house plants available for your consideration is staggering. For every combination of conditions your home can offer, including heat, light, and humidity, there are literally thousands of suitable house-plant varieties, offering a virtually limitless selection of sizes, forms, colors, patterns and textures, growth patterns, and flowering habits. You have only to survey the conditions that your home can offer, and then make your plant selections, within those limits, to suit your own tastes.

The house plants selected for inclusion in this book are only representative of far greater numbers. I have included nearly all of the most common plants, and I have tried to avoid those difficult to grow. All the old favorites are here, as well as some newer varieties and unusual plants which can add zest to your collection.

IV - 2

The plants have been divided into three main groups: foliage plants, cacti and other succulents, and flowering plants. Within each group, individual plants are listed alphabetically by their common names, followed by (in parentheses) their scientific (or Latin) designations. The scientific name usually comprises both the genus and species names. For example, the scientific name for the common boxwood is Buxus (the genus) sempervirens (the species). After a genus name is introduced, it is thereafter abbreviated. Thus Buxus sempervirens, if mentioned again, becomes B. sempervirens. there may be a third part to the scientific name which designates a further subdivision of the species, usually called a subspecies or a variety. The popular Japanese boxwood, for example, is B. microphylla japonica.

IV - 2a

In addition, some breeders have given their creations patented variety names, such as English ivy 'Pixie'; in this book, all such names will be indicated by single quotes.

Although I have attempted to maintain an informal tone in these pages by using common names whenever possible, the scientific nomenclature has obvious benefits. Many species are known by different common names in different parts of the country; different species of a genus are often called by a single common name; and a single common name may be applied even to varieties of completely different genera. The only sure way to identify any plant, then, is by referring to its scientific name.

For each plant listed, you will find information on its individual preferences for growing temperature, light, soil moisture and air humidity, and window placement.

IV-3

Please remember that these are rough guides and not inflexible demands. Many plants have a wide range of tolerance and will thrive in a variety of conditions. Many plants which are said to prefer an east window will do just as well in a shaded south or a west location. Do not hesitate to try a plant of your liking because you cannot provide its exact needs—but neither should you attempt a plant if you can provide none of them. Experimentation is both valuable and enjoyable.

WHERE TO BUY HOUSE PLANTS

It is best to buy house plants from growers who know their own plants and who will be able to offer sound advice on their culture. If there is no grower in your area, the next best source is your local flower shop or nursery center. Whichever place you choose, talk to the owner or the owner's representative about house plants. Ask for precise identification of a plant that interests you. Ask for specifications of the plant's needs for light, soil, temperature, and humidity. Ask how large the plant is apt to become and whether or not it produces flowers, even if you know the answers to these questions. If it becomes apparent that the person you are talking to doesn't know very much about the plant or about house plants in general, then ask to talk to someone who can answer your questions in greater detail, or seek another source.

Plants found in supermarkets and discount houses are usually not bad, although many, that you see flowering in the store may have been grown quickly and forced into bloom under ideal green-

IV-4

house conditions that you cannot hope to match in your home, and large plants offered at bargain prices are often severely underrooted. However, most plants offered by these sources are likely to be common varieties that are quite tolerant of adverse conditions. It is hard to go wrong with grape ivy or a climbing philodendron.

Plants stored outside at garden centers or shopping centers may carry insects or disease, particularly if they are resting close to flats of outdoor vegetable or flower seedlings. Examine them closely before purchasing, and isolate them for one or two weeks at home before putting them with other house plants.

Wherever you buy your plants, look for young and sturdy specimens with rich color and a generally healthy appearance. Examine particularly carefully large and mature plants which carry high price tags. These may have been growing for too long a time in ideal conditions. Generally, you will have better luck with a younger plant, and you will have the added pleasure of bringing it along to maturity in your own home.

IV-5

Chapter 4: FOLIAGE PLANTS

In this chapter, we will survey many of the house plants grown primarily for their foliage. Some of them, under favorable conditions, will flower from time to time, although few should be selected for their flowering abilities. Nearly all of these plants are fairly easy to grow and maintain, giving even the beginner a wide variety of plants from which to choose.

The plants are listed in alphabetical order, according to their common or popular names. If there is no popular name for a plant, or if there are two or more none dominant, the plant is listed by its scientific or Latin name. The index, which includes both common and scientific names, provides a convenient means of cross-checking names.

The special symbols accompanying each plant name will provide a quick and convenient guide to that plant's requirements. Remember, however, that these are guides and not sharp demands. Many of these plants are tolerant by nature, will take to an east window as well as a west window, and can tolerate some direct sunlight even if none is recommended. Most crucial, perhaps, are the guides to humidity and moisture, since overwatering is one thing that virtually no plant will tolerate.

[Table 2 here]

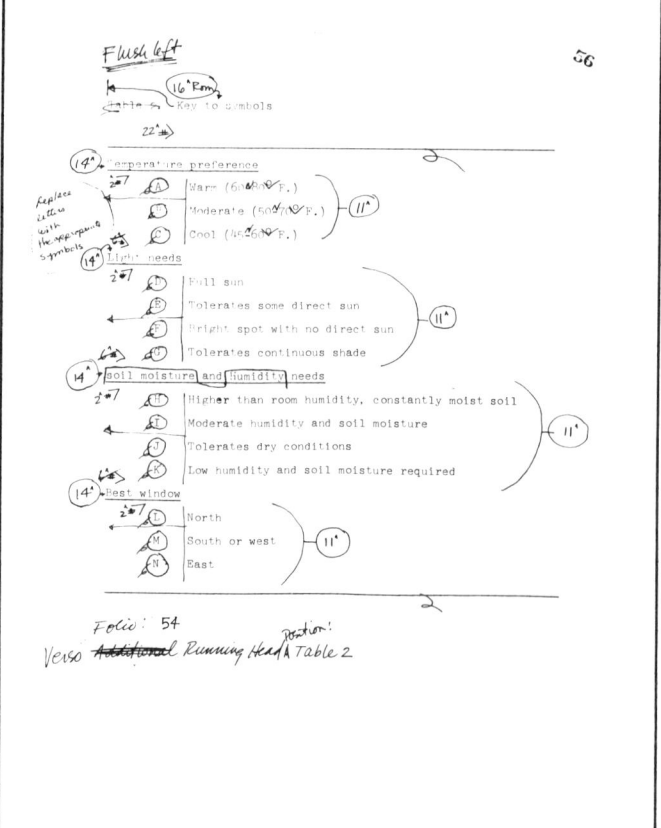

IV-6

African Boxwood (*Myrsine africana*)
A slow-growing plant with red stems, but otherwise similar to regular Boxwood (q.v.). Many people think it is even more graceful. African Boxwood is a good plant for terrariums, if the atmosphere is not too hot.

Aluminum plant. See Pilea.

Aralia (*Fatsia japonica*)
Sometimes sold as *Aralia sieboldii*. Beautiful bright green, leathery, maple-like leaves highlight this cheerful plant. In appearance, it is similar to the castor-oil plant, and in fact is sometimes called false castor-oil plant. It thrives in a cool spot. Aralia can easily grow leggy and so should be pruned annually in order to encourage it into bushy growth. It will attain a height of four feet at maturity.

F. japonica crosses with ivy (*Hedera*) to form a striking hybrid. *Fatshedera lizei*, a climbing plant with maple-shaped leaves, which is tolerant of adverse conditions.

There is also a plant called false Aralia (*Dizygotheca elegantissima*), which has graceful and feathery foliage. It bears no resemblance to the true Aralia and is difficult to grow.

Artillery plant. See Pilea.

Asparagus
There are three kinds of Asparagus suitable for growing as house plants. Fern Asparagus (*A. plumosus*), with slender, needle-like, dark green leaves, forming a feathery green appearance; *A. asparagoides* (smilax), a trailer; and *A. sprengeri* (emerald feather), a climber, which has thicker, yellow-green leaves and drooping stems. The latter makes a good

IV-7

plant for hanging baskets and produces red berries at Christmastime. These plants like some sun in the summer and full sun in the winter and can grow to a height of about two feet.

Aspidistra. See Cast-Iron plant.

Australian Laurel (*Pittosporum tobira*)
A tolerant and slow-growing plant whose leaves, glossy and leathery, resemble those of Rhododendron. Australian Laurel will grow vigorously bushy and does not ask much attention. Florists often use the leaves in floral arrangements.

An interesting variegated form is *P. tobira variegata*.

Australian Umbrella Tree (*Schefflera actinophylla*)
A very attractive and vigorous-growing tree with rich-looking, green glossy leaves that radiate like umbrellas from the ends of several leaf stalks. It is a tough and rewarding plant, growing to six feet, which can be propagated by air-layering.

Australian Umbrella Tree is also sold as *Brassaia actinophylla*. A dwarf variety, *B. actinophylla compacta*, is also available.

Baby's Tears (*Helxine soleirollii*)
A low creeper, also called Irish Moss. It likes a constantly moist (but not soggy) soil and higher than average humidity. It makes a good ground cover for terrariums but will also grow in a pot if adequate humidity is provided. Baby's Tears may appear to die in the colder months, but after

IV-8

an adequate rest period the plant will spring back to life.

Black Pepper (*Piper nigrum*)
Not an especially attractive plant, but one which produces real peppercorns which may be used at the table and is a good conversation piece for that reason. The plant's green berries later turn red, then dry up and turn black. Pick the dried-up black corns, dry them thoroughly for several weeks in an open spot, then use them in your pepper grinder. The care for Black Pepper is about the same as that required for Philodendron. It is not a demanding plant.

Boxwood (*Buxus*)
The same plant which grows the most prized hedges outdoors can make a very attractive house plant. Boxwood is slow-growing, which has glossy, bright green leaves, and dependable, a good subject for bonsai, the ancient Oriental art of growing dwarf trees and shrubs. *B. sempervirens* and *B. microphylla japonica* (Japanese Boxwood) are the two popular species.

Bromeliads
There are more than eighteen hundred varieties of this popular group, many of which are suitable for growing as house plants. Some of them produce attractive flowers, but most are grown for their striking and variegated leaf patterns. One distinctive feature of the Bromeliads is the rosette leaves which form a small water cup, which the plant uses to hold reserve

IV-9

supplies of water in its natural habitat in the crotches of trees in Central and South America; the water cup is an evolutionary survival characteristic. In the home, keep the cup filled with water, changing it weekly to keep it fresh.

A few of the more common genera of Bromeliads are *Aechmea*, *Ananas* (Pineapple), *Billbergia*, *Cryptanthus*, *Dyckia*, *Tillandsia* (Spanish Moss), and *Vriesia*.

Caladium
Caladiums, with their spectacularly colored and variegated leaves, are equally at home in the garden or on the window sill. They are ideal additions to plant groupings on porch or patio in the summer and early autumn. Give them bright light, but not long periods of direct sun in summer, if you want the brightest leaf colors.

Caladiums are grown from tubers, which can be divided easily to produce new plants. Start the tubers in regular potting soil at a very warm temperature 80°–90°F, and move the young plants to a cooler spot when they have appeared. They will attain a height of about one foot.

Cast-Iron Plant (*Aspidistra elatior*)
Perhaps the easiest plant in the world to grow, as its name suggests. It is virtually impossible to neglect it to death. It is also called Saloon Plant, since it was one of the few that could survive in Victorian taverns, and it was made immortal by George Orwell in his novel *Keep the*

IV - 10

Aspidistra Flying. If you cannot grow the Aspidistra, you may safely conclude that you have a purple thumb, hopelessly irredeemable.

The Cast-Iron Plant (which grows about two feet tall) seems to thrive even better when kept slightly potbound, and it will benefit from having its leaves washed occasionally. A white-striped species is called *A. elatior variegata*.

Chinese banyan. See Ficus.

Chamaeranthemum igneum A—F H N

A low, spreading herb that has attractive dark green leaves with reddish-yellow veins. It is suitable for hanging baskets or as a low contrast in large plant groupings. It does like warm temperatures and high humidity, however, and may not be suitable for dry apartments.

Chinese Evergreen (Aglaonema) A—F I L

An attractive and low-growing plant that is very easy to grow. It will stand abuse almost as easily as Cast-Iron Plant.

There are at least ten commonly found species of the *Aglaonema*, the most popular of which, *A. modestum*, has interestingly mottled leaves. Perhaps the most attractive, however, is *A. pseudobractaetum*, which is sometimes difficult to find in stores and greenhouses.

IV - 11

Cissus A—E I N

A vine plant that offers a number of interesting and attractive species. Most are vigorous climbers, suitable for training on a trellis or for adding to hanging baskets.

Among the more popular species are *C. rhombifolia* (Grape Ivy), which is one of the most popular of all house plants; *C. antarctica* (Kangaroo Vine), which prefers a small pot; *C. antarctica minima* (Miniature Kangaroo Vine); *C. rotundifolia*; and *C. discolor* (Begonia Ivy), which is perhaps the most spectacular of the genus, although difficult to grow.

Of all the Cissus, Grape Ivy is the easiest to grow, a fact that doubtless accounts for a large share of its popularity.

Coleus A—D H M

An old favorite with velvety leaves sporting bright splashes of reds, pinks, purples, and yellows. There are a seemingly endless number of varieties of Coleus, nearly all of them interesting, most growing twelve to eighteen inches in height. Most garden varieties are varieties of *C. blumei*.

Coleus is equally happy outdoors, grown as an annual in temperate areas, or in the window garden. It can be grown easily from seed, and stem tip cuttings can be taken from established indoor plants. If you grow Coleus outdoors in summer, take some cuttings before the first autumn freeze and root them for growing as house plants.

The soil for Coleus should be kept damp but not soggy. Pinch back plants often to encourage bushy growth.

For "trailing coleus" see *Plectranthus*.

IV - 12

Copper Leaf (Acalypha wilkesiana) A—D H M

A member of the Spurge family which features (chenille plant) copper-colored foliage. A close relative, *A. hispida*, is described as a flowering plant in Chapter 6.

Copper Leaf may be propagated easily by taking cuttings late in the summer. The plant is susceptible to attack by spider mites, and proper precautions should be taken against this menace.

no extra #

Dichorisandra reginae A—F I N

An attractive, slow-growing plant with interesting leaf markings. It resembles Wandering Jew, except that it grows upright. Give it warm temperatures and not too much direct light, but do watch room humidity.

IV - 13

Dieffenbachia A—F J N

A popular plant with many species, often called Dumbcane. It is prized for its large leaves with interesting markings, usually variations of cream and white on dark green. Dieffenbachias are fairly tough plants, not too difficult to grow. Most varieties attain a height of eighteen to twenty-four inches, although growth is slow.

D. arvida 'Exotica' is very popular because it is even more durable than other members of the family. Other well-known species include *D. picta*, *D. amoena*, *D. sequina*, and *D. bowmannii*.

There are no special cultural requirements, although the Dieffenbachia does best in a warm spot and should have its foliage cleaned regularly. The plant may be propagated by taking stem cuttings and rooting them in moist and warm peat.

Caution: Eating or nibbling on the leaves of the Dieffenbachia can cause severe swelling of the tongue and mouth tissues; hence the popular name, Dumbcane. It is not a plant to grow in a home with toddlers.

Dracaena A—E I N

Many available species, which vary so greatly in appearance that some appear to be unrelated. Most grow tall—five feet or more—on sturdy stalks.

IV - 14

They are very tough plants, tolerant of a surprising amount of neglect, all in all one of the most dependable house plants.

Some varieties to investigate are D. deremensis Warnecki, D. fragrans (which has corn-like leaves), D. fragrans massangeana (whose leaves feature yellow stripes), D. marginata (a truly exciting plant, with grass-like, cream-colored foliage, edged in red; sometimes sold as D. marginata tricolor), D. sanderiana (with white-banded leaves), D. godseffiana, D. draco (the "Dragon Tree" of the Canary Islands), and many others, some of which will doubtless by offered by any good supplier. These mentioned, however, are some of the most attractive and also some of the easiest to grow. See also Pleomele.

Dumb cane See Dieffenbachia.

Episcia

A genus, offering many species and subspecies, which is related to the African Violet and requires largely the same culture, although it does demand a little more light. Episcias are among the easiest plants to grow successfully and should be tried only after success has been attained with some of the others listed in these pages. The leaves are a rich green, most varieties tinged with copper, some with variations of silver, blue, purple, and bronze. The veins often offer striking color contrasts. Episcias are trailing plants, a natural selection for hanging baskets. They send out runners that may be used for propagation.

IV - 15

Most species produce small and attractive flowers, in the color range of red-orange-yellow, but the plant is generally grown for its delightful foliage. If you do not wish to strive for blossoms, a north window will suit an Episcia well enough.

The most popular species is E. cupreata (Flame Violet), which has soft hairy, copper-tinged leaves and comes in several attractive varieties. Also investigate E. dianthiflora, which produces white flowers, and E. lilacina 'Cuprea,' with lavender-colored flowers. Many other species and subspecies are easily available, all of which have fascinating foliage variations and some of which will bloom quite profusely.

Fatshedera, see Aralia.

Fatsia japonica (see Aralia.

Ferns

ferns are the oldest plants on the evolutionary scale, that you are likely to cultivate. They are predated only by the algae and the mosses. Everyone knows and admires ferns for their graceful and feathery fronds. They are among the few house plants that reproduce by spores rather than seeds. Some ferns grow regally upright, while others trail with modesty and grace. There are many sizes of ferns, from miniature plants suitable for the window sill, all the way to the seven-foot-tub plants that can add a touch of class

IV - 16

to entryways, patios, and conservatories.

The secret to the successful raising of ferns is in offering them an environment matching, as nearly as possible, that of their natural habitat. They need warmth, a decent degree of room humidity (not under 30 percent) and a moist and humusy soil (at least 50 percent organic matter). They appreciate bright light but will be affected adversely if allowed to stand for long periods of time in direct sun.

There are a great many ferns from which to choose. One of the smaller ones is

Adiantum, the Maidenhair Fern, which is available in several varieties; it sends forth fragile-looking fronds in sprays; needs good light and high humidity.

Other smaller ferns include

Pteris multifida (Brake Fern), Woodwardia orientalis (Chain Fern), and Polypodium aureum (Hare's-Foot Fern). There are many, many others. For asparagus fern, emerald feather, and smilax, see Asparagus.

Among the larger ferns are the following:

Cyrtomium falcatum (Holly Fern), which has frond leaflets resembling the shape of holly and with a similar gloss.

Asplenium nidus (Bird's-Nest Fern), with broad, lance-shaped fronds.

IV - 17

Nephrolepis exaltata, which has long, sword-shaped fronds and is often called Sword Fern.

N. exaltata bostoniensis, the ever-popular Boston Fern.

Platycerium bifurcatum (Staghorn Fern), whose fronds are usually attached to a piece of bark or other support, and which can become parched quite easily in a dry atmosphere.

The world of ferns is a large one, full of interest, and extremely rewarding. No house-plant collection should be without at least one or two representatives.

Ficus

A large family of indoor plants, whose best-known member is the Rubber Plant. Ficus species range from large, tree-like plants to small-leafed trailers. Although they are not difficult plants to grow, the large species are especially sensitive to both overwatering and sudden temperature changes and will react to either by dropping their leaves.

There has been much improvement in the Rubber Plant (F. elastica) since World War II. The best now is perhaps F. elastica 'Robusta,' which is remarkably trouble-free. There are many decorative varieties, as well, including F. elastica 'Doescheri,' which has light and dark green patched leaves and cream-colored leaf margins, and F. elastica

'Schryveriana,' another mottled-leafed variety. F. elastica 'Decora,' from which 'Robusta' was developed, is still a popular slow-growing variety. Rubber plants will grow as tall as any room but may be cut back to encourage bushiness. Chinese Banyan (F. retusa), another tree-like Ficus, showers forth with a profusion of small, leathery leaves. F. retusa nitida, Indian Laurel resembles mountain laurel.

The Fiddle-Leaf Fig (F. lyrata) is a tough and attractive tree-like species, with large dark green, fiddle-shaped leaves. It needs warmer conditions than other Ficus. Weeping Fig (F. benjamina) is another Ficus tree which has small, dense-growing foliage.

There are, as well, many small plants in the genus. Most popular, perhaps, is Creeping Fig (F. pumila), a small-leafed creeper which has been developed to include several variations, such as F. pumila minima (slower-growing and smaller), and F. pumila variegata, a variegated variety. All will adhere to rough surfaces, sending out aerial roots similar to those of ivy, and are thus easily trained.

The tree-type Ficus are propagated by air-layering, while the small-leafed climbers and trailers may be reproduced easily by simple division.

Firebrand. See Ti plant.
Flame violet. See Episcia.
Friendship plant. See Pilea.
German Ivy (Senecio mikaniodies), an easy-to-grow plant that is similar to the true ivies in both appearance and requirements. A handsome relative is S. macroglossus variegatus (Cape Ivy). Treat them in every way like Ivy (q.v.) for success.

Ginger (Zingiber officinale), a fact that the same ginger used in cooking, makes the plant even more interesting than its appearance would indicate. The untreated rhizomes sold in specialty food and gourmet shops can be planted directly in potting soil to produce plants (root in water, as for an avocado, then plant with just the tip of the root showing) or established plants may be divided easily. The plants have reed-like stems and interesting grassy foliage, truly exotic in appearance. Success as a house plant depends upon giving ginger plenty of sunlight and warm temperatures. Keep the soil constantly damp but never soggy for long periods of time. As an added bonus, healthy plants will bear colorful clusters of flowers.

Golddust Plant (Aucuba japonica), a modest plant that features dark green leaves spotted with yellow-gold markings. Its main attribute is that it will withstand very cool temperatures, all the way down to freezing. It is good for unheated winter porches in all but the coldest parts of the country. Two popular varieties are A. japonica variegata and A. japonica goldeana. Indian laurel. See Ficus. Irish moss. See Baby's tears.

Ivy (Hedra), surely one of the most popular of house-plant species, both easy to grow and cheerful and attractive in appearance. There are a great number of varieties, with new improvements coming along all the time.

English Ivy (Hedera helix) is the most popular of the true ivies and is available in more than fifty varieties to suit nearly any taste. There are varieties with large leaves or with small, fast or slow growing habits, plain green or variegated. The best way to choose an English Ivy to your liking is to visit some flower shops and greenhouses, or to beg a few cuttings from a friend who has a plant that appeals to you.

Propagation of Ivy is easy, and in fact the plant does half of the job for you. Small rootlets will form on the stem of the plant, just below the leaves (the Ivy uses the rootlets to attach itself to rough surfaces, helping it to climb.) Make cuttings just below the rootlets and plant these cuttings directly in potting soil or a sterile rooting medium.

It would be the sheerest folly to attempt to recommend all the good varieties of English Ivy. For a starter, however, you might investigate H. helix conglomerata (Japanese Ivy), an upright-growing plant with small, densely growing leaves; 'Curlilocks' and 'Ivalace' with curled leaf margins; 'Green Ripples,' 'Maple Queen,' 'Merion Beauty,' 'Needlepoint,' 'Pittsburgh,' 'Pixie,' 'Rochester,' H. helix scutifolia, and 'Shamrock,' the last of which likes more than average moisture and is good for terrariums.

Among the variegated English Ivies, try 'Golddust,' 'Glacier,' and 'Goldheart,' the last of which has dark green leaves with sharply contrasting bright yellow centers.

Canary Islands Ivy (H. canariensis) also known as Algerian ivy, is another easy-to-grow Ivy, which has larger leaves than English Ivy. It is often trained around a piece of bark, much like a Philodendron, to form a striking plant with a very bushy appearance. More popular than the basic green-leafed variety is the variant H. canariensis variegata, also known as 'Gloire de Marengo,' whose leaves are slate-green to cream in color.

IV-21a

For grape ivy and begonia ivy, see Cissus; for German ivy and cape ivy, see German ivy; for Swedish ivy, see Plectranthus.

Japanese sweet flag (Acorus gramineus) A-F-H-N
A moisture-loving plant that grows only two inches tall. It will do best in a terrarium.

Joseph's Coat (Alternanthera) A-E-I-M
These low-growing dwarf plants that are good for terrariums. Their multicolored foliage adds interest to any plant grouping. Joseph's coat needs warm temperatures and a moist soil. Codiaeum (leaf croton) is also sometimes called Joseph's coat, because it, too, has colorful foliage. However, Codiaeum grows to a height of ten feet. The name "Joseph's coat" is also applied to various other plants.

Jungle plant. See Maranta.
Kangaroo vine. See Cissus.

Maranta A-F-H-N
a genus of plants that has striking foliage. They are easy to grow and impressive in appearance. Marantas will grow to about eight inches in height. M. leuconeura kerchoviana (Prayer Plant) is perhaps the most popular of the Marantas and is so named because its leaves fold up at night, as if in prayer. The leaves are large and oval-shaped, and the plant requires a fairly humid atmosphere. In the autumn, the leaves may begin to die out.

IV-22

If so, do not be alarmed. Cut off the affected leaves and reduce watering until late winter, when new growth begins; then water normally.

A red-veined variety, even more striking, is M. erythroneura. Another with red veins is M. leuconeura erythrophylla (Jungle Plant), which has olive-green leaves. Still another striking variation is offered by M. leuconeura massangeana.

Most house-plant growers will want to include at least one Maranta among their collections. The key to success with this plant is in giving it lots of bright light, but no direct sun at all.

Miniature Holly (Malpighia coccigera) C-E-I-M
not a true holly but a bushy evergreen shrub with dense, holly-like foliage. The leaves are shiny, dark green, and have spiny teeth. Miniature holly does produce small flowers, but it is grown primarily as a foliage plant. It is propagated easily from cuttings.

Nephthytis A-F-I-L
an attractive plant, but difficult to identify, since there is great confusion over what is and what is not a Nephthytis. Experts say that many plants sold as Nephthytis are really from the genus Syngonium. Since the two genera are difficult to tell apart, however, no one cares very much except

---

IV-23

the experts. Whatever they are, they are tough plants, able to withstand adverse conditions. Nephthytis and Syngoniums have large, arrow-shaped leaves and are either trailers or climbers. Used as climbers, they will have to be offered some support, such as that used for Philodendrons. Propagation may be achieved by taking stem cuttings.

Among several available species, the most popular is Syngonium podophyllum (Goosefoot Plant).

Norfolk Island Pine (Araucaria excelsa) A-E-I-N
A popular evergreen, graceful and symmetrical, seen with increasing frequency. It will hold up well under adverse conditions, although its branches will droop in dim light. Give it a damp, but not soggy, soil, for it is very susceptible to overwatering. It seems to do well when kept slightly potbound.

Norfolk Island Pine is a slow grower and should never be pruned. It will grow gracefully to a height of about six feet, after which it tends to become ungainly.

Palms B-F-I-m
a plant family full of nostalgia for many people. In Victorian times and right up through the 1930s and 1940s, the potted palm was a symbol of exotic elegance, bringing a bit of the tropics to shivering Northerners. No movie made before 1950 was complete without a detective peering out from behind a potted palm.

The elegant palms lost much of their allure after

IV-24

World War II, but now they are making a modest comeback. You can achieve success with palms by giving them bright light (even though they will endure shade), water, and no plant food during the winter months. Palms, actually, seem to thrive on inattention, doing well when slightly potbound. They are slow-growing, in any case.

The palms are a plant family. Palmae is the scientific name of the family, which comprises many genera and far more species. Few, however, are both attractive and manageable as house plants. Among the palms you might wish to investigate are the following:

Chamaerops (Fan Palm) has fan-shaped leaves on long stalks and will become quite large at maturity.

Cocos is an attractive coconut palm, the best species C. weddelliana. Its proper name is actually Howea is the Palm Court Palm, the most popular of all indoor large palms. H. belmoreana, the most attractive species, will eventually grow to ten feet or more in height.

Neanthe is an attractive and easy-to-grow dwarf which can tolerate a dry room.

Phoenix, the Date Palm, can be grown easily from the stone of a fresh date. Plant the stone in potting soil, keep it warm (70 to 80°F), and it should germinate in about a month. It is slow-growing during the first year or so, but within ten or fifteen years it will become as tall as any room.

Pellionia

Pellionia, a colorful, slow-growing, creeping plant, fine for hanging baskets and a good filler plant for groupings. It features small, oval-shaped leaves with interesting variegated patterns. There are two popular varieties: P. daveauana and the more compact P. pulchra.

Pellionia is not difficult to propagate. As it creeps along the soil it sends down roots from the stems. Just cut the stems into sections and root them in potting soil.

Peperomia

There are many varieties of this popular and cheerful little plant (eight inches or less in height), most of which are low and upward-growing, some with deeply ridged leaves. It is the ridging that gives these peperomias their distinction in a world of larger and more spectacular house plants. They are tough plants, tolerant of most conditions, although they will rot at the groundline if the top of the soil is not allowed to dry out between waterings. Peperomias like bright light, but not direct sun in the summer.

Among the more popular varieties are these:

P. caperata (Emerald-Ripple peperomia) has deeply ridged, heart-shaped leaves; the tops of the ridges are green and the valleys are brown, giving an interesting effect.

P. rotundifolia is a low grower with thick, light green leaves.

P. obtusifolia (Oval-leaf peperomia) has solid green leaves, while P. obtusifolia variegata is the variegated form of the same species.

P. sandersii (Watermelon peperomia) is identified by its red petioles and silver-striped leaves.

P. grieseo argentea hederaefolia has ridged, glossy leaves, silver-hued, and purple-olive veins.

There are many other varieties of peperomia, many of which may be seen at your local flower shop or greenhouse.

Philodendron

Philodendron, probably the most popular group of house plants in America today. There are many, many species and varieties, with leaves ranging from small to very large, in an interesting variety of shapes offered by no other house plants. Most are climbers and will appreciate a support that can be kept moist, such as that described in Chapter 2.

Philodendrons are not difficult plants to grow, unless you disregard the rules. Growth will be stunted by poor light, and the leaves can turn yellow and drop from lack of water, too small a pot, low temperatures, or poor drainage. The plants will benefit from a monthly washing with a mild soap (not detergent) solution. Cut back the growing tips if you wish to encourage bushy growth, and use the tip cuttings to form new plants.

Some of the more popular varieties include:

P. scandens (heart-leaf philodendron), a very popular climber which can withstand the dry air of a typical apartment.

P. oxycardum, the most commonly grown form, which has heart-shaped leaves very similar to those of P. scandens. It is often grown in water or wet moss.

P. dubium (Cut-leaf philodendron), a slow grower with star-shaped leaves.

P. panduraeforme (Fiddle-leaf philodendron), which has irregularly shaped, olive-green leaves.

P. pertusum, also known as Monstera deliciosa, has perforated leaves, irregularly shaped. The older plants have broad, thick leaves with many perforations.

P. squamiferum (Anchor-leaf philodendron), which has leaves and petioles that are covered by red hairs. The leaves are shaped like daggers.

P. bipinnatifidum (Twice-cut philodendron), a large-leafed variety; the leaves resemble those of the smaller P. dubium in shape but are more deeply notched.

P. selloum, another cut-leaf variety, the cuts becoming more pronounced as the plant reaches maturity. This species will tolerate temperatures down to freezing with no apparent harm.

P. wendlandii is another large-leafed species, very tolerant of a wide range of temperature and humidity. Its leaves are long and narrow.

Piggyback Plant (Tolmiea menziesii)

Piggyback Plant (Tolmiea menziesii), native to the West Coast of the United States; a modest-sized plant that can be grown outdoors in the warmer regions of the country. Its name is derived from its unusual habit of bearing young plantlets from the junction of the leaf and the petiole. These can be rooted easily to grow new plants. The leaves are toothed and lobed, covered with down. It is an easy plant to grow.

Pilea

Pilea, a genus that includes at least four cultivated house plants, none of which grows more than a foot in height. They are rather unusual-looking plants. All like moist soil, warm temperatures, and full sun in the winter. The plants become less attractive as they grow older, but cuttings are easily made, so that older plants may be discarded when desired. Fertilize liberally when growth is active.

P. cadiere (Aluminum Plant) has dark green leaves with striking aluminum-colored markings. A dwarf variety, P. cadiere minima, is preferred by many, as is P. cadiere nana, a compact variety.

P. microphylla (Artillery Plant) is fine in texture with bright green, fern-like leaves. When its flowers are dry, pollen literally explodes from the blossoms, hence its common name.

IV - 29

P. involucrata (South American Friendship Plant) is bushy in growth and has coppery leaves. It can be made to appear even bushier if several cuttings are taken, then rooted in the same pot, to the sides of the parent plant.

P. 'Silver Tree' has bronze-hued leaves with silver markings.

Pineapple. See Bromeliads.

Plectranthus

Various species of this genus are often called trailing Coleus or Swedish Ivy. Some are upright in growth, while others are trailers, making good subjects for hanging baskets.

P. australis, a trailer, has waxy-green leaves, round in shape with saw-tooth edges.

P. australis variegatus is similar in leaf shape, with added white markings.

P. purpuratus is an upright-growing plant with purple coloring on the undersides of its leaves.

There are other interesting varieties, including P. oertendahlii, a flowering trailer with bronze-hued leaves and silvery veins.

Pleomele

an interesting group of plants with cultural requirements similar to those of Philodendrons.

P. reflexa variegata (Song of India) is now included in the genus Dracaena. Its attractive, spear-shaped leaves are gold-and-green striped, borne in clusters on branching stems. It will grow to tree size in ten or fifteen years.

IV - 30

P. reflexa gracilis has dense foliage; its recurved leaves have translucent edges.

P. thalioides has waxy-green leaves, ribbed lengthwise.

Pothos (Scindapsus)

Pothos is very similar in appearance and growth habits to the heart-leaf Philodendron, P. scandens, except that it needs less water and warmer temperatures—not below 65°F. It likes bright light but cannot stand direct sun. Pothos is a natural trailer, although it can be trained upward along a support, again like Philodendron. The leaves are heart-shaped and green, with pale yellow markings. Pothos is not as easy to grow as most plants listed in this book.

The most popular species is S. aureus, which offers several variegated varieties, some of which require even warmer temperatures.

Prayer plant. See Maranta.

Rubber plant. See Ficus.

Ruellia makoyana

an old favorite, not seen as often today as in the 1930s. It is a free-spreading plant that has glossy, pale green leaves with silvery veins. It likes a warm, moist environment, shaded from the sun.

Sanchezia nobilis glaucophylla

a member of the same family as the Aphelandra. It grows to a height of four feet and has large, glossy, sword-shaped leaves with yellow veins.

IV - 31

Screw Pine (Pandanus)

An old favorite that will withstand most adverse conditions. It is recognized by its long, arching, sword-like leaves, which have saw-toothed edges.

P. veitchii has green-and-white-striped leaves. Often preferred, however, is P. veitchii compactus, a dwarf variety with clearly variegated leaves. P. baptistii has no marginal spines, as do the other species. All Screw Pines like moist, but never soggy, soil. They can take some direct sun, except in the heat of summer, although they do best in a bright location out of direct sun altogether.

Selaginella

fernlike plants, including some small creepers, some erect-growing species, and some trailers. All offer bright green, feathery foliage.

S. kraussiana is a low creeper, perfect for terrariums.
S. emmeliana is an erect-growing plant.
S. willdenovii is a vigorous climber with unusual blue leaves. S. apus is a trailer, good for hanging baskets.

Sensitive Plant (Mimosa pudica) (prefers dry soil but high room humidity)

a fascinating plant for both adults and children

IV - 32

because its delicate and feathery leaves and petioles droop and fold up instantly (and temporarily) whenever it is touched, lighted, or even if a match is held close to it. Seeds from which plants will grow easily are often available in stores. The plant becomes leggy and gets out of hand after about a year, but it is not difficult to grow more plants at any time.

Silk Oak (Grevillea robusta)

a pleasant plant with graceful, feathery foliage similar to that of the False Aralia. It will grow to three feet in height. Silk Oak likes cool, moist conditions and can spend the summer outdoors with benefit. It does tend to get leggy if unchecked, so it should be cut back at the growing tip fairly regularly. Silk Oak will react badly if its soil becomes very dry.

Snake Plant (Sansevieria)

seldom thought of as such actually a succulent but It has long been very popular, probably because of its great tolerance to adverse conditions. It is also called Mother-in-Law Tongue and Bowstring. Like the Cast Iron Plant, it can grow perfectly well in hot, dry, and dim locations (including, it seems, most old hotel lobbies in the country). The leaves are thick and sword-shaped, usually upright, growing to eighteen inches or more in height, but in some varieties ground-hugging. It is propagated easily by division of the rootstock or by taking leaf cuttings. (Be careful not to turn the leaf cutting upside down when setting it in the rooting medium, for roots grow only from the downward portion of the cutting.)

There are many varieties available, including:

S. trifasciata laurenti (Variegated Snake Plant) with handsome yellow bands along its leaf margins.

S. trifasciata, similar in form, but without the yellow bands.

S. trifasciata laurenti compacta (Dwarf Congo Snake Plant), with shorter leaves and yellow margins.

S. trifasciata hahni (Hahn's Dwarf Snake Plant), with light and dark green bands along the leaves.

There are many other interesting variegated varieties of this old standby.

Song of India. See Pleomele.
South American friendship plant. See Pilea.
Spanish moss. See Bromeliads.
Spathe Flower (Spathphyllum)

an easy-to-grow, tough plant, suitable for the homes of most novice green thumbs. It has glossy, sword-shaped green leaves. White blossoms will sometimes surprise you in the winter, but do not depend on their appearance.

There are two popular species, S. clevelandii and S. floribundum.

Spider Plant (Chlorophytum comosum)

Spider Plant is one of the most popular of house plants. It has grassy leaves, variegated cream and green in color, which arch gracefully from either pot or hanging basket. Mature plants produce perfectly formed baby plants on the end of long runners, which resemble spiders hanging from a thread. Propagation is simply a matter of rooting one of the "baby spiders" in a rooting medium. The Spider Plant can store water in its tubers and can take dry soil for a fairly long time because of this characteristic.

Strawberry Geranium (Saxifraga sarmentosa)

trailing plant, also called Strawberry Begonia and Mother-of-Thousands, good for both hanging baskets and terrariums. All it really asks is a woodsy soil containing plenty of organic matter, and a cool location. Leaves of the Strawberry Geranium resemble those of the true geranium, and it sends out runners just as strawberry plants do. The leaves of the standard variety are deep olive in color, with silver-gray markings. An interesting variant, S. sarmentosa tricolor, has dark green leaves marked with white and pink and is considerably more difficult to grow.

Syngonium, see Nephthytis.

Ti Plant (Cordyline terminalis)

C. terminalis is only one of many species of Cordyline, but it is certainly the most popular. Also called Firebrand, it will last for only one to three years and grow to two feet in height, before dying out, but its spectacular young life is certainly worth your placing this plant on your list of house-plant candidates. It has long, upward-reaching leaves, cerise, purple, and green, which grow from a cane trunk. Another popular species is C. australis, which features long, slender leaves. The Ti Plant is very popular in Hawaii, where its colorful grassy leaves are used in making grass skirts. It is sold there in tourist shops as a "Ti Log." In recent years, breeders have developed several variations of the original plant, including a dwarf and a variegated variety, which go under various names.

Umbrella flatsedge (Cyperus alternifolius)

a popular exotic plant with narrow, pointed, grasslike leaves that grow in clusters. It will grow up to two feet tall in a pot. Constant moisture is essential, and propagation is a simple matter of root division.

Related species include C. papyrus, which is similar in appearance and requirements but grows to seven feet in height, and a dwarf variety, C. alternifolius gracilis.

Velvet Plant (Gynura)

This is a vigorous-growing plant with dark red, velvety leaves. It will offer a fine contrast to your green plants. It is best to train the Velvet Plant to some support, to keep it in bounds, or to pinch it back often to encourage bushy growth.

There are two common varieties, G. aurantiaca, which is upright in growth habit, and G. sarmentosa, a smaller and loosely-twining plant. The flowers of both have a horrible scent and should be removed immediately upon appearance.

Wandering Jew (Tradescantia; Zebrina)

Tradescantia and Zebrina both claim the common name of Wandering Jew, and the two genera are so similar that they are →

commonly interchanged. Both include easy-to-grow, tolerant, vigorous trailers of many varieties, perfect for hanging baskets. Feed them regularly for good growth. Propagation is simplicity itself. Simply take cuttings of growing tips and root them in water.

Among very many interesting species are the following:

T. fluminensis, the original Wandering Jew, has silver markings, but there are many species of different markings and colors available today.

T. albiflora has bluish-green leaves with white stripes.

Z. pendula is an excellent house plant whose leaves have purple undersides. Again, there are several interesting variegated varieties.

Yew (Podocarpus)

Yews are prized outdoor plants in many parts of the country and can be made into attractive house plants anywhere. These hardy evergreens can provide a welcome contrast to tropical plants. They are slow-growing and tolerant of adverse conditions. They will withstand low temperatures and may require frequent repotting because of vigorous growth. They can become quite large and bushy.

P. macrophylla angustifolia (Southern Yew) can be pruned to a pleasing shape and will respond with even more vigorous growth. Other similar species include P. macrophylla 'Nagai' and P. macrophylla 'Maki'.

Note: If we were really publishing this book, the following correspondence would ensue.

1. CIP form to the Library of Congress, as soon as manuscript is in production. New copyright page, with LC number and other CIP information, as soon as CIP slip returned by LC.

2. Letter to author explaining production schedule, as soon as schedule is available, with request for notification if he will be unable to meet given deadlines. (Follow-up letter or phone call if any changes in schedule become necessary at this end.)

3. If illustrations prepared here, Xerox copies to author for his approval before they go to printer.

4. One set of galleys to author, with the attached proofreading instructions. Phone call to author to say that galleys are coming and be sure he can still meet deadline for returning them. Check-up phone call near deadline to be sure they are coming on time, if there is any reason for doubt. (Proofreading against copy done by Press proofreader since this is a trade book. Author's changes, if allowable, transferred to master proofs by Press proofreader or editor. If this were a scholarly monograph rather than a trade book, author would be expected to read galleys against copy.)

5. Pages to author for indexing, with Chicago indexing guide (if not sent earlier). Phone call to author to say pages are coming and be sure he can meet schedule. Index in this case would need to include common and scientific names of all plants discussed in book, with cross referencing. Index would be checked by editor against style cards prepared during editing. Index proofs checked here.

6. If illustrations not included in indexing pages, Xerox copies of repros with illustrations to author for approval when ready. Approval by phone if possible. (Except in unusual cases, authors don't see vandykes or blues.)

All the above-mentioned correspondence with author, by letter and telephone, would be handled by the manuscript editor and progress reported in weekly editorial report.

TRANSMITTAL SHEET (Editorial Checklist)   House Editor: ITH
                                           Date: 8/1/76

Author/~~Editor/Translator:~~ Pruvis Mulch

Title: NO TIME FOR HOUSEPLANTS: A Busy Person's Guide to Indoor Gardening

Series: None   FAC Approval Date: July 15, 1976

Length of MS. 170 ms. pp, not including index & illustrations	One-edition book: yes/no For discussion
Trim size: ~~5¼x8"~~ ~~5½x8½"~~ 6x9" ~~For discussion~~	Paperback possibility: yes/~~no~~ For discussion
Release attached: yes/~~no~~	Duplicate MS herewith: yes/~~no~~	Original to MS Editor: yes/~~no~~

Prelims & end matter: Check items now in manuscript. If items are to follow, mark each with estimated MS pages. Cross out those items not to be included.

Half title	Illustrations in text:
~~Series title~~	Number of line drawings: 100
Title	Number of halftones:
Copyright	No. of charts, graphs, maps:
~~Dedication~~	No. of separate plates:
~~Foreword~~	
Preface	
Contents	Binding: Cloth: one/two/three piece
List of Illustrations	stamping: one/two hits
List of tables	
~~Introduction~~	
Acknowledgements	Jacket: Number of colors: 3
Appendix(es) 11	Line drawing/~~halftone/type~~
~~Glossary~~	Good varnish/laminate/plain
Bibliography	
~~Notes~~	
Index? : yes	Paperback: Number of colors:
Index to be done by: author	

Quantity - first printing: Cloth: 5000 min.	Paper:	2nd prtg. probable: yes/~~no~~
Proposed publishing price: $6 - $7	Required return, 1st prtg.: %	
Discount: trade	Required return, 2nd prtg.: %	

Market: World rights: yes   Limited territory (specify):

No. of free copies: 10/10   Offprints: yes/no   No. per contributor:

Royalty terms: 5% net receipt proceeds 1-3000, 7½% net receipt proceeds 3001-5000, 10% net receipt proceeds beyond 5001

Permission/other fees: none	Subsidy: none
Target pub. month: March 1977	MS, proofs to: author

Copies: (1) Production   (2) MS-Editing   (3) Bookfolder

Preproduction Meeting Notes   August 10, 1976

Present: Acquisition and Copy Editors, Production Manager and Staff, Business Manager, Marketing Manager and Staff, and Director

Title: NO TIME FOR HOUSE PLANTS
Subtitle: A Busy Person's Guide to Indoor Gardening
Author: Purvis Mulch
Press ed.: CW   Acqu. ed.: ITH
Designer: RH   ISBN: 0-292-FANTAS-Y
Fund: uncertain (Corrie Herring Hooks?)   Series: No
Category B (inexpensive trade book)   Subsidy: No
No. of pp.: 170 ms. pp., not including index & illustrations; castoff 128
Size 6 x 9   Jacket: yes, trade
Ads on jacket: no, descrip. of book instead with possible blurb from someone like Thalassa Cruso (in catalog, book should be placed with *Roadside Flowers of Texas*).
Illustrations: yes—opinion expressed by ITH and agreed to by others that the book is not "cute" as are many similar books, and while in some ways this works to its advantage, at the same time it needs the distinction that good new illus. would add—BNS also points out that more illus. are needed to help the reader identify plants—therefore we will do our own new illus.—mostly line drawings (Ed Lindlof will do sample). Designer to discuss no. and type of illus. needed with copy editor. The point was made, however, that in dealing with a book of this type a decision would have been made and settled in the acquisition phase.
Proofreading: in house   Typesetting: in house
Index: yes, necessary   AA's/blue pencil changes: no
Direct to pp.: no
Books in warehouse: (edited copy to author this week or early next wk.) ca. 7 months from time edited copy goes to author
Print: tent. 7500 cloth only
Cost estimate: $13,275   Unit cost: $1.77
Price: $6.95   Discount: trade
Author information: Author bio. has been requested by CCW; to come.
Editorial comments: CCW described contents and distributed copies of a table of contents. A trade book. PDJ points out that in the case of a trade book the audience must be defined before making production, marketing, etc., plans. Need to check prices of similar books, size of audience, etc., to make it competitive with the many others on the market. RH and CCW define this as a general trade book for the beginner, ordinary people raising house plants. To be treated as a national trade book. Large no. of very low-cost mass market paperbacks in this field emphasized by several. CT and others point out that in actuality this press would not do this book—this will be pointed out in the project log.
Marketing plans: Sell rights to paperback ed., book club also (CA will do sample letters). Market as if this were the lead title in our catalog in any season. Ads in suitable gardening mags., *Better Homes and Gardens*, perhaps organic gardening mags. Point out that Mulch describes both organic and inorganic methods. Marketing to circulate a sheet descriptive of ad methods, as usual.
Discussion: Question of omitting subtitle raised. Decided to retain subtitle lest the book be mistaken for a humorous book a la Erma Bombeck. Possibility of humorous cover described by RH, however; by Sally Blakemore, of a busy person attempting to deal with flourishing house plants.

EDITORIAL FACT SHEET

Date 8/1/76

To: All concerned

From (House Editor): ITH

You are hereby officially notified that

    (X) The following book has been contracted, and the manuscript has been transmitted to Manuscript Editing and Production.

    ( ) The following book has been contracted will be imported from (foreign publisher):

Author: Purvis Mulch
Title: NO TIME FOR HOUSE PLANTS
Series: Not applicable   Translation: No

Author's background:
Purvis Mulch received his B.A. from the University of Iowa in 1961. He is the editor of Vigor magazine and an associate editor of Organic Gardening & Farming. His books include the _____ Garden Guide and The Earthworm Book.

Description of book--reason for publishing:

This is a basic book on house plant care; it is directed to the busy person who has little or "no time" for attending to his/her plants. The book must be distinguished from others on the market by striking illustrations throughout which we will commission.

Production information

Number of (MS/printed) pages: 170 ms. pp. not incl. index & illustrations
Number of illustrations: 100
     Halftones _____ Line cuts _____
Binding:

Marketing information

Proposed month of publication: March 1977
Proposed price: under $7.00
Proposed discount: Trade/Specialist/Text
Rights: World/Other
Special marketing prospects (book club, Overseas, etc.):
Gardening book clubs, magazine excerpts. We might consider a calendar using the illustrations.

Ed.: CCW
EDITORIAL/PRODUCTION TRANSMITTAL SHEET

170 ms.
Category A (B) C D

Author Purvis Mulch   ~~Illustrator~~
Title No Time for House Plants
Subtitle A Busy Person's Guide to Indoor Gardening
~~Translator~~
~~Series/sub/joint pub/new ed~~   ~~Intro or Foreword author~~
Date to Production 9-14-76   ISBN number: 0-292-FANTAS-Y
Proofreading time: galleys 10 working days   pages 5 working days
    (Includes mailing time)
Index to be done by author (X) ~~(enclosed)~~ 15 working days (Includes mailing time)
Proofreading time for index page proofs 2 working days

Number of proofs needed (total) galleys 3 sets, pages 4 sets
galleys: master, author, shelf; pages: master, indexer, sales, shelf
Cross out items which do not apply. Check items submitted with manuscript and indicate which are to come and when. Indicate position in book if possible:

~~Series~~
~~Dedication~~   Halftitles 3
~~Foreword~~   Subheads: No. of levels 1
Preface X   Line illusts: ~~No.~~ yes
~~Acknowledgments~~   Halftones: ~~No.~~ number to be determined in production
~~Introduction~~   ~~Colorplates No.~~
~~Epigraph~~   ~~Frontispiece No.~~
~~Time-note~~   ~~Maps No.~~
~~Abbreviations~~   Tables: No. 3
Appendices (no.) 11
~~Glossary~~
Bibliog X
~~Notes~~
Index to come
~~Other~~
Extracts ~~(yes)~~ (X) no
~~Notes (end of book~~ ( ) end of article ( ) at foot of page
Foreign language: no
Special characters needed: 4 symbols, to be created in production.
Special instructions: If designer prefers, the 11 appendices may be treated as "special boxes" and placed throughout the text. If this is done, "Appendices" in Contents should be changed to "Boxes."

ESTIMATED COSTS

Date: 8/4/76 By: NB

Title: NO TIME FOR HOUSEPLANTS
Author: Purvis Mulch
Quantity: HB 7500   PB
Pages: Castoff 128   Actual _____   Trim size 6 x 9
Paper: 60# Warrens Old Style

Binding costs based on: A grade cloth, plain endsheets, stamping one hit on spine, individual shrinkwrapping

Additional binding costs for: multicolor endleaf

Suppliers: Composition: In-house
           Printing: Kingsport
           Jacket/Covers: P.D.
           Binding: Kingsport

Plant Costs:

Composition:	$ 750
10% A.A.'s & misc. type:	$ 75
Illustrations:	$ 2625
Photographs: stats	$ 150
Paste-up:	$ 750
Re-design of artwork:	$
Stamping dies:	$ 50
Subtotal:	$ 4400

Manufacturing Costs:

Quantity:	7500 HB		
Printing:	$ 2500	$	$
Paper:	$	$	$
Halftones/Illustrations:	$	$	$
Color Section:	$	$	$
Jackets/Covers:	$ 525	$	$
Binding:	$ 5175	$	$
Freight:	$ 675	$	$
Subtotal:	$ 8875	$	$
Total:	$ 13,275	$	$
Unit cost:	$ 1.77	$	$

Comments: This includes 100 illustrations.

Differences

Texts — Structural relocation of pages to be used as an intro —

- Reworking of material not as extensive as MIT.

M.I.T.   ok
Printed cover overboards
Hard Bound Copy
Simple comprehensive guide
to plants
Primary Market
Retail Bookstores
College Bookstores,
wholesaler and jobber accounts
$6.95
p 64 — Related Books
p 65 — Home Crafts —

TEXAS
Cloth Binding
$6.95
128 pps
7500 print

— 198 Structural Suggestions

University of Texas Press Box 7819, Austin Texas 78712

COMPOSITION SPECIFICATIONS

Author/Title Purvis Mulch NO TIME FOR HOUSEPLANTS Date September 17, 1976

Trim size 6 x 9" Overall text page 29x46 picas

Margins: top 7/8"
gutter 5/8"

Main text: In justified setting use thin space bands. In ragged right setting use tight and uniform word spacing.

11/11 Goudy Old Style (VIP). Ragged right. Double column.
14 picas maximum, a-prox 12 picas minimum. OK to hyphenate. One pica column space

Text 47 lines per page   OK 1 line long/short facing pages
Paragraph indent one em, except flush left after heads   ☐ figures   ☐ oldstyle   ☒ lining
Folios 10/10 Goudy Old Style lining figs, flush outside at bottom.
Running heads 10/10 Goudy Old Style italic clc, flush left bottom recto pages only.
Lead to first text line --

Extract None

Lead above   Lead below

Chapter openings
Begin ☐ recto or verso as it falls   ☒ recto only
Folios ☒ will show on chapter opening pages   ☐ will not show on chapter opening pages

Chapter number: 10/10 Goudy Old Style italic, clc, flush left bottom (same position as running head).
Chapter title: 16/16 Goudy Old Style clc, flush left. Align with base of first text line.
Sink first text line 55 points from top margin.

Subheads
Level 1: 14/14 Goudy Old Style italic clc, flush left. 28 picas maximum. Do NOT hyphenate
Lead above 30 points   Lead below 11 points
Begin first text line following flush left.

Level 2: 11/11 Goudy Old Style italic clc, flush left. Run in.
Lead above   11 points   Lead below --
Begin first text line following run in.

Level 3: (captions) 9/9 Goudy Old Style italic clc, flush left.
Lead above cutting space   Lead below   cutting space
Begin first text line following --

Title/Author NO TIME FOR HOUSEPLANTS/Mulch

Halftitle 18 Goudy Bold clc, lead 4 pts, flush left.

Series title None

Title page 18/22 Goudy Bold, 18/22 Goudy Old Style, 11/22 Goudy Old Style. See layout.

Copyright 11/22 Goudy Old Style, flush left.

Dedication None

Contents 11/22 Goudy Old Style ragged right 29 pi max. Folios one word space from titles. Part titles 14/22 Goudy italic.

List of Illusts 11/11 Goudy Old Style ragged right 14 pi max. Folios one word space from titles.

Preface Same as main text.

Introduction None

Part titles 18 Goudy Old Style clc, flush left at top.

Notes None

Bibliography 11/11 Goudy Old Style, ragged right 29 pi max. Turnovers indent one em.

Index ☐ Oldstyle figures ☒ Lining figures
10/10 Goudy Old Style, ragged right, 14 pi max, OK to hyphenate.
Runover lines indent one em   Lead 10 pts between alphabetic sections

Other instructions No widow lines at the top of page.
All display matter to be set with tight word spacing.

Appendices: 11/11 Goudy Old Style, double column. Each 14 pi max.
Publisher will supply complete makeup instructions on dummy.

Manuscript to compositor September 20, 1976	Galleys:	3 sets
Galleys complete to Texas Press October 15, 1976	Corrected galleys:	3 sets
Galleys returned to compositor November 1, 1976	Pages:	4 sets
Pages complete to Texas Press	(Xeroxes of dummy)	
Pages and Index manuscript to compositor SEE ATTACHED SCHEDULE	Repros:	1 sets
Index pages to Texas Press		
Index pages returned to compositor		
Repros complete to Texas Press January 7, 1977		

Production / Design / Texas / 227

University of Texas Press

Date January 14, 1977

SPECIFICATIONS FOR PRINTING

Book title NO TIME FOR HOUSEPLANTS   Author PURVIS MULCH

Quantity 7500   Trim size 6 x 9"   Pages 128

Margins: top 7/8"
gutter 5/8"

Ink Black throughout

Stock 60# Warrens Old Style white wove   ☒ supplied by printer   ☐ supplied by Texas Press

Illustrations 100 line illustrations in place on repros

Special Instructions

Bound books needed in Austin not later than April 1, 1977

One set of silverprints folded and trimmed for approval before printing.
Provide 3 sets folded and gathered sheets as soon as ready
☐ for approval before casing in ☒ for Texas Press use only, do not wait for OK

Please provide a schedule for shipping silverprints, F&G's, bound books as soon as possible.

BINDING SPECIFICATIONS

Casebound books

Quantity 7500   ☐ perfect bind   ☒ smyth sewn   Sew in ☐ 32's ☒ 16's   ☐ round back ☒ flat back

Crash & paper, no stain, square edges, headbands in green & white

Endleaf: Multicolor Carioca Green

Cloth: One piece Columbia Bayside Linen BSL 4647

80 point genuine binders board

Stamping: Black foil on spine only

Repro for stamping die provided by Texas Press. Bindery to provide dies.
Jackets supplied by Texas Press as flat untrimmed printed sheets.
☐ sample case to Texas Press for approval before casing in ☒ sample case not necessary

Paperback books

quantity NONE   ☐ perfect bound   ☐ smyth sewn in ☐ 32's ☐ 16's

Covers provided as flat, untrimmed printed sheets by Texas Press. If books are combined run (smyth sewn casebound and perfect bound paperbacks), the paperbacks may be slightly narrower to allow for loss in binding.

ALL BOOKS TO BE INDIVIDUALLY SHRINK WRAPPED.

Shipping

Pack in 275 lb. test cardboard cartons. Mark each carton with title and number of copies contained. Ship skid packed via prepaid motor freight to Austin, Texas. Have driver call 471-3634 or 471-7233 upon arrival in Austin for further delivery instructions.

6 advance copies to be sent as soon as books are bound (6 casebound and 6 paperbacks if combined run).

Manuscript to compositor	September 20
Galleys to Texas Press	October 15
Galleys returned to compositor	November 1
Corrected galleys to Texas Press	November 5
Dummy to compositor for page makeup	November 19
Xerox of dummy to indexer	November 19
Index manuscript to compositor	December 14
Index pages to Texas Press	December 20
Index pages to compositor	December 23 (allow 1 week extra because of holiday)
Complete repros to Texas Press	January 7, 1977
Illustrations due from illustrator	November 5
Illustration photostats ready	December 14
Complete repros to printer with line illustrations in place	January 14
Book blues due from printer	February 11 (ca.)
Books due in Austin	not later than April 1

	Manuscript		Galleys			Pages			Index			
	to prod	to comp	to ed	from ed	to comp	to ed	from ed	to comp	to prod	to comp	to ed	from ed
due			10/15	11/1	11/1	11/19	12/14	12/14	12/14	12/14	12/20	12/23
in	9/14	9/20										

Author: MULCH **Title:** NO TIME FOR HOUSEPLANTS **Bound bks due:** April 1, 77 **Pub date:** May 77

	OK pgs/repros			Blues OK	F&Gs recd	Ja/cover copy recd	Art to printer	Vandyke OK	Ja/cover shipped	Die art sent	
	to ed	fm ed	to printer								
due	1/11	1/12	1/14			12/14	1/28		2/18	1/14	
in											

Category: A (B) C D

Corrected galleys due from comp.: 11/5
Complete dummy made up by: 11/19 (xeroxes to editor for indexer, to comp for pasteup)
Illustrations due from Lindlof: 11/5
Illustration photostats done: 12/14

Editor CCW **Designer** EW **Illustrator** Lindlof **Trim size** 6 x 9" **Pages** ca 128 **Print run: HB** 7500 **PB** --

Compositor In house (Manley) **Printer** Kingsport **Binder** Kingsport

Typefaces and leading 11/11 Goudy Old Style (VIP) **Stock** 60# Warrens Old Style

Binding cloth Bayside Linen BSL 4647 **Endleaves** Multicolor Carioca Green

Illustrations ca. 100 line illusts

Jackets: quantity 7800 **printer** PD **Designer** EW **Price** $6.95 **Discount** trade **Fund** --

Series -- **ISBN NO:** 0—292— FANTAS-Y **Estimated manufacturing cost** $13,275

No Time for Houseplants

University of Texas Press
Austin & London

A Busy Person's Guide to Indoor Gardening

No Time for Houseplants

by Purvis Mulch

International Standard Book Number 0-292-FANTAS-Y
Library of Congress Catalog Card Number 76-PLANT
Copyright © 1977 by the University of Texas Press
All rights reserved
Printed in the United States of America

Contents

Preface ix

One/Understanding House Plants

1. The Secrets of No-Work House-Plant Success 3
2. Basic Needs of House Plants 7
3. Plant Troubles and Cures 41

Two/Introducing the House Plants 49

4. Foliage Plants 53
5. Cacti and Other Succulents 95
6. Flowering House Plants 105
7. Special Indoor Gardens 127

Appendices

1. The ABCs of Artificial Light 147
2. Should You Send Your Plants to Summer Camp? 150
3. Can Your Plants Survive Your Vacation? 152
4. Plants for Cool Conditions 153
5. Plants for Medium Temperatures 154
6. Plants for High Temperatures 155
7. Plants for Greatest Tolerance 156
8. Plants for Dry and Semi-Dry Conditions 157
9. Vines and Trailing Plants for Totem Poles 158
10. Plants for Hanging Baskets 159
11. Suggestions for Large-Tubbed Specimens 160

Bibliography 161

Index 169

Basic Needs of House Plants

Every plant has its own preferences and requirements for soil type, light, temperature, ventilation, humidity, and several other factors that are within our power to control, or at least to mitigate. It is vitally important for you, as a busy indoor gardener, to understand the basics of each, since a prior understanding will enable you to avoid much work later on while achieving routine success in growing plants.

In addition to understanding these basic needs, you will want to know something about pots and other containers, repotting plants, propagation, and a few other matters which, while not vital to immediate success, will help you to gain further enjoyment in raising better plants.

The Basic House Plant

The major difference between a house plant and an outdoor plant is one of location. All house plants could live and flourish outdoors, in the proper climate. All are derived from forebears which lived, reproduced, and died outdoors, whether on a forest floor in Central Europe or on the bough of a tree in a South American rain forest. Over many centuries of adaptation and evolution, each plant species embraced those characteristics that enabled it to survive; and, even today, every house plant carries within its genetic structure the characteristics of its distant progenitors. Thus the maranta will lose some of its leaves each autumn, even though autumn's weather does not come to the top of the bookshelf where the plant rests, and a cactus, no matter how long it has been fed and watered with unfailing regularity, will continue to hoard food and water within its swollen stems. In plants, old habits may recede, but they are never forgotten.

At no time are these innate plant characteristics more noticeable than during the autumn and winter, when many plants—particularly those from temperate regions—enter a period of dormancy. Then new growth ceases and the plant takes on a listless and washed-out appearance. Other plants, including many of tropical origin, will maintain their bright appearance but will stop growing completely for several months each year, emulating the natural rest periods of their forebears. You will do well to watch for these signs of dormancy and rest and respond to each plant's needs at that time. When any plant enters a dormant or rest period, water should be reduced and fertilizer withheld completely until new growth begins, usually in the late winter or early spring. At that time, water the plant freely and give it normal doses of fertilizer once again, in order to encourage new growth. By your proper treatment of the plant at this time, you will emulate the advent of spring, working with the plant in carrying out its rhythmic cycles.

Chapter 2

Bromeliads

Some plants also are naturally short-lived and will last no more than a year or two in your home despite your careful attention, because their genetic structure dictates a finite life span. Garden annuals, for instance, will germinate, grow to maturity, flower, produce seeds, and die, all in as little as six months. For this reason, very few annuals are selected as house plants. Although a few short-lived plants are cultivated indoors for their unusual characteristics, such as the sensitive plant, which is easily grown from seed, the house plants that have been cultivated over the generations are most often those that will give years of pleasure. Some house plants, in fact, can live to be hundreds of years old.

Still other house plants are attractive when young but grow ungainly or otherwise unattractive when they approach maturity. The only plants of this kind I have chosen for inclusion in this book are those that are very easy to propagate from cuttings, so that the parent plant may be discarded after a year or two, to be replaced by its children.

From the hundreds of thousands of plant species in the world, those traditionally cultivated as house plants are the relatively few that have shown a wide tolerance to conditions of heat, light, moisture, humidity, and ventilation—in other words, those that can withstand a human environment. They are both attractive to the eye and tough. Still, if you are looking for success with house plants—and particularly success without working hard at it—then you should take some time to learn the characteristics of each plant, recognizing its individual needs and fulfilling them to the best of your ability.

How a Plant Feeds

A plant manufactures nearly all of its food by itself—and not from the "plant food" that you buy for it. Commercial plant food is no more than a combination of certain chemicals (sometimes in an organic base) that are essential to the plant's basic functioning, much as vitamins are essential to human nutrition. But the bulk of a plant's food—the sugar it uses for energy and growth—is manufactured by the plant itself. In the presence of light, the leaves of the plant draw carbon dioxide from the air and water from the roots, converting these into sugar that is then used for energy production or stored for future use.

During this sugar-manufacturing process, known as *photosynthesis*, several other things happen within the plant. While carbon dioxide is being absorbed, oxygen is being released from the *stomata* (pores) of the leaf surface. (Plants produce not only all of the world's food but most of its atmospheric oxygen as well.) During darkness hours, the process is reversed; some of the atmosphere's oxygen is recaptured by the plant and used to convert stored sugar to energy for growth. Generally, a plant manufactures growth food during the day and does its actual growing at night.

Often, the plant converts its newly manufactured sugar to starch and stores it, reconverting it to sugar as the need arises. Although the starch can be stored in almost any area of the plant, certain plants have developed specialized storage areas just for this purpose. Cacti and succulents have enlarged stems and leaves for the greatest above-ground storage capacity of any house plant, while other plants have developed underground storage apparatus for this purpose, including bulbs, tubers, corms, and rhizomes. A *bulb* is simply an enlarged underground bud, such as is found with hyacinths, tulips, and onions. A *tuber* is nothing more than an enlarged stem or root: a common potato is a tuber; gloxinias, caladiums, dahlias, and many other common plants are grown from tubers. A *corm* is the enlarged base of a stem. And a *rhizome* is simply a laterally growing, enlarged stem, usually underground. All are used by the plant for food storage, and all can be used to propagate plants, too.

Water is constantly being drawn up through the plant. As it transpires through the stomata of the leaves, a "pulling" action draws more water up through the roots. The water carries with it mineral salts, including all the elements which the plant needs to carry out its complex chemical processes. The transpiration which takes place in the leaves is similar to perspiration in humans, and it serves a similar purpose—to cool the plant. With house plants, it would be difficult for you to notice this cooling effect. But it is readily apparent when a group of large trees carry out the transpiration process. The cool and fresh feeling you enjoy in a thick woods in summer is primarily the product not of the shade itself but of the transpiration of the millions of leaves overhead.

A plant can seldom absorb too much water, since its vessels and cells can accommodate only so much at a given time; however, the overwatering of a plant can exclude oxygen from the root system, causing wilting of the top portion of the plant. If water is withheld, on the other hand, the plant's cells will gradually collapse, causing wilting of the entire plant. All plants do have protective mechanisms that conserve water in times of drought, however, and can withstand a temporary dry spell. Most wilted house plants will quickly spring back to a normal state when water is again provided.

Parts of the Plant

Stem. The stem serves to support the plant and to contain and direct the vessels that transport water from the roots, and food from the leaves, to every other part of the plant. Most house plants, including philodendron, ivy, and spider plant, have *soft stems*. Such plants must either climb or crawl, since their stems are not strong enough to support an upward-growing structure of significant height. Other plants have soft but thick stems that enable them to attain good height, although their stems are apt to be subject to breakage. *Woody-stemmed* plants, such as the avocado, poinsettia, and boxwood, are far more sturdy and are usually derived from trees or shrubs of the temperate region. *Canes* are thick stems with hollow or pithy centers. Bamboo is an example of a cane with

Spider mite

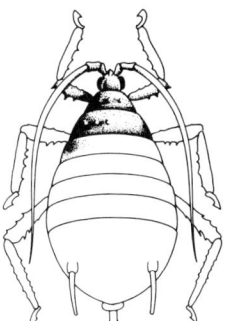

Spider mites, or red spiders, are probably the most virulent attackers of house plants. They thrive in the warm and dry atmosphere of your home and will readily take up residence among your prize plants. Spider mites are too small to be seen with the naked eye. Small white spots on plant leaves may be evidence of spider mite activity, the result of the mites having sucked juices from the leaf surface. If the infestation is sizeable, leaves will gradually take on a fine webbed appearance, have a vaguely fuzzy feeling on their undersides, and eventually feel crumbly. The attack, if unchecked, can prove fatal.

Since spider mites thrive on warmth and dryness, control rests on making them cold and wet. At least in the early stages, they can be eliminated by washing the plant with a mild soap (not detergent) solution, then spraying the entire plant vigorously with cold water, being sure to hit the undersides of leaves where the mites are usually harbored. Repeat this process weekly until the infestation has ceased, and in the meanwhile spray plants daily with a fine mist, preferably in the morning, again being sure to reach the undersides of leaves. If the infestation is truly severe, a solution of rotenone and/or pyrethrum may be used. Both are of low toxicity to warm-blooded creatures, including children, dogs, and cats. (Caution—rotenone is very toxic to fish.) As a last resort, you might choose to use malathion or some other powerful chemical.

Key to symbols

Temperature preference

- ▮ Warm (60–80F.)
- ▮ Moderate (50–70° F.)
- ▯ Cool (45–60° F.)

Light Needs

- ○ Full sun
- ◐ Tolerates some direct sun
- ◑ Bright spot with no direct sun
- ● Tolerates continuous shade

Humidity and soil moisture needs

- ◆ Higher than room humidity, constantly moist soil
- ◆ Moderate humidity and soil moisture
- ◇ Tolerates dry conditions
- ◇ Low humidity and soil moisture required

Best window

- ▲ North
- ➤ South or west
- ► East

Table 2 /Foliage Plants

Bromeliads

Caladium

There are more than eighteen hundred varieties of this popular group, many of which are suitable for growing as house plants. Some of them produce attractive flowers, but most are grown for their striking and variegated leaf patterns. One distinctive feature of the bromeliads is the rosette leaves which form a small water cup, which the plant uses to hold reserve supplies of water in its natural habitat—the crotches of trees in Central and South America. The water cup is an evolutionary survival characteristic. In the home, keep the cup filled with water, changing it weekly to keep it fresh.

A few of the more common genera of bromeliads are *Aechmea, Ananas* (pineapple), *Billbergia, Cryptanthus, Dyckia, Tillandsia* (Spanish moss), and *Vriesia*. ▮ ○ ◆ ►

Caladiums, with their spectacularly colored and variegated leaves, are equally at home in the garden or on the window sill. They are ideal additions to plant groupings on porch or patio in the summer and early autumn. Give them bright light, but not long periods of direct sun in summer, if you want the brightest leaf colors.

Caladiums are grown from tubers, which can be divided easily to produce new plants. Start the tubers in regular potting soil at a very warm temperature—80–90° F.—and move the young plants to a cooler spot when they have appeared. They will attain a height of about one foot.

▮ ◐ ◆ ➤

Plants for Cool Conditions
50°–60° at night

Aloe
Aspidistra
Australian Laurel
Azalea
Baby's Tears
Black Pepper
Boxwood
Bromeliads
Cacti
Calceolaria
Camellia
Cape Ivy
Christmas Begonia
Chrysanthemum
Cineraria
Citrus
Creeping Fig
Cyclamen
Easter Lily
English Ivy
Fatshedera
Fiddle-Leaf Fig
Flowering Maple
Freesia
Fuchsia
Geranium
German Ivy

Honeysuckle
Hyacinth
Jasmine
Jerusalem Cherry
Kalanchoe
Kangaroo Vine
Lily-of-the-Valley
Lithops
Miniature Holly
Mother of Thousands
Narcissus
Oxalis
Primrose
Sensitive Plant
Silk Oak
Snake Plant
Spindletree
Tulip
Vinca
Wandering Jew
White Calla Lily

Appendix 4

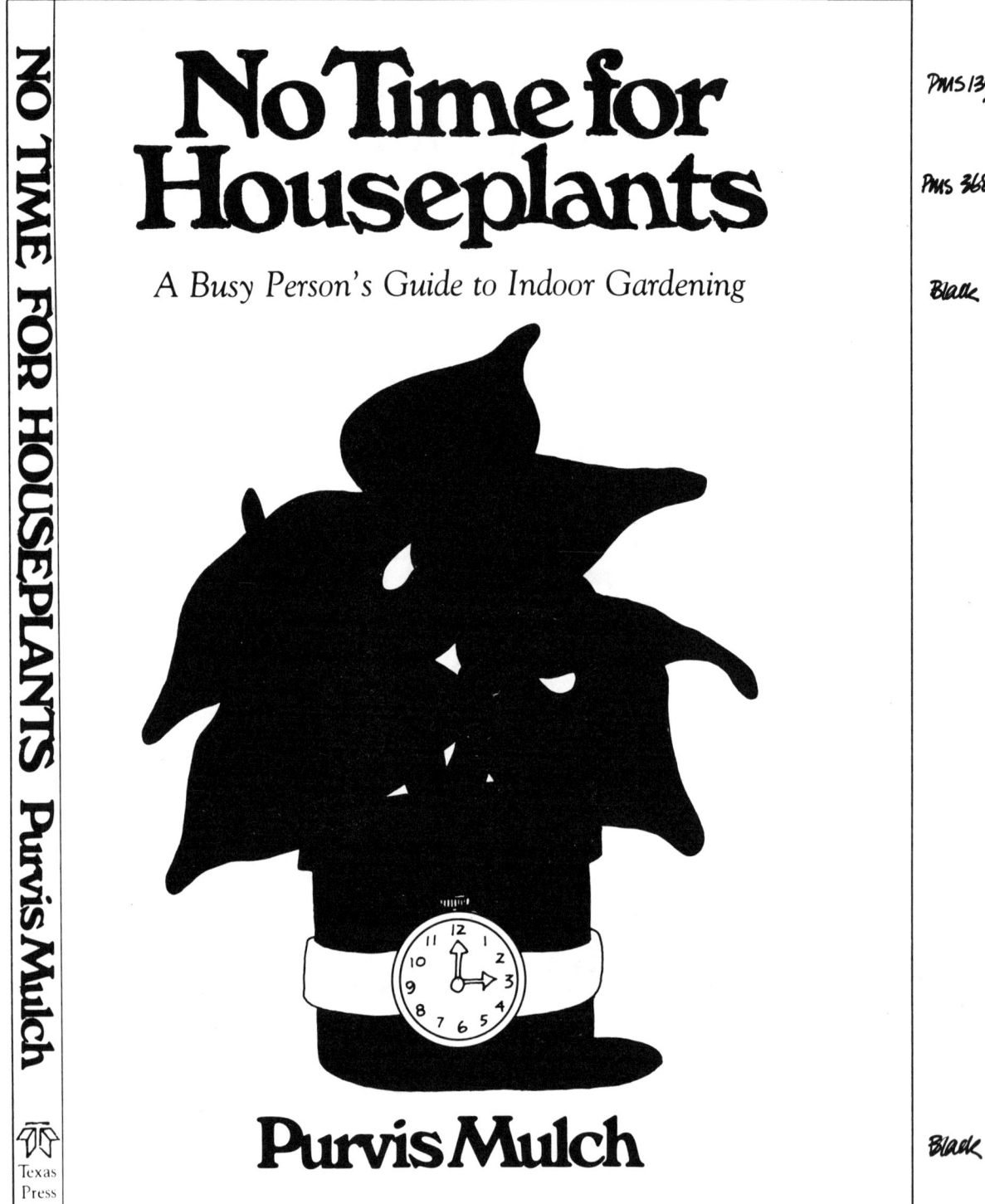

PMS 139
PMS 368
Black

Black

Drawing in black. pot in PMS 139. Plant in PMS 368

University of Texas Press

Date: January 28, 1977

DUST JACKETS/PAPERBACK COVERS PRINTING SPECIFICATIONS

Title: NO TIME FOR HOUSEPLANTS

Job must ship not later than: February 18, 1977

Dust Jackets

Quantity: 7800
Trim Size: 20 x 9 1/4"
Stock: 80# Lustro Offset Enamel Gloss Text
Ink: PMS 139, PMS 368, Black   plus full bleed varnish

Paperback Covers

Quantity: NONE
Trim Size:
Stock:
Ink: plus full bleed varnish

Description

Front panel: First line of title and flower pot in PMS 139
Second line of title and flower in PMS 368
All else in black including drawing outline.
Spine: Pressmark in PMS 368
Back panel: Pot in PMS 139, flower in PMS 368
Flaps in black

Provide a ☐ vandyke or blue print   ☒ 3M or equivalent
☒ Not necessary to check color with University Press. Match PMS color exactly.
☐ Call   to check color

Allow approximately 1/4" all around for copies sent to bindery.
We have allowed 1/8" on artwork for bleeds.

Ship __7500__ flat and untrimmed to bindery
Ship __300__ trimmed to size to University Press as soon as job is ready.
Call for labels and shipping instructions.

Production / Design / Texas / 235

```
BA300V    TEXAS PRESS, UNIVERSITY OF TEXAS AT AUSTIN        WORK-IN-PROGRESS                    DATE  1/31/78     PAGE   1

ISBN  10-999997    NO TIME FOR HOUSEPLANTS                    REVOLVING PUB. FUND
SNWR  104-600      CARD  AN    DSCNT  1     LIST PRICE  6.95    NET PR    4.93
                   CARD  AU    SUB-TITLE   NO TIME FOR HOUSEPLANTS        AUTHOR OR EDITOR   PURVIS MULCH
                               SUBSIDY      0  SOURCE                     SERIES
                   CARD  AK    CAT YEAR    577    PAGES  128   PRINT   7,500   BIND   7,500   MFG COST    13,275

       WORKS-IN-PROGRESS           NO TIME FOR HOUSEPLANTS

                NUMBER UNITS  P   7,500   B  7,500     EST MFG COST     13,275.00     EST SUBSIDY              0.00

       DATE        JOURNAL           DESCRIPTION              CDE  TC     MFG EXP       OTH EXP      TOT EXP    SUB REC
       12/15/76      159       ED LIDLOF STUDIOS              551   1    2,658.79          .00     2,658.79        .00
       12/29/76      176       EMPRESSION                     551   1      752.00          .00     3,410.79        .00
       1/11/77       222       WALLACE ENGRAVING              551   1       20.00          .00     3,430.79        .00
       1/08/77       357       WALLACE ENGRAVING              551   1       54.00          .00     3,484.79        .00
       1/12/77       382       CATHERINE LENOX                551   1      148.00          .00     3,632.79        .00
       2/23/77      1229       KINGSPORT PRESS                551   1    9,110.75          .00    12,743.54        .00
       12/14/77     5669       UNIVERSITY PRINTING DIV        551   1      525.00          .00    13,268.54        .00

       1/31/78                 TOTAL PRODUCTION EXPENSE                 13,268.54          .00    13,268.54        .00

                               EDITORIAL EXPENSE                             .00
                               PRODUCTION EXPENSE                            .00
                               MANUFACTURING EXPENSE                   13,268.54
                               PROMOTION EXPENSE                            .00
                               OTHER EXPENSE                                .00
                               AUTHORS EXPENSE                              .00

       TOTALS            EST MFG COSTS    13,275.00   ACT MFG COSTS   13,268.54   EST SUBS   .00   SUB REC   .00

       FUND TOTALS       EST MFG COSTS    13,275.00   ACT MFG COSTS   13,268.54   EST SUBS   .00   SUB REC   .00

                                                 XXX END-OF-REPORT XXX
```

Summary of Promotion Plan: No Time for House Plants

No Time for House Plants will be the lead title in the catalog the season it is published. It will be treated as a general audience trade book. We will try to reach "busy" young singles and professionals as well as the more traditional home gardening market through our promotional efforts. We will emphacize the "no-time" aspect of this book in an effort to differentiate it from the hundreds of other plant books on the market.

ROUTE SLIP--SPACE ADVERTISING

Job Number **7700 SP**
Journal & Issue **Texas Monthly**
Specifications **4 5/8" x 4 7/8" CRC**
Date Needed **a.s.a.p.**

Route: Advertising Manager __CB 12/1__
Marketing Manager __CPS 12/1__
Senior Editor __lost 12/1__
Director __CJ 12/2/76__
Advertising Manager __CB 12/2__
Manuscript Editor _____
Advertising Manager _____

Special Instructions to Production:

Treat "No Time for House Plants" as headline.

7700 SP

No Time for House Plants

A Busy Person's Guide to Indoor Gardening

By Purvis Mulch

The "no-time" gardener can raise *a houseful of healthy, interesting* ~~as many as twenty different house~~ plants without spending more than five minutes daily and a half hour every other week caring for them. No Time for House Plants tells you exactly how to do it.

(bibliographic material to come)

University of Texas Press
Post Office Box 7819
Austin 78712

Direct Mail

Copy for mailing piece will be drawn from catalog copy with emphasis on busy people market and information about author's background.

It will offer 46% discount if the establishment orders the tabletop display dump (holds 20 books). The order blank will have no provision for charge cards.

Mailer cost:

$500   production
$195   mailing
$695   total

print 5,000

Mail to:

900 to Texas Assn. of Nurserymen (test mailing)
2000 to selected bookstore (Bowker list)
1000 to selected department store book departments (Bowker list)

Dump Display
Order 500 initially at $1.50 ea.
cost: $750

Direct Sales

Bookstores and major plant stores in major Texas cities

Major bookstores in major cities in New Mexico, Arizona, California, Washington, Oregon and the Northeast.

University of Texas Press
Post Office Box 7819
Austin, Texas 78712
512-471-7233

11/29/76

DS, ITH (et al), PDJ, BS, CG

Catalog copy for NO TIME FOR HOUSE PLANTS.

- Same copy for jacket
- no ads on jacket

No Time for House Plants
A Busy Person's Guide to Indoor Gardening
By Purvis Mulch

No matter what color your thumb and no matter how hectic your schedule, you can brighten your home with healthy, growing plants.

There are two crucial rules the "no-time" indoor gardener must follow: ¢hoose tolerant, hardy plants↓ and then give them the right conditions to grow without your constant attention. No Time for House Plants tells you exactly how to do it. Purvis Mulch begins by explaining how plants work and what they need for success, including potting mixtures, fertilizing (either organic or chemical), containers, watering, humidity, ventilation, temperature, light, and pruning. When these conditions are met at the beginning, countless hours will be saved later in nursing plants or attempting to track down troubles.

The book lists over (100) beautiful and interesting no-time plants, including foliage plants, flowering plants, and succulents. Each listing is accompanied by a description, a finely detailed line drawing, and a set of read-at-a-glance symbols indicating temperature, light, moisture, and window placement preferences. There are graphic illustrations of processes like potting and pruning which might be unfamiliar to the beginning gardener, and the chapter devoted to plant ailments and cures includes drawings of the most common insect pests. There are also special sections on summer care, artificial light, and maintaining plants while you're away.

The no-time gardener can raise as many as twenty different house plants without spending more than five minutes daily and a half hour every two weeks caring for them. For those who enjoy a little fussing, there is detailed information on repotting, propagation, training, dish gardens, planters, bottle gardens and terrariums, kitchen scrap gardens, and indoor vegetable gardening.

Purvis Mulch is a very active person who has been gardening and writing for over twenty years. He is the author of _____ Garden Guide and The Earthworm Book.

For catalog:

6 x 9 in., ca. 000 pp., 000 line drawings, 00 black-and-white photographs.
Pub. date   LC 00-000   (00000-0) $00.00.

For jacket front:

No Time for House Plants
A Busy Person's Guide to Indoor Gardening
Purvis Mulch

For jacket spine:

No Time for House Plants
Purvis Mulch
Texas Press

Advertising

Texas Monthly

4 5/8 x 4 7/8 $660 - 15% agency discount $561

Apartment Life (mail order section)

2 1/4 x 5 $1200 - 15% $1020

Better Homes & Gardens (mail order section)

2 1/4 x 2 1/2 $463

Saturday Evening Post (classified)

25 words @ $2 per word $50

Publishers Weekly

Will share full page with other trade titles
in announcement issue $250

Newspaper advertising in major dailies in conjunction with
author parties and television appearances $600

TOTAL: $2944

REVIEW LIST

Title _No Time for House Plants_

Author or editor _Mulch_

Publication date _0/0/77_

Date to Business Office _0/0/77_

Date shipped _0/0/77_   Postage _____

Total number of books _132_

Special Instructions:

Send one book each unless otherwise indicated on label.

All books outside U.S. and Canada should be sent Air Mail.

— Review cards as usual
  $00.00 cloth

— News release w/ each book

Authorized by _Chris Gray_
_0/0/77_

Flower & Garden
Ms.
Playboy
Sphere
Vogue
Esquire
Good Housekeeping
National Observer
New Woman
Plants Alive
News & Information Service-UT Austin

House Beautiful
Mademoiselle
House & Garden
Town & Country
Cosmopolitan
Glamour
Avant Gardener
Home & Country
National Gardener
Plants & Gardens
   (Brooklyn Botanical Garden)

REVIEW LIST (continued)

Cumulative Book Index
Citizen Journal, Arlington, Tx
The El Paso Times
San Antonio Light
Albuquerque Tribune
Chicago Sun-Times
Hartford Times
Memphis Commercial Appeal
Pittsburgh Press
Seattle Times
Mr. John Dawson, AUPG, London
Abilene Reporter News
Corpus Christi Caller-Times
Houston Chronical
Victoria Advocate
Texas Monthly
Scrooge & Marley, Gene Shalit
The Arizona Republic
Chicago Tribune
Indepen. Press-Telegram
Miami Herald
The Plain Dealer
San Francisco Chronicle
Blackwell North America
A L A Booklist
Amarillo News-Globe
Courier-Times-Telegraph
Fort Worth Star-Telegram
San Angelo Standard Times
Waco News Tribune
Mother Earth News
Charlotte Observer
Detroit News
Los Angeles Times
The News, Birmingham, Alabama
San Francisco Examiner
Bro-Dart Books
The Kirkus Service, Inc.
Daily Texan
El Paso Herald-Post
San Antonio Express & News
Books West
Baltimore Sun
Christian Science Monitor
Kansas City Star
Minneapolis Tribune
Richmond Times-Dispatch
Tulsa World

Austin American-Statesman
Dallas News
Pasadena News-Citizen
Atlantic Monthly
Boston Globe
Denver Post
LA Herald-Examiner
The New Mexican
Rocky Mountain News
Washington Post
Choice
Austin Citizen
Fort Worth Press
Saunders Book Store
John Barkham Reviews
Book Review Critics, NY Times
United Press International
Boston Herald American
Detroit Free Press
Little Rock Gazette
New Orleans Times-Picayune
Southern Exposure
The Baker & Taylor Co.
Library of Congress
Library Journal
Avalanche-Journal
Dallas Times Herald
Houston Post
Southwest Books
Bookletter
Atlanta Journal-Constitution
Cleveland Press
Oklahoma City Oklahoman
Milwaukee Journal
Portland Oregonian
Star-Tribune Publications
Publisher's Weekly
Beaumont Enterprise
Galveston News
Palestine Herald-Press
American Scholar
Universal Features
Chicago Daily News
Hartford Courant
Louisville Courier-Journal
Philadelphia Inquirer
Seattle Post-Intelligencer
Book People

University of Texas Press

POST OFFICE BOX 7819, AUSTIN, TEXAS 78712, (512) 471-7233

AUTHOR INFORMATION

The promotion of a book is necessarily a mutual effort. The effectiveness of our promotional copy—for jacket, catalogue, publicity releases, flyers, brochures, and space advertising—depends directly upon the thoroughness with which you complete this questionnaire. We urge you to develop your replies to whatever extent necessary to give us adequate information. Please fill out this form on the typewriter if possible. If for any reason you cannot supply portions of the requested information, please indicate your omission so we will know you have not overlooked the item. Return the completed form as soon as possible. Thank you.

Date August 9, 1976

1. Name (a) in full (required for copyright registration)

   (b) as you wish it to appear on title page

2. If the title page is to carry the names of any other authors, editors, or contributors, please supply their names here as used on title page

   none

3. Title of book (or manuscript)

   No Time for House Plants: A Busy Person's Guide to Indoor Gardening

4. Series (if applicable) none

5. Required for copyright registration: legal address, citizenship, and place of birth. Please indicate which address is to be used for correspondence concerning this book.

   (a) Office address and zip code   Office phone

   (b) Home address and zip code   Home phone

(c) Citizenship USA
    If not native, when did you come to the USA? When?
    Naturalized citizen?

(d) Place and date of birth

6. Social Security number

7. Present academic connection, position, or occupation

8. Previous positions (with dates)

9. Education (please include dates of degrees) and honors

10. Learned and honorary societies to which you belong. Please separate present from past and include all relevant offices held.

    none

11. Special research, experience, or travel for this book; relevant military, government, or other official positions. Also include countries, cities, and states in which you have lived, with approximate dates.

    No field research for this book. Lived in Pennsylvania, 1933-1957; Iowa, 1957-1961; Pennsylvania, 1961-1963; New Jersey, 1963-1965;

12. Special fields of interest. Any other pertinent biographical data for use on book jackets, etc.

    Organic gardening; solid waste recycling; environmental issues

Sales / Promotion / Texas / 245

13. Titles of your publications (including forthcoming) and publishers. Indicate (with *) which two or three of your books and articles are most important. Attach list if lengthy. (Please indicate book club adoptions, paperback reprints, serializations, and foreign editions).

Title   Publisher   Year   Approx. Sale
* WISCONSIN GARDEN GUIDE, Wisconsin House, Ltd., 1975; 15,000 in print
* THE EARTHWORM BOOK, Rodale Press, Inc., scheduled for 1977
  "The Earthworm Czar," Organic Gardening & Farming, Sept. 1976
  "Gardening for the Late Bloomer," Mother Jones, June 1976
  "To Garden in the City, Organize Community Plots," House Beautiful, April 1976
Other articles in Camping Journal, Mobile Life, other magazines

14. Description of your book that might be used to inform its potential readers (literate nonspecialists as well as students in the field) about its subject matter, the reasons for its importance, your method of approach to that subject matter, and your conclusions (300 or more words). We hope you will bear in mind that this information will be our primary source for preparing jacket, catalogue, and advertising copy. Please do not merely refer us to your preface or other parts of your manuscript, for the manuscript is often unavailable at the time the information is needed.

I have been gardening and writing about gardening for more than twenty-three years. In this time, my major emphasis has been on outdoor plants, particularly vegetables. I have always had a few indoor plants, but never took much interest in them and, so, had very limited success.

In 1973, with the purchase of a new house, I was determined to increase my house plant population. Still, I realized that, with my busy schedule, I would not have much time to devote to indoor plants. I was frequently gone for long periods of time, and many days, even while in town, I simply have no time to fuss with plants.

I therefore sought to find methods to raise interesting and beautiful house plants with the least amount of effort. All the house plant books I checked, however, were apparently written by enthusiasts who spent unending hours in careful watering, potting, repotting, propagating, tying up, inducing to flowering, humidifying, bathing, and even talking to their plants, in an effort to get them to grow. There was no book for the casual house plant grower.

There is now such a book. By researching many sources, and with the aid of personal experimentation and past experience, I have narrowed down the crucial requirements for a "no-time" indoor house plant population. The research yielded two cardinal rules: "Choose plants that are tolerant of adverse conditions, and then give them the right conditions to grow without your constant attention.

The implementation of these rules form the crux of this book. I explain how to choose plants, tell which are the easiest to grow, and explain the conditions of light, soil moisture, humidity, and temperature that each of more than a hundred indoor plants requires. I explain, in short, how your house plants can live well without your constant attention and painstaking devotion.

(more, separate sheet attached)

[14, continued]

The chapter on understanding house plants is critically important to the "no-time" system, since it details the initial requirements plants need for success, including potting mixtures, fertilizing, containers, watering, humidity, ventilation, temperature, light, and pruning. When these conditions are met at the very beginning, countless hours will be saved later in nursing plants or attempting to track down troubles.

There is a separate chapter devoted to plant troubles and cures, and special sections on artificial light, summer care, and lists of plants for various conditions of light and temperature. For those who wish to devote a little more time to raising house plants, there is detailed information on repotting, propagation, training, dish gardens, planters, bottle gardens and terrariums, kitchen scrap gardens, and growing vegetables indoors.

The bulk of the book, however, comprises listings of more than a hundred "easy" foliage plants, flowering plants, and succulents including cacti, giving light, soil moisture, and humidity requirements for each.

For the home owner or apartment dweller who wants to raise several dozen attractive house plants while spending only a few minutes a day in caring for them, this book will tell everything that is necessary to know in order to achieve success.

15. Particular points to be emphasized in promotion, including details on new material or new interpretation of old material as compared with previously published studies in the field. (This is very important for a variety of sales and promotional purposes.)

    There are hundreds of house plant books in print; this is, so far as I know, the first to take this approach.

16. Does any section of your book lend itself to excerpting? Have any sections been previously published? If so, by whom?

    Chapter 2 could be excerpted, as a short guide to the care of house plants in general.

17. Artwork. Specify illustrations, figures, photos, etc. that might be used in advertising to stimulate interest.

    The photos on hand are not spectacular. The ones depicting bottle gardens are perhaps the most interesting.

18. Audiences for your book: be as specific as possible and list in order of importance. Also list names and addresses of persons whose good opinion of the book might broaden its audience—those to whom, for instance, advance copies of the book might be sent by us for comments that could be quoted in advertising. Endorsements from both foreign and domestic scholars and critics should be considered.

    Single people, working people, apartment-dwellers would constitute the major audience for the book.

19. Other books on the same subject (with dates of publication and publisher if possible; compare with yours if possible).

    There are dozens of books on house plants published each year. It would serve no purpose to list them all, even if I could.

20. Courses for which your book might be used as a text or collateral reading. Please list those professors and their institutions that should be approached with a view to the classroom adoption of the book.

    The only course for which I could foresee this book's adoption is a short course in growing house plants. It is meant for a lay audience and not suitable for students in botany and/or horticulture, who will have advanced far beyond this book's scope.

21. Special groups to circularize. Please give us the names and addresses of professional societies and organizations that will be interested in the book. Include, if possible, the names and addresses of persons to whom we can apply for very specialized lists; indicate (with *) which lists you can supply yourself. *Your efforts in this area can be especially valuable to our marketing success.*

    Apartment Ideas subscription list; other general magazines with a young, professional, and largely single audience—Mother Jones, Esquire, Ms, Rolling Stone, Playgirl, etc.

22. Individuals to circularize. Attach to this form. You may supply as many names and addresses of individuals as you wish.   none

23. At which association conventions might it be appropriate to exhibit your book? Which conventions do you normally attend?

    ALA, ABA

24. How many circulars could you use for your own purposes?
    100

25. Suggested advertising media. Please list magazines and scholarly journals that accept advertising, where notice of your book might be especially effective. List in order of importance. (Include publications outside the USA—especially Canada and Europe.)

    Professional Journals   General Magazines

                                   NYTBR
                                   Apartment Ideas
                                   Mother Jones
                                   Organic Gardening & Farming
                                   Ms
                                   Esquire
                                   Better Homes & Gardens
                                   House Beautiful

26. Reviewing media. List the most important scholarly and general publications that might review your book. You may attach a list of publications of secondary importance if you wish.

Scholarly Publications   General Publications

Organic Gardening & Farming   Milwaukee Journal
Horticulture   Chicago Tribune
Flower & Garden   Los Angeles Times
Better Homes & Gardens   Village Voice
House Beautiful   Mother Jones
House & Garden   Rolling Stone

27. Hometown or other newspapers (and editors, columnists) to whom you or your book is news.

28. Bookstores and/or radio/TV commentators to whom you or your book is known.

29. Prizes and awards for which your book might be eligible.

don't know of any

30. Photograph. Please supply one or more copies of whatever recent black-and-white photograph (preferably 5 x 7 inches or larger) that you would prefer we use for promotion purposes. Note: Many prizes and award competition entries must be accompanied by photograph. Photograph will not be returned. Photo enclosed _____ (or date when we can expect one).

call when needed

Thank you,

Marketing Department
University of Texas Press

NO TIME FOR HOUSE PLANTS

Book Club Rights

After receiving docket material, the editorial fact sheet, and other pertinent information on the book (through various discussions with the acquisitions editor and marketing), the rights and permissions manager would decide if book club rights should be sought.

As a trade title with a projected large audience, the book seems a likely candidate. At the earliest possible date, I (the r&p manager) would request extra sets of galleys to be ordered by the production department. Then, inquiries would be sent to the appropriate book clubs when galleys are received. A covering letter would accompany the (bound) set of galleys explaining the general content of the ms. with a brief note about the author and why we feel it would appeal to the book club membership. Since this manuscript is a basic introduction to house plants, I would stress its simplistic style and easy comprehensible nature as well as elaborating on the excellent quality of the book's illustrations which most plant enthusiasts find to be useful and desireable. I would also emphasize its potential value for the working man or woman with an interest in plants but a heavy schedule which leaves little time to devote to plant care. Finally, the letter would include the list price, bound book date, publication date, and the (deadline) date by which we would need a response from the book club if they intend to print with us. Although a response might take six to eight weeks, a follow-up letter or phone call would be made perhaps two weeks before the actual deadline (if no response has been received at that time).

Possible book clubs to investigate would be the American Garden Guild Book Club, Better Homes & Gardens Crafts Club, Woman Today Book Club, Organic Gardening Book Club, and, perhaps, one of the subsidiary clubs from, say, Prentice Hall, Inc.

In actuality, I would not be too hopeful of selling these rights. The field is already flooded with books on most every aspect of growing house plants and acceptance by a book club would require a very strong and distinguished manuscript. This particular manuscript does not seem to be especially unique or enlightening from what has previously appeared on the market.

AUTHOR PARTY

We assume for our purposes that Mulch is willing to pay his way to Texas in order to promote the book.

The author appears in major plant stores (those that stock plant books) in Houston, San Antonio, Dallas, Fort Worth, and Austin. He will be available at the store all day Saturday to autograph books and to give plant buyers advice on how to care for their plants the "no-time" way. The announcement will stress that Mulch will be there to give his expert advice to anyone who has questions about plants. The plant stores will use their lists for the announcements, and the Press will pay for printing and postage.

We will also send news releases to local media. We will try to get Mulch on noon time chat shows the Friday preceeding the autograph day to talk about the book, the autograph party and to demonstrate some of the processes explained in the book.

UNIVERSITY OF TORONTO PRESS

Table of Contents

Acquisitions and Administration

Notes on Log / 253
Decision to Publish / 254
Publishing Budget / 255
Contract / 256
Manuscript / Project Information Sheet / 259

Editorial

Memo / 260
Edited Manuscript / 262
Correspondence with Author / 269

Production and Design

Breakdown of Production Costs / 272
Composition Specifications / 273
Printing and Binding Specifications / 274
Manuscript and Proof Routing Form Schedule / 275
Composition Instructions / 276
Page Layout / 277
Sample Pages / 278

Sales and Promotion

Correspondence with Author / 286
Author's Information Sheets / 287
Outline of Sales and Promotion Campaign / 290
Promotion Budget / 295
Cover Copy / 295
Catalog Copy / 296
News Release / 297
Autobiographical Sheet / 298
Review Copies List / 299
Ad Copy / 302

Some Notes on Toronto's Log

No Time For House Plants would not have been seriously considered by Toronto for publication in real life, and we would have recommended to Purvis Mulch that he approach a commercial house. As a result, and also because of the constraints imposed by the limited number of pages available for the log, certain steps in our procedures are omitted altogether.

When a manuscript first arrives in house it is immediately logged and a preliminary publications docket opened for it. It is then placed with the house editor into whose area of responsibility it falls, who is responsible for acknowledging to the author its arrival and giving a first indication of what will follow. Frequently a manuscript is rejected outright after an editorial reading for any of a number of valid reasons and the author so informed. If the house editor sees possibilities for us in the manuscript it will be sent to a first outside reader for a report. Depending on the nature of this report and on whether subsidy is to be sought for the work from one or other of the sources of such subsidy, a second reader may be sought or the manuscript sent to one of the subsidizing councils for their scrutiny and report.

When the house editor is satisfied with the reports, a decision to publish form is started (page 254) and this is sent, together with the manuscript and the readers' reports, to the sales and promotion departments. The sales manager makes a marketing assessment of the book, usually in more than one combination of price, discount and quantity, notes the special requirements if any, and passes to the promotion manager who notes if any special promotional costs may be involved and also any special promotional requirements.

The manuscript and copies of the decision to publish form are then circulated to the internal committee (representing management, sales, promotion, editorial, production and design) for approval. The Production Manager obtains an estimate and the last page of the decision to publish form is completed so that the full picture of the marketing possibilities and costs can be seen in the one form. The house editor presents the manuscript, the reports and the financial picture to the Manuscript Review Committee. If the work is approved, the house editor draws up a contract with the author, and editing and production proceed.

Numerous internal forms are not to be seen in the log. Such forms include the production record, the form circulated with the jacket design, blurb, the final proofs and etc. and the card controlling the final quantity to be printed, bound, or held unbound, and the complete promotion record.

A final word about the change in sex of the author, a thoroughly 'unreal' event. In this case it was occasioned by a memo from the University of North Carolina Press which gave the author's sex as female, and it was accepted happily by our promotion manager as a means of greatly expanding the promotional possibilities of the book at minimum expense.

Editorial comments (including strengths, weaknesses, special features, origins, of ms)

Author is a plain practical person who knows how to choose house plants that are easy to look after and is confident, as I am, that there are a great many people who would benefit from her knowledge. The main problem is that she cannot express herself clearly, mostly because her knowledge of grammar is faulty. But we have here a short, practical book which with severe editing should enjoy a long life and have a reasonable share of a large market.

Information about the author (notable qualifications, honours, previous publications, etc.)

Previous outdoor gardening book very well received.

Readers' names and present affiliations (with date report received)
T.H. Everett, Senior Horticulture specialist, New York Botanical Gardens
D. Levine, Owner, The Potted Plant, Chapel Hill, N.C.

Physical description of manuscript   Number of manuscript pages 136
Illustrations supplementary to text [XX] essential [XX] can be grouped [ ] must be through text [XX]
                          number of halftones ____ number of line illustrations 15
                          special artwork required ____
Tabular material   number of tables ____ Formula setting none [ ] limited [ ] extensive [ ]
Special design/production considerations (including any use of colour)

Markets expected for this book
Will appeal particularly to the well-educated and serious reader. Big city and college market particularly. Good library possibilities also.
Sales experience of comparable books published by UTP
  Author   Title   ISBN   Pub date   Price   1st yr 2nd yr 3rd yr Total to date
            Not Applicable

Competitive books from other publishers
(Author, title, publisher, publication date, page length, price, sales history if known)
Numerous, particularly from specialized publishers such as Sunset Books.

How does this manuscript differ from such competition?
This work will appeal to serious people as it is well organized and amusingly written and conveys much essential information in a short space.
Recommendations re subsidiary rights, special promotion, prepublication prices, etc.
Some opportunity for Book Club sales.

_____ _____
Date   Area editor

University of Toronto Press
Decision to Publish

Author(s) /Editor(s) Purvis Mulch   Date started 25 Nov 1976
with affiliations
                                                  Docket 1234
Title
  tentative [ ] final [XX] No Time for House Plants: a   Printed pages (per
                            Busy Person's Guide to Indoor estimate) 136
  Series   Gardening
Brief description
This is a sprightly short book clearly and amusingly written and the sub-title A busy person's guide to indoor gardening well explains its purpose. The market for the work covers all of North America but it will have a particular appeal to the well educated and should enjoy a particularly good sale in university communities. There are a number of books of a similar nature, of course, and it will be necessary to ensure that the promotion of the book is clearly aimed at the most likely elements of the market - such as university communities. This work is not like any other in our list but fits well into our general program of publishing good books for the general public on a commercial basis.

Projected schedule: manuscript complete in house now [XX] anticipated date ____
                     recommended publishing season Spring 1977

Outside assistance: subsidy available [ ] anticipated [ ] to be applied for [ ]
                     from HRCC [ ] SSRCC [ ] block grants [ ] other ____
                     amount (if firm) $ ____
                     totally underwritten (sponsored) by ____
                     co-publication government [ ] import [ ] rights available all

On the basis of projections in this form, addition of this title to the List of Publications following Option ____ is recommended by:

  Comments   Date _____ _____
                                                   Area editor

                            Date _____ _____
                                                   General Editor

                            Date _____ _____
                                                   Manager, Sales and Distribution

                            Approved by
                            Date _____ _____
                                                   Associate Director

                            Approved by
                            Date _____ _____
                                                   Director

Approved by Manuscript   Agreement concluded   ISBN cloth _____ paper _____
Review Committee
                          Date _____   Subject classification _____
Date _____

Appraisal of manuscript editing requirements, given current state of ms _____

Ms editing budget in-house hours __60__ freelance fees _____

Projected schedule, assuming ms will be complete in house on anticipated date editing to begin __Dec. 1, 1976__ edited ms ready for production __Jan. 21, 1977__
(Revised projected schedule to be circulated when complete ms received)

Extraordinary costs for ms editing ☐ artwork ☐ to be absorbed by UTP ☒ charged to author charged against royalties ☐ other _____ Est. amount $ _____

_____ _____
Date   Executive Editor

_____ _____
Date   General Editor

SALES—OPTIONS

	Cloth			Paper		
	1	2	3	4	5	6
Price/Discount	10.95	9.95				
	40	40				
Wholesalers	750	1,000				
Bookstores (incl. flower shops)	5,000	6,500				
College Bookstores	1,000	1,500				
Libraries	500	500				
Edition						
Export (other than U.S.)						
Other						
Total Sales	7,250	9,500				
Frees	250	500				
Printing run	7,500	10,000				

SALES FORECAST

First year	4,000	6,000			
Second year	2,000	3,000			
Third year	1,250	500			
Sub-Total	7,250	9,500			
Fourth & Fifth year					
Total					

Recommended publication date __Spring 1977__ published when 12 months - 2 years
Paperback prospects __excellent__
Need for advance ~~jackets~~ covers, 250 page proofs 6 sewn copies 25 other
Subsidiary markets ☒ book clubs ☒ serialization ☐ translation ☐ excerpts ☐ co-publication
Special plans and budget requirements

Promotion } ~~Extra $2,500 (Total $5,000)~~
Advertising
Direct Mail __nil__

_____ _____ _____
Date   Manager, Promotion   Date   Manager, Sales & Distribution

---

MULCH

PUBLISHING BUDGET

	CLOTH			PAPER		
	OPT. 1	OPT. 2	OPT. 3	OPT. 4	OPT. 5	OPT. 6
Suggested list price	$10.95	$9.95	$	$	$	$
Average discount	38 %	38 %	%	%	%	%
Net proceeds	$6.79	$6.17	$	$	$	$
Sales in units	7,250	9,500				
Sales	$49,220	$58,615				

	OPT. A	OPT. B	OPT. C
Sales income - cloth	49,220	58,615	
- paper			
Total	49,220	58,615	
Costs:			
Production			
Copy editing (78 hrs @ $11.75)	920	920	
Design (40 hrs @ $15.00)	600	600	
Production (30 hrs @ $15.00)	450	450	
Mfg. cost - compilation	5,244	5,244	
- variable	11,837	15,466	
Other			
Total production	19,051	22,680	
Selling			
Special promotion	2,500	2,500	
Royalties @ 10 %	4,922	5,862	
Overhead @ 40 %	19,688	23,446	
Commission @ % of sales 5000/65000	3,285	3,881	
Mark-up 10	4,922	5,862	
Total selling	35,317	41,551	
Total costs	54,368	64,231	
Net income (shortfall)	(5,148)	(5,616)	
Edition sale, if any			
Total net income (shortfall)	$	$	$
Subsidy required, if any			
Sources of subsidy			
Subsidized publications budget	$19,688	$23,446	
Other	5,148	5,616	
Overhead			
Less UTP subsidy			
Net contribution to overhead	$14,540	$17,830	

Date __25/1/77__   _____ Publications Co-ordinator

Title No Time for House Plants: A Busy Person's Guide to Indoor Gardening

Memorandum of Agreement

between

Purvis Mulch, ... Box 1379, ...

Hereinafter referred to as the Author

OF THE ONE PART

and

UNIVERSITY OF TORONTO PRESS

Hereinafter referred to as the Publisher

OF THE OTHER PART

WHEREBY IT IS MUTUALLY AGREED BETWEEN THE PARTIES HERETO for themselves and their respective executors, administrators, assigns, or successors as follows:

1. The Author hereby grants and assigns to the Publisher the sole and exclusive world rights to copyright, produce, and publish in book form and in machine hereinafter provided, subject to the following conditions, the literary work at present entitled and described as follows:

No Time for House Plants: A Busy Person's Guide to Indoor Gardening

2. The Author , if .... not already done so, agree to deliver to the Publisher, within .... from the date of this agreement the manuscript of the said work in its final form properly prepared for the press, including illustrative material as follows:

Receipt of the manuscript is hereby acknowledged.

3. The Author hereby undertakes that the material submitted for publication is (will be) original and free from any copyright restrictions, or where not original with the Author, that it will be free from copyright restrictions except as may be set forth in writing to the Publisher at the time of submission. The Author further guarantees that he will indemnify and hold harmless the Publisher from and against all claims, demands and actions that may be made against the Publisher, and against all costs, damages, expenses and liability sustained or incurred by the Publisher, by reason of any unlawful or libellous matter contained in the said work.

4. The Publisher undertakes, subject to his editorial approval, to publish the said manuscript at his own expense in such style or styles as he deems best suited to its sale, provided however that the cost of making Author's corrections or revisions in the text after typesetting may be charged against the Author's future royalties. However such charges shall not include those for correcting deviations from copy by the compositors, which shall remain the responsibility of the Publisher.

5. The Publisher agrees to deliver to .... the Author on publication six (6) copies of the published work free of charge, and to supply additional copies for the Author's personal use at the full trade discount from the list price at which the book is currently being sold. Two free copies shall also be delivered by the Publisher to the National Library, Ottawa.

(*i*) On any income from rights not otherwise set forth in this agreement, fifty per cent (50%) of the amount received, said percentage to be distributed in the proportions indicated in 8(*a*) where there is more than one author.

9. The Publisher shall render annual statements of account to the Author for each year ending the thirtieth day of ~~June~~ <ins>September</ins> or before the first day of ~~September~~ following, and shall at the same time make any payments due to the Author hereunder in respect of the preceding accounting period.

10. This agreement shall not be deemed to have been completed until two copies (or more if so provided for elsewhere in this agreement) have been duly completed by all parties to it and one copy has been actually received at the editorial and administrative offices of the Publisher.

11. Where the work referred to in this agreement has been approved for publication under subsidy from the Publications Fund of the Publisher, the Publisher's obligation to publish shall be conditional on such subsidy being available from the Publications Fund at the time of publication.

12. Should sales of the work referred to herein fail to justify, in the opinion of the Publisher, its re-publication, the Publisher may cancel this contract by forwarding a written notice to this effect by registered mail to the last known address of the Author. On receipt of such notice the Author shall have the right to purchase from the Publisher at half the cost of original production the plates of the said work if such are in existence and at the disposal of the Publisher. It is understood that cost of original production of the plates shall include the cost of typesetting. If the Author shall decide to exercise this right he must also purchase at the same time from the Publisher the bound stock of said work then on hand at one-third of the current catalogue or retail price of said work, and the sheet stock at one-fifth of such price. If there are no plates of said work in existence, but if the type of the said work is standing, then the Publisher shall make said type available to the Author at one-half the cost of setting and compilation plus the full cost of the type metal. If the Author has not exercised his rights under this provision within three months of the mailing of the notice as specified herein, the Publisher may destroy the plates and/or distribute the type and/or dispose of the stock as he sees fit without royalty or other compensation to the Author. If the Publisher for any reason should subsequently decide to reissue said work, he may do so, but only under the royalty provisions and other conditions specified in this agreement.

6. Should it at any time in the future, in the opinion of the Publisher, become necessary to offer a revised edition of the said work the Author agrees to prepare at his own expense the manuscript of such revision as may be necessary, and should the Author by reason of death or otherwise be unable or unwilling to prepare such a revision then the Publisher may charge any editorial payments he may have to make for such revision by another editor or editors against the Author's future royalties.

7. The Publisher will have the right to make such editorial revisions as in his opinion may be considered necessary to render the finished work suitable for publication.

8. In consideration of the rights herein granted, the Publisher agrees to pay to the Author or to his duly authorized representatives the following royalties on books sold by him ~~except as otherwise provided in this contract~~:

(*a*) Ten per cent (10%) of the list price on the first 5,000 (five thousand) copies sold; twelve and one-half per cent (12 1/2%) of the list price on the next 5,000 (five thousand) copies sold; and fifteen per cent (15%) on all copies sold thereafter.

(*b*) Where bound copies or sheets are sold for export from Canada at less than the domestic booksellers' normal <ins>net price in situ</ins> the total royalty payable under this agreement shall be calculated at ten per cent (10%) on the price actually received by the Publisher (after deduction of selling discounts and commissions,) said royalties to be divided in the proportions indicated in 8(*a*) where there is more than one author.

(*c*) On sales of all or of parts or digests of the said work, subsequent to publication, to newspapers or periodicals for publication therein, fifty per cent (50%) of the amount received, said percentage to be divided in the proportions indicated in 8(*a*) where there is more than one author.

(*d*) On sales of the right to publish in countries outside Canada for a lump sum or royalty all or parts of said work fifty per cent (50%) of the amount received after commissions if any, said percentage to be divided in the proportions indicated in 8(*a*) where there is more than one author.

(*e*) On sales of all or parts of the said work, subsequent to publication, for reprint in other books, fifty per cent (50%) of the amount received, said percentage to be divided in the proportions indicated in 8(*a*) where there is more than one author.

(*f*) On sales of editions for a lump sum or a royalty to Book Clubs, fifty per cent (50%) of the amount received, said percentage to be divided in the proportions indicated in 8(*a*) where there is more than one author.

(*g*) On sales of dramatic, motion and talking picture, and broadcasting rights fifty per cent (50%) of the amount received, said percentage to be divided in the proportions indicated in 8(*a*) where there is more than one author.

(*h*) No royalties shall be payable on copies supplied free of charge by the Publisher in the course of promoting sales of the published work.

(*i*) On sales of the right to translate into foreign languages, fifty per cent (50%) of the amount received, said percentage to be divided in the proportions indicated in 8(*a*) where there is more than one author.

PROVISION FOR PAPERBOUND EDITION OF

Purvis Mulch, 'No Time for House Plants: A Busy Person's Guide to Indoor Gardening'

With respect to the publishing agreement for the above work dated it is further agreed as follows:

In the event that the Publisher issues in addition to a regular case-bound edition of the said work, and/or in addition to case-bound reprinted editions of the said work, whether or not the latter be similar in format to the original edition, a paperbound edition of the said work at a catalogue price of *less than one-half* the original catalogue price of the first case-bound edition of the said work, then the royalties and/or other income payable on the sales of copies or sheets of *the paperbound edition (only)* shall be calculated at one-half of the rates provided in this agreement with respect to sales of the first case-bound edition, it being further understood and agreed:

(*a*) that the numbers of copies or sheets sold in such a paperbound edition shall not be counted as part of any formula for accelerated royalty percentage payments on sales of the regular edition where such an accelerated royalty formula keyed to accumulated sales may have been provided for under the original agreement, and

(*b*) that all other terms and conditions respecting the first case-bound edition shall apply to the paperbound edition, and

(*c*) that "paperbound edition" as used in this supplementary agreement shall include any paperbound edition offered *bona fide* by the Publisher, his agents, or customers as a part of a series of generally similar paperbound books, whether or not acetate or similar transparent lamination is used on such paper bindings, provided however that case-bound editions, whether or not paper is used as the binding material, shall not be treated as "paperbound" editions for the purpose of this supplementary agreement.

IN WITNESS WHEREOF the parties hereto have hereunto set their hands and seals this 27th day of December 1976

.... AUTHOR

UNIVERSITY OF TORONTO PRESS

.... PUBLISHER

IN WITNESS WHEREOF the parties hereto have hereunto set their hands and seals this 27th day of December 1976

.... AUTHOR

UNIVERSITY OF TORONTO PRESS

.... PUBLISHER

Manuscript / Project Information Sheet   Date 12 Dec. 1976
                                                   revised

author Mulch, Purvis   citizenship/residence U.S.
title   No Time for House Plants: a busy person's guide to indoor working/final
                                                         gardening   number
series n/a
subsidy: UTP   other   manufacture required: UTP   USA X   other
total no of ms pages 168   no to come   expected run 7,500
other

Preliminary Pages
half title   title X   frontis   copyright X   dedication
series list   contents X   list of illustrations X   list of abbreviations
preface X   foreword   acknowledgments
other   estimated no of printed prelim pages 6

Text
total no of chapters 7   no to come   no of parts   part titles
footnotes   notes: at end of chapter   at end of book X   captions yes
headings 8   no of levels   tabular matter   mathematical setting
charts of graphs   maps   extracts   poetry
foreign language setting   kinds
special symbols X   other

Further Comments

End Matter
total no of appendixes   to come (length)   notes   series list
bibliography X   to come (length)   glossary   to come (length)
index   number   estimated no of printed pages
other

Illustrations
no of halftones 30   estimated no of pages   to come   colour
no of line cuts   estimated no of pages   to come
artwork required   diagrams and line drawings
other

MS Pages with Special Problems   Other Notes

Editor

Mr. Marshall

re: No Time for House Plants

This experiment is proving to be more interesting than even I had expected it to be. At this stage it has indeed assumed a larger dimension. I greatly hope that this exchange of correspondence, containing the author's response to the readers' reports, will be shown to directors and accountants, for it illustrates a problem in appraisal which cannot be solved, and is in fact made far worse, by indiscriminate budgetary constrictions.

The author of "No Time for House Plants" is clearly a plain, practical man who knows how to choose house plants that are easy to look after and is confident that there are a great many people who would benefit from his knowledge. (He is right. There are, and I number myself among them.) His main problem is that he cannot express himself clearly, mostly because his knowledge of grammar is faulty. I have thought of him up to this point as a sensible, even-tempered fellow, not self-conscious about his knowledge but concerned rather to share it effectively, and I have assumed that he would be open to suggestions about his writing out of natural respect for a branch of knowledge which he does not command.

The editor at University of North Carolina Press who handled this appraisal has my sympathy. The second reader turned out to be a judge of the blunt and scornful sort. (I had supposed that these irascible persons were largely confined to the field of

2

bibliography, but I now see that I was naïve.) The appraising editor, left to his own devices, would undoubtedly have chosen to incorporate this reader's criticisms in a letter of his own composition, suggesting and persuading rather than challenging and denouncing. But if he had done that, he would have incurred severe criticism for running up the costs of appraisal. So he decided, resignedly, to send the author a copy of the report in its raw state. The result is an author so self-conscious and tetchy that it is going to be very difficult to get him to listen to suggestions about his writing. To make matters worse, the effect of the third report is to lend support to the notion that photographs and line drawings can compensate for lack of clarity in the text. They cannot, and the belief that they can is the reason why most handbooks are so frustrating to use. I would expect that a book published by a university press would set a new standard.

I have not got the manuscript beside me as I write, but I remember from my first reading that the account of double-potting was impossible to understand. Hence it is only too likely that readers would think the author meant them to sit out in the backyard waiting for the pail to fill with rainwater, as he so vehemently protests in this response. They will in fact interpret this as a humane suggestion, a lovely restful thing to do while trying to recover from the effort of carrying bathtubs around the house. I refer to the sentence beginning on page 2 of the response to the second reader: "Using the bathtub as the container, anyone can carry 20 to 25 plants into the bathroom and immerse them in five minutes." I remark, with some

3

feeling, that even if I had a free-standing bathtub (but mine is built into the wall and floor) I would not be strong enough to carry it around my apartment even if it would go through the doors, but it wouldn't. Another confusing description is contained in the next sentence: "After a half-hour or so of soaking, the water is drained...." Water is by nature soaked; what does it need to be soaked some more for? To carry the care of plants to this extreme is only going to discourage people who would profit by this prospective book.

The result of skimping on the rightful costs of appraisal is plain to see. More money will be spent on the copyediting than would otherwise have been necessary. The appraisal editor knows that and feels bad about it. The copyeditor will soon know it and will feel bad too, but not quite so bad, for he knows he is just the PBI.

Respectfully submitted

AQS

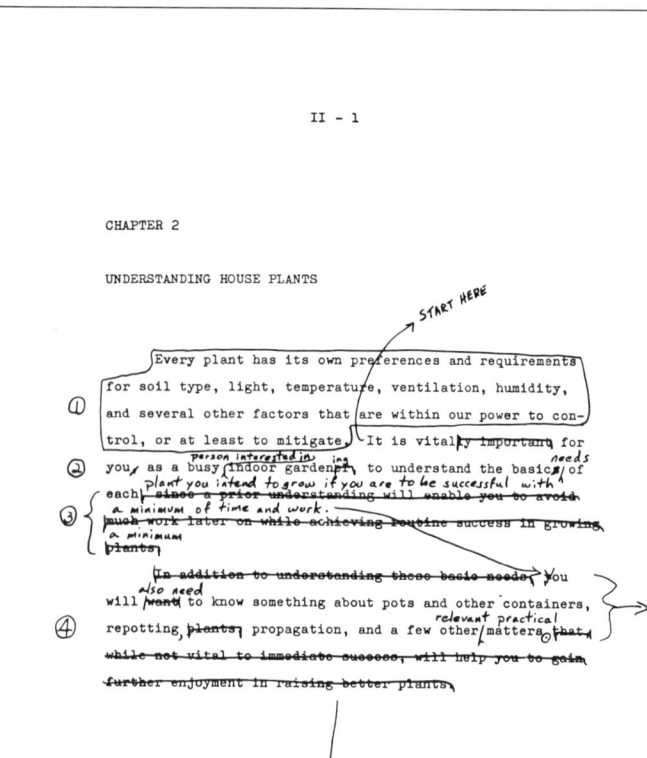

II-1b

each year, ~~emulating the natural rest periods of their forebears.~~ It is ~~You will do~~ well to watch for these signs ~~of dormancy and rest~~ and ~~respond to each plant's needs at that time. When any plant enters a dormant or rest period,~~ to make the appropriate response. Water should be reduced and fertilizer withheld completely, until new growth once again begins, usually in ~~the~~ late winter or early spring. ~~At that time, water~~ The plant should then be ~~freely and~~ given its normal doses of water and fertilizer once again, ~~in order to encourage new growth. By your treatment of the plant at this time~~ proper in emulation of ~~you will emulate~~ the advent of spring, so as to ~~working~~ with the plant in carrying out its rhythmic cycles.

Some plants ~~also are naturally short-lived, and will~~ last no more than a year or two indoors ~~in your home~~ despite ~~your~~ careful attention, because their genetic structure dictates a ~~finite~~ short life span. ~~Garden annuals, for instance, will~~ Very few, because they germinate, grow to maturity, flower, produce seeds, and die, all in as little as six months. ~~For this reason, very few annuals are selected as house plants.~~ Although a few short-hyphen lived plants are cultivated indoors for their unusual char- acteristics, such as the Sensitive Plant which is easily grown from seed, most of the house plants that ~~we~~ have been cultivated over the generations are ~~most often~~ those that ~~will~~ give years of pleasure. Some house plants, in fact, live to be literally hundreds of years old.

Still other house plants are attractive when young,

II - 1b

① Right you are — The term 'dormancy' having been defined on its first appearance (see pink slip on previous page) there is now no need to give it repeated stress — hence the suggested omissions. Also, the influence of forebears has been fully explained already.

② OK — Good — This word seems open to unfortunate misconstruction given the widely varying needs for water and the tendency of owners to over-water. The editorial suggestion is to put more weight on the word 'normal' in the same line.

③ Don't agree, but will accept — The occasional use of 'you' and 'your' gives a warm human touch, but frequent use makes the impression that the author is giving orders — but that would be totally out of character. Would you agree that an impersonal tone is somewhat better in this passage (and below) as suggested?

④ Not needed here — see lower in paragraph.

⑤ Good point — True enough, but not the meaning you wish to convey in this passage. All spans of life are (to the best of our knowledge) finite, but in this instance you are concerned with plants whose span of life is too short to make it very rewarding to grow them indoors.

II-1c

but grow ungainly or otherwise unattractive when they approach maturity. The only plants of this kind I have chosen for inclusion in this book are those that are very easy to prop- agate from cuttings, so that the parent plant may be discarded after a year or two, to be replaced by its children.

Of the hundreds of thousands of plant # species ~~From~~ in the world, those traditionally cultivated as house plants are the rela- tively few that have shown a wide tolerance to conditions of heat, light, moisture, ~~humidity,~~ and ventilation, in the ground and in the air, in other words, those plants that can withstand a human environment. They are both attractive to the eye and ~~they are~~ tough. Still, their natural adaptability and resilience do need human fostering. ~~If we are looking for success with house plants—and particu- larly success without working hard at it—then we should spend some time to learn the characteristics of each plant, recog- nizing its individual needs and fulfilling them to the best of our ability.~~

HOW A PLANT FEEDS

~~A plant manufactures nearly all of its food by itself—and not from the "plant food" that you buy for it.~~ Commercial plant food is no more than a combination of certain chemicals (sometimes in an organic base) that are essential to the plant's basic functioning, much as vitamins are essential to human nutrition. But the bulk of a plant's food—the sugar it uses for energy and growth—is manufactured by the plant itself. In the presence of light, the leaves ~~of the plant~~

II - 1c

① Good — The terms 'moisture' and 'humidity' seemed to require clearer differentiation.

② OK — This point is weakened by repetition (see II 1), and should only be touched on very lightly here.

③ OK — This same point is made at the bottom of the page. Better to delete this sentence.

④ Good point — The distinction between chemical food and naturally grown food is not made clear in this passage. I would suggest omitting the sentence about chemical food because (1) it seems out of place here and (2) it is dealt with at length later in the book.

II-1d

draw carbon dioxide from the air and water from the roots, converting them into sugar, *a process which is known as photosynthesis.* ~~that is then used for energy production or stored for future use.~~

During this ~~sugar manufacturing~~ process, *something else is happening* ~~known as photosynthesis;~~ ~~several~~ ~~other things happen~~ within the plant. *the leaves are absorbing carbon dioxide through their stomata (or* While ~~carbon dioxide is being absorbed, oxygen is being re-~~ *pores) they are also releasing oxygen.* ~~leased from the pores of the leaf surface.~~ (Plants produce not only all of the world's food but most of its atmospheric oxygen as well.) During *the* ~~darkness~~ *of* hours, the process is reversed; some ~~of the atmosphere's~~ oxygen is recaptured *from the atmosphere* ~~by the plant,~~ and used to convert *the* stored sugar ~~to~~ *into* energy ~~for growth.~~ Generally, a plant manufactures ~~growth~~ food during the day and does its actual growing at night.

Often, the plant converts its newly-manufactured sugar *into* ~~to~~ starch and stores it, reconverting it *into* ~~to~~ sugar as the need arises. ~~Although the~~ *Part, but* Starch can be stored in almost any ~~area of the plant,~~ certain plants have developed specialized ~~storage~~ areas, ~~just for this purpose.~~ Cacti and succulents *have in the form of* ~~have~~ enlarged stems and leaves ~~for~~ the greatest above-ground storage capacity ~~of any house plant,~~ while others ~~have~~ *have developed underground storage apparatus* ~~for this purpose,~~ including bulbs, tubers, corms, and rhizomes. A bulb is simply an enlarged underground bud, such as is found *on* ~~with~~ hyacinths, tulips, and onions. A tuber is nothing more than an enlarged root; a common potato is a tuber; gloxinias, *caladiums*, dahlias, and many other common plants are grown from tubers. →

II - 1d

OK ① Repetition of previous sentence, and should be deleted. The reason for the insertion is to move the definition up to the first place where it is mentioned.

OK ② The use of 'several' seems excessive, and is likely therefore to be confusing.

Light ③ Again, a definition moved back, this time from II 1c, line b.

OK ④ Best to avoid using nouns as adjectives, because they make such a jolt in the natural rhythm of the sentence, as in this case.

Light ⑤ Hyphen not needed: 'newly' is an adverb which is already modifying 'manufactured' and so does not need a visual link.

II-1e

→ A corm is the enlarged base of a stem. And a rhizome is simply ~~a laterally growing~~ *an* enlarged underground stem *that grows laterally.* *All these* ~~methods~~ are used by ~~the~~ plants *to store food* ~~for food storage,~~ and all *of them* can be used to propagate plants, too.

① ~~Water is constantly being drawn up through the plant.~~ *water* As ~~it~~ transpires through the stomata ~~(pores)~~ of the leaves, a "pulling" action draws more water up through the roots. The water carries with it mineral salts, including all the elements which the plant needs to carry out its complex chemical processes. ~~The~~ Transpiration ~~which takes place~~ *of plants* in the leaves is similar to perspiration in *the skin of* humans and ~~it~~ serves a similar purpose — to cool ~~the plants. With house plants, it~~ *The cooling effect of* transpiration is difficult to detect in house plants ~~would be difficult for you to notice this cooling effect.~~ But it is readily apparent *in* ~~when~~ a group of large trees ~~carry out the transpiration process.~~ The cool and fresh feeling ~~you~~ *of* ~~enjoy in~~ a thick woods in summer is not primarily the product of the shade itself, but *of* the transpiration of the millions of leaves overhead.

③ A plant cannot absorb *more* ~~too much~~ water *than it needs because* ~~since~~ its vessels and cells can accommodate only so much at a given time; however, ~~the~~ overwatering ~~of a plant~~ can exclude oxygen from the root system, ironically causing wilting of the top portion of the plant. When *no watering is done,* ~~water is withheld~~ the plant's cells ~~will~~ gradually collapse, ~~causing wilting of~~ *and wilts* the entire plant. *All* plants do have protective mechanisms that conserve water in times of drought, however, ~~and~~ *they* can withstand a temporary dry

---

II - 1e

OK-Good ① This statement seems to be a contradiction of the statement at the bottom of II 1c a and the top of II 1d - that water is only drawn up during the hours of light. I would suggest that the first statement be made comprehensive and that this statement be omitted, repetition being unnecessary.

OK ② See comment on II 1d re moving definition back.

③ I suggest this change because in common speech nowadays, 'too' is misused to mean 'very,' and so your statement could be given a wrong meaning, even though it is correct.

Upon receiving new evidence, I now suggest: "A plant can rarely absorb more water than it can use profitably because its vessels...etc."

IV - 6

African Boxwood (Myrsine africana)   B-C-A-C

① ~~This slow-growing boxwood~~ has red stems, ~~but otherwise~~
~~is~~ similar to regular Boxwood (q.v.). *except that it* Many people think it
is even more graceful. ~~African Boxwood is~~ A good plant for
terrariums, if the atmosphere is not too hot.

Aralia (Fatsia japonica)   C-B-B-C

~~It~~ Sometimes sold as Aralia sieboldii. Beautiful, bright- *hyphen*
green, leathery, maple-like leaves highlight this cheerful
plant. In appearance, it is similar to ~~the~~ Castor Oil Plant ②
and in fact is sometimes called False Castor Oil Plant. It
thrives in a cool spot. Aralia can easily grow leggy, and ~~too~~
~~it~~ should be pruned annually in order to encourage it into
bushy growth. *It will attain a height of four feet at maturity.*

A striking hybrid, Fatshedra lizei, crosses F. japonica
and ~~Ivy~~ Hedra *(Ivy) to produce* ~~forming~~ a climbing plant with maple-shaped
leaves, which is tolerant of adverse conditions.

There is also a plant called False Aralia, which has
graceful and feathery foliage. It bears no resemblance to
the true Aralia and is difficult to grow.

Asparagus   A-B-B-B

There are two kinds of Asparagus suitable for growing
as house plants, Fern Asparagus (A. plumosus), with slender,
needle-like, dark-green leaves, ~~forming a~~ *giving a* feathery appearance,
and A. sprengeri (Emerald Feather) which has thicker yellow- *hyphen*
green leaves and drooping stems. The latter makes a good

What if someone refers to this species alone?
↓
The q.v. directs them

① Not needed here because included in description of regular Boxwood (IV 8). It is best to mention only the characteristics that are different.

Good idea

② Should you not supply the botanical name of the Castor Oil Plant for the sake of precision (and consistency)?

IV - 7

plant for hanging ~~plants~~ *baskets*, and produces red berries at Christmastime. Both like some sun in the summer and full sun in
the winter, *and both can grow to a height of about two feet.*

Australian Laurel (Pittosporum tobira)   C-B-A-B

A tolerant and slow-growing plant whose leaves, glossy
and leathery, resemble those of Rhododendron. ~~Australian~~ ①
It ~~Laurel~~ will grow vigorously bushy and does not ~~ask~~ *need* much
attention. Florists often use the leaves in floral arrangements.

An interesting variegated form is P. tobira variegata.

Australian Umbrella Tree (Schefflera actinophylla)   A-A-B-A

Here is a very attractive and vigorous-growing tree
with rich-looking, ~~and~~ glossy leaves that radiate umbrella-like
from the ends of several leaf stalks. It is a tough and
rewarding plant, *growing to six feet,* which can be propagated by air-layering.
~~Australian Umbrella Tree is~~ Also sold as Brassaia
actinophylla. ¶ A dwarf variety, B. actinophylla compacta, is
¶ also available.

Baby's Tears (Helxine soleirollii)   B-B-A-B

This low creeper is also called Irish Moss. It likes
a constantly moist (but not soggy) soil, and higher than
average humidity. It makes a good ground cover for terrariums,
but will also grow in a pot if adequate humidity is provided.
Baby's Tears may appear to die in the colder months, but after

---

That is the botanical name. There are many species.

① Insert botanical name?

IV - 8

an adequate rest period it will spring back to life.

Black Pepper (Piper nigrum)   A-C-B-C

This is not a ~~horribly~~ very attractive plant, but it produces real peppercorns which you may use at the table, and is a good conversation piece for that reason. The plant's berries ~~begin as~~ green, later turn red, then dry up and turn black. Pick the dried-up black corns, dry them thoroughly for several weeks in an open spot, then use them in your pepper grinder. ~~The care for Black Pepper is~~ the same care as ~~that required for~~ Philodendron. It is not a demanding plant: it needs.

Boxwood (Buxus)   C-A-B-B

The same plant which grows the most prized hedges outdoors ~~with glossy, bright-green leaves~~ can make a very attractive house plant. ~~Boxwood~~ The ancient Oriental art of growing dwarf trees and shrubs is slow-growing and dependable, a good subject for bonsai. It has glossy, bright-green leaves. B. sempervirens and B. microphylla japonica (Japanese Boxwood) are the two popular species.

Bromeliads   A-B-B-C

There are more than 1,800 varieties of this popular group, many of which are suitable for growing as house plants. Some of them produce attractive flowers, but most are grown for their striking and variegated leaf patterns. One distinctive feature ~~of the Bromeliads~~ is the rosette leaves which form a small water cup ~~which the plant uses to hold reserve~~

IV - 9

[artificial habitat of a house]   [used to hold reserve supplies of water.]

~~supplies of water in its~~ natural habitat of ~~since~~ the plant is ~~lives in~~ the crotches of trees in Central and South America, and the water cup is an evolutionary survival characteristic. In the ~~home, keep~~ the cup should be kept filled with water, which is changed ~~it~~ weekly ~~to keep it fresh~~.

A few of the more common Bromeliads are Aechmea, Ananas (Pineapple), Billbergia, Cryptanthus (Zebra Plant), Dyckia, Tillandsia (Spanish Moss), and Vriesia.

Caladium   A-B-B-C

Caladiums, with their spectacularly colored and variegated leaves, are equally at home in the garden or on the window sill. They are ideal additions to plant groupings on porches or patios in ~~the~~ summer and early autumn. Give them bright light, but not long periods of direct sun, ~~especially~~ in summer, if you want them to show their brightest ~~leaf~~ colors.

Caladiums are grown from tubers, which can be divided easily to produce new plants. Start the tubers in regular potting soil at a very warm temperature—80° to 90°—and when appear, move them the young plants to a cooler spot ~~when they have appeared~~. They will attain a height of about one foot.

Cast Iron Plant (Aspidistra elatior)   A-C-B-C

This is perhaps the easiest plant ~~in the world~~ to grow, as its name suggests. It is virtually impossible to neglect it to death. It is also called Saloon Plant, since it was one of the few that could survive in Victorian taverns, and it was made immortal by George Orwell in his novel Keep the

---

IV - 10

Aspidistra Flying. If you cannot grow the Aspidistra, you may safely conclude that you have ~~a~~ an purple thumb ~~hopelessly~~ irredeemable.

Cast Iron Plant, which grows about two feet tall, seems to thrive even better when kept slightly pot-bound, ~~and~~ but it will appreciate having its leaves washed occasionally. ¶ A white-striped species is called A. variegata.

Chamaeranthemum igneum   A-C-A-C

This low, spreading herb has attractive, dark green leaves with reddish-yellow veins. It is suitable for hanging baskets or as a ~~low~~ contrast of in large plant groupings. It does like warm temperatures and high humidity, however, and might not be suitable for dry apartments.

Chinese Evergreen (Aglaonema)   A-C-B-A

Here is an attractive, and low-growing plant that is very easy to ~~grow~~ look after. It will stand abuse almost as easily as Cast Iron Plant.

There are at least ten commonly found species of ~~the~~ Aglaonema, the most popular of which, A. modestum, has interestingly mottled leaves. Perhaps the most attractive, however, is A. pseudobractaetum, which is sometimes difficult to find in stores and greenhouses.

IV - 10

Good point   ① Not needed, because irredeemable means hopeless.

OK   ② The term 'low contrast' seemed awkward and its meaning obscure. As the plant has already been described as 'low' in the first line of the description, I thought it could be deleted here, thus solving the problem.

Must be a variety with which I am unfamiliar. Can we cut "low"?

③ 1) Would not simply 'low' be just as expressive, and neater?
2) Would you consider qualifying this point? A friend of mine has a Chinese Evergreen that is two feet tall, and quite bushy. Perhaps height varies with species?

CAPTIONS

Cast Iron Plant (Aspidistra).
A selection of succulents — easy to grow and infinite in variety.

Anthurium andreanum and A. crystalinum.
A good example of double-potting. The sphagnum moss between the two pots reduces the need for watering.

A selection of begonias for indoor growing.

Decorative containers without drainage holes can be used sucessfully if the plant is double-potted. This Prayer Plant (Maranta) has been potted in a clay pot, which was then inserted into the decorative container on a layer of gravel. Moss occupies the space between the two pots, assuring constant moisture for the plant's roots.

Large-leafed plants will appreciate an occasional bath. Use a mild soap solution and rinse thoroughly with clear water — both at room temperature.

Stem cuttings should be made just below a node, the point where a leaf originates. The cut should be sharp without damaging the stem, since many plants already have embryonic root systems at the nodes which develop rapidly when placed in water. For this purpose, a sharp pair of pruning shears is adequate, although a sharp single-edge razor blade is even better, since it will not crush the stem.

CAPTIONS 2

The cuttings of many house plants can be rooted easily in water. The roots of this Aluminum Plant are at a stage where the plant can be potted. Many of these plants, including this one, can also be grown permanently in water.

Any plant and soil ball may easily be separated from its pot by turning it upside-down and rapping the rim of the pot sharply against the end of a bench. If the plant is not sufficiently potbound to require repotting as this one is not—then the soil ball may easily be replaced with no harm and little mess.

Overwatering is the most common cause of house plant failure. This device prevents overwatering. Use a pot with a hole in the bottom. Then get a piece of plastic tubing one inch in diameter. Stop up the end and drill 1/8-inch holes up and down the tube. Set the tube vertically in the pot, add soil, and fill the tube with sand. When watering, simply fill the tube.

special box No. 1

THE ABCs OF ARTIFICIAL LIGHT

The recent introduction of fluorescent tubes meant especially for plant growing has been a great boon for indoor gardeners. With the aid of artificial light, we can now grow lush, green plants in areas where they would never grow before. A windowless bathroom, which might offer ideal humidity and temperature conditions, can now be made into an ideal plant-growing environment. Plants growing on a drab northern window sill can now receive supplemental light during winter's short and dark days. Dim corners of any room can be transformed into green showplaces. Cuttings and seedlings can now make faster and surer progress than ever, under artificial light, and we can even grow vegetables in the dead of winter in the bedroom or kitchen. Artificial lighting is not essential for house plant success, but it certainly does broaden our horizons and increase chances for maximum rewards.

The old incandescent bulb does offer some help to growing plants, although the heat it produces makes it impossible to offer plants the amounts of light they need without drying or burning the plants. Also, incandescent bulbs offer a very short spectrum of light wavelengths, falling far short of simulating the beneficial rays of the sun. Ordinary daylight or cool white fluorescent lights are far better for growing plants, since they have not only a wider and more effective

special box No. 1, add 1

light wavelength, but also produce light with three times as much efficiency as incandescent bulbs, thus reducing heat by fully two-thirds. Not until the past decade, however, have we had fluorescent tubes made to meet exactly the needs of growing plants. These lights, sold under names such as Gro-Lux, Plant-Gro, and Plant-Light, cost more than ordinary fluorescent tubes, but they are long-lasting and they can solve virtually any light problem for the indoor gardener. By attaching them to a twenty-four hour timer, you can control light exposure perfectly, even for such tricky operations as forcing plants to bloom out of season.

The best way to start out with artificial light is the most simple way. Purchase two forty-watt plant-growing tubes with the proper fixture, and hang it over a table where you wish to begin your experiments. Be sure you have some method of raising and lowering the fixture, for you will want to adjust the lighting intensity to meet different plant requirements. Ferns and snakeplant, for instance, have low light requirements, so that the tubes should be placed twelve to eighteen inches above them, while succulents, ivy, most flowering plants, and all vegetables have high light requirements, requiring the lowering of the tubes to eight inches or less above the plants. The lowest you can bring the tubes and still avoid injury from heat is three inches above the plants. There are guidebooks giving the exact light requirements of most common plants, available from the tube manufac-

(20)

special box No. 1, add 2

turers] There are also some excellent books on artificial
light gardening, which are most likely in the collections of
and some of these are probably
your public library.

If you enjoy artificial light gardening and the gratifying results it brings, you will have no problem in expanding your activities in this area. Manufacturers have introduced a wide variety of special plant-growing stands, some with several tiers capable of holding dozens of plants, others decorative enough to enhance the beauty of any room. Your choices are limited only by your imagination and your checkbook balance.

(21)

special box No. 4

PLANTS FOR COOL CONDITIONS (50°–60° at night)

Aloe	Creeping Fig	Kangaroo Vine
Aspidistra	Cyclamen	Lily-of-the-Valley
Australian Laurel	Easter Lily	Lithops
Azalea	English Ivy	Miniature Holly
Baby's Tears	Fatshedera	Mother of Thousands
Black Pepper	Fiddle-Leaf Fig	Narcissus
Boxwood	Flowering Maple	Oxalis
Bromeliads	Freesia	Primrose
Cacti	Fuchsia	Sensitive Plant
Calceolaria	Geranium	Silk Oak
Camellia	German Ivy	Snake Plant
Cape Ivy	Honeysuckle	Spindletree
Christmas Begonia	Hyacinth	Tulip
Chrysanthemum	Jasmine	Vinca
Cineraria	Jerusalem Cherry	Wandering Jew
Citrus	Kalanchoe	White Calla Lily

(22)

special box No. 5

PLANTS FOR MEDIUM TEMPERATURES (60°–65° at night)

Achimenes	Copper Leaf	Pilea
Aechmea	Crown of Thorns	Peperomia
Amaryllis	Cryptanthus	Poinsettia
Ardisia	Dracaena	~~Rose~~
Asparagus Fern	Easter Lily	Rubber Plant
Aspidistra	Echeveira	Shrimp Plant
Avocado	English Ivy	Silk Oak
Begonia	Gardenia	Snake Plant
Bird's Nest Fern	Grape Ivy	Staghorn Fern
Browallia	Hibiscus	Ti Plant
Chenille Plant	Hydrangea	Tuberous Begonia
Christmas Cactus	Maranta	Umbrella Tree
Chrysanthemum	Norfolk Island Pine	Velvet Plant
Citrus	Palms	Wax Begonia
Coleus	Philodendron scandens	Wax Plant
		Weeping Fig
		Yellow Calla Lily

UNIVERSITY OF TORONTO PRESS

University of Toronto, Toronto, Canada M5S 1A6

EDITORIAL DEPARTMENT

1 December 1976

Professor Purvis Mulch
c/o Wisconsin University Press
Box 1379
Madison, WI 53701

Dear Professor Mulch

My last duty as appraisal editor of your manuscript, 'No Time for House Plants,' is to send you the two official forms which are enclosed with this letter. The first is the Memorandum of Agreement. I hope that you will find the terms agreeable, and if you do, please date and sign both copies, keeping one in your file and returning the other to me. The Author's Information Sheets which are also enclosed have been devised by our Promotion Department as a help to them in reaching the largest possible market for our books. They are rather a chore to fill out, but I suppose you will not mind that very much, especially as your book is expected to have an unusually wide appeal and therefore needs special promotion.

Ordinarily I would at this stage have handed the manuscript and its file to our Executive Editor, who would have arranged for it to be edited and shepherded through to publication by one of our copyeditors (someone keen about house plants, needless to say). But I had become so interested in your manuscript and had discussed it so thoroughly with my colleagues and other friends that to give it up seemed uneconomic and frustrating - so much explaining to fill in the background and what I had learned about this genre during appraisal. Besides, the explaining would not likely have been satisfactory anyway.

I still have a bad conscience over sending you the report of Reader B in its original state instead of selecting his important criticisms and suggestions and incorporating them in a letter of my own. To be faced with such abrasiveness and irascibility was upsetting for you, and the effects on the manuscript have been more far-reaching and subtle than I realized until I examined this latest version closely. On such a tight schedule, though, it seemed necessary to save time by taking any possible shortcuts.

..../2

Professor Purvis Mulch   -2-   1 December 1976

In one of his characteristics - his literal-mindedness - Reader B has to be reckoned with as being in a curious way representative of the prospective readers of your book. To be sure, they are not going to be wilfully dim (as I greatly suspect Reader B of being) but on the contrary receptive and keen to learn. For that very reason they will come close to B's literal-mindedness in their wanting a handbook of this kind to be direct and compact, and for the additional, equally strong reason that they are on your own definition very busy people who have very little time to spend on this hobby. They will want an efficient book - the book you describe in your Preface as 'a collection of solid and practical information, trimmed of excess detail and shaped for a single purpose,' and, as you mention in the next paragraph, portable, so that it can be carried on trips to florist shops and gardening centres. The damage done by B is to lead you to question your original confidence in the ready intelligence of your readers, and to use repetition as a method of making information stick in their heads. This reaction, though understandable, is a grave mistake, for it will simply perpetuate the irritation caused by B. Most of the editing I have done is aimed at obviating the sharp retort, 'I caught that the first time; why are you telling me again?' and to work towards exactitude of expression as the best means of imparting information in a lasting way. A great many authors of handbooks and guidebooks obviously do think that repetition is necessary, but the sample testing I have done on a liberal cross-section of users of such books confirmed my impression that this method is a source of irritation and even resentment.

My markings are intended as suggestions for you to consider, not as cut and dried changes. When I have put a fence like this ⌐ ⌐ over a word or passage, I mean to suggest that it be omitted. Suggested rewording is written above the fence. Explanations and questions are written on the pink slips attached to the pages; please write your answers and comments, sacred or profane, on the back of the slips. A simple yes, or no, or a note in the margin will be enough to show me your reaction to the changes, and I'd be grateful if you would leave all the tidying up for me to do rather than change my markings, for otherwise a considerable amount of confusion could result.

I have greatly enjoyed your manuscript and will certainly buy a copy of the book for my shelves when it is published. I wonder if there is any chance of your coming to Toronto when all this rush is over. I should very much like to meet you, and so would Albert, who sends you a leaf as a token of his affection. He was sold to me as a fruit sage, but I'm not sure if that is right, and I have no notion of his botanical name. I do not think I could honestly recommend him for inclusion in your book, for although he is immensely good-natured and a great sire - our Sales Manager has Son of Albert, our Editor (Modern Languages) has Albert II, and an author on the west coast has III and IV - he has a drinking problem,

..../3

Professor Purvis Mulch   -3-   1 December 1976

especially on weekends. No amount of soaking satisfies him, and practically every Monday morning he is in a thoroughly dejected state of dehydration. I am pretty sure he has never heard of storing food, or if he does store any he uses it up right away - growing taller and bushier. Then he gets claustrophobia and when he is repotted promptly gets agoraphobia. So, altogether, and even though he is so handsome and sheds such a lovely scent in my office, I must conclude, with sadness, that he is just a little bit too temperamental to qualify.

Yours sincerely

Agatha Q. Sigglesthwaite
Agatha Q. Sigglesthwaite
Editor (Environmental Arts)

AQS:sm
Encl.

December 28, 1976

Ms. Agatha Q. Sigglesthwaite
Environmental Arts Editor
UNIVERSITY OF TORONTO PRESS
University of Toronto
Toronto, Canada M5S 1A6

Dear Ms. Sigglesthwaite:

Thank you for your good letter of December 1, for the Memorandum of Agreement, and for the Author's Information Sheets and the edited copy from my manuscript, No Time for House Plants. I return, herewith, the last three of these, properly completed.

I appreciate your acting not only as appraisal editor but also as executive editor and copyeditor for my work. (From your description, the only duty of the executive editor is to receive manuscripts from the appraisal editor and pass them along to the copyeditor. Should a vacancy ever occur in that position, please call me.)

I believe the less said about Reader B, the better.

I think you did a superb job of editing this section, operating along unshakeable principles of logic. My only concerns are that (1) some of the flow, the character, of the language—good or bad as it might have been—has been interrupted or clouded, and (2) some of the repetitions deleted might have served a good purpose when the reader turns to the work in order to seek the answer to a particular question. The editorial logic employed here appears to assume that each reader will read the entire work at a sitting, absorbing and retaining everything he reads. If that assumption were true, then there would be no need for repetition. In a reference work such as this, however, I do question the assumption. Nevertheless, the editing was the most thorough I have seen.

Last, I have become intrigued by Albert, whom I have as yet not identified. Could I ask that you cut a growing tip from him, wet it down thoroughly, seal it in a plastic bag, and send it to me? I would like to root it.

Ms. Agatha Q. Sigglesthwaite, December 28, 1976, page 2

Again, thank you for your enthusiasm and concern for my manuscript, and for the exceeding care that you have given it. I appreciate your efforts, and look forward, along with you and Mr. Marshall, to its swift and successful completion.

Best wishes.

Sincerely,

Purvis Mulch

(page 1)

University of Toronto Press, Publications Production Department

BREAKDOWN OF PRODUCTION COSTS

Author **MUCH**   Docket **01676**   Date **Jan 24/77**
Title **No Time For House Plants**
Anticipated date of receipt of edited MS _____ Mark-up for lapse of time _____
Trimmed page size **7 x 9**   Length (pp.) **136**   Process **VIP/OFFSET**
Significant features of production and special circumstances to be noted:
30 H/T'S, APPROX. 55 SMALL DIAGRAMS, 15 LINE DRAWINGS

Suppliers A _____ B _____

COMPILATION

Copy preparation
Editorial costs **78** hrs copy editing @ $11·75 _____ appraisal _____ hrs @ _____   **920·00**
Design costs **40** hrs @ $15·00   **600·00**
Production costs **30** hrs @ $15·00   **450·00**
Proofreading   **150·00**
Charges for (special artwork) photography (for **55 DIAGRAMS + 15 DRAWINGS**)   **400·00**
Other special requirements (_____)

Composition
Typesetting **100** pp @ _____ per page (by **VIP TO GALLEYS (ALPHA GRAPHICS)**)   **1800·00**
$18·00
Tabular, formulae or special setting to pages ☐ galleys ☐
Page assembly **136** pp @ **4·00** per page (by _____)   **544·00**
Proofing _____ copies @ _____ per copy
Strip-up for offset   **757·00**
Line negatives and offset plates
Making blues
Author's alterations (**10** %)   **180·00**

Purchases (one time)
Outside type or repros, stats, photo prints and binding stamps   **400·00**
Line negs. _____ fine-line negs. _____ (from _____)
Halftone or duotone film _____ (from _____)   **400·00**
Colour separations/colour proving _____ (from _____)

TOTAL COMPILATION   **6601·00**

Unit costs of compilation
7500 copies   **10,000** copies _____ copies _____ copies
·880 unit   **·660** unit _____ unit _____ unit

(page 2)

University of Toronto Press, Publications Production Department

BREAKDOWN OF PRODUCTION COSTS

Author **MUCH**   Docket **01676**   Date **Jan 24/77**
Title **No Time For House Plants**
Suppliers: A **ALPHA / T.H.BEST**   B _____

	A (7500)		( )	( )	(10M)	B
COMPILATION (see page 1)	660·00	·880			·660	660·00
PRESS PREPARATION	525·00	·070			·053	525·00
RUNNING COSTS (per **7500** copies)						
Paper	2400·00					3325·00
Presswork	750·00					875·00
Bindery						
(to **FLAT SHEETS**)		·420			·420	4200·00
SUBTOTAL	3150·00					
CASING-IN (including **SEWING SECTIONS & PRINTING CLOTH DUOTONE**) (**7500** copies)	8775·00	1·170			1·135	11354·00
JACKET Compilation						
Running (_____ copies)						
PAPERBINDING						
(_____ copies)						
COVER Compilation						
Running (_____ copies)						
OFFPRINTS						
_____ copies each of _____						
SHIPPING						
(_____ copies)						
TOTAL (**7500** copies)	19051·00	2·54			2·27	22680·00

Prelim specs: ___ Final specs: **x** ___ Date: **1 December 1976**

Author & Title: **Mulch: No Time for House Plants**

Prelim docket **01676** ___ Typesetting/printing docket ___

Trim page size **7" x 9"** ___ Margins: head **3 picas** gutter **3½ picas**

University of Toronto Press

TYPESETTING SPECIFICATIONS

Typeface: text **VIP Sabon** ___ display **Sabon, Vivaldi**

Type area: **32½** picas X **44** picas (plus r/h) ___ Text lines per normal column: **44**

Running head: **x** ___ Sample r/h: left page **folio   r/h** ⎫ flush left ___ Foot folio: ___

Space below r/h: **1 pica** ___ right page **folio   r/h** ⎭ ___ Space above foot folio: ___

Chapters start: right only **x** left or right ___ Lines per chapter opening page: **31**

Notes: end of chapter ___ end of book ___

SIZES OF TYPE AND LEADING

Text: **10 on 12 x 16 picas** ___ Title Page: **see ms**

Extracts: ___ Part number: ___
Space above: ___
Space below: ___ Half title: ⎫ **10/12 caps L space**
Footnotes: ___ Part title: ⎭ **1 unit**
End notes: ___ Initial: ___
Bibliography: **10/12 x 16** ___ Chapter number: **10/12 caps**
Appendix: **10/12 x 16** ___ Chapter title: **42 pt Vivaldi / 12'**
Index: ___ Subheads (1): **Bold rom. ulc**
10/12 s.c. with o/s figs.
Running head: ___ Space above: **18'**
___ Space below: **4'**
Tables: ___ Sub-subs (2): **italic ulc. 12'**
___ Space above: **see ms**
Captions: **9/12 x 16** ___ Space below: **see ms**
Folios: ___ Sub-sub-subs (3): **10/12 s.c.**
Reference guide - see ___ Space above: **12 '**
Other: **appendix** ___ Space below: **12'**

```
TIGHT WORD SPACING

REQUIRED THROUGHOUT

4-to-em mono

thin bands lino

TIGHT VARIABLE

SPACING
```

SPECIAL STYLE NOTES

Ellipses: |...| ___ En dash: |-| ___ Figures: old style **x** ___ modern ___
___ Quotes: single **x** ___ double ___
Close up space around initials ___ Headings: centered ___ flush left **x**
(i.e. G.H. Smith) ___ Caps: letterspace **1 unit** average
___ small caps: letterspace **1 unit** average

Text setting - **16 picas tight ragged right throughout will appear as 15½ picas average line in final printing.**

Editor: **A.Q.T.** ___ Designer: **W.R.**

A MOUNTED COPY OF THIS FORM MUST ACCOMPANY MANUSCRIPT FOR TYPESETTING

Production / Design / Toronto / 273

BOOK SPECIFICATIONS   Prelim specs: final specs: x   date: 1 December 1976

Author & Title   Mulch: No Time for House Plants

Trim page size   7" x 9"   Pages not known at time of estimate

COMPOSITION: See separate sheet for typesetting specifications

ILLUSTRATIONS   Production to check)

line   halftone   colour

print with text, or separate   print with text

if separate, indicate tip-ins, wraps, inserts, sections, and number of pages

_____

PRINTING

letterpress   offset x

Ink: text black   illustrations black   endpaper

Paper: text   opaque offset stock of your choice

Paper: illustrations   "

Paper: endpaper   Multicolor Carioca Green

~~JACKET / COVER~~ CASE   Duotone printing with foil stamping (front and spine)

No. of colours   2   letterpress   offset x

~~paper (jacket)~~: _____   inks: (1) black
~~paper (cover)~~: _____   (2) green - PMS 582
Print duotone so that light to mid-grey areas   (3)
are predominantly green, and dark to black areas (4)
~~BINDING~~   are predominantly black. Minimum 150 line screen halftone.

Cloth Riverside Linen RL 334   Headbands x   tailbands x   colour white

                                 Back: rounded x   square

Stamp: front & spine x   spine only   foil glitter gold

Print cloth: letterpress   offset x   ink(s)

Collate separate illustrations as

FOR PRODUCTION USE:

Paper binding: perfect bound   sewn

Trim size after perfect binding

274 | Toronto | Design | Production

Author MULCH   Editor
Title No Time For   Docket
      House Plants
Series   Delivery MAY 30/77

		SCHEDULED 1977	ACTUAL
MANUSCRIPT	to Production	14/1	
	to Design		
	to Editorial		
	to Supplier		
GALLEYS	to Editorial	31/1	
	to Design		
	to Production	7/2	
	to Supplier	8/2	
REVISED GALLEYS	to Editorial		
	to Design		
	to Production		
	to Supplier		
PAGE PROOFS	to Editorial	21/3	
	to Design	24/3	
	to Production	25/3	
	to Supplier	28/3	
REVISED PAGE PROOFS	to Editorial	5/4	
	to Design		
	to Production		
	to Supplier		
FINAL PROOFS OK'd	by Editorial	8/4	
	by Design	15/4	
	by Production	15/4	
	to Supplier	15/4	
CAMERA COPY	to Supplier	20/4	
BLUES OK'd	to Editorial	28/4	
	to Design	28/4	
	to Production	28/4	
	to Supplier	28/4	
SEWN COPY OK'd	by Design	19/5	
	by Production	19/5	
BOUND COPY OK'd		30/5	

MS & PROOF ROUTING

Author __MULCH__   Date __Sept. 30, 1976__
Title __No Time for House Plants__   Docket _____
Dept __Production__   FOR
                                           Process _____

(Circle present stage) MS GALLEYS FIRST PP REVISES/REPROS FINAL PP BLUES

FROM   TO
Name __Pru Potts__   Name __HSM__
Dept __Production__   Dept _____

HEREWITH (list all accompanying material)

1. Manuscript
2. Preliminary specifications and layouts
3. Guesstimate
4. Rough schedule

COMMENTS

unless marked otherwise

RULES FOR TYPOGRAPHIC

COMPOSITION FOR PUBLICATIONS

OF UNIVERSITY OF TORONTO PRESS

These rules are based on the principle that legible typography depends upon the careful use of space. Strict adherence to these rules will not always be possible because of differences between the major keyboard systems. However, the principle remains as a constant, and the more rules that are followed the better will be the over-all composition.

TEXT COMPOSITION

WORD SPACING
All text composition must be closely word spaced. In mono setting, the average word space should be 4-to-the-em (minimum 5-to-the-em, maximum 3-to-the-em); in lino setting use minimum space bands. Divide words at the ends of lines in preference to loose word spacing. No more than normal word spacing should be used after punctuation and, in certain situations, the word spacing can be omitted (see *periods*). When setting unjustified material, line lengths should not fluctuate more than 1 pica. Never use an en-quad for spacing.

WORD DIVISION
Letters retained at the end of the line should forecast the portion of the word turned over. Do not divide the last word in a paragraph.

LOWER CASE ROMAN AND ITALIC
Text setting of roman or italic must never be letterspaced.

PARAGRAPHS
Do not indent the first line of the first paragraph of any text or separate section thereof. Indent following paragraphs 1 em of the text type size.

LEADING
No extra space should be placed between paragraphs. When extra space is required between sections of the text, such space should be ½, the same as, or a multiple of, the type size plus the leading. For example, space above and below set-down copy should be approximately ½ line each.

SMALL CAPITALS
Use small capitals in text setting for degrees / LL D, PH D, MA, P ENG, B SC, B PAED, D PHIL / abbreviations / BNA USA CBC MP / and Roman numerals / Richard III, George V, Chapter X.

FIGURES
Use old style, non-aligning figures with small caps and, wherever possible, in text settings. Use modern, aligning figures with capitals. Divide date and page sequences with an en dash without extra space. Always use the fewest possible figures / 306–9, 1946–7, but 1914–18.

PUNCTUATION

DASHES
Always use an en rule, preceded and followed by the word space of the line. Centre dashes and hyphens on capital height when used in conjunction with capitals or lining figures.

PERIODS
Use sparingly and omit after the following abbreviations and contractions / Mr / Mrs / Messrs / Dr / St / Co / Ave / Inc / 8vo / No / am / pm /. Spacing following the period must approximate the rest of the word space in the line. No word spacing is required after the period when it is followed by the capitals A J T V W Y. Equalize visual space around initials in names / H.C. Jones / John L. Smith.

APOSTROPHES
Not required in plural forms of such contractions as 1920s. Where small capitals are used for abbreviations insert hair space between final cap and s / MPs.

COLONS AND SEMI-COLONS
Should be preceded by a hair space only.

EXCLAMATION AND INTERROGATION MARKS
Should be preceded by a thin space only.

ELLIPSIS
This mark of omission consists of three periods set without spaces, but preceded and followed by the word spacing of the line. No further punctuation is required.

QUOTATIONS
Opening quotes must be followed by a hair space except before the capitals A, C, G, J, and the lower case a, c, d, e, g, i, j, m, n, o, p, q, r, s, u, v, w, x, y, z. Closing quotes must be preceded by a hair space except after a comma or a period. When a paragraph commences with a quotation, the quote mark must be considered part of the indentation space.
Either single quote style [' " " '] or double quote style [" ' ' "] should be used consistently through each book. UTP manuscripts will be marked at the front for style to be followed, and quote style will be indicated on manuscript style sheet. Punctuation goes inside or outside closing quotes, as marked on manuscript.

SPECIAL SETTING

CAPITALS
Words in full capitals will not appear within text setting, but may be used in headings or display. Words in capitals must always be visually letterspaced. The goal is to secure the appearance of even spacing. The same rule applies to small capitals used in headings or display setting.

TABLES
Avoid double rules. Use 1 or 2 pt rules for head and foot of table, hairline rules within. Avoid vertical rules.

FOOTNOTES
When footnote reference figures are required in text, use superior fraction figures preceded by a thin space. Either modern or old style fraction figures may be used provided they are in harmony with the face used for the text. Do not use modern fraction figures in any old style fount and vice versa. Use full figures, not superior fraction figures, for numbering of the footnotes themselves.

SET-DOWN QUOTATIONS, EXTRACTS
If possible, extracts should begin flush left, with subsequent paragraphs indented one em of text size. Spacing between text and set-down material should be approximately ½ line of text size plus leading.

PAGE MAKE-UP

FACING PAGES
Facing pages should be made equal in depth. Fractional differences should be corrected by varying slightly the space around subheadings or set down material, or between text and footnotes.

WIDOWS
Lines of less than half the full measure are considered to be widows, and should not appear as the first line of a page. This can usually be avoided by increasing or decreasing the number of lines of type on facing pages. A pair of facing pages may be one line longer or one line shorter than a standard text page, but should not vary more than one line from preceding or following pages.

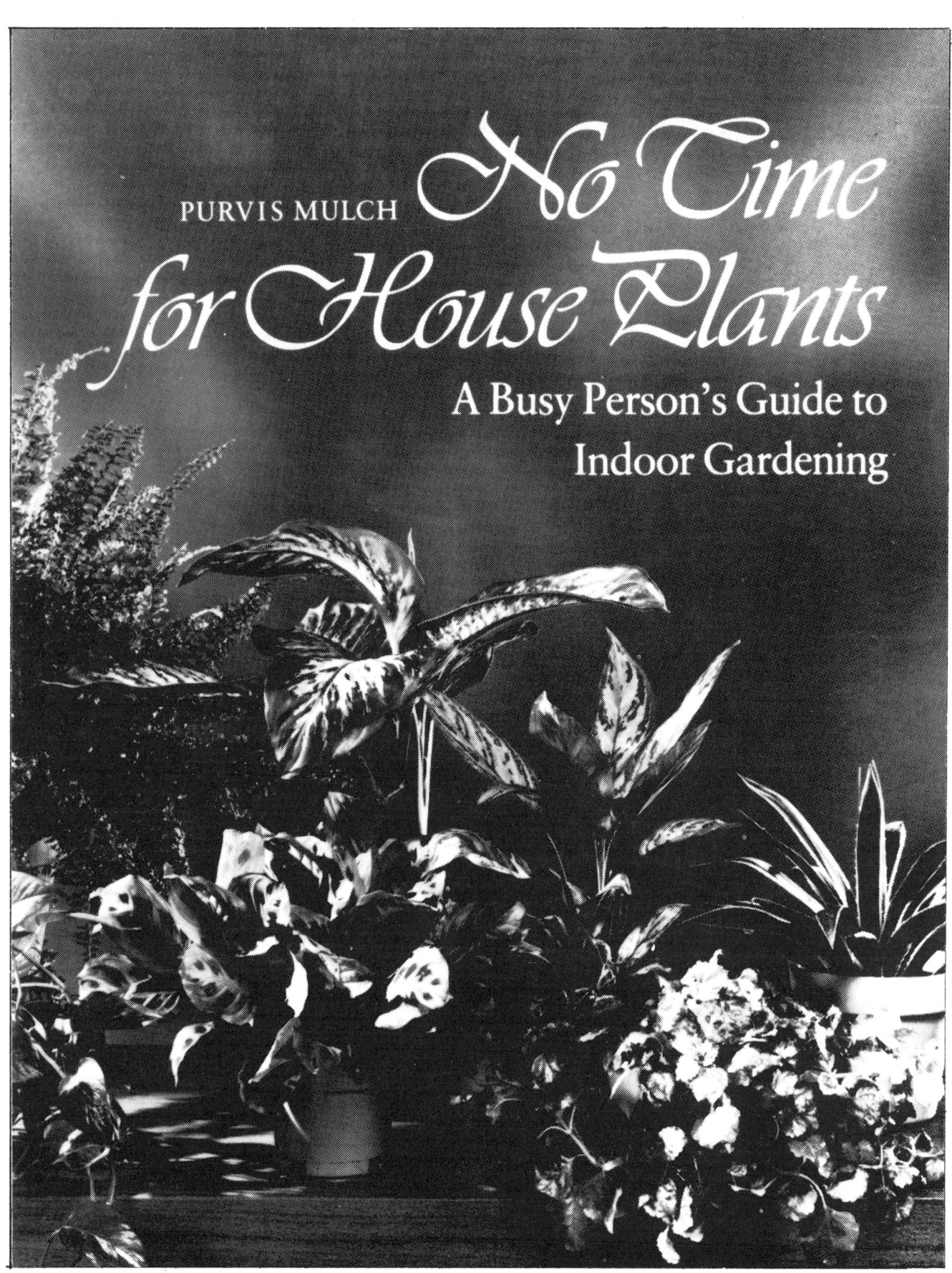

NO TIME FOR HOUSE PLANTS A Busy Person's Guide to Indoor Gardening

Specifications

Trim page size: 7" x 9"
Margins: head – 3 picas, gutter 3½ picas

TYPESETTING
Typeface: VIP Sabon with Sabon and Vivaldi display
Type area: 32½ by 44 picas (plus r/h)
44 lines per full column
Chapters start right only
Text: 10/12 x 15½ picas tight ragged right 31 lines per chapter opening column
Bibliography: 10/12 x 15½ picas
Running head: 10/12 s/c + o/s figures x 15½ picas
Captions: 9/12 x 15½ picas
Reference guide: 10/12 x 15½ picas
Title page: see ms
Half title: 10/12 caps + 12 upper and lowercase
Chapter number: 10/12 caps
Chapter title: 42 Vivaldi
Plant reference headings: 12/14 ulc
sub heads: 10/12 s/c

SPECIAL STYLE NOTES
Ellipses: [...]   En dash: [–]
Figures: old style
Quotes: single
Headings: flush left
Caps and small caps: letter space 1 unit

ILLUSTRATIONS: (Production to check)
Print with text

PRINTING
Offset; black ink
Paper: 70 lb Warren's 1854 (or similar opaque stock)
Endpaper: Multicolor Carioca Green

BINDING
Case printed two colours (duotone): black + PMS Green (colour to come)
Stamp glitter gold foil on front and spine
Cloth: Riverside Linen RL 334
Rounded back

This signature was printed by Kingsport Press, Kingsport, Tennessee.

PURVIS MULCH

No Time for House Plants

A Busy Person's Guide to Indoor Gardening

UNIVERSITY OF TORONTO PRESS Toronto and Buffalo

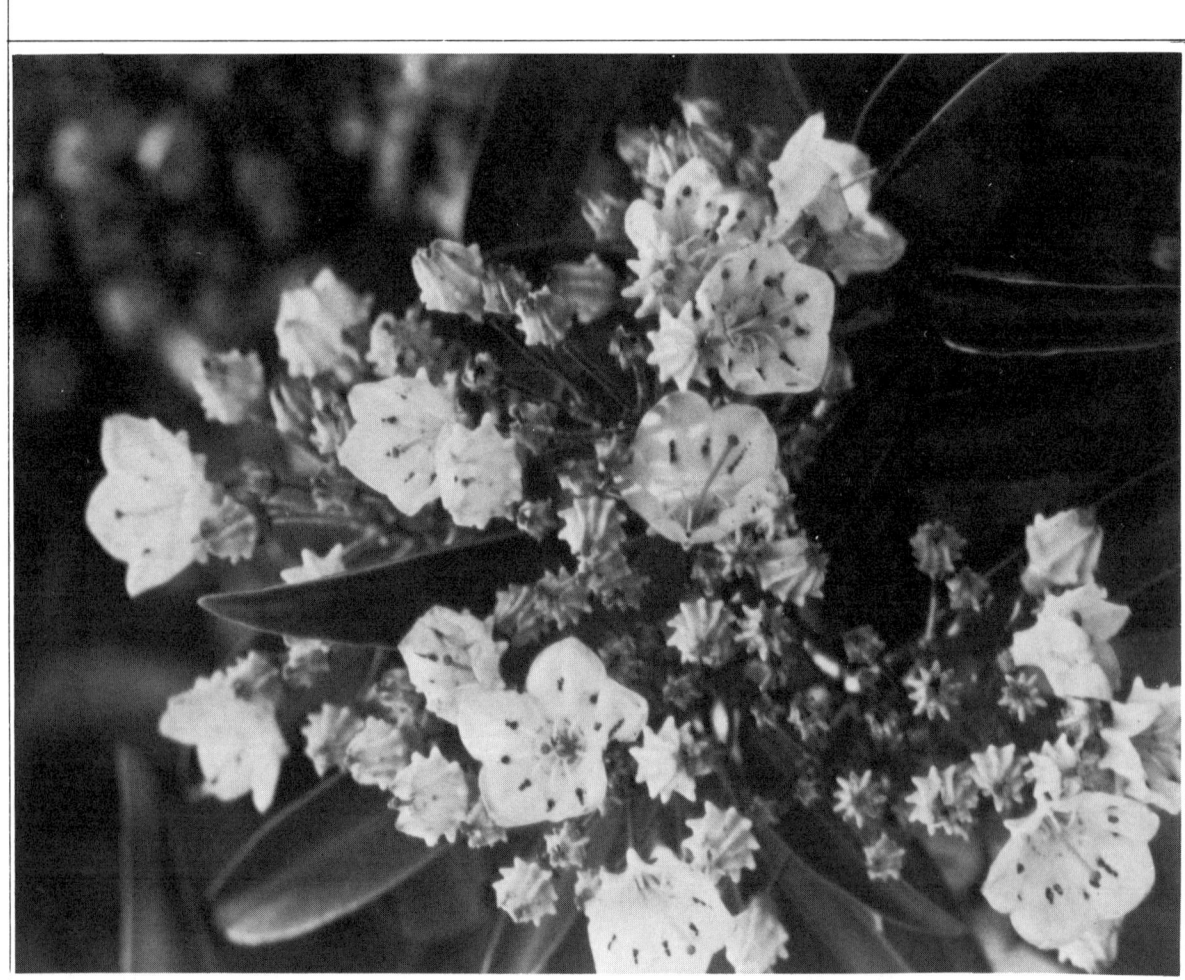

© University of Toronto Press 1977
Printed in USA
ISBN 0-8020-2214-7

Library of Congress Cataloguing in Publication Data

Mulch, Purvis
No time for house plants: a busy person's guide to indoor gardening
Bibliography
Includes index
1. House plants I. Title
SB126.K7   635'.9'54   76-26057

Contents

Preface vii

1
The Secrets of No-Work House Plant Success 3

2
Understanding House Plants 17

The Basic House Plant 17
How a Plant Feeds 18
Parts of a Plant 20
Soil 24
Acidity/Alkalinity 27
Potting Mixtures 31
Nutrient Maintenance 32
Containers 34
Watering 37
Humidity 39
Ventilation 43
Temperature 45
Light 47
Pruning and Training 48
Repotting 51
Propagation 54

3
Plant Troubles and Cures 55

Improper Handling and Care 55
Insect Foes 57
Diseases 61

4
Introducing the Foliage Plants 63

Where to Buy House Plants 64
Foliage Plants 69

5
Cacti and other Succulents 75

Care of Cacti and Succulents 83
Potting Soil for Cacti 89
Introducing the Cacti 94
The Unusual Succulents 99

6
Flowering House Plants 105

Forcing Spring Bulbs 112
Care of Gift Plants 122

7
Special Indoor Gardens 131

Dish Gardens and Planters 140
Bottle Gardens and Terrariums 151
House Plants from Kitchen Scraps 159
An Indoor Kitchen Garden 164

Handy Reference Guide 170

The ABCs of Artificial Light 171
Should You Send Your Plants to Summer Camp? 176

CHAPTER TWO

Understanding House Plants

It is vital for you as a busy person interested in indoor gardening to understand the basic needs of each plant you intend to grow if you are to be successful with a minimum of time and work. You will also need to know something about pots and other containers, repotting, propagation, and a few other relevant practical matters.

THE BASIC HOUSE PLANT

Every house plant carries within its genetic structure the characteristics of its distant progenitors that lived out of doors. Thus the Maranta loses some of its leaves each autumn, even though autumn's weather does not come to the top of the bookshelf where the plant sits, and a cactus, no matter how long it has been fed and watered during its growing season, keeps hoarding food and water within its swollen stems. Old habits may recede, but they are never forgotten.

At no time are these innate characteristics more noticeable than during the autumn and winter, when many plants enter a period of dormancy, or rest. New growth ceases, and some plants, particularly those from temperate regions, take on a listless appearance. Other plants, including many of tropical origin, maintain their bright appearance but stop growing completely for several months each year. It is well to watch for these signs, and to make the response. Water should be reduced and fertilizer withheld completely until new growth once again begins, usually in late winter or early spring. The plant should then be given its normal doses of water and fertilizer once again in emulation of the advent of spring, so as to work with the plant in carrying out its rhythmic cycles.

Some plants last no more than a year or two indoors despite careful attention, because their genetic structure dictates a short span of life. Very few garden annuals are selected as house plants because they germinate, grow to maturity, flower, produce seeds, and die, all in as little as six months. Although a few short-lived plants are cultivated indoors for their unusual characteristics, such as the Sensitive Plant which is easily grown from seed, most of the house plants that have been cultivated over the generations are those that give years of pleasure. Some house plants, in fact, live to be literally hundreds of years old.

Large-leafed plants will appreciate an occasional bath. Use a mild soap solution and rinse thoroughly with clear water – both at room temperature.

18 NO TIME FOR HOUSE PLANTS

Still other house plants are attractive when young, but grow ungainly or otherwise unattractive when they approach maturity. The only plants of this kind I have chosen for inclusion in this book are those that are very easy to propagate from cuttings, so that the parent plant may be discarded after a year or two, to be replaced by its children.

Of the hundreds of thousands of plant species in the world, those traditionally cultivated as house plants are the relatively few that have shown a wide tolerance to conditions of heat, light, moisture in the ground and in the air, and ventilation; in other words, those plants that can withstand a human environment. They are both attractive to the eye and tough. Still, their natural adaptability and resilience do need human fostering.

HOW A PLANT FEEDS

The bulk of a plant's food – the sugar it uses for energy and growth – is manufactured by the plant itself. In the presence of light, the leaves draw carbon dioxide from the air and water from the roots, converting them into sugar, a process which is known as photosynthesis.

During this process, something else is happening within the plant. While the leaves are absorbing carbon dioxide through their stomata (or pores) they are also releasing oxygen. (Plants produce not only all of the world's food but most of its atmospheric oxygen as well.) During the hours of darkness, the process is reversed; some oxygen is recaptured from the atmosphere and used to convert the stored sugar into energy. Generally, a plant manufactures food during the day and does its actual growing at night.

Often, the plant converts its newly manu-

Any plant and soil ball may easily be separated from its pot by turning it upside-down and rapping the rim of the pot sharply against the end of a bench. If the plant is not sufficiently pot-bound to require repotting – as this one is not – then the soil ball may easily be replaced with no harm and little mess.

factured sugar into starch and stores it, reconverting it into sugar as the need arises. Starch can be stored in almost any part, but certain plants have developed specialized areas. Cacti and succulents have the greatest above-ground storage capacity, in the form of enlarged stems and leaves, while others, including bulbs, tubers, corms, and rhizomes, have developed underground storage apparatus. A bulb is simply an enlarged underground bud, such as is found on hyacinths, tulips, and onions. A tuber is nothing more than an enlarged root: a common

19 UNDERSTANDING HOUSE PLANTS

Decorative containers without drainage holes can be used successfully if the plant is double-potted. This Prayer Plant (*Maranta*) has been potted in a clay pot, which was then inserted into the decorative container on a layer of gravel. Moss occupies the space between the two pots, assuring constant moisture for the plant's roots.

potato is a tuber; gloxinias, caladiums, dahlias, and many other common plants are grown from tubers. A corm is the enlarged base of a stem. And a rhizome is simply an enlarged, underground stem that grows laterally. All these methods are used by plants to store food, and all of them can be used to propagate plants, too.

As water transpires through the stomata of the leaves, a 'pulling' action draws more water up through the roots. The water carries with it mineral salts, including all the elements which the plant needs to carry out its complex chemical processes. Transpiration in the leaves of plants is similar to perspiration in the skin of humans and serves a similar purpose – to cool. The cooling effect of transpiration is difficult to detect in house plants but it is readily apparent in a group of large trees. The cool and fresh feeling of a thick woods in summer is not primarily the product of the shade itself, but of the transpiration of the millions of leaves overhead.

A plant can rarely absorb more water than it can use profitably because its vessels and cells can accommodate only so much at a given time; however, overwatering can exclude oxygen from the root system, ironically causing wilting of the top portion of the plant. When no watering is done, the plant's cells gradually collapse, and the entire plant wilts. Because all plants do have protective mechanisms that conserve water in times of drought, however, they can withstand a temporary dry spell. Most wilted house plants quickly spring back to normal when water is again provided.

PARTS OF THE PLANT

Stem. The stem serves to support the plant and to contain and direct the vessels that transport water from the roots, and food from the leaves, to every other part of the plant. Most house plants, including Philodendron, Ivy, and Spider Plant, have soft stems. Such plants must either climb or crawl, since their stems are not strong enough to support an upward-growing structure of significant height. Other plants have soft but thick stems that enable them to attain a good height, although their stems are apt to break. Woody-stemmed plants, such as the Avocado, Poinsettia, and Boxwood, are far more sturdy and are usually derived from trees or shrubs of the temperate region. Canes are thick stems with hollow or pithy centres. Bamboo is an

68 NO TIME FOR HOUSE PLANTS

African Boxwood
(Myrsine africana) 🌡 ○ □ ⊞

Similar to regular Boxwood (q.v.) except that it has red stems. Many people think it is even more graceful. A good plant for terrariums, if the atmosphere is not too hot.

Aralia
(Fatsia japonica) 🌡 ● □ ⊞

Beautiful, bright-green, leathery, maple-like leaves highlight this cheerful plant. In appearance, it is similar to *Ricinus communis* (Castor Oil Plant) and in fact is sometimes called False Castor Oil Plant. It thrives in a cool spot. Aralia can easily grow leggy, and should be pruned annually in order to encourage it into bushy growth. It will attain a height of four feet at maturity.

Sometimes sold as *Aralia sieboldii*.

A striking hybrid, *Fatshedra lizei*, crosses *F. japonica* and *Hedra* (Ivy) to produce a climbing plant with maple-shaped leaves which is tolerant of adverse conditions.

There is also a plant called False Aralia, which has graceful and feathery foliage. It bears no resemblance to the true Aralia and is difficult to grow.

Asparagus 🌡 ● □ ⊞

There are two kinds of asparagus suitable for growing as house plants – *A. plumosus* (Fern Asparagus) with slender, needle-like, dark-green leaves, giving a feathery appearance, and *A. sprengeri* (Emerald Feather) which has thicker yellow-green leaves and drooping stems. The latter makes a good plant for hanging baskets, and produces red berries at Christmastime. Both like some sun in the summer and full sun in the winter, and both can grow to a height of about two feet.

Australian Laurel
(Pittosporum tobira) 🌡 ○ □ ⊞

A tolerant and slow-growing plant whose leaves, glossy and leathery, resemble those of Rhododendron. It will grow vigorously bushy and does not need much attention. Florists often use the leaves in floral arrangements.

An interesting variegated form is *P. tobira variegata*.

Australian Umbrella Tree
(Schefflera actinophylla) 🌡 ● □ ⊞

Here is a very attractive and vigorous-growing tree with rich-looking, glossy leaves that radiate umbrella-like from the ends of several leaf stalks. It is a tough and rewarding plant, growing to six feet, which can be propagated by air-layering.

Also sold as *Brassaia actinophylla*.

A dwarf variety, *B. actinophylla compacta*, is also available.

Baby's Tears
(Helxine soleirollii) 🌡 ● □ ⊞

This low creeper is also called Irish Moss. It likes a constantly moist (but not soggy) soil, and higher than average humidity. It makes a good ground cover for terrariums, but will also grow in a pot if adequate humidity is provided. Baby's Tears may appear to die in the colder months, but after an adequate rest period it will spring back to life.

Black Pepper
(Piper nigrum) 🌡 ● □ ⊞

This is not a very attractive plant, but it produces real peppercorns which you may use at the table, and is a good conversation piece for that reason. The plant's green berries later turn red, then dry up and turn black. Pick the dried-up black corns, dry them thoroughly for several weeks in an open spot, then use them in your pepper grinder. It is not a demanding plant: it needs the same care as that required for Philodendron.

Boxwood
(Buxus) 🌡 ○ □ ⊞

The same plant which grows the most prized hedges outdoors can make a very attractive house plant. It has glossy, bright-green leaves and is slow-growing and dependable, a good subject for bonsai, the ancient Oriental art of growing dwarf trees and shrubs. *B. sempervirens* and *B. microphylla japonica* (Japanese Boxwood) are the two popular species.

Bromeliads 🌡 ● □ ⊞

There are more than 1,800 varieties of this popular group, many of which are suitable for growing as house plants. Some of them produce attractive flowers, but most are grown for their striking and variegated leaf patterns. One distinctive feature is the rosette leaves which form a small water cup. The natural habitat of the plant is in the crotches of trees in Central and South America, and the water cup is an evolutionary survival characteristic, used to hold reserve supplies of water. In the artificial habitat of a house the cup should be kept filled with water which is changed weekly.

A few of the more common Bromeliads are *Aechmea*, *Ananas* (Pineapple), *Billbergia*, *Cryptanthus* (Zebra Plant), *Dyckia*, *Tillandsia* (Spanish Moss), and *Vriesia*.

Caladium 🌡 ● □ ⊞

Caladiums, with their spectacularly coloured and variegated leaves, are equally at home in the garden or on the window sill. They are ideal additions to plant groupings on porches or patios in summer and early autumn. Give them bright light, but not long periods of direct sun in summer, if you want them to show their brightest colours.

Caladiums are grown from tubers, which can be divided easily to produce new plants. Start the tubers in regular potting soil at a very warm temperature – 80° to 90° – and when the young plants appear, move them to a cooler spot. They will attain a height of about one foot.

Cast Iron Plant
(Aspidistra elatior) 🌡 ● □ ⊞

This is perhaps the easiest plant to grow, as its name suggests. To neglect it to death is virtually impossible. It is also called Saloon Plant, since it was one of the few that could survive in Victorian taverns, and it was made immortal by George Orwell in his novel *Keep the Aspidistra Flying*. If you cannot grow the *Aspidistra*, you may safely

Cast Iron Plant (*Aspidistra*).

Handy Reference Guide

The ABCs of Artificial Light

The recent introduction of fluorescent tubes meant especially for plant growing has been a great boon for indoor gardeners. With the aid of artificial light, now grow lush, green plants in areas where they would never grow before. A windowless bathroom, which might offer ideal humidity and temperature conditions, can now be made into an ideal plant-growing environment. Plants growing on a drab northern window sill can now receive supplemental light during winter's short and dark days. Dim corners of any room can be transformed into green showplaces. Cuttings and seedlings can now make faster and surer progress than ever, under artificial light, and we can even grow vegetables in the dead of winter in the bedroom or kitchen. Artificial lighting is not essential for house plant success, but it certainly does broaden our horizons and increase chances for maximum rewards.

The old incandescent bulb does offer some help to growing plants, although the heat it produces makes it impossible to offer plants the amounts of light they need without drying or burning the plants. Also, incandescent bulbs offer a very short spectrum of light wavelengths, falling far short of simulating the beneficial rays of the sun. Ordinary daylight or cool white fluorescent lights are far better for growing plants, since they have not only a wider and more effective light wavelength, but also produce light with three times as much efficiency as incandescent bulbs, thus reducing heat by fully two-thirds. Not until the past decade, however, have we had fluorescent tubes made to meet exactly the needs of growing plants. These lights, sold under such names as Gro-Lux, Plant-Gro, and Plant-Light, cost more than ordinary fluorescent tubes, but they are long-lasting and they can solve virtually any light problem for the indoor gardener. By attaching them to a twenty-four hour timer, you can control light exposure perfectly, even for such tricky operations as forcing plants to bloom out of season.

The best way to start out with artificial light is the most simple way. Purchase two forty-watt plant-growing tubes with the proper fixture, and hang it over a table where you wish to begin your experiments. Be sure you have some method of raising and lowering the fixture, for you will want to adjust the lighting intensity to meet different plant requirements. Ferns and snake-plant, for instance, have low light requirements, so that the tubes should be placed twelve to eighteen inches above them, while succulents, ivy, most flowering plants, and

171 HANDY REFERENCE GUIDE

Plants for Cool Conditions (50° – 60° at night)

Aloe
Aspidistra
Australian Laurel
Azalea
Baby's Tears
Black Pepper
Boxwood
Bromeliads
Cacti
Calceolaria
Camellia
Cape Ivy
Christmas Begonia
Chrysanthemum
Cineraria
Citrus
Creeping Fig
Cyclamen
Easter Lily
English Ivy
Fatshedera
Fiddle-Leaf Fig
Flowering Maple
Freesia
Fuchsia
Geranium
German Ivy
Honeysuckle
Hyacinth
Jasmine
Jerusalem Cherry
Kalanchoe
Kangaroo Vine
Lily-of-the-Valley
Lithops
Miniature Holly
Mother of Thousands
Narcissus
Oxalis
Primrose
Sensitive Plant
Silk Oak
Snake Plant
Spindletree
Tulip
Vinca
Wandering Jew
White Calla Lilly

Plants for Medium Temperatures (60° – 65° at night)

Achimenes
Aechmea
Amaryllis
Ardisia
Asparagus Fern
Aspidistra
Avocado
Begonia
Bird's Nest Fern
Browallia
Chenille Plant
Christmas Cactus
Chrysanthemum
Citrus
Coleus
Copper Leaf
Crown of Thorns
Cryptanthus
Dracaena
Easter Lily
Echeveira
English Ivy
Gardenia
Grape Ivy
Hibiscus
Hydrangea
Maranta
Norfolk Island Pine
Palms
Philodendron scandens
Pilea
Peperomia
Poinsettia
Rubber Plant
Shrimp Plant
Silk Oak
Snake Plant
Staghorn Plant
Ti Plant
Tuberous Begonia
Umbrella Tree
Velvet Plant
Wax Begonia
Wax Plant
Weeping Fig
Yellow Calla Lily

UNIVERSITY OF TORONTO PRESS

University of Toronto, Toronto, Canada M5S 1A6

November 24, 1976

Professor Purvis Mulch

Dear Professor Mulch:

We are all of us enthusiastic about No Time for House Plants and I have just come from the second conference devoted to it.

Our ambition is to produce your book initially in a clothbound edition priced at less than $10.00 in a format that will be as economical as possible and which will lend itself to a large run cheap edition in due course.

We recognize that your book is going to appeal to a very particular section of what is a large market and it is one which we are quite accustomed to reaching, for it is the market for good general scholarly books. We see the particular merit of your book being in the fact that it is amusingly and well written but, most particularly, that it condenses a very great deal of information into a short space. It should be an ideal book for literate people who want all the necessary information provided to them in the most compact and easily digested form possible. We think we can achieve this well with your excellent little work.

You will be receiving from the editorial department a form of contract and an author's information sheet which will be invaluable to us in planning the detailed promotion of the book. Naturally, we will see that a simple and inexpensive announcement about the book goes out very widely with our general direct mail program to scholars but we will also, of course, have to place appropriate advertisements in quite a variety of places. Your thoughts as to what will be most effective will be very helpful to us for we will be working with a budget that will be far from inexhaustible.

Professor Purvis Mulch   - 2 -   November 24, 1976

Our production department is anxious to have a set of the drawings that we know you can provide us and I would be grateful if you could send them to me at your earliest convenience.

I look forward to associating with you over the next few months and, particularly, when we publish in the spring of next year.

Yours sincerely,

Hilary S. Marshall,
Manager,
Sales and Distribution.

HSM:ir

Author's Information Sheets

University of Toronto Press
Sales & Promotion Department
Toronto M5S 1A6, Ontario
Telephone (416) 928-2250

Author: Purvis Mulch

Title of Book: No Time for House Plants: A Busy Person's Guide to Indoor Gardening

Form sent: 1 December 1976   Form received back:

Sponsoring Editor: Agatha Q. Sigglesthwaite   Manuscript Editor: the same
Editor (Environmental Arts)

The Sales and Promotion Department of the University of Toronto Press is responsible for finding the greatest possible market for your book. To do this, many different methods of promotion are used, the chief of which are:

1 Distribution of review copies to suitable media

2 Description in the appropriate seasonal catalogue and listing in our complete catalogue of books in print. These catalogues are distributed to librarians and booksellers throughout the world

3 Description in a brochure which will be mailed to librarians, scholars, booksellers and appropriate professional groups

4 Listing in Bowker's *Publishers' Trade List Annual* and *Books in Print*, two of the most important reference tools for booksellers and librarians

5 Book exhibits at meetings of academic, library and professional groups

6 Advertising in scholarly journals

7 Advertising in metropolitan daily newspapers, and mass-circulation magazines (for books of interest to the general reader)

8 In the case of a book with textbook possibilities, distribution of desk copies to appropriate department heads and instructors

9 Special promotions applicable to the individual book

It should be noted that not all these methods are necessarily used for every book, although with rare exceptions the first two are used for every book. As we believe that the author, with his intimate knowledge of the content and style of his book, is in an excellent position to assist us in reaching the largest possible market, we ask you to complete as fully as possible the information requested on the following sheets. Please note that while portions of your description of the book, and your biography, may be used verbatim in jacket and catalogue descriptions and in mailing pieces, this material will not be attributed to the author, and will be revised if necessary to suggest that it has been written by a member of the Press staff.

PLEASE return the attached sheets as soon as possible. If we have these details at an early stage, it ensures that the many people dealing with your book are fully and accurately informed.

ALTHOUGH SOME OF THE ITEMS MAY BE IRRELEVANT TO YOUR BOOK, PLEASE ANSWER ALL THOSE QUESTIONS YOU CAN.

Author's Information Sheets

A BIOGRAPHY Please fill in ALL the information requested below

Author, editor, translator, introducer. Please give your name here in exactly the form you wish it to appear in the book's advertising.

Purvis Mulch

Title (or working title) of book

No Time for House Plants: A Busy Person's Guide to Indoor Gardening

Working address (including postal code and telephone number)

University of Wisconsin Press   608: 262-7756
Box 1379, Madison, Wisconsin 53701 USA

Home address (including postal code and telephone number)

315 N. Franklin St.
Madison, Wisconsin 53703
608: 255-6065

Please indicate which is to be used for correspondence concerning your book

WE ARE REQUIRED BY LAW TO PROVIDE THE FOLLOWING INFORMATION TO THE NATIONAL LIBRARY OF CANADA FOR COPYRIGHT PURPOSES

Name in full   Purvis Sphagnum Mulch

Maiden name if applicable   (current maiden)

Year and place of birth   1933, Crackersport, Pennsylvania, USA

Nationality   U.S.

If Canadian, is it by birth or residence?

1 Present academic connections or occupation and official title
Freelance garden writer, lecturer, and plant exorcist

2 Education and professional training, degrees, honorary degrees. Please give dates.
No professional training, no degrees, no honorary degrees

3 Prizes, honours, scholarships, fellowships, medals, membership in honorary societies. Please give name and purpose of award, name of organization awarding and year.   No recognition whatsoever

4 Reference books (i.e. *Who's Who*) in which you are listed.
Listed in no reference books

5 Titles, dates, and publishers of other books you have written, edited, or worked on in some capacity / magazines which have published your work.
A Crackersport Garden Guide (1975); Encyclopedia of Organic Gardening (contributing editor, 1960); articles in House Beautiful, Organic Gardening & Farming, Mother Jones, Camping Journal, etc.

6 Other writing you are engaged in at present.
The Earthworm Book (for Rodale Press, 1977)

7 Television and radio programmes you have appeared on.
No TV or radio

(9-continued)

cents a pound in grocery stores, mangoes and guavas were going for a dime apiece. In 1948, he became convinced that a large greenhouse might be the answer to the recurring frost problem. He finished the greenhouse on August 12, 1950, the day before the greatest hail storm in local memory, and spent the next three years in constructing glass mobiles for the tourist trade. All this while, mother commanded top wages in the steel mill, commuting between the farm and Bethlehem six days a week. She organized the steel workers union at Bethlehem and is still remembered there for once dispatching four goons in an alley behind a tavern. A folk song about her exploits never sold well.

From this background, I developed a sensitivity to growing things as well as a respect for the inner toughness that often sees us through life's cloudy days. The fact that I once assaulted a six-foot dieffenbachia in the Brooklyn Botanical Gardens is not without developmental roots.

After childhood, my life's direction was fairly well set. I educated myself in both library and garden, and at the age of 28 developed a theory that organic fertilizer was the answer to communism. My first published article, "Marx or Manure: America's Choice for the 50s", appeared in the Philadelphia Inquirer Sunday garden supplement of March 2, 1955. On the strength of that piece, I began to write and lecture full-time, paying special attention to mangoes and left-wing bureaucrats at the U.S. Department of Agriculture.

With the waning of the communist scare, my interests turned more to companion planting, varieties of hairy vetch, bacterial control of brown rot on sour cherry trees, and earthworms as the guardians of modern civilization.

My first book, A Crackersport Garden Guide, was well received throughout Lehigh County, selling out its first edition of 114 copies within a year and a half. This latest effort, No Time for House Plants, was written in a desperate effort to make money quickly.

Author's Information Sheets

3

8 What is your attitude to personal publicity, i.e. are you prepared to be interviewed by journalists and broadcasters if your book lends itself to this treatment?

I'll try anything once.

9 Please give us a short autobiography. The Press, the booktrade, and the public are always interested in 'human interest' material concerning the lives of authors. (Childhood, travels, special interests, professional life, writing experience, and, in particular, activities connected with the subject of your book.) Attach a separate sheet if you require more space.

I was born in Crackersport, Pennsylvania during the Great Depression, of Pennsylvania Dutch parents. We were not poor, but honest--good country folk. My father, Marvin Mulch, was a farmer who specialized in mangoes and guavas. My mother Roxanne worked at the open hearth furnaces at Bethlehem Steel. I believe that I inherited my love for plants and my romantic streak from my father, and my intensely practical nature from my mother. Father's history still remains a frazzled thread in the family fabric. He spent twenty-three years in trying to grow tropical fruits in the middle of the best potato-growing land on the Eastern Seaboard. Naturally, his young trees died every year around Thanksgiving. During one unusually warm year, in 1939, he nursed a guava until three days before Christmas before it fell to mice. Dad's reasoning was that, while potatoes were selling for four (continued)

10 Can you supply, if requested, a photograph of yourself suitable for book jacket or promotion?

Yes--available later.

B YOUR BOOK

1 What are the particular characteristics of your book which you think will help us in promoting it? What led you to write it? What is the single most significant point of this book? What is the first point we should emphasize in telling others about your book?

This is the only book written for the working person or couple who wants to raise a few house plants successfully, but have little time to devote to the task. It is not for rank beginners, as many house plant books are, but for someone who might have some experience but wishes to learn short-cuts, proper plants to buy, etc.

2 Are there any circumstances connected with the book that may have possible news value? Are there any centenaries, festivals, exhibitions, or other occasions with which we could link our publicity?

It would make a dandy Christmas present for anyone who has half a dozen sickly house plants around the house.

3 Are there any forthcoming conferences or seminars to which the book has particular relevance?

No.

4 Please list recent books, with prices and publication dates if possible, (or any you know of that are in active preparation) that could be said to compete with yours, noting any significant differences.

"There are many "beginning" house plants--but none competing directly.

5 For whom is your book intended? Be as specific as possible, and if applicable please list professors and their institutions that might be approached with a view to classroom adoption of the book. Name courses to which it might apply.

(explained above)

Author's Information Sheets

6 With these people' in mind, please describe your book.

a short description (20 to 50 words,in one or two sentences)

This book explains how anyone can raise several dozen house plants with a minimum of care, by centering on two areas: How to choose easy-care plants to begin, and how to give them the proper conditions initially that will encourage them to grow successfully.

b long description (300 to 400 words). Your summary or précis will assist us in preparing a good description of your book for the jacket and for other promotional material. Please do not refer us to your preface or other parts of your manuscript, for this is often unavailable when the information is needed.

In 1973, with the purchase of a new house, I was determined to increase my house plant population. Still, I realized that, with my busy schedule, I would not have much time to devote to indoor plants. I was frequently gone for long periods of time, and many days, even while in town, I simply have no time to fuss with plants.

I therefore sought to find methods to raise interesting and beautiful house plants with the least amount of effort. All the house plant books I checked, however, were apparently written by enthusiasts who spent unending hours in careful watering, potting, repotting, propagating, tying up, inducing to flower, humidifying, bathing, and even talking to their plants in an effort to get them to grow. There was no book for the casual house plant grower.

There is now such a book. By researching many sources, and through past personal experience and experimentation, I have narrowed down the crucial requirements for a "no-time" indoor house plant population. The research yielded two cardinal rules: Choose plants that are tolerant of adverse conditions, and then give them the right conditions to grow without your constant attention.

The implementation of these rules forms the crux of this book. I explain how to choose plants, tell which are the easiest to grow, and explain the conditions of light, soil moisture, humidity, and temperature that each of more than a hundred indoor plants requires. I explain, in short, how your house plants can live well without your constant attention and painstaking devotion.

The chapter on understanding house plants is critically important to the "no-time" system, since it details the initial requirements plants need for success, including potting mixtures, fertilizing, containers, watering, humidity, ventilation, temperature, light, and pruning. When these conditions are met at the very beginning, countless hours will be saved later in nursing plants or attempting to track down troubles.

There is a separate chapter devoted to plant troubles and cures, and special sections on artificial light, summer care, and lists of plants for various conditions of light and temperature. For those who wish to devote a little more time to raising house plants, there is detailed information on repotting, propagation, training, dish gardens, planters, bottle gardens and terrariums, kitchen scrap gardens, and growing vegetables indoors.

The bulk of the book, however, comprises listings of more than a hundred "easy" foliage plants, flowering plants, and succulents, including cacti, giving light, soil moisture, and humidity requirements for each.

For the home owner or apartment dweller who wants to raise several dozen attractive house plants while spending only a few minutes a day in caring for them, this book will tell everything that is necessary to know in order to achieve success.

Author's Information Sheets

C PROMOTION

Questions A.7 and A.8 are also relevant. Where you suggest the name of a contact, please mark with an asterisk if we may NOT say that we are telephoning/writing at your suggestion.

1 Local

a Have you any contacts with your local press, broadcasting, or television? Please give names and addresses.

I have no local contacts of value.

b Please list chronologically (with dates) any places where you have lived for any length of time; any places which might have a special interest in you or the subject of your book.

Crackersport, Pa. (1933-57)
Iowa City, Ia. (1957-61)
Emmaus, Pa. (1961-63)
Newark, N.J. (1963-65)
Madison, Wis. (1965-present)

2 National

a Please suggest any television or radio programmes you consider suitable for the promotion of your book.

Many local stations have weekly gardening programs. I have no list of them.

b Can you suggest any newspapers, magazines, periodicals (lay or specialized) which we might approach to do a feature on your book, print extracts from it, or interview you? Please give names of any contacts you have with these papers.

Try *Organic Gardening & Farming* (M. C. Goldman), *Mother Jones* (Jeffrey Klein), *House Beautiful* (Elvin MacDonald), and *Countryside* (Heather Tischbein), all of which I have written for.

3 Abroad

a Which countries might be *particularly* interested in your book?

Possibly Great Britain and Australia.

b Please give names of foreign publishers who have translated or bought rights of any work of yours not published by us. Please also give names of any contacts.

None.

c Please give similar information concerning any other foreign publishers who might be interested in publishing translations of this book.

None that I know of.

4 Please list scholarly journals, magazines, and newspapers which you believe are most likely to carry a review of your book and mark with an asterisk those most suitable for possible display advertising. (Attach another page if necessary.)

NYTRB, Apartment Ideas, Apartment Life, Mother Jones, Organic Gardening & Farming, Ms, Esquire, Better Homes & Gardens, Playboy, other magazines geared to the single and/or working life.

Memo to: H. S. Marshall   From: A. Livernois

OUTLINE OF SALES AND PROMOTION CAMPAIGN

No Time for House Plants
by Purvis Mulch

After closer examination of the manuscript, discussions amongst ourselves and with sales representatives, a sampling of the media and the trade, we concluded that No Time for House Plants has a wider market potential than originally anticipated. Our campaign therefore will be directed toward a general audience of intelligent, busy people; it will be aggressive but in good taste. We will not attempt to compete with the low-priced books which tend to provide only basic information, but will stress that No Time for House Plants provides complete information on the selection and care of appropriate house plants which will help the reader raise healthy plants with a minimum of time and care, and a maximum of pleasure.

April 1 has been chosen as publication date, after due consideration of production timing versus suitable release date. This will catch the market just prior to the outdoor planting season (in our area at least), in time for various gift periods, and will avoid the busy fall book season. Finished books will be ready two months in advance of publication. The following is a general outline of sales and promotion plans:

Book Clubs

Submissions for possible book club sale:

American Garden Guild Book Club, New York,
Organic Gardening Book Club, Emmaus, PA.

Excerpts

Approach the following magazines and journals for possible excerpting, those asterisked because Purvis Mulch has written articles for them, the others because of their large distribution to the potential market:

Author's Information Sheets

5 Please give the dates, places, and sponsoring organizations of any forthcoming speaking engagements.

None.

6 Are there any societies or other organizations likely to be interested in you or the subject of your book? Are mailing lists available from them and from whom?

None that I know of.

7 At which association conventions might it be appropriate to exhibit your book?

ALA, ABA.

8 If you feel it appropriate, please list in order of importance, names and addresses of individuals whose good opinion of the book might broaden its audience—those to whom, for instance, advance copies of the book might be sent by us for comments that could be quoted in advertising. Add a brief note of explanation where necessary.

Try M. C. Goldman, Managing Editor, Organic Gardening & Farming

9 Give the name and address of any booksellers or librarians who might take a special interest in your book. Add a brief note of explanation where necessary.

All bookstores know me through my first work.

10 Please list names and addresses of personal friends, relatives and colleagues to whom you wish copies of your book sent (with 'compliments of the author cards) and charged to you at author's discount of 40% from the list price, plus mailing costs.

Mrs.   54 Farragut Dr., Palm Coast, Fla. 32037 (mother)
Mr.   2414 Fairview St., Allentown, Pa.

11 Please indicate how many copies of the mailing piece you will want for your own distribution to friends and colleagues.

100

PLEASE ADD ANY OTHER PROMOTION IDEAS AND FURTHER INFORMATION WHICH YOU THINK MIGHT BE USEFUL.

Thank you,

Sales and Promotion Department
University of Toronto Press

- 2 -

Excerpts (continued)

```
         *Organic Gardening and Farming
         *Mother Jones
         *House Beautiful
         *Countryside
          Cosmopolitan  )   and to other similar magazines should
          Playboy       )   these not be interested
          Canadian Homes Magazine
          Today's Woman
```

Sales Particulars

1.   We will concentrate on the areas in which we have sales representation: the northeast, middle west, and western states, as well as every province in Canada. (Promotion and distribution in the United Kingdom and Europe will be handled by our agent, Books Canada Limited.)

2.   In addition to covering their regular book and department store accounts, sales representatives will call on the larger indoor plant shops and nurseries in their areas. They will recommend the most appropriate location for Author Demonstrations in the cities on the publicity tour, and provide a list of accounts for poster distribution. They will arrange their itineraries so that they will be available to assist Purvis Mulch when she visits the cities in their areas.

3.   Co-operative advertising, on a 50/50 basis, will be offered to stores holding Author Demonstrations. It is necessary that stores liaise with the Promotion Department regarding timing and shared costs.

4.   The following escalating discount schedule will apply to all trade orders:

```
          1 -   24 copies        40%
         25 -   99 copies        42%
        100 -  249 copies        44%
        250 -  999 copies        46%
       1000 up                   50%
```

.../3

- 3 -

These discounts should induce quantity buying and allow the sales representative to get the books into appropriate wholesalers.

5.   Our plans envisage a paperback edition, but it will not appear until at least one year after publication.

Promotion Particulars

Purvis Mulch is an attractive, articulate woman in her early 40s - an expert on house plants, with a good sense of humour and a quick wit. She is fairly well known through her articles and lectures on gardening and she is willing to do all she can to promote her book.

The promotion budget has been set at roughly $5,000 -- made up of $2500 based on our usual calculations and another $2500 built into the price of the book, since we felt $5000 was the minimum amount required to promote No Time for House Plants. Should initial orders suggest a larger printing, or should reprinting be necessary at a later date, additional promotional dollars will be made available. Therefore we are including one or two extras, which we may or may not be able to finance. A breakdown of the budget is attached. (A)

The following is an outline of promotion plans:

Catalogues

No Time for House Plants will be announced in the spring and summer seasonal catalogue, with a photograph of the jacket. Copy is attached. (B) It will appear as well in the Complete Catalogue of Books in Print. Catalogues are distributed to booksellers (trade and college), libraries (public and university), and the media in the United States, Canada, the United Kingdom and Europe. They are also given away at exhibits and on request.

.../4

- 4 -

Advance Material

Pages will be sent to Publishers' Weekly and Kirkus Review. Since we have planned a two-month lead time, finished books can be sent to all other reviewers.

Release

Copy for a release is attached. (C) The release will be sent to all garden columnists prior to the review copy. Also to bookstores, indoor plant shops, and nurseries with the poster; to general columnists at time of publication; to radio and TV shows and columnists who are approached for interviews. (For the latter group, a biographical sheet (D) has been prepared as well.)

Review Copies

At a cost of $2.54 each, review and publicity copies will be our least expensive method of promotion and will be distributed generously. (The cost of frees does not come out of the book budget.) We toyed with the idea of being gimmicky and sending a pot containing one of the hardiest and healthiest of house plants to major garden columnists, but decided that this had been overdone, not to mention the difficulty of delivering the plants in a healthy condition.

The review list is attached (E); the publicity list has not been prepared in detail as yet, but a general plan is included as part of the review list. A clipping service will be retained for this book, since many of the columnists are likely to omit mention of the publisher.

Review copies will be sent in three groups:

(1) Journals and magazines - two months before publication date
(2) Newspapers - 5 weeks prior to publication date
(3) Publicity - 4 weeks prior to author's visit

.../5

- 5 -

Direct Mail

Initially, there will be no direct mail campaign for No Time for House Plants. Later, if more money becomes available, an inexpensive circular may be produced and included in mailings of other circulars. Costs therefore would be kept to a minimum, including only the cost of the circular and of the extra insertion.

Author's Publicity Parties

We do not plan to spend promotion dollars on publicity parties, thinking that little publicity would result from such parties that we cannot get in other less expensive ways.

Advertising

(Copy and layouts attached)

1. Announcement advertisements in: (F)

    Publishers' Weekly,
    Quill and Quire
    American Nurseryman
    Organic Gardening and Farming

2. Co-operative advertising with stores holding Author Demonstrations. (G)

3. Original plans called for small advertisements in such magazines as Apartment Life, House Beautiful, and New Yorker. Advertising rates proved prohibitive, however, and we had to abandon this plan. We would like to run a series of classified advertisements in these and other consumer magazines such as Playboy and Cosmopolitan, but even these prove too expensive for the initial promotion budget. Classified advertisements therefore become (H) part of the second stage of promotion which becomes possible if advance sales permit a larger printing and a concomitant increase in promotion budget.

Posters

Approximately 2500 will be distributed to popular bookstores, indoor garden

.../6

- 6 -

shops, and nurseries. While posters are a costly item, they are extremely useful for this type of book, especially where the book cover design is used for maximum recognition and impact. To avoid the expense and waste of a large haphazard poster mailing, sales representatives will provide distribution lists. Copy and layout attached. (I)

Publicity Tour

Purvis Mulch lives in   ; thus we plan a publicity tour that will take her to seven major cities between there and New York City. The cities on the itinerary, and tentative dates, are:

Home City	March 31
	April 3 & 4
Near-by City	April 6 - 8
Chicago, Illinois	April 10 - 12
Cleveland, Ohio	April 13 - 15
Toronto, Canada	April 17 - 19
Boston, Massachusetts	April 20 - 24
New York City	April 25 - May 2
Philadelphia, Pennsylvania	May 3 - 5
Home (via New York)	May 6

Fortunately, Purvis Mulch is a popular lady with friends in all of these cities who have offered her their hospitality. Thus living expenses during the publicity tour will be minimal. Much as I would like to accompany Purvis Mulch on this tour, the budget will not allow it. However we will provide detailed itineraries well in advance to the author, sales representatives, stores in the particular area, and ABA Newswire. Sales representatives will schedule their itineraries so that they can assist Ms. Mulch. They will not have to spoon feed her of course; she is a competent woman, accustomed to travel and interviews, and quite capable of getting herself from interview to interview, when necessary. Sales representatives should be at the Author Demonstrations, however.

.../7

- 7 -

Activities in each city will fall into the following areas:

1. Television Interviews

These and the following interviews have yet to be set up. Early research and contact will indicate who is likely to be interested in interviews.

To these we will send release, biographical sheet, photograph of Purvis Mulch, and a copy of No Time for House Plants, accompanied by an individual letter. Follow up and final arrangements will be made by telephone.

Television interviews, both national and regional, will be scheduled on appropriate talk, garden, and general interest shows. In some cases, plants and props, or possibly photographs, will be provided for demonstration and discussion.

2. Radio Interviews

Radio interviews will include garden and general interest shows, as well as phone-in discussion and advice programs.

3. Newspaper Coverage

In each city we will attempt to get feature articles in one or more of the leading newspapers and magazines. These interviews are likely to be done by by-line columnists. However, Ms. Mulch will talk to garden and book columnists as time permits, following up the review copy sent in February. Photographs of Author Demonstrations will be sent to newspapers and may get some additional space.

4. Author Demonstrations

So called for lack of a better description. In actual fact these demonstrations will combine:

(i) Demonstration of plant selection and care
(ii) Clinic to which people are invited to bring their plant problems or even their sick plants if they wish
(iii) Autographing books.

.../8

- 8 -

With the help of sales representatives, demonstrations will be arranged at the best possible location in each city, which could be a department store with both book and plant departments, a major indoor gardening shop, or a large nursery. Alternatively, a Demonstration could tie in with a garden show or convention.

Demonstrations will be scheduled on the last day in each city if this is possible, in order to take advantage of newspaper, radio, and television publicity. Ms. Mulch will be instructed to mention Demonstrations whenever possible.

Demonstrations will be supported by:

(i) Co-operative advertising (50/50) which must be co-ordinated with the Promotion Manager, and the cost approved. Repros will be available. (Layout and copy attached.) (G)

(ii) Posters, those provided by us, and others announcing the Demonstration.

(iii) Prescription slips (Layout and copy - see attached). (J) These prescription slips are double duty - to advertise No Time for House Plants and provide a space for Ms. Mulch's advice.

(iv) Plant stakes (See attached.) (K) This is an extra, and part of Stage 2, i.e. increased promotion budget. The sticks would be ideal for use both at Demonstrations and by plant shops afterwards. The idea of course is that the dye-cut plant stake sticks into the soil of the plant -- No Time for House Plants is advertised on one side, and the other side is left blank for plant identification.

(v) Each store will be encouraged to offer its own special inducement during the Demonstration, such as a particular hardy plant at discounted price with purchase of the book.

Special Television

One area in which Purvis Mulch has been very successful is in plant exorcism. We want to reserve this performance for a really big talk show, such as Mike Douglas, or if the 'Tonight Show' people could be persuaded to pay Ms. Mulch's expenses to Los Angeles, then that would be our first choice.

.../9

- 9 -

One exorcism is all we plan since it is extremely exhausting for Purvis Mulch and the show will probably want an 'exclusive'.

Exhibits

No Time for House Plants will be shown at every exhibit which we ourselves attend; the people who visit our booth are as likely to be interested in house plants as in their own discipline. In addition, we will include it in major co-operative displays.

Lectures

Whenever Purvis Mulch speaks on the subject of indoor gardening in future we will arrange that her book is available for display and sale, if possible. Naturally she will refer to it herself at every opportunity.

Outside Back Cover Copy

No Time for Houseplants

A busy person's guide to indoor gardening

Purvis Mulch

This delightful and entertaining book is the first guide to indoor gardening written specifically for the indoor gardener. It offers a recommended list of plants that will thrive under various conditions of light and temperature and explains the basic rules for caring for them without spending more than five minutes every other day. The busy homeowner or apartment dweller will find No Time for Houseplants an ideal guide.

'A simple and sensible guide to indoor gardening. It should demolish, once and for all, the myth of the green thumb.'   M.C. Goldman, Organic Gardening and Farming

'Refreshing and welcome ... a Mulch-needed publication.' Weekend Gardener

Purvis Mulch is the author of A Crackersport Garden Guide and has written numerous articles on gardening and related subjects. She is presently working on The Earthworm Book.

ISBN 0-8020-2214-7

LC 76-10000

University of Toronto Press

Cover photograph by Ken Bell

A

PROMOTION BUDGET

No Time for House Plants

by Purvis Mulch

3500 copies Release	
3500 copies Autobiographical Sheet	$ 200.00
Announcement ads	1,270.00
Purvis Mulch Travel Expenses	500.00
Meals and Miscellaneous (no accommodation and only some meals)	700.00
Posters 2500	800.00
Prescription Slips	60.00
Co-operative Advertising re Author Demonstrations	1,500.00
Miscellaneous	300.00
	$5,330.00
Stage 2	
Classified Advertisements	$1,000.00
Plant Stakes	800.00
Direct Mail: Inexpensive Circulars plus small handling cost	700.00
	$2,500.00

NB
Cost of frees and mailing are not included in individual book budgets.

Catalogue copy

No Time for House Plants
A busy person's guide to indoor gardening
Purvis Mulch

This delightful and entertaining book is the first guide to indoor gardening written specifically for the casual gardener. It explains the basic rules for selecting and caring for plants that need a minimum of attention.

Purvis Mulch, a busy person herself, has developed this successful approach to easy-care gardening through research, experience, and experimentation. The principles of the 'no-time' system are simple: first, choose plants that can tolerate some neglect, and then provide the right conditions for them to grow without constant attention. She outlines the initial requirements that plants need in order to thrive, requirements which, if met from the start, will save hours of identifying and correcting problems.

A separate chapter covers the diagnosis and treatment of plant ailments. Special sections are devoted to artificial light and summer care. The book lists over a hundred easy care foliage plants, flowering plants, and succulents, including cacti, giving light, soil moisture, and humidity requirements for each. Special lists of plants suited to various conditions of light and temperature enable indoor gardeners to select plants that will grow in any part of the country or in any corner of the house.

B

For those who find that this easy-care system leaves time for more ambitious adventures in gardening, Mulch provides detailed information on repotting, propagation, training, dish gardens, planters, bottle gardens and terrariums, kitchen scrap gardens, and growing vegetables indoors.

For the homeowner or apartment dweller who would like to raise several dozen attractive house plants without spending more than a few minutes a day in caring for them, No Time for House Plants is an ideal guide.

Purvis Mulch is the author of A Crackersport Garden Guide and has written numerous articles on gardening and related botanical subjects. She is currently working on The Earthworm Book.

RELEASE   C ___

University of Toronto Press

TORONTO / ONTARIO / CANADA M5S 1A6

For Immediate Release

PURVIS MULCH demolishes the myth that house plants require a lot of time, effort, and a very green thumb in her new book, No Time for House Plants.

Many people - singles, working couples, harassed mothers, college students, anyone whose daily living pattern leaves precious little time for indoor gardening - would enjoy the beauty and companionship of luxuriant green house plants. However, past failures and fruitless excursions into gardening books that confuse while trying to explain have convinced them that they had neither the time nor the expertise to raise plants successfully. 'Nonesense,' maintains Purvis Mulch, 'anyone can raise beautiful and healthy plants.'

'The secrets to success are simple,' Ms. Mulch continues. 'Choose plants that are easy to grow and give them the conditions they must have to thrive.' Explaining her approach to easy-care gardening in No Time for House Plants, she recommends and describes more than one hundred plants and plant groups (comprising several thousand individual varieties) which have demonstrated tolerance of the human environment.

Every plant has its own requirements for soil type, light, temperature, ventilation, humidity - factors that are within our power to control, or at least to mitigate. Purvis Mulch fully describes the preferences of each plant; also, through a system of unique symbols, she provides an at-a-glance profile of their needs.

Before growing any plant, however, Ms. Mulch advises the indoor gardener to take some time first to understand it, to learn what the plant needs and to decide whether that is easily provided, and to choose the spot in which the plant will be most comfortable. Then, as many as twenty different house plants can be raised by spending no more than five minutes with them every other day, and perhaps a half-hour every two weeks in pruning,

.../2

- 2 -

tying climbers, bathing leaves, spraying, and fertilizing.

The recommended plants are divided into four broad groups - foliage plants, cacti and other succulents, flowering house plants, and bulb plants. Amongst the known and lesser known varieties are Asparagus, Bromeliads, Cast Iron Plants, Dieffenbachia, Ferns, Ficus, Ivy, Umbrella Sedge (foliage plants) and the Aloes, Echeverias, Crassulas, Kalanchoes, Spider Plant, Snake Plant, and Sedums (succulents). Flowering house plants include Achimenes, African Violets, Amaryllis, Begonia, Chenille Plant, Gloxinia, Wax Plant, and Zebra Plant. The bulb plants are Crocuses, Hyacinths, Tulips, and Daffodils. Within each group, the plants are listed alphabetically by their common names, followed by their scientific (Latin) names in parentheses.

For those who find this easy-care system leaves time for more ambitious adventures in gardening, Purvis Mulch provides chapters on pots and other containers, repotting plants, propagation, problems and their cures, special gardens such as planters, bottle gardens and terrariums, and growing vegetables indoors.

Busy people will find No Time for House Plants the ideal guide for adapting indoor gardening to their lifestyles.

Purvis Mulch is well known for her articles and lectures on gardening and for her bestselling book, A Crackersport Garden Guide.

NO TIME FOR HOUSE PLANTS: A Busy Person's Guide to Indoor Gardening
$9.95, publication date April 1, 19--, published by University of Toronto Press

Contact Audrey M. Livernois
416-978-2052

University of Toronto Press

TORONTO / ONTARIO / CANADA M5S 1A6

D

Autobiographical Sheet

PURVIS MULCH   (Author of No Time for House Plants)

[Purvis Mulch tells her own story so well that we have decided to provide an Author's Autobiographical Sheet, rather than the usual Biographical Sheet.]

'I was born in Crackersport, Pennsylvania during the Great Depression, of Pennsylvania Dutch parents. We were not poor, but honest, good country folk.

'My father, Marvin Mulch, was a farmer who specialized in mangoes and guavas. My mother Roxanne worked at the open hearth furnaces at Bethlehem Steel. I believe that I inherited my love for plants and my romantic streak from my father, and my intensely practical nature from my mother. Father's history still remains a frazzled thread in the family fabric. He spent twenty-three years in trying to grow tropical fruits in the middle of the best potato-growing land on the Eastern Seaboard. Naturally, his young trees died every year around Thanksgiving. During one unusually warm year, in 1939, he nursed a guava until three days before Christmas before it fell to mice. Dad's reasoning was that, while potatoes were selling for four cents a pound in grocery stores, mangoes and guavas were going for a dime apiece. In 1948, he became convinced that a large greenhouse might be the answer to the recurring frost problem. He finished the greenhouse on August 12, 1950, the day before the greatest hail storm in local memory, and spent the next three years constructing glass mobiles for the tourist trade. All this while, mother commanded top wages in the steel mill, commuting between the farm and Bethlehem six days a week. She organized the steel workers' union at Bethlehem and is still remembered there for once dispatching four goons in an alley behind a tavern. A folk song about her exploits never sold well.

'From this background, I developed a sensitivity to growing things as well as a respect for the inner toughness that often sees us through life's cloudy days.

.../2

Purvis Mulch - Autobiographical Sheet -- Page 2

The fact that I once assaulted a six-foot dieffenbachia in the Brooklyn Botanical Gardens is not without developmental roots.

'After childhood, my life's direction was fairly well set. I educated myself in both library and garden, and at the age of 28 developed a theory that organic fertilizer was the answer to communism. My first published article, "Marx or Manure: America's Choice for the 50s", appeared in the Philadelphia Inquirer Sunday garden supplement of March 2, 1955. On the strength of that piece, I began to write and lecture full-time, paying special attention to mangoes and left-wing bureaucrats at the U.S. Department of Agriculture.

'With the waning of the communist scare, my interests turned more to companion planting, varieties of hairy vetch, bacterial control of brown rot on sour cherry trees, and earthworms as the guardians of modern civilization.'

Publisher's Note

Purvis Mulch has become well known through her lectures and articles on gardening. Her tongue-in-cheek autobiography is typical of the humor for which she is also known. She has two previous books to her credit: A Crackersport Garden Guide (author) and Encyclopedia of Organic Gardening (contributing editor), and numerous articles in such magazines as House Beautiful, Organic Gardening and Farming, Mother Jones, Camping Journal, and Countryside. She is presently working on a new book to be entitled The Earthworm Book. Purvis Mulch has been married twice. Currently unmarried, she remains 'good friends' with her ex husbands. She has three children all of whom wholeheartedly support her earthy interests.

REVIEW COPIES LIST
(120)

CODE: SBN 8020 - 2214-7
TITLE: No Time for House Plants
AUTHOR: Purvis Mulch
PUB. DATE: April 1, 19--
PRICE: $9.95

Sheet No: 1 of _____ sheets.

DATE	State / Province	PUBLICATION
February 1		U.S. Newspapers
	California	Los Angeles Times, Carolyn Murray, Home Columnist
		San Francisco Chronicle, Ruth Miller, Women's Interest
		San Francisco Examiner, Marie Hammock, Garden Columnist
	Colorado	Denver Post, Clark Secrest, Garden Columnist
	Connecticut	Hartford Courant, John Massaro, Garden Columnist
		New Haven Register, Marion McDonald, Women's Interest
	DC	Washington Post, Tom Stevenson, Garden Columnist
		Washington Star News, Wilbur H. Youngman, Garden Columnist
	Florida	Miami Herald, Fecilce Dickson, Garden Columnist
	Illinois	Chicago Daily News, Richard Delano, Garden Columnist
		Chicago Sun Times, Eldred E. Green, Garden Columnist
		Chicago Tribune, Arthur Kozelka, Garden Column.st
	Indiana	Indianapolis News, Richard Creem, Garden Columnist
	Iowa	Des Moines Register, Fleeta Woodruffe, Garden Columnist
	Massachusetts	Boston Globe, G. D'Alfonso, Women's Interest
		Christian Science Monitor, Millicent J. Taylor Garden Col.
		Boston Herald American, Maureen Taylor, Women's Interest
		Worcester Telegram, Nicholas Zook, Garden & Home Columnist
	New Jersey	Newark Star Ledger, John Van de Water, Garden Columnist
		Trenton Sunday Times, Sally Lane, Garden & Home Columnist
	New York	Buffalo Evening News, Ed Collins, Garden & Home Columnist
		Rochester Democrat & Chronicle, Home & Family Department
		Syracuse Sunday Herald, Edward Sabine, Garden Columnist
		New York Times, Joan Lee Faust, Garden Columnist
		New York Times Book Review (2 copies)
		New York News, R. Marie Burke, Women's Interest
	Maryland	Baltimore Sun, Francis Rackemann, Garden & Home Columnist
		Baltimore News American, Tom Stevenson, Garden Columnist
	Michigan	Detroit Free Press, Dorothy Weddell, Garden Columnist
		Detroit News, June Hicks, Garden Columnist
		Grand Rapids Press, Charles Johnson, Garden Columnist
	Missouri	St. Louis Post-Dispatch, Joan Dames, Garden & Home Col.
		Kansas City Star, Mary Hobbs, Garden Columnist
	Minnesota	Minneapolis Tribune, Mary Hart, Women's Interest
		St. Paul Dispatch, Robert Phillips, Garden Column.st
	Ohio	Cincinnati Enquirer (Sun), Elliw Rawnsley, Garden Col.
		Cleveland Plain Dealer, Irma W. Bartell, Garden Columnist
		Cleveland Press, Paul Young, Garden Columnist
		Dayton Daily News, Linda Heffley, Home & Family Columnist

E

REVIEW COPIES LIST

CODE: SBN 8020 - 2214-7
TITLE: No Time for House Plants
AUTHOR: Purvis Mulch
PUB. DATE: April 1, 19--
PRICE: $9.95

Sheet No: 2 of _____ sheets.

DATE	State/Province	PUBLICATION
February 1		U.S. Newspapers Continued
	Pennsylvania	Philadelphia Sunday Bulletin, Patricia Spollen, Garden Col.
		Philadelphia Inquirer, Florence Bahar, Garden Columnist
		Pittsburgh Press, Newton Georg, Garden Columnist
	Texas	Dallas Morning News, Neil Sperry, Garden Columnist
		Dallas Times Herald, Edith McRoberts, Garden Columnist
		Houston Post, May Del Flagg, Garden Columnist
		Richmond Times Dispatch, Mrs. Jerry Williams, Garden Col.
	Virginia	Seattle Times, Clayton Hay, Garden Columnist
	Washington	Seattle Post Intelligencer, Ed Hume, Garden Columnist
	Wisconsin	Madison Capital Times, Mary B. Hopkins
		Madison State Journal, Carmen Elsner, Book Editor
		Madison Progressive, Mary Sheridan, Managing Editor
		Milwaukee Journal, Gerald Van Ryzin, Garden Columnist
		Milwaukee Sentinel, David Kitchen, Garden & Home Columnist
		U.S. Magazines, Journals, Book Review Service
		Publishers' Weekly (also pages)
		Kirkus Review (also pages)
		Library Journal
		Booklist
		John Barkham Reviews
		Chicago Seed
		New Home Books
		American Home
		American Nurseryman
		Apartment Ideas
		Apartment Life
		Better Homes and Gardens
		Budget Decorating
		Cosmopolitan
		Countryside
		Esquire
		Family Circle
		Harpers
		Home Lifestyles
		House and Garden
		House Beautiful
		The Homemaker
		Horticulture
		Interior Design
		Ladies' Home Journal
		Leisure Living

REVIEW COPIES LIST

CODE: SBN 8020 - 2214-7
TITLE: No Time for House Plants
AUTHOR: Purvis Mulch
PUB. DATE: April 1, 19--
PRICE: $9.95

Sheet No: 3 of ___ sheets.

DATE	State / Province	PUBLICATION
February 1		U.S. Magazines, Journals, Book Review Service (cont'd)
		McCall's
		Mother Jones
		Ms.
		National Gardener
		New York Magazine
		New Yorker
		New Woman
		Plants & Gardens
		Playboy
		Playgirl
		1000 + 1 Decorating Ideas
		Organic Gardening and Farming
		Todays Woman
		Vogue
		West Coast Review
		Women's Circle
		Workbasket
		Woman's Day
		Canadian Newspapers
	British Columbia	Vancouver Sun, R. Nicholson, Garden Columnist
	Alberta	Calgary Herald, Walter Webber, Garden Columnist
		Edmonton Journal, B. Andrews, Garden Columnist
	Saskatchewan	Regina Leader Post, Family Editor
		Saskatchewan Star Phoenix, Ted Hainworth, Family Living
	Manitoba	Winnipeg Free Press, M.W. Chestnut, Garden Columnist
	Ontario	Ottawa Citizen, Steve Jonescu, Garden Columnist
		Toronto Globe and Mail, Lenore MacDonald, Family Section Ed.
		Toronto Star, H. Fred Dale, Garden Columnist
		Toronto Sun, Joan Sutton, Women's Interest
	Québec	Montréal Star, Paul Pouliot, Garden Columnist
	Nova Scotia	Halifax Mail Star, Lorna Inness, Columnist
		Canadian Magazines, Journals, Miscellaneous
		Canadian Press
		John Bradshaw, syndicated horticulturalist
		Canadian Book Review Annual
		Canadian Field Naturalist
		Canadian Living

REVIEW COPIES LIST

CODE: SBN 8020 - 2214-7
TITLE: No Time for House Plants
AUTHOR: Purvis Mulch
PUB. DATE: April 1, 19--
PRICE: $9.95

Sheet No: 4 of ___ sheets.

DATE	State / Province	PUBLICATION
		Canadian Magazines, Journals, Miscellaneous (cont'd)
		Canadian Homes (supplement to Canadian Magazine)
		Chatelaine
		Homemaker's Magazine
		Nature Canada
		Quest
		Readers' Club of Canada
		Miscellaneous Additions

Classified ad copy

```
                    1 3/4
             ┌──────────────┐     H
2 char. sp. -│ 34 characters│- 2 char. sp.
             └──────────────┘
                               1 3/4
```

PLANT expert Purvis Mulch tells
all you need to know about plant
selection and care to grow healthy
house plants and spend no more than
five minutes every other day doing
it. Order her book
NO TIME FOR HOUSE PLANTS
$9.95 from plant and book stores
or from
University of Toronto Press
33 E Tupper St., Buffalo, NY 14203

LIBERATED GARDENERS

You can raise as many as twenty
different house plants without
spending more than five minutes
every other day. Purvis Mulch tells
how in her book
NO TIME FOR HOUSE PLANTS
$9.95 from plant and book stores
or order from
University of Toronto Press
33 E Tupper St., Buffalo, NY 14203

REVIEW COPIES LIST

(allowance 100 publicity copies)

PUBLICITY LIST

Sheet No: 5 of _____ sheets.

CODE: SBN 8020 - 2214-7
TITLE: No Time for House Plants
AUTHOR: Purvis Mulch
PUB. DATE: April 1, 19--
PRICE: $9.95

Generous distribution of books to interview possibilities in the following cities, re publicity tour during April

Tentative Dates	City	
March 31, April 3 and 4	Home city	
April 6 - 8	Near-by city	
April 10 - 12	Chicago	Detailed schedule will be provided well in advance to: Sales Representatives Author Bookstores, Nurseries, Indoor Plant Shops in area ABA Bookings
April 13 - 15	Cleveland	
April 17 - 19	Toronto	
April 20 - 24	Boston	
April 25 - May 2	New York	
May 3 - 5	Philadelphia	
May 6	Home (via New York)	To: Newspaper Columnists for feature article Magazine Columnists for feature articles or short notes Television Shows - garden, talk, general interest Radio Shows - garden, talk, general interest, phone in

You can raise as many as twenty different house plants by spending no more than five minutes with them every other day.

PURVIS MULCH

PURVIS MULCH
No Time for House Plants
A Busy Person's Guide to Indoor Gardening

Lorem ipsum dolor sit amet, consectetur adipiscing elit, sed diam nonnumy eiusmod tempor incidunt ut labore et dolore magna a erat volupat. Ut enim ad minim veniam, quis nostrud exercitatio ut aliquip ex ea commodo consequat. Duis autem vel eum irure in reprehenderit in volupante velit esse molestaie consequat, vel dolore eu fugiat nulla pariatur. At vero eos et accusam et iusto o dignissim qui blandit praesent luptatum delenit aigue duos dolor molestias excepteur sint occaecat cupiditat non provident, simil s culpa qui officia deserunt mollit anim id est laborum et dolor fug harumd dereud facilis est er expedit distinct. Nam liber tempor c soluta nobis eligend optio comgue hinil impedit doming in quodr placeat facer possim omnis voluptas assumenda est. Omnis dolor aut tum rerum necessit atib saepe eveniet ut er repudiand sint et t Itaque earud rerum hic tenetury sapiente delectus au aut prefer c dolorib asperiore repellat. Hanc ego cum tene senteniam, quid e

University of Toronto Press

otest fier ad augendas cum conscient to factor tum poen

F

Ad copy for
Publishers Weekly, Quill & Quire, American Nurseryman,
and Organic Gardening and Farming (minus the discount line)

"You can raise as many as
twenty different house plants
by spending no more than five
minutes with them every other day."

                        Purvis Mulch

<u>No Time for House Plants</u> is the first guide to indoor greenery written specifically for the casual gardener. Informative and entertaining, it outlines a simple approach to easy-care gardening. In it, Purvis Mulch recommends and describes more than one hundred plants, comprising several thousand individual varieties, and shows through a unique system of symbols the conditions required for each. She discusses pots and potting, propagation, problems and cures, and other matters that will increase the indoor gardener's understanding and enjoyment of plant raising.

"Choose plants that are easy to grow, give them the conditions they need to thrive," advises the author, "and you can grow house plants anywhere in the country, any time of the year, in any corner of the house."

                        $9.95

          Generous discounts on quantity orders

             UNIVERSITY OF TORONTO PRESS
                Buffalo, NY   Toronto, Canada

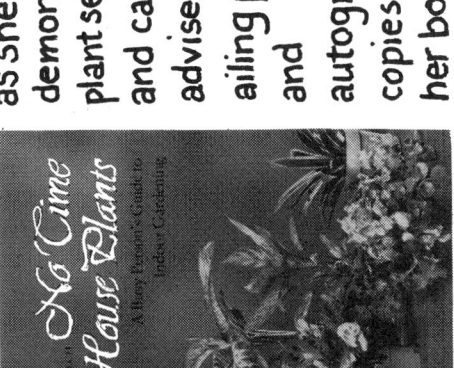

Bring your plant problems and meet PURVIS MULCH, author of *No Time for House Plants: A Busy Person's Guide to Indoor Gardening* as she demonstrates plant selection and care, advises on your ailing plants, and autographs copies of her book

---

Cooperative Ad

G

Date and time space block (large)

Bring your plant problems
and MEET plant expert
    PURVIS MULCH
    author of

    ┌─────────────┐
    │   cut   │
    │   of   │
    │   book   │
    └─────────────┘

        as she

- demonstrates plant selection and care
- advises on your ailing plants
- autographs copies of her book

space block for name and address of
sponsoring store (large)

Instructions

2 cols. X
up to a maximum of 100 lines,
preferably 75
Strong ad please,
with border.

Prescription Slip (J)

Plant Stake (K)

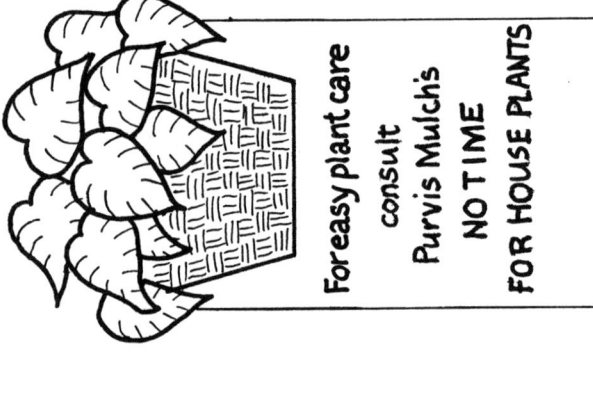

Poster (I)

Size 10 1/4 x 15

2 colour, reverse title

jacket reproduced 9 3/4 x 12 3/4

Copy

If you can spare five minutes every other day
welcome to the pleasures of indoor gardening.

$9.95

University of Toronto Press

Afterword

*What Do You Make
of a "Make-believe" Book?*

*One Book Six Ways:
The University of Oklahoma Press*

Afterword

ONE BOOK/FIVE WAYS has told its own story very well so far, but a number of things remain to be said. Clearly, as Chandler Grannis noted in his Introduction, "There is more than one way to make a book." But what may not be so clear (even though some of the harsh economic realities of publishing are evident, directly or indirectly, in the foregoing pages) is that book publishing is "a slow way to make a fast buck"—at least for the vast majority of publishers and authors. Furthermore, there are interesting and entertaining facts regarding the development and publication of ONE BOOK/FIVE WAYS which have not been presented elsewhere and which deserve to be shared. These and a number of other incidental topics that concern book publishing in general and education for publishing in particular are included here in the spirit of the rest of the book. It is our hope that many readers with differing interests will be provided with some additional insights and food for ongoing thought.

Critic Herbert Mitgang noted recently in *The New York Times* that "America's university presses do not publish just for college students and professors. Quite often these days, they are putting out books that almost any regular trade house would be proud to include on its list." I would add that for some time now, university presses have been publishing books that are far more interesting, imaginative, useful, and substantial in every way than are the largest numbers of books published by the regular trade houses. University presses also help conceive and develop good books that are published eventually by a trade house or by some other commercial publisher, rather than by one of their own number. ONE BOOK/FIVE WAYS is a case in point, to which all of the foregoing assertions apply.

In his Introduction to this book, which was written well before any plans for commercial publication were made, Chandler Grannis also noted, "It is a valuable contribution to the literature of education for publishing . . ." The opinions of Chandler Grannis, a lifelong observer of book publishing, are not to be taken lightly; Mr. Grannis has served as Editor-in-Chief of the leading trade journal, *Publishers Weekly*, to which he is now a Contributing Editor. He is also a book editorial consultant to the R. R. Bowker Company, "the publishers' publisher". He has written extensively on bookmaking, book design, and university presses, and he is also the editor of two books: HERITAGE OF THE GRAPHIC ARTS and WHAT HAPPENS IN BOOK PUBLISHING.

Given the importance of ONE BOOK/FIVE WAYS and the existence of so many excellent university presses as possible publishers, why has this book been published by William Kaufmann, Inc.—a commercial publisher—rather than by one of the participating presses; or, for that matter, by any one of the scores of others?

The answer to the question is simple. We are the publisher because we made a proposal for the book that was acceptable to the "author"—in this instance, the Association of American University Presses, Inc., which acted as "agent" in behalf of the participating presses and others in the Association who were involved in the project. This is the simple procedure by which most books get signed up by publishers in the first place. Publishers discover (or are shown) book proposals or manuscripts at various stages of completion. If they find any of these proposals appealing from the vantage point of their own editorial needs, the publishers offer the authors or their agents an agreement for publication. If the terms are found to be acceptable to all parties concerned, a formal contract for publication (much like any of those in this book) is concluded.

But, as may be imagined, there were unusual elements leading to the publication of ONE BOOK/FIVE WAYS. My own involvement with this extraordinary enterprise began with a telephone call in June 1976 from Walter Sears, the Director of the University of Michigan Press. He briefly described a project which was under way, which he called "The Manuscript Project", and invited me to speak about it from a commercial publisher's point of view at the Annual Meeting of the Association of American University Presses, scheduled to take place in Asheville, North Carolina, June 26-29, 1977. I accepted his invitation, but was not fully aware of what I had let myself in for until many months later.

Early in March 1977 I received a complete xerox copy of the press-ready pages (reproduction proofs) for what had by then become known as ONE BOOK/FIVE WAYS. It was to be printed for distribution as a "workbook" for all of the delegates to the upcoming Annual Meeting. Even in a small edition of fewer than 1,000 copies it would be less expensive per copy to print than to reproduce by xerox or other copying methods, and of course much more convenient to use.

By the time I had gone through all those xerox pages, I knew that here was something truly original, something remarkable, something that should be published for broader distribution. It seemed to me that this would be a unique book, completely unprecedented. Such a book is (as everyone in publishing knows) a rare and almost miraculous event. Who else but the university presses would be willing or able to assign the talent and make a comparable expenditure of the time and money and the multiple creative efforts that had so obviously gone into its development and production? (The "sedate spoofery", wit and good humor throughout that are characteristic of the entire venture come as sheer bonuses to the reader, even though the thorough and serious explication of the entire publishing process is the chief contribution of this superbly educational book.) And, from a competitive marketing point of view, it seemed clear to me that ONE BOOK/FIVE WAYS fulfilled its aims so well that it was unlikely that anyone else would even try to match its achievement for a long time to come.

Following the AAUP Meeting in Asheville, the Canadian Book Trade Journal *Quill and Quire* published a long account in which the reporter pointed out that there is ". . . much to learn from ONE BOOK/FIVE WAYS. The logs contain complete sets of forms for handling a manuscript from acquisition to printing and reveal methods of costing, contracts and royalty schemes that no trade publisher would let out of his office . . . a wealth of material on publishing procedures." It was just those aspects of this book that had "hooked" me as a publisher when I first saw it in xerox copy form. As "one of commercial publishing's strongest advocates for publishing education" (*Publishers Weekly's* designation), I have been active in the development of various courses, seminars and conferences about publishing, at

Stanford University, at campuses of the University of California, Berkeley, Davis and San Francisco, and in other West Coast educational centers. It has also been my privilege to serve on the Committee on Education for Publishing, which was established in 1975 by the Association of American Publishers in response to the growing recognition, among leaders in the regular trade, textbook, reference and other commercial publishing houses, of the vital importance of fostering better education for (and about) publishing. It is satisfying to see publishing education beginning to receive the attention it merits.

Different people concerned with publishing have their own, perhaps different, reasons for considering education for publishing to be so important. But there are two major reasons why I do. First, I regard the publishing of good books (or journals or magazines) as a very high calling indeed, one for which the opportunity for continuing education is highly desirable, if not absolutely necessary, with potential benefits for those who work in publishing as well as for many who do not—librarians, booksellers, teachers, and other "book consumers" of all sorts. In his book, *Dr. Johnson's Printer*, J. A. Cochrane said that publishing

> ". . . was and is no ordinary trade . . . It is practised by men no more intelligent than those engaged in other lines of business; its rewards are, commercially, trifling in relation to the industry and shrewdness it calls into play; as an occupation it entails fully as much of the humdrum drudgery, the pettiness of detail, as is exhibited in any manner of earning a living. But the book trade is distinguished from any other by the fact that its fundamental staple is ideas, even though the tangible expression o those ideas is bought and sold like other commodities. This is the reason for its intrinsic interest and for the fascination it exerts upon those who work in it and so rarely desert it; this is what gives the market place its curious atmosphere, in fluctuating proportions, of idealism and commercial practicality."

On the occasion of the 500th Anniversary of The Oxford University Press, John Russell commented, in *The New York Times Book Review*,

> "Publishing (ideally, at any rate) has to do with genius . . . It has to do with gambling of a lofty but nonetheless desperate kind. It calls for insight, imagination, great technical address and a superfine sense of social and political realities . . . To the layman, it might seem that a university press is the easiest thing in the world to run . . . These are delusions. A university press is, if anything, even more difficult to run than an independent publishing house. . ."

The second reason for placing so high a value on education is related to the first. Given the fundamental importance of reading and books in our society, it is essential that people involved in publishing be given the chance to keep up with the challenges that new techniques and technologies, new ideas, new legislation and social changes will inevitably bring to their work. If they can gain and maintain a broader understanding of the whole world of books they themselves, as well as the important commodities they deal in, can compete more successfully in an increasingly competitive world. Samuel S. Vaughan, Publisher and President of the publishing division of Doubleday and Company, noted in his 1976 Bowker Lecture:

"... forty of the finest people I know in publishing are at work today on education for publishing, education in publishing, and education about publishing. They believe that to help educate the world, we and those who follow had better educate ourselves further.... Publishers first have to understand better what it is we do and then take less time to gossip and more time to explain."

Fortunately, there is a growing (even if still terribly insufficient) appreciation of the importance of reading and books—including their economic importance—to contemporary society. The *mini-industries*, including film and television "tie-ins", that have literally been founded on some recent books, such as *Jaws* and *Roots*, as well as on various series such as those from Time-Life, Inc., the National Geographic Society, and others that could be mentioned, are astonishing. The combined economic impact of certain scholarly monographs and textbooks, not to mention various automotive books, cookbooks, craft books, survival books and other kinds of "how-to-be-successful-at-this-or-that" books is enormous. Incidentally, in 1975, "How-to-do-it" books occupied about 20 pages of *Books in Print*, the Bowker book trade "bible", representing some 1200 titles—and this includes only those whose titles begin with "How To..."! But of course economic power is hardly a new phenomenon in the world of books. For centuries, the Bible and other religious publications in many lands have provided countless people with their daily "bread", as well as with inspiration.

The distinguished publishing consultant, Datus C. Smith, Jr. (himself a former Director of the Princeton University Press and President of the AAUP, 1947-48) spoke eloquently of some of these issues (in a different context) in his 1977 report for UNESCO:

"Unawareness of the basic economic facts of book publishing is astonishingly prevalent among book people—even including book publishers themselves—in all countries. That lack of understanding is found not just in developing areas but also in the publishing industries of the countries preening themselves on their sophistication in both technology and economics . . .

"And if the publishers themselves are uninformed . . . it would be remarkable if the governments of their countries should have any better grasp of the facts and concepts. Yet the welfare of book institutions—publishing houses, printing plants, bookstores, libraries—can be powerfully affected for good or ill by those governments. The need for educating the government—and the public to which the government is supposed to be responsive—is overwhelming if there is to be any true understanding of the national interest in book development . . .

"The first step toward mobilizing public and governmental support for any program in book development is therefore full understanding of their own field by book people themselves. . ."

Amen. My own powerful convictions about the importance of publishing and publishing education are as an almost inevitable consequence of my background and training in educational publishing, especially under the gifted tutelage of William H. Freeman, founder of the San Francisco publishing company that bears his name, during the 1950's. Science education in particular was burgeoning then, and some of the world's leading scientists were writing introductory textbooks, monographs and other expository works (as distinguished from their research reports) in unprecedented numbers. To my surprise, many of these scientists reported that they were learning more about their own special subject matter whenever they undertook to write popularizations or introductory textbooks than they had in almost any other way. It turned out that this was an unexpected "dividend"—a by-product of the stringent requirement that they survey an entire field or discipline thoroughly, and at the same time explain it simply, clearly and accurately to readers who presumably knew little or nothing about the subject. Some authors even undertook to write books for the express purpose of learning. Dr. John R. Pierce, a professor of engineering at the California Institute of Technology in Pasadena, recently recalled just such an occasion, writing in *Science* magazine about Dr. Edward E. David Jr., President-Elect of the American Association for the Advancement of Science, who had served as science advisor to President Richard Nixon and as director of the U.S. Office of Science and Technology. Dr. Pierce relates that, when they first met, Dr. David was at Bell Laboratories, in charge of acoustics research, which included fundamental work on speech and hearing. "Because neither he nor I knew much about this," Pierce said, "we wrote a book . . . which taught us a great deal. . ."

But I later learned that this was hardly new. Nearly a century ago, one of America's earliest and most distinguished entomologists, Leland O. Howard, contributed the entomological terms to the *Century Dictionary*. Later on, he wrote regarding this task,

> "The whole work was extremely interesting and had a high educational value. Things that I learned then have been of service to me in many ways. Then, too, the extra money was a great help."

Fiction writers also have commented on this educational aspect of book writing. For example, California author Peter S. Beagle has observed:

> "There's a very odd relationship between me and a piece of paper . . . I'll start a chapter without knowing what's in it. Things come to flower that I have no idea I'm thinking about . . . I seem to write books to find out what it is I'm writing about. In each case, with every book I've done, I've been wrong about what I thought it was. About two-thirds of the way through, I find out what book I'm suppose to be doing . . ."

As my own publishing experience grew during the 1960's, I became increasingly aware of how narrowly trained many of the people I met in publishing seemed to be, and how circumscribed were their special jobs within their companies. They often seemed unnecessarily cut off from access to any overall view of the publishing process from beginning to end. Gradually I found myself assuming the role of an advocate for more effective communication among all people in publishing and for more and better channels for publishing education.

This, then, was some of the background that ensured the firing of my enthusiasm about ONE BOOK/FIVE WAYS when those xerox copies arrived. Coincidentally, our company had concluded publishing arrangements for a related book (see Bibliography) just a few months earlier, and it seemed to us that these two books would complement one another nicely. Although we could not be certain of the size of the market for either book, we were confident that they were both going to be valuable and important working tools for many individuals employed in the various departments of publishing companies, as well as for authors. They would also be useful references for many of the other "book people" mentioned earlier, who have either a professional interest in book publishing or merely some degree of curiosity about our profession. My enthusiasm for publishing these books and the different problems inherent in producing and selling them reminded me of a favorite passage from *Now, Barabbas*, William Jovanovich's delightful book:

> ". . . a publisher should commit himself only to those books that engage him most seriously and thus confine his excesses to his interests. This suggests that there are sound personal reasons for the existence of many different kinds of publishing, and it may explain why publishing does not tend to follow a uniform procedure. The uniqueness of a book, any book, argues against the refinement of those skills based on repetition of effort. It is for this reason that my colleagues and I seem to approach each book as if we had never made one before."

The observation that publishing does not tend to follow a uniform procedure is confirmed again and again in the pages of ONE BOOK/FIVE WAYS, where different approaches to the same project at so many stages of its development are demonstrated by the participating presses. It should be apparent to authors that the insights and comparative data contained in this book will be of great value to them, too—especially any who may be contemplating "self-publishing". As self-publication has become a more respectable and feasible alternative route to publication, more and more individual authors will need to avail themselves of the kinds of detailed knowledge offered here. (I can report from first-hand experience that anyone contemplating either self-publication or the launching of his or her own publishing company is going to find either experience an incomparably effective way—if an unexpectedly strenuous and expensive one—to obtain an education about publishing!)

From the outset of the meetings in Asheville, one of the questions that engaged the attention of most participants was, "Who *is* Purvis Mulch?" The true identity of Purvis Mulch, the pseudonymous author of *No Time for Houseplants*, the manuscript used for this unprecedented educational experiment with comparative publishing procedures, was not revealed until the second day of the Asheville meeting. The further adventures of his now-famous manuscript are related below, but before coming to those matters, further information regarding the background of the entire project is essential. I am indebted to Hilary Marshall of the University of Toronto Press for permission to borrow freely from the lively and informative remarks he presented at the AAUP Meeting in Asheville regarding the early evolution of ONE BOOK/FIVE WAYS. I only regret that space does not allow for a complete presentation of all the rich intellectual fare presented by Hilary and the others who participated in the program—particularly Jack Putnam, Executive Director of the AAUP, and J. G. Bell, Associate Director of the Stanford University Press, whose Introduction to the entire program at the Sunday Evening Plenary Session was a masterpiece of wit and wisdom.

In Hilary Marshall's words, then, here is how it all began:

"Ten years ago our annual meeting was held in Toronto. Approximately two years before that I was asked to be responsible for the arrangements for the Toronto convention. Perhaps it was while I was working on them that the idea that we now see realized as ONE BOOK/FIVE WAYS came to me.

The basic idea was quite simply that if you were to present exactly the same manuscript to a number of different publishing houses, each of them would see in it a different book and, quite possibly, a different market. I thought that different editors would probably treat the manuscript differently, I knew I could count on the designers to come up with different designs, and I was pretty certain that sales people would also see different ways of getting to the market, given the right manuscript.

There were a lot of things I did not consider, of course, and some of these come close to being impossible to achieve. How, for example, could one ever find an author prepared to deal with five or six different presses, fill in all their different forms, carry on correspondence with editors, sales and promotion people, read all the edited versions, make comments on them, and spend hundreds of hours of time, all for the good of the cause? How could one find five or six presses prepared to donate the time and effort and money to put through this purely experimental idea, in the hope that it would be educational?

Somehow this idea came to be mentioned at a meeting of the Education and Training Committee some five or six years ago, and, at a meeting soon after that, Joyce Kachergis told me that the 1977 convention would be taking place under the aegis of North Carolina—and they were going ahead with the project.

Immediately all the problems that one could possibly think of with a project like this began to come into my mind, but once Joyce picks up an idea, she is just about impossible to stop. In no time at all she had six presses agreeing to do the work. We lost only one of them subsequently, and that was for very good reasons.

By the middle of January 1976, the final version of a manuscript entitled "No Time for Houseplants," by a pseudonymous author known as Purvis Mulch, came into being. A great deal of the preparatory work on the manuscript, and the time and energy the author and many staff members of the presses gave to the project does not show up in ONE BOOK/FIVE WAYS . . . The manuscript was subjected to a normal critical appraisal both in-house and outside. Malcolm Macdonald, who was then executive editor of the University of North Carolina Press, read it in first draft and made many wise and constructive comments on it. These are to be found in the North Carolina log, but it should be understood that the other presses benefitted from them. Not many of the exchanges of the author and the Press can be included here, for reasons of space, but some excerpts may help give the flavor. For instance, on January 6 1976, the author sent the following information to North Carolina: "Did you know that, 200 years ago today my great-great-great-great-grandfather cooked schnitz and knep because his wife Emma had strained herself on the way to the outhouse? It all happened in Lehigh County, Pennsylvania. . ." (The importance of such information to a promotion department at the beginning of a bicentennial year can easily be discerned.)

The final version of the manuscript was sent to two outside readers by the University of North Carolina Press. Reader A, a very senior horticulturalist, liked the manuscript instantly and said so. He described it as generally meritorious, offering much sound information and advice, and having the makings of a good book. But he warned that good editing was going to be needed.

Afterword / 313

Reader B did not like the book. The owner of a large shop selling household plants, Reader B wrote a single-spaced, six page review in which he attempted to pull the book to pieces. The author's response ran to 16 pages and consisted of a line by line (literally word by word) refutation of about 90% of Reader B's comments and an acceptance of the balance. Reader B caused some anxiety at North Carolina so the manuscript went to a third reader.

Reader C was an academic in the Department of Botany at the University. He made a short report and a number of editorial comments. His main concern seemed to be the market for the book, a concern of the publisher just as much as the author. The author was grateful for the helpful suggestions but disturbed that Reader C apparently did not see the purpose of the book and responded "It is, I hope, brevity, directness and a sense of purpose that will distinguish this manuscript from others. I think that the reader to whom the book is directed will find this book of value."

It was with all this background that the four other presses concerned with this project started to work on their individual editions."

ONE BOOK/FIVE WAYS details most of the consequences of this work in the preceding pages, but in concluding his remarks, Hilary Marshall also revealed to us the "confidential" evaluations Purvis Mulch had made of each of the university presses on the basis of his own experiences with them throughout this exercise. With the initial diffident remark, "I know so little about design I hesitate to comment on any of the five, except to say that each is lovely in its own way." Mulch made the following observations:

One of the early communications I received from Chicago informed me that a meeting had just been held, among eleven top executives, discussing plans for my manuscript. I think of this as "The Chicago Meeting," and I had the idea that awsome and irresistible forces were at that time set into motion, over which I had no control. After that, each Chicago department went about its business in a perfectly routine and professional manner, and I felt that I shouldn't interfere in any way. Catherine Seybold's editing was assertive, reasonable, and free from needless tinkering. My style was preserved. I saw Chicago as an aspidistra—tenacious, fearless, strong, and utterly dependable.

The people at MIT exuded a spirit of self-confidence and pride bordering on cockiness. This attitude bothered me at first, but it was soon justified by their cool and professional execution in all areas. Of the five presses, they were the last in getting started; but, after having begun, they brought the task to fruition in short order. Their editing was crisp and reasonable, their marketing and production plans bold and assertive. The MIT staff is, in my mind, a fiddleleaf philodendron—strong, clean in line, fully assured, and reaching without doubt for the sky.

The North Carolina treatment of my manuscript was, it seems to me, fraught with grave concern for both the manuscript and my well being. Barbara Reitt's copyediting, arriving in the mail, was like a hand extended across the miles, offering a pat of encouragement, perhaps an apology, and, afterward, a warm handshake—probably in relief that I had agreed to most suggestions with a struggle. In the end, the Chapel Hill product was a thing of beauty, competent and graceful in every way. North Carolina was a paradise palm—slow-growing and occasionally uncertain, but, in the end, branching out strongly with more than a touch of grandeur.

Texas provided, I think, the most thorough job of editing of all the five presses—so thorough, in fact, that I feared for the very character of the manuscript. The structure was attacked, the anthropomorphisms plucked, the non sequiturs properly sequitured. My manuscript was returned, adorned with dozens of gummed tabs holding queries. I answered the queries on more gummed tabs, and stuck them onto the pages. I was most relieved finally to be finished with Texas—but I knew also that Carolyn Wylie's gentle persuasion had produced a better manuscript, and that her task was greater than mine. Texas was a morning glory—worrysome, but beautiful.

Toronto is a grape ivy—strong and deep-rooted, exploding forth unabashedly, slightly impish in its behavior. The enthusiasm of both the editorial and marketing staffs came through without reservation or hesitation. The forms were, in themselves, things of beauty. In working with Toronto, I felt that my worries were over, that these were professional publishers with enough self-confidence to laugh occasionally at themselves. I would enjoy, late on a Friday afternoon, having a glass of sherry with Toronto, perhaps exchanging some choice repotting stories.

Purvis Mulch then concluded his observations:

"My dream is to see my little book, in each of its five beautiful forms, displayed in every bookstore in the United States and Canada. The customer, then, could choose the design that best suits his or her personality—and I could built up oh-so-lovely a royalties account."

The expressed "dream" of Purvis Mulch was not to be, but there was a happy outcome after all. As a result of the Asheville meeting and the AAUP's "workbook" version of ONE BOOK/FIVE WAYS, the interest of the University of Oklahoma Press in *No Time for Houseplants* had been aroused, and arrangements for publication were concluded with "Purvis Mulch", who had by now—undoubtedly with great relief—reassumed his true identity: Jerry Minnich, Assistant Director of the University of Wisconsin Press. May his little book—and all good books—fulfill their authors' and their publishers' fondest dreams.

We are deeply grateful to the University of Oklahoma Press for its cooperation in providing information comparable to that of the other presses represented in this volume relating to the publication of *No Time for Houseplants*. The appearance of that book in the fall of 1978 under the Oklahoma imprint marks the ultimate realization of the visionary ideas of Hilary Marshall and Joyce Kachergis and the fulfillment of the greatest expectations of the other dedicated and generous participants in "The Manuscript Project". From beginning to end, this project stands as a benchmark in the developing field of education for publishing. It is a pleasure to record our gratitude to all of the other participants in this volume, to thank everyone involved for giving us the opportunity to become participants ourselves, and to express the hope that ONE BOOK/FIVE WAYS will serve the interests of our magnificent profession long and well.

William Kaufmann
21 April 1978

UNIVERSITY OF OKLAHOMA PRESS

Table of Contents

General Statement / *318*

Acquisitions and Administration

Readers' Reports / *323*
Contract / *324*
Manuscript / Project Information Sheet / *326*

Production and Design

Manufacturing Cost Estimate / *327*
Sample Pages / *328*

UNIVERSITY OF OKLAHOMA PRESS

General Statement:

Unlike the presses involved in the One Book Five Ways project, the University of Oklahoma Press was interested in the actual possibility of publishing <u>No Time for Houseplants</u>. We have always carried a number of general trade titles on our list, particularly the how-to-do-it types of books, and this seemed a natural addition.

ACQUISITION PROCESS

The idea of our publishing the book was first raised by our Marketing Manager at one of our July 1977 biweekly editorial board meetings. (Any one of our seven member editorial board may make acquisition recommendations.) At this meeting it was decided to ask Jerry Minnich to submit the manuscript to us for formal consideration.

The editor telephoned Mr. Minnich; the manuscript arrived, was logged in, and was immediately assigned to an in-house reader for evaluation of style, suitability for our list, and potential market. The in-house reader reported favorably on the manuscript; the editorial board decided to seek an outside expert's opinion; the outside reader was contacted; the manuscript was sent out accompanied by our standard Reader's Report form; and within a couple of weeks the reader's report arrived recommending publication pending some minor revisions.

At this point a cost estimate was requested from our Production Department, to be based on producing 5,000 copies, paperback only, in a 6x9 trim size. The estimate returned from production; the editor completed a preliminary pricing analysis; and the project, with in-house reader's report, outside reader's report, cost estimates, and preliminary pricing information, was again considered for a final publishing decision at our late August 1977 editorial board meeting.

It was agreed at this meeting that the Press should offer Mr. Minnich a contract to publish the book, pending the revision suggested by the readers. The editor sent a contract memorandum to the Director, detailing the terms of the contract as agreed upon by the editorial board. The Director prepared and signed the contracts, sent them to the Business Manager for second signature, and the Business Manager forwarded them to the Editor for negotiation with the author.

The Editor prepared a contract letter to the author, detailing the conditions of publication, and sent the contracts, relevant portions of reader's reports, and an Author Information form to the author. The author accepted the terms of contract, returned the contracts signed, and informed the Editor that the revision would be completed and the final manuscript submitted in mid-October 1977.

EDITORIAL

The final manuscript was received on November 16, 1977, and was assigned to a house editor to prepare a physical inventory of the manuscript; to note any missing materials (the illustrations--line drawings--were noted as missing at this point); to determine any potential editorial or production problems; to prepare the manuscript for copyediting; and to make recommendations on print quantities, binding, price, and preferred publication season.

The house editor's "Report on Contracted Manuscript Received" was considered at our early December 1977 editorial board meeting, and it was decided to publish the book early in the Fall of 1978. A first printing quantity of 5,000 copies, all paperback, and a price of $5.95 was set at this time, based on a second cost estimate from the Production Department, and a second pricing analysis by the Editor. The Editor contacted the author to determine a date for receipt of final artwork, and contracted with a freelance editor for the copyediting of the manuscript. The manuscript was sent to the freelance editor with a set of detailed instructions on editorial preparation of the manuscript.

The edited manuscript returned from the freelance editor, and the finished artwork arrived from the author in late January 1978. A house editor checked the editing of the freelancer, prepared and placed the artwork, prepared frontmatter copy, and running head copy, and completed a transmittal form for design and production.

The manuscript, artwork, transmittal form and related materials were turned over to the Director for final analysis and approval of the publication plan. The Director then sent the manuscript to design and production.

SALES AND PROMOTION

Publication date: September 30, 1978

Bound Book arrival date: August 15, 1978

Summary:

The emphasis of our promotional effort on this publication will be through bookstores and trade wholesalers. We will rely heavily on our publicity department to see that consumers hear/read about No Time for Houseplants. There will be minor efforts made in advertising (mostly classified), subsidiary rights, and exhibits. The Marketing Manager has asked for estimates on print runs of 5000, 7500, and 10,000 paperbacks. While we feel there may be a market for some cloth, the competition in this field is very great (see UNC Press list of competition), thus a low-price paperback is in order. Marketing Assignments are listed in left column.

(SM)=Sales and Marketing Manager (R&PM)=Rights & Permissions Manager
(PM)=Publicity Manager   (BM)=Business Manager
(TSM)=Trade Sales Manager   (RM)=Review Copy Manager
(DMM)=Direct Mail Manager

(PM) 1. Poster: colorful (2-or3-color), distribution to 2500 bookstores (including chain stores)

    2. Circular:
- (DM) (a) 15,000 with 1-page sales letter (with order blank) mailed in envelope to Nursery people. States: CA, CT, IL, MA, NY, NY BOROS, OH, OK, TX
- (DM) (b) 3,000 with 1-page sales letter (with order blank) mailed in envelope to florist. States: CA, CT, IL, MA, NY, NY BOROS, OH, OK, TX
- (TSM) (c) 100 stuffers to each account of B. Dalton, Waldens, Doubleday, Brentanos, and Coles.
- (TSM) (d) 100 stuffers to each: top 250 O.U. Press accounts.
- (BM) (e) Single stuffers inserted in each of our statements for 2 months (i.e. Sept/Nov)
- (DMM) (f) 500 to author
- (SM) (g) piggyback circulars in One Book Five Ways (Kaufman Publishing Company)
- (SM) (h) 4,000 circulars to our exhibit program
- (DMM) (i) 3,000 misc. use

TOTAL 152,500

(TSM) (3) Counter-pre-pack: 10 copies each. TOTAL: N/A at this time. Quantity depends on advance sales orders to bookstores.

(TSM) (4) Trade Sales efforts: (a) special approaches by Sales Representatives to B. Dalton, Brentanos, Coles, Doubleday, Hunters, etc. (Alpha order) (b) special emphasis on promotion plans to sales force (consist of 16 commission sales representatives in each of the 50 states.)

(TSM) (5) Complimentary copies: Sent to 250 bookbuyers. Selected on basis of total net business (1977) with OU Press. This will hopefully promote book store awareness of this publication in an already crowded field of houseplant books, thus increasing sales when a customer asks for suggestions.

(RPM) (6) Bookclub adoptions: These will be sought through appropriate book clubs. (i.e. Quality Paperback Club, American Garden Guild Book Club, Organic Gardening Book Club, etc.)

(SM) (7) Two quotes from famous (but busy) individuals will be sought. Examples might be Jane Pauley or Sylvia Porter. These will be used in promotional copy and back-cover copy. Unlikely but worth a small amount of effort.

(RPM) (8) Excerpts: We will approach selected magazines and journals for possible excerptions. (List available on request.) Examples: Organic Gardening and Farming, Mother Jones, House Beautiful, Cosmopolitan, Today's Woman.

(SM) (9) Exhibits: OU Press regularly attends 35-40 exhibits per year (discipline, Library, historical society, etc.). We will feature No Time for Houseplants at each of these as a "bonus" consumer item. In this manner we will reach many professional people (teachers, librarians, etc.) who have house plants but "no time". We will also emphasize that No Time for Houseplants would make a nice, inexpensive gift.

(AM) (10) colorfully announced in Publishers Weekly seasonal ad (fall announcement)

(AM) (11) Classified ads will be arranged in selected magazines. List available on request. Examples: New York, Los Angeles, New Times, Texas Monthly, New Yorker.

(AM) (12) Space advertising: ads will be arranged in selected magazines, journals, and newspapers. List available on request. Emphasis will go to magazines in the North (shortest outside growing season) and magazines read by professional people (rather than horticultural magazines). Examples: various apartment magazines, New Times, New West, New York.

(PM/RM) (13) Newsrelease plus book (for review purposes): These copies to selected Garden Editors and life style editors (newspapers and magazines). Emphasis on this being the perfect house plant book for professional people. Newspaper list selected from Editor and Publisher; available on request.

(RM) (14) Selected copies to book reviewers but not many. List available on request. Hold to 75 copies.

(PM) (15) Review copies (plus letter) to 25 selected TV shows covering plants, flowers, and horticulture in general. (This might boost sales representative results in 25 area markets.) List available on request.

(TSM) (16) Newsrelease circular to <u>selected paperback jobbers</u> (wholesalers) not on OU Press account listing. List available on request.

(PM) (17) Advance page proofs to 25 selected newspapers and magazines. List available on request. Examples: <u>Publishers Weekly</u>, <u>New York Times</u>, <u>Better Homes & Gardens</u>, <u>House & Garden</u>, <u>House Beautiful</u>, <u>New Times</u>, <u>New West</u>, <u>New York</u>, (selected), <u>Chicago Sun</u>.

(DMM) (18) <u>No Time for Houseplants</u> will be included in our Fall and Winter 1978 seasonal catalog (8½x11). Distribution to 40,000 institutions and individuals (previous OU Press book buyers).

Contract sent 8/30/77 *(rushed to Helen 10-17-77)*

MANUSCRIPT TITLE: NO TIME FOR HOUSEPLANTS

PHOTOGRAPHS AND ILLUSTRATIONS (Give number): ~~Being compiled~~ 180-p. MS; illust. to come

AUTHOR: Jerry Minnich (Purvis Mulch)   ADDRESS: P.O. Box 1379, Madison, WI 53701

DATE RECEIVED: 11-16-77   ACKNOWLEDGED 11-17-77   RETURNED: Rejection / Revision / Correction / After publication

READERS:

Name	Date taken	Date returned
Doris Morris	11-17-77	12-7-77
Su Emry	12-16-77	1-10-78

TO AUTHOR: Date taken: Date returned:

TO SHOP: Date taken: Date returned:

PROOF   Date taken: Date returned:

UNIVERSITY OF OKLAHOMA PRESS : NORMAN

First Reader's Report On NO TIME FOR HOUSEPLANTS: A BUSY PERSON'S GUIDE TO INDOOR GARDENING
by Jerry Minnich

Summary of the Manuscript: 180 pages of manuscript, with perhaps as many as 50 pen and ink drawings to come. The subtitle is pretty descriptive: this is a guidebook for those people who want to have greenery in their living environment, but do not have the time or inclination to spend a lot of time and effort caring for plants. The first three chapters deal with general problems associated with care of plants; the remaining four chapters treat specific types of plants and plant environments: Foliage Plants; Cacti and other Succulents; Flowering Houseplants; and Special Indoor Gardens. Chapters 4, 5, and 6, list specific plants in alphabetical order, detailing their special characteristics, and providing through the use of special symbols the pertinent information concerning the necessary temperature range, humidity, amount of sunlight, and exposure.

Qualities of Style: The style is fine for its intended readership--the general trade. There is little or no scientific detail. There are numerous typos; some lapses in syntax; and much switching from singular to plural and back creating some problems in subject-verb agreement.

Suitability for List: As suitable as any of our other guide books.

Adaptability to Series: Not adaptable.

Probable Reader Appeal: It should have a wide appeal, but the competition is pretty stiff. It will need special promotion that points up its strengths over competing titles (it _is_ simple, easy to follow, and specific plants or specific problems are easy to find.)

Recommendations: That we get an opinion from an outside reader knowledgeable both about houseplants, and about the potential market for the book. If the reading is favorable, I would recommend offering to publish.

Date: 8/2/77

First Reader ___Wilson___

READER'S REPORT

UNIVERSITY OF OKLAHOMA PRESS

AUTHOR Jerry Minnich   **TITLE** NO TIME FOR HOUSEPLANTS: A BUSY PERSON'S GUIDE TO INDOOR GARDENING

To the Editor:

In reply to the question—Is this manuscript a contribution to the field?—it is my opinion that
It is a contribution in the sense that it is well organized, complete, and easy to follow. It should make a very handy reference for anyone who wants to have attractive plants around the house, but do not want to go to the kind of trouble necessary to grow the more exotic and sensitive sorts of plants.

In reply to the question—Is the scholarship of this manuscript sound?—it is my opinion that
This question does not really apply, because this is not intended as a scholarly work. However, within the framework of the intent of the manuscript, it is certainly sound. The material on plant diseases, cures, and general descriptions of plant environments and needs is quite accurate.

In reply to the question—Does this manuscript have a readable style?—it is my opinion that
The style is very good. It is a warm, personal style; there are numerous anthropomorphisms that fit well with the sort of intimate relationship the author obviously has with plants.

In reply to the question—If you were a publisher of scholarly books, would you consider the publication of this manuscript a worthy addition to your list?—I would say that
It is not a scholarly book, but it is a useful book. It is certainly never going to be considered a seminal work. It is, though, similar to other books that the Oklahoma Press publishes for the general market.

My opinion of the market for such a work is The potential market is enormous, but so is the competition. It will require a very special promotion effort on your part, to get ahead of the rather elaborately illustrated competing volumes.

Remarks: This was really a pleasure to read, and has been helpful to me already; I will look forward to receiving a bound copy.

My final reaction to this manuscript is that I would—would not—publish it. I would definitely publish it.

(Signed) Duard Leafrot, Ph.D.

Date
Place

For your information: PLEASE BE FRANK IN YOUR OPINION. IT WILL BE HELD STRICTLY CONFIDENTIAL. NEITHER YOUR NAME NOR YOUR OPINION WILL IN ANY CASE BE REVEALED TO THE AUTHOR OF THE MANUSCRIPT UNDER CONSIDERATION. WHAT WE WANT IS YOUR HONEST OPINION OF THE MERIT OF THIS MANUSCRIPT AS A CONTRIBUTION TO SCHOLARSHIP OR TO THE FIELD TO WHICH IT PERTAINS.

Afterword / 323

UNIVERSITY OF OKLAHOMA PRESS
PUBLISHING DIVISION OF THE UNIVERSITY

PUBLISHERS' CONTRACT

A contract is hereby entered into by and between the UNIVERSITY OF OKLAHOMA PRESS, SALES DIVISION, hereinafter referred to as the PUBLISHERS, and Jerry Minnich (Purvis Mulch)   , of P.O. Box 1379, Madison, Wisconsin   53701   ,

hereinafter referred to as the AUTHOR, for the publication of a manuscript entitled NO TIME FOR HOUSEPLANTS   ,

according to the terms and conditions hereinafter set forth.

I. The PUBLISHERS promise:

1. To publish such manuscript, subject to the availability of funds, within a period of two years from the date of the receipt by the said PUBLISHERS of a completed copy thereof, ready for the editorial marking and printing thereof, in such book form and edition, or editions, and at such price as the PUBLISHERS deem best suited for the successful marketing thereof, and to keep such in print as long as the demand for such work reasonably justifies;

2. If such work be subject to copyright, to secure, in the name of the PUBLISHERS, a copyright in the United States, together with copyrights in such foreign countries as the PUBLISHERS deem necessary to protect all rights in such work, and to secure a renewal of such copyright or renewals of such copyrights as is or are necessary so long as this contract remains in force and effect;

3. Upon the publication and distribution of such work to:

a) supply said AUTHOR with five (5) copies thereof;

b) furnish, at the discretion of the PUBLISHERS, copies for review, publicity, or other business purposes;

c) pay to the said AUTHOR a royalty ~~of~~ on the cloth edition of 10 per cent of the retail (list) price of the said work on the first five thousand (5,000) copies thereof sold and distributed; 12½ per cent of the retail (list) price of the said work on the next five thousand (5,000) copies sold and distributed; and 15 per cent of the retail (list) price on all further copies sold and distributed of the cloth edition; and, in addition, pay to the said AUTHOR a royalty on any paperback edition issued by said PUBLISHERS of 5 per cent of the retail (list) price on the first five thousand (5,000) copies sold and distributed; 6¾ per cent of the retail (list) price on the next five thousand (5,000) copies sold and distributed; and 7½ per cent of the retail (list) price on all further copies sold and distributed of any paperback edition issued by said PUBLISHERS; with the exception of copies of the said work which are sold outside the territorial limits of the fifty states of the United States, which shall be considered overseas sales, for which the royalties payable to the said AUTHOR shall be one-half of the foregoing rates;

provided, however, that no royalty shall be paid or payable upon such copies of said work as are distributed under subparagraphs a) and b) above, or upon such copies as are damaged or unsalable, or upon such copies as are distributed under the provisions of subparagraph d) below;

d) pay to the AUTHOR 50 per cent of the net profits accruing in the event any first or second serialization, motion picture, television, radio production or transcription, or dramatic or musico-dramatic production of such work for the stage is arranged or contracted for by the PUBLISHERS or the work is selected and contracted for by any book club, reprint house, or other agency of publication, for all of which purposes the said PUBLISHERS are hereby solely empowered by said AUTHOR to contract;

e) submit to the said AUTHOR on or before each May 1   following the publication of the said manuscript provided for herein, during the life of this contract, a statement of account of the sales made and contracts consummated by the said PUBLISHERS on account of the said publication for the annual period preceding as of   April 1   ;

f)   remit to the said AUTHOR on or before each   May 1   following the publication of the said manuscript provided herein, during the life of this contract, such royalties and profits as may have accrued in his favor on the basis provided in subparagraphs c) and d) hereof and as are shown by the aforesaid statement of account;

g)   permit the said AUTHOR, upon written request, to examine by certified accountant the books of account of the PUBLISHERS in so far as they relate to the said publication, which examination shall be at the expense of the AUTHOR, unless errors adverse to the said AUTHOR shall be discovered in such accounting amounting to fifteen (15) per cent of the total sum properly payable to the AUTHOR in any annual accounting period commencing   April 1   as aforesaid, in which case the PUBLISHERS shall bear the reasonable expense of such examination;

h)   permit the AUTHOR, upon written consent of the PUBLISHERS, to assign by written assignment all rights reserved by the AUTHOR in such work.

4. The AUTHOR does hereby grant, assign, transfer, and convey to the PUBLISHERS the sole and exclusive right, title, and interest in such work, including the right to arrange for, market, and contract for any first or second serialization, motion picture, television, radio production or transcription, or dramatic or musico-dramatic production of such work for the stage, and to arrange for, promote, or contract for any book club, reprint, or other selection of such work.

II. The AUTHOR hereby promises to:

1. Furnish to the PUBLISHERS, within a reasonable time after the execution of this contract and ready for publication, a manuscript, to the satisfaction of the PUBLISHERS;

2. Supply at his own expense all illustrations for such publication;

3. Make an index for said publication, if such be required by the PUBLISHERS.

4. Remit to the PUBLISHERS, within thirty (30) days following publication of such work, any costs or expense incurred on the part of the PUBLISHERS, which said PUBLISHERS are hereby expressly authorized to incur, arising from the typing or retyping of all or any portion of such manuscript furnished by said AUTHOR required to comply with the stipulation, hereby made, that it be typewritten, double-spaced, with no longhand insertions, on paper eight and one-half (8½) by eleven (11) inches in size, and to conform otherwise to the Manual of

324 / Afterword

Style of the PUBLISHERS or to one designated by the PUBLISHERS, or arising from any changes, except typographical errors, made by the AUTHOR in the proofs thereof;

5. Return to said PUBLISHERS all proofs within five (5) days after the receipt thereof by the AUTHOR;

6. Accept as complete and full compensation under this contract for his work in preparing said literary work for publication the royalty and net profit payments to be made him by the said PUBLISHERS as provided in Part I, paragraph 3, subparagraphs c), d), and f) of this contract;

7. Co-operate with the said PUBLISHERS in expediting in every way possible the production and publication of the said literary work.

III. The AUTHOR does hereby warrant that:

1. The manuscript to be furnished by him hereunder when submitted will be complete and ready for publication, that he will be the sole author thereof, and that he has full power to enter into the within contract;

2. The manuscript to be furnished by him hereunder when submitted will be free from any and all libelous or otherwise unlawful or objectionable matter;

3. He will hold the said PUBLISHERS harmless against any suit, claim, or recovery upon any proprietary right, copyright, or libelous or other unlawful or objectionable matter as regards such literary work, and will, at his own expense defend any such suit, claim, or recovery in his own behalf and in behalf of the PUBLISHERS;

4. The manuscript to be furnished by him hereunder has not previously been published in whole or in part by anyone, and that it is therefore to be considered by the PUBLISHERS to be a new work and subject to copyright by the PUBLISHERS as a book now published for the first time in the United States of America.

IV. It is further mutually promised and agreed between the PUBLISHERS and the AUTHOR that:

1. The title of such manuscript to be produced and published hereunder shall be NO TIME FOR HOUSEPLANTS

and such title shall be changed only by mutual consent of the parties expressed in writing;

2. Such changes may be made by the PUBLISHERS in the text of the manuscript submitted by the AUTHOR as may be required to conform to the PUBLISHERS' Manual of Style or one designated by the PUBLISHERS, and otherwise conform to the prerequisites of the PUBLISHERS for publication;

3. Notice of copyright or copyrights, if copyrightable, shall be printed in all copies of such work sold and distributed;

4. If, after three (3) years from date of publication, fewer than twenty-five (25) copies of such work shall have been sold in any one (1) year, to be computed as and from respective anniversaries of the publication date, the PUBLISHERS may offer, at a remainder price, free of royalties, to the AUTHOR, the remaining part of the edition, and in the event that the AUTHOR does not, within sixty (60) days from receipt of such offer, notify the PUBLISHERS in writing of his agreement to purchase same, the said remaining part of the edition may be destroyed by the PUBLISHERS or disposed of as waste paper, without payment of any royalty, as hereinbefore provided, on the portion thus destroyed;

5. In the event of any suit arising from publication of such work, the signatories and agents of the UNIVERSITY OF OKLAHOMA and the STATE OF OKLAHOMA whose signatures are affixed hereto, and the members of the BOARD OF REGENTS OF THE UNIVERSITY OF OKLAHOMA, in their individual capacities shall in no manner, individually or collectively, be liable for any damages to anyone, and that any suit or claim hereunder shall be filed against the BOARD OF REGENTS OF THE UNIVERSITY OF OKLAHOMA in a corporate capacity, or against the STATE OF OKLAHOMA, as duly provided by the laws of the STATE OF OKLAHOMA.

In witness hereof, the undersigned have hereunto affixed their signatures.

UNIVERSITY OF OKLAHOMA PRESS

By _____
    Director

By _____
    Service Manager

_____
AUTHOR

Executed this _____30th_____ day of __August__, 19_77_, at Norman, Oklahoma.

```
                                                                    Date    3/9/78
                                                                Pub Date    Fall 1978
                                                               House Ed.    LW

Author (s)      Jerry Minnich
Editor (s)      _____
Translator (s)  _____
Forwarder (s)   _____
Prefacer (s)    _____
  → Introducer (s)  _____
Illustrator (s) Dian Wehrle Hjertman
Other (s)       _____

Title  NO TIME FOR HOUSEPLANTS: A Busy Person's Guide to Indoor Gardening

Series _____                        No. _____

MS pages (total) 180

Accents _____

Special Features  Scientific names of plants. Following each plant there will
                  appear four symbols (art) identifying the temperature, moisture, humidity,
                  and sunlight needs of each plant. These will have to be photographed and stripped
Design Suggestions in for each of about 80 plants.

Jacket Suggestions  Cartoon of busy people rushing out of the house, briefcases
                    in hand, watering a plant on the way.

Schedule  rush.

Comments  There are several items missing: dedication, acknowledgements page,
          explanation of symbols (which will appear in two places in the book), and
          some art.

                         Editor            Director         Art Department
Print Order              3,000             _____           _____
  Text                   _____
  B&W Illustrations      _____
  Color Illustrations    _____

Bind Order               3000
  Bind                   _____
  Leave flat sheets      _____
  Leave sewn sheets      _____

List Price               4.95 paper
Discount Price
Mfg. Cost/Copy
Margin
```

```
            REPORT ON CONTRACTED MANUSCRIPT RECEIVED

AUTHOR: Jerry Minnich           DATE CONTRACTED: 10-17-77

TITLE: "No Time for House Plants"   DATE RECEIVED: November 16, 1977

Physical inventory of the manuscript: 180 pp.

   Prelims
   Text
   Appendix
   Bibliography (alph. order under topics--may not be best--i.e., easiest to use--format)

Missing materials:
   1. To be supplied by author: illustrations; explanation of plant key (see
Chap. 3), index*

   2. To be supplied by the Press (finished artwork, etc.):

Problems:
   1. Editorial:
Light editing (check for mechanics, grammar). Au caps & ital genus when also common
name (resolve w/au). Some sections have already been minimally edited. Resolve w/au
organization of Bibliography.
   2. Design and production:
Tables (few) 4 values subheads: 1 ctr, 1 run in, in plant-lists 2 sep-line side
heads (1 for plant groups in list--see Chaps. 3 & 4)

Recommendations:
   Print: _____ cloth; _____ paper
   Bind:  _____ cloth; _____ paper
   Price: $_____ (editor's recommended price)
   Publication season: _____

Other comments: Will need a good index. Garden books often lacking good ones. Include both common
and scientific names, types (e.g., "Ferns")

Date: _____                    by: _____
```

SPECIFICATIONS FOR MINNICH: NO TIME FOR HOUSEPLANTS

```
Trim size:          5½ x 8¼ inches.
Text type:          11/12 Patina on 24 picas.
Display type:       Palatino Semibold and Arboret.
Runningheads:       7-point Patina caps.
Folios:             11-points Patina.
Type measure (overall page):  24 x 42 picas.
Head margins:       3 picas.
Inner margins:      4½ picas.
All composition by Alphatype and Phototypositor.
```

 # Cacti and Other Succulents

Many house plant fanciers are completely indifferent to cacti and the other succulents, and some express a distinct dislike for them. Still others are completely enthralled with these unusual and diverse plants, giving them attention to the exclusion of all others.

Whatever your individual preferences, there is no denying that the succulents (and cacti are but one group of succulents) are remarkably colorful and interesting subjects, easy to care for, and responsive to special attention. They are, further, ideal plants for the no-time gardener, since they require less attention than other plants. Most succulents ask little more than a sunny window, occasional water, and very occasional fertilizing. There is no pruning, no tying up, no staking, no repotting. They are slow growing and thoroughly dependable.

There are literally thousands of species in this plant category, including more than two thousand cacti alone. Of these, several hundred, both attractive and suitable for indoor culture, are bred and sold as house plants.

Although cacti are succulent plants, the two are treated as separate groups in common practice, and in these pages we will follow that practice. Botanists classify cacti according to their flower characteristics, although most of us recognize may appear to die in colder months, but after an adequate rest period it will spring back to life. It is very sensitive to fertilizer burn and salt accumulation.

BLACK PEPPER (*Piper nigrum*)

This is not an especially attractive house plant, but it produces real peppercorns that you may use at the table and is a good conversation piece for that reason. The plant's green berries eventually turn red, then dry up and turn black. Pick the dried black corns, dry them thoroughly for several weeks in an open spot, and then use them in your pepper grinder. The care for black pepper is the same as that required for *Philodendron* (see below). It is not a demanding plant.

Note: Be sure that you have this plant and not one of the so-called black peppers of the deadly nightshade family!

BOXWOOD (*Buxus*)

The same plant that grows the most prized hedges outdoors can make a very attractive house plant. Boxwood, with its glossy, bright green leaves, is slow growing and dependable, a good subject for bonsai, the ancient oriental art of growing dwarf trees and shrubs. Japanese boxwood (*B. microphylla japonica*) and (*B. sempervierns*) are the two most popular species.

BROMELIADS

There are more than eighteen hundred varieties of this popular group, many of which are suitable for growing as house plants. Some of them produce attractive flowers, but most are grown for their striking and variegated leaf patterns. One distinctive feature of a bromeliad is the rosette of leaves

Afterword / 329

Bibliography

Books About the Book Industry

This selection was made by Chandler Grannis for the Committee on Professional Education for Publishing of the Association of American Publishers and is reproduced here (with several additions) by permission of Chandler Grannis and the Association of American Publishers, Inc. One Park Avenue, New York, N.Y. 10016.

BOOK INDUSTRY—GENERAL

Benjamin, Curtis G. A CANDID CRITIQUE OF BOOK PUBLISHING. (N.Y., Bowker, 1977)
  A distillation of the observations and opinions of a person who has been an eloquent spokesman and a major force in the publishing world for several decades.

BOWKER LECTURES ON BOOK PUBLISHING. (N.Y., Bowker, 1957)
  The first of the R. R. Bowker Memorial Lectures, each by a distinguished authority, reviewing a specific area of the book industry.

Burack, A. S., ed. THE WRITERS HANDBOOK. (Boston, The Writer, Inc., 1975 ed.)
  Collection of articles by authorities about writing, writers, and their relations with publishers and audiences.

Dessauer, John P. BOOK PUBLISHING: WHAT IT IS, WHAT IT DOES. (N.Y., Bowker, 1974)
  A concise introduction to the industry, giving basic facts about virtually every operation in the sequence of book publishing.

Grannis, Chandler B., ed. WHAT HAPPENS IN BOOK PUBLISHING. (N.Y., Columbia University Press, 2nd ed. 1967)
  Twenty chapters by experts in the principal functions and major subdivisions of book publishing.

Hill, Mary and Cochran, Wendell. INTO PRINT: A PRACTICAL GUIDE TO WRITING, ILLUSTRATING, AND PUBLISHING. (Los Altos, CA, William Kaufmann, Inc. 1977)
  Two experienced authors and editors make the entire publishing process understandable. A step-by-step, easy-to-use handbook designed to make it easier for authors, publishers, editors, artists, typesetters, printers, and all others involved in the publishing process to communicate successfully with one another.

Greenfield, Howard. BOOKS: FROM WRITER TO READER. (N.Y., Crown Publishers, 1976)
  This up-to-date volume, including glossary, bibliography and index, is unique in its description of every step in general book publishing, from author and agent to bookseller and reader, not only in text but with extensive, directly informative illustrations; the writing is clear, does not omit essential technicalities, and is apparently meant for readers from a sophisticated secondary school level on up.

Kujoth, Jean Spencer, comp. BOOK PUBLISHING: INSIDE VIEWS. (Metuchen, N.J., Scarecrow Press, 1971)
  Trends and issues in publishing, 1962-1970, in 50 articles by experts and observers of the book industry.

Smith, Datus C. Jr. A GUIDE TO BOOK PUBLISHING. (N.Y., Bowker, 1966)
    Fundamentals expressed in simple, step-by-step style, with special note of the needs of the book trade in developing countries.

Smith, Roger H. ed. THE AMERICAN READING PUBLIC: WHAT IT READS, WHY IT READS. (N.Y., Bowker, 1961)
    With emphasis on the reader, 20 authorities examine schools and the reader, commercial publishers, university publishing, the reader and the book, mass media, book reviewing.

Tebbel, John. OPPORTUNITIES IN PUBLISHING CAREERS. (Louisville, Ky., Vocational Guidance Manuals, Inc., 1975)
    A concise, brightly written, up-to-date outline of the nature of book publishing, its main branches, jobs available, how to get started.

MANAGEMENT

Bailey, Herbert S., Jr. THE ART AND SCIENCE OF BOOK PUBLISHING. (N.Y., Harper & Row, 1970)
    The application of management science to all branches of book publishing, by the director of Princeton University Press.

Bohne, Harald, and Harry van Ierssel. PUBLISHING: THE CREATIVE BUSINESS. (Toronto, University of Toronto Press, 1973)
    Specifics of the business operations of publishing management; major housekeeping functions; accounting for all operations; wise financial procedures.

Huenefeld, John. HOW TO MAKE MONEY PUBLISHING BOOKS. (Bedford, Mass., Vinebrook Publications, 1974)
    Detailed, comprehensive guide and reference for managing small book publishing houses.

Naggar, Jean V., ed. THE MONEY SIDE OF PUBLISHING: Fundamentals for Non-Financial People, Report of a 1976 Conference sponsored by the General Publishing Division, Association of American Publishers. (N.Y., AAP, 1976)
    Proceedings of the February 19, 1976 conference discussing such topics as working capital and cash flow, analyzing an operating statement, controlling production costs, negotiating a contract, and more.

EDITORS, AUTHORS, AGENTS

Appelbaum, Judith and Evans, Nancy. HOW TO GET HAPPILY PUBLISHED. (N.Y., Harper & Row, 1978)
    Written by two professional editors, this book contains indispensible information, advice and "tricks of the trade" that provide new insights into writing and publishing that even the most experienced authors should have. It concludes with a unique "Resources" section.

Balkin, Richard. A WRITER'S GUIDE TO BOOK PUBLISHING. (N.Y., Hawthorn, 1977)
    A useful reference to every phase of the author-publisher relationship, from manuscript submission and contract negotiation through editing, design, publication and marketing.

Bluem, A. William, and Jason E. Squire. THE MOVIE BUSINESS. (N.Y., Hastings House, 1972)
    Includes chapters on literary agents, story editors, and negotiating rights for books and screen plans.

Gross, Gerald, ed. EDITORS ON EDITING. (N.Y., Grosset & Dunlap, 1962)
    The editor in action, shown in 25 articles, speeches, sets of letters portraying the thinking and functions of editors in many branches of book publishing.

Perkins, Maxwell E. EDITOR TO AUTHOR: The Letters of Maxwell E. Perkins Selected and Edited by John Hall Wheelock. (N.Y., Charles Scribner's Sons, 1950)
    Correspondence of a famous editor with Hemingway, Wolfe, Fitzgerald, Galsworthy, and other renowned writers.

Reynolds, Paul R. A PROFESSIONAL GUIDE TO MARKETING MANUSCRIPTS. (Boston, The Writer, Inc., 1968)
> Addressed to authors, but equally a guide for publishers, on all aspects of author-publisher business matters.

THE WORLD OF TRANSLATION. (N.Y., P.E.N. American Center, 1971)
> Compilation of 39 conference papers on world problems of translation of literary manuscripts and on author-translator-publisher relations.

DESIGN AND PRODUCTION

Bruno, Michael H., ed. POCKET PAL (N.Y., International Paper Co. 11th ed., 1974)
> Comprehensive illustrated guide to printing and graphic arts practice, backgrounds, trends, procedures, and materials.

Klemin, Diana. THE ILLUSTRATED BOOK: ITS ART AND CRAFT. (N.Y., Clarkson N. Potter, distributed by Crown, 1970)
> A survey of the work and methods of 74 book artists, with examples and commentary, by a distinguished art director and designer.

Lee, Marshall. BOOKMAKING: THE ILLUSTRATED GUIDE TO DESIGN AND PRODUCTION. (N.Y., Bowker, 1965)
> A detailed, sequential instructional guide on book design and production.

Williamson, Hugh. METHODS OF BOOK DESIGN: THE PRACTICE OF AN INDUSTRIAL CRAFT. (N.Y., Oxford University Press, 2nd ed. 1966)
> Highly detailed guide to production processes, especially as known in British practice.

Wilson, Adrian. THE DESIGN OF BOOKS. (Salt Lake City, Peregrine Smith, Reprint ed., paper, 1974)
> Not only basics of book design, but many design approaches and solutions to varied problems are presented by a master designer.

CHILDREN'S BOOK PUBLISHING

Arbuthnot, May Hill, and Zena Sutherland. CHILDREN AND BOOKS. (N.Y., Lothrop, Lee & Shepard - Morrow, 4th ed., 1976)
> Heavily illustrated, extremely comprehensive work on children's needs and interests in reading, and analyses of books and authors.

Colby, Jean Poindexter. WRITING, ILLUSTRATING AND EDITING CHILDREN'S BOOKS. (N.Y., Hastings House, 1967)
> Comprehensive description of all aspects of children's book publishing, including editor-author-illustrator relations and dealing with the diversity of the field.

Lanes, Selma G. DOWN THE RABBIT HOLE. (N.Y., Atheneum, 1971)
> Subtitled "Adventures and Misadventures in the Realm of Children's Literature," this volume is one of the most informative and stimulating of many available books assessing contemporary children's literature.

Klemin, Diana. THE ART OF ART FOR CHILDREN'S BOOKS. (N.Y., Clarkson N. Potter, distributed by Crown, 1966)
> Pages from more than 60 contemporary books with comments on how the artists complemented the texts.

McCann, Donnarae, and Olga Richard. THE CHILD'S FIRST BOOKS: A CRITICAL STUDY OF PICTURES AND TEXTS. (N.Y., H.W. Wilson, 1973)
> Picture story books of young children are analyzed for conception and components, effectiveness, and children's response.

MASS MARKET PAPERBACKS

Petersen, Clarence. THE BANTAM STORY: THIRTY YEARS OF PAPERBACK PUBLISHING. (N.Y., Bantam Books, 1975)
> A sparkling account of the largest firm in the field, its history and current practice, but also including overall U.S. paperback publishing development.

Smith, Roger H. PAPERBACK PARNASSUS. (Boulder, Co., Westview Press, 1976)

A broad, detailed survey of the mass market paperback industry, its current condition, structure, and relations with the rest of the book industry and with authors.

SCHOLARLY PUBLISHING

Hawes, Gene R. TO ADVANCE KNOWLEDGE: A HANDBOOK ON AMERICAN UNIVERSITY PRESS PUBLISHING. (N.Y., American University Press Services, Inc., for AAUP, 1967)

> A full guide for workers in or entering scholarly publishing, examining objectives, history, problems, audiences, economics and authors.

MARKETING HANDBOOK FOR SCHOLARLY PUBLISHERS. (N.Y., American University Press Services, Inc., for AAUP, 1973)

> Authorities give detailed chapters on every step in the promotion and marketing of scholarly books and books for the professions.

Nemeyer, Carol A. SCHOLARLY REPRINT PUBLISHING IN THE UNITED STATES. (N.Y., Bowker, 1972)

> Development, structure, audiences, economics and other aspects of a special field, highly important in the library market.

LIBRARIES

THE LIBRARY MARKET. Reprint from *Publishers Weekly*, June 16, 1975. (N.Y., Bowker, advt. dept., 1975)

> A special survey in eight articles and extensive statistical charts of recent and projected figures; topics are book selection, school libraries, special libraries, sales, professional books, libraries and the bookseller.

Mathews, Virginia. LIBRARIES FOR TODAY AND TOMORROW. (N.Y., Doubleday, 1976)

> What publishers and their staffs need to know about American library services, their nature, how they came about, how they are funded, the problems they face. Clarifies the immensely complex library funding legislation; offers suggestions for the near future; includes extensive statistical data supplied by *PW* and other sources.

BOOKSELLING

Anderson, Charles B., G. Royce Smith and Sanford Cobb, eds. American Booksellers Association MANUAL OF BOOKSELLING. (N.Y., Harmony Books, distributed by Crown, 2nd ed., 1974)

> Greatly enlarged and revised edition, with 47 articles by experts in all aspects of bookselling operations and management.

COPYRIGHT

Wincor, Richard. LITERARY PROPERTY. (N.Y., Clarkson N. Potter, distributed by Crown, 1967)

> "An intelligent layman's guide" to authors' rights and literary property law.

Wittenberg, Philip. PROTECTION OF LITERARY PROPERTY. (Boston, The Writer, Inc., 1968)

> Extensive account of the laws and regulations on copyright and the ownership and use of literary property.

FREEDOM TO READ

Levy, L. W. FREEDOM OF THE PRESS. Vol. 1, From Zenger to Jefferson. (Indianapolis, Bobbs-Merrill, 1966)

> Anthology of primary documents, in two volumes.

Nelson, H.L. FREEDOM OF THE PRESS. Vol. 2, From Hamilton to the Warren Court. (Indianapolis, Bobbs-Merrill, 1967)

> Anthology of primary documents.

Rembar, Charles. THE END OF OBSCENITY. (N.Y., Simon & Schuster, 1970)

> The trials of "Lady Chatterley," "Tropic of Cancer" and "Fanny Hill" by the lawyer who defended them.

REPORT OF THE COMMISSION ON OBSCENITY AND PORNOGRAPHY. (N.Y., Bantam Books, 1970)

> Majority and minority statements and documents of the National Commission established by Congress.

BACKGROUNDS OF THE BOOK INDUSTRY

Anderson, Charles B., ed. BOOKSELLING IN AMERICA AND THE WORLD. (N.Y., Quadrangle Books, 1975)
   History of American and world bookselling and of the American Booksellers Association, by several authorities, with many literary excerpts on the subject; prepared for ABA's 75th anniversary.

Canfield, Cass. UP & DOWN & AROUND: A PUBLISHER RECOLLECTS THE TIME OF HIS LIFE. (N.Y., Harper's Magazine Press, 1971)
   A publisher for major literary artists, statesmen and other public figures since the mid-20s recounts his dealings with them in succinct, instructive, straight-to-the-point essays.

Chappell, Warren. A SHORT HISTORY OF THE PRINTED WORD. (N.Y., Alfred A. Knopf 1970)
   A handsomely illustrated account of top events and personalities in printing history, by a distinguished designer and artist.

Comparato, Frank E. BOOKS FOR THE MILLIONS. (Harrisburg, Pa., Stackpole Books, 1971)
   History of book manufacturing to the present day, emphasizing decisive inventions.

Doran, George. CHRONICLES OF BARABBAS 1884-1934. (N.Y., Holt, Rinehart & Winston, 2nd ed., 1952)
   A great publisher tells of the pains, fun and achievements of his profession, with many anecdotes of a brilliant period.

Doubleday, F.N. THE MEMOIRS OF A PUBLISHER. (N.Y., Doubleday, 1972)
   Frank Nelson Doubleday recounted here, in 1926, his early years with Scribner's, the founding and growth of Doubleday, work with famous persons, problems of the industry; also, essay by Christopher Morley.

Exman, Eugene. THE HOUSE OF HARPER. (N.Y., Harper & Row, 1967)
   Entertaining, authoritative account of a major firm's 150 years, its ups and downs, mistakes and successes.

Gilmer, Walker. HORACE LIVERIGHT: PUBLISHER OF THE TWENTIES. (N.Y., David Lewis, 1970)
   The meteoric career of a flamboyant publisher who presented many outstanding new writers to a large public, and whose firm was the training ground for several later leaders of the industry.

Gross, Gerald, ed. PUBLISHERS ON PUBLISHING. (N.Y., Grosset & Dunlap, 1961)
   The background of today's publishing told in 36 articles and excerpts by British and American publishers from the mid-1880s but mostly modern; selections arranged according to the functions of publishing.

Hackett, Alice Payne. SEVENTY YEARS OF BEST SELLERS, 1895-1965. (N.Y., Bowker, 1968)
   A reference volume tabulating best sellers of each year; social and historical setting for each year; supplementary indexes.

Henderson, Bill, ed. THE PUBLISH-IT-YOURSELF HANDBOOK. (Yonkers, N.Y., Pushcart Book Press, 1973)
   Pieces by writers and others who have put out their own books without commercial or vanity publishers. Unconventional procedures; facets of contemporary literary history.

Jovanovich, William. NOW, BARABBAS. (N.Y., Harper & Row, 1964)
   Incisive, thoughtful essays on the publisher and editor and their relation to writers, readers, sellers, reviewers, government and the public interest; by the head of Harcourt Brace Jovanovich.

Lehmann-Haupt, Hellmut, Lawrence C. Wroth and Rollo G. Silver. THE BOOK IN AMERICA. (N.Y., Bowker, revised ed., 1951)
   The definitive single-volume history on the making and selling of books in the U.S., 1630-1950.

Madison, Charles A. BOOK PUBLISHING IN AMERICA. (N.Y., 1966; Bowker (reissue) 1974)
   Developments and representative publishers from colonial times to 1965.

Madison, Charles A. IRVING TO IRVING: AUTHOR-PUBLISHER RELATIONS, 1800-1974. (N.Y., Bowker, 1974)
> Specific cases show, often amusingly, how contracts, copyright agreements and other business arrangements among authors and publishers have evolved.

Steinberg, S.H. FIVE HUNDRED YEARS OF PRINTING. (N.Y., Penguin, revised ed., 1974)
> The leading, handy, one-volume work on the subject, especially on the printing of books, including 20th century production.

Stern, Madeleine B. IMPRINTS ON HISTORY: BOOK PUBLISHERS AND AMERICAN FRONTIERS. (N.Y., AMS Press, reprint, 1975)
> The pioneering activity of 17 publishers on various American frontiers, including some that became important in the 20th century.

Targ, William. INDECENT PLEASURES. (N.Y., Macmillan, 1975)
> Acute observations, anecdotes, recollections of famous writers, and advice about publishing make up a witty book by a top level contemporary editor and publisher, one-time seller of rare books.

Tebbel, John. A HISTORY OF BOOK PUBLISHING IN THE UNITED STATES. Vol. 1, "The Creation of an Industry, 1630-1865;" Vol. 2, "The Expansion of an Industry, 1865-1919." (N.Y., Bowker, Vol. 1, 1972, Vol. 2, 1974)
> The most extensive history of American publishing; thorough, but entertainingly written.

Unwin, Sir Stanley. THE TRUTH ABOUT PUBLISHING. (N.Y., Bowker, 7th ed., 1960)
> An outspoken, widely respected English publisher produced this complete textbook of sound publishing practice.

EDITORIAL REFERENCES

Jordan, Lewis. MANUAL OF STYLE & USAGE. (N.Y., Quadrangle Books, 1975)
> A leading reference that sets high standards for journalistic style.

A MANUAL OF STYLE. (Chicago, University of Chicago Press, 12th ed., 1969)
> A major authority, especially in the book industry and in scholarly usage.

Skillin, Marjorie E., and Robert M. Gay. WORDS INTO TYPE. (N.Y., Appleton, revised ed., 1964)
> One of the references most favored by book editors.

UNITED STATES GOVERNMENT PRINTING OFFICE STYLE MANUAL. (Washington, D.C., U.S.G.P.O., revised ed., 1973, Order from Supt. of Documents, Washington, D.C. 20025, by title and catalog No. GP 1/4: St 9/073.)
> Major and thorough reference, especially valuable in handling information about government.

TOOLS OF THE TRADE

BOOK BUYER'S HANDBOOK. (N.Y., American Booksellers Association, annual.)
> Available to publisher-associates as well as to ABA members; complete looseleaf directory of all publishers' terms and arrangements.

BOOKS IN PRINT. (N.Y., Bowker, annual. Various prices, depending on year.)
> Two volumes each of author and title indexes, of all books from 3500 or more U.S. publishers; over 400,000 titles. Companion publications are annual SUBJECT GUIDE TO BOOKS IN PRINT, PAPERBOUND BOOKS IN PRINT, and bi-monthly FORTHCOMING BOOKS.

THE HORN BOOK. (Boston, The Horn Book, Inc., bi-monthly)
> The definitive journal of children's book editing, illustrating, writing and publishing.

LITERARY MARKET PLACE WITH NAMES AND NUMBERS. (N.Y., Bowker, annual)
> Extensive directory of publishers and their personnel, also manufacturers and trade services, review media, etc.

Peters, Jean, ed. THE BOOKMAN'S GLOSSARY. (N.Y., Bowker, 5th ed., 1975)

    Completely revised and heavily enlarged, this volume explains some 1,600 terms used in publishing, bookselling, printing, the antiquarian book trade and the contemporary technology of book production.

PUBLISHERS WEEKLY. (N.Y., Bowker)

    The comprehensive magazine of the book industry; trade news, trends, personnel notes and advance reviews of more than 5,000 trade books per year.

SCHOLARLY PUBLISHING. (Toronto, University of Toronto Press, quarterly)

    This "journal for authors and publishers" covers the broad range of North American editing and publishing while focusing on the university and other learned presses.

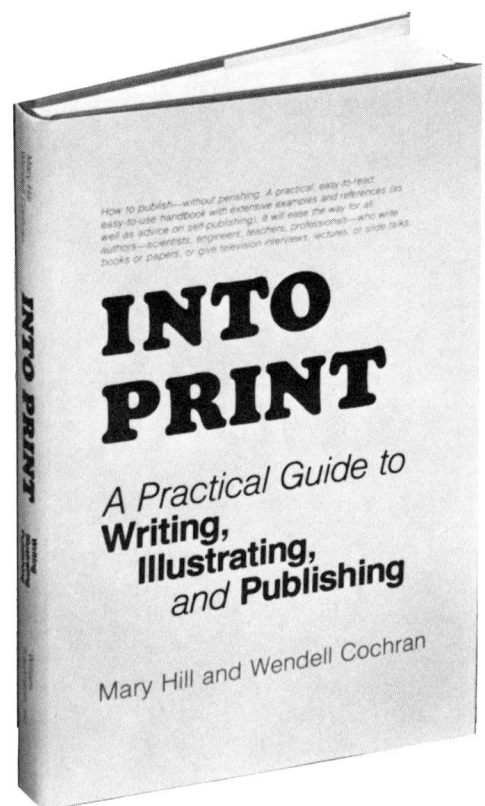

"They touch all the bases..."
—Publishers Weekly

Two experienced editors of non-fiction have written a practical, easy-to-use handbook for those who work with publishers, printers and artists on books, papers, speeches and other presentations. **Into Print** is richly illustrated, with extensive examples and references, and includes advice on self-publishing.

"They touch all the bases from front matter to index, from cautions to number manuscript pages to how to write a press release."
—**Publishers Weekly**

"From their opening chapter, dealing with appropriate choice of subject matter and how to market your product, the authors present step-by-step instructions on the art of rewriting, preparing an attractive manuscript, how to illustrate your work, and the important but often overlooked job of keeping accurate records of money spent on the preparation of your manuscript . . . **Into Print** is an excellent buy and should provide the information and encouragement would-be writers need to get published."
—**Asbury Park Press**

"Invaluable for printophiles."
—**San Francisco Examiner**

INTO PRINT:
A Practical Guide to Writing, Illustrating and Publishing

Mary Hill and Wendell Cochran

176 pages, illus., index, 1977.
LC # 77-4083
paperback $6.95 ISBN 0-913232-44-0
hardcover $12.00 ISBN 0-913232-43-2

CONTENTS

Previewing: looking toward publication
Recording: keeping track of money and facts
Writing: writing it right
Rewriting: revising and improving
Reviewing: weighing the words of others
Preparing: typing and labeling the manuscript
Illustrating: evaluating types of illustrations
Photographing: selecting camera and film
Lighting: illuminating the subject
Searching: making, finding and handling photographs
Drawing: preparing drawings and diagrams
Charting: making graphs and charts
Mapping: constructing maps
Listing: making tables
Finishing: adding front and back matter
Marketing: finding a publisher
Publishing: doing it yourself
Printing: working with editor and publisher
Proofing: copyediting and proofreading
Indexing: preparing an index
Advertising: writing advertising copy and press releases
Speaking: presenting speeches and giving interviews
Showing: selecting a projector
Telling: making and showing slides
Continuing: beginning the next edition

An important addition to any publishing library

Sample pages from the "one book" of One Book/Five Ways

Sets of 16-page sample signatures—including title pages, contents and chapter openings—from the unique educational exercise which produced *One Book/Five Ways* are available from the publisher. The sturdy envelope includes representative pages from each university press version of *No Time for Houseplants*, actually printed and trimmed to the specifications of the University of Chicago Press, MIT Press, University of North Carolina Press, University of Texas Press, University of Toronto Press. These "hands-on" samples provide a unique opportunity to further study and compare the dramatically different book concepts developed by the participants in this extraordinary publishing experiment.

Write William Kaufmann, Inc., One First St., Los Altos, CA 94022 for price information.